Advanced Research on Asian Economy and Economies of Other Continents – Vol. 9

Economic Development of Taiwan

Early Experiences and the Pacific Trade Triangle

Advanced Research on Asian Economy and Economies of Other Continents

(ISSN: 1793-0944)

Series Editor: Manoranjan DUTTA
(Rutgers, The State University of New Jersey, USA)

Published

Vol. 1 Asian Economic Cooperation in the New Millennium: China's Economic Presence
Edited by Calla Wiemer (East Asian Institute, National University of Singapore) & Heping Cao (Peking University, China)

Vol. 2 China's Industrial Revolution and Economic Presence
by Manoranjan Dutta (Rutgers, The State University of New Jersey, USA)

Vol. 3 International Economic Integration and Asia
Edited by Michael G Plummer & Erik Jones (Johns Hopkins University SAIS-Bologna, Italy)

Vol. 4 Economic Dynamism of Asia in the New Millenium: From the Asian Crisis to a New Stage of Growth
Edited by Yoshinori Shimizu (Hitotsubashi University, Japan)

Vol. 5 Future Perspectives on the Economic Development of Asia
by John Malcolm Dowling (Singapore Management University, Singapore)

Vol. 6 Asean Economic Integration: Trade, Foreign Direct Investment, and Finance
by Michael G Plummer (Johns Hopkins University, SAIS-Bologna, and East-West Center, Italy)

Vol. 7 EU-Asia and the Re-Polarization of the Global Economic Arena
Edited by Lars Oxelheim (Lund University, Sweden & Research Institute of Industrial Economics, Sweden)

Vol. 8 Resilient States from a Comparative Regional Perspective: Central and Eastern Europe and Southeast Asia
by Bafoil François (Sciences Po Paris, France)

Vol. 9 Economic Development of Taiwan: Early Experiences and the Pacific Trade Triangle
by Frank S. T. Hsiao (University of Colorado, Boulder, USA) & Mei-Chu Wang Hsiao (University of Colorado, Denver, USA)

Advanced Research on Asian Economy and Economies of Other Continents – Vol. 9

Economic Development of Taiwan

Early Experiences and the Pacific Trade Triangle

Frank S T Hsiao
University of Colorado at Boulder, USA

Mei-Chu Wang Hsiao
University of Colorado at Denver, USA

World Scientific

NEW JERSEY • LONDON • SINGAPORE • BEIJING • SHANGHAI • HONG KONG • TAIPEI • CHENNAI

Published by

World Scientific Publishing Co. Pte. Ltd.
5 Toh Tuck Link, Singapore 596224
USA office: 27 Warren Street, Suite 401-402, Hackensack, NJ 07601
UK office: 57 Shelton Street, Covent Garden, London WC2H 9HE

Library of Congress Cataloging-in-Publication Data
Hsiao, Frank S. T.
Economic development of Taiwan : early experiences and the Pacific trade triangle / Frank S.T. Hsiao, University of Colorado, Boulder, USA, Mei-Chu Wang Hsiao, University of Colorado, Denver, USA.
pages cm. -- (Advanced research on Asian economy and economies of other continents ; 9)
ISBN 978-9814618502 (hardcover : alk. paper)
1. Economic development--Taiwan. 2. Taiwan--Economic conditions. 3. Taiwan--Commerce. 4. Industries--Taiwan. I. Hsiao, Mei-Chu Wang. II. Title.
HC430.5.H717 2015
338.951249--dc23
2014040782

British Library Cataloguing-in-Publication Data
A catalogue record for this book is available from the British Library.

In-house Editor: Rajni Gamage

Typeset by Stallion Press
Email: enquiries@stallionpress.com

In the memory of
our parents

Contents

Part III Early Postwar Economic Development 407

Sources of the Chapters

Part I Overview of Economic Development of Taiwan

Chapter 1. "Taiwanese Economic Development and Foreign Trade", is mostly based on the working paper of the same title published in William C. Kirby and J. Megan Greene (eds.), *Harvard Studies on Taiwan*, Vol. I, *papers of the Taiwan Studies Workshop*, 1995, 199–270. Cambridge, MA: John King Fairbank Center for East Asian Research, Harvard University. Revised in John Y. T. Kuark (ed.), *Comparative Asian Economies*, Contemporary Studies in Economic and Financial Analysts, Vol. 77 (Part B), An International Series of Monographs, 1996, 211–302. Greenwich, CT: JAI Press. This chapter is the book length manuscript, *Taiwanese Economic Development and Foreign Trade*, 1996, as listed in the References section of Chapter 1. It is an expanded and extended version of the Harvard paper.

Chapter 2. "Taiwan in the Global Economy: Past, Present, and Future." In Peter C. Y. Chow (ed.), *Taiwan in the Global Economy-From an Agrarian Economy to an Exporter of High-Tech Products.* Westport, CT: Praeger Publishers, 2002, 161–221.

Chapter 3. "Taiwan in the Global Economy: End of the 'Miracle'?", reprinted and expanded from "Taiwan in the Global Economy: End of the 'Miracle'?" (by FSTH). In Shyu-tu Lee and Jack F. Williams (eds.), *Taiwan's Struggle: Voices of the Taiwanese.* Lanham, MD: Rowman & Littlefield Publishers, 2014, 235–253.

Part II Colonial Linkages

Chapter 4. "Colonialism or Comparative Advantages? — On Agricultural Development in Colonial Taiwan" (by FSTH). *Proceedings of the National Science Council, Part C: Humanities and Social Sciences*, 7(4). National Science Council, Taipei, Taiwan, October 1997, 497–513.

Chapter 5. "Colonial Linkages in Early Postwar Taiwanese Economic Development." In William C. Kirby and Michael S. Weiss (eds.), *Harvard Studies on Taiwan*, Volume II, *Papers of the Taiwan Studies Workshop.* Cambridge, MA: The John King Fairbank Center for East Asian Research, Harvard University, 1998, 91–117.

Chapter 6. "The Historical Traditions of Taiwanese Small-and-Medium Enterprises." In Fu-san Huang and Ka-im Ang (eds.), *Taiwan's Commercial Traditions Collected Papers.* Institute of Taiwan History, Academia Sinica, Taipei, Taiwan, May 1999, 464–524.

Chapter 7. "The Economic and Cultural Backgrounds of Taiwan's 228 Incident — An Application of Social Expectation Theory" (by FSTH). Originally written in English, translated in Chinese by Yi-Hsiong Lin (Colorado, USA) and published in Yong-hsing Chen (ed.), *Proceedings of 1991 Conference on Research on the 228 Incident.* The U.S.-Taiwan Cultural Exchange Foundation, 228 Citizen's Study Group, and Modern Research Foundation, Taipei, Taiwan, 1992, 77–113.

Part III Early Postwar Development

Chapter 8. "Product Life-Cycle and Diffusion of Technology — The Taiwanese Case." In B. W. Poulson, C. M. Becker and A. Rapport (eds.), *International Economic Integration: Lessons from the 1980s and Prospects for the 1990s.* Proceedings of the Economics Institute 2nd World Banking and Finance Symposium and the North American Economics and Finance Association (NAEFA) 5th International Congress, Joint Program, July 1989, University of Northern Iowa, 1991, 809–822.

Chapter 9. "Direct Foreign Investment, Technology Transfer, and Industrial Development — The Case of Electronics Industry in Taiwan" (by MCWH). In M. Dutta (ed.), *Asian Economic Regimes: An Adaptive Innovation*

Paradigm. Research in Asian Economic Studies, A Research Annual, Vol. 4, 1992 (Part A). Greenwich, CT: JAI Press, Inc., 145–164.

Chapter 10. "Globalization of the Taiwanese Economy and U.S.-Taiwan Trade Relations." In C. F. Lee (ed.), *Advances in Pacific Basin Business, Economics, and Finance*, Vol. I. Greenwich, CT: JAI Press, 1995, 197–214.

Chapter 11. "Japanese Experience of Industrialization and Economic Performance of Korea and Taiwan — Tests of Similarity." In Sheng-Cheng Hu and C. F. Lee (eds.), *Advances in Financial Planning and Forecasting Supplement 1, Taiwan's Foreign Investment, Exports, and Financial Analysis.* Greenwich, CT: JAI Press, 1989, 157–190.

Chapter 12. "Economic Liberalization and Development — The Case of Lifting Martial Law in Taiwan." In *The Transformation of an Authoritarian Regime: Taiwan in the Post-Martial Law Era.* Taiwan Studies Promotion Committee, Academia Sinica, Taipei, Taiwan, January 2001, 353–379.

Chapter 13. "Diminishing Returns and Asian NIEs — How They Overcome the Iron Law." In *Conference Proceedings on Economic Development in Memory of Professor Mo-Huan Hsing.* The Institute of Economics, Academia Sinica, Taipei, Taiwan, October 2001, 239–286.

Acknowledgments

In the process of preparing the chapters for publication in this book, we are grateful to the original publishers of our papers, as listed in the Sources of the Chapters section, for their quick response to our requests for copyright transfer, and to Professors Sheng-cheng Hu and William Kirby for writing the blurbs for us.

Spanning several decades, our research has focused on careful examination of the data and relevant literature. We particularly appreciate many institutes and organizations for regularly sending us their data and publications enabling us to keep up with current economic and social progress in Taiwan and other countries. They include: Professors Wan-an Yeh and Sheng-cheng Hu, formerly the Council of Economic Planning and Development, Executive Yuan, Taiwan; Drs. Sheng-yen Lee and Kuo-shu Liang, formerly the Central Bank of China, Taiwan; Mr. Chi-Ching Wang, formerly the Bank of Taiwan; the Institute of Economics, Institute of European and American Studies, and Institute of Taiwan History, all of Academia Sinica, Taiwan; Economics Department, National Taiwan University; Taiwan Institute of Economic Research, Taiwan; Taipei City Government; The American Chamber of Commerce in Taipei; The Association of Korean Economic Studies; International Monetary Fund (IMF); Federal Reserve Banks of Dallas and San Francisco; The International Centre for the Study of East Asian Development (ICSEAD), Kitakyushu, Japan; Economic Department, Chiba University, Japan; Japan Focus publisher, among others.

In conducting the related research over the years, the first author was granted a Fullbright-Heys Research Fellow at Hitotsubashi University and National Taiwan University. He was a visiting scholar at the Fairbank

Center for Asian Research, Harvard University (twice); Korea Development Institute; Hong Kong Baptist University; Kansai University and Nagoya University, Japan. In addition, both authors had opportunities to visit and do their research as visiting scholars/researchers at the Hoover Institute of Stanford University; the Institute of Economics, Academia Sinica, Taiwan; Chung-Hua Institution for Economic Research, Taiwan; and ICSEAD, Japan. We appreciate the hospitality and research environments provided by these institutes.

We are also very fortunate to be acquainted with many friends, teachers, and students. For many years, Professor Manoranjan Dutta of the Rutgers, the State University of New Jersey, encouraged us to study East Asian economies by inviting us to his annual conferences in various countries and to submit papers to the journal, which he was the editor. The exchange of academic publications and correspondence, along with their long friendship, although we might differ in viewpoints, with Professors Teruo Asamoto, Peter C. Y. Chow, Natsuki Fujita, Song-Ken Hsu, Hiroshi Ishida, Teng-hui Lee, Kuo-Shu Liang, Ta-hou Lin, Shin-kei (Jin-qing) Liu, Michael Luzius, Robert McNown, Motoaki Moriya, Yuzin Chiau-tong Ng (Sho-do Ko), Masao Oda, Michael G. Plummer, John P. Powelson, Eric D. Ramstetter, Hiroshi Setooka, Jaw-yann Twu (Muraoka), Henry Y. Wan, Jr., Wen-hsing Wu, Tsong-min Wu, and Tzong-shian Yu, were very helpful and greatly appreciated. The Dean's Office of the Leeds School of Business, University of Colorado at Boulder, and its many faculty members, provided us an excellent environment to work on this book. Many current and previous staff members of the Editorial Office, especially Rajni Nayanthara Gamage, the Desk Editor, and David Sharp, of World Scientific Publishing Co. and Imperial College Press, spent a long time to see this book published. We are grateful for their patience and advice. Naturally, all errors of commission and omission are ours.

Finally, we wish to express our sincere and deep gratitude to our parents, who saw the importance of having us receive the best education we could. We also wish to express our profound appreciation to our teachers who taught us rigorous economic analysis; and to our children for their patience and understanding throughout our research and teaching careers.

About the Authors

Frank S.T. Hsiao, Professor Emeritus of Economics, Department of Economics, University of Colorado at Boulder, is an Associate Editor for the *Journal of Asian Economics*. He received his B.A. and M.A. in Economics from National Taiwan University, Taipei, Taiwan, and M.A. and Ph.D. in Economics from the University of Rochester, Rochester, NY. From 1966 to 2007, he was a full-time professor in the Department of Economics, University of Colorado at Boulder, U.S.A.

Mei-Chu Wang Hsiao, Professor Emerita of Economics, Department of Economics, University of Colorado at Denver. She received her B.A. in Accounting and Banking from National Taiwan University, Taipei, Taiwan, and M.A. and Ph.D. in Economics from the University of Rochester, Rochester, NY. From 1981 to 2008, she was a full-time professor in the Department of Economics, University of Colorado at Denver, U.S.A.

Introduction

In the 1970s and 80s, Taiwan, along with Korea, attracted the attention of the world as they followed Japan to economic success. However, since the late 1990s, as the Chinese economic and political influence increases, the world's attention has been increasingly focused away from Taiwan. Nevertheless, in recent years, scholars and institutes, both inside and outside Taiwan, have renewed their interest in Taiwan for a variety of reasons. Taiwan has a diverse culture, unique history, and ethnically mixed society. Its computer and information technology industry has grown significantly. It has undergone a democratic transformation from one of the world's worst dictatorship. Moreover, its precarious political, economic, social, and linguistic relations with China are of particular interest to sinologists and social scientists.

This book is a collection of our papers published mostly between 1989 and 2002 on the early experience of Taiwanese economic development. Several colleagues of ours have been encouraging us to publish this collection as it presents what we think are unique and comprehensive Taiwanese viewpoints of the early experiences of Taiwan's economic development. While these papers are closely related one another, they are scattered across special issues of workshop or conference proceedings, and are not easy to find. Among them, two papers were invited papers published in *Papers of Taiwan Studies Workshops* of the Fairbank Center for East Asian Research, Harvard University, three papers were invited papers published in conference proceedings of Academia Sinica, Taiwan, and one paper from National Science Council Proceedings, Taipei, Taiwan. Other papers were presented at the conference sponsored by the American Committee of Asian Economic Studies, etc. Most of them were refereed. Although these institutes are one of the most, if not the most, prestigious ones in each country, the papers are not widely distributed.

Unlike the popular Western view that Taiwan's economic success was led by "wise" government policies ("put the government back" or "development dictatorship"), this book emphasizes the historical importance of the Japanese colonial legacy. While recognizing the importance of other factors, the perspective of the Japanese colonial linkages ("put the history back") and the Pacific trade triangle ("put the people back") during the early Taiwanese economic development are brought forward systematically in this book in large part because they have been overlooked in other works.

Furthermore, we integrate the above linkages and triangle relations with the social and political effects of the U.S. Aid Program and the tragedy of the 228 Incident to the early experiences of Taiwanese economic development. Our studies of history debunk the myth of postwar rags to riches story as well as the myth of "wise" government policy. Our stress on the trade triangle highlights the role of Taiwanese people in generating postwar economic growth. Most importantly, we emphasize the importance of Taiwanese small-and-medium enterprises in the exports oriented open economy during Taiwan's economic transformation.

By putting history and people back, early Taiwanese experiences of economic development can be a valuable paradigm for other Asian and African developing countries. These are explained in the following three sections.

Preview of Chapters

The basic theme of the entire book is laid out in Chapter 1. In 1996, we planned to publish a book on *Taiwanese Economic Development and Foreign Trade, the Miracle Reexamined* (as listed in the References section of Chapter 1). The abridged version (reduced to about two-third) of the book was presented at the Taiwan Studies Workshop at the Fairbank Center for East Asian Research, Harvard University. It was very well received and published in the Fairbank Center's *Papers of Taiwan Studies Workshops, 1995*, and later as an article in *Comparative Asian Economics*, JAI Press, 1996. Chapter 1 of the current book contains the published part of the *Papers of Taiwan Studies Workshop* and the unpublished part in the original book, including additional explanatory charts and tables, the methods of data analysis, and detail sources of data. We have preserved the original formatting and writing as much as possible. However, we have changed the endnotes to footnotes, and moved the charts and tables inside the text to make that information more accessible.

The other chapters of this book extend and expand the topics presented in Chapter 1. Thus, topics in Chapter 1 that are closely related to topics in later chapters are indicated with "Ref." The readers are advised to refer to that chapter in this volume for a more systematic or detailed exposition. We also use this "Ref." in the References section of other chapters to refer to the papers collected in this book.

The three chapters in Part I provide an introductory survey of the Taiwanese economy covering three significant but different periods. Chapter 1 covers from 1920's to mid-1990, with emphasis on 20 years before and after the WWII. In particular, we have described in detail the postwar émigré regime as a continuation of Japanese colonial rule. The first part of Chapter 2 supplements Chapter 1 by extending the discussion of the Taiwanese economy up to 19th Century, and emphasizes the role of Taiwan's geographical location in its history and development. We also see the increase of Taiwan's foreign direct investment, especially in China. Chapter 3 examines the current Taiwanese economy from a global perspective and as a continuation of the earlier development. We present the overview of recent development of the Taiwanese economy. While Taiwan is already an advanced country comparable to any developed countries in the world, the overreliance on the Chinese market for its outward foreign direct investment and exports resulted in "rich companies and poor country," namely, uneven distribution of the benefits of growth, persistent high unemployment, and the stagnation of the average wages.

Part II discusses the prewar and postwar linkages of *agriculture* (Chapter 4), which laid the foundation of the postwar development; of *industry* (Chapter 5), which was the basis of postwar industrialization until the mid-1960s; and finally, of Taiwanese *small-and-medium enterprises* (Chapter 6), which has played a crucial role in the Pacific trade triangle until the 1980s and probably beyond. Since Taiwan's 228 Incident was a pivotal turning point in the Taiwanese view of the Japanese and the Chinese, and it affected the Taiwanese economic behavior, we also added a unique chapter, Chapter 7. It explores the great discontinuity and disruption of economic and cultural expectations between prewar and postwar periods.

The six papers in Part III recount Taiwan's internal and external economic development after mid-1960s. During that time, Taiwan resumed its regular economic growth and reconnected to the "normal" growth of mid-1930s. The result was steady growth of exports and inward foreign direct investment. In Chapter 8, we explain product life-cycle theory and diffusion of technology in Taiwan's early industrialization, using the production of black-and-white television in Taiwan as an example. In turn, Chapter 9 considers the role of inward direct foreign investment in bringing foreign technologies (especially Japanese technologies) to Taiwanese electronic industries. Chapter 10 calculates Taiwan's globalization indicators, increase in exports, and discusses long-run US trade deficits with Taiwan. Chapter 11 studies whether the economic development of Taiwan, and also Korea, is "similar" to, or has "learned" from, that of Japan by studying their output and trade structures.

Taiwan's authoritarian regime and rigid economic system ended when the 38-year long martial law (since 1949) was lifted in 1987. Taiwan then entered a new era of rapid economic and political reforms. At the same time, the roles of its Japanese legacy and the Pacific trade triangle faded gradually. In their place, the Chinese economic and political factors and the government policy began playing an important role in the Taiwanese economic development (Ref. Chapter 3). With the popular election of a Taiwanese president in 1996 and the election of the opposition Taiwanese party to government in 2000, the characteristics of colonial émigré regime continued to degenerate and the process of Taiwanization advanced. Hence, Chapter 12 studies the economic transition before and after 1987.

The last chapter broadens the view from Taiwan to other three fast developing Asian economies, South Korea, Singapore and Hong Kong, namely, the Asian Newly Industrializing Economies (NIEs). We discuss Krugman's contention that growth of NIEs has been input-driven. In particular, we examine the notion that the law of diminishing returns will eventually set in, and result in the demise of the Asian Century. In Chapter 13, we show in detail that levels of education and openness had been increasing; that technology did transfer to Taiwan and other NIEs; and that their exports upgraded with time. These were studied through the components of imports, exports, and foreign direct investment. However, in retrospect, it appears that technological progress, as measured by improvements in total factor productivity, does not capture the degree of innovation. In recent years, Taiwan's economic progress has fallen behind that of South Korea, as South Korea's innovative capability surpassed that of Taiwan (Ref. Chapter 3). This chapter also didn't foresee the rapid growth of China as the world's source of manufactured goods and its impact on NIEs and Japan. Some recent China factors are discussed briefly in Chapter 3.

We plan to expand and extend our discussions in Chapter 13 in a separate volume. Our next work will discuss the recent economic development of NIEs and ASEAN by examining the relationships among Gross National Products, Foreign Trade, and Foreign Direct investment after 1980s.

Features of This Book

1. In this book, we point out that by the end of the 1920s, Taiwan's agricultural sector was so productive it already achieved primary export–led growth (Ref. Chapters 1 and 4). Taiwan then plunged into the period of controlled wartime economy of national mobilization in the 1930s until 1945. During this period, Taiwan became self-sufficient through import-substitution and quickly industrialized (Ref. Chapter 2). By the end of WWII, the Taiwanese economy was already at the stage of "precondition to take-off," and "institutional readiness" for rapid growth (Ref. Chapters 2, 7). However, the rapid growth was resumed only in the middle 1960s after US Aid was terminated.
2. We emphasize that, after the war, the Chinese émigré regime adopted the Japanese economic and social system, and continued, with the help of U.S. Aid, the rigid Japanese wartime national mobilization (Ref. Chapters 1 and 5). The regime confiscated the assets of Japanese firms and transformed those businesses into government-owned or the government-party-owned enterprises. Land reform measures expropriated Japanese owned land and distributed it to Taiwanese farmers. This is one of the important reasons for the success of the Chinese émigré regime.
3. On the cultural front, we pointed out the economic effects of the regime's national language policy. This policy created the Taiwanese the "silent majority" literally and figuratively, and lasted until the mid-1980s when the postwar generation of Taiwanese started to assert political and economic freedom and rights. A unique feature of this book is that we analyzed economic and political impacts of the 228 Incident, and introduced a simple Social Expectation Theory to explain the Incident (Ref. Chapters 1 and 7). The incident paved the way for postwar private cooperation between the Taiwanese and the Japanese (Ref. Chapter 8, 9), and Taiwanese economy grew along with Japan's (Ref. Chapter 11).
4. We discussed and illustrated in detail the composition of US Aid to Taiwan, one of the largest in the post-WWII world, and its impacts on the Taiwanese economy and its government policy (Chapter 1). To

show the need of austerity for the émigré regime, we estimate, for the first time in the literature, the burden on the Taiwanese people to support the Chinese refugees and soldiers (Ref. Chapter 1). We illustrate in detail the elaborate scheme of government exploitation (or the process of "original accumulation" of capital) of rice farmers (the *rice-for-fertilizer barter system*) and sugar cane farmers (the *sugar sharing system*) (Ref. Chapter 1). Despite the contrary assertions, our analysis of government budgets showed how little the government spent on local construction and education (Ref. Chapter 1) in the early Taiwanese economic development.

5. Heavy government protection of the textile industry, partly through "the *commissioned spinning and weaving system*" and U.S. Aid on cotton, is illustrated in Section 1.7.3.5 of Chapter 1. By 1960, the value of textile exports exceeded the value of raw cotton imports. In 1965, textile exports replaced sugar as the number one export item, ending the dominance of sugar exports in Taiwanese economic history. It also ended the postwar economic recovery and reconnected and resumed its prewar growth of 1930s. Taiwan then entered into the outward looking export-oriented open economy. Using a World Bank study, we refute the assertion that Taiwan became outward looking economy due to "small domestic markets and a shortage of natural resources" (Ref. Section 1.11 and Appendix 1A, Chapter 1), rather, the policy reform came as a result of external factors like the termination of the U.S. Aid program, basic characters of the uprooted émigré regime, along with the hindrance of upward movement of the Taiwanese small-and-medium size enterprises (SME) in the domestic market, helped by Japanese shoshas.
6. From 1965 to early 1990s, we divide the process of Taiwanese economic development in three stages: Take-off and Export Promotion Period (1964–1973), Second Import Substitution Period (1974–1980), and Accelerated Growth and High Tech Industrialization Period (1980–) (Ref. Chapter 1). The leading export items during the 1960s and the 1970s were textile products, and those during 1980s and 1990s were machinery and electric products (Ref. Chapter 1, 2, 13), and high tech products, including information and communications, in later years (Ref. Chapter 3).
7. The success of the exports promotion policy was helped mainly by the Pacific trade triangle, namely, Taiwan, Japan, and the USA Nexus (Ref. Chapters 1, 2, 8, and 9). The formation of the Pacific

triangle was supported by the dual industrial structure, outward looking Taiwanese small-and-medium size enterprises, Japanese linkage, Japanese investment and technology transfer, and Japanese marketing agencies (Ref. Chapters 1, 2, 8, 9), along with high social mobility of the Taiwanese society, and the Taiwanese spirit of the settlers (Ref. Chapters 1, 6).

8. Using the textile industry as an example, we have illustrated Taiwan's industrial structure in the 1970s (Chapter 1). The monopolistic government/KMT party controlled public enterprises monopolized the upstream industries. The oligopolistic larger private enterprises functioned as midstream. The furiously competitive Taiwanese small-and-medium enterprises are at the downstream, and engaged in exports. The exact role of the public enterprises and the government on the economy is not clear. Further study is called for.
9. We found that government help of the Taiwanese small-and-medium size enterprises was minimal both internally and externally (Ref. Chapters 1, 6). We have shown the resilience, adaptability, persistence, and ingenuity of the Taiwanese small-and-medium Enterprises. Our findings appear to be inconsistent with the "development state" advocacy in the popular literature. In general, the official government position has been that "Taiwan was returned happily to China after WWII, Taiwanese are Chinese, and the government is benevolent to the people." We take a more flexible position. We try to be as objective as possible, and find that the theme is untenable if we take a serious and honest look at Taiwan's development history, at least in the early postwar period (Ref. Chapter 1).
10. There are many perspectives on Taiwanese economic development. Some are pro-KMT government, some are anti-KMT government, as observed by Robert Wade (*Governing the Market*, Princeton, 1990). Some are macroeconomic policy oriented, some are microeconomic and industry oriented. One of the reasons for these different views is due to the background of the researchers, and whether the researcher reads Japanese, Chinese, and/or English references, and whether they are economists, sociologists, political scientists, or historians. We have tried to review the Taiwanese economic studies in these three languages, with the added advantage of our own experience in Taiwan during the 1950s and 1960s.
11. As pointed out in the previous section (Ref. Chapter 12), the roles of Japanese colonial legacy and the Pacific trade triangle, especially the

former, have faded gradually in the 1980's. As the second generation of the Taiwanese who were educated under the Chinese system started to rise, and China has rapidly become one of the major economic and political power houses in Asia and the world, international economic conditions started to change. Thus, the study of Taiwanese economic development depends on its stage of development, and should consider changes in domestic and international economic conditions at each stage.

12. There are debates on whether Taiwanese economic development can be viewed as economic development under "Development Dictatorship" from the end of World War II until the mid-1960s or before the lifting of Martial Law in 1987. We think it depends on the definition of the term. If the term refers to a benevolent dictatorship, where there is "development by dictatorship for the benefit of its own people;" it was clearly not the case. Under the émigré regime before the mid-1960s in Taiwan (Ref. Chapter 1), the whole nation was used by the dictator and his followers (outsiders) solely for their own ends, namely, "Counter-Attack and Regaining the Mainland." In this sense, we submit that it was a dictatorship, but not a "Development Dictatorship." The rigid policy was relaxed somewhat and was gradually reduced in severity from 1970s to the end of martial law in 1987 (Ref. Chapter 12). This period may be considered the period of "limited development dictatorship." After 1987, when martial law was lifted and the dictatorship ended, Taiwan entered a new era of economic, social, and democratic political development. However, Taiwan is not completely emancipated from the shadow of the émigré regime, as the old Constitution, with all its flaws and impediments which was brought into Taiwan by the Chinese émigré regime and pretends to govern China (the so called Mainland China), is still in effect. This, however, is outside the scope of our studies.

Lessons for Developing Countries

Lastly, an important question is: Would Taiwan's experiences of economic development be a useful paradigm for other developing countries? The answer is yes, and there are plenty of reasons.

1. Colonialism has unexpected positive consequences. For instance, after independence, India turned away from Britain and tried to learn from the Soviet Union, without much success. Despite the negative

effects of colonization, the Taiwanese did learn much from Japan (Ref. Chapter 11), Taiwanese recognized those elements of the Japanese system that were superior, and incorporated them into their own governmental and business procedures (Ref. Chapters 1, 6, 7, 9), and they succeeded.

2. As Malaysia celebrates 30th years of its Look East Policy, the Malaysian Government boasted that about 15,000 Malaysians were educated or trained in Japan, learned Japanese work ethics, discipline, and their value system. Besides the positive effect that having such a cadre of Japanese trained professionals has on attracting additional Japanese foreign direct investment and technology transfer to Malysia, these professionals are expected to be the leaders of the Malaysian economic development and modernization. This number is almost the same as the 18,000 Taiwanese graduates of secondary vocational schools at the end of WWII when the Japanese left from Taiwan, in addition to about 25,000 graduates of two- and three-year lower level vocational schools (Ref. Chapter 1). They were the pioneers of Taiwanese "Laobans," the managers and owners of the Taiwanese small-and-medium size enterprises, which were the backbone of the Taiwan's economic development (Ref. Chapter 1, 6, 9). Malaysian Prime Minister Mahathir Mohamad, who initiated the Look East Policy in 1982, can learn from the Taiwanese experiences, as can other developing countries, including those in Africa.
3. We have illustrated with charts and tables the effects of the unique and elaborate scheme of extracting surplus (original accumulation or exploitation) in the agricultural sector for capital accumulation by the émigré regime. These policies included: the *375 rent-reduction land reform*, the *rice-for-fertilizer barter system*, the *sugar sharing system*, and the *commissioned spinning and weaving system* (Ref. Chapter 1). These naked exploitation systems were initiated and executed under the new émigré regime and the white terror. Nevertheless, the very process of effectively extracting agricultural surpluses, white terror aside, under democracy and human right consideration can serve as useful examples of what to do and what not to do for other developing countries with a commitment to human rights.
4. The effective administration of economic and military aid programs by the Taiwan government and American agencies, as well as the timely advising of national government policy makers, can be studied and emulated by other donor and aid recipient countries. Few economists

realize that the rapid self-sustained economic development of Taiwan occurred only after the US aid program was terminated in 1964, and accelerated only after mid-1970s (see Figures 1.11 and 1.12 of Chapter 1). This will be a lesson for the dependency theory of economic development. It appears that the foreign aid program should have a starting date as well as ending date, so that the economic planners will not overly depend on foreign aid and plan for the future after foreign aid program terminates.

5. We have discussed the émigré regime's efforts to integrate its ethnic and linguistic groups into the broader Taiwanese society by instituting a national language and cultural policy. The experience of the local Taiwanese participants during Taiwan's economic development and growth (Ref. Chapter 1) may provide a valuable albeit negative lesson on the effect of culture on economic growth and policy for other multilingual countries.
6. The development process of Taiwan's television industry provides an interesting and useful example of the product life-cycle theory of diffusion of technology (Ref. Chapter 8, 9). It also provides an exemplary paradigm for how an adoption of new products can create forward and backward linkages among industries in Taiwan, and contribute to Taiwanese industrialization. Our analysis points out that, while the right government policy is important, the policy may not be successful without inventiveness, progressiveness, vitality, ingenuity, and diligence of the Taiwanese people. As it is said, one may drag a horse to water, but one may not force the horse to drink. Our analysis shows the importance of the people.
7. Taiwan's early postwar development strategy incorporated a strong "Look East Policy." Relying heavily on the private sector (although the government in the early stage tried to disengage it), Taiwan's development process was enhanced by its relationships with its neighbors, Japan and the United States, in the Pacific trade triagle (Ref. Chapter 10). Other Asian countries have also adopted Look East Policy. India's Look East Policy was initiated in 1991 during the government of Prime Minister P.V. Narasimha Rao. However, unlike Taiwan, its purpose has been to strengthen economic and strategic relations with ASEAN, and less with Japan, Korea and Taiwan. Our analysis of early Taiwanese experiences indicates that India, like Malaysia, should extend its Look East Policy to these three Asian countries and take note of, if not emulate, their economic development processes, as well as their

culture, and value systems, but with modern emphasis on democracy and human rights. Moreover, other developing countries in Asia, Africa, and Latin America could also benefit from studying Japan, Korea and Taiwan's examples.

8. Despite living under the rule of the dictatorial émigré regime, the continuing international isolation, and the existential military threat from China, the Taiwanese were able to achieve significant economic gains. They were able to change from primarily an agrarian economy in the prewar and early postwar period (Ref. Chapter 1, 3, 4) to one of the world's major exporters of textiles in the 1970s (Ref. Chapter 1), television and electric machinery in the 80s (Ref. Chapters 8, 9), computers and electronics in the 90s (Ref. Chapter 13), and high tech information and communication technology industries in the 2000s and 2010s (Ref. Chapter 3). The Taiwanese have come a long way in climbing the technological ladder in their industrialization process, achieved within just two generations. The trajectory of industrial transition during each decade since the 1920s serves as an excellent example of textbook studies of economic development and growth theory in the postwar period. In addition, the Taiwanese experience provides a valuable paradigm for all the developing countries in the world, probably more useful and interesting than that of Japanese and Korean experiences.
9. Early theory of economic development emphasizes the agricultural base of industrial development in the form of original accumulation in the agricultural sector. As shown in Chapter 4 and the first part of Chapter 1, Taiwan achieved high and advanced development of the agricultural sector during the prewar and early postwar period, supporting the Japanese war efforts in the prewar period, feeding massive refugees from China, and eventually triggered industrial development in the postwar period. The study of long-run Taiwanese economic development will provide the role of agricultural sector in the traditional theory of industrial development.
10. In recent years, however, Taiwanese economic development has appeared to reach its peak and there are discussions and concerns of the end of the "miracle" inside and outside Taiwan (Chapter 3). Studies of what factors and policies which have caused its economic stagnation, especially overreliance of a large country like China, and inquiries of how to revitalize and recover from economic decline, especially compared with apparently ever growing economies of nearby South

Korea and China, will provide interesting and helpful lessons for other developing and developed countries.

11. Our studies (Chapters 3 and 13) suggest that the recent shift of Taiwanese trade and investment from the United States and Japan to China, along with the failure to establish Taiwan's own brand names, may have contributed to recent economic stagnation, as this shift has led to the demise of the Pacific trade triangle. Other empirical studies show that a country's choice of trade and investment partners is important in increasing a developing country's productivity (Chapter 13). Our observation may also explain the catching up of the South Korean economy with that of Taiwan, as well as development dynamics in China and Asia, in comparison to developing countries in other regions. While more analysis is called for, the Taiwanese case provides an interesting theoretical and empirical example.
12. In addition to changes in the political economy arena, the second generation Taiwanese were able to attain a political change from a dictatorial émigré regime to a democratic government without bloodshed. It was also called Taiwan's "Political Miracle." Rapid economic reform and liberalization followed. We have shown that political change occurred almost abruptly, but the economic reform has been a continuous process (Rev. Chapter 12). The abrupt process of changes in political regime and the ensuing political economy of interactions between politics and economics should be studied carefully and could provide a useful paradigm for other developing countries striving for economic development and democracy.
13. Despite more than a half century of governing under the Chinese émigré regime, after a long isolation from China (Ref. Chapter 2), and notwithstanding the resumption of social and economic contacts with China, the majority of Taiwanese have developed a sense of independence from China and Chinese culture. Nevertheless, the coexistence of Chinese traditional culture in Taiwan with Taiwanese modernity (Ref. Chapter 3) and the strong influence of Japanese and American cultures and institutions (Ref. Chapters 3, 7, 10), may provide interesting materials for sociological and anthropological studies of social and economic change induced by rapid economic development.
14. On the other hand, in view of economic, political, and social awakenings of the second generation postwar Taiwanese, the Taiwanese themselves are yet to develop their own interpretation of their history, their culture,

or their own identity, and have yet to define their position in the history of the world (Ref. Chapter 2). While the development process is still evolving, we submit that the problems mentioned above are common in post-colonial societies, especially about national identity. Consequently, we think that Taiwanese experiences may provide a very useful paradigm for study.

We submit that all of these features of Taiwanese economy, society, political system, and history, in addition to Taiwan's geopolitical position in East Asia, have contributed to recent resurgence of Taiwan Studies in major universities and institutes. This book has advanced only part of the broader phase of Taiwan Studies. We hope more research in the directions presented in this book will continue in the future.

Part I

Overview of Economic Development of Taiwan

Chapter 1

Taiwanese Economic Development and Foreign Trade

1.1 Introduction

Taiwan, along with South Korea (hereafter Korea), Hong Kong, and Singapore, is one of the Asian Newly Industrializing Countries (NICs). In 1979, an OECD report defined the NICs as those countries "whose share in world industrial output and in world exports of manufactures has increased rapidly since the early 1960s and particularly during the 1970s" (OECD, 1979, 6). Ten NICs were identified in the report. In addition to the four "Asian NICs," the group included Portugal, Spain, Yugoslavia, and Greece in Southern Europe, and Brazil and Mexico in South America. After more than a decade, it turns out that only the four Asian NICs, along with Spain and Portugal, which were already in the OECD group, remained NICs (WDR, 1992, 245). Among the four Asian NICs (renamed as NIEs, Newly Industrializing Economies), however, development economists tend to put aside the significance of the achievements of Hong Kong and Singapore because they are small "city-states." Thus the rapid growth of Taiwan and Korea are considered truly "miraculous," showing the exemplary success of an outward-looking development strategy, and the workings of a market economic system.

Generally speaking, the economic performance of Taiwan and Korea has been similar (Hsiao and Hsiao, 1983, 52; 1993, 240), and their development resembles the Japanese experience of industrialization (Hsiao and Hsiao, 1989, 185). However, the beginning of Taiwanese development occurred earlier than that of Korea (Fei *et al.*, 1985), and it is as much as ten years more advanced than the development of Korea (Ko, 1988, 21–22). The Taiwanese per capita GDP has been consistently higher than that of Korea (see each issue of WDR before 1980, and each issue of TSDB after 1981). Thus, Taiwan, followed closely by Korea, is expected to be the second country after Japan since the end of WWII to become a developed country, joining the group of prestigious OECD countries (Ranis, 1992, 1).

The purpose of this paper is to offer some critical reviews of the "miracles" of Taiwanese economic growth and to examine whether such "miracles" can be "learned" by other countries. Numerous papers and books have been written about the economic development of Taiwan. However, we feel that we still can contribute, in this paper, to several aspects of the studies of Taiwanese economic development.

In Section 1.2, we introduce a brief historical background of Taiwan. Section 1.3 presents the different stages of Taiwanese economic development during the last ten years before World War II. We emphasize that the import substitution phase of development had already taken place prior to the war. The use of stages of economic development is to highlight the gradual advancement of Taiwanese industrialization during the later period of the Japanese occupation. A more accurate characterization of the Japanese period seems to be "First half period, Agriculture, second half period, Industrialization" rather than the usual slogan of "Industrial Japan, Agricultural Taiwan."

The Japanese legacy is analyzed in Section 1.4 with the historical perspective of phases in economic development. In Section 1.5, the impact of the February 28 incident of 1947, martial law, and the government's language policy on Taiwanese economic development are considered for the first time. We emphasize that government officials in the émigré regime do not speak Taiwanese. They use a different language, literally and figuratively. Without these factors, sociopolitical stability and smooth implementation of economic policy could not be justified. In a sense, the 2-28 Incident is a source of Taiwanese "miracle." For the first time, we have calculated the burden on the Taiwanese, especially the farm workers, imposed by the Chinese refugees and soldiers. We have also tried to compare the pre-1949 general government corruption and its land reform failure in China and the post-1949 government cleansing and the success in Taiwan.

We also emphasize the importance of the U.S. aid program as a stabilizing factor in Taiwanese society and economy, as the supplier of the foods and raw materials for industries, and then later as a promoter of private enterprises and exports. The initial conditions when the

Taiwanese economy started to recover in the early 1950s are examined in Section 1.6.

The structure of government finance reveals that the government took Taiwanese economic development seriously only after the 1970s. In addition to the macroeconomic linkages, we also study the microeconomic industry-wise linkages of the prewar and postwar periods in Section 1.7. We have examined some major public enterprises, such as the electric power, fertilizer, and sugar processing industries, along with some private industries such as textile and cement. The dominance of public enterprises and the rise of private enterprises are appraised. The schemes of government exploitation in the agricultural sector is surveyed. The rise and fall of the agricultural sector is examined in the context of specific social and economic circumstances.

The process of original accumulation for Taiwanese economic development was roughly completed by the mid-l960s. Taiwan then entered a new era of export-oriented economy which was restructured in accordance with, and subject to, an international division of labor in world production. In Section 1.8, we review briefly the early postwar economic development of Taiwan. Then, in Section 1.9, we first give a bird's-eye view of some macroeconomic indicators and foreign trade performance within the Taiwanese economy after the war with the help of diagrams. The steady and rapid growth after 1970 of Taiwan's current and real per capita GNP, real GDP, exports, and the balance of trade is the basis of Taiwan's so-called "miracle."

Section 1.10 continues to present the overall economic and political changes by dividing economic development after 1964 into three periods, take-off and export promotion period (1964–1973), second import substitution period (1974–1980), and the accelerated growth and high-tech industrialization period (1980 and after). The Ten Major Construction Projects of 1974 are reviewed briefly.

Taiwanese economic growth is attributable to the export-oriented strategy. In Section 1.11, we point out that, through international comparison, this strategy is driven less by market glut than by the very character of the émigré regime. The subsequent Section 1.12, reports some primary features of Taiwanese exports, imports, and its major trading partners. In Section 1.13, we confirm the existence of a Pacific trade triangle in which Taiwan plays as an intermediary between Japan, the Taiwan's number one importing country, and the United States, Taiwan's number one exporting country. The next section, Section 1.14, then emphasizes the contribution of technology transfers through direct foreign investment by Japanese and American multinationals. Section 1.15, shows that Taiwanese small and medium enterprises (SMEs) are the backbones of Taiwanese economic development and foreign trade. This fact has not been examined systematically in the literature. In Section 1.16, the emergence of entrepreneurs of SMEs as a massive social group and the sources of vitality of Taiwanese industrial activities are traced to the historical Japanese linkage, spill-over effects of Japanese economic growth, technology transfer and international marketing though multinationals and foreign buyers, high social mobility, and a reaction to the government control of domestic markets. Contrary to popular opinion, we have found that the role of government in nurturing the SMEs has been minimal. The true "miracle" is, despite all of the domestic and international handicaps, Taiwanese SMEs still could achieve rapid economic growth through foreign trade.

Section 1.17 presents a brief summary of later postwar economic development since 1964, and the last section concludes with some remarks on whether the Taiwanese experience is applicable to other developing countries. The Taiwanese economy had a huge gap from the mid-l930s when it started import substitution phase of development to the mid-l960s when it completed the first phase of import substitution and started export promotion phase. If Taiwan were an independent country and were not dragged into WWII and the civil war in China, Taiwan could have developed much faster.

We have tried to synthesize two major approaches (or trends) in the study of Taiwanese economic development. One is more critical, political and socioeconomically oriented, looking at microeconomic studies of individual industries. This approach is primarily propagated by economists affiliated with the Tokyo University in Japan. The other is a more complimentary, economic growth oriented, macroeconomic approach to the economy. This type of analysis is more common with scholars in Taiwan and in the United States.

Our purpose is to build a scenario or a model of Taiwanese economic development based on statistical facts and the results of research in the literature as objectively as possible. Our search for a satisfactory explanation of the events leads us to look into sociopolitical as well as historical-cultural factors influencing Taiwanese economic development. Without these factors, a scenario or model would be partial and superficial. The relationship between the events are carefully considered and commented on in order to reach supportable conclusions as we explain the economic development of Taiwan. We hope that we have answered some criticisms of economists by other social scientists (Winckler and Greenhalgh, 1988), and have demonstrated both "breadth and depth" for the study of Taiwanese economic development. Many topics raised in this paper are elaborated on elsewhere in this book.

1.2 A Brief Historical Background of Taiwan

Taiwan is an island located some 100 miles east of the Mainland China, isolated by the Formosa Strait. The land area is 36,000 km^2, or 13,814 square miles. It is a mountainous island, slightly smaller than the Netherlands, yet slightly larger than Maryland and Delaware combined. In 1991 Taiwan had a population of 20.5 million, slightly less than that of Canada or California. The Taiwanese people are primarily of Han decent (about 95%), with a small number of aborigines (approximately 5%). The latter are of Malayan-Indonesian origin. Approximately 85 percent of the Han people emigrated from the southern part of China, initially as trader-pirates and famine-stricken people during the last century of the Ming Dynasty (1368–1644), then as refugees, rebels, and displaced persons from the early Ch'ing (Qing) Dynasty (1644–1911). These Han immigrants probably outnumbered the aborigines by the end of the seventeenth century.[1] The rest of the Han émigré (about 15%) are new Chinese refugees who fled to Taiwan when the Chinese communists took over power in China in 1949.

The Portuguese called Taiwan "Ilha Formosa" (The Beautiful Island) around 1550 (Oh, 1970, 11). Taiwan was a colony under the Dutch regime from 1624 to 1661. It was taken over by a Fukienese general, Koxinya, and his family from 1661 to 1683, then conquered by the Ch'ing Dynasty in 1683. Taiwan was made a Fu, or a prefecture, of Fukien Province in 1684 (ibid., 58). After two centuries of loose Mandarin rule and oppression, Taiwan became a province in 1887 (ibid., 80). Taiwan was ceded to Japan in 1895 after China was defeated in the first Sino-Japanese War (1894–1895). The local Taiwanese revolted and established the "Republic of Taiwan," which fell within half a year to invading Japanese forces (Ng, 1970; Lamley, 1968). Taiwanese-armed rebellions against the Japanese, which lasted from 1895 to 1915, were brutally and cruelly suppressed (Oh, 1970, 91–94, 104–112). Taiwan was a Japanese colony from 1895 to 1945.

[1] See Oh (1970). The English sources on Taiwanese history may be found in the references cited in Chen and Reisman (1974).

1.3 Industrialization under the Japanese Regime

Under the Ch'ing government, Taiwan was a traditional agricultural society. It exported rice and sugar, the main staples, across the Formosa Strait to China and imported daily necessities and equipment from China. Under Japanese colonialism, Japanese capitalists invested heavily in developing Taiwanese agriculture, especially rice and sugar, which were exported to Japan proper. In return, Taiwan became a market for Japanese industrial products, thus completing the usual pattern of colonialism (Ho, 1978, 29; Ranis, 1992, 208). This historical picture is generally agreed upon, at least through the mid-1930s. The literature on post-WWII Taiwanese economic development stops at this point. However, few works have examined the years after the outbreak of the Manchurian Incident between China and Japan in 1931 when the situation changed considerably. Taiwan's industrialization started in earnest after the incident, with various plans for industrial development being put forward by the Japanese. As the Pacific War broke out in 1941, Taiwan was to be industrialized with heavy industry and the Taiwanese were to be "Japanized" and to serve as the vanguard of the Japanese "Southward Movement" (Kusui, 1944, 47; F. Hsiao, 1992, 83, Ref. Chapter 7).

Taiwanese economic development under the Japanese regime may be divided into five periods.[2] The last three periods correspond to the period of Japanese militarism.[3] They are explained briefly as follows.

1.3.1 *The Initial Period (1895–1905)*

This is the preparation phase for transferring the traditional Chinese-oriented Taiwanese economy into the sphere of the Japanese market system. During this period, Taiwan's colonial government undertook several important policy and development initiatives. For example, it conducted land surveys, land registration, and (the first) land reform were completed (Chang and Myers, 1963), thus increasing the tax base for the colonial government.

The government also monopolized salt, cigarettes, camphor, and opium. It eliminated the treaty tariff, which had been under British control. In addition, it standardized weights and measures in accordance with the

[2]The first two periods are based on the classification of Sumiya *et al.* (1992, Chapter 1).
[3]See Kusui (1944), 40–42. It may also be divided as the pre-quasiwar period (before 1931), the quasi-war period (1931–37), and the war period (after 1938). Also see Okurasho (1949), 209.

Japanese system. These policies led to an increase in government revenues which in turn led to fiscal independence of the colonial government from the Central Government in Tokyo. The Bank of Taiwan was established in 1899. It then financed the improvement of transportation and communication system, including the north-south highway and railroad, modern harbors, government buildings, and so forth, by issuing public bonds. (Sumiya *et al.*, 1992, 9–13; Lin, 1973, 14–15).

1.3.2 *The Intermediate Period (1905–1931)*

Taiwan's industrialization started with the cane sugar industry with the introduction of modern refinery techniques at the turn of the twentieth century. At the beginning, modern Japanese sugar firms existed side by side with the traditional native factories. They eventually replaced the latter during the 1910s. A decade later, the sugar industry was completely under Japanese control.

As in Japan, the outbreak of WWI in 1914 stimulated the development of sugar and other related industries within Taiwan. During the fifteen year period from 1914 to 1929, the value of industrial products increased nearly five-fold from 79.8 million yen to 382.5 million yen. (Shinohara, 1972, Table 1.13). However, its composition in the total gross value of national production increased only from 34.0 percent to 41.3%. This was because the value of output of other sectors such as agriculture, fishing, forestry, and mining also increased at more or less the same rate as industrial products (manufacturing) during the same period (Grajdanzev, 1942, 91). There are two qualifications to such a rapid growth.

First, the bulk of industrial output, 70 to 75 percent, consisted of food processing, especially sugar (Shinohara, 1972, Table 1.17). Second, other products such as chemicals, machinery, and textiles, were also related to the sugar processing industry. More specifically, they included alcohol, sugar refinery machines, machine repairing, and hemp and jute bags as containers for sugar and rice. The rest of the industrial products were produced by small-scale firms for local use, like cement, bricks, buckets, and so forth (Takahashi, 1937, 423–430).

On the other hand, Taiwanese agricultural productivity, after a slow start, increased considerably in the 1920s through applications of new genetic technology (like introduction of Holai rice), chemical fertilizer, irrigation techniques, and organization of rural institutions (Thorbecke, 1979, 136; Ishikawa, 1967, 102–108; Ho, 1978, Chapter 3; Lin, 1973, Chapter 2).

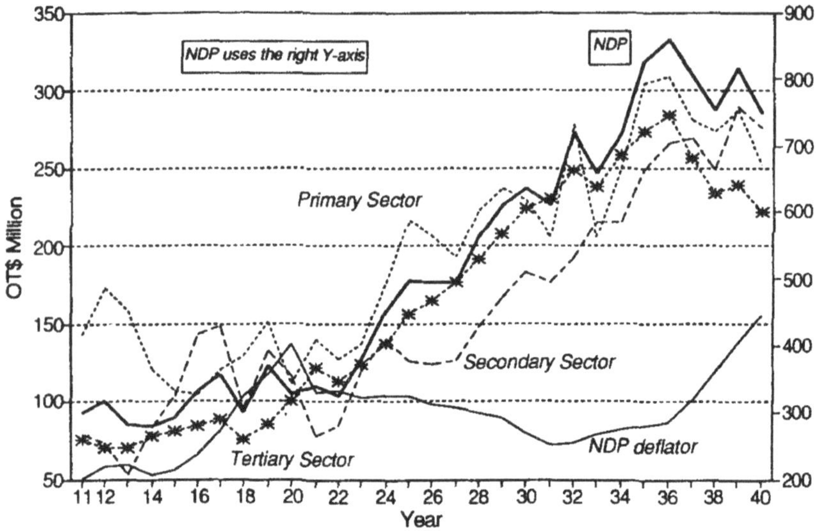

Figure 1.1: National Income Estimates, Taiwan
Lee's Estimates of NDP in 1937 Price

This "Green Revolution" is illustrated by the sudden increase in the output of the primary sector in Fig. 1.1.[4] All rice and most sugar cane (about 80%) were produced by small Taiwanese farms. However, in the sugar processing industry, production and distribution were monopolized by the Japanese. The native Taiwanese firms dominated rice processing and marketing in Taiwan, while Japanese firms controlled rice exports to Japan (Sumiya *et al.*, 1992, 18). This pattern of production and marketing was a practice that continued even after WWII by the Japanese Shosha.

1.3.3 *The Quasi-War-Stage of Industrialization (1931–1937)*

From 1931 to 1937, the industrialization process proceeded slowly. Perhaps because industrialization was still heavily biased toward agriculture, particularly the production of sugar and rice, and it emphasized export processing industries for sugar, tea, fruits, canned pineapples, etc.

[4]Figure 1.1 is drawn from the T. H. Lee's estimate of Net Domestic Product as listed in Ho (1978), 284.

By 1935, the only large modern industries other than the sugar processing industry were camphor, opium, and alcohol production, all of which were monopolized by the government (Kusui, 1944, 65–66). The major industrial development in this period was the completion of the 100,000 kw Sun-Moon Lake hydraulic power plant in 1934, tripling Taiwan's electricity output to 150,000 kw (Takahashi, 1937, 420). The abundant power supply led to the development of an aluminum factory in the southern part of Taiwan (1935) and an iron alloy factory in the north (1935). The availability of electricity also stimulated other new industries. Shipping (in 1936), pulp (in 1935), fertilizer (in 1937), and oil and fats (in 1935) (Kusui, 1944, 69–74) all grew during this period. About one third of total agricultural output (including almost half of the rice output), and 85 percent of agricultural processed output (including over 90 percent of sugar output) was exported, almost all to Japan (Ishikawa, 1972, 16–17; Ho, 1978, 31).

Economic growth resulted in such a dramatic increase in demand for electricity that, by the end of the period, a doubling of electricity output was planned (Takahashi, 1937, 421). It has been estimated that, between 1935 and 1939, agricultural output per farming household in Taiwan was 50 percent higher than that of Japan proper, and output per hectare was about 80 percent of that of Japan proper (Ishikawa, 1972, 17–19). Thus, in general, farmers in Taiwan appeared to be more affluent than those in Japan.

1.3.4 *The First War-Stage of Industrialization (July 1937 to December 1941)*

From mid-1937, the three basic political slogans in Taiwan were "industrialization" (Kogyoka), "Japanization" (Kominka), and "South-ward Advancement" (Nanshinka) (Kusui, 1944, 85). The basic industrial policy was laid out in the Five-Year Plan of Productivity Expansion, which was implemented in 1938. The emphasis was on metal processing and refinery, machinery (including weapons, airplanes, and automobiles), petroleum, chemical, and pharmaceutical industries (Kusui, 1944, 158, 168). At the same time, light industries of daily necessities, such as light bulbs, glass, ink, pencils, porcelain, radios, leathers, nail, agricultural machinery, and so on, were developed with the purpose of wartime self-sufficiency (Sumiya *et al.*, 1992, 21). As a result of this vigorous industrialization, a real problem during this period was a shortage of Taiwanese labor. There was a strong argument for importing Chinese labor and using the abundant electricity to develop heavy and chemical industries as an alternative to the light industries (Takahashi, 1937, 410).

Taiwan's agriculture was forced to reorganize, in large part, due to an increase in rice productivity in Japan and accessibility of sugar cane in Southeast Asia. The emphasis in agricultural production shifted toward specialty crops, like cotton, hemp, jute, castor oil, and sweet potatoes. In addition, agriculture's share in the domestic products decreased. With vigorous promotion of the Five-Year Plan under the Japanese government, the value of industrial output exceeded that of agricultural output for the first time in Taiwanese economic history in 1939, a milestone, that is, a turning point, in Taiwan's economic development. It remained mostly so afterward during the first part of 1940s (Kusui, 1944, 157; also see Sumiya *et al.*, 1992, 21).

The Taiwanese economy entered a new phase of sustained growth. Figure 1.1 presents the changes in the sectorial distribution of Taiwan's national income during the colonial period. The output value of the secondary (industrial) sector increased steadily after 1927. The tertiary (service) sector also expanded steadily after 1920 and decreased after Japan plunged into the Second Sino-Japanese War in 1937.

The shifting in the sectorial distribution of the value of output was also attributed in part to the pressures from Japanese territorial expansion and availability of resources from China and Southeast Asia. The agricultural sector was forced to readjust. After the Sino-Japanese War in 1937, the average growth rate of agricultural output decreased about 5 percent each year (Thorbecke, 1979, 135).

1.3.5 *The Second War-Stage of Industrialization (January 1942 to August 1945)*

After the outbreak of the Pacific War in December 1941 Taiwan achieved economic independence from Japan proper. There were a couple of reasons for this. First, the war made shipping goods from Japan and other countries difficult. Second, the war effort intensified within Japan itself, leading policy makers to emphasize a move toward Taiwanese self-sufficiency. The policy emphasis was on metal and machinery industries. Some miscellaneous goods, including candies, soy sauce, milk products, batteries, and so on were now also to be produced on the island (Kusui, 1944, 379–381). Thus, in this period, Taiwan entered the import-substitution phase of economic development.

The greatest achievements in this period were the beginning of construction of the Daikokei (Tachiasi) River Power Plant and the Takken (Ta-Chian) Dam in western Taiwan, the scale of which was reported to be several times larger than the Sun-Moon Lake Power Plant. The cement industry expanded and the iron and steel factories merged as steps toward the establishment of heavy industry in Taiwan (Kusui, 1944, 383–387).

Due to wartime secrecy much less data were available than from other periods. However, the highest industrial activities were reached in 1940. Even in 1944, although industrial production started slightly declining due to supply chain bottlenecks arising from the war efforts, production of petroleum products (for naval airplanes and ships), mica, asbestos, and alcohol exceeded the production targets by more than 60 percent on average, while foodstuffs and textiles had been sacrificed.[5]

After 1944, because many plants (like the three new cement plants) were constructed by moving old facilities from Japan to Taiwan and the difficulty of shipping capital equipment and materials during the later part of the war, accompanied by intense air raids by the Allied Forces in 1945, the industrialization program eventually came to a halt. Production plummeted, as is shown in Table 1.1.

1.4 The Japanese Legacy

Taiwan's real annual growth rate of industrial output from 1912 to 1940 averaged an estimated 5.86 percent, almost the same as that of Japan from 1905 to 1930 (Shinohara, 1972, 72). However, despite all the efforts of industrialization, food processing still accounted for 65 to 80 percent of total manufacturing output throughout the colonial period. This, despite the fact that metal and machinery outputs increased from 3.3 percent in 1912 to 10.8 percent of total manufacturing output in 1940 (Shinohara, 1972, 68).

From 1912 to 1940, 55 percent of total Taiwanese exports was sugar and about 30 percent was rice (Shinohara, 1972, 72). Just as with the United States, Canada, and Australia at the turn of the century, Taiwanese industrialization during the prewar period was achieved through primary

[5]For a collection of Taiwan's prewar statistics, see TSS (1946). The industrial statistics part is summarized in Chang (1980) and, more systematically in Chow (1958). Although, Chang, to a lesser degree, Chow, as Chinese, tries to minimize and degrade Japanese achievement on Taiwan, the statistics show themselves, they are simply "awesome" in that period. See Table 1.4, and later paper by Hsiao and Hsiao (2003).

Table 1.1: Production and Price Indexes of Taiwan, 1934–1950 (in %)

Year	Sector Indexes Agricul	Fishery	Industry	Mining	Prod Index	Price Index	Rate of Inflation
1934					69.56	82.03	
1935					85.85	83.47	1.8
1936					97.15	86.33	3.4
1937	100	100	100	100	100	100	15.8
1938	101.83	92.89	104.78	105.09	101.05	116.6	16.6
1939	108.03	105.81	90.14	135.27	109.81	133.9	14.8
1940	96.86	193.7	75.01	139.53	126.28	151.3	13.0
1941	86.77	98.89	60.69	133.93	95.07	164.6	8.8
1942	97.31	68.42	48.11	112.66	81.63	162.7	−1.2
1943	80.28	47.03	72.2	95.13	73.66	274.2	68.5
1944	61.62	21.96	15.7	91.41	47.67	460.1	67.8
1945	34.23	14.88	2.7	44.33	24.04	2360.3	413.0
1946	36.42	53.15	20.12	55.02	41.18	9456.6	300.7
1947	56.43	61.01	37.79	73.3	57.13	15600.5	65.0
1948	58.91	74.54	90.87	81.3	76.41	379566.2	2333.0
1949	82.92	72.85	84.96	69.21	77.49		
1950	79.52	83.05	91.91	77.4	82.97		

Source: From Tables 1 and 2 in Xia (1951). The rate of inflation is calculated from $[(P_t - P_{t-1})/P_0] * [1/(P_{t-1}/P_0)] * 100$, where P_t/P_0 is the index given in the table.

export-led growth. It is a classic example of economic development (Gillis *et al.*, 1992, Chapter 15). The modern sugar industry started quite small in size and gradually expanded over a thirty-year period, providing the time for the Japanese capitalists in Taiwan to learn the production techniques. The products were exported to the protected market in Japan as the demand for sugar in Japan also increased with economic growth. The steady increase in the supply of sugar in Taiwan and its demand in Japan created backward linkages in Taiwan, stimulating the development of related industries in Taiwan, such as the sugar refinery machines, chemical fertilizer, and so on in the early period of industrialization.

Some of the huge trade surpluses from sugar and rice undoubtedly spilled over to the construction of infrastructure (overhead capital) in Taiwan. Examples of this were the opening of the north-south cross-country railroad (1909), sugar company railroads and highways (to transport sugar cane and passengers), dam and irrigation networks, schools, and above all, cheap electricity (they were part of fiscal linkages). This may be seen in Fig. 1.2 from the increase in investment expenditure along with the increase in the trade surplus (the balance of trade, BOT) since 1915. In 1938, per capita real Gross Domestic Expenditure (GDE) in Taiwan

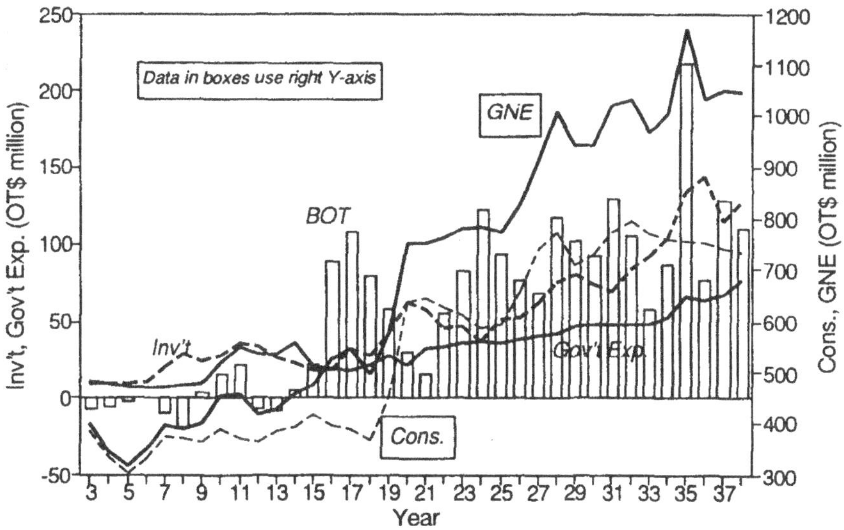

Figure 1.2: Gross National Expenditure
In Constant 1934–36 Average Prices

was about 57 percent of that in Japan proper (Tables 3B and 4B in Mizoguchi and Nojima, 1981). Despite all the talk of colonial exploitation, this was probably the highest relative ratio of GDE to Japan that the Taiwanese have ever enjoyed. Japanese per capita income has increased much faster than Taiwanese per capita income since WWII. In fact, even given the emphasis on postwar industrialization and rapid economic growth, and in spite of imported human and physical capital (as described subsequently), the postwar Taiwanese have never had an opportunity to come closer than to one third of the Japanese standard of living (TSDB, each issue).

In Fig. 1.2 private consumption (Cons.) is measured from the right Y-axis, and investment (Inv't), government expenditure (Gov't Exp.), and net exports (BOT, in bar chart) are measured from the left Y-axis.[6] Taiwan experienced trade surpluses every year from 1915 to the mid-1940s. Although the surpluses fluctuated considerably, they had upward trends over the years, and they surpassed investment and government expenditures in Taiwan.

[6]Figure 1.2 is drawn from the data estimated by Mizoguchi (1975), 150, also reproduced in Ho (1978), 286.

In addition to the tangible improvements of the economy and the welfare of the society as a whole, the Japanese legacy left an important intangible asset to the Taiwanese. By the end of the war, 81 percent of the boys and 61 percent of the girls among Taiwanese school-aged children were enrolled in elementary schools (OS16, 1944, 16). Furthermore, by the end of the war, there were about 25,000 graduates of two-and three-year lower level vocational schools and about 18,000 graduates of secondary vocational schools.[7] After the war, they emerged as the backbone of private small and medium enterprises in Taiwan. About 10,000 Taiwanese received higher education, although they consisted of merely 0.16 percent of the population[8] in 1943. They included 1,661 graduates of medical schools, 7,314 graduates of teacher's schools, and 161 graduates of the only university in Taiwan, the Taihoku Imperial University (Wu, 1986, 101–106). In addition, there were about 2,500 Taiwanese enrolled in colleges and universities in Japan by the end of the war[9] (Tsurumi, 1977, 128).

In retrospect, it does appear likely that if Taiwan had been an independent country in the late 1920s and had had massive Japanese foreign investment, the backward linkages and fiscal linkages created by the primary export-led growth would have enabled Taiwan to advance to the next phase of economic development. In moving to the phase of import substitution, as early as the late 1920s when agricultural productivity surged, Taiwan's economic growth might have surpassed Japanese growth. Unfortunately, this phase did not take place. Most of the wealth from the successful primary export-led growth was transferred to Japan. This was done by the colonists in the form of shipping charges, remittances, and deposits in the Japanese banks (Lin, 1973, 24), which in turn helped the economic development of

[7]Estimated from Tables D1 and D2 of Appendix D in Tsurumi (1977), listing only the even year enrollment data from 1922 to 1944. We estimated the odd year enrollments by using the mean of two adjacent even years. We also assumed that, on average, each year the two-year vocational schools graduated one-half of their enrollments, totaling 28,989. If all the vocational schools programs lasted three years, those schools graduated one third of their enrollments each year, totaling 19,326. Taking the average, we obtain the number in the text. Similarly, since the secondary vocational schools had three year program (ibid., 85), we assumed that each year, one-third graduated.

[8]This percentage is low by today's standard. However, it is not clear whether it is exceptionally low as compared to the situation in Japan or China, or for that matter, in any other country in the early 1940s.

[9]Another obvious Japanese heritage is the tradition and habit of collecting statistical data. The data are widely collected and compiled in Taiwan. We are not aware that this is the case in other developing countries, nor in the People's Republic of China, nor in the period of Republican China.

Japan. Taiwan was then forced into World War II, and the turmoil after the war lasted into the 1950s.

1.5 Economic Development Immediately after World War II

After the defeat of Japan in August 1945, control of Taiwan was transferred to China (for the legal problem and disputes, see Chen and Reisman, (1974)),[10] and was again made a province. When the war ended in 1945, the Taiwanese economy was in ruin, as shown by unofficial estimates in Table 1.1. If the year 1937 is used as the base year, industrial production came to a standstill in 1945. The industrial index was a mere 2.7 percent of the 1937 level. Agricultural and fishery industries fell to 34.23 and 14.88 percent, respectively, of the 1937 level. The price index shot up more than 23 times as compared with the price level in 1937. Production recovered somewhat in 1946, rising to 41 percent of 1937 level.

1.5.1 *The Chaotic Period (August 1945–1949)*

War destruction and the release of pent-up demand left the Taiwanese economy in ruin, but no worse than many other countries immediately after the war. It was certainly in better shape than in Japan or China.[11] Recovery could have been swift, and the Taiwanese expected a better and happier life without the Japanese governance. However, the Chinese immigrants who came to take over the island on October 25, 1945, acted as despotic foreign conquerors (Su, 1980, 701–702; Kerr, 1965, 52; Newman, 1961, 270; Sumiya *et al.*, 1992, 29; Fairbank, 1967, 75).

As Kerr (1965), 53, witnessed in the early months of 1946, there was a general pattern of looting of businesses and villages in Taiwan:

> "China's coastal cities were war-starved, Taiwan was comparatively rich. Busy gangs sent back their plunder to the continent as fast as possible. They made no distinction between Japanese and Formosan shops and properties, looting... especially foodstocks. At the lowest level in this scavenging period, the National garrison troops–a tattered

[10]There may be some international legal problem on Taiwan's status. Formosa's "legal title had not passed to China with Japan's defeat. The Nationalists should properly have acted as custodians... and rendered accounting of their stewardship to the United Nations" (Clubb, 1964, 274, 317; also Chen and Reisman, 1974).

[11]We have compared Taiwan's war damage in a later paper (Hsiao and Hsiao, 2003).

lot–ill-clothed, ill-fed, and poorly disciplined, simply wandered about, sometimes far into the countryside, picking up what they wanted."

There was official plundering of foodstuffs and smuggling of sugar, rice, and machinery out of Taiwan to China (Fairbank, 1971, 256; Chen *et al.*, 1991, 79, 93). All of the major industries developed under the Japanese regime after the 1930s, such as sugar refinery, petroleum, electric power, aluminum, fertilizer, soda, machinery, ship-building, cement, paper, financial institutions, and so on, were confiscated and reorganized as public enterprises in Chinese hands (Liu, 1975, 29). Mismanagement, corruption, and atrocities by the occupying Chinese alienated the Taiwanese people.[12]

Thus, the Taiwanese economy and society was again transformed into a system that blended the systems of two colonial masters. In terms of then popular Marxist terminology,

> "The Japanese monopoly capital was transformed at once as... state capital monopoly system,... which is nothing but the bureaucratic capital nourished and settled in the soil of semi-feudalistic Chinese society since the 1920s.... (However) there was a limit of the bureaucratic capital, which is characterized by the collusion between the capital and semi-feudalistic power, to engage pre-modern bureaucracy to manage the modern industries... The new rulers simply had no ability to manage Taiwan's modern industries" (Sumiya *et al.*, 1992, 27–29).

Within four months after the Chinese government took over the Japanese regime, Japanese books and magazines were banned, Japanese movies were censored. Only one year later, Japanese editions of newspapers in Taiwan were also eliminated. The use of Japanese in high schools was also prohibited. This is in great contrast to the policy under the Japanese regime of respecting local culture and language, as Taiwanese language was taught in common (elementary) schools during the initial period of

[12]See Lai *et al.* (1991), Chapter 3; F. Hsiao (1989). Similar episodes of plundering, except for the language policy, occurred on the Chinese mainland, especially in Manchuria, immediately after the war, leading to the Chinese Nationalists' loss of the Mainland (see Clubb, 1964, 274–275, Chapter 8, especially, 283; Pepper, 1986, 738–750). Also see People's University (1979), Chapter 9, Chapter 12 for the role of "bureaucratic capital" in China. For corruption and atrocities in Taiwan, also see recent reports by Lee (1986) and Chen (1991).

the Japanese occupation (Tsurumi, 1977, 40), and the Taiwanese language schools (Shobo) existed even after the Sino-Japanese war in 1937.

Because the Japanese and the Taiwanese languages are quite different from the Chinese language, these and other measures made effective communication among the Taiwanese, and also between the Taiwanese and the Chinese, very difficult, if not impossible. Under the pretense of "returning to the motherland," few Taiwanese intellectuals at that time protested. The Taiwanese became the silent majority. The language problem eased gradually only after the next generation of Taiwanese, who were educated under the Chinese system, started being socially active in the mid-1970s.

The upholding of the Chinese language as the official language gave the Chinese government a convenient excuse to fill the higher ranking, better paid, and more responsible government positions with Chinese "carpetbaggers" (Kerr, 1965, 52; Fairbank, 1971, 256). No decision-making positions were delegated to the local Taiwanese (Wang *et al.*, 1984, 40–42), despite the fact that Taiwanese leaders were generally well-educated (in the Japanese system). The Chinese simply replaced the Japanese as "new colonists" in this newly acquired "old territory" (Su, 1980, 702; Sumiya *et al.*, 1992, 29; Fairbank, 1967, 75).

In addition to the cultural shock, there were also economic shocks. Despite the departure of 335,000 Japanese (Kusui, 1944, 301), Taiwanese were unemployed and underemployed (Oh, 1970, 140). It is estimated that unemployment reached 800,000 (Su, 1980, 738; Chen, 1991, 96). When another 100,000 young repatriated Taiwanese soldiers and militia sent to the war front overseas by the Japanese regime were added, unemployment reached almost 15 percent of the population. Runaway inflation and massive unemployment after the war under the Chinese regime had been unheard of under the Japanese regime.

In less than a year and a half under Chinese administration, the Taiwanese revolted in what is known as the "2-28 Incident" on February 28, 1947. The unrest was primarily confined to the cities, and involved mostly young people. The island almost fell into the revolters' hands. On March 9th, Chinese reinforcement troops arrived, and started random killings (Lai *et al.*, 1991, 147). Ten to twenty thousand civilians were massacred (see Kerr, 1965, 310; Newman, 1961, 43, 67, 270; Lai *et al.*, 1991, 160, which estimated the number as 8,000). The tragedy of the incident and its aftermath has been well-documented (Lai *et al.*, 1991; Chen, 1991; Kerr,

1965; Su, 1980, 699–798; Wang *et al.*, 1984). Martial law was implemented on February 28 and lifted on May 16, 1947 (Sasamoto and Kawano, 1968, 918, 926). Massive arrests and murders of the Taiwanese elite continued, and the investigation of the incident was not closed until May 1950 (Lai *et al.*, 1991, 183).[13]

The incident had a profound effect on the Taiwanese attitude toward politics and the economy thereafter. "Political activity became associated with a violent end. As they have been the brutal Japanese military take over fifty years earlier, the reconquered Taiwanese again became leaderless, atomized, quiescent, and apolitical. It was learned behavior, not a cultural trait" (Gold, 1986, 52). Now Taiwanese parents wanted their children to be doctors, scientists, engineers, or businessmen, but never a politician.[14]

Without independent Taiwanese politicians representing the interests of the Taiwanese, Chinese policymakers had free reign to implement their economic policy, like land reform, or for that matter, any policies they chose in Taiwan. As we will see, this incident also reduced the Taiwanese enmity toward the Japanese and paved the way for joint ventures and expedited technical cooperation between the Taiwanese and the Japanese.

1.5.2 *The Transition Period (1950–1953)*

While the Taiwanese were recuperating from the March 1947 massacre and the economy was still depressed, three domestic and international events significantly changed the course of Taiwan's future. They are (1) monetary and land reforms, (2) the establishment of the Republic of China on Taiwan, and (3) the Korean War and U.S. aid to Taiwan. Each of these exerted a

[13]Lai *et al.*, ibid., asserts that "there is no basis for the common claim that the Nationalists killed all or most of the Taiwanese elite.... We can assume around 325,000 people...were...elite. If we conclude that 8,000 persons at most were killed and that half that number were members of the elite...we can surmise that 0.012 percent of the elite were killed." The correct proportion here should be 1.2 percent. From Wu's (1986), 101–106, estimation of the Taiwanese elite group, as mentioned later on, even the "conservative" estimation of Lai, *et al.* implies that the incident wiped out almost all Taiwanese intellectuals if teacher's school graduates were excluded. The controversy has an important bearing on the relationship between the local human capital and economic development.

[14]Listed in the order of general preference. Few people have noticed that Taiwan produced a Nobel Prize winner in Chemistry in 1986, Dr. Yuan T. Lee of the University of California at Berkeley. He returned to Taiwan, and became the President of Academia Sinica in 1994.

considerable influence on the Taiwanese economy and its future course, as will be described briefly.

1.5.2.1 *Monetary and Land Reforms*

Two major economic reforms were carried out during the transition period.

Monetary reform. The first reform was that the Bank of Taiwan issued a new currency, called the Old Taiwan Dollar (OT$), and exchanged it one to one to replace the Japanese yen on September 1947.

During this period, the internal war between the Chinese Nationalists and the Chinese Communists was blazing in China, the inflation that was rampant in China was also transmitted to Taiwan. After all, Taiwan had to import industrial necessities from China. The deficit financing that was used to restore public enterprises added to the fuel of inflation (Lin, 1968, 31). Prices shot up 23 times in 1948 from the previous year, as shown in Table 1.1, forcing the second monetary reform.

The second reform was issuance of the New Taiwan Dollar (NT$) on June 15, 1949 to stop inflation inflicted on Taiwan from China (One NT$ was exchanged for 40,000 Old Taiwan Dollars, and five NT$ for one U.S. dollar). The government imposed a strict control over widespread speculation and prevalent underground financial organizations, as well as over the money supply and the budget.

With the separation of Taiwan from China after the fall of Shanghai at the end of May 1949, the rampant inflation started subsiding, and the stability of economy was gradually restored (Sasamoto and Kawano, 1968, Chapter 10).

Land reform. Despite its failure in the era of Republican China in China per se, land reform was introduced in Taiwan because of the need to pacify disgruntled Taiwanese farmers (Sasamoto and Kawano, 1968, 163), and to establish the authority and control[15] of the Taiwanese in the aftermath of the "2-28 Incident," especially at the time the retreat of the Kuomintang (KMT) government to Taiwan was apparently imminent.[16] It was also an attempt to show the difference between the KMT method of land reform

[15]Land reform was often used by the Chinese Communist Party to establish authority in the conquered area before and after the establishment of the PRC (Fairbank, 1971, 338–339).

[16]See a brief but vivid description of the last days of KMT in China in Clubb (1964), 294–297.

and that of the Chinese Communist Party in China. It was implemented[17] with financial help and advice of the Americans.[18] This was the second land reform in Taiwan. As such, unlike land reforms in China, land reforms in Taiwan were more effective. The basic land survey and registration that had already been implemented during the first land reform under the Japanese regime made the second set of reforms that much easier. The landlord-tenant relationship in Taiwan after the war was no longer feudalistic, as was the case in Republican China.

In fact, Chinese villages before 1949 seemed much worse off than those in Taiwan (Belden, 1967), and yet during the long Republican period (1911–1949), the KMT failed to introduce meaningful land reform" in China.[19] In contrast, land reform was vigorously pursued with a "success" in Taiwan for several reasons, as expounded below.

It proceeded in three stages, as illustrated in Fig. 1.3. The three stages in Fig. 1.3 below are denoted as (1), (2), and (3) in the chart.

The first stage was "375 Rent Reduction." Starting from May 1949, 302,000 farm families signed 393,000 lease contracts in which rental rate was limited to no more than 37.5 percent of the annual main crop yield (Chen, 1961, 27; see (1) of Fig. 1.3).

The second stage was the "Sale of Public Land" in June 1951. In the six sales from 1948 to 1958, the government sold about 39.5 percent of public

---

[17]Several other specious arguments, like maladjustments in land distribution, worsening of the tenancy situation, Sun's teaching, and so on were commonly given (Chen, 1961, 7–10). The arguments failed to explain why the Chinese Communist Party, not the KMT, was recognized as the "agrarian reformers" (Fairbank, 1971, 274) while the KMT was in power in China before 1949.

[18]There is a discrepancy in who did what. Fairbank (1971), 321–322 stated that the joint Commission on Rural Reconstruction (JCRR), set up by the China Aid Act of 1948, ... secured the backing of the provincial government and was able to build on the Japanese structure of Farmer's Associations. It carried through ..." land reform. However, in Chen (1961), 68–69, 100, JCRR merely performed some minor "technical assistance and financial support" (also see Jacoby (1966), 171–172; Kerr (1965), 419–420).

[19]Belden (1967), 310–327; Kerr (1965), 419. Note that the main reason for the KMT failure of land reform in China may be seen in the statement by Belden: "The Chiang regime could not reform as long as it dared not attack the landlords. And it dared not attack the landlords because in essence it represented feudalism itself." (as quoted in Schurmann and Schell (1967), 314). In contrast to Taiwan, land ownership pre-war China was limited to the ruling group, the "Four Families" (namely, Chiang Kai-shek, Chen Li-fu, H.H. Kung, and T.V. Song) Their holdings in their home provinces were "staggering" (ibid., 312).

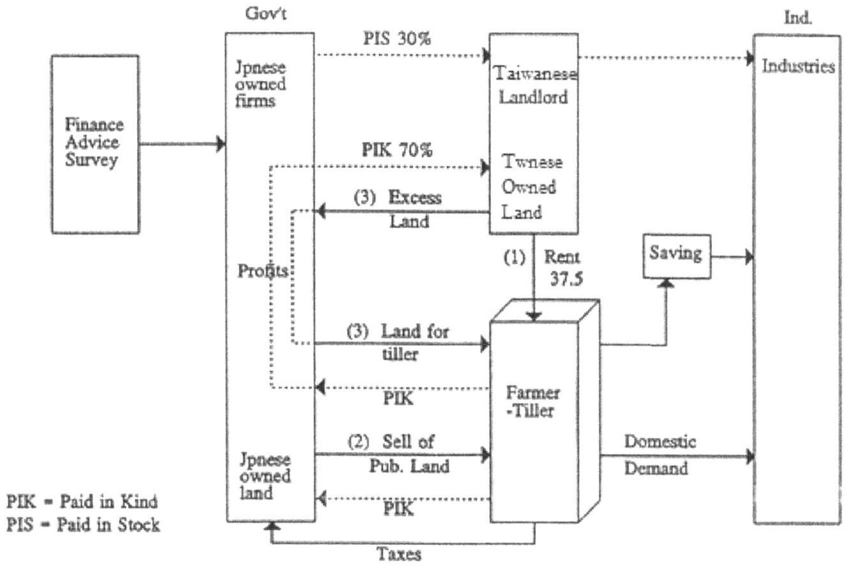

Figure 1.3: Impacts of Land Reform on the Industrialization of Taiwan

land (171,763 acres) to 139,688 incumbent tenant families (ibid., 63–64; also see (2) of Fig. 1.3), averaging about 1.23 acres per family.

The third stage was the "Land-to-the-Tiller" Program in November 1952. By the end of 1953, a total of 344,092 acres, or 56.5 percent, of private tenanted lands were compulsorily purchased by the government ((3) of Fig. 1.3). These purchases, held by 59.3 percent (106,045 owners) of larger landlords, with holdings in excess of 3 hectare of medium grade paddy field along with its improvements, were sold at the greatly undervalued fixed price of 2.3 times the annual main crop yield ((3) of Fig. 1.3),[20] a price less than one half to one third of the market value of the land (Ho, 1978, 166). The value of the crop yield was determined by using the average prices (rice and sweet potatoes) prevailed in Taiwan in December 1952 (Sasamoto and Kawano, 1968, 171).

The government paid a lump sum to landlords. This comprised of 70 percent (PIK in Fig. 1.3) in commodity bonds (paddy rice and sweet potatoes) at a low 4 percent real interest rate, and 30 percent in the stocks

[20]Chen (1961), 75; CYB (1972–73), 218; Sasamoto and Kawano (1968), 166–167; Lin (1973), 57. By 1952, the land price fell to about one-third of 1948 price (Lin, 1973, 53).

of four overvalued inefficient government enterprises (PIS in Fig. 1.3),[21] namely, Cement, Industrial and Mining Development, Pulp and Paper, Agriculture and Forestry Corporations. The landlords were losers in all respects.[22]

The land was not only vastly undervalued, the real interest rates paid on the commodity bonds were substantially lower than the market rates in 1953. In fact, the real interest rate on a secured bank loan at that time could run as high as 26 percent per year (32 percent for the nominal rate), and the prevailing rate for a non-bank loan was 32 percent per year (Hsiao, 1960a; Chen, 1972b, 42, 48). The future prospects of the transferred enterprises were so pessimistic that most of the landlords sold their stocks of the four overvalued government enterprises quickly at substantial losses (Ho, 1978, 167).

The lands were then resold by the government at the same fixed price to 194,823, or 64.1 percent, of the farming families ((3) in Fig. 1.3). The purchasers made payments in kind in 20 installments over 10 years at an interest rate of 4 percent per year. "Yearly payment for the purchase price plus land taxes; water fees and other expenses a purchaser had to bear was about equal in amount of the annual 37.5 percent land rent the tenant would have had to pay had the farmer continued to be a tenant" (CYB, 1972–1973, 218). Thus in terms of farmers' payments, the government had actually replaced the old landlords, although the farmers now owned the land.

Table 1.2 summarizes the balance sheet of land reform for the government from 1953 to 1962. The total gross profit is considerable. Not excluding administrative costs, the total gross profits of this land reform from the sales of public land (Step (2)) and the land-to-tiller program (Step (3)) amounted to about 36 percent of the paddy rice production and 43 percent of the sweet potato production, respectively, of 1953 (see the last row). In the second stage (2) of Land reform, the KMT government sold the public land which had been confiscated from the Japanese to the

[21]The companies were revalued in June 1949. During the following decade, the last two corporations never paid any dividends, the dividends of the Cement Corporation were almost the same as the inflation rate, and the second corporation only provided small nominal dividends (Sasamoto and Kawano, 1968, 176; also, Lin, 1973, 57).

[22]The companies were revalued in June 1949. During the following decade, the last two corporations never paid any dividends, the dividends of the Cement Corporation was almost the same as the inflation rate, and the second corporation only provided small nominal dividends (Sasamoto and Kawano, 1968, 176; also, Lin, 1973, 57).

Table 1.2: Government Profits from Land Reform, 1953–62

(Unit: in equivalent 1000 metric tons)

		Paddy Rice		Sweet Potato
		Paid in kind (PIK)		Paid in cash(PIC)
Sales of Pub. Land (Step (2))				
Gross Profit		330		882
Land-to-Tiller Program (Step (3))				
Buying from Landlords	1,272		434	
Sales to Owner-Farmers	1,525		519	
Gross profits (diff of above)		253		85
Total gross profits		583		967
1953 Annual Output (a)		1,642		2,277
% of total 1953 Output		35.5		42.5

Sources: CYB (1972–73), 217–18. Steps (2) and (3) refer to Fig. 1.3. (a) see Chang, K. (1968), 157.

Taiwanese farmer. No question was asked how the Japanese obtained the land in the first place, and the confiscated land was never returned to the pre-war Taiwanese owners, but rather sold to the new set of Taiwanese farmers.

To the KMT government "Land-to-the-Tiller" program was costless. The Americans helped with the technical and financial aspects of the program. The land sold as public land to the Taiwanese farmers and the four "public" corporations sold to the Taiwanese landlords were all confiscated from the Japanese after the war (see LHS of Fig. 1.3). One reason that land could be compulsorily bought and land reform could be "smoothly" implemented (Li, 1988, 61) was that the Chinese-speaking carpetbagger government officials did not hold any piece of land in the newly acquired territory. The transformation of land ownership was touted by the government as "peaceful and harmonious" (Chen, 1961, 78) and a great success (ibid., Preface). The 106,000 landlords who bore the bad name of "exploiters" and who were treated unfairly by the government (Lin, 1973, 57; Ho, 1978, 166) never raised a voice of complaint or opposition, although they were generally well-educated (in the Japanese system) and were leaders of Taiwanese villages.

Few economists and writers have noticed that the "success" of land reform was achieved only two years after the February 28, 1947, massacre of the Taiwanese (Hsiao, 1992, 101). The society was still in fear of government retribution (Lee, 1986, 252–254). The fear was aggravated by daily newspaper reports of the cruelty of the communist peasants in China who "struggle to settle accounts (Qingsuan Douzheng)" with the landlords via killings and executions. Another important "coincidence" was that when the tenants were signing new leases, a general house-to-house probe (supposedly to flush out communist insurgents) of the whole island was carried out (on May 1, 1949). More than 1,500 people were reported to have been arrested (ibid., 254), enough to quell any disobedience. Furthermore, martial law was re-imposed three weeks later on the whole island on May 20, 1949.

The government vowed to suppress any disturbances ruthlessly. They issued such statements as: "Under the law, those who disturb public peace will be executed" (ibid., 254; Sasamoto and Kawano, 1968, 956–960). Thus few landlords resisted. They even "volunteered" under such an authoritarian atmosphere. When it was reported that the landlords in Taizhong area would not sign the new lease, the Taiwan Provincial Governor Chen Cheng came to tour Taizhong. During his tour, Chen uttered the following: "Somebody may be mischievous and doesn't care about the face, but I am sure nobody doesn't care about his life." "This one sentence solved the problem of signing the new lease" (ibid., 252). The landlords knew Governor Chen's threats were credible. For instance, his ruthlessness was amply demonstrated by his mass arrest of students during that period (Kerr, 1965, 369).

1.5.2.2 *Establishment of the Republic of China on Taiwan*

During this period, domestic war was razing on the Chinese mainland, and in October 1949 the People's Republic of China (hereafter called the Chinese Government) was established. The KMT government fled to Taiwan in December of that year and in March 1950 Chiang Kai-sek declared himself the President of the Republic of China on Taiwan (hereafter called the KMT government). These events had several profound economic effects.

Economic independence. With the establishment of The People's Republic of China, Taiwan became a de facto independent country, completely separated from China politically and economically.

The effects were profound. Taiwan had lost both of its closest trading partners, Japan and China, immediately after the war, forcing it to reorganize its economic and trade structures. In retrospect, although Taiwan lost these two export markets, the losses were blessing in disguise. The separation from Japan prevented Japanese goods from flooding Taiwanese markets, thus protecting Taiwan's infant industries. The separation from

China, on the other hand, prevented the plundering of Taiwanese resources by the Chinese "central" government.

Taiwan's independence created abundant investment opportunities in light industries producing daily necessities for the vastly increased population after the war. Another advantage of independence was that, unlike the Japanese colonial time, any profits and export surpluses could be retained in Taiwan for reinvestment.

Overlapping government structures. The KMT's "Government of the Republic of China on Taiwan" has overlapped with "The Taiwan Provincial Government." Both controlled exactly the same area of Taiwan, the only difference being that the former also controls China's two offshore small islands, Quemoy and Matsu (CYB, 1972–1973, Chapter 8). Thus, on Taiwanese soil, there are in effect two "central" governments competing the same tax bases and sphere of operations, resulting in redundancy and inefficiency (Gold, 1986, 59–61).

At the beginning, there was confusion between the two governments concerning which was really in charge of economic policy (Lin, 1968, 40). However, as the prospect of "recovering the mainland" dimmed, the KMT regime started settling down in Taiwan and took charge of Taiwan's economy.

Chiang Kai-sek and his followers, complete with the Chinese government organizations and "National Assembly" elected in China before 1949, now moved into the building of the Government-General, the symbol of the Japanese colonial empire, literally and figuratively. The carpetbaggers ran the government with an iron hand, and spoke a language different from the Taiwanese or the Japanese. Taiwan was considered a temporary base for these Chinese. At least for the first fifteen years, "recovering the mainland" from communist control was the ultimate purpose of government policy. Economic development and social progress in Taiwan were of secondary importance (Jacoby, 1966, 137, 144, 169, 221, 223). In fact, serious economic reconstruction of Taiwan occurred only in the mid-1970s when the government announced the "Ten Great Reconstruction" program.

One-family oligarchy. Fortunately for Taiwan's future, three of the KMT ruling group's corrupting "Four Families" (People's University, 1979, Chapters 9, 12; Jiang, 1985, 293–323) and many of the KMT leaders did not follow Chiang to Taiwan (Clubb, 1964, 310, 274; Kerr, 1965, 384). The KMT regime in Taiwan "had become a One-family oligarchy instead of a Four-Family hierarchy" (Clubb, ibid., 310).

To be sure, there were differences in opinion among the Chinese bureaucrats about the direction of economic development of Taiwan (Gold, 1986, 124). However, the dominance of the one family oligarchy was never threatened. With less significant conflicts of interest among the ruling groups and less "exploitation" by "bureaucratic capital" of the nation's wealth, implementation of Taiwan's national economic policy was much easier than it would have been otherwise.[23]

Imported human capital. Among Chiang's loyal followers were Western-educated, English-speaking, engineer-turned-economic technocrats.[24] Most of them were ranking officials of the Ministry of Finance, the Ministry of Economic Affairs, the Council for U.S. Aid (CUSA, 1948–1962), Council for International Economic Cooperation and Development (CIECD, 1963–76) (Tien, 1989, 125–29).

They were able to communicate with, and learned from, the American experts (Jacoby, 1966, 61, 132–133). These followers of Chiang were given semi-autonomous status to develop economic policies. They functioned outside of the regular ministries (ibid., 60–61, 222–223; Lin, 1973, footnotes in 75, 83, 84; Gold, 1986, 67–69). These technocrats were the human capital imported directly from China that were able to contribute to Taiwanese economic development.[25]

Refugees and soldiers. As Chiang's family fled to Taiwan at the end of 1949, large numbers of Chinese civilians and soldiers also immigrated to Taiwan (we will call them the Chinese). Table 1.3 presents an estimate of the population of Chinese civilian refugees (Civ) and soldiers (Sld) in

[23]As an example, at the time of this writing (April 6, 1993), the newspaper reported that the long awaited President Clinton's $16.3 billion economic stimulus package failed to pass the Senate as a result of Republican filibusters, showing the importance of consensus in policy making.

[24]Kirby (1990), 123; Fairbank (1967), 74. Incidentally, the professional economists in Taiwan at that time were not quantitatively trained. Many of them were either disguised Marxists or anti-Marxists, and few were Keynesians.

[25]To explain "the riddle" of Hong Kong's rapid economic growth in ten years after the war, and to compare it with the slow growth of the Taiwanese economy, it was observed (Szczepanik, 1958, 5) that "the newcomers to Taiwan . . . had difficulty in merging with the predominantly Fukienese indigenous population, speaking different language and thinking in different political terms." There are two kinds of Chinese, ". . . the refugees who went to Taiwan were . . . a group ready to rule or fight but not to work. Refugees in Hong Kong were determined to survive through toil." It seems that there was a third kind of Chinese refugee who was suited very well to the U.S. AID Mission and made contributions.

Table 1.3: Estimation of Chinese Refugees in Taiwan after WWII 1946–1961

	TtlPop(1000)		Chinese pop							Taiwanese pop and burden					
	Total	Total				%ttl		Gr rates		Twnse Pop			Twnse Farm labor		
	with	with	No.	No.	No.	%	%	%	%	No.	%	%	No.	%	%
	Civ	Sld	Civ	Sld	Ttl	Sld	Chi	Pop	Chn		Sld	Chi		Sld	Chn
Col	a	b	c	d=	e=	f=	g=	h	i	j=	k=	l=	m	n=	o=
yr				b-a	c+d	d/b	e/b	fm b	fm e	a-c	d/j	e/j		d/m	e/m
46	6091	6151	32	60	92	1.0	1.5			6059	1.0	1.5	1555	3.9	5.9
47	6495	6542	59	47	106	0.7	1.6	6.4	15.2	6436	0.7	1.6	1662	2.8	6.4
48	6806	6853	127	47	174	0.7	2.5	4.8	64.2	6679	0.7	2.6	1666	2.8	10.4
49	7397	7708	417	311	728	4.0	9.4	12.5	318.4	6980	4.5	10.4	1717	18.1	42.4
50	7554	8056	525	502	1027	6.2	12.7	4.5	41.1	7029	7.1	14.6	1731	29.0	59.3
51	7869	8471	601	602	1203	7.1	14.2	5.2	17.1	7268	8.3	16.6	1738	34.6	69.2
52	8128	8730	650	602	1252	6.9	14.3	3.1	4.1	7478	8.1	16.7	1735	34.7	72.2
53	8438	9041	714	603	1317	6.7	14.6	3.6	5.2	7724	7.8	17.1	1754	34.4	75.1
54	8749	9350	766	601	1367	6.4	14.6	3.4	3.8	7983	7.5	17.1	1754	34.3	77.9
55	9078	9691	853	613	1466	6.3	15.1	3.6	7.2	8225	7.5	17.8	1737	35.3	84.4
56	9390	10003	945	613	1558	6.1	15.6	3.2	6.3	8445	7.3	18.4	1718	35.7	90.7
57	9690	10303	1014	613	1627	5.9	15.8	3.0	4.4	8676	7.1	18.8	1710	35.8	95.1
58	10039	10649	1096	610	1706	5.7	16.0	3.4	4.9	8943	6.8	19.1	1705	35.8	100.1
59	10431	11031	1191	600	1791	5.4	16.2	3.6	5.0	9240	6.5	19.4	1739	34.5	103.0
60	10792	11392	1279	600	1879	5.3	16.5	3.3	4.9	9513	6.3	19.8	1755	34.2	107.1
61	11149	11749	1361	600	1961	5.1	16.7	3.1	4.4	9788	6.1	20.0	1781	33.7	110.1
Average %, 1946–61								4.4	33.7						
Average %, 1950–61											7.2	17.9	1738	34.3	87.0
Average Taiwanese Burden, 1950–61											13.9	5.6		2.9	1.1

Notes: Col. a. The civilian population, including the Taiwanese and Chinese. Col. c. Chinese civilian population (civ) in Taiwan. Both cols. a and c are based on *Statistical Abstract of the Republic of China*, 1966, Directorate-General of Budgets, Accounts, and Statistics, Executive Yuan, 38–39. Also see "Summary of Household Statistics of the Taiwan Province" 1962, as quoted in Sasamoto and Kawano (1968), 77. Col. b. Total Population including soldiers. From Ho (1974), 314. Col. j the Taiwanese population, not including the Chinese refugees and soldiers. Col. m. Population of the Taiwanese farmers, taken from Chang, K. (1968), 176. Col. i. Bordered cells indicate a sudden increase in population for each event. Growth rates in cols. h and i are annual discrete growth rates calculated from cols. b and e.

cols. c and d, respectively, and the total Chinese immigrants in col. e. Taiwan's total civilian population (including the Chinese civilian) is in col. a and Taiwan's population including the Chinese civilian and soldiers are in col. b.

In six years, from 1945 to 1951, Taiwan's total population (including Civ and Sld) increased from 6.059 million[26] to 8.471 million (col. (b)). The population density in 1951 was 613 persons per square mile, one of the highest in the world (Sasamoto and Kawano, 1968, 77; Hsiao and Hsiao, 1983). The nearly 2.4 million increase during this period comprised of about one half from natural growth of the resident Taiwanese population, the other half to immigrants from China (col. (e)). Among these Chinese, half were civilians and half were soldiers (cols. (c) and (d)). During the 1950s, the new immigrants constituted approximately 14 to 16 percent of the total population (col. (g)), 5 to 7 percent of which were soldiers (col. (f)). Column h shows the growth rate of total population, and col. i shows the growth rate of Chinese population. Most of the Chinese immigration occurred from 1947 to 1951, with increase of 318 percent (728,000) in 1949 when the Chiang Kai-sek's government retreated to Taiwan. The bordered cells in col. i show the surge of Chinese population in the 1950s. The surge tapered off after 1960.

Columns (k) and (l) show the percentages of Chinese soldiers and the total Chinese population as the proportion of Taiwan's population from 1946 to 1961. The columns shows that, in 1951, Chinese soldiers consisted of 8.3 percent, and the total Chinese including the soldiers consisted of 16.6 percent of the local Taiwanese population. It even went up to 20 percent of the Taiwanese population in 1961.

This means that after 1950, on average, every 5 to 6 Taiwanese had to support one Chinese, and about every 14 Taiwanese had to support one Chinese soldier (Calculated as $100/7.2 = 13.9$ in the last two rows) (Hsiao and Hsiao, 1996).

The burden is staggering when only the Taiwanese farm laborers were taken into account. The last two columns show the percentages of soldiers and Chinese as compared with the number of the Taiwanese farm laborers. The last row shows that after 1950, every 3 Taiwanese farm laborers had to support an average of one Chinese soldier, and every 1.1 farm

[26]In 1943, the Taiwanese population was 6.134 million (not including 0.397 million Japanese), see OS16 (1949), 4–5. From 1946 number in Table 1.3, we estimate that the 1946 Taiwanese population was $6.091 - 0.032 = 6.059$ million.

labor supported approximately one unproductive Chinese soldier, refugee, or bureaucrat. By 1958, the number of Chinese immigrants is the same as the number of the farm laborers (col. (o)). The Chinese immigrants exceeded the Taiwanese farm labors afterward, as shown by percentage larger than 100 in the last column, further increasing the burden of the farm labors.

This was the real burden for the Taiwanese when Taiwan was reprocessed into China after WWII. For the KMT government, securing a steady supply of food for these Chinese was the utmost political concern during the recovery period.

By the end of 1961, a total of about 2.0 million Chinese immigrated to Taiwan[27] (col. (e)). The poor refugees lived in shantytowns in vacant spaces around major cities all over Taiwan, adding an even greater burden to the already fragile Taiwanese economy.

Aside from the soldiers, the civilian refugees after 1949 were generally more educated. We have estimated that among the 650,000 Chinese civilian refugees between 1946 to 1952 (see col. (c)), about 8.5 percent (or 55,000) of the immigrants were college educated and about 43 percent (or 279,000) had high school education.[28] Before immigrating, they had been landlords or village bosses in China. Thus it is reasonable to conclude that at least in

---

[27]Column i of Table 1.3 shows that in addition to the immigration wave in 1949, Chinese immigrants surged in 1953, 1955, and 1958. In 1953, many communist Chinese prisoners from the Korean War arrived in Taiwan. In 1955 the Ta-chen Islanders arrived after their islands were evacuated, and 1958 some Quemoy islanders evacuated to Taiwan. See Sasamoto and Kawamoto (1968), 78.

[28]This is estimated as follows. In 1946 when the massive Chinese immigration had barely started, there were 19,000 people in Taiwan with college education, and 183,000 with high school education (Lin, 1973, 52). The numbers in 1952 were 86,000 (an increase of 352.63 percent over the six years) and 564,000 (208.2 percent increase), respectively; in 1958 they were 139,000 (+61.68%) and 878.000 (+55.67%); in 1964 they were 225,000 (+61.87%) and 1,511,000 (+72.1%), respectively (TSDB, 1977, 6). Hence we may reasonably assume that the "natural" increase from 1946 to 1952 was 61.63 percent for college graduates and 55.67 percent for the high school graduates.

If this is the case, the "excess" rates of increase from 1946 to 1952 would be 291 percent and 152.52 percent, respectively. From 1946 data, this implies that 55,000 of college graduates and 279,000 of high school graduates could be accounted for by the inclusion of Chinese immigrants. From col. (c) of Table 1.3, the Chinese civilian immigrants from 1946 to 1952 were 650,000. This gives the percentages in the text.

Note that the first number in the 1946 data by Lin above is consistent with Wu (1986) estimate of the Taiwanese college graduates at the end of the War, as we quoted at the end of Section 1.4. The second number seems too high compared with our estimation in the same section.

the early 50s, about half of the refugees in Taiwan were educated, staunchly anti-communist middle class Chinese.

Most of them were employed at all levels within the government, the military forces, and various public enterprises. Although they may also be regarded as imported human capital, they were very much isolated from the general Taiwanese community. It is not clear how much of a contribution they made to Taiwanese economic development. Undoubtedly, however, their existence has reinforced the political power of the KMT government and contributed to the stability of Taiwanese society.

Martial law. As mentioned earlier, in May 1949 the KMT government suspended the constitution and ruled the country by martial law. It lasted for 38 years until July 1987. At the same time, the KMT continued to maintain approximately 600,000 combat-ready soldiers, along with a massive staff of policemen and other security personnel.[29] The Pao-chia system of the Japanese colonists was maintained and expanded after the war, a system in which citizens watched their neighbors closely on behalf of the government (Chen, 1975).

For almost forty years, labor unions were strictly regulated and controlled by the government. Labor unrest and strikes were, in effect, illegal (Deyo, 1989, 115–118, 133–134; Arrigo, 1984, 9). Local objection to pollution and environmental concerns was simply ignored or suppressed. These were some of the important factors involved in attracting direct foreign investment to Taiwan. The terror under martial law and the tension from the warring state with China was generally felt (Arrigo, 1984, 8) until martial law was lifted in 1987.

Infusion of Chinese textile capital. Among the Chinese refugees were technicians and entrepreneurs (Ho, 1978, 105). In 1961, there were 22 large cotton textile companies in Taiwan. Eleven firms were established between 1948 to 1951, and ten of them were owned by the Chinese from Shanghai (Sasamoto and Kawano, 1968, 663). The other eleven firms were established between 1954 and 1960, six of them were Chinese-owned.[30] All of the nine wool textile companies and some of the synthetic fiber companies were also

[29]There is a network of nine security agencies including: Investigation Bureau and Taiwan Garrison Command, and numerous covert activities (see Gold, 1986, 62–63).

[30]At the end of the war, there were six textile companies, with a total of 10,664 spindles and 400 looms. The main products were low quality hemp textiles. According to the Japanese classification, a company with less than 50,000 spindles is called small and medium scale; with 500,000 spindles, a super company; in-between is called large

started by the Chinese in this period (ibid., 1968, 664–669). These Chinese-owned firms were vanguards of the new import-substitution policy. They solved, at least in part, the domestic needs of importing textile products after the Taiwanese economy was separated from Japan and China. At the same time, they stimulated the establishment of local Taiwanese-owned textile firms.

1.5.2.3 *U.S. Economic Aid*

While Taiwan was in great turmoil in 1949 and threatened by the prospect of a Chinese invasion (Clubb, 1964, 337), the Korean War broke out on June 25, 1950. The United States responded immediately by sending the American Seventh Fleet to patrol the Formosa Strait, and resumed U.S. aid to the Republic of China.[31] Taiwan was considered essential in the U.S. policy of containing communist expansion. From June 1951 to June 1965, US$1,465 million of economic aid was earmarked for Taiwan, averaging about $100 million a year (Jacoby, 1966, 38), about 6 percent of Taiwan's GNP during this period (Chang, 1974, 81).

U.S. aid to Taiwan was very generous. In fact, among the Asian developing countries, from 1950 to 1959, annual per capita U.S. aid was $8.56 for Taiwan, next only to Korea ($10.04), Vietnam ($19.90), and Laos

(Sasamoto and Kawai, 1968, 676). Thus the "large" textile firms in Taiwan are some of the smallest firms in Japan.

In addition to the textile plants, large amounts of money in the form of foreign exchange and gold and silver flew into Taiwan. From September 1948 to December 1948, the Chinese remitted 300 billion Old Taiwan Dollars from Shanghai to Taiwan. This amount is 30 percent higher than the currency issued by the Bank of Taiwan at the end of the year. Although most of the money were for military uses, where the money came from and went to was a mystery (Liu, 1975, 213).

[31]As early as in 1945, the Republic of China was aided by the United Nations Relief and Rehabilitation Administration (UNNRA) with US $658 million, 72 percent of which was contributed by the United States. "UNNRA was often diverted to fatten the account of Chinese officials, or else rusted or rotted in warehouse." (Clubb, 273, 276). In April 1948, the U.S.Congress passed the China Aid Act. After the publication of the China White Paper in August 1949, the United States, refraining from interfering the internal war in China, halted the military aid in January 1950. However, Taiwan continued to receive about $18 million worth of U.S. Aid from 1948 to February 15, 1950, and another $8.5 million from February 15, 1950 to June 30, 1950 (Sasamoto and Kawno, 1968, 291). From June 1952 to June 1962, U.S. Aid was based on the Mutual Security Act (MSA) of October 20, 1951, and from June 1962 to June 1965, on the Act for International Development of September 1961. Congress also passed the Agricultural Trade Development and Assistance Act of 1954 (commonly called Public Law 480 Program) to make agricultural aid (ibid., 291–296).

($23.30), and was followed by Cambodia ($7.68). All other countries in Asia received less than $3.00 per capita.[32]

In addition, total US military assistance to Taiwan over the fifteen-year period (1951–1965) amounted to about US$2.5 billion. This averaged about $170 million a year (Jacoby, 1966, 118). Altogether, U.S. economic and military aid consisted of about 4 percent of total U.S. foreign aid of US$100 billion during 1945–1965 (ibid., 3).

The American military and civilian presence in Taiwan had three major consequences. Externally, the Seventh Fleet kept the KMT regime from attempting an armed invasion of China (ibid., 137). At the same time it protected Taiwan from Chinese invasion, ensuring peace in the Taiwan area by force (ibid., 115). The lower part of Fig. 1.4 dramatizes the importance of the American fleet.

Internally, the watchful eyes of the American big brothers supervising U.S. Aid in Taiwan, along with the deep reflection of the ignominious failure of the KMT on the mainland, probably contributed to the relatively successful administrative reform of the KMT government.[33] U.S. personnel also exerted a strong influence on government policies (Ibid., 11, 24, 134–135, 244). Crude corruption and explicit plundering disappeared. "Democracy" and "freedom," at least officially, were upheld to please the Americans and to distinguish the KMT regime now from the oppressive communist regime in China. Furthermore, the aid program contributed political and economic stability in Taiwan. It paved the way for rapid economic growth during and after the 1960s (see the upper part of

---

[32]Economic Survey of Asia and Far East. 1961, 49, as quoted in Chang, II (1974), 81. From 1946 to 1966, in terms of total amount of AID economic assistance, Korea received $2,647 (all the following numbers are in million U.S. dollars), Japan, $22. Other large receivers included West Germany ($1,472), Italy ($1,650), Turkey ($1,741), Pakistan ($1,844), Vietnam ($2,670), India ($2,795), France ($3,190), and U.K. ($3,835). In terms of total amount of non-AID economic assistance, Taiwan received $341 from Food for Peace (Public Law 480) program (the first number below), plus $580 from other non-AID program (the second number below). Korea received $753 + $860, and Japan, $170 + $2,708. Other large receivers were Italy ($464 + $1,666), France ($19 + $1,942), and U.K. ($0.3 + $4,175). See AID (1967), Tables No. 1 and 2, 284–289. Thus Taiwan was not the largest receiver of U.S. Aid.

[33]For the KMT reform and party system in Taiwan, see Tien (1989, Chapter 4). Deep reflection alone may not make the government effective (see Kerr, 1965, Part 4, Appendix). U.S. Aid alone may not be effective either, as demonstrated by the experiences of U.N. and U.S. development assistance in pre-1949 China, as well as in other countries.

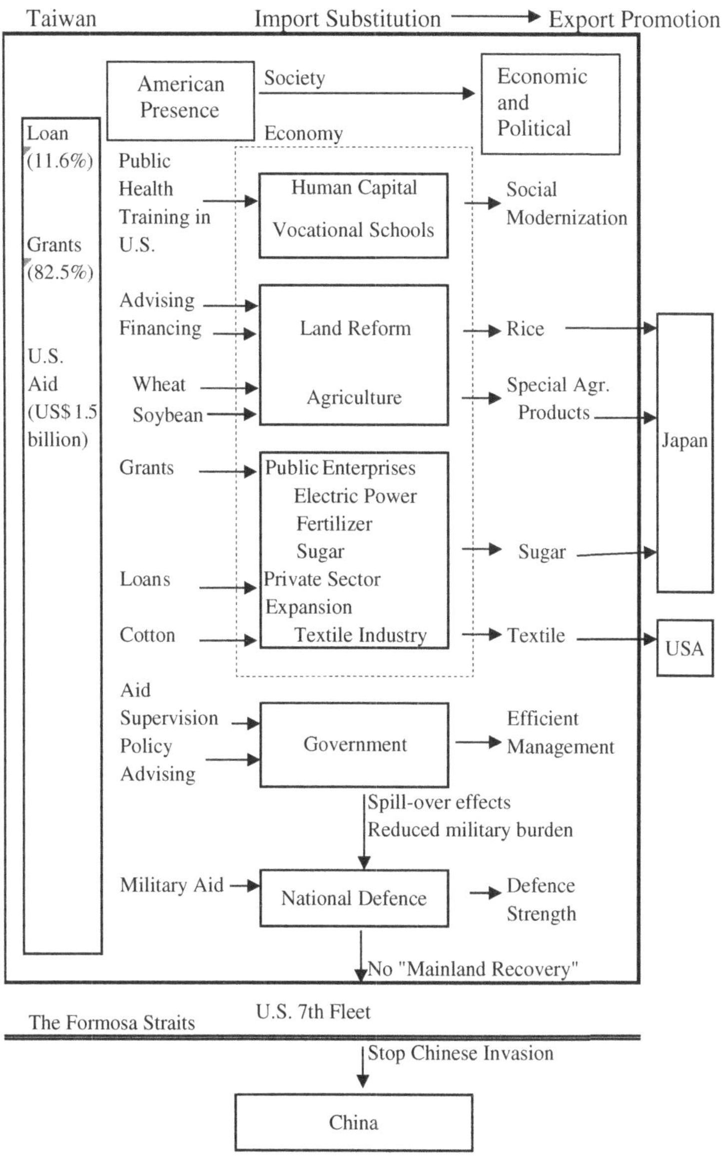

Figure 1.4: The Effects of U.S. Aid on the Taiwanese Economy 1951–65

Fig. 1.4). U.S. aid had other consequences, as will be explained in the following sections on military and infrastructure (Section 1.7.2), the textile industry (Section 1.7.3.5), its role in developing Taiwan's private industries, economic planning (Section 1.7.3.7), and Taiwan's trade policy reform in the early 1960s (Section 1.11).

1.6 Initial Conditions

Economic recovery began in the early 1950s after the chaotic period. We have shown that, before the war, an advanced agricultural sector completed the phase of primary export-led growth, while an industrial sector was already in the initial stage of the import-substitution phase, during which an economic policy of self-sufficiency was adopted. The island was still fertile and productive, and the Taiwanese people were well disciplined, educated, and diligent. Basic social and economic infrastructure like modern transportation (highways, railroads, and harbors), communication (telephones and telegraphs), schools for all levels of education, irrigation and flood control, and electric power and facilities were already in place, saving the KMT government considerable initial investment in infrastructure at the beginning of the post-war economic recovery (Chang, II, 1974, 79).

The infrastructure built by the Japanese was overused due to the sudden influx of Chinese refugees and the large natural increase in the Taiwanese population after the war. Furthermore, despite U.S. advice recommending military reduction (Jacoby, 1966, 122), the KMT government maintained 600,000 soldiers during and after the U.S. aid period. In 1953, Taiwan had one of the largest military forces in the world, 6.3 percent, measured as a percent of the population. (ibid., 118). Maintaining such a large military proved burdensome. In fact, "During 1951–65, military expenditures averaged 9 to 11 percent of the GNP, even more than in the rich and advanced economy of the United States. They consistently formed about 85 percent of the outlays of the national government, and around 50 percent of the combined outlays of government at all levels" (ibid.). The government had huge deficit spending (Chiang, 1971, 2) and Taiwan's fiscal future appeared bleak.

Under these initial conditions, the natural approach for survival was to return to the phase of primary export-led growth of the colonial period. This entailed earning foreign exchange by exporting traditional products of sugar and rice while also developing the existing industries and encouraging and protecting the new import substituting industries, such as textile and fertilizer, to save precious foreign exchange. Domestically, with U.S. aid on one hand and the KMT's iron hand on the other, the government implemented schemes that taxed consumers heavily and extracted contributions from (or exploited) Taiwanese farmers and laborers. We now explain the processes involved at the inception of economic development during this period.

We have shown that up to the mid-1950s, in terms of the production structure, labor composition, and the trade structure, Taiwanese industrialization was an expansion and extension of the industrial base already established during the Japanese regime. It might be useful to put the Taiwanese economy into international perspective. Table 1.4 shows per capita GNP of Taiwan in comparison with the Republic of Korea (Korea), Japan, China, Brazil, and the Netherlands. In 1961, Taiwan, along with Korea, was ranked in the fifth category (from US$100 to US$250), Japan and Brazil were in the fourth (US$250 to US$500), and China was in the lowest, or sixth, category (below US$100).

Similarly, the Harbison-Meyer Human Resource Development Composite Index (HRDCI for secondary and higher education) put Taiwan and Korea in Level III (semi-advanced, along with 21 other countries), while Japan and the Netherlands were in Level IV (advanced, 16 countries).

Table 1.4: Some Development Indicators of Taiwan (in U.S. $)

Year	Taiwan	Korea	Japan	China	Brazil	Netherland
PER CAPITA GNP						
1961 (a)	116	106	383	83	268	954
Rkg (a)	V	V	IV	VI	IV	III
1961 (b)	145	73	502			
1990 (c)	7954	5400	25430	370	2680	17320
1965–90 (d)	(15.5)	7.1	4.1	5.8	3.3	1.8
HUMAN RESOURCE DEVELOPMENT COMPOSITION INDEX						
HRDCI (e)	53.9	55	111.4	19.5	20.9	133.7
Rkg (e)	III	III	IV	II	II	IV

Sources: (a) Higgins (1968), 852, (b) Adelman and Morris (1967), 88, (c) the Taiwanese data are from TSDB (1992), 30. Others are from WDR (1992), Table 1. (d) Taiwan's growth rates are calcualted by the authors as the average annual growth rate of per capita GNP in US Dollars, taken from TSDB (1992), 30. The source of other data is the same as (c), (e) Harbison-Myers' HRDCI is taken from Higgins (1968), 22.

China and Brazil were in Level II (partially developed, 21 countries). Level I consisted of 17 underdeveloped countries (Higgins, 1968, 22).

Although we don't have data prior to 1953, when Taiwanese economic development began in earnest, we are certain that Taiwan already had developed economically and socially in 1953 in comparison to many other developing countries.[34] An interesting observation is that in both sources cited in Table 1.4, Japan was classified as an "underdeveloped" country, only slightly more advanced than Taiwan and Korea. This is consistent with our earlier observation that Taiwan and Japan were close in terms of living standards immediately after the war.

1.7 Recovery and Import Substitution Period (1953–1963)

We use 1953 as the start of the recovery period, for in this year the "Land-to-the-tiller" program had been completed. The economy had recovered from war damages (see Table 1.1), and inflation subsided considerably. The first four-year plan was implemented in this year, indicating that the economy had settled down and the government had started to take economic development rather seriously.

1.7.1 *Government Tax and Revenue System*

As in many other countries, the first and the foremost tool for supporting heavy government expenditures would be tax revenues. In a small country like Taiwan, there are four levels of government: central, Taiwan provincial, hsian and municipal, and village and town. The government revenues increased on average 15 to 30 percent every year from 1955 to 1990 (see Table 1.5. The figures in col. (3), Table 1.5, are five year average annual growth rate), on average, more than doubling every five years (col. (2)). This is due to rapid growth in the Taiwanese economy. However, the tax burden as percentage of GNP, that is, the tax ratio (col. (10)), did not decrease. Instead, it increased steadily from 15 to 20 percent over the 35-year period, however, the ratio of total government expenditures to GNP increased rather slowly from 20 to 28 percent (col. (9)). These proportions

[34] An extensive ranking of Taiwan in terms of social, political, and economic indicators during the 1950s, along with other 74 developing countries, can be found in Adelman and Morris (1967). Their data were used to compare the initial conditions of Taiwanese and Indian economic development (Hsiao and Hsiao, 2005).

Table 1.5: The Structure of the Government Finance

	Total		Cntrl Gov't		Local Gov. Subsidies			Ratio	
	Rev All lvl	Av.an. Gr rate	% of tt Rev.	Av.an. Gr rate	Prov.	Hsien Muni	Village &Town	Tax/GNP	Exp/GNP
(1)	(2)	(3)	(4)	(5)	(6)	(7)	(8)	(9)	(10)
	b NT$	%	%	%	%	%	%	%	%
1955	7.8		49.6					19.8	15
1960	15.4	19.1	51.4	20.6	4.4		47.1	21.0	14.9
1965	26.5	14.6	56.6	18.1	1.8		40.7	21.0	14.3
1970	57.2	23.1	59.8	25.6	3.6	37.8	25.8	23.4	17.4
1975	142.1	29.7	58.8	28.8	12.6	45.2	35.8	22.8	17.6
1980	371.7	32.3	64.1	37	21.3	49.9	36.1	25.9	19.6
1985	653.8	15.2	64	15.1	21.2	39.4	32.3	23.0	16.1
1990	1180.6	16.1	67.2	17.9	26.4	37.7	51.4	28.1	20.4

Sources: 1955–65, from Statistical Abstract of Republic of China, 1966, 1969. 1970–1990, from Sumiya (1992), 243, 246. Col. (3) is five year growth rates divided by 5 to obtain 5 year average annual growth rates. Col. 4 is derived from 100 percent minus the sum of the three local government subsidy percentage distribution from the Central Government obtained in ibid., 246. Col. 5 is obtained in two steps. A. multiply col. (2) by col. (4) to obtain the revenue of Central Government. B. From the results in A, we calculate the five year growth rates of the Central Government revenue divided by 5. Column (6) to (8) are from ibid., 243. Col. (9), TSDB (1975), 148; (1992), 159. Col. (10), TSDB (1975), 155; (1992), 166. Note that there are slight discrepancies in the data listed in TSDB (1975) and (1992).

were relatively high among developing countries, almost twice as high as that of Japan, and comparable to that of the United States (WT, 1976, 444–445). Since tax revenues were also increasing, central and local governments have had common surpluses almost every year since 1965 (TSDB, 1992, 154; Yu and Chen, 1982, 195).

The central government increasingly grabbed 50 percent to 67 percent of total government revenues (col. (4)). This revenue usage is generally lower than other developing countries, but higher than most developed nations (WT, 1976, 444). The central government's revenues also grew faster than total government revenues (col. (5)). With its control of revenues, the central government exerts enormous influence on local governments through subsidies. For example, the Taiwanese provincial government has received about a quarter of its budget in subsidies in recent years (col. (6)). The subsidies at the lowest level of government amounted to one third to one

Table 1.6: The Structure of the Central Government Finance

(in %)

Yr	REVENUES (100%) Taxes Total tax (c) %		Drct tax	Indirect tax sum	Cust. Duty	Commodity	Other taxes	Monopoly	Public Enterprises	Other rev (a)	EXPENDITURES (100%) Dfnce & Gen Adm Total Exp (1)	(c) %	Defence (2)	Gen. Adm (3)	Social Sec. (4)	Econ. devpmt. (5)	(c) %	Edu. Sci. Cul. (6)	(c) %	Sub. to local gov. (7)	Others (b) (8)
1955	55	(62)	*		*	*	*	20	3	22	81	(64)	-	-	-	1	(11)	2	(14)	11	6
1960	55	(57)	7	48	17	11	19	17	7	21	85	(61)	-	-	1	1	(14)	3	(14)	4	6
1965	51	(51)	7	44	14	13	17	14	12	23	69	(54)	-	-	2	2	(19)	4	(13)	2	21
1970	61	(60)	9	52	27	19	6	12	11	16	66	(49)	58	9	10	7	(18)	6	(16)	2	9
1975	68	(63)	17	51	29	17	5	10	14	8	55	(39)	40	14	11	18	(30)	6	(16)	6	5
1980	70	(64)	18	52	26	19	7	7	12	11	44	(39)	39	6	13	26	(32)	7	(15)	7	3
1985	59	(61)	21	38	19	15	4	8	20	14	45	(35)	38	7	17	18	(25)	12	(20)	3	6
1990	59	(66)	25	34	13	10	10	5	14	22	40	(29)	31	8	19	16	(26)	15	(20)	2	9

Sources: 1955–1965, from Chiang (1971), 7, 17. 1955, 1960, and 1965 data are the average of 1953–56, 1957–60, and 1965–68, respectively. Thus they are not stricly comparable with the yearly data of the later years. *These columns for 1960 and 1965 are yearly data calculated directly from Statistical Abstract (1966). 1970–1990 data are yearly, taken from Sumiya *et al.* (1992), 244, 254. (a) = 100 − (Tax + Mono + Pub). (b) = 100 − ((1) + (4) + ⋯ + (7)). (c) The number in the parenthesis is the pecentage of the corresponding column on the left for *all* levels of governments, taken from TSDB (1992), 156, 158.

half of their budgets (cols. (7) and (8)). Under such a tight fiscal control, one may wonder what kind of self-governing and local construction could be performed by the local people.

In the early 1950s and even until recently, the government relied heavily on indirect taxes. Table 1.6 presents the composition of central government revenues and expenditures along with the corresponding figures for all levels of government. Most of them are custom duties ("Cus.Du" in the Table) and commodity taxes (denoted as "Commodity"). The main commodities taxed are sugar, cotton threads, cement, wood, etc. (Sasamoto and Kawano, 1968, 263).

Monopoly revenues are also a form of a regressive sales tax levied on liquor, cigarettes, and salt. They are some of the "evil" taxes inherited from colonial days. If indirect taxes and monopoly revenues are added, then Taiwan has had one of the highest indirect tax burdens in the world

(WT, 1976, 436). In recent years, direct taxes (including those on income, land, housing, mining lot, estate, and deeds) have increased to about a quarter of total revenues. However, direct tax revenues are still far behind the indirect revenues.

Enterprise revenues include profits from public enterprises and public utilities. They are also a form of indirect taxes. During the 1950s, public enterprises were so inefficient that they contributed only 3 to 7 percent of the government revenues. During the mid-1970s, thanks to a few successful public enterprises, enterprise revenues surpassed monopoly revenues and became second only to total tax monies in revenue generated.

The bulk of Central Government expenditures (as well as total government expenditures) in the 1950s was on the defense and general administration, 81 percent (or 64 percent of the total) in 1955 (col. (1) on the right hand side of the table). It was one of the highest proportions in the world (WT, 1976, 437). The central government had absolute power and it maintained a huge armed force and employed refugees. This led to bloated military and government bureaucracy.

Central Government expenditures on economic development (col. (5)) was a mere 1 percent until 1960, 2 percent in 1965, and 7 percent in 1970. It maintained at about 20 percent from 1975 to 1990 (col. (5) of the RHS of Table 1.6). In terms of overall government expenditure (see the number in the parentheses next to col. (5)), the percentages are slightly higher. They are 11, 14, 19, and 18 percent, respectively, indicating that more economic development programs were implemented by the local governments. The central government expenditures on education, science, and culture (Col. (6)) have also been meager until the mid-1970s–2 percent in 1955, 7 percent in 1980, and 15 percent in 1990. The corresponding expenditures for overall governments are 14, 15, and 20 percent, respectively. In general, these figures show clearly that the burden of economic and social development was on the local governments, which have a higher proportion of these expenditures in the local budgets. The statistics disclose once again that, for the KMT government, developing Taiwan was only a secondary priority until the mid-1970s.

1.7.2 *Importance of U.S. Aid*

In the 1950s and the 1960s, even with 70 to 85 percent of the central government budget (or 55 to 65 percent of the total government budgets) being devoted completely to defense, an average soldier could receive only

US\$300 to US\$350 per year.[35] Since per capita GNP was between US\$100 to US\$200 per year at that time, the soldiers could barely survive with such a small allocation. Equipping the 600,000 soldiers with modern weapons was completely out of the question. Thus, U.S. aid was indispensable. "Most heavy military equipment, such as planes, ships, and vehicles, was supplied by the U.S. as a grant" (Jacoby, 1966, 118). It amounted to about US \$4,100 per soldier for the 15-year period. Such a large amount of military aid must have had a considerable spill-over effect on economic development. However, a systematic study of its effects are still not available.

In addition to U.S. military aid, as stated in a previous section (Section 1.5.2.3), U.S. economic aid amounted to about US \$1.5 billion from 1951 to 1965. The characteristics of aid may be viewed in five ways, as shown[36] in Fig. 1.5 and explained below.

In the first categorization US aid is classified as projects, non-projects, agricultural or non-agricultural. Under this approach slightly above one quarter (27%) of it was project-type assistance. This aid provided funds to import construction materials, plants, and technology for a specific project, to send domestic technicians abroad for learning, or to invite foreign specialists for consulting (Sasamoto and Kawano, 1968, 302). From 1951 to 1965, the project distributed funds to electric power industry (36%), mining and manufactures (24.2%), transportation (13.2%), agriculture (9%), education (2.4%) and Health and sanitation (1.8%) (TSDB, 1992, 232).

The first column also shows that the other three-fourths (73%) of U.S. economic aid was non-project type assistance applied to purchasing agricultural goods (56%) or non-agricultural materials (17%). From 1951 to 1968, the largest item in non-project-type assistance was raw cotton (24%), wheat (22%), and soybeans (11%). Other agricultural goods included tallow (3%), milk powder (2.5%), wheat flour (2.2%), leaf tobacco (1.6%), etc. The main non-agricultural (industrial) goods included fertilizer (4.6%), metals

[35]In 1955, 1960, and 1965, the budget for defense and general administration was NT \$4.2, 7.4, and 8.6 billion, respectively (TSDB, 1992, 157). We assume all the defense expenditures were used on soldiers during that period (equipment was supplied by US Aid). The (buying) exchange rate for U.S. dollar was NT \$21.5, 40, and 40, respectively (TSDB, 1975, 166). Hence, converting the budget in terms of U.S. dollars, and dividing the number of soldiers listed in col. d of Table 1.3, we arrive at expenditures for 1955, 1960 and 1965 of US \$319, 308, and 358 per soldier.

[36]Columns (1) and (2) of Fig. 1.5 were drawn from Jacoby (1966), 41, 175, cols. (3) and (4) from 175, and col. (5) from 46. Figures in cols. (3) and (4) consist of both U.S. dollar project aid and NT dollar project aid, 1951–1963.

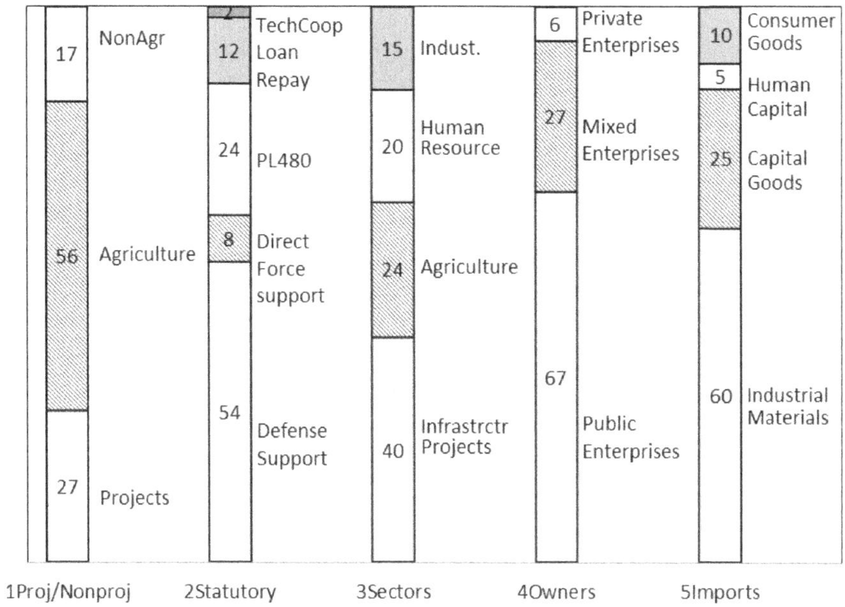

Figure 1.5: Allocation of U.S. Economic Aid
By Kinds of Aid and Sectors, 1951–1965

and manufactures (4.1%), machinery and tools (3.7%), lubricant (3.4%), chemicals (3.0%), pharmaceutical (2.3%), textile products (1.3%), vehicle and parts (1.2%), etc. (TSDB, 1992, 230–231).

The second column of Fig. 1.5 classifies U.S. aid by statutory sources. The largest statutory source was defense support (54%). It was used in financing the commodity import program (Jacoby, 1966, 42). The next largest item was Public Law 480: Food for Peace program (24%), Grant and Loan (12 percent), Direct Forces Support (8 percent), and Technical Cooperation (2%). Thus the main purpose of economic aid is to maintain the KMT government's military forces, although it also had effects on economic development.

The third column classifies aid by sectors of the economy. Funds were distributed to infrastructure, such as electric power projects (40%), to agriculture (24%), to human resources (20%), and to industry (15%). Thus the main purpose of economic aid was to revitalize infrastructure and industry, the main part of which were confiscated from the Japanese after WWII, with minimum maintenance after the war. This lead to the fourth column, which shows that two-thirds (67%) of the funds went to public enterprises, including electric, fertilizer, chemical, and agricultural industries. 27 percent of aid went to (public and private owned) mixed enterprises. Only 6 percent went to help privately owned firms (mostly small and medium Taiwanese enterprises).

The last column classifies aid by imports: Industrial materials for domestic processing (60 percent), capital goods (25%), human capital (knowledge) (5%), and consumer goods (10%). They were complemented by Taiwan's non-aid imports by the KMT government (Jacoby, 1966, 46).

Thus, from the first two categories of the chart, we can see that majority of the US Aid program was directly and indirectly related to the defense supports through imports of industrial materials, including row cotton, for mostly public and also some mixed enterprises, laying the foundation of Taiwan's early industrialization through exporting textile products. Note that the US Aid program was mutually advantageous to both Taiwan and USA economy and defense.

In addition to the original aid in U.S. dollars, there was a local requirement that the recipient country "pay" for aid imports by depositing its currency in a local currency aid fund, jointly overseen by agencies of both governments (Jacoby, 1966, 46–48). From 1952 to 1964, NT$26.8 billion of the local fund was spent on "direct military force" (34%). Agriculture accounted for 16 percent of the local fund, electric power 13 percent, mining and manufactures 9 percent, transportation 7 percent, health and sanitation 4 percent, education 3 percent, community development 2 percent, and others 14 percent (TSDB, 1965, 131; also Sasamoto and Kawano, 1968, 311). A large amount of other items was probably used to close the gap in fiscal deficits (Sasamoto and Kawano, 1968, 310). In both the original U.S. aid and its derived local fund, electric power facilities received the lion's share.[37]

In general, at the beginning of economic development, investment in infrastructure would mean to invest in flood control, irrigation, and drainage of farm land (Ishikawa, 1967, 70), and in basic social construction, like the establishment of a national education system, railroads and highways, telephone and telegraph, etc. However, as we have seen in Section 1.3, these basic structures were already undertaken by the Japanese regime. Thus U.S. aid, which is closely coordinated with the first three of the four-year economic plans of the KMT government, could then concentrate

[37]For the role of electric power industry in economic development in Japan and China, see Kanemaru (1993), 30.

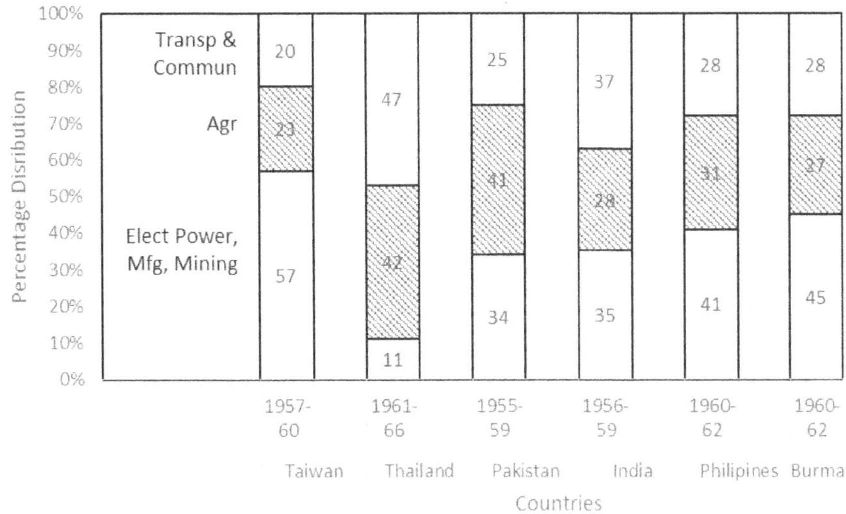

Figure 1.6: Public Investment Planning
Some Asian Countries, in %

Source: UNECFE, *A Decade of Development Planning and Implementation in the ECAFE Region*, Conference of Asian Economic Planners, Session 1, 1961. Taken from Chang, II (1974), 90.

on investments in electric power, mining and manufactures (Chang II, 1974, 89). Figure 1.6 testifies the relative advantage of Taiwan's initial conditions clearly.[38] Among the six developing countries in Asia, the proportion of public investment in Taiwan from 1957 to 1960 in (a) electric power, mining and manufactures was the highest, and its investments in (b) agriculture and (c) transportation and communications are lowest, among these six Asian countries.

1.7.3 *Industrial Development*

This section reviews briefly some major industries during this period. They are three public-owned industries: electric power, fertilizer, and sugar processing, and two private-owned industries: textile and cement. The link between the prewar and the postwar periods in each industry has been

[38]UNECAFE, *A Decade of Development Planning and Implementation in the ECAFE Region*, Conference of Asian Economic Planners 1 Session 1961, taken from Chang, II (1976), 90.

considered. We also examine the dominance of public enterprises and rising of private enterprises.

1.7.3.1 *The Electric Power Industry*

We have seen that the Japanese developed electric power plants in Taiwan before the war. After the war, 24 Japanese hydroelectric and 9 thermoelectric power generating plants were reorganized as government-owned "Taipower" (CEA, 1958, Chapter 2). From 1943 to 1944 before the war, Taipower produced about 1.2 billion kW of electricity, supplying 445,000 households (ibid.), which was about 40 percent of the total households in Taiwan. This was a very respectable number in that period.[39]

From 1952 to 1964, Taipower completed nine hydroelectric plants with 353 million kW capacity and six thermoelectric plants with 458 million kw capacity. Almost all of the projects received U.S. aid, totaling NT$4 billion (for details, see Sasamoto and Kawano, 1968, 702). This aid was almost as much as central government revenues in 1955, about 50 percent of all government revenues in that year. Without U.S. aid, expansion of Taipower was impossible.

In 1952, Taipower produced 1.4 billion kW of electricity. Apparently it took more than five years to recover completely from the war-time destruction. In 1964, about 82 percent was used by industries, and 18 percent by commercial and residential users (Jacoby, 1966, 178). Taipower's production expanded steadily over the years. By 1991, it produced almost 90 billion kW of electricity (TSDB, 1992, 87). Despite the fast and steady growth of electricity output, it appears that demand for electricity outstripped Taipower's ability to supply it. During the U.S. Aid period, Jacoby reports that Taiwan's economy was still plagued by shortages of electricity (Jacoby, 1966, 177).

As in the previous period, development of electricity had strong forward linkages.[40] The availability of inexpensive electric power primarily benefitted (or was used by)[41] large-scale industries, such as fertilizer (21%),

[39]The number of Taiwanese households in 1940 was 1,038,883, which is an increase of 7.27 percent over that of 1937 (OS16, 1949, 8). Assuming the same growth rate, we estimate households in 1943 at around 1,114,410.

[40]Strong forward linkages of electric power industry occurred in Japan but failed in Jiangsu, China, before 1924 (Kanemaru, 1993, 75).

[41]The percentages are the proportions of electric power production used in the industry in 1965 (Chang, 1974, II, Table 12, 92).

iron and steel (9%), aluminum (9%), textile (7%), cement, paper, and caustic soda (each 6%) (Sasamoto and Kawano, 1968, 704).

1.7.3.2 *The Fertilizer Industry*

Development of the fertilizer industry follows the usual pattern of import substitution. Before 1964, the Taiwan Fertilizer Corporation was a government monopoly which consisted of four confiscated Japanese plants (Sasamoto and Kawano, 1968, 683). In 1950 fertilizer production filled only 16 percent of the domestic demand (0.367 million tons), and the remainder had to be imported (Chang, II, 1974, 95). In that year, Taiwan imported US$18 million worth of fertilizer, constituting about 15 percent of Taiwan's total imports. Among them, 60 percent was imported through U.S. aid (Sasamoto and Kawano, 1968, 686). In 1964, the rate of self-sufficiency increased to 79 percent (1.1 million tons, Chang, 1974, II, 95; ibid., 686). However, the production rate remained between 1.5 to 2.0 million tons per year until recently (from 1964 to 1990, TSDB, 1992, 88).

In general, Taiwan relied on rice and sugar exports to earn foreign exchange. The need for international currencies and the pressures of population growth on agriculture required expansion of the fertilizer industry to help conserve foreign exchange. The development of Taiwan's fertilizer industry evolved slowly until 1955. However, by 1964, with the joint venture of the China Petroleum Corporation, Socony Mobil Oil Company and Allied Chemical, the industry developed into one of the foremost large-scale industries in Taiwan (Sasamoto and Kawano, 1968, 687). U.S aid to the fertilizer industry was practically discontinued after 1964 (TSDB, 1992, 230).

From 1949 to 1964, about four-fifth (78%) of fertilizer was used in the rice production, 15 percent in sugar cane, and 7 percent in other crops like sweet potato, wheat, banana, pineapples, oranges, tea, etc. (Sasamoto and Kawano, 1968, 685).

In the early stage of economic development, the fertilizer industry played several important roles. It not only increased agricultural productivity, but also stimulated the development of the machinery and repair industry. As an import substitute, it saved Taiwan's foreign exchange. As a government monopoly, it was a tool to exploit farmers through the rice-fertilizer exchange program (see Section 1.7.4.2). As a heavy industry, it induced forward and backward linkages, leading to the development of synthetic resins, synthetic seasonings, plastics, printing, dyeing, medicine, and machine tools.

1.7.3.3 *The Sugar Industry*

The development of the electric power industry and fertilizer industry directly benefitted the Taiwan Sugar Corporation. The Taisugar was organized from four large confiscated private Japanese sugar companies which operated 42 plants at the end of the war (ibid., 591, 599). The highest prewar production rate was 1.4 million tons achieved in 1938–1939 (ibid., 603). Due to air raids by the Allied Forces, more than half of the plants were damaged, but they recovered quickly and completely by 1948 (ibid., 600).

Immediately after the war, Taisugar was already export-oriented. In 1953, it produced 0.9 million tons, 92 percent of which were exported. The exports were valued at US$90 million, and comprised 67 percent of Taiwan's total value of exports that year (Chang, 1974, I, 96; TSDB, 1986, 90, 221).

Sugar exports consisted of more than 30 percent of the yearly total Taiwanese exports until 1964. They helped the government earning precious foreign exchange which, unlike U.S. aid, could be used to import capital goods and materials of the government's choice. Thus sugar played its major role as leading commodity of the primary export-led growth.

After 1964 Taiwan started the export promotion policy. The proportion of the value of sugar in the total Taiwanese exports decreased quickly afterward, and sugar production slowed and then started decreasing after 1977 (TSDB, 1992, 87). By 1985, sugar exports consisted of mere 0.1 percent of the total exports (ibid., 221).

1.7.3.4 *On Public Enterprises*

Electric power, sugar, and, to a larger degree, fertilizer industries were the three major monopolies of the KMT government during the import substitution period. In fact, in the 1950s the KMT government either monopolized or controlled three major sectors of the Taiwanese economy: production, distribution, and finance. They are shown as the public enterprises in the fourth column of U.S. Aid in Fig. 1.5, and its postwar trends are illustrated in Fig. 1.7.

In production, the KMT government has monopolized liquor, beer, tobacco, cigarettes, cigars, sugar, molasses, yeast, salt, and about 90 percent of petroleum and petroleum products. It had a majority of shares in the production of food, chemicals and chemical products, metal and metal products, and "others," which include shipbuilding and bagasse board (SA, 1966, 189–229). These government-operated public enterprises were generally much larger and more machine-intensive than private enterprises.

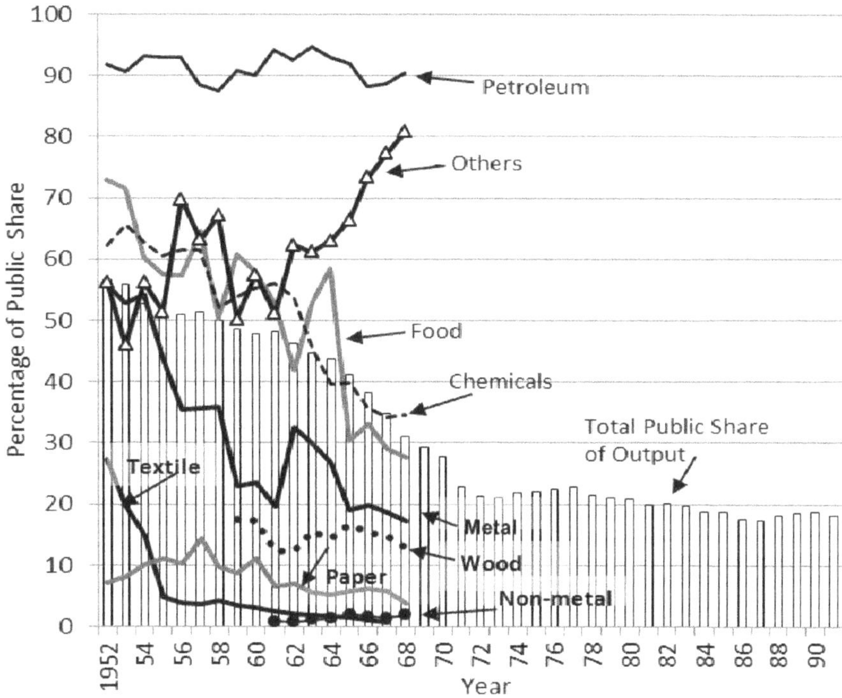

Figure 1.7: Public Share of Industrial Output
Selected Industries, 1952–68

More than 75 percent of the public enterprises used more than 15 horsepower in the 1954 census (the RHS of row (8), Table 1.7). In contrast, only 7 percent of the private enterprises were in the same category (the RHS of row (7), Table 1.7).

In the distribution sector, the government monopolized railroads and all the communication facilities. It had major control of foreign trade and shipping by the Commerce Bureau, of foods by the Food Bureau, of general agricultural products by the Taiwan Supply Bureau. In financial services, except for one commercial bank (The Overseas Chinese Bank), the government monopolized all the commercial and development banks, in addition to the central and local government banks before 1964 (Liu, 1975, 108–135).

The weight of the government monopolies and industrial controls in production and foreign trade has decreased over the years, as shown by the column chart (labeled Total) in Fig. 1.7, overshadowed by the growth of

Table 1.7: The Size of the Textile Industry

Enterprises (in no. and %)				*Classification by Number of Workers (in %)*						
Row	Year	Industry	Total	%	1-3	4-29	30-99	100-299	300-999	>=1000
(1)	1954	Txtl (a)	2117	100	59.3	28.6	8.7	2.3	0.7	0.3
(2)		**Mfg ttl (b)**	**42288**	**100**	**72.5**	**25.1**	**1.8**	**0.4**	**0.1**	**0.0**
(3)	1961	Txtl (a)	2183	100	64.8	23.5	6.8	2.7	1.6	0.5
Power Usage (in no. and %)				*Classification by Horse Powers (in %)*						
	Year	Industry	Total	%	0	< 5	5-19	20-149	150-999	>=1000
(4)	1954	Txtl (a)	2117	100	64	12	17	6	2	0
							28.0			2.2
(5)		**Mfg ttl (b)**	**42288**	**100**	**66.0**		**30.8**	**2.6**		**0.6**
				%	0	0.1-3	3-15	15-100	100-1000	>=1000
(6)	**1953**	**Total (h)**	**13538**	**100**	**26**	**35**	**31**	**6**	**2**	**0**
(7)		Private (h)	13254	100	26	35	32	6	1	0
(8)		Public (h)	284	100	19	0	5	25	33	18
(9)	1961	Txtl (a)	2183	100	59	14	15	8	3	1
Type of Organization (in no. and %)										
	Year	Industry	Total	%	Coop		Prtnrship		Indiv	Others
(10)	1933	Txtl (c)	60	100	6.7		1.7		91.7	0.0
(11)	1938	Txtl (c)	83	100	7.2		0		90.4	2.4
(12)	1954	Txtl (d)	2013	100	4.3		6.8		88.9	0
(13)	**1954**	**Mfg ttl (e)**	**39748**	**100**	**1.1**		**4.2**		**94.1**	**0.6**
(14)	1961	Txtl (d)	2212	100	13.8		4.6		81.5	0.1

Sources: (a) Sasamoto and Kawano. (1968), 667–668. (b) Hsiao (1960b), 2–3. Both data use "1954 Census of Industry and Business in Taiwan Province." (c) From Okurasho (1949), 202, 203, 215. (d) Sasamoto and Kawano (1968), 671. (e) Hsiao (1960b), 2. (f) Note the difference in the range of classification. (g) Foreigners were mostly Chinese. (h) Hsiao (1960), 3. The data came from Taiwan's Cities and Industries, compiled by US Aid Mission and National Taiwan University, 1956(?).

private enterprises.[42] However, public enterprises persistently maintained about 20 percent of the share of industrial output since 1971. In recent

[42]The proportion of total public-enterprise industrial production in Fig. 1.7 is taken from TSDB (1992), 84. The data for individual industries are based on Hsing (1971), Table A.35, 304.

years, the various national construction plans have reinforced the weights of public enterprises in the economy. Even in the early 1990s, the total assets of the 27 central government enterprises were worth US$200 billion, and those of the 34 provincial enterprises, about US$70 billion. The combined total assets of government enterprises in Taiwan are eight times the combined assets of the top 500 private companies in Taiwan.[43] Despite the privatization plan of 6 "national" and 14 provincial firms and banks in 1989 (Yu and Chen, 1982, 208; Pang and Chen, 1993; Chen *et al.*, 1991, 51–52), the plan has yet to be implemented. Public enterprises still exert an enormous influence in the domestic market.

1.7.3.5 *The Textile Industry*

At the end of Section 1.5.2.2, we have noted that when the KMT government was established in Taiwan at the end of 1949, the Chinese textile industry relocated to Taiwan from the Shanghai area. This movement was equivalent to a massive infusion of grants of turn-key plants. They also came with free imported capital to operate, and skilled and experienced executives to manage, using local Taiwanese labor. It was indeed a timely establishment. Clothing was scarce due to the sudden increases in population, the import markets were closed after Taiwan was isolated from Japan and China, the government was more than eager to reward the loyal entrepreneurs who had relocated in Taiwan (instead of remaining in China or relocating to Hong Kong), and raw cotton could be obtained from U.S. aid (see Fig. 1.4 on U.S. Aid).

The government actively protected the textile industry through various measures. It assured the existing firms' monopolistic position from 1954 to 1960, and restricted or imposed high tariffs on textile imports.

Government policies in support of the textile industry included limiting the total number of existing weaving machines at 10,000. The government also restricted the annual increase of cotton spindles to 20,000, thus effectively excluding the entrance of new textile firms (Sasamoto and Kawano, 1968, 665). It also allocated scarce foreign exchange to the textile industry to facilitate importation of machinery and raw materials. In addition, Taiwan's government granted a favorable foreign exchange rate

[43] Since many of these 61 mammoth government enterprises reinvest in major private enterprises, the government control of the economy extends beyond the officially registered government enterprises (Chen *et al.*, 1991). "Some analysts argue that, dating back to the early 1950s, Taiwan has had the largest public-enterprise sector outside the Communist bloc" (ibid.)

similar to that of importing goods for public enterprises, and it maintained low prices of foods and other agricultural products so that wage rates could be kept low (Chang, II, 1974, 97).

One ingenious measure of the government patronizing large textile firms was the "commissioned spinning and weaving system." This system involved the government commissioning selected textile firms to spin and weave raw cotton obtained with U.S. aid, and then paid the firms very generously. The scheme is illustrated in Fig. 1.8.

After firms received raw cotton (2) through U.S. Aid program (1) (see the numbering in Fig. 1.8), they then produced yarn and cloth for the government and received about whopping 138 percent of the same cotton as the processing fees and profits in kind (3). The firm then processed its earned cotton into cloths and sold it to consumers (4). The government, on the other hand, either sold yarn at a fixed price to other textile firms or sold cloth to farmers (5) in exchange for rice (6), or to the households (7). It was estimated that, during the two years, about 60 percent (US $12 million) of imported U.S. cotton aid was "paid" to the textile firms in this fashion as fees (Liu, 1975, 222). The low price of clothing also help maintain low rice prices (8), which in turn keep low wages (9) and high profits for industries, in particular, the textile industry.

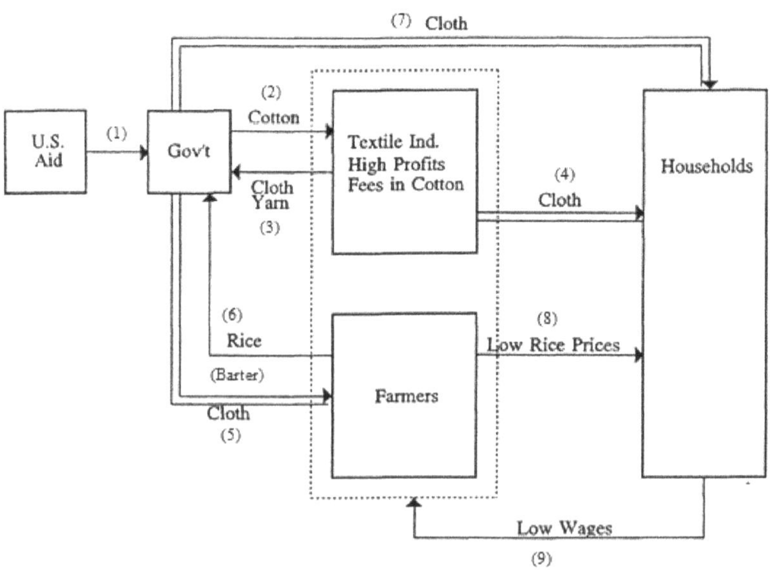

Figure 1.8: Original Accumulation in the Textile Industry

The processing fees in kind were converted to fees in cash from June 1952 to June 1953, but the generous fee scheme was unchanged (ibid., 222–223). The government contracted out only to certain privileged firms. It guaranteed these firms the source of raw materials, the product market, and exorbitant profits. This scheme extricated the privileged textile firms during the most difficult initial years, and undoubtedly fostered the original accumulation in the textile industry.

Thus, in a relatively short period, the textile industry saturated the domestic market. By 1954, the industry exported NT$ 16 million worth of textile products (1.1% of total exports), its export value more than doubled to NT$ 46 million in the following year (2.2% of total exports), and, in 1961, the textile exports jumped 27 times to NT$ 1,178 million, 15 percent of the total exports that year. As explained in Fig. 1.13, textile exports (which later included garment) continued to increase and had been number one export item until 1986 to 1988 when the electric and electronic products substituted its position (TSDB, 1975, 1993). It played a crucial role in Taiwan's export-oriented industrialization after the fall of rice and sugar exports.

In addition to the large imported Chinese-owned textile plants and capital, there were numerous smaller local Taiwanese textile firms. They were built during the days of Japanese occupation. The lower part of Table 1.7 shows that there were 83 textile firms in Taiwan in 1938 (row (11)), an increase of 38 percent over 1933. Among them, only six Japanese firms were incorporated (7.2%), and 90.4 percent of the firms were individually owned small companies. The total number of the textile firms increased 24 times to 2,013 in 1954 (row (12)). Most of them were very small. Only 83 (4.3%) of them were incorporated, and 89 percent of them were individually-owned family firms.

However, compared with the manufacturing industry as a whole (row (13)), the textile industry was still larger and probably more prosperous than the other manufacturing industries in 1954. The textile included more firms that were incorporated (4.3% vs 1.1%) and it included more partnerships (6.8% vs 4.2%) compared to the manufacturing sector as a whole (rows (12) and (13)). On the other hand, the textile industry had relatively fewer individual proprietorships (88.9% of textile firms as compared to 94.1% manufacturing firms). By 1961, when the government relaxed entry restrictions for textile firms, the proportion of Taiwan's firms with over 100 workers increased, while the proportion of firms with less than 100 workers decreased (rows (1) and (3)), although deregulation also increased many small firms hiring less than three workers (from 59.3% to 64.8%).

The smallness of the firm size was also reflected in the number of workers and the use of horsepower as shown in the upper part of Table 1.7. Almost 60 percent of the local textile firms hired only 1 to 3 workers (row (1)), and about 64 percent did not use any motors (row (4)), while only 7 textile firms (0.3%) hired more than 1000 workers (row 1), and only 11 (0.5%) textile firms used more than 1000 H.P. in 1954. Still, comparing textile industry with the manufacturing industry as a whole, the textile industry had more medium-sized firms (row (1)) than the other manufacturing industries (8.7% vs 1.8%). From 1954 to 1961, more textile firms were mechanized (compare row (9) with row (4)).

These smaller Taiwanese firms also apparently benefited from the heavy government protection of larger Chinese textile firms. The spillover effect can be seen from the following statistics of Taiwan's textile industry. According to Sasamoto and Kawano (1968), 667, based on the census survey of 1954 and 1961, the number of firms increased only 3 percent and number of workers increased 35 percent. However, during that same period, wages increased 139 percent, fixed assets, 420 percent, capital 338 percent, power usage 150 percent, output 143 percent, and value-added, 75 percent.

In conclusion, in less than five years from 1950, the textile industry saturated the domestic market, and as early as in 1954, it went from an import-substitute to an export-expansion industry in a short time period. Man-made fibers were introduced in 1957 and developed rapidly throughout the 1960s and the 1970s. Their value exceeded cotton yarn production in 1972, and also the value of cotton fabrics in 1983 (TSDB, 1984, 84). In the area of international trade, by 1960 the value of textile exports exceeded the value of raw cotton imports (TSDB, 1984, 214, 224; Sasamoto and Kawano, 1968, 673–74), and started earning export surpluses. In 1965, textile replaced sugar as the number one export item (TSDB, 1984, 214), ending the dominance of sugar exports in Taiwanese economic history. Taiwan entered a new era of industrialization through exporting textile products.

1.7.3.6 *The Cement Industry*

The cement industry represents a different breed of private enterprise in Taiwan. Since Taiwan produces quality limestone, the cement industry started as early as 1915. By the end of WWII three monopolistic cement companies produced about 0.3 million tons of cement (Sasamoto and Kawano, 1968, 676). These three were confiscated and reorganized as the government-owned Taiwan Cement Company, which monopolized the market until 1955. It recovered from the wartime destruction quickly and its production exceeded the prewar level after 1950. In 1954, its stocks were transferred to Taiwanese landlords as compensation for their land sold to the government. Thus, it is an exemplary example of the transformation of "feudalistic land capital" to modern "industrial capital."

Until 1961, Taiwan's cement industry catered mainly to domestic military and civilian demand (import substitution). In contrast, by 1963, the industry had grown to ten companies and produced 2.3 million tons of cement, 44 percent of which were exported (ibid., 677). This production represented about 6.5 percent of the value of Taiwan's total manufactures produced and about 3.8 percent of the value of Taiwan's total exports. In the early 1960s, most of exports went to South Vietnam (41%), Hong Kong, Philippines, and Korea, and other Southeast Asian countries (ibid., 680).

Although the Taiwan Cement Company is privately owned, its sales and prices were strictly controlled by the government. The government sets the priority of its sales in the following order: uses in military, electric power, reservoir and irrigation, transportation, public buildings, air defense, and lastly, general civilian consumption. The government also fixed the civilian prices and the military prices, the latter was only about a half of the former (Liu, 1975, 246). Since demand generally exceeded supply, a black market in cement emerged. As might be expected, the price of cement on the black market was about 30 percent higher than the fixed civilian prices, resulting in much higher industry profits from the black market than the regulated market (ibid., 247).

Under strong government protection, the company grew steadily with the Taiwanese economy. By 1991, it produced almost 20 million tons of cement (TSDB, 1992, 88).

Other private industries expanding during the recovery period were the canned pineapple industry, chemical seasoning, iron and steel, non-iron metals, metals, machinery, electric equipment, and transportation services (Sasamoto and Kawano, 1968, 690–699).

1.7.3.7 *Development of Private Enterprises*

Developing private enterprises did not fit the KMT government's basic ideology of "developing state capital and controlling private capital." This dogma was advocated by the KMT's Founding Father, Sun Yet-sen, at the beginning of the twentieth century.[44]

The inexorable rise of private enterprise may be attributable to several sources. First and foremost of these was the influence of the Agency of International Development (AID, 1967) which handled the U.S. aid program (Jacoby, 1966, 174–176; Ho, 1978, 117). Although 67 percent of U.S. aid went to public enterprise, this was in the area of infrastructure and agriculture. Investment in electricity, highways, railroads, harbors, and communication helped create favorable external economies for private enterprises. Another impetus for private enterprise was the inefficiency and corruption that existed in most public enterprises. Public enterprises were enclaves for Chinese refugees, overstaffed, and run by retired Chinese bureaucrats or generals with little knowledge of modem management (Tien, 1989, 136). With the exception of Taipower, the China Petroleum Corporation, and the Monopoly Bureau of Tobacco and Wine which made huge monopoly profits, public enterprises lost money almost every year. Subsidies only added to the already excessive government expenditures (Liu, 1975, 206–207). In order to survive and to increase employment, the government had no choice but to encourage private enterprise.

More directly, the U.S. Aid Small Industrial Loan Fund, totaling about US$10 million and NT$401 million (also equivalent to about US$10 million), made "medium-term loans available at below market interest rates to small private industrial firms, to enable them to expand output, improve quality, and raise productivity" (Jacoby, 1966, 191). It was medium-term loans for a one to four years duration (Hsiao, 1960a, 22). From 1954 to 1964, some 413 firms had received U.S. dollar loans, and 483 firms had received NT dollar loans (Jacoby, 1966, 191).

Table 1.8 shows that the actual interest paid by the surveyed firms, on average, was mere 10.08 percent for US Aid loan, as compared with 21.60 percent for the bank and 39.6 percent for the private bank. The lower part of Table 1.8 shows the effects of aid loans on the textile and manufacturing

---

[44]Jacoby (1966), 136–137; Chen *et al.* (1991), 31. In fact, Sun and his KMT Party was strongly influenced by now-bankrupt communist ideology (Moody, 1992, 17). Liu (1975), Chapter 2 even pointed out that, in view of the kinds of indiscriminate monopoly and monopolistic holdings in almost all major areas of the Taiwanese economy, Taiwan's public enterprises were rooted in the colonial heritage, worsened by political greed, and established through confiscation of Japanese assets. It is apparent that the rhetoric of "developing state capital" is only an excuse for political and economic controls of Taiwan by Chiang's family and the KMT Party.

Table 1.8: Sources of Indebtedness of Firms Received US Aid
(in No., NT$ million, %)

	Year	Industry	Firms no.	Total debt mNT$	total Int rate	Bank 21.60%	USAid 10.08%	Prvt 39.60%	Others
					Debt composition				
(1)	1954	Txtl	10	93.2	100	33.2	0.0	18.1	48.7
(2)		**Mfg**	**177**	**337.4**	**100**	**25.7**	**8.1**	**21.0**	**45.2**
(3)	1957	Txtl	13	236.2	100	23.2	1.5	15.1	60.2
(4)		**Mfg**	**204**	**907.2**	**100**	**19.6**	**9.3**	**24.9**	**46.2**

Sources: Interest rate is the average nominal rate paid by the firms surveyed. Hsiao (1960a). Based on the survey of the results of the US Aid Program of Small Loans to private manufacturing industru in Taiwan during the Accounting Year 1954–1957.

industries as a whole by surveying firms in 1954, before the loans were made, and surveying them again in 1957, after the loans were made. There were 10 and 13 textile firms surveyed; and 177 and 204 manufacturing firms surveyed, respectively. The firms included in the survey were classified as medium-sized, having 30 to 99 workers.[45] The fact that they were chosen as the target of U.S. Aid implies that they were rather well-off promising upper middle-sized firms, as compared with the numerous smaller firms shown in rows (2) and (3) of Table 1.7.

Row (2) of Table 1.8 shows that, in 1954, the 177 manufacturing firms surveyed had debt of NT$ 337.4 million. Among those firms, 25.7 percent of the debt was borrowed from commercial banks, 8.1 percent directly from U.S. Aid, and 21.0 percent were from private sources in the underground, informal financial markets. It was estimated that the nominal interest rates for these debts were 21.60 percent, 10.08 percent, and 39.6 percent per year, respectively (Hsiao, 1960a). The "Other Debts" consisted of such items as account payables, check payables, and temporary financing by the firm owners, etc. In 1957, after receiving the U.S. loans, the debts of these firms increased almost three times to NT$ 907.2 million (row (4)), possibly due to expansion. The bank loans decreased to 19.6 percent of the total debts, the U.S. aid loan increased slightly, and private borrowing and other debts increased. Similar conditions hold for the textile firms (rows (1)

[45]These firms consisted of about 1.8 percent of the total manufacturing firms in 1954, see the upper part of Table 1.7 (Hsiao, 1960a, 18; 1960b, 2). Note the unusually high interest cost of borrowing in early Taiwanese economic development in Table 1.8.

and (3)), except that, in general, the textile firms were still better off than the manufacturing firms in general in the sense that they received more bank loans than other manufacturing firms in the survey, all of them government-controlled, at almost half of the private loan rates.[46]

The government-controlled commercial banks were either unable or not interested in helping private enterprise (Hsiao, 1960b, 3). Smaller Taiwanese-owned firms were on their own. As we have pointed out, these 177 or so firms were still the healthier ones. There were 72.5 percent (30,658) of firms with 1 to 3 workers, and 25.1 percent (10,614) with 4 to 29 workers (row (2) of Table 1.7). These smaller Taiwanese firms were out of luck in receiving government or US Aid assistance. They had to face the harsh reality that business expansion must be financed through informal financial markets with excessively high interest rates or from the owners' pockets (see the last two columns of Table 1.8). Government assistance could hardly be expected (Chen, 1972a, 10). The situation did not improve from the 1960s (Chen, 1972b, 42) through the 1980s.

Given the government's lack of assistance, U.S. loans to private enterprise, although limited in amount and scope, undoubtedly gave greater promise to many successful private firms, almost all of them were Taiwanese-owned. It also encouraged the establishment of a bookkeeping system and modern management techniques. Furthermore, the American system of free enterprise and competition directly countered the government-centered bureaucratic Chinese officials, who did not speak Taiwanese,[47] and infused fresh air into the heavily armed Taiwanese society in the 1950s.

By the end of the decade, using U.S. aid as leverage, the Americans were able to go a step further "to induce changes in Chinese government policy." They initiated "the 19-Point Program of Economic and Financial Reform" (Jacoby, 1966, 134) in January 1960. It was an extended version of the 8-Point Program proposed by the AID Mission director the previous year. The plan was subsequently adapted by the KMT officials in the Third

[46]In view of the KMT mentality on state capital and its previous practice in China, where about 40 percent of textile products was produced by government-owned firms (Liu, 1975, 231), the textile firms might as well have become government-owned. One reason they have stayed private was that "much of the Chinese textile capital was also the KMT bureaucratic capital," which also tries to woo the native Taiwanese capital by helping its development (ibid., 204).

[47]They also disliked businessmen (Gold, 1986, 77), probably the latter did not understand the Chinese lofty call for "recovering the Chinese mainland."

Four-Year Economic Plan, 1961–1964, which was announced at the same time. The plan overhauled current monetary, fiscal, foreign exchange, and trade policies to encourage private investment. Furthermore, it called for the liberalization of trade controls, the curtailing of government bureaucracy, and the promotion of exports. In short, AID puts "steady pressure on the Chinese government to improve the climate for private investment." Thus U.S. "Aid was the catalytic financial element in such new industries as glass, synthetic fibers, polyvinyl plastic, hardboard, soda ash, and cast iron pipe" (ibid., 138). Other new industries supported by AID included the manufacturing of monosodium glutamate, flat glass, fluorescent lamps, and the assembly of compact cars (Lin, 1968, 300). The 19-Point Program paved the way for the next phase of Taiwanese economic development, the phase of export expansion after 1964 (Lee and Liang, 1982, Chapter 10).

1.7.4 *Agricultural Development*

In Section 1.5.2.2, we saw that the mass influx of Chinese refugees into Taiwan, placed additional burdens on the Taiwanese people. We also saw that the government addressed the basic need for clothing by heavily protecting the textile industry and helped its import-substituting expansion by guaranteeing its exorbitant profits. However, people must have food as well as clothing. How did the government secure the food supply, especially rice, for the refugees and soldiers? In a vivid contrast to its treatment of firms in the textile industry, the government secured the food supply by heavily exploiting the Taiwanese farmers.

Taiwan's agricultural sector was so productive that it not only supplied foods to the households (thus sparing the necessity of food imports and saving foreign exchange), it also supplied raw materials to the food processing industry, contributing to export earnings. It performed its role of providing "original accumulation" for industrialization.

1.7.4.1 *Agricultural Productivity*

In 1952, 52 percent of Taiwan's population was employed in the agricultural sector. This proportion declined steadily to 45 percent in 1965 (TSDB, 1984, 57). At the same time, the agricultural population, including farm labor, increased during this period (see col. m of Table 1.3). In 1955, 34 percent of farmers cultivated less than 0.5 hectare of land and 45 percent of them cultivated between 0.5 to 1.5 hectares. These statistics have not changed much during the past forty years. As with the firms in the manufacturing sector, most of the Taiwanese farms are very small (Sumiya *et al.*, 1992, 63).

In 1951, the four sectors, agriculture, industry, commerce, and others, contributed 36 percent, 18 percent, 19 percent, and 27 percent, respectively, to net domestic product (NDP). The structural composition of NDP changed to 27 percent, 28 percent, 17 percent, and 28 percent, respectively, in 1965 (TSDB, 1984, 34). Thus, although the weight of the agricultural sector was decreasing and that of industrial sectors was increasing steadily, Taiwan was still predominantly an agricultural society during the recovery period.

In 1952, 38 percent of farmers owned land, and 36 percent were tenants (TSDB, 1992, 66). After land reform, 67 percent of farmers owned land, and the tenant population was reduced to 13 percent (ibid.). By 1990, the proportion of farmers who owned their land increased to about 85 percent while the proportion of tenant farmers decreased to 6 percent (ibid.). Overall, however, farms in Taiwan were small. The area of cultivated land per farm family was reduced from 1.3 hectares to 1.1 hectares in 1965 (ibid., 67).

From 1953 to 1962, agricultural production grew an average of 4.8 percent per year, far less than the 11.7 percent for industrial production (TSDB, 1984, 2). However, the growth of agricultural production still exceeded the 3.5 percent population growth rate (ibid., 2). During this period, 1952 to 1962, the output of almost all crops increased, including rice (129%), sweet potatoes (135%), bananas (147%), peanuts (159%), cotton (183%), tea (166%), citrus fruits (229%), pineapple (281%), wheat (295%), and soybeans (304%) (ibid., 61–65). Because Taiwan's cultivated land is almost saturated, increases in outputs were brought about by increasing productivity, ranging from 106 percent for citrus fruits to 195 percent for wheat (ibid., 61–65). In addition, new products, like asparagus and mushrooms were introduced in 1963. Sugar, canned food, rice, and bananas were the major agricultural exports during this period.

There were several reasons agricultural outputs grew so rapidly. First was the high degree of responsiveness of Taiwanese farmers to changes in the demand and supply relationship, and the incentives of higher returns from crop diversification (Jacoby, 1966, 91, 208). This responsiveness was inherited from the farmers' responses to rice and sugar price changes during the prewar period. Farmers had to choose between rice and sugar cane cultivation, adopt new type of seeds, use chemical fertilizer, and work extra hours in order to increase productivity (Chang, II, 1974, 64). This was supported by the high literacy rate among farmers (in 1960, 57% of farmers had some formal education)[48] and the accessibility of reading materials and others (Ho, 1978, 179). The extensive farmers' associations and credit cooperatives, which were restored and improved from the colonial period, also helped disseminate information (ibid.).

Second, land reform, especially the land ownership program, gave incentive to the business-minded farmers to work harder and increase their incomes. In fact farmers were better off than urban dwellers during the 1950s (K. Hsiao, 1987). Third, "increases in the amount of capital investment in fertilizer, pesticides, seeds, hand-powered tillers, water resources, and improvements in agricultural technology, mainly financed with U.S. aid" (Jacoby, 1966, 90–91; Ho, 1978, 175–178). Fourth, all of these efforts might have been in vain if the land was not fertile, as in some African countries. Fortunately, Taiwan is located in the subtropical zone, endowed with fertile land and blessed with the ability to supply many different crops and fruits.

Rapid industrial growth in Taiwan has been discussed in previous sections. Here we may add contributions from the agricultural sector. The increase in the agricultural production stimulated the establishment of the food-processing industries (Chang, I. Chapter 1), and the increase in farm income contributed to the expansion of domestic markets for the industrial sector.

Note that, the increase in agricultural productivity itself did not mean that the government could procure sufficient foods for the Chinese bureaucrats and soldiers. At the same time, the government had to maintain low food prices to feed the refugees, to keep consumer prices low, and to keep the wage rate low for industrialization. More specifically, to secure rice and to maintain general price stability, the government "squeezed" the Taiwanese farmers through in kind taxes and by practicing a pre-modern barter system in rural areas. In what follows, we give two prominent examples to illustrate the barter economy in Taiwan during the recovery period.

[48]Also see Sasamoto and Kawano (1968), 78. Those who received a Japanese education were in their thirties during the 1950s and the 1960s. In a private conversation, Professor T.H. Lee (who later became the President of Taiwan) of JCRR (Joint Commission of Rural Reconstruction) once remarked to the first author in a gathering in the late 1950s that the Taiwanese farmers read Japanese magazines, even before the JCRR experts, to diversify and improve their farming methods. The KMT government banned importing all Japanese books and magazines except technical and agricultural publications.

1.7.4.2 *Rice Production*

Rice is produced almost everywhere in Taiwan; it is one of Taiwan's main staples. After wartime damage, its output recovered to the prewar high in 1950 (Sasamoto and Kawano, 1968, 457). In 1952, rice production was 1.6 million (metric) tons (TSDB, 1993, 69). Production increased slowly but steadily afterward, reaching 2.7 million tons in 1976. Rice output then decreased slowly until recently. Since 1952, the area of land planted in rice decreased continuously almost every year until 1992. However, over the same period, rice yield per hectare increased steadily from 2,000 kg per hectare in 1952, reaching a peak of 4,241 kg per hectare in 1991 (ibid., 69). In contrast, the value of rice exports has fluctuated considerably. In 1953, US$13 million of rice were exported, but almost none was exported in 1975 and 1976, despite the large amount produced. Rice exports increased to a peak of US$94 million in 1983 and have decreased thereafter (TSDB, 1986, 222).

The KMT government not only inherited the prewar economy, it also acquired much of Japanese colonial policy of law and order. As early as October 1945, the government adopted the wartime foods control and distribution system of the prewar Japanese period, promulgating the "Temporary Measure of Foods Control." In November 1946, it then established the "Taiwan Provincial Food Bureau" to manage and control Taiwan's food production, marketing, and consumption (Liu, 1975, Chapter 2).

A land tax in kind was started in 1946. In the following year (July 1947), a compulsory purchase system of rice was put in effect. To secure more rice to feed the army and government employees, the government announced a rice for fertilizer barter system in September 1948. The government monopolized production and distribution of chemical fertilizer, and used one ton of fertilizer in exchange for one ton of paddy rice at the government determined barter ratio. In this way, the government "taxed" the farmers by one third to one half of rice procured through the barter system (Liu, 1975, 148–149; Sasamoto and Kawano, 1968, 499–500; K. Hsiao, 1987, 86). A barter system involving rice for cotton fabrics, as well as rice production loans that were payable in kind were also introduced.

The government's rice price policy was successful. Up to 1960, the rice price in Taiwan was about 30 percent less than general price levels in Taiwan. These prices were also cheaper than all other rice producing countries (Sasamoto and Kawano, 1968, 499). After 1960, the price of Taiwanese rice started to increase, surpassing that of Burmese rice. The government could maintain the low rice prices because it controlled the

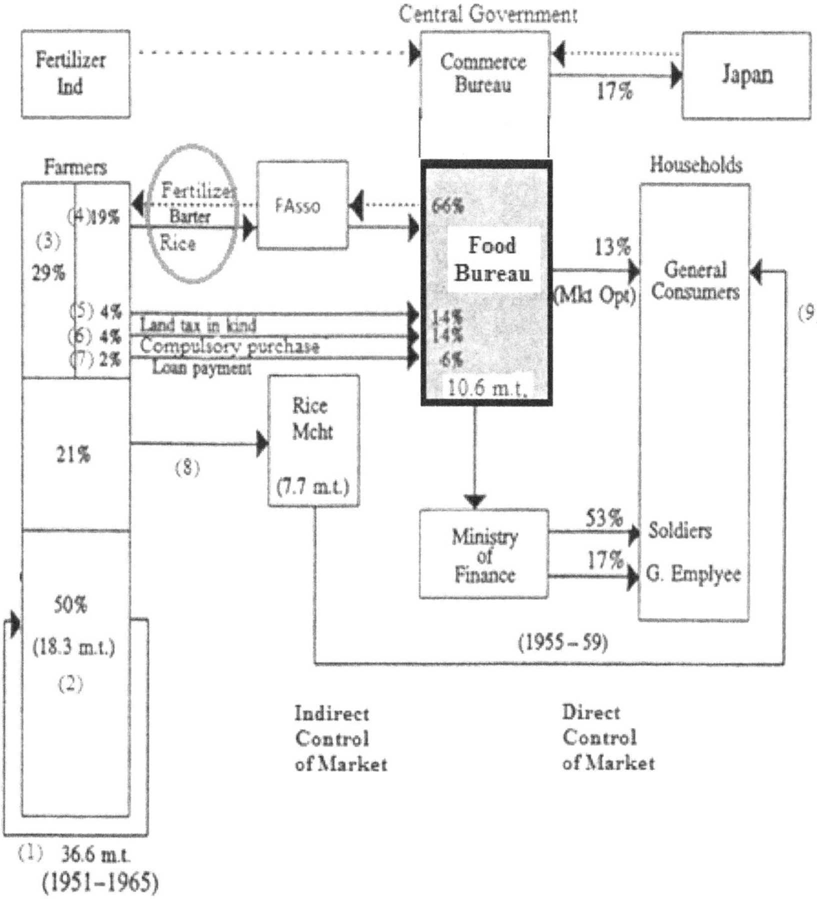

Figure 1.9: Distribution of Rice

The Rice-fertilizer Barter System

market under martial law and through U.S. aid by importing wheat and soybean into Taiwan as rice substitutes. The low rice price became the basis of Taiwan's low-wage labor-intensive industrialization during the 1960s and the 1970s.

Figure 1.9 illustrates how these explicit and implicit taxes amounted to an elaborate scheme of exploitation in Taiwan.[49] It was estimated that,

[49]Figure 1.9 is revised from Fig. 10 in Liu (1975), 150, and also from Fig. 1 in Sasamoto and Kawano (1968), 284.

from 1951 to 1965, the total paddy rice production of the 15-year period was 36.6 million tons (1).[50] Among them, we assume that 50 percent of it was retained as seeds and consumption in the agricultural sector (2). For the rest, 10.5 million tons, or 29 percent of the total production, went to the government (3),[51] either through rice-fertilizer barter (19%) (4), which was handled by the Farmers' Association (FAsso), or land taxes in kind (4%) (5), compulsory purchases (4%) (6), and loan repayment in kind (7). The rest, 21 percent (8), were refined by the rice merchants (Rice Mcht) and sold to general consumers (9).

From 1953 to 1959, there were about 10,000 to 15,000 small overly competitive rice merchants in the country, thus profiteering through hoarding and speculation were out of the question (Sasamoto and Kawano, 1968, 488). To enforce the control, the government required that, every region which had more than three rice merchants had to organize a trade association, and every trade association had to support the government's food policy (ibid., 491). In general, among the 50 percent of the total rice output available for the consumer market, as shown on the upper left hand side of Fig. 1.9, about 60 percent (29% of 50%) was directly controlled by the government, and the other 40 percent (21% of 50%) was indirectly but strictly regulated. In this way, rice and food prices could be kept as low as possible, as explained in details below.

The major "unequal exchange" or "exploitation" by the government came from the **rice for fertilizer barter system**, which consisted of 66 percent of part of the total government rice procurement (10.6 million tons, see the circled part and the shaded box in Fig. 1.9). The system was compulsory since all chemical fertilizer was either imported only through the government or manufactured by the government-owned company and distributed through the Commerce Bureau, as shown in the middle part of Fig. 1.9. The barter exchange rates depended on the types of fertilizer.

Taiwanese farmers use about 50 percent of ammonium sulfate and about 25 percent of phosphate (Liu, 1975, 146). From 1951 to 1965, the government-determined barter ratio was one ton of paddy for one ton of ammonium sulfate. The ratio fluctuated somewhat yearly (ibid.). However,

[50]See Sumiya *et al.* (1992), 72 and Liu (1975), 140. The following estimations differ somewhat from Ho (1978), 180–182. Similar analysis has been given in Kuo (1983), 34–36.

[51]Ho (1978), 182, estimated that average annual collection by the government was around 0.75 million metric tons of paddy, or about 25 percent of Taiwan's annual rice production.

the market price of ammonium sulfate was in general only about two-third of that of rice, and its import price was only one-half of the rice price. Thus the government "taxed" the farmers by one-third to one half of rice procured through the barter system (Liu, 1975, 148–149; Sasamoto and Kawano, 1968, 499–500; Hsiao, K., 1987, 86). The barter ratios were reduced several times after 1970. The government yielded finally to farmers' complaints, and the system was discontinued only in 1973.

Another source of exploitation was the compulsory purchase of rice, the system of which was also inherited from the Japanese colonial days (Ho, 1978, 180). As in those days, the farmers and the landlords were required to sell 12 kg of every yen of land tax (ibid.; Liu, 1975, 142). The purchase price was determined by the government, and was generally about 25 percent to 30 percent lower than the market price (ibid.; Liu, 1975, 144). Similarly, the pre-harvest loans to rice farmers had to be paid back with interest in kind after rice harvest. The rice price was again fixed by the government.

Soldiers and government employees receive the lion's share of the government rice at a discounted market price. From 1955 to 1959, the government rice collected by the Food Bureau was distributed to soldiers (53%) and government employees (G. Emplyee, 17%) at a price on average about 20 percent cheaper than the market price. The rest (17%) was exported mainly to Japan through the Commerce Bureau in exchange for fertilizer, and partly retained in the Food Bureau (13%) to stabilize and maintain the low rice price in the consumer market (Liu, 1975, 150).

1.7.4.3 *Sugar Cane Production*

Sugar cane is the raw material of the sugar industry. The government did everything possible to stabilize supply sources and maximize the collection of sugar cane.

The harvest area of sugar cane was reduced about two thirds after the war. This was primarily due to competition for space with other crops, and also due to sales of some Taisugar (see below)-owned public land in land reform during the transition period. In contrast, the per hectare sugar cane harvest increased about 15 percent, a feat made possible by seed improvements and better cultivation methods (Sasamoto and Kawano, 1968, 596, 602–603). In the 1950s, the land productivity of sugar cane in Taiwan was one of the best in the world (ibid., 619).

As in the prewar period, the Taiwan Sugar Company (Taisugar) produced about 20 percent (to 30%) of the nation's sugar cane. The rest had to be supplied by "contract farmers." The contract farmers are small yet are more numerous than rice farmers. Their numbers have fluctuated widely over the years. During the 1950s, there were about 13,000 to 16,000 sugar cane cultivating families, constituting about 20 percent to 25 percent of total farming families. About 80 percent of them cultivated less than 0.6 hectare of land (ibid., 607), making mechanization difficult (ibid., 616).

The government collected sugar cane from the contract farmers using a pre-modern fees-in-kind method called "**Sugar Sharing System**." This payment method was used in the Ch'ing Dynasty and later abandoned by the Japanese (Sumiya *et al.*, 1968, 77; Liu, 1975, 162).[52] The system enabled Taisugar to collect hidden taxes on the farmers at a rate of about 42 percent, as explained below. This percentage is much higher than the highest rent of 37.5 percent touted by the KMT government as a reason for initiating land reform, as noted earlier.

The "Sugar Sharing System" worked as follows. The sugar cane farmers took the sole risk in planting sugar cane (the government claimed that the farmers were their "own masters"). They then brought the harvest to the local Taisugar factory to process sugar cane into sugar. The farmers paid a certain ratio of sugar as processing fees. The "sharing" ratio between farmers and Taisugar was, as usual, fixed by the government, and fluctuated slightly year to year. However, on average, the government's fixed ratio was 50–50 (see 1Share, col. 2, Fig. 1.10). Since 20 percent of sugar cane was produced by Taisugar (TSProd (1)), this means that 80 percent of Taiwan's total sugar production by the farmers was shared equally among the contract farmers' production (FaShare (2)) and that by the government (TSShare (3)).

Note first that this ratio is almost the same as the one used by local sugar processing firms during the non-mechanized pre-modern days under the Ch'ing Dynasty over 60 years earlier. In fact, it is estimated that, with modern facilities, the actual processing cost should not have exceeded 13 percent of processed sugar (Sumiya *et al.*, 1992, 77). This is denoted

[52]The Japanese used "Pricing-by-Weight Method." The sugar company determines the sugar cane purchase price with reference to the rice price, and writes contract with the sugar cane farmers. The company then buys the sugar cane at the pre-determined price after harvest. "Naturally, this method is much closer to the modern form of management than the "sugar sharing system" (Liu, 1975, 154).

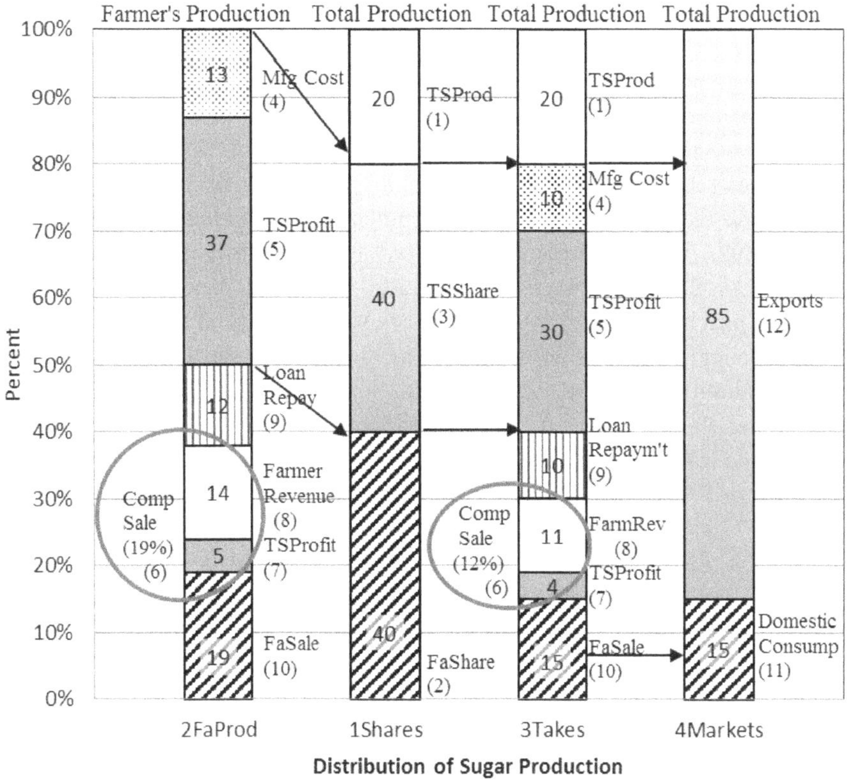

Figure 1.10: Sugar Production and Distribution — The Sugar Sharing System

as manufacturing cost (Mfg cost (4)) in Col. 2FaProd, by taking farmers' production as 100 percent. Thus the government exploited the farmers at about a whopping 37 percent (50% − 13%) of the farmers' processed sugar, denoted as Taisugar profits (TSprof (5)) in Col. 2FaProd.

In terms of the total sugar production, the 13% Mfg cost is equivalent to about 10 percent (=80% × 0.13) of the total sugar production ((4) of Col. 3Takes), and 37 percent of TSprof in turn is equivalent to about 30 percent (=80% × 0.37) of Taiwan's total sugar production ((5) of Col. 3Takes).

The government exploitation of farmers did not stop here. Although, officially, the other 50 percent of contract farmers' sugar, that is, 40 percent of the total sugar production, belonged to the farmers, as shown in the lower part of Col. 2FaProd or Col. 3Takes, the farmers even could not keep all of their share. There is a government-imposed "holding limit." According to the regulation, about 38 percent of the farmers' production (that is, taking farmer's production as 100%), or, equivalently, about 19 percent (=50% × 0.38) of the contract farmers' share ((6) of Col. 2FaProd), or, 15 percent (40% × 0.38) of the total sugar production ((6) of Col. 3Takes), had to sell to the Taisugar at a government-fixed purchase price (Sumiya *et al.*, 1992, 76). This amount is denoted as "compulsory sale" (6) (Comp sale) in Col. 2FaProd with a circle and also (6) in Col. 3Takes with a circle.

The purchase price of this compulsory sale depends on the international price of sugar, which is converted to local currency through an exchange rate at about 20 percent to 30 percent lower than the general exchange rate under the fixed exchange system (Liu, 1975, 162). If the international price is too low to provide the farmers an incentive to cultivate sugar cane, a "guaranteed" price would be used. Although officially the latter guaranteed "average" revenue of the sugar-cane farmers, it was determined as low as possible depending on the Taisugar's raw material policy, its financial condition, and also the KMT government's fiscal conditions (ibid., 164).

If the farmers' exchange rate or government's guaranteed price is estimated about 25 percent less than the general exchange rate or the market price, then 9.5 percent (=38% × 0.25) out of farmers' compulsory sale of 38 percent of farmers' share, or about 5 percent of total sugar the farmers produced, is Taisugar's profits. This part is denoted as "TSProfit" (7) in Col. 2FaProd and also (7) in Col. 3Takes. The rest, 14 percent of the farmers' production (FaRev (8) in Col. 2FaProd), or, equivalently, 11 percent of the total production, (FaRev (8) in Col. 3Takes), will be the farmer's revenue.

Furthermore, from farmers' total production, the farmers had to pay about 12 percent of their output (LoanRepay (9), Col. 2FaProd)), or about 10 percent of total sugar production (LoanRepay (9), Col. 3Takes), to Taisugar to defray costs of transportation, harvesting, and pre-harvest loans. Thus, at the end, the farmers could retain and sale only 19 percent of their share (FaSale (10) in Col. 2FaProd), namely, about 15 percent of total sugar production (=80%*0.19) (FaSale (10) in Col. 3Takes). This amount then could be sold to the domestic market by the farmers ((11), Col. 4Markets). The other 85 percent, 20 percent of which were produced by the Taisugar ((1) of Col. 1Shares or (1) of Col. 3Takes) and 65 percent by the contract farmers (from Col. 3Takes, 10% + 30% + 10% + 11% + 4%), would be exported to earn precious foreign exchange (12).

In conclusion, from Col. 2FaProd, the total "profit" or exploitation of the sugar farmers by the Taisugar appeared to be whopping 42 percent (37% + 5% in Col. 2FaProd) of total farmers' production. In spite of such a heavy exploitation, few farmers protested or even raised a question under authoritarian regime.

1.7.4.4 *The Decline of the Agricultural Sector*

Under such severe exploitation and unequal exchange conditions, one may wonder why the farmers should care to cultivate sugar cane at all, since they still had the freedom of choosing crops, at least theoretically. One explanation that has been given (Liu, 1975, 159) is the effect of pre-harvest loans. Sugar cane farmers required loans to purchase inputs and maintain their families. Sugar cane requires on the average 15 months to harvest. Since many farmers are small and poor, after being wooed to cultivate sugar cane with an unrealistic rosy profit expectation, after harvest, many farmers probably had to borrow more to maintain a living. They were thus tied to sugar cane cultivation, and couldn't emancipate themselves from such unequal exchanges.[53] The situation might even be aggravated by the fact that most farmers spoke only Taiwanese, which is different from the official Chinese language spoken by the Chinese bureaucrats, and under martial law any protests and strikes were severely punished. To determine whether this was really the case requires further research.

Another possible explanation is that Taiwan's farm land was so fertile and/or the fertilizer was so effective that the farmer still received reasonable prices and income. Thus, although heavily exploited, the promise of higher future returns and ownership of their own land provided incentives for farmers to increase production.

Heavy exploitation of the rice and sugar-cane farmers brought about drastic changes in Taiwanese agriculture after the 1960s. These changes were prompted by shifts in the international agricultural markets, along with rapid domestic industrialization.

[53]Liu (1975), 159. This may not be an isolated case. A banana farmer in Davao, Philippines, had to pay 75 percent of his monthly salary for debts and 21 percent for fertilizer, etc. After the reduction, he had to borrow more to maintain his living, thus he is tied to harvesting bananas for his life time. Under Philippine's martial law, strikes were prohibited, and those who resisted were simply murdered by the owners of banana plantation. See David *et al.* (1981), as quoted in Tsurumi (1982), 153–154. I am indebted to late Professor Natsuki Fujita for the reference.

The proportion of both rice and sugar in Taiwan's total exports was surpassed by other exports in 1959, and the proportion decreased steadily thereafter. By 1985, both rice and sugar consisted of a mere 0.1 percent of total exports (TSDB, 1986, 221). Rice and sugar production has catered only to domestic consumption in recent years.

Instead, the agricultural sector has become diversified and specialized, and farm income pluralized (Kuo, 1983, Chapter 3). With help from the Joint Commission on Rural Reconstruction (JCRR) of the U.S. Aid Mission, various agricultural improvements and innovations were introduced (Ho, 1978, 178). New crops, like asparagus and mushrooms were introduced in the mid-l960s (TSDB, 1992, 73). By the 1980s, there was a shift in agricultural exports to fishery products like pawns and eel, and livestock products such as hogs, poultry, and chicken eggs (ibid., 78–79). These were produced by specialized farmers using modern large-scale management systems. In 1989, most of these new products, like pawns (97.7%), eel (97.9%), and pork (99.8%), were exported to Japan (Sumiya *et al.*, 1992, 82).

Even with diversification and specialization, the agricultural sector has been shrinking (ibid., 88–90). There are several reasons for this. First, diversification and specialization brought about environmental pollution and destruction. The social costs outweighed the merits of earning foreign exchange. Second, the compulsory purchase system of rice and sugar combined with the guaranteed price system only increased the government's budgetary burden. Third, there were adverse effects to trade liberalization on agriculture. In response to massive exports of manufactured goods to the United States, the U.S. Government has been pressuring Taiwan to buy more U.S. agricultural products. In 1989, 87.3 percent of wheat, 93.5 percent of soybean, and 93.9 percent of corn consumed domestically were imported from the United States. Furthermore, as relations between Taiwan and China improve, there is the threat of cheap agricultural imports from nearby China.

From 1966 to 1989, the average per family net income from farming decreased about 50 percent. To supplement the declining income from farming, pluralization took place. More farmers worked only part-time and became factory workers. In fact, farmers' wage income, and therefore income from non-farming activities, doubled during this period (ibid., 84). Although the overall average per family farm income increased 11.2 times in 1989 from NT$ 32,320 in 1966 (ibid., 84), farmers' income relative to non-farmer's income (taking non-farmers' income as 100%) decreased from 94.8 percent in 1966 to 72.2 percent in 1970, and further to a mere 66.4 percent in 1989. Thus, Taiwan's agricultural sector has been declining steadily.

There have been several government proposals to revitalize the agricultural sector. Government policies to assist domestic agriculture have proved to be fragmented, inconsistent, and slow in implementation. The end result has effectively been a disregard for the welfare of the farmers.[54]

We can now put Taiwan's land reform and its early industrialization and agricultural development into a historical perspective. Although the Taiwanese landlords lost almost everything, they can still take some comfort in the fact that the land was not completely confiscated and people were not executed as in China. Meanwhile, the traditional local power structure in the villages were virtually destroyed, forestalling potential rural unrest and political opposition. Many landlords became entrepreneurs, the bosses ("Lau Bang" in Taiwanese) of the Taiwanese small and medium enterprises, and the backbone of the Taiwan's economic miracle. These Taiwanese landlords in villages were replaced by cadre of Farmers' Associations, which are directly or indirectly controlled by the government (Tien, 1989, 47–48), and most of them became conservative supporters of the KMT government.

1.8 A Review of Early Post-War Development

Up to now we have shown that Taiwanese economy had already completed the phase of primary export-led growth by the 1920s and entered the import substitution phase in late 1930s. The outbreak of the Sino-Japanese War and the entrance of WWII stimulated Taiwanese industrial development, but eventually led to the destruction of its economy by Allied air raids.

Immediately after the war, the Taiwanese economy was again disrupted by the incompetent Chinese government, and by the internal war in China. When the internal war was over in China in 1949, Taiwan was under the direct and strict control of the KMT émigré regime. The government officials could not speak Taiwanese, and major policies were made without

[54]Even up to 1987, a health insurance system for farming communities in Taiwan had not been established. The three government-monopolized television stations were allowed to use only one and a half hours to broadcast programs in the Taiwanese language per day. Most of the farmers cannot understand Chinese. While the Chinese in Taiwan depend on the Taiwanese farmers for food, they nevertheless depict the farmers on television as second rate citizens in society (K. Hsiao, 1987, 97–100).

much consideration of the welfare of the Taiwanese people. For almost ten years after the war, the KMT regime was preoccupied with the "Recovery of the Chinese mainland". Economic development of Taiwan was only a secondary or no priority, as evidenced from the allocation of government expenditures, resource allocations in the cement industries, and the relentless schemes of rice and sugar cane procurements.

The Americans contributed in financing and maintaining economic growth and the armed forces, and advising on the development policies during the most crucial post-war period. The Chinese contributed in human capital and textile capital and technology, ruled the island under a one-family oligarchy and maintained political stability at least on the surface. The Taiwanese were the silent majority of timid tillers and toilers, generally educated, hardworking, but leaderless and apolitical. With these four sources of contributions, Taiwan's initial conditions for take-off were not exactly "underdeveloped." Its starting point already is much higher than most of the developing countries in that period.

The Chiang government confiscated large Japanese firms and plants after the war, and made them public enterprises. The public enterprises dominated the economy in the 1950s but gradually lost their dominance to private enterprises after 1960s. While laissez faire prevailed for the small and medium enterprises, the large private enterprises, like the large textile firms, were nourished and protected by the government though various laws of encouraging investment.

The government adopted a barter system, "the commissioned spinning and weaving system" in the textile industry, the in-kind land tax, rice-fertilizer barter system in rice production, and the "sugar sharing system" for the sugar cane farmers. The first system was used to subsidize the textile industry to secure foods for its employees, it nevertheless pushed the economy one step backwards, and distorted the market economy. The unequal exchange and barter system could be implemented because of the dictatorial character of the government with a tight security system.

In general, Taiwanese economic development, at least up to 1963, was filled with many unique characteristics which are hardly shared with the other developing countries. In recent years, the role of the state in economic development has been one of the major topics in the economic literature. The KMT government in Taiwan may fit into the success model of "development dictatorship" (although it depends on the definition of the term). Among the countries in the world in the 1990s, dictatorship, not democracy, has been a rule rather than an exception, but only a few succeeded in economic development. Thus, the Taiwanese history is rather an exception.

But, then, few countries had inherited a well-organized social structure and economic infrastructure from Japanese colonialism, nor received massive infusion of U.S. foreign aid and advisers in the initial fifteen crucial years after the war. Furthermore, few countries had the new émigré regime which spoke a different language, both literally and figuratively, without any ties to the local society, and which tried hard to overcome failure in the past and determined to succeed in the future. These were unique combined features which none of the other developing countries seem to have, and will be, ever experienced.

We also feel that the major impact of the 228 incident, one-family oligarchy, white terror under martial law, and the KMT's language policy on Taiwanese economic development has been that the policy-decision making process has degenerated into a simpler one in which few problems of conflict resolution were encountered. Since the success of government policy in a democratic country is a process of conflict resolution, the Taiwanese case under dictatorship does not seem to present much interesting experience. Furthermore, if one argues that the above sequence of events was necessary for securing economic stability and progress, then in terms of social cost, human right violation, jailing, even execution of opponents, and, with the benefit of hindsight, more people probably would choose a more democratic society but less rapid economic growth. A case in point is that if the local Taiwanese people, not the carpetbagger bureaucrats, had had some inputs in economic planning and decision-making some decades ago, the severe problems of pollution and environmental devastation in Taiwan (Bello and Rosenfeld, 1990, 131) today could have been mitigated or even alleviated.

We have seen the external contributions of the Japanese, the Americans, and the Chinese to Taiwanese economic development up to the early 1960s. Based on this foundation, the Taiwanese economy then entered into the phase of export expansion, in which the local Taiwanese people and the foreign direct investments by the multinational corporations started playing a prominent role. The examination of this phase, which will be rather technical, will be the topic of the following sections.

1.9 Some Basic Indicators of Economic Development

The process of original accumulation for Taiwanese economic development was roughly completed by the mid-1960s. Although economists and politicians of Taiwanese studies generally agree that the decade of the 1950s was the period of recovery and import substitution, and the decade of 1960s was the period of take-off and export-led growth (Chen, 1982, 80), they differ in the exact year each period began and ended. This is understandable since both trade policies coexisted during these two decades. The period after the mid-1960s presents a marked difference from the previous period, as foreign trade began to play a vital role in Taiwanese economic development. The Taiwanese economy was restructured and subjected to an international division of the production process. The vitality of the economy was bolstered by direct foreign investments and a boom in small-and medium-sized Taiwanese enterprises.

Taiwanese economic development after 1964 may also be divided into several stages. This will be done in the next section. We first give a bird's-eye view of the macroeconomic performance of the postwar Taiwanese economy.

Some of the basic macroeconomic indicators of economic development are gross domestic product (GDP), real GDP growth rates, real and nominal per capita Gross National Product (GNP), price indexes, inflation rates, exchange rates, exports, imports, the balance of trade, and export and import dependencies.

1.9.1 *Gross Domestic Product and Wholesale Price Index*

The basic indicators of Taiwanese economy are summarized in Figs. 1.11 and 1.12. The Taiwanese data source on GDP is given at 1986 prices (that is, real GDP) in New Taiwan dollars (NT$, TSDB, 1993, 25). We have converted it to U.S. dollars by dividing it by the exchange rate for U.S. dollar (ibid., 152), taking the average of the buying and the selling rates. This is what we call real GDP (denoted as rGDP in upper right corner of Fig. 1.12). Starting from real GDP of US$10 billion in 1952, it decreased first and fluctuated slightly due to inflationary pressure. It recovered in 1964 and has grown steadily afterward even during the two oil crises of 1973 and 1979, and the world depression in the 1980s. Overall, it shows a rather smooth and steady increase over the past 40 years. The growth rates of real GDP are shown as the empty bars in Fig. 1.11, denoted as percentage changes using the right Y axis. With few exceptions, the real GDP growth rates are positive after 1960, except 1982. Although the growth rate in 1982 dipped, it recovered quickly and achieved the highest real growth rate, 40 percent, in 1987.

The original Taiwanese trade statistics are given in current U.S. dollars. To eliminate the influence of price fluctuations, they are converted into real

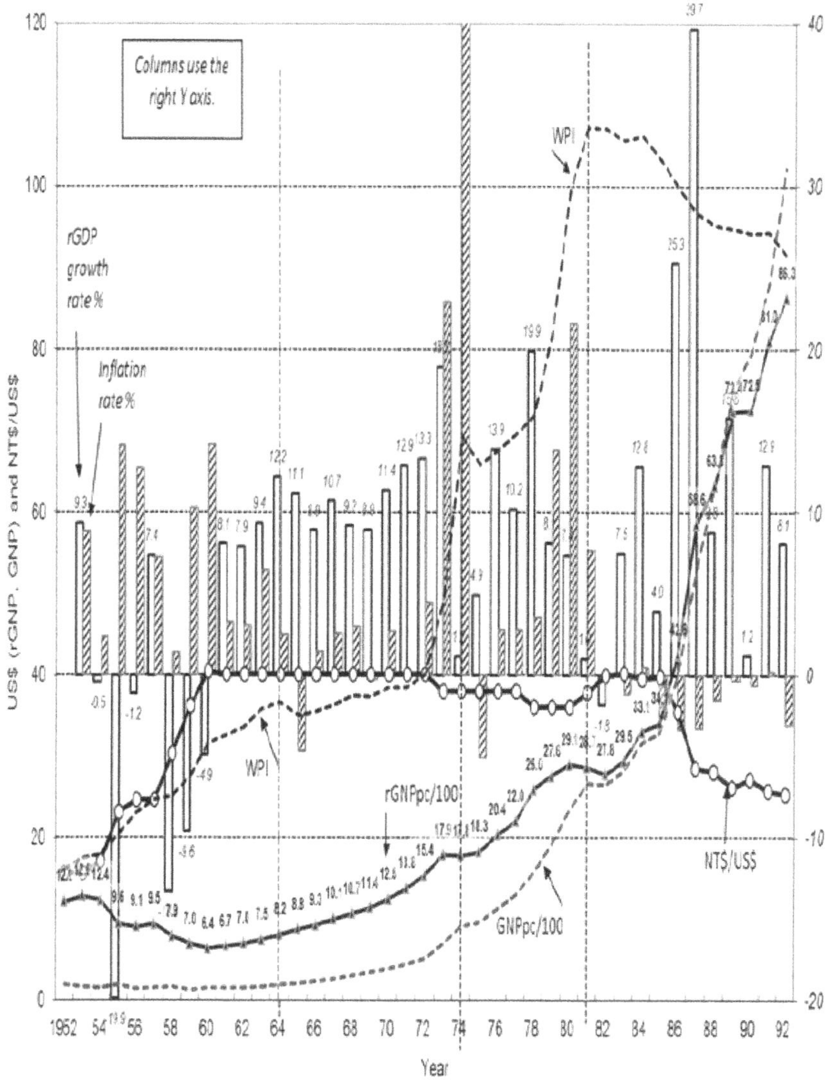

Notes: r = real, pc = per capita, rGNPpc/100 = real per capita GNP divided by 100.

Figure 1.11: Some Basic Indicators of Taiwan

GDPpc, rGDPpc, WPI, Exchange Rate, rGDP Growth and Inflation Rates

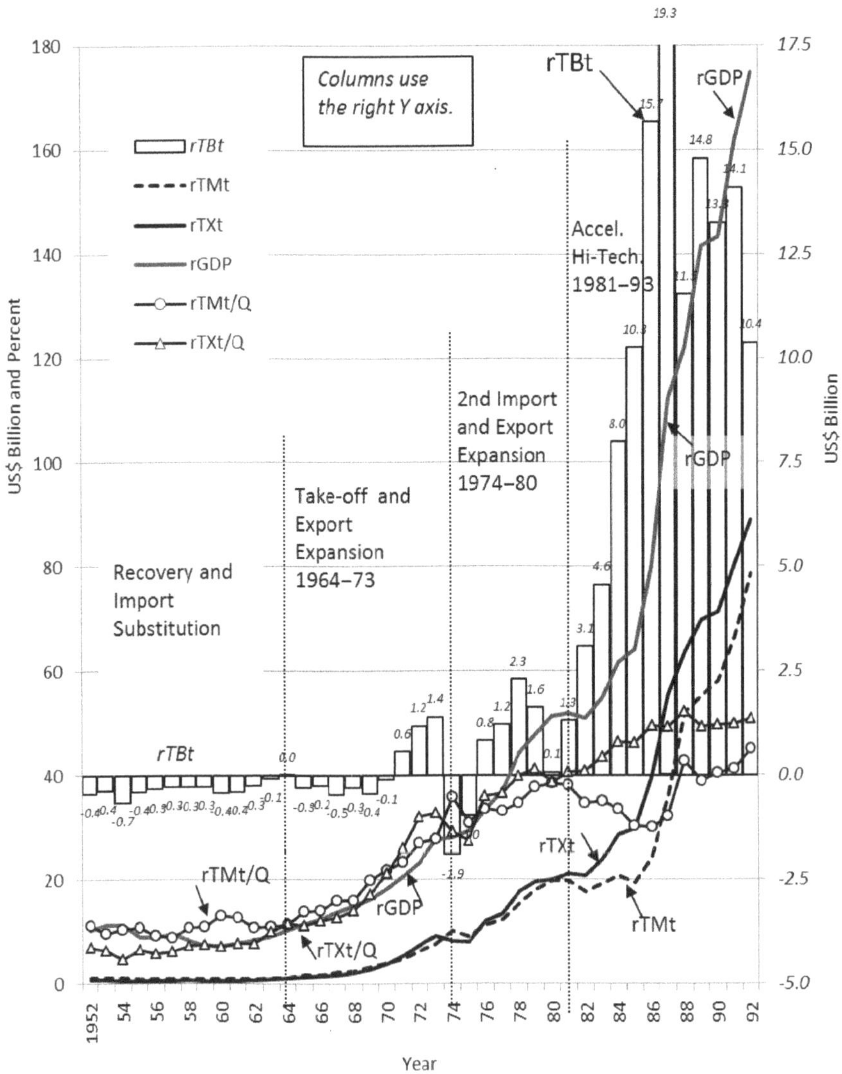

Notes: T = Taiwan, r = real, t = total, X = Exports, M = Imports, B = Balance of Trade, /Q = Divided by rGDP

Figure 1.12: Some Basic Indicators of Taiwan

Taiwan's Real, GDP, Total Exports, Imports, BOT, and Exports and Imports Dependencies

values in U.S. dollars by dividing them by Taiwan's wholesale price index (WPI), taking l986s wholesale price as 100 (TSDB, 1993, 167). The results are then multiplied by 100 to obtain the price adjusted real value in U.S. dollars. The WPI is shown as the heavy dotted line in Fig. 1.11. The WPI, instead of the consumer price index (CPI), is chosen, since exports and imports are generally managed by wholesalers.

The WPI increased sharply during the 1970s, and tended to decrease in the 1980s. The percentage change of WPI, which is an indicator of inflation rate, is shown as the columns right of the rGDP growth rate with upward sloping pattern using the right Y-axis. The light solid line (NT$/US$) is the exchange rate of the U.S. dollar at the end of each year, measured in NT$ from the left Y-axis. It was NT$15.6 at the end of 1952 (TSDB, 1975, 166). The government devaluated it to NT$40 in 1960, which was maintained until December 1972. After 1972, it gradually evaluated again to NT$25.4 for one U.S. dollar in December 1992 (TSDB, 1992, 152).

The light dotted line (GNPpc/100) at the bottom of Fig. 1.11 is gross national product (GNP) per capita in current U.S. dollar (TSDB, 1993, 30) divided by 100 (just to fit into the scale of the left Y-axis). It started at US$196 (shown as 1.96 in Fig. 1.11) in 1952, US$217 (2.17 in Fig. 1.11) in 1965, US$964 in 1975. It increased to US$10,215 (102.15 in Fig. 1.11) in 1992. As shown by Fig. 1.12, the sharp increase is apparently fueled by the evaluation of New Taiwan dollar and decrease in WPI.

The light solid line (rGNPpc/100) on its left side shows real GNP per capita, obtained from dividing real GNP per capita in New Taiwan dollars at 1986 prices (ibid.) by the exchange rate of U.S. dollars, which is given as the heavy solid line (NT$/US$) in Fig. 1.11. The numbers are again divided by 100 to fit into the scale of the Y-axis. The real GNP per capita tells a quite different story. In real terms (using 1986 prices), Taiwanese GNP per capita in 1952 already reached US$1,216 (12.16 in Fig. 1.11), more than six times larger than per capita GNP in nominal value, thanks to overvaluation of the dollar. It increased to US$1,287 (or 12.87 in Fig. 1.11) in the following year, and then started decreasing to the bottom of US$642 (6.42) in 1960. It surpassed the 1953 record only in 1970 with US$1,248 (12.48). Considering the very slow recovery, or even stagnation, of real standard of living, this observation of real GNP per capita seems to be consistent with the finding that Taiwan's real consumption expenditure surpassed the prewar level only around 1960 (Mizoguchi, 1975, 23, 28).

After 1971, real GNP per capita (rGNPpc) took off and increased steadily to US$8,630 (86.30 in Fig. 1.11) in 1992, which is about 85 percent of the nominal GNP per capita, shown by the light dotted line in Fig. 1.11. After 1981, the discrepancy between real GNP per capita and nominal GNP per capita narrowed considerably.

1.9.2 *Foreign Trade Performance*

In Fig. 1.12, the lower heavy solid line (rTXt) shows Taiwan's real total (denoted by t) exports, and the heavy dotted line (rTMt) presents Taiwan's real total (t) imports. The line with triangle markers (rTXt/Q, where Q is real GDP) is the export dependency ratio, and the line with circle markers (rTMt/Q) is the import dependency ratio. The bars show the real balance of trade (rTBt = rTXtr − rTMt), measured from the right Y-Axis. The steady and rapid growth after 1970 of Taiwan's current and real per capita GNP (see Fig. 1.11), real GDP, exports, and the balance of trade (Fig. 1.12), are the foundation of Taiwan's so-called "miracle."

As shown in Fig. 1.12, both real total exports (rTXt) and imports (rTMt) started with about US$1 billion each in 1952. Imports are consistently larger than exports before 1970 and smaller thereafter. After 1964, both imports and exports increased, each passing the US$50 billion mark in 1987–1988. By 1992, real total exports reached US$ 89 billion, and real total imports reached US$ 79 billion. In terms of current prices, however, they are higher due to decrease in WPI. They were US$81 billion and US$72 billion, respectively, in 1992 (TSDB, 1993, 190).

Unlike the colonial days (see Fig. 1.12), Taiwan had persistent trade deficits from the end of the war until 1975, except 1964 and 1971 to 1973. The deficits were large for the size of Taiwanese economy during the 1970s, ranging from US$83 million in 1963 to US$1.9 billion in 1974 in real terms (US$30 million and 1.3 billion, respectively, in nominal terms). They are shown by the negative bars measured from the right Y-axis. The negative bars look small because of the scale of measurement. Admittedly, the earlier stage of import substitution policy (for fertilizer, metal, machinery, and chemicals), and export promotion strategy (of textiles, etc.) required substantial amounts of raw materials and capital equipment. Thus, like other developing countries, Taiwanese trade deficits in the early stage of economic development were understandable. What makes it unusual is that it took thirty long years since 1945 to turn the tide. Without U.S. aid, the economy would have collapsed. Apparently increased population and military burden took a heavy toll. The government had great difficulties or was only half-hearted in imposing its development policy until the middle of the 1960s. The trade turned to have surpluses every year since 1976.

We look at dependency ratios on the left Y-axis, which is now measured in percentage. A dependency ratio is a ratio of exports or imports to GDP in percentage form (rTXt/Q or rTMt/Q). They also have been increasing steadily. They were both about 11 percent in 1964, 32 percent and 27 percent, respectively in 1973, both 39 percent in 1980, and 50 percent and 45 percent, respectively, in 1992 (TSDB). This indicates that the importance of trade in the Taiwanese economy increased over the years. These ratios are found to be relatively high compared with other developing countries (Riedel, 1992, 260), exposing Taiwanese economy to fluctuations of external economic conditions.

1.10 Stages of Economic Development after 1964

The period after 1964 is divided into three parts. The take-off and export promotion period, 1964–1973, the second import substitution period, 1974–1980, and the accelerated growth and high-tech industrialization period, 1981–1993 (see Fig. 1.12). They are explained briefly in this section.

1.10.1 *Take-off and Export Promotion Period (1964–1973)*

By the mid-1960s, despite the termination of the U.S. Aid Program, the economic and political pessimism of the 1950s was "replaced by a popular sense of confidence and prosperity" (Liang and Liang, 1982, 237). This was in a great contrast to the chaos of "Great Cultural Revolution" in China during the same period (1966–1976). Admittedly, since history is a continuous process of events, the exact time of demarcation does not make much sense. However, the following events before and after 1964 may be noted.

Gross Domestic Product. As shown in Fig. 1.12, Taiwan's real gross domestic products (rGDP) fluctuated downwards slightly between 1952 and 1963. It recovered to the 1952 level of US$ 10 billion in 1964. After 1964, real GDP increased steadily to US$28 billion in 1973, and then to huge US$ 175 billion in 1992.

As shown in Fig. 1.11, measured from the right Y-axis, Taiwan's average annual percentage growth in real GDP (rGDP growth rate in Fig. 1.11) jumped from 9.4 percent in 1963 to two digits growth rate (12.2%) in 1964 for the first time since the War (TSDB, 1993, 26). The Taiwanese economy entered a period of mostly double digit high growth rates until slowing down in 1973.

The Structure of Labor in the primary industry showed a definite sign of steady decrease to less than 50 percent of the total employment after 1964 (ibid., 16), indicating the change in the labor structure. The unemployment rate decreased drastically from about 4.0 percent in and before 1964, to 3.3 percent in 1965, 1.5 percent in 1972, 1.2 percent in 1980, and then 1.5 percent in 1992 (ibid.).

Industrial Structure. The industrial share of GDP exceeded the agricultural share in 1963. Few economists noted that this was the second occurrence in Taiwanese economic history after a lapse of 24 years (since 1939). After 1964, the difference increased steadily. This indicates the recovery of production structure of the Taiwanese economy from the prewar period in the mid-1960s. The agricultural share in GDP decreased steadily from 23.6 percent in 1965 to 12.1 percent in 1973, and to a mere 3.5 percent in 1992. On the other hand, the industrial share in GDP increased from 30.2 percent in 1965 to 43.8 percent in 1973, and then remained in the range of 40 percent to 48 percent afterward (ibid., 42).

Trade Structure. The trade structure also started to shift around 1964. The export share of industrial products exceeded the share of raw and processed agricultural products in 1962 (TSDB, 1984, 199). However, from 1963 to 1964, sugar prices soared rapidly due to the Cuban Crises, reducing the industrial share to less than 50 percent, namely, 41.1 percent, 42.5 percent, and 46.0 percent, respectively. The industry share in total exports jumped to 55.1 percent in 1966, increased steadily to 84.6 percent in 1973, and reached 95.7 percent in 1992 (TSDB, 1993, 194). Thus, 1964 may be considered the dividing year of changing from dominant agricultural exports to dominant industrial exports.

Meanwhile, the share of sugar in the total value of exports dropped to 20.9 percent in 1962, but recovered to 30.8 percent in the following year. It maintained almost at the same rate (29.6%) in 1964, but decreased steadily and drastically immediately after 1964. It was only 9.8 percent in 1966, and merely 2.0 percent in 1973 (ibid., 1984, 213), rapidly ending the long era of the dominance of sugar in Taiwanese economy since the Japanese days.

Direction of Trade. In 1964, for the first time, Taiwan's imports (in real value) from Japan exceeded those from the United States. In 1967, Taiwan's real exports to the United States exceeded exports to Japan, completing the role reversal between Japan and the United States and establishing the Pacific trade triangle as will be explained subsequently.

Balance of Trade. For the first time after the war, the real balance of trade registered a surplus of US$ 5 million in 1964. Although it was negative from 1964 to 1971, the 1964 surpluses boosted the morale of the government and business community that the export promotion policy during previous years has been working.

Direct Foreign Investment. The approved direct private foreign and overseas Chinese investment increased drastically in 1963 from a slump in 1962. It then increased almost steadily after 1964. The first export processing zone (EPZ) was opened in December 1966, and two more were opened in 1971 (Li, 1988, 92–100), symbolizing the determination of export promotion policy of the government and steady internationalization of Taiwanese economy.

By the end of 1980, the three EPZs hired 79,000 workers, about 3.7 percent of the manufacturing employment, exported US$ 1.46 billion, or 7.4 percent of the total exports, while the value of imports amounted to only US$ 0.75 billion (Li and Yeh, 1982, 117). Like land reform, it was deemed a success by the government officials (Li, 1988, 94), although it appears that this success was rather small. There are several studies of the plight of young female workers in the EPZs by sociologists (Arrigo, 1980, 1984; Cartwell, Luce, and Weinglass, 1978, 12–15), however, there seems to be no systematic and critical evaluation of the economic effects of the EPZs.

The beginning years of the 1970s probably were the darkest period of the KMT government. In October 1971, Taiwan's archenemy, China, was admitted to the United Nations, and Taiwan withdrew its membership. In 1972, Nixon visited China, and Japan recognized China and severed diplomatic relations with Taiwan. Despite the diplomatic setbacks, the Taiwanese economy nevertheless held up high growth rates between 1970 and 1974, with a low inflation rate (see the columns of Fig. 1.11). Helped by relatively stable import prices and the devalued New Taiwan dollar (MOEA, 1991, 244), exports and trade surpluses continued to increase (see the columns of Fig. 1.12). The economic crisis, however, came at the end of 1973 when oil prices shot up and the world economy plunged into a recession. A new era for the Taiwanese economy started in 1974.

1.10.2 *Second Import Substitution Period (1974–1980)*

The impact of the first oil crisis appeared in 1974. As shown in Fig. 1.12, both exports and imports flattened out and the current balance of trade registered deficits of US$ 1.3 billion, the largest after the war. Fig. 1.11 shows that the real GDP growth rate plunged to a mere 1.2 percent per year in 1974 compared with 19 percent the previous year. At the same time, the inflation rate shot up to 41 percent per year, as compared to 23 percent the previous year. The government responded with an economic stabilization program at the beginning of 1974. In the following year, the trade deficits were cut in half, inflation subsided, and real GDP growth rate quadrupled to 4.9 percent. The balance of trade returned to surpluses in 1976. Despite this, the recovery was rather erratic, as shown in Fig. 1.11 by the zigzag empty bars of real GDP growth rates after 1975. However, helped by the appreciation of the Japanese yen, disregarding the subsequent cycles of world recession, recovery, and then recession again, Taiwanese trade surpluses increased tremendously each year (see the columns of Fig. 1.12).

1.10.2.1 *Ten Major Construction Projects*

Despite recession, or because of it, the KMT government went ahead to implement, in 1974, the "Ten Major Construction Projects," which was conceived in the-1972 Sixth Four-Year Economic Plan. The projects total cost was about US$ 5.8 billion. They included the development of the Giant Kaohsiung Shipyard (4.0% of the project cost), an integrated steel mill (17.6%), petrochemical complexes (15.4%), a nuclear power plant, the North-South Freeway, railroad electrification, Taoyuan International Airport, North-Link Railroad, the Taichung Harbor, and the Suao Seaport. The first three projects belong to what is called the heavy and chemical industry. The rest belongs to transportation infrastructure. Not all of the projects were new. The first part of construction was completed between 1977 and 1979.

We have seen that the U.S. aid construction program was imposed and financed from the outside. In contrast, these projects represented the first and foremost demonstration that the government was now serious about Taiwanese economic development by investing heavily on the projects, although more than 50 percent of the fund was borrowed from abroad (Wu, 1992, 166). The results of the projects were very much mixed.

1.10.2.2 *Evaluation of the Projects*

After the war, the Japanese ship repairing and building facility in Kaohsiung was reorganized as the government-owned Taiwan Shipbuilding Company (TSC). In 1973, a private-owned China Shipbuilding Company was established as a joint venture with the government. Despite heavy project investment by the government, the private partners withdrew in 1977. The government took over, and merged with the TSC in 1978 (Chen *et al.*, 1991, 47). Since then, the shipbuilding industry has been constantly troubled with mismanagement, misjudgment, and technical and parts problems.

The shipbuilding project ended disastrously, sustaining the largest loss every year among the public enterprises under the Ministry of Economic Affairs (ibid., 48). As the shipbuilding project went awry, the project on an integrated steel mill lost its steam. Before the 1970s, the government was negligent in developing the iron and steel industry (ibid., 46). There was one large steel mill and about 100 private non-integrated mills using raw steel recovered from shipbreaking. In the early 1970s, the Taiwanese shipbreaking industry was number one in the world. The government-owned China Steel Corporation started operating in 1978, using virgin raw materials (King, 1993, 43). Although domestic steel production in 1991 reached 12.5 million metric tons, supply still lagged behind the demand. Steel imports as a percentage of consumption rose from 22.6 percent in 1985 to 30.5 percent in 1991 (ibid., 47). The domestic output was of low-and middle-level quality, and high-quality steel still depended on imports (Sumiya *et al.*, 1992, 128).

The most successful project was the development of a petrochemical complex. Investment in this industry completed the second import substitution phase of up-stream and mid-stream industries for Taiwan's two most important exports: textile and plastic products. After 1980, Taiwan was even able to export petrochemical raw materials. The success of building transportation infrastructure was also mixed. For example, the last two projects, development of Taichung Harbor and the Suao Seaport, did not achieve the expected results (Wu, 1992, 160).

The petrochemical industry will be re-examined in Section 1.15.4 in relation with the textile industry. Due to the problems of price uncertainty in petroleum imports and, more importantly, high environmental pollution, which is the sources of numerous street protests in the 1980s, future development of petrochemical industry seems precarious and uncertain.

In general, the ten major construction projects merely upgraded the already well-protected public enterprises. Their effects on the development of private enterprises were at most indirect. To be fair, the projects have raised the industrial structure to a certain degree. However, the Taiwanese economy was hardly transformed to a more advanced stage of industrialization like Korea. The government blames the smallness of the Taiwanese market and has changed its objective of developing heavy and chemical industry to the "high-tech" industry.

1.10.3 *Accelerated Growth and High-tech Industrialization Period (1980-)*

The period of the 1980s was a politically flurried and restless decade for Taiwan. In 1975, President Chiang Kai-sek died. His son, Ching-Kuo, became the president in 1978. In the following year, the United States recognized China and severed diplomatic relations with Taiwan. Taiwanese youths educated under the Chinese system have become active socially and politically.

1.10.3.1 *Steps toward Democracy*

In 1986, the previously informal Taiwanese political "ex party" (Dangwai) was reorganized formally as the Democratic Progressive Party in 1986. It adopted the party platform of "Taiwanese Independence" in 1991. The 37 year old martial law was lifted in July 1987, and political parties and street demonstrations sprouted like bamboo shoots (H. Hsiao, 1990).

Communication between the postwar second generation Taiwanese and the second generation Chinese improved after the 1980s. Some second generation Chinese, most of them speak fluent Taiwanese, even organized the "Association of Supporting Independence of Taiwan" in 1992. Thus, distinction between the two groups was becoming ambiguous.[55] Exchange programs with China among the Chinese on both sides of the Formosa Straits were gradually allowed.

Chiang Ching-Kuo died in January, 1988, and the native-born Professor T.H. Lee became the President in 1989. Lee nominated the "National Unification Committee" in 1990 to study Taiwan's relation with China.

[55]Naturally some Taiwanese are also Sinicized. From our observation of Chinese culture, however, it is not clear whether these Taiwanese still can be identified with Chinese culture and the Chinese nation (Hsiao and Sullivan, 1979, 460).

In 1991, the "Period of National Mobilization for Suppression of the Communist Rebellion" was terminated, ending the 42-year long state of war with China, and beginning an era of democracy in Taiwan. For the first time, the government acknowledged in 1991 the tragedy of the 228 Incident of 1947. It published an official report in the following year.

Taiwan applied to join the General Agreement on Tariffs and Trade (GATT) organization in 1990 and granted an observer status in 1992. It also applied to join other international organizations, including the United Nations in 1993, which was hindered by opposition from China. Taiwan's political and economic situations changed rapidly during this period, prompting numerous studies on Taiwan in recent years.

This period starts from 1980, following the 1979 second oil crisis. The effects of oil price increase is that the world plunged again into deep recession and Taiwan's balance of trade dipped to mere US$ 0.08 billion. Unlike the first oil crisis, however, it did not become negative (see Fig. 1.12). The real GDP growth rate still maintained at 7.4 percent per year. The world recession eventually caught up in Taiwan and the growth rate dipped to mere 1.0 percent in 1981 and became −1.8 percent in 1982 (Fig. 1.11). Many people felt that the Taiwanese economy was in a great trouble, and condemned it as a "shallow dependency economy."

1.10.3.2 *Recovery from the Second Oil Crisis*

To the surprise of the world, the Taiwanese economy recovered quickly from the second oil crisis (Figs. 1.11 and 1.12). It attained an annual real GDP growth rate of 25.3 percent in 1986 and a whopping 39.7 percent in 1987, the highest rate ever accomplished after the war. The extremely high growth rates were achieved with negative inflation −3.34 percent in 1986 and 3.25 percent in 1987 (Fig. 1.11). From 1980 to 1992, the growth rates were very uneven, but the wholesale price tended to be declining (Fig. 1.11). The average real GDP growth rates during this 13 years was 10.97 percent, all this with wholesale price change a mere 1.05 percent.

The performance in the foreign sector during this period was even more remarkable. The United States pressured Taiwan to revaluate the NT dollar against the U.S.dollar. As shown in Fig. 1.11, the NT dollar indeed evaluated steeply by 36 percent, to the great disadvantage to the Taiwanese exporters, from about NT$40.00 per U.S. dollar in 1982–1985 to NT$25.4 in 1992. In spite of currency revaluation, Taiwanese real exports increased so fast that the real balance of trade hopped and jumped from US$ 1.3 billion in 1981 to a whopping US$ 19.3 billion in 1987 (Fig. 1.12), an increase of 15 times in six years. It decreased to US$ 10.4 billion in 1992 (Fig. 1.12), due to an increase in imports. The increase in imports seems to be caused by faster growth in real GNP. The pressure from the United States to open up the domestic markets also played an important role.

The continuous positive balance of trade during the last decade enabled Taiwan to amass an immense amount of foreign reserves. By April 1991, Taiwan had foreign exchange reserves of more than US$ 76 billion, the biggest in the world (Rafferty, 1992, 216), even surpassing those of Germany and Japan.

Within 11 years, from 1981 to 1992, the decline in the wholesale price index and reevaluation of the New Taiwan dollar worked to increase real GDP 3.4 times, from US$ 51.8 billion to US$ 174.8 billion (Fig. 1.12), and real per capita GNP three times, from US$2,870 to US$8,630 (see rGNPpc/100 in Fig. 1.11). In terms of current per capita GNP, the increase is even greater; it increased 3.8 times, from US$ 2,670 to US$ 10,215 (see GNPpc/100 in Fig. 1.11). Clearly Taiwan has matured into a developed country in this period.

1.10.3.3 *Capital- and Skill-Intensive Industrialization*

Capital and skill industries include chemicals, chemical products, basic metal products, machinery, electrical and electronic equipment, and precision instruments (Lee, 1993, 30). Their share in total manufacturing production increased 11 percent from 1981 to 1991: 30.1 percent in 1981, 36.2 percent in 1986, and 41.2 percent in 1991. The upgrading of the industrial structure is also reflected in the trade structure. The export share of labor intensive products in total Taiwanese exports decreased steadily by 7.6 percent from 1982 to 1992, from 47.2 percent in 1982 to 39.6 percent in 1992. During the same period, the export share of capital intensive products increased 10.6 percent, from 18.3 percent to 28.9 percent, and the export share of high-tech products increased 12.1 percent, from 25.3 percent to 37.4 percent (ibid., 30–31).

The employment structure also shifted heavily from other sectors to services. The employment share of services increased steadily from 39 percent in 1981 to 47.8 percent in 1992. The employment share of the agricultural sector decreased steadily from 18.8 percent in 1981 to 12.5 percent in 1992. At the same time the employment share of manufacturing industries increased first from 32.2 percent in 1981, up to 35.2 percent in 1987, and then decreased steadily afterward to a mere 30.2 percent in 1992 (ibid., 31).

1.10.3.4 *The Six-Year National Development Plan*

After completion of the first phase of the Ten Major Construction Projects, government investment in infrastructure and heavy industry declined again. From 1976 to 1987, government investment (including investment by the public enterprises) contributed on average only 0.4 percent of the annual GDP growth rate (Kuo, 1993, 4). Combined with rapid economic growth, this decline in government investment results in a shortage of electricity and water, deterioration in transportation facilities and environments (ibid., 5), and a lag in various cultural and social welfare programs (Pang and Chen, 1993).

Thus in 1991, the government launched an immense US$ 300 billion Six-Year National Development Plan, one of the most ambitious construction plans in the world (Lee, 1993, 36). The plan called for 775 hastily assembled projects (Pang and Chen, 1993), including urban mass transit systems, nuclear power plants, public housing, welfare services, and pollution controls. It was intended to make Taiwan a leader in high technology, a regional and world financial center, and regional transport hub (Rafferty, 1992, 216).

We have seen the overall economic and political development after 1964. In the following sections, the relationship between foreign trade and economic development will be examined in detail.

1.11 Trade Policy Reform

The period of 1964 to 1973 was also a period of export substitution, namely, exports of industrial products substituted exports of agricultural commodities, especially rice and sugar for Taiwan. Some authors take 1960 as the beginning of Taiwan's export era. This is rather misleading since the need for a vigorous export sector started only soon after Taiwan's industries recovered from the damage inflicted during World War II.

By the end of the 1940s and early 1950s, Taiwanese markets were already flooded with over 100 traditional agricultural products and handicrafts which were traditionally exported to Japan (Lin, 1973, 72). By 1959, many plants were operating at 23 percent to 67 percent of capacity (Liang and Liang, 1982, 223). The government was in strict control of foreign exchange and foreign trade. The shortage of foreign exchange and the needs for importing raw materials and capital goods for public enterprises drove the government to maintain strict import control, a substantially overvalued exchange rate, and a multiple exchange rate structure (see Fig. 1.11). Rent seeking activities were rampant (Liang and Liang, 1982, 222). However, trade policy reform in Taiwan came passively and slowly.

At first the government subsidized 20 selected products for export in 1952. Tax rebates were implemented in 1954, and a system of exchange entitlement was introduced in 1956 (Lin, 1973, 74, 85). Finally, prodded by the U.S. Aid Mission (Jacoby, 1966, 140), a major foreign exchange reform was announced in April 1958. It simplified the foreign exchange regulations and reduced the multiple exchange rate system to a dual rate system. With a reward by the U.S. Aid Mission of an extra US$20–30 million of U.S. aid for prompt implementation (Jacoby, 1966, 135; Gold, 1986, 77), the "19-Point Economic and Fiscal Reform" and the "Statute for Encouragement of Investment" were promulgated in February and September, 1960, respectively. In 1961, the central government held a high-level conference for the first time to hear the views of major business leaders (Lin, 1973, 84), mostly Taiwanese. A single exchange rate was declared in 1961 with the rate of NT$40 to one U.S. dollar (Jacoby, 1966, 140), which was maintained throughout this period until 1972 (TSDB, 1984, 185, see Fig. 1.11). The era of vigorous export promotion and rapid economic growth had begun.

The outward looking trade policy. Probably due to the geographical position of Taiwan, sandwiched between two populous countries, Japan and China, people in Taiwan tend to envision themselves as "small" in everything. In actuality the Taiwanese population, and so the domestic market, is not small compared with most other countries (Hsiao and Hsiao, 1981, 1983). To our knowledge, however, all those who write about the Taiwanese economy assert or agree that the smallness of domestic markets and shortage of natural resources necessitated the shifting of the import-substitution policy to the export-promotion strategy. The fallacy of the argument in both respects was revealed in a World Bank study (WDR, 1987).

World Bank study. According to the study (see Appendix 1A), Burundi and El Salvador both have populations and land area much smaller than those of Taiwan, and yet they took inward-oriented strategies from 1963 to 1985. Six out of ten moderately outward-oriented countries changed to moderately inward-oriented strategies from 1963–1985. Three out of 12 moderately inward-oriented countries even changed to strongly inward-oriented strategies. Eight countries in the moderately inward-oriented strategy category did not change their strategies at all. Why were these countries so oblivious to the benefits of export promotion policy and either reversed or maintained a policy which is supposed to be inferior? Eleven countries maintained strong inward-oriented strategies throughout the three decades. Again, this happened in spite of all the evidence of the advantages of outward-oriented strategies (WDR, 1987, Chapter 5). (See Appendix 1A)

Thus, while the market glut was real, the smallness of domestic markets and shortage of natural resources were not a sufficient condition to drive Taiwan to shift from inward-oriented import substitution strategies to outward-oriented export promotion strategies. The major reason for the shift was likely the influence of the U.S. Aid Mission, which was eager to prove the strength of free trade and the free market system. Although it has been argued that the major obstructions of trade reform were massive unemployment during the process of transition (WDR, 1987, 106), as well as the strong resisting raised by the previously protected vested economic interests (ibid., 95), these were moot points in Taiwan during the early 1960s. The unemployment rate was already high (TSDB, 1984, 14); the major industries were government-owned enterprises which provided "iron rice bowls" to the mostly Chinese immigrant employees, freeing them from the fear of unemployment; and the economy and the whole island were under strict control of the authoritarian émigré regime; few dared to raise objection to the national policy. We submit that, one of the reasons is, as was pointed out earlier, the regime itself never had a root in Taiwan, and was basically "outward looking." It looked to either the "recovery of the mainland," the United States for assistance, or the overseas Chinese, if not other governments, for support of its legitimacy as "the sole Government of China."

Taiwan's trade policy reform. Toward the end of the 1950s, the voice for an outward-looking strategy was strongest in the textile industry. Its large firms and the KMT government were, as we have seen, "intimate comrades in adversity," as both were imported from China. The textile firms had been heavily protected by the government, and yet it was these firms that wanted to have trade reform. Because no harm would be done to the government monopoly of power and public enterprises, the government was more than willing to oblige. Furthermore, the prospect of the termination of the. U.S.

aid program in 1965 also played a decisive role in policy reform. The central government desperately needed foreign exchange to buy arms to counter the Chinese threat of "liberating" Taiwan by force.[56] "With the help from strict regulations and harsh penalty, as well as the total [government] monopoly of banking system, all foreign reserves acquired from exports came under the full control of the Central Government" (Pang and Chen, 1993).

Once the policy shift received a nod from the highest level of the regime[57] the changes took place smoothly (Li and Yeh, 1982) with the help of the Western-trained English speaking economic bureaucrats. In conclusion, while government policy on trade reform might be important in smoothing out the transition, the transition itself was brought out by external influences.[58]

A smooth transition to an export-oriented policy is one thing; sustaining the reform is another. Many countries probably had also tried trade reform but failed eventually. What are the factors that makes the Taiwanese trade reform successful? We submit that the essential factor is the formation of the Pacific trade triangle, as will be explained.

1.12 Development and Trends of Foreign Trade

In economic literature, there is a continuing debate on trade as an "engine" of economic growth or a "handmaiden" of growth. Econometric tests suggest (M. Hsiao, 1987, 157) that there is no unidirectional causal relation between exports and GDP. Indeed, the two variables are interrelated: either a feedback relationship between them or no causal relationship between them. So far as Taiwan and South Korea are concerned, "the rapid economic

---

[56]Amsden (1985) tried to explain why the military went along with the export-oriented policy. Her major difficulty was, like in almost all other similar papers, which foreign trade and the role of Japan in Taiwanese economic development are not considered, or are not put in historical perspectives.

[57]"The autocratic K.Y. Yin pushed the reforms, backed by Chiang Kai-sek and Ch'en among other leaders" (Gold, 1986, 77). According to Professor Henry Wan, Jr., Chiang probably was persuaded by his adviser, Ta-chung Liu, an econometrician at Cornell University. However, the timing of advising was not clear. In addition to the bureaucrats, the KMT government was also advised by some Chinese-American economists in the United States (see Tien, 1989, 126; Tsiang, 1985, Appendix). The local people call them the "Air-borne troop" and "hit-and-run experts" (see Wang, 1959, 11).

[58]American influences might also be important in Korea's policy reform, although no country will admit that its policy was swayed by the American "imperialists." Taiwan's reform started several years earlier than that of Korea (Fei, Ohkawa, Ranis, 1985 and Hsiao, 1989, 160–61). Probably because of Taiwan's outward looking strategy, Korea followed suit.

growth is not only achieved with the export promotion policy, but also derived from the domestic growth of industries and import substitution" (ibid.). In this section, we first discuss the commodity composition of trade, and then Taiwan's major trading partners. The discussion leads us to Taiwan, Japan, and the U.S. nexus.

Since the performance of Taiwanese foreign trade sector has been well documented, we will explain with diagrams, which may be more appealing. The numerical values behind all the diagrams may be found in various issues of TSDB.

1.12.1 *Commodity Composition of Trade*

As the country becomes industrialized, the commodity composition of exports and imports also changes, as will be explained.

1.12.1.1 *Commodity Composition of Exports*

Figure 1.13 shows the five major exports of Taiwan[59] taken in 1992 and 1980, respectively. The left Y-axis is measured in two scales. For the data in 1965 and thereafter, it is measured in billion US$. For the data from 1952 to 1964, since the five exported commodities taken at 1980 were almost negligible or nonexistent during this period, we have reduced the left Y-axis to units of 10 million, instead of billions of US$. Thus, for this early period, 10, 20, and so on along the left Y-axis should be read as US$100 million, US$200 million, and so on.

The commodity classification used in the figures is based on the Chinese Commodity Classification (CCC) system, which is different from the SITC (Standard International Trade Classification) code.[60] Some commodity items have continued since 1969, some were discontinued and substituted by others, as Taiwanese industrialization progressed. In Figs. 1.13 and 1.14, an extra column is inserted between 1980 and 1981. If an item has continued from the previous period, we fill the blank between 1980 and 1981 with data from 1980 (that is, repeated once). If an item was discontinued after 1980, we left it blank resulting in the collapse of those items which is discontinued between 1980 and 1981. The continued items are shown at the bottom layers of the figures with 1980 figure repeated between 1980 and 1981.

---

[59] For the data in 1992, see TSDB (1993, 208–209). For the data in 1980, see TSDB (1982, 204–205).

[60] For comparison, see various issue of SA.

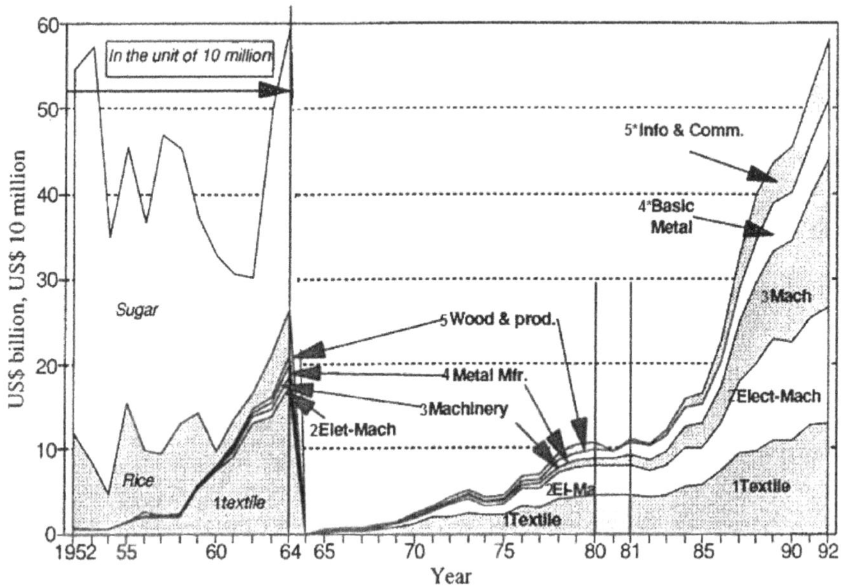

Figure 1.13: Major Exports of Taiwan
1980 and 1992, 1986WPI = 100

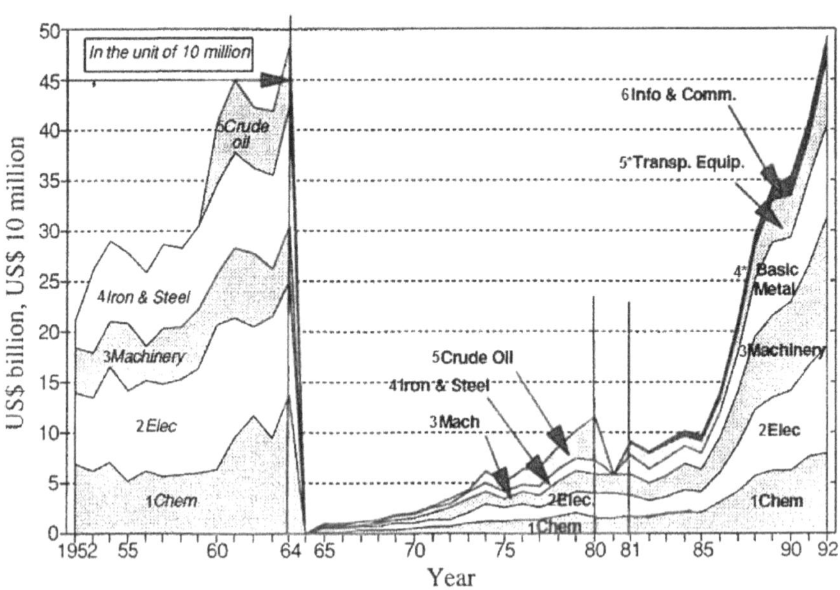

Figure 1.14: Major Imports of Taiwan
1980 and 1992, 1986WPI = 100

The first series is exports of textile products (1Textile in Fig. 1.13). These increased steadily over time. After 1981 textile products have consisted of garments (US$3 billion in 1992. Abbreviated simply to 3b hereafter) and other textile products (9b).[61] Exports of electrical machinery and apparatus (2Elect-Mach in Fig. 1.13), including televisions, sound recorders, and so forth started only around 1960, and became significant only after 1970. After 1981, exports of electrical machinery and apparatus (2Elect-Mach) are calculated as the sum of electronic products (8.7b), electrical machinery products (2.8b), and household electrical appliances (1b), which are listed separately in TSDB (1993). The third series is machinery (3Mach). These exports were also negligible in the early period, becoming significant (16b) only after 1981.

The fourth and fifth series split into two different categories in 1980. Before 1980, the fourth series was exports of 4Metal Manufactures (0.9b in 1980). After 1981, it was replaced by 4*Basic Metals and Articles Thereof (6.5b). Similarly, the fifth series prior to 1980 was exports of 5Wood and Products (0.8b in 1980). After 1981, it was replaced by 5*information and Communication Products (6.4b).

The 5Wood and Products exports series was negligible before 1964. For this reason we have shown "Rice" exports in the fifth series from 1952 to 1964 (0.02b in 1964). Exports of "sugar" (0.lb) are shown above "rice." Notice the irregular fluctuations of primary exports as compared to exports of manufactured goods. This shows a real disadvantage of primary goods exports. By comparison, export levels of manufactured goods are much more stable. As we have observed before, exports of both sugar and rice experienced significant decline after 1964.

1Textiles, which includes garments, has consistently played an important role in Taiwanese exports and industrialization in the postwar era. By 1990, Taiwan was the seventh largest textile exporting country in the world,[62] with a world market share of 6 percent. Although textile exports have been increasing steadily over the years, they were eventually

[61] All the numbers in parentheses are the 1992 current (instead of real) values of exports in US$ billion, unless otherwise specified. In 1990, Taiwan exported textile products worth of US$ 10.3 billion. The major items were man-made filaments (2b), man-made staple fibers (1.6b), knitted or crocheted fabrics (1b), apparel and clothing accessary (3.5b). See MOEA (Feb. 1991), Vol. 258, 105–109. For detailed statistics, see MESI (1991).

[62] Following Hong Kong (14%), Italy (13%), Germany (12%), China (10%), Korea (8%), and France (6%), and followed by Belgium (5%) and the United States (5%). The world share is in the parentheses (Yu and Chen, 1982, 123).

superseded by exports of 2Electrical Machinery and Apparatus in 1988 (all measured in real terms). If 5*Information and Communication Products is added to the latter, then 2Electrical Machinery and Apparatus overtook 1Textiles in 1986. In view of the competition from ASEAN, other Asian NICs, and China (Itaya, 1991, 5–40), it is likely that the Taiwanese textile industry has reached its peak. Continued growth of this industry seems to depend on whether Taiwanese industries can upgrade to produce more high-tech and high value-added textile products.

Figure 1.13 is important as it shows Taiwan's industrialization process from 1952 to 1992. It comfirms Taiwan's steady industrialization by climbing the technology ladder. It illustrates the advancement of export commodities from agricultural goods and agricultural processed goods (rice, sugar, canned foods, etc.) to low technology manufactured goods (textile, metal manufactures, machinery), and then to high technology manufactured goods (electronic products, electrical machinery products, information and communication products, etc.).

Indeed, Taiwan's export record is staggering amid its rapid growth. Taiwan could claim more than two dozens of exporting items as "Taiwan as Number One" in the world. In 1983, Taiwan exported 520 million pairs of plastic shoes, one pair for every nine persons in the world; 11 million dozens of umbrellas, one for every 40 persons in the world; and more than 6 million tennis rackets. In addition, it exported 3.16 million sets of sewing machines, having 80 percent of world sewing machine exporting market; 240 million units of mini-motor, having 70 percent of world mini-motor exporting market; 80 million bicycle tires, having 50 percent of world bicycle tire exporting market (Duan, 1989, 313). In 1986, Taiwan produced the world's largest number of computer terminals, printed circuit boards, surveillance cameras, recreational boats, electronic calculators, telephones, and so on (MOEA, 1991, 239). These are mostly labor intensive products of small-and medium-size enterprises.

1.12.1.2 *Commodity Composition of Imports*

Figure 1.14 shows the five major imports of Taiwan[63] in 1980 and 1992. The left Y-axis is the same as that of Fig. 1.13. The commodity composition of imports is rather stable, remaining nearly constant from 1952 to 1980. From

[63]For the data in 1992, see TSDB (1993), 219–220. For the data in 1980, see TSDB (1982), 213–214.

1981 to 1982, however, the fourth series, 4Iron and Steel (US$1.3 billion in 1980. Denoted as 1.3b hereafter in this and the following paragraphs) is replaced by a broader category of 4*Basic Metals and Articles Thereof (8.4b in 1992), and the fifth series, 5Crude Oil (4b in 1980) is replaced by 5*Transportation Equipment (6b in 1992). In order to compare with export categories, 6Information and Communication Products (2b in 1992) is added as the sixth series in this last period. 5Crude Oil (3b in 1992) was an important item before 1980. However, after 1981, it was superseded by imports of manufactured goods.

Included in imports of 2Electrical Machinery and Apparatus from 1980 to 1992 (11.6b in 1992. Hereafter the numbers in this paragraph are for 1992 imports.) are electronic products (9b), electrical machinery products (2b), and household electrical appliances (0.6b). Other major imports shown in Fig. 1.14 are 1Chemicals (7b),[64] 3Machinery (l0b), and 4*Basic Metals and Articles Thereof (8b). A comparison of Figs. 1.13 and 1.14 shows that imports and exports of the three series, 2Electrical Machinery and Apparatus, 3Machinery, and 4Basic Metals have a surprisingly similar pattern of growth. The similarity is also observed in 6Information and Communication Equipment in both diagrams. So far as these four commodity categories are concerned, the industrialization of Taiwan depended heavily on original equipment manufacturing (OEM), product assembly, and labor intensive processing industry.

In other words, even during the 1980s and early 1990s, when the secondary import substitution phase of industrialization was supposed to be completed, especially in the area of machinery, iron and steel, and petrochemicals (Chen, 1988, 48), Taiwan's rapid economic growth was still attained mainly by providing Taiwanese labor as a chain in vertical integration of world production, at a higher level of sophistication, as carried out by multinational companies. A more detailed classification and comparison of exports and imports in 1990, item by item, will confirm our observations (see Appendix 1B and Ref. Chapter 11).

1.12.2 *Major Trading Partners*

Figures 1.15 and 1.16 are area diagrams characterizing major Taiwanese trading partners rather dramatically. Both figures show that the United

---

[64]The 1990 current value of imports of chemicals was US$ 5.8 billion. It included organic chemicals (3b), miscellaneous chemical products (0.8b), inorganic chemicals, isotope, and radioactive materials (0.6b) (MSEI, 1991, 146–149).

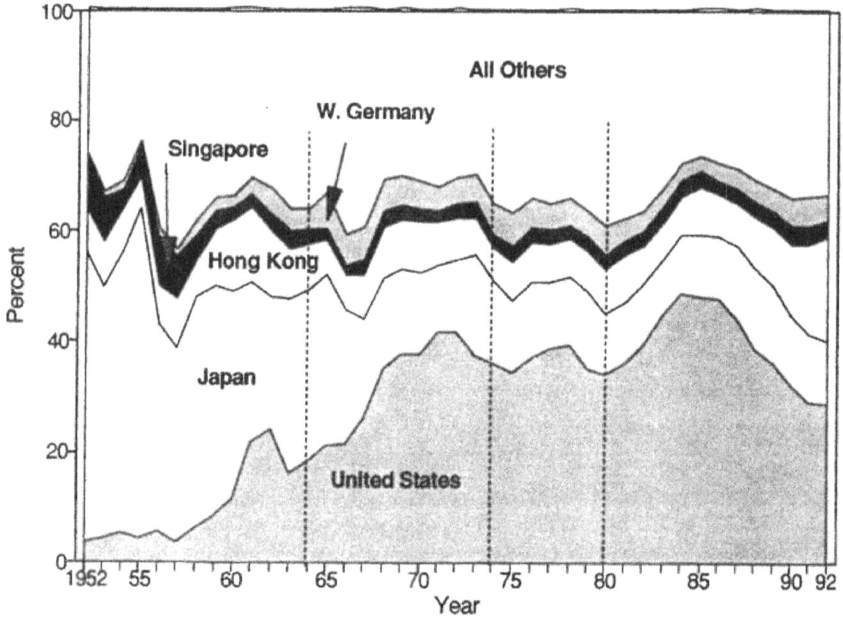

Figure 1.15: Direction of Taiwanese Exports
Percentage Shares of Total Exports (1986WPI = 100)

States and Japan are the two largest trading partners throughout the postwar period. Figure 1.15 shows that Japan was the largest export market for Taiwan until 1966. Japan's export share in total Taiwanese exports (measured as TXJ/TXt, where TXt is Taiwan's total, denoted by small letter t, exports) ranged from 60 percent in 1955 to only 18 percent in 1967. After 1967 the United States became Taiwan's largest export market. The U.S. share of Taiwanese exports (TXU/TXt) ranged from 49 percent in 1984 to 29 percent in 1992. Since 1990, exports to Hong Kong has exceeded those to Japan. Hong Kong has become the second largest export market for Taiwan. In 1992, Hong Kong's export share was 19 percent, and exports to Japan were only 11 percent. The bulk of the increase in Taiwan's trade with Hong Kong was due mostly to indirect trade with China. Like the United States, Taiwan has a hard time cracking the Japanese domestic markets. Despite Taiwanese efforts in attaining a diversification of trading partners, Fig. 1.15 shows that the relative export shares of Singapore, which is the entrepot to the ASEANs, and West Germany, which is the gateway to Europe, and others remain almost constant, although exports to these

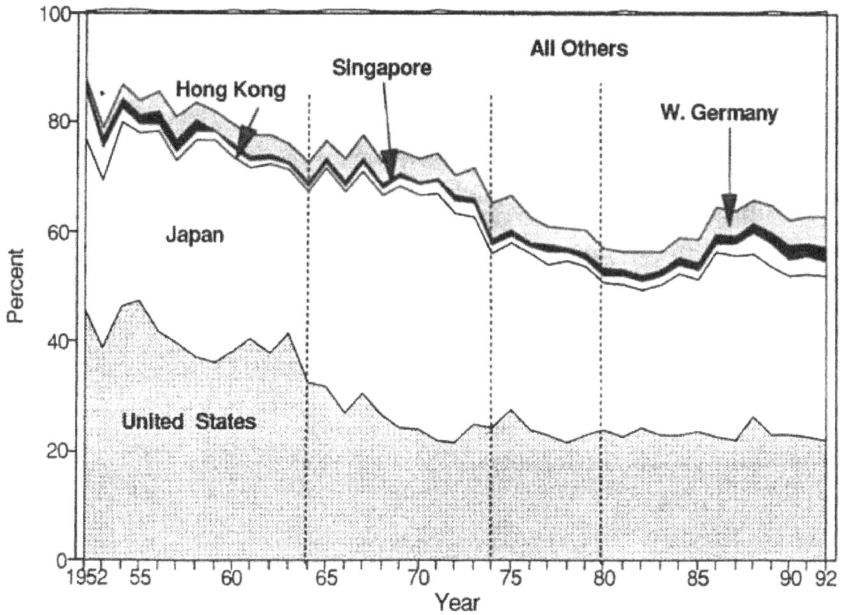

Figure 1.16: Direction of Taiwanese Imports
Percentage Shares of Total Imports (1986WPI = 100)

countries have accelerated since 1985 (TSDB, 1993). This means that trade with these countries has increased only at the same pace as with trade with Japan and the United States.

The major importing partners are just reversed from the major exporting partners. Figure 1.16 shows that, prior to 1963, Taiwan imported primarily from the United States. Japan was busy with its economic reconstruction and the United States was the only major partner helping Taiwan's reconstruction with the huge aid program. The role of the United States and Japan reversed in the mid-1960s when the U.S. economic aid program was terminated. The U.S. share in total Taiwanese imports ranged from 47.5 percent in 1955 to 36.1 percent in 1959. After 1964, however, imports from Japan has become dominant. Japan's share in Taiwanese imports ranged from 45 percent in 1971 to 25 percent in 1982, while the U.S. share ranged from 32 percent to 22 percent. The latter has decreased gradually.

Since 1952, 40 to 65 percent of Taiwanese total exports went to the United States and Japan. Imports from these two countries ranged from

50 to 80 percent of Taiwanese total imports. Here lies the dependency criticism of Taiwanese economic development. Both Japan and the United States constantly played very important roles in Taiwanese economic development.

1.13 Taiwan, Japan, and the U.S. Nexus

Figure 1.17 dramatizes Taiwan's trade relationship with the United States and Japan. As shown in the lower part of the diagram, from 1952 up to

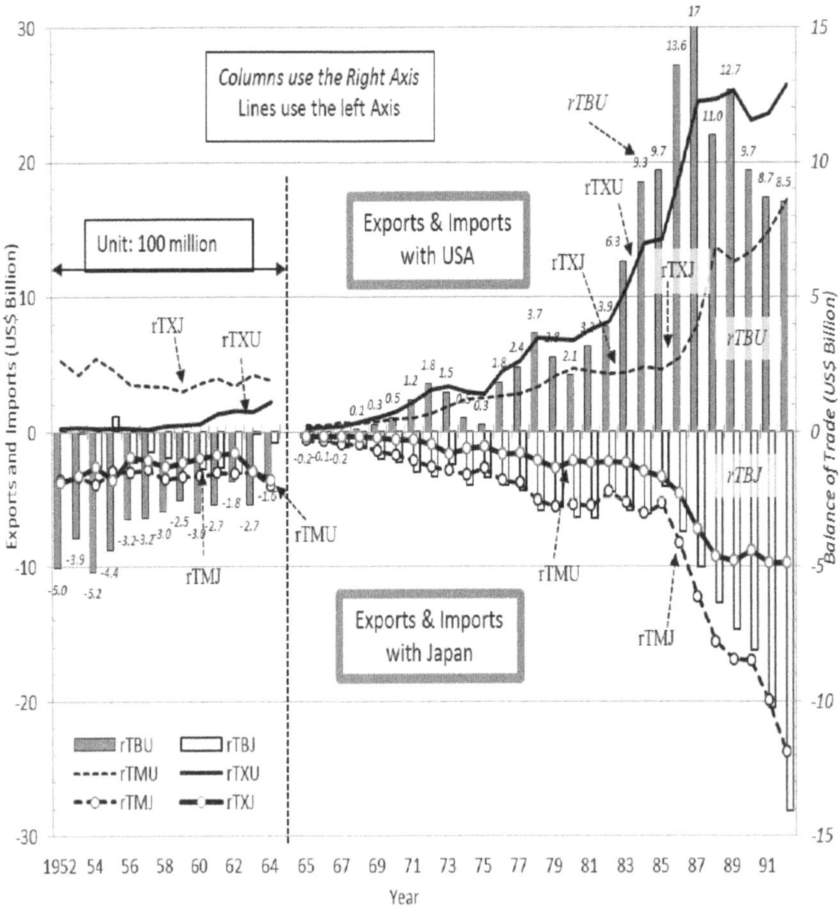

Figure 1.17: Taiwan/USA/Japan Trade Relations
Real Exports, Imports, and BOT (1986WPI = 100)

1992, Taiwan's real imports from Japan (rTMJ, the dotted line in the lower chart) are consistently higher than Taiwan's real exports to Japan (rTXJ, the solid line in the lower chart). This means Taiwan has consistently had a negative balance of trade with Japan since 1953 (except 1955) even up to 1992. This is shown by the empty bars in the lower part on the right Y-axis. Note that deficits with Japan during 1952 to 1964 are so small, much less than US$100 million, that they are almost invisible.

The situation is quite different with the United States. Before 1967, Taiwan also had trade deficits with the United States every year (see the negative tipped bars measured from the right vertical axis). Figure 1.17 shows the deficits in real terms with the United States from 1952 to 1964 by filled bars with black tip. After 1968, Taiwan's real imports from the United States (rTMU, the dotted line in the upper chart) have been consistently lower than her real exports to the United States (rTXU, the solid black line in the upper chart), bringing about real trade surpluses (rTBU) with the United States. This is shown by the lightly filled bars in the upper part of the chart measured from the right Y-axis.

After 1965, both deficits with Japan (rTBJ) and surpluses with the United States (rTBU) have increased over time with the progress of Taiwan's industrialization. In Fig. 1.17, this is illustrated as explosion to the two sides of the horizontal axis like a broom. After 1986, exports to both the United States and Japan slowed (see the black curves on both sides), while imports from both countries continued to increase (see the dotted curves on both sides). In fact, real commodity imports from Japan accelerated (the dotted line below the origin), indicating that the more Taiwan tries to increase its exports, whether to the United States or other countries, the more and deeper Taiwan has to rely on imports of materials and capital equipment from Japan. Despite almost desperate efforts by the KMT government,[65] Taiwan simply cannot get Japan off her back!

Real trade surpluses with the United States peaked at US$17 billion in 1987 and then started to decrease (see the tipped bars), while trade deficits

[65]The following episode is illuminating. In February 1982, to reduce US$ 3.2 billion trade deficits with Japan, Taiwan surprised the world by unilaterally banning imports from Japan: more than 1,500 commodities for an indefinite time and heavy trucks and diesel engines for one year. Tokyo threatened to cancel Taiwan's preferential tariff and trade status. The ban inflicted serious damage to Taiwanese exports and its national economy. As Tokyo also could not wage a trade war simultaneously with the United States and the EEC, both sides reached a compromise and the ban on half of the goods was lifted by November of that year (for details, see Arnold (1985), 194–196; Aoki (1985), 157).

with Japan (see the lower empty bars) continued to increase. The deficits with Japan reached an all-time high at US$14 billion in 1992. However, as we have seen in Fig. 1.12, Taiwan still has managed to achieve a huge positive overall real balance of trade with all countries in recent years (see the bar chart of Fig. 1.12). (For the composition of Taiwan's exports and imports with Japan and the United States, and the proportion of traded commodities, see Chapter 13).

1.13.1 *A Pacific Trade Triangle*

From these discussions, we may derive several characteristics of Taiwanese trade:

a. Taiwanese trade relies very heavily on the United States and Japan. Taiwan relies more on the U.S. markets for exports and on Japan for imports.
b. In the 1980s, Taiwanese trade with both the United States and Japan exploded. At least until 1990, its increases in exports to the United States were paralleled by increasing imports from Japan.
c. After 1964, Taiwan has persistently had trade surpluses with the United States and trade deficits with Japan, although the overall trade balance with all traded countries is positive. Despite many serious attempts to reverse the trade deficits with Japan (see reports by Shi and Li, 1978; Liu and Jian, 1983), the government has never succeeded. Figure 1.17 illustrates this point. In real terms, the deficits with Japan have worsened greatly in recent years.
d. 1Textile in the 1960s and the 1970s as well as 2electrical equipment and 3machinery products in the 1980s were the leading export items (Fig. 1.13). Taiwan's industrialization also centered on these three leading commodities.
e. There has been a virtual explosion of exports in 3machinery products and 2electric equipment. Exports to the United States and its imports from Japan are especially dramatic (not shown in the figures) (Ref. Chapter 11). A less dramatic export increase can also be observed in Basic Metals and Articles.
f. The machinery products and electric equipment are significant in both exports and imports in the 1980s. This can be seen immediately by imposing Fig. 1.13 over Fig. 1.14. This characterizes, again, Taiwan's economic development as largely the process-type or OEM contracts industrialization. The persistent and ever-increasing needs of importing

both items for processing, and then exporting the finished products of the very same items, also indicate that the government generally failed in establishing intermediate and heavy up-stream industries for these commodities, which also depend on the success of research and development. Therefore, despite all the talk of heavy and high-tech industrialization, the secondary import substitution phase, until recent years, did not seem to succeed in general.

g. From the figures, the following trade patterns emerge. Taiwan imports intermediate goods and raw materials from Japan and exports manufactured goods to the United States. Taiwan also imports agricultural goods and intermediate goods from the United States for its industries, and exports its locally produced agricultural goods and some miscellaneous manufactured goods to Japan. These triangular relations among Taiwan, Japan, and the United States are summarized in Fig. 1.18, in which the number in parentheses is the 1992 trade figure in US$ billion.[66] The share of agricultural goods in exports and imports were much larger in the earlier period of Taiwan's economic development.

In the 1980s, the value of exports of machinery and electrical equipment to the United States were about 5 to 10 times higher than that the value of those items exported to Japan. However, during the same period, the value of imports of the same items from Japan are only about 2 to 3 times higher than that the value of those items that were imported from the

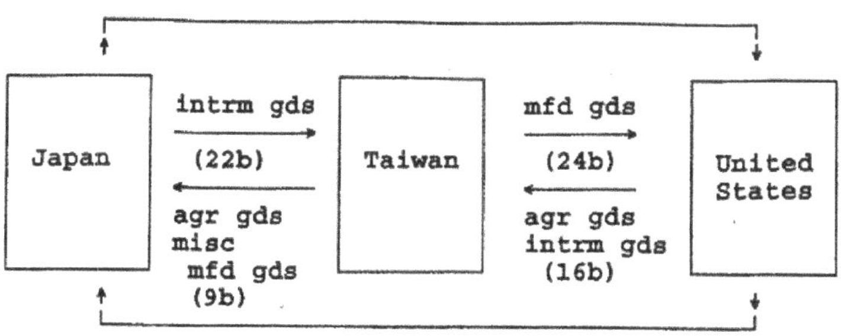

Figure 1.18: Taiwan, Japan, and the United States Nexus

[66]In fact, Taiwan and Korea form two of the three vertexes of the Pacific triangle between Japan, Taiwan, and the United States, as shown by the upper and lower arrows in the diagram. For simplicity, we ignore the details of Japan-U.S. connection (Sumiya *et al.*, 1992, 48; Kwan and Kitamura, 1988.)

United States. This indicates that the Taiwanese firms generally imported from Japan more intermediate materials and capital goods, especially in machinery and electrical equipment, and exported more finished products of these items to the United States. In other words, in the system of world trade, Taiwan played the role of an intermediary between those two trading parties.

1.13.2 *On Sustainable Growth*

Here is the answer to the important question of how Taiwan's outward-oriented strategy can be sustained. It is due to special geographical and historical circumstances.

a. Taiwan was already an export-oriented country under the Japanese regime. Although traded goods at that time were primarily agricultural and processed agricultural products, a majority of the population were farmers. Thus the Taiwanese were very much accustomed to the notion of "production for exports" for living and profits. As soon as the Taiwanese economy recovered from war damages and the society recuperated from the terror of February 1947, Taiwan started exporting traditional goods like sugar, rice, bananas, tea, and canned foods to Japan. When the KMT government started its export-promotion policy around 1960, the Taiwanese already had almost two generations of successful experience with exports as a modern business practice.
b. In the early 1960s, textile products, lumber and timber products, plywood, electrical and machinery apparatus, chemicals, and basic metals were added to rice, sugar, and bananas for exports (TSDB, 1975, 190–191). Much to the dismay of the Chinese bureaucrats in Taiwan (Shi and Li, 1978), the historical tie between Taiwan and Japan persisted and strengthened: first, Japan as the number one export market for Taiwan, then as the number one country from which Taiwan imported intermediate goods and capital goods.
c. One of the major hurdles of export business is international marketing. A country may produce goods, but may not find markets in which to sell them. In Taiwan, even during the 1970s and the 1980s when the KMT government encouraged the establishment of native "large trading companies," 60 percent of the total exports was handled by either foreign-owned or foreign and Taiwanese jointly-owned trading companies. Furthermore, most of these foreigners were Japanese. Remaining exports were divided almost evenly: 20 percent by the manufacturers/traders

and the government-owned Central Trust, and 20 percent by the 36,000 small Taiwanese trading companies (Yajima, 1986, 107). Thus Taiwanese exports were actually helped by Japanese general trading companies, multinational companies, and foreign importers (Chou, 1988, 186; 1992, 1080). Through Japanese joint ventures and trading companies, Taiwanese firms were able to solve most of their marketing problems with Japan. This avenue also proved successful for conducting trade with the United States and other countries.[67] In the early period, many of these Taiwanese entrepreneurs spoke and read Japanese. Japanese customs and habits were not completely alien to them. This undoubtedly removed major hurdles[68] to trade between Taiwan and Japan after the war.

d. On the other hand, through generous U.S. Aid and the Seventh Fleet, the American influences were omnipresent in the 1950s and the 1960s, and many of the decision making bureaucrats of that time were "English speaking" and studied abroad, especially in the United States. They were familiar with the United States. Thus, to them, it was natural for them to develop an outward looking trade strategy that targeted the richest country in the world, the United States.

e. Other factors, such as the availability of cheap labor, the rise of multinational companies and international division of labor, the Vietnam War, long prosperity and growth in the world economy, especially in Japan and in the United States, and advocacy and encouragement of free trade and free markets by world organizations like the International Monetary Fund and the World Bank, all helped to make Taiwan's drive to export a success. However, we consider that these amenities were of secondary importance since they were also available to all other countries. Thus, we submit that it was an outward-looking propensity of the Taiwanese people and the Chinese bureaucrats in Taiwan, along with the triangle relationship with Japan and the United States, spurred by the decreasing value of the American dollar that sustained the outward-looking strategy and made it a success even until today.

---

[67]In addition to marketing, Sogo Shosha also helped in financing, foreign exchanges, organizing, and consulting (Steven, 1990, 70). Their actual operations in Taiwan were never studied.

[68]Barriers to exporting are culture, language difference, special customs requirements, market information (particular markets, availability, usefulness, and awareness), product design and specification requirements, government policy, etc. (Brooks and Frances, 1991, 102).

1.14 Direct Foreign Investment and Economic Growth

Japan and the United States are not only Taiwan's most important trading partners, Japanese and American manufacturers also invested directly and heavily in Taiwan, supplementing Taiwan's domestic investment at the beginning of her industrialization. While critics like to label direct foreign investment (DFI) as the vanguard of imperialist capitalism[69] and foreign control of the host economy, it is also considered as a major channel to bring technological know-how to the host country, creating backward and forward linkages which stimulate the local development of industry (Hsiao and Hsiao, 1984). The latter is exactly what happened in Taiwan.

1.14.1 *An Overview of DFI in Taiwan*

In the early 1950s, when the newly independent former colonies, and semi-colonies such as China, were still recovering from the horror of exploitation and imperialism,[70] Taiwan was probably the only country in the world that invited the much-suspected DFI with open arms. In retrospect, although one may explain that such an unusual policy may be inherited from the Republican China's general guidelines of industrialization in the 1930s, which call for the help from foreign capital (Kirby, 1984, 78–81), it is also consistent with our observations explained earlier. The émigré regime had no roots in Taiwan and wanted to break its isolationism internationally and domestically. While the KMT government in China failed to attract massive foreign investment during the 1930s (ibid., 81), the KMT government in Taiwan succeeded in attracting DFI. Seeing Taiwan's success, Korea followed suit, along with other developing countries, China and the ASEANs.

Direct foreign investment in Taiwan started as early as 1953 (Hsiao and Hsiao, 1984). In 1952, Taiwan and the United States exchanged an agreement on "Guaranty of American Investment of Private Capital in Taiwan," insuring against the loss of American investments due to

[69] Among the numerous works by Marxists, the latest one probably is Steven (1990), 4–5. Incidentally, there are two basic forms of private foreign investment. It may take the indirect form (called portfolio investment), in which the foreign firms invest only in financial assets of host countries, or the direct form, in which foreign firms control at least partially, enterprises in host countries. Up to the 1980s, indirect foreign investment was rare in Taiwan.

[70] China's unequal treaties ended only in 1943 and Chiang Kai-sek published *China's Destiny* "to show the harm they had done to China" (Fairbank, 1967, 62).

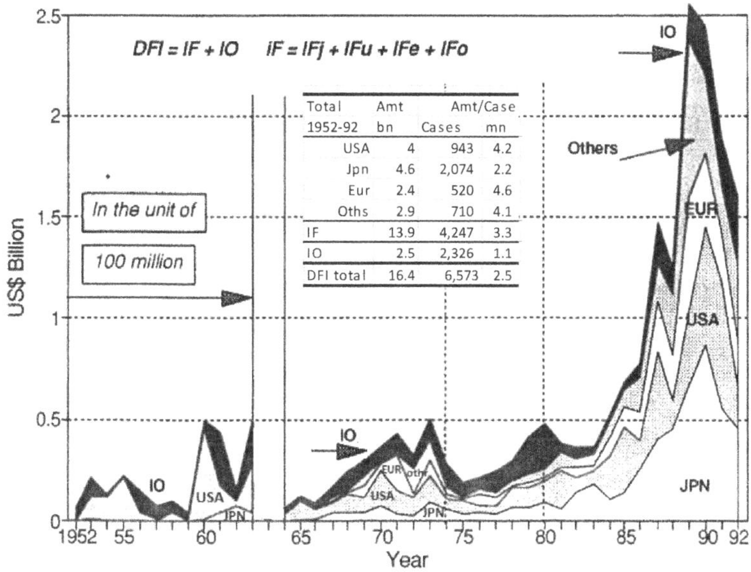

Figure 1.19: Direct Foreign Investment in Taiwan (Amount Approved, 1952–1992, 1986WPI = 100)

foreign exchange inconvertibility, expropriation of assets, war, revolution, or insurrections (Wu *et al.*, 1980, 27). In Taiwan, the government statistics divide DFI into private investment by foreign nationals (denoted as IF, the light area, in Fig. 1.19) and overseas Chinese investment (IO, the black part), which is also foreign investment. In 1953, there were US$1.7 million (12 cases) of investment by overseas Chinese (IO) and US$2.04 million (2 cases) of investment by foreign nationals (IF). In July 1954, the government announced the "Statute for Investment by Foreign Nationals," which was followed by the "Statute for Investment by Overseas Chinese" (November 1955). As shown in Fig. 1.19, the effects were small at the beginning, probably due to Taiwan's dismal future prospects as well as the fact that activities of multinational corporations were still just beginning. In December 1970, a more attractive and comprehensive "Statute for Encouragement of Investment" was announced (Wu *et al.*, 1980, 29). These statutes have been amended several times since their publication. These special treatments combined with other economic and social factors explained below have attracted a massive inflow of investment in Taiwan from foreign countries.

Figure 1.19 shows the approved amount of direct foreign investment in Taiwan from 1952 to 1992. As in the case of trade statistics, we have converted the data into real terms, that is, all data are divided by Taiwan's WPI with 1986's wholesale price being taken as 100 (TSDB, 1993, 167). IO is shown in the upper dark band in Fig. 1.19. The rest of the chart shows IF, consisting of DFI from Japan (IFj), the United States (IFu), Europe (IFe), and other countries (IFo) (IF = IFj + IFu + IFe + IFo). IO consists of investment mainly from those overseas Chinese residing in Hong Kong and Japan. Before 1964, IO was an important source of DFI. The weight of IO in total DFI decreased after 1965, taken over by IF from the United States. After 1982, IO's weight in total DFI decreased drastically. IF from the United States started in 1953 and was superseded by IF from Japan most of the time after 1982. As with trade relations, Japanese and American investments have dominated DFI in Taiwan since 1966. The two oil shocks in 1973–1974 and 1979–1980 eventually spurred, rather than depressed, DFI.The largest amount of annual DFI was achieved in 1989: 478 cases approved with the value of US$2.2 billion in IF (US$ 641 million from Japan and US$344 million from the United States) and 70 cases with the value of mere US$ 0.18 billion in IO were approved. Altogether, from 1952 to 1992, 6,573 cases (16.5b) of DFI were approved (see the last row of the inserted table in Fig. 1.19). Among them, there were 4,247 cases (worth US$ 14 billion. Denoted as 14b hereafter in this paragraph) of IF and 2326 cases (2.5b) of IO. Among IF, Japan is the largest contributor with 2,074 cases (4.6b), followed closely by the U.S.A., accounting for 943 cases (4.0b), Europe, for 520 cases (2.4b). Other countries were responsible for 710 cases (2.9b) (TDFB, 1993, 244–246). In general, the average scale of DFI is US$2.5 million. The European had largest investment per case (US$ 4.7 million on average), followed closely by the Americans (4.3 million), the Japanese (2.2 million), and lastly the overseas Chinese (1.1 million).

The reasons for a steady increase in direct foreign investment may be seen from two opinion surveys of foreign enterprises in Taiwan. In 1969, Zhang (1969) found that the investment motives of about 38 percent (336 firms) of foreign firms in Taiwan (including IF and IO) were, in order of decreasing importance: (1) political stability, (2) low wage rate, (3) rapid economic growth and an improving domestic market, (4) higher educational levels, diligence and reliability of workers, (5) low cost of electricity and natural gas, (6) the five-year tax holiday, and so on. For the American firms surveyed in 1980 (Wu *et al.*, 1980, 51), the sequence was the same except that "an improving domestic market" (in (3)) was dropped to eighth place, while the five-year tax holiday moved up to third place. The sixth inducement for American firms to come to Taiwan was to "beat international competition." Apparently, martial law, the relentless government policy of low wages, U.S. aid investment in infrastructure, and encouragement of private enterprises were working together to attract DFI in the 1960s.

However, the first two major reasons listed here seem unable to explain the great rush of DFI in the 1980s, as shown in Fig. 1.19. In the 1980s, and especially in the second half, factory wages were high, independent labor unions were sprouting, and opposition political parties were allowed to demonstrate on the streets before and after the abolition of martial law in July 1987. So far as Japanese investment is concerned, geographic proximity, historical ties, and socio-linguistic similarity might have played a more important role than the political stability.[71] In any case, a new explanation of the dramatic rise of DFI in Taiwan during the 1980s is called for.

In general, from 1952 to 1992, 28 percent of Taiwan's DFI has been in electronic and electric products, totaling almost US$ 4 billion. This is followed by chemicals, 21 percent, US$ 2.9 billion; services, 10 percent, US$1.4 billion; and machinery, equipment, and instruments, 9 percent, US$ 1.3 billion. Metal products and foreign trade services have 7 percent each, with about US$ 1 billion (TSDB, 1993, 247). None or very few DFIs were in agriculture, fisheries and livestock, paper and paper products. The last decade registered significant increases in the service industry: banking and insurance, foreign trade, and services, in addition to metal products and machinery, equipment, and instruments.

1.14.2 *The Effect of DFI on Taiwan's GDP*

For a developing country like Taiwan, the major objective of inducing direct foreign investment is to increase the nation's economic activities. In a previous paper (M. Hsiao, 1992, 151. Ref. Chapter 9), it is shown that, using the 1967 to 1987 data set, the real growth of DFI has had a significant and positive effect on the real growth of Taiwan's GDP. When the real growth rate of DFI increases by 1 percent, it may generate a 0.11 percent increase in the growth rate of Taiwan's GDP.

---

[71] This was the case after the June 1989 Tiananmen Massacre in China. The society and politics were hardly stable after 1989, and yet DFI in China increased, especially from Taiwan. Note that Japanese investment in Taiwan and Taiwanese investment in China are not protected by their governments.

When we disaggregated the DFI into IF and IO, we found that the DFI by foreign nationals (IF) has a greater effect than the DFI by overseas Chinese (IO) on the growth of Taiwan's GDP. This is consistent with the facts that IF concentrates investment in high-tech and heavy industries, generating more economic activity for the Taiwanese economy. On the other hand, IO has an emphasis in service industry investment, which is unlikely to have a strong and lasting effect on the Taiwanese economy. We found that none of the lagged variables of DFI had a significant effect on the GDP. This may imply that most of the DFI in Taiwan was in short-term high-tech industries rather than long-term heavy industries.

1.14.3 *DFI and Technology Transfer*

There are two kinds of technology: engineering/production technology and management/marketing technology. Both are relevant and important to developing countries. They may be transferred in four ways: through imitation, direct foreign investment, royalty and licensing, and free information (Johnson, 1968). In this section[72] our emphasis is on technology transfer through DFI.

In 1973, 311 large firms in five industries, textile, clothing, plastic and plastic products, metal and its products, and electronic and electric products were surveyed. These firms were fast-growing exporters with at least one million dollars of annual exports, and 80 to 90 percent of their outputs were exported (Schive, 1983, 477). Thirty-nine percent of the firms reported that they adopted foreign technology either through technical cooperation or royalty and licensing agreements. The electronic and electric products industry has the largest share of the foreign investment. The percentage of firms using foreign technology almost doubled in this particular industry to 76 percent of the 62 firms.

Among the 311 firms, the proportions of firms that adopted foreign technology in national firms, minority foreign-owned firms, and majority foreign-owned firms were 8 percent (out of 185 firms), 61 percent (out of 23 firms), and 91 percent (out of 103 firms), respectively. For the electronic and electric products industry, the proportions of the three ownership categories increased to 24 percent (out of 62 firms), 71 percent (out of 7 firms), and 100 percent (out of 38 firms), respectively. This is what we call "slanted structure" in technology transfer (M. Hsiao, 1992, 154. Ref. Chapter 9).

[72]The following two sections are taken from M. Hsiao (1992), 143–159. Ref. Chapter 9.

The pattern is the same in the 1978 survey of 199 major firms in Taiwan, which included eight industries, namely, automobiles and parts, chemicals, and machinery, with the five industries mentioned previously (Schive, 1983, 479). Foreign firms have a tendency to be three to seven times more likely than the national firms to adopt foreign technology. In terms of the percentages of national and foreign firms that produced new products, foreign firms (54% of 68 firms) are in general only somewhat more active in adopting foreign technology than the national firms (42% of 131 firms), and twice more active in electronic and electric products industry (63% vs 30%).

The survey also found that, among the firms that did adopt foreign technology, 64 percent of them used it to produce new products, rather than improve the existing technology. Among those that adopted foreign technology, more national firms (68%) introduced new products than foreign firms (63%), although there seems to be no major difference. This may imply that some foreign firms are part of a division of labor in vertical integration with the foreign company and therefore do not require the introduction of new products. Similarly, in the electronic industry, among 54 firms that adopted foreign technology, 59 percent introduced new products. Among them, 50 percent of the 30 national firms and 61 percent of the 24 foreign firms introduced new products. The difference is not as large as expected. This seems to indicate that, so far as product innovation is concerned, the Taiwanese firms are as innovative as the foreign firms.

The most effective way of transferring technology is probably through foreign personnel employed in the foreign firms. In 1982, about 1,765 foreign citizens worked for the foreign firms in Taiwan. About half of them were in the area of general administration and the other half worked as technicians. They made up about two percent of the total administrators and technicians of the foreign firms. Undoubtedly, through personal contacts with the local administrators and technicians, this influx of foreign personnel, especially through interactions between the Japanese and the Japanese-speaking Taiwanese, has played an important role in transferring engineering/production technology as well as management/marketing technology.

The unusually high influence of Japan on Taiwan can be seen from an international comparison (M. Hsiao, 1992, 158. Ref. Chapter 7). Table 1.9 shows the number of cases of technical cooperation in some Asian countries. From 1952 to 1983, there were 1,871 cases in Taiwan (col. 1). Japan is the major supplier of technology (65.5%), followed by the United States (21.4%), and other advanced countries, mainly from Europe (13.1%). In

Table 1.9: Sources of Technology Transfer in Some Asian Countries
(Unit: Percent)

Receivers	Taiwan	S. Korea	Singapore	Malaysia	Thailand	Philippines
Suppliers	1952–83 (1)	1962–85 (2)	1983 (3)	1960–81 (4)	1981 (5)	1978–79 (6)
Japan	65.5	54.6	25.0	30.5	36.3	20.7
USA	21.4	23.2	24.4	14.7	18.8	46.0
UK	0.0	3.8	9.4	13.5	7.7	6.7
Other Adv. Countries	13.1	18.3	41.2	25.9	25.5	22.7
Developing Countries	0.0	0.0	0.0	15.5	11.6	4.0
Total (cases)	1871	3397	541	348	388	150

Source: Mostly based on the data from Institute of Developing Economies, as shown in Du (1986), 155.

Taiwan and South Korea, most of the older people read and speak Japanese. This historical background may explain the unusually high proportion of technology transfer from Japan to these two countries (65.5% and 54.6%, respectively, see cols. 1 and 2). The 11 percent difference between Taiwan and South Korea probably reflects the general attitude toward the Japanese in the two countries.[73]

1.14.4 *The Television Industry*

The television industry created the forward and backward linkages among industries in Taiwan, and thus contributed to Taiwanese industrialization. It is an example of life-cycle product theory in international trade and shows how an industry went through the stages of imports, to import substitution, and then to exports (Ref. Chapters 7 and 8).

The first black-and-white television broadcasting station in Taiwan appeared in 1962 with help from Japan's NHK (Japan Broadcasting Association). At that time, Taiwan's domestic consumption of televisions depended completely on imports. Taiwan imported 6,000 units in 1962 and 18,000 units in 1963 of black-and-white televisions. At the same time, there were two local firms and one joint venture (that is, Tatung with the Japanese) working to produce televisions. The production of black-and-white televisions started in 1964. In that year, three joint

[73]When Japan annexed Korea in 1910, Korea was an independent country and Koreans resisted fiercely throughout Japanese occupation. The Taiwanese nemesis toward the Japanese virtually ceased after the "228 Incident" (Ref. Chapter 7).

ventures with Japan (Sanyo, Matsushita, and Sharp) and two national firms were established. The eight firms together produced about 30,000 units and none were exported. Their initial purpose was to sell in Taiwan's domestic market. The government imposed high tariffs to protect the infant industry.

Within three years, in 1967, the exports of black-and-white televisions totaled 2,000 units. In the next year, production was boosted to 630,000 units and the exports increased to 56,000 units when RCA and Admiral of the United States joined in Taiwanese production for the sole purpose of exports (Yeh, 1980; Schive and Yeh, 1980). Apparently, the industry started with OEM (original equipment manufacturing) type assembly. From then on until 1980, the black-and-white television industry in Taiwan grew rapidly at an average rate of about 50 percent per year. In 1980, production reached the peak level of 5.58 million units, nearly all of them were exported to the world markets. After 1980, production and exports started to decline because of the substitution by the demand for color televisions. By 1988, Taiwan produced and exported only about 1.3 million units of black-and-white televisions. The technological know-how to produce black-and-white television soon led to the technology of producing color television in Taiwan (the forward linkage) in 1969. From 1970 to 1984, the average growth rate of color television production and exports was about 60 percent per year, higher than that of black-and-white television.

With the development of the television industry, its parts industry also sprouted (the backward linkage). In the late 1960s, imported black-and-white television picture tubes were gradually replaced by domestic production. By 1973, the exports of picture tubes exceeded imports, which became negligible by 1978. The process of change from imports, to import substitution, and then to exports also occurred in the production of television tuners. In this case, the exports of tuners exceeded imports in 1975. Color television picture tubes are much more difficult to build. Until l978, Taiwan still imported a large quantity of color television picture tubes. It is reported that Taiwan RCA and Taiwan Admiral have 150 subcontractors, and Zenith has more than 50 local firms supplying television parts. These local subcontractors received technical assistance from the parent companies in the United States (Saito, 1981, 49), and also imported parts from Japan. Japan provided slightly more than half of the cases of foreign technology assistance (39 cases), followed by the United States (21 cases), and then Holland (5 cases), and one case from another country. (Ref. Chapters 8 and 9).

1.14.5 *Vitality of Taiwanese Industrial Activities*

We have seen that product innovation is found to be almost the same between native firms and foreign firms. This reflects the vitality and progressiveness of the Taiwanese people and society. It is a source of rapid economic growth experienced by the Taiwanese economy. The Taiwanese were able to absorb foreign technology for production and exports, which in turn improved their living. This has allowed them to meet the changing demands of domestic and world markets. Taiwan also started developing the parts industry to support the domestic production. The television production technology is now applied to build computer terminals and monitors (Chang, 1986).

Taiwan's television industry started in 1962. However, according to the United Nations statistics (Yeh, 1980, 165), by 1976, the Taiwanese share of the world television production was 7.1 percent (out of the world production of 45.82 million sets). It ranked fourth in the world, only after Japan (30%), the United States (13.8%), and the USSR (13.3%). The Philippines started producing televisions in 1956, Mexico and Brazil in 1955. Nevertheless, their world shares remained almost constant at about 0.2 percent, 1.3 percent, and 2.9 percent, respectively, during the same period. Despite Taiwan's limited natural resources and small land area, the rise of Taiwan to a giant in world television production is truly extraordinary. What are the sources of such vitality and progressiveness of the Taiwanese? What made the Taiwanese television industry different from Mexico, Brazil, and Philippines? We would like to examine these questions after analyzing the basic structure of Taiwanese industries.

1.15 The Basic Structure of Taiwanese Industry and Trade

In Section 1.7, we have shown that in the early 1952s, the large public enterprises dominated Taiwanese economy, and that, except the four companies which were transferred to landlords as partial payment of land after land reform (see Section 1.5.2.1), and some burgeoning textile firms which were transplanted from China, most Taiwanese private enterprises were very small.

In 1954 among 42,288 manufacturing firms, 72.5 percent had one to three workers, 25.1 percent had only four to 29 workers, and just 1.8 percent had 30 to 99 workers (row (2) of Table 1.7). The small Taiwanese firms, however, continued to grow over the years. The statistical definition, and hence, the base of consistent government policy on "small-and medium-scale enterprises (SMEs)" did not exist until September 1967. In 1967, an SME was defined as "a manufacturing enterprise having total assets of less than NT$5,000,000 with not more than 100 persons regularly employed; or a commercial firm having an annual turnover of not more than NT$5,000,000 with less than 50 persons regularly employed" (Chou, 1992, 1069). The definition changed five times (1973, 1977, 1979, 1982, and 1991). In 1973, the maximum capital increased four times to NT$20 million, and in 1977, the maximum employees increase three times to 300. In 1982, the total assets limit increased six times again to NT$120 million (Chou, 1992, 1070; MOEA, 1991, 12).

1.15.1 *The Dual Industrial Structure*

Taiwan's economic structure is very similar to that of Japan in the early postwar period, with much more pronounced duality among the large and small enterprises.

1.15.1.1 *Public and Private Enterprises*

The extreme dual structure of public and private enterprises in Taiwan's manufacturing industry has not changed much since the 1950s. Row 7 (LHS) of Table 1.10 shows the scale of operation by ownership for 1966 and 1976. In 1966, there were only 43 (0.16%) public enterprises (row 7). On average, they had assets of NT$ 613 million, employed 1,854 persons, with sales of NT$ 433 million, and value-added of NT$ 149 million. In a vivid contrast, there were 27,666 (99.84%) private enterprises. On average, they had assets of mere NT$ 2 million, employed 18 persons, with sales of NT$ 1.8 million, and value-added of NT$ 0.6 million. Public enterprises are, on average, about 300 times larger in assets, 100 times larger in employment, and 240 times larger in sales than the corresponding items in private industry. However, despite government's monopolistic position and government protection, the value-added per employee in public enterprises (NT$0.08 million = VA/Empl) is merely about 2.7 times that in private enterprises (NT$0.03 million). Herein lies the criticism of the inefficiency of public enterprises.

Among private enterprises, only 15 percent were incorporated (rows 10 and 11, LHS). The other 85 percent are unincorporated enterprises, employing an average of only seven persons (row 11). In fact, col. j (row 6) of Table 1.10 shows that 72.2 percent of private enterprises hired less than nine persons in 1966, probably a slight improvement over the 1954 census data

Table 1.10: Ownership, Scale of Operation, and Exports

1	Item	Total	Average Size of				1966	Number of firms				
3	Ownership		Assets	Empl	Sales	VA	Size	PubE		PvtE		
4	Units	No.	NT$m	prsn	NT$m	NT$m	Persons	no.	%	no.	%	
5	1966	a	b	c	d	e	f	g	h	i	j	k
6	Mfg	27709	3	21	2.5	0.8	0-9	1	2.3	19975	72.2	
7	Public E.	43	613	1854	433	149	10-49	9	20.9	6197	22.4	
8	Private E	27666	2	18	1.8	0.6	50-99	6	14.0	747	2.7	
9	Private E.						100-499	11	25.6	636	2.3	
10	Corporat	4227	13	82	9.9	3.2	>=500	16	37.2	111	0.4	
11	Non-Cor	23439	0.258	7	0.4	0.1	sum	43	100	27666	100.0	
12	1976	No.	Assets	Empl	Sales	K/L		Average of				
14	Total mfg	69517	15.1	27	11.3	559	1976	No.	Assets	Empl	Sales	K/L
15	Public E.	89	3474	1493	1445	2327	Forgn E.	988	119	266	138	449
16	Private E	69428	11	25	9	557	Group E	673	376	446	290	842
17	SME**	67767	5	17	5	555						

		a	b	c	d	e	f	g	h	i	j	k
18		Sales of top 100 firms				Top 100 exporters			Exports of top 500 firms (e)			
19		1982(a)		1987(b)		1981(c)	1986(d)	1986(d)			Export share	
20	Ownership		Sales		Sales	Exp Share		Exp Share			1976	1980
21		No.	%	No.	%	%	No.	%			%	%
22	Public E.	15	59	23	53	3.2	0	0	500 Enterprise		25.0	24.0
23	Private E	67	34	77	47	8.3	63	10	500 Exporters		11.7	12.9
24	Foreign E	18	7	(5?)		8.5	37	8	500 Frgn firms		28.6	26.3
25	Sum	100	100	100	100	20.0	100	18			65.3	63.2

Notes: E. = Enterprise. *Calculated from (avg)x(total number) and deducting other items from total mfg. **Does not include foreign and group enterprises.

For rows 18 to 24: (a) Chou (1988), Table 3. (b) Sumiya *et al.* (1992), 133. (c) Chou (1988), 183–4. (d) Sumiya *et al.* (1992), 141. NT$ was converted to US$ by exchange rate 35.5, and then divided by 1986 exports of US$ 39,862. (e) Chou (1988), Table 4.

Sources: All the original data are based on Industrial Census. For rows 1 to 17: 1966 data are from Yeh, Tables 2, 3, 11 (for cols. a to e), and Tables 4 and 5 (for cols. f to j). 1976 data are in Chou (1988), Tables 2, 3.

(Row 2, Table 1.7). In terms of value-added per employee, corporate private enterprises are slightly more than twice as efficient as the non-incorporated private enterprises.[74]

1.15.1.2 *Comparison Over Time*

After ten years of development, the basic industrial structure still remained the same. Row 15 in Table 1.10 shows that the number of public enterprises more than doubled (from 43 to 89), the average value of assets increased more than five times, and average sales more than tripled. On the other hand, employment in public enterprises fell by 20 percent. The growth of private enterprises is more dramatic. Row 16 shows that the number of private enterprises increased more than 2.5 times, and both the average value of assets and average sales increased more than five times. Employment increased about 40 percent, to 25 persons per enterprise, showing an increase in the scale of operation.

Note that the value added per employee for both public and private enterprises increased considerably. Value added per employee in public enterprises increased 19 times to NT$ 1.6 million per employee. In contrast, value added per employee in private enterprises increased a whopping 700 times to NT$ 22 million per employee. Here again the vitality of the Taiwanese small and medium d enterprises is demonstrated.

From the 1976 census data, we find the characteristic of foreign enterprises and "group enterprises." The group enterprises are similar to those in other developing countries (Chou, 1988, 177). These are the most effective form of organizations for small-and medium-size enterprises, and consist of, and are linked by, nepotism or family. In Taiwan, group enterprises emerged during the 1960s after economy grew to a more advanced stage. However, as the enterprises grew with the economy, many group enterprises simply could not adapt to modern management techniques and fell behind the competition (Sumiya *et al.*, 1992, 138). After decades of competition, there were only six Taiwanese group enterprises and two Chinese group enterprises that were prominent in Taiwan during 1973 to 1983 (ibid., 138–141). The largest group was the Taiwanese-owned Formosa Plastics, with 18 enterprises, 33,000 employees, and US$2 billion sales in 1983 (ibid., Table 2.19).

---

[74]That is, NT$ 0.04 million and NT$ 0.017 million, respectively (VA/Empl, rows 10 and 11, LHS, Table 1.10).

1.15.1.3 *Size of Foreign Firms in Taiwan*

Rows 15 and 16 of RHS Table 1.10 show that, in 1976, there were 988 foreign enterprises and 673 group enterprises. On average, a firm in these two categories had asset value of NT$ 119 million, and NT$ 376 million, hired 266 and 446 workers, with sales of NT $138 million and NT$ 290 million, respectively. Thus, unlike in some other countries, foreign enterprises have not had an overwhelming presence in Taiwan. In fact, employment of less than 300 workers and an asset value of NT$ 60 million was defined as small and medium enterprises in Taiwan in 1977.

Columns (e) and (k) show the capital intensity (capital-labor ratio, K/L) of each kind of enterprise. Foreign enterprises have typically had the lowest capital intensity (NT$449 per worker), indicating they came to Taiwan with labor intensive industries to take advantage of lower wages and high-quality labor. In contrast, the capital intensity of group enterprises is twice as large (NT$842 per worker), and that of public enterprises, five times as large (NT$2,327 per worker). Since public enterprises include capital intensive electric, gas, and water companies, without separating them, it is difficult to say whether unusually high capital intensity in public enterprise is appropriate for capital-scarce developing countries like Taiwan.

Row 17 calculates the number and the value of assets, employees, sales, and capital intensity of private SMEs after deducting from total manufacturing industry (Row 14) the corresponding items from public, foreign, and group enterprises. Compared to the same items (in Row 8) in 1966, in which foreign and group enterprises were too few to separate, the average scale of SMEs (Row 17) still show a large increase (two and a half times) in their assets and sales, with a slightly reduced number of employees (18 vs 17). This again reflects the vitality of Taiwanese private economic activities as compared with the public enterprises, which are mostly, if not all, operated by the Chinese bureaucrats.

1.15.1.4 *Exports of the Top Enterprises*

The last part of Table 1.10 is a continuation of the change in industrial structure in recent years. Columns (a) to (d) in the last part of Table 1.10, from rows 18 to 24, present the changes in number and sales of the 100 largest public and private enterprises in Taiwan from 1982 to 1987. In 1982, there were 15 public enterprises, 67 domestic private enterprises, and 18 foreign enterprises. They had sales of 59 percent, 34 percent, and 7 percent, respectively. In 1987 among the 100 largest enterprises in

Taiwan, the number of public enterprises increased to 23, and the domestic and foreign private enterprises decreased[75] to 77. However, the sales of public enterprises decreased to 53 percent and those of private enterprises increased to 47 percent, indicating again the relative increase in scale and efficiency of the private sector among the largest enterprises.

Columns (e) to (k) in the last part of Table 1.10 show the export share of the largest enterprises in Taiwan. If the top 100 exporters are taken, then in 1981 the export share of public enterprises was only 3.2 percent of the total exports and the share of the private enterprises was 8.3 percent, and of the foreign enterprises was 8.5 percent. Despite their mammoth size in assets, employment, and sales, public enterprises contributed less than 3.2 percent of Taiwan's total exports! Among the public enterprise exports, 0.6 percent came from sugar and 0.1 percent from rice (Chou, 1988, 182). Thus, exports by public enterprises have declined along with the sugar industry. By 1986, none of public enterprises was listed in 100 largest exporters. There were 63 private enterprises, contributing merely 10 percent of total exports, and 37 foreign enterprises, with an 8 percent of trade share. Foreign enterprises are twice as export oriented as the private enterprises. Altogether, these three kinds of enterprises within the top 100 exporters only took up about 20 percent of the total Taiwanese exports in 1981 and 1986. This means that the bulk (80%) of exports was done by small and fragrant exporters/manufacturers (row 25).

Columns (j) and (k), rows 22 to 24, show that, at the end of the 1970s and early 1980s, the export share of the top 500 enterprises was only about 25 percent of total exports, and that of the top 500 exporters was merely about 12 percent, while that of top 500 foreign firms was about 27 percent. This again indicates that the Taiwanese exporters are generally small and medium enterprises. The foreign firms came to Taiwan, not to compete domestically with the local public or private business, but mainly for export purposes. Here again we see the relatively small contribution of these large private enterprises and exporters to Taiwanese exports. Indeed, the SMEs are the backbones of Taiwanese exports and economic growth.[76]

---

[75]The list in Sumiya *et al.* (1992), 132–133, shows that there were five foreign firms ranked among 50 of the largest enterprises. The list does not give information on those firms between number 51 and number 100.

[76]For Taiwanese SMEs in action, Japanese multinationals, the effects of the "228 Incident," and the difference between the first and the second generation mainlanders, and so on, see a documentary film directed by Eaton (1991).

1.15.1.5 *Expansion of SMEs in Selected Individual Industry*

The structure of individual industry also shows a similar pattern of massive expansion of SMEs, except those industries where the government enterprises monopolize the field. Table 1.11 shows the structure of the 2machinery and 3electrical equipment industries, Taiwan's leading exports in 1966, 1983 and 1987 (see Fig. 1.13). The seven manufacturing categories are arranged in the order of the number of SMEs in 1987, and show the dramatic increase of SMEs in the major industries. In 1966, among the seven industries listed in Table 1.11, the machinery industry had only 24 large and very large enterprises (LLE) and 2,107 SMEs, consisting 98.9 percent of the total firms in this industry. In 1983, SMEs in that industry increased only about 3.4 times to 7,177. The largest winner in 1983 was the 5primary metal products industry (bordered). There, the number of SME increased by a factor of nearly 37. This was followed by similarly impressive increases in the 1fabricated metal products industry (16 times), and the 3electrical and electronic equipment industry (11 times). This change in industrial production structure was also reflected in export and import structures, as we have seen in Section 1.12.1. In contrast, the numbers of LLEs were at most doubled from 1966 to 1983, and LLEs in the machinery industry

Table 1.11: SMEs of Selected Industries in Taiwan 1966, 1983, 1987

Year	1966			1983					1987				
Industry	Total		Share	Total		Share	*GR 83/66*		Total		Share	*GR 87/83*	
(Arranged in the	SME	LLE	SME	SME	LLE	SME	*SME*	*LLE*	SME	LLE	SME	*SME*	*LLE*
order of 1987 SME)	a	*b*	*c*	d	e	*f*	*g*	*h*	i	j	*k*	*l*	*m*
Unit	No.	No.	%	No.	No.	%	*d/a*	*e/b*	No.	No.	%	*i/d*	*j/e*
1Fabrctd Mtl Prods*	1,630	24	98.5	26,690	53	99.8	*16.4*	*2.2*	31,389	126	99.6	*1.2*	*2.4*
2Mach, excl. EE Eqp.	**2,107**	**24**	**98.9**	**7,177**	**22**	**99.7**	***3.4***	***0.9***	**8,321**	**93**	**98.9**	***1.2***	***4.3***
3Elctr/Eltro (EE) Eqt.*	516	59	89.7	5,857	126	97.9	*11.4*	*2.1*	7,773	315	96.1	*1.3*	*2.5*
4Textile Mill Prods				**6,783**	**181**	**97.4**			**7,713**	**305**	**96.2**	***1.1***	***1.7***
5Primary Mtl prod*	159	35	82.0	5,856	71	98.8	*36.8*	*2.0*	6,254	147	97.7	*1.1*	*2.1*
6Apparel & others				7,140	29	99.6			6,025	49	99.2	*0.8*	*1.7*
7Transp Equipment	957	34	96.6	2,647	46	98.3	*2.8*	*1.3*	3,879	87	97.8	*1.5*	*1.9*

GR = Growth rate, LLE = Large and very large enterprises
Sources: Data on 1966 are from Kao (1969), Table II.
*In Kao, 1 is listed as Metal Products, 2 as Machinery Mfg., 3 as Electrical Equip, 5 as Basic Metal. Data on 1983 and 1987 are from Chou (1992), Table 5.

even decreased by 10 percent. Undoubtedly, some of SMEs in 1966 grew up to LLEs in 1983. However, from the figures, we may see that the increase of LLEs are very few and very slow during this period as compared with SMEs. As we will see below, this might have something to do with the government policy.

However, the number of LLEs increased dramatically by 1987. In as short a period as four years, the number of LLEs in the 2machinery industry quadrupled, and that in the 5primary and 1fabricated metal products industries, as well as 3electrical and electronic equipment industry, more than doubled, while SMEs in these industries increased only 10 percent to 30 percent. In view of massive increase in direct foreign investment both in cases and amount during this period (see Fig. 1.19), we suspect that most of increase in LLEs came from joint venture with foreign investment (FI). Even so, the number of SMEs are still over 96 percent of each industry, an enormous number considering the size of Taiwanese economy in this period (see rGDP in Fig. 1.12).

The limited data of Table 1.11 shows the enormous growth of the SME in Taiwan from 1960s to 1980s in almost all manufacturing sectors. This can be seen by comparing the number of SMEs in 1966 with that in 1987. In 1966, there were only 1630 SMEs in 1fabricated metal products firms, it grew to 31,389 in 1987. As we will see below, the Taiwanese SMEs swarmed into these new, profitable and growing industries like bees. This exposed them to fierce competition with other SMEs in those industries and in turn forced them to explore the foreign markets.

1.15.2 *The Kingdom of Small and Medium Private Enterprises*

Few studies of Taiwanese economic development have taken into consideration the existence and contributions of SMEs during Taiwan's industrialization and trade. Most macroeconomic analyses merely exhibit some aggregate statistics such as exports, GNP, investment and savings, government policies, and so on. These studies often arrive at a conclusion as if the KMT government is the only government in the world that knows how to manage the economy for rapid growth. The people who are behind these statistics, the Taiwanese, are simply overlooked.

In Section 1.14.5, we saw that the Philippines started producing television sets in 1956, and Mexico and Brazil began in 1955. Were the governments of these countries really so unenlightened that they did not know how to set up high tariffs to protect the infant industry? Why did they not give economic incentives to the firms, encourage production, and even promote exports to earn foreign exchange? What was so different that made the Taiwanese (and the Koreans) successful? Apparently, so far as Taiwan is concerned, there is something much more important than government policies.

1.15.2.1 *Postwar Growth of SME in Taiwan*

Figure 1.20 characterizes[77] the Taiwanese SMEs over the last three decades. The lower solid line (1) shows the number of SMEs in thousand in the

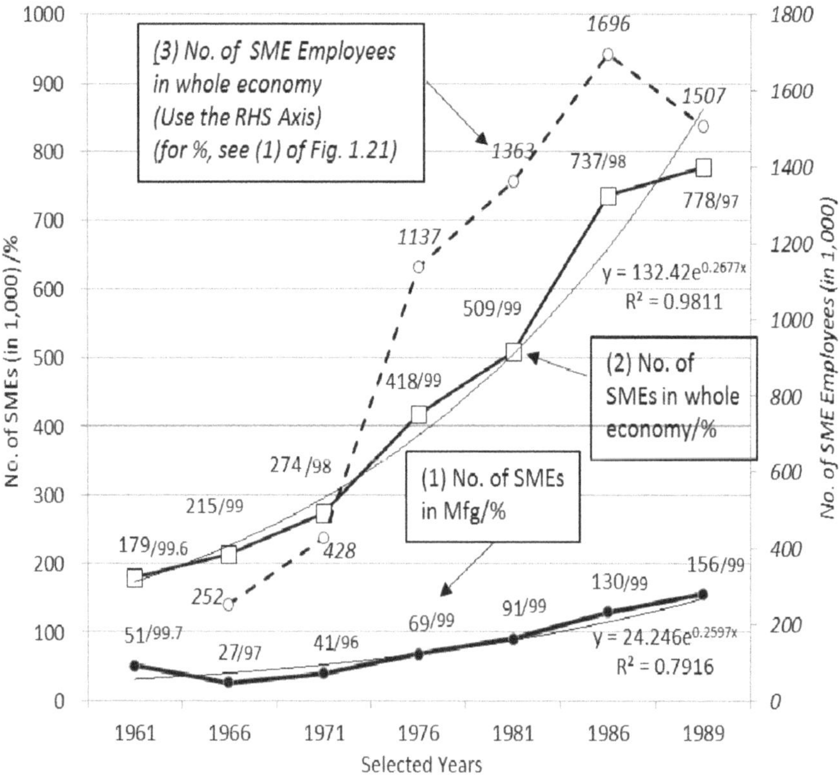

Figure 1.20: SMEs in Manufacturing and Whole Industry
Number of Firms and Employees

[77]Data in Figs. 1.20 and 1.21 are taken from Tables 5 and 9 in Lin and Hu (1992), and also from Tables 2, 6, 7 in Wu and Chou (1988).

manufacturing industry, in all industries (upper solid line (2)), and the number of SME employees in manufacturing (the dashed line (3)). It is not clear why the number of SME firms (1) dipped from 51,000 in 1961 to 27,000 in 1966, especially since there were no changes in the definition of SMEs in this period. The upward trend fit well with an exponential growth regression line. From 1961 to 1989, the number of SME in manufacturing grew at continuously compounded growth rate of about 26 percent. The number after the slash line from 1961 to 1989 shows the percentage of SMEs in manufacturing. It was 99.7 percent in 1961 and 99 percent in 1989. In general, except in 1966 (97%) and 1971 (96%), the percentages are close to 99 percent.

Similarly, the upper solid line (2) shows the number of SME in the total industries, including primary and tertiary industries.[78] In 1961, they counted at 179,000 firms, about 99.7 percent of total enterprises. They have increased steadily with the increase of population, and in 1989, they grew more than four times to 778,000 firms, about 97 percent of total enterprises. For other years, the percentage of SMEs also ranges from 98 percent to 99 percent. The continuous compound growth rate from 1961 to 1989 was 27 percent, slightly higher than that of the manufacturing industry, implying the vitality of the Taiwanese SME is not restricted to manufacturing industry.

In terms of the number of employee in SME of the manufacturing industry (3), in 1961, they counted mere 252,000, but it increased quickly and greatly to 1,507,000 in 1989, an increase of whopping 7 to 8 times during this period, with continuously compounded growth rate of 39 percent. Clearly, growth of the number of employees in SME outstripped the growth of the number of the SME firms. This indicate that, thanks to SMEs, Taiwan achieved low unemployment rate and low income inequality, all due to the vitality of Taiwanese SME activities. In terms of SME employment in the total employment, the second number of the dotted line (3) shows that SMEs in manufacturing contributed about 36 percent (1971) to 68 percent (1986 and 1989) of total manufacturing employment.

It should be noted that, since the definition of SMEs broadened over the years, the average size of SMEs in 1989, measured in terms of assets

---

[78]The data include 1. Mining and quarrying, 2. Manufacturing, 3. Electricity, gas and water, 4. Construction, 5. Commerce, 6. Transportation, and communication, 7. Financing, real estate, and business services, 8. Other profit organizations (Wu and Chow, 1988, Table 2).

and employees, was three times larger than SMEs in 1961. Furthermore, the decrease in SMEs as a proportion of total enterprises, about three percent to 97 percent in 1989 (see (2)), indicates the growth of larger private industry in non-manufacturing industry during the 1980s. The majority of SMEs came from commerce sector (not shown in Fig. 1.20), which over the years has the number of SMEs about four times larger than the number of SMEs in manufacturing.

Figure 1.21 presents various percentage measures of SME contribution to the economy. The dotted line (2) shows that SMEs in manufacturing contributed 27 percent (1971) to 47 percent (1976 and 1986) of total

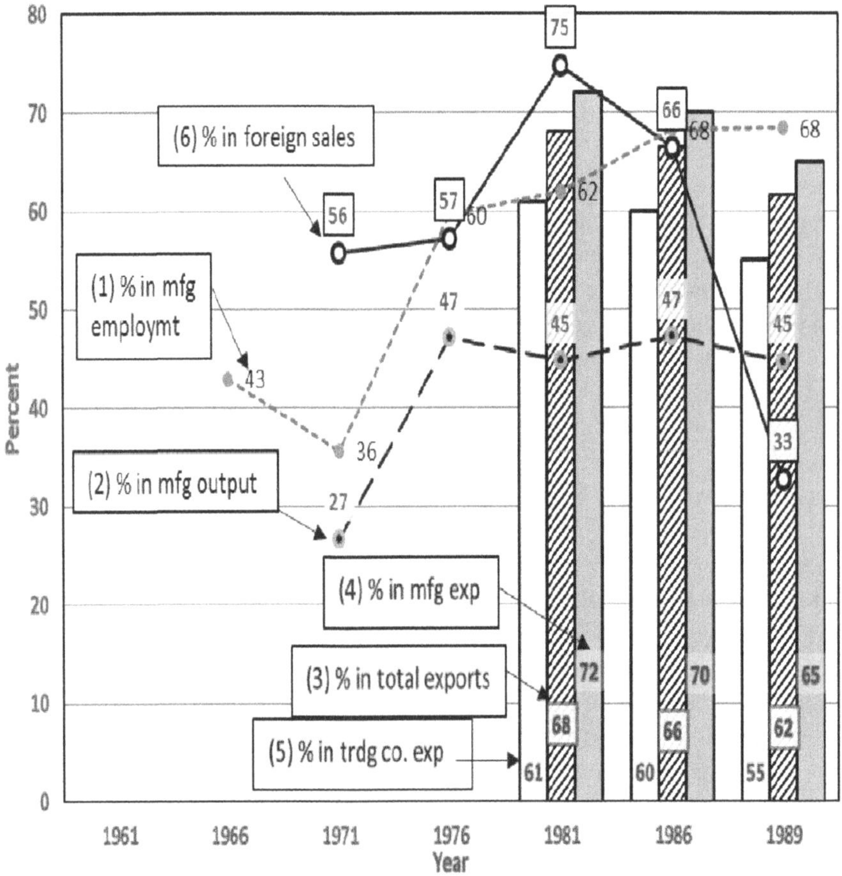

Figure 1.21: SMEs in Manufacturing and Whole Industry
Percentage in Foreign Sales, Exports, Mfg Employment, and Output

manufacturing output. In fact, the SME contributions to the commerce sector (not shown in Fig. 1.21) are even much higher, ranging from 96 percent in 1966 to 73 percent in 1986 for employment, and from 90 percent in 1971 to 61 percent in 1986 for output (Lin and Hu, 1992). In recent years, percentages of SMEs in both employment and output contributions increased again.

1.15.3 *Contribution of SMEs to Exports*

Unlike Japan, Korea, and many other countries, the major exporters in Taiwan are the SMEs, namely, the small and medium sized enterprises. In Fig. 1.21, the middle bars (3) shows the percentage of SME in the total exports. About two-third of Taiwan's total exports was contributed by the SMEs: 68 percent in 1981, 66 percent in 1986 and 62 percent in 1989. This percentages are calculated from the sum of two parts, exports by SMEs of manufacturing companies (4) and exports by SMEs of trading companies (5) (Wu *et al.*, 1980, Table 6). If the former (4) is taken alone, then the percentage of total exports contributed by SMEs of manufacturing companies was even higher. It was 72 percent, 70 percent, and 65 percent for 1981, 1986, and 1989, respectively. The SME contributions to exports by trading companies (6) are slightly lower, 61 percent, 60 percent, and 5 percent during in the 1980s.

On the other hand, in terms of SME sales revenue, more than half of SMEs sale revenue were derived from foreign markets. The heavy solid line (6) in the upper part of Fig. 1.21 shows that in 1981, the sale revenue of SMEs from foreign markets reached as high as 75 percent of the total SME sales. However, the SME revenue structure changed drastically in 1989. Its foreign revenue decreased to mere 33 percent, although, as we have seen above, the SMEs' contribution to total exports still maintained 62 percent. This is achieved by increase in the number of SMEs and possibly in the productivities of SMEs.

The drastic change in the revenue structure (6) in 1989 may be attributable to a shift in the importance of domestic markets. This shift was spurred by a number of trends and events in Taiwan: a sudden increase in Gross Domestic Product (see rGDP in Fig. 1.12); the revaluation of New Taiwan dollars (see Fig. 1.11) which discouraged exports; increased protectionism in the United States and European countries; increased competition in the foreign markets from developing countries like the ASEANs and China (Lin and Hu, 1992, 20); and new outward foreign direct investment by the Taiwanese SMEs to other developing countries like China, Malaysia, Indonesia (MOEA, 1991, Chapter 6). The foreign direct investment by Taiwanese firms in turn reduced the volume of exports to these countries. Whether this change is permanent or temporary, is not clear since the time period involved is so short.

In any case, we have shown that SMEs have been the drivers of growth in Taiwanese industry and trade. In large part, this is because Taiwanese SMEs are export oriented. On the other hand, government enterprises made almost no direct contribution to exports in the 1970s and the 1980s. Similarly, government enterprises and large private enterprises generally dominate the production of non-traded goods and domestic markets, and are monopolistic or monopolize the domestic markets (Chou, 1988, 181). Thus the vanguard of exports expansion and economic growth is the Taiwanese SMEs, mostly supported by either imports of intermediate goods, raw materials, and capital equipment from foreign countries, strengthened by technology transfer from direct foreign investment, and helped by the foreign trading companies, especially from Japan.

1.15.4 *SMEs, Exports, and Growth — The Textile Industry Again*

In Section 1.14.4, we have shown that development of the television industry was initially helped by Japanese companies and later mostly by Japanese technology. As we will see below, the Japanese also played a prominent role in the development of the textile industry, the mainstay of Taiwan's industrialization until the mid-1980s. To put the role of SMEs, exports, and economic growth in perspective, we will use the textile industry as an example.

In the early 1950s, the bulk of textile exports consisted of cotton fabrics, primarily manufactured by SMEs. Then in 1961, the United States restricted her imports of cotton fabrics. The restriction stimulated the development and exports of man-made fabrics in Taiwan, using man-made fibers and yarn, see Fig. 1.22, (1) and (2) on the lower right-hand side, which, unlike cotton, had to be imported mainly from Japan (3). Increasing imports of man-made fibers and yarn by SMEs triggered backward linkages. Domestic production of mid-stream petrochemical products for the raw materials of making man-made fibers, such as ethylene glycol (EG, (4)), purified terephthalic acid (PTA (5)), and caprolactam (CPL, (6)), became profitable (see Fig. 1.22). The companies producing the mid-stream

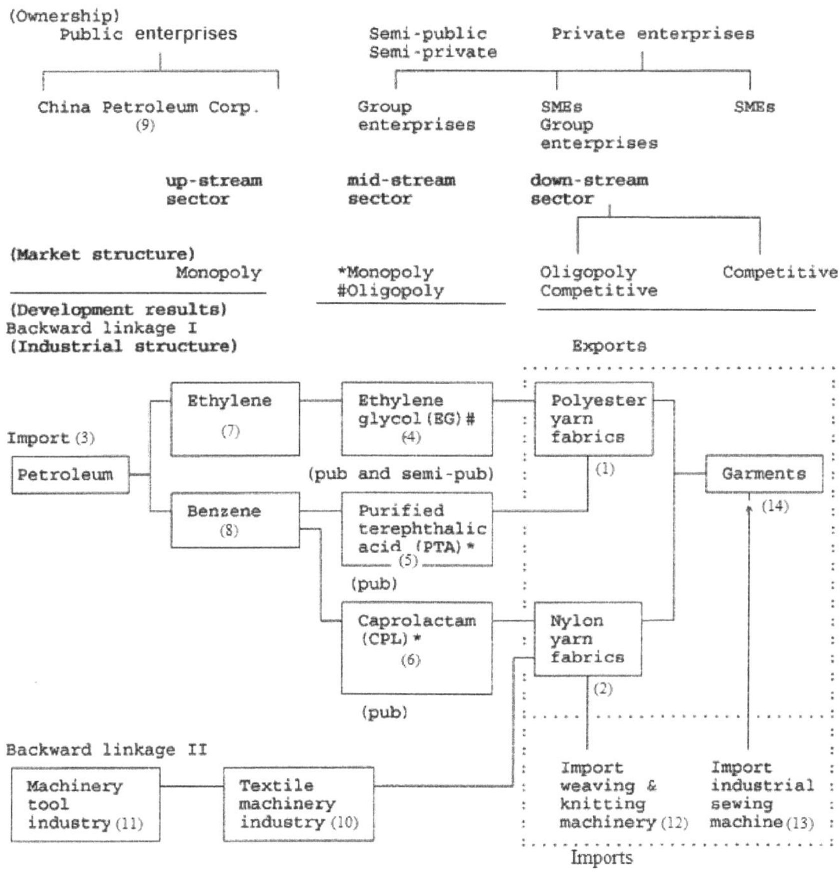

Figure 1.22: Market and Industrial Structure of the Textile Industry

petrochemical products are either directly owned by the government (like PTA, (5), and CPL (6)) or indirectly owned by the government through investment by public enterprises (like EG, (4)). The latter ones are in effect semipublic and semiprivate enterprises (Chen *et al.*, 1991, 45, 105). Import substitution of man-made fibers started in 1958 and was completed in 1978 (Lin, 1992, 148).

When the input demand for mid-stream petrochemical products reached the minimum scale for domestic production, it stimulated the production of up-stream products like ethylene (7), benzene (8), and so on (Fig. 1.22). In Taiwan, the up-stream petrochemical products are monopolized by the government-owned China Petroleum Corporation (9)

(Chen *et al.*, 1991, 105; Wu, 1992, 158). See the upper part of Fig. 1.22. It protects the government's direct and indirect investment by selling raw materials to the firms in the mid-stream industry with prices less than production cost (Chen *et al.*, 1991, 46), especially during the periods of the oil crises. The government then claims that public enterprises are "helping private enterprises" to pull through the crisis.

There is a second backward linkage arising from the development of the textile industry. Taiwan's textile machinery industry started as repair shops of imported machines, mainly from Japan. Then the import-substitution phase took place (see the lower part of Fig. 1.22). Taiwan produced her own textile machines by either imitating Japanese machines or by joint ventures entered around 1966 with Japanese companies (including Iwama, Toyota, and Sakamoto). By 1971, there were about 120 firms producing different types of textile machinery (10), which in turn stimulated the development of the machine tool industry (11) (Lin, 1992, 149).

By 1990, Taiwan was the seventh largest textile exporting country in the world. Despite the development of the machinery industry, Taiwan still could not master advanced production technology. She had to continue importing textile machinery from other countries, mainly from Japan. Even as late as 1987, with all the government talk of Taiwan's heavy and high-tech industrialization in the period of the 1980s, Japan supplied 51 to 73 percent of Taiwan's imports of weaving and knitting machinery (12) each year. This was valued annually from US$42 to 170 million (Itaya, 1991, 42). For example, in 1987 alone, her textile machinery imports increased three times, up to US$292 million: 58 percent came from Japan, 20 percent from Switzerland, and 9 percent from West Germany. Other countries which supplied textile machinery to Taiwan were Belgium and Luxembourg (8%), Italy (3%), and the United States (2%) (ibid., 42).

Among the Taiwanese exports of textile products from 1978 to 1988, 72 percent consisted of garments (ibid., 10; TSDB, 1989, 229–230), almost all were produced by Taiwanese SMEs. It is an irony that while Taiwan was the world's largest producer and exporter of household sewing machines in 1983, grabbing 80 percent of the world export market (Duan, 1989, 313), its industrial sewing machines (13) were imported from Japan. From 1968 to 1978, Taiwan imported industrial sewing machines from Japan worth of about 18 billion Japanese yen (0.4 million sets). From 1979 to 1989, the imports not only didn't decrease, they almost tripled to 52 billion Japanese yen (0.6 million sets) (Duan, 1989, 60). Apparently, other industries have the same problem despite the seemingly successful government plan of upgrading Taiwan's industrial structure. Here again we confirm that Taiwanese SMEs produce household sewing machines mostly with the help from the multinationals, and have grown to the largest exporter in the world. However, basic industrial machinery and equipment used in export products, such as simple weaving, knitting, and sewing machines used by Taiwanese SMEs still have to rely on imports. It is not surprising that Taiwanese total imports from Japan accelerated in recent years as its exports to other countries increased, as shown on the right-hand side of Fig. 1.17.

The unit price of imports of industrial sewing machines (13) may be considered an indicator of the quality of garment products produced within a country. During the first period (1968 to 1978), the unit price of Taiwanese imports of the sewing machine was lowest among other Asian countries, only about 75 percent of that of Korea and 28 percent of that of China, indicating that the imports were used mainly by the Taiwanese under-capitalized SMEs. During the second period (1979 to 1989), Taiwan's unit price of imported sewing machines exceeded Hong Kong, Singapore, Thailand, Indonesia, Philippines, and Malaysia, but still trailed its major competitors, Korea and China, by 22 percent and more than 50 percent, respectively. Korea and other Asian developing countries have been importing high valued multi-purpose specialized sewing machines, indicating that other countries are aiming at producing high value-added garment products (12) for exports (Itaya, 1991, 60–64).

1.16 The Sources of Taiwanese Vitality

In Taiwan, as early as 1954, the census of industry and business already showed that 99.4 percent of the manufacturing enterprises (42,034 enterprises) were SMEs, employing less than 99 workers. The number of SMEs doubled in 1980, and almost doubled again just before 1990, consistently maintaining about 99 percent of the manufacturing enterprises. As we have noticed before, the definition of SMEs has changed over time. Therefore, it is not clear whether the cottage industry, which has only one to three employees, grew during this period. In any case, according to the experience of other countries, the growth of SMEs may be characterized as "multi-births, multi-deaths, and enlarging reproduction process" (Kiyonari, 1970, 30).

In a dynamic growing economy, technical progress introduces differentiated products, and increases in income enable consumers to purchase a variety of commodities. The deepening of the social division of labor creates more fields for the SMEs, and more new SMEs enter the market. In these new fields, large enterprises most likely are still not dominant, the average profit rate is high, and accumulation of capital is possible. This enables, as Alfred Marshall once observed, "a broad movement from below upwards." On the other hand, in a declining industry, or in an industry using obsolete technology, many enterprises will fail. Hence the faster the industrial structure changes, the more the phenomenon of multi-births and multi-deaths will occur, and in a growing economy, new births outrun the deaths of old enterprises (ibid., 31).

The growth of Taiwanese SMEs is nothing unusual in light of the dynamic changes facing Taiwanese industry. What makes them unique is that, as we will see, they are, as with the agricultural sector, inherited from the Japanese educational system, helped by postwar Japanese technology and the Japanese marketing network. The Taiwanese SMEs are very much on their own, and their upward movements are hindered by the government monopoly of up-stream and mid-stream industries and the banking system.

1.16.1 *Japanese Linkage Once Again*

The emergence of entrepreneurs of SMEs as a massive social group in the 1950s and the 1960s can only be explained by educational advancing in the Japanese period. As noted in Section 1.4 (Japanese Legacy), the existence of 40,000 or so graduates of lower and secondary vocational schools and another 10,000 or so graduates of normal schools and professional schools, in addition to millions of primary school children who received Japanese education by the end of the war were essential. They were in their productive prime period[79] from the 1960s to the 1980s. We have seen that the 2-28 Incident in 1947 taught them to be apolitical (Section 1.5.1). Civil servants had a language barrier and low status (Section 1.5.1), and cultural activities along with social works were underdeveloped. Thus, many talented Taiwanese youths chose to open their own shops and engage in business and manufacturing. "Basically, machinery and electrical

[79]We may use the current seventy-year old President of the KMT Government as an example. President T.H. Lee was born in 1923 in Taipei. He was a freshman at the Kyoto Imperial University in 1943 and became a sophomore at the National Taiwan University in 1946, a year after the war. The bearers of the Taiwanese industrial development mostly belonged to his generation, probably five to ten years younger, finishing at least primary education under the Japanese regime.

manufacture and repair work can be carried out on a variety of scales. Anybody with some mechanical skill can start a business of his own in this field" (Kao, 1969, 7). It seems that few developing countries have developed these SMEs into a massive vital export sector. Clearly there must have been some special background in Taiwanese development.

One important characteristic is that many of these entrepreneurs came from rural areas (Sumiya *et al.*, 1992, 161), either as youths seeking better opportunities in industry, or as displaced, better-educated landlords. For almost two generations since the 1920s, the farmers and villagers were accustomed to the idea of production for exports. Unlike the Western plantation system in other parts of the world, Taiwanese rice farmers and the majority of the sugar cane farmers have been independent producers. They could choose the cash crop they would plant. They knew how to use chemical fertilizer and adopt new technology to enhance production. As we have seen earlier, the farmers were faced with very sophisticated government schemes of taxation and exploitation when they calculated revenues from the alternatives and predicted the possible profits (Sections 1.7.4.2, Fig. 1.9, and 1.7.4.3, Fig. 1.10). They knew the importance of savings and plowed back their profits for further expansion. In general, they were modern farmers who took risks, seized opportunities, and made decisions. Undoubtedly, these traits could be carried on to the management of SMEs in the process of industrialization.

Furthermore, like their counterparts in Korea, the rapid economic recovery of Japan after the war and advancement of "Japan as Number One" (Vogel, 1979) have probably stimulated the Taiwanese to imitate, follow, and work harder to catch up with those they feel to be arrogant but not unsurpassably bright former colonists (Tsurumi, 1977, 211). "If the Japanese can do, we can do too" has been a common catch phrase among many Taiwanese (and Korean) entrepreneurs and businessmen. They imported Japanese technology, read Japanese books on management, and found directions by looking to the Japanese (Hsiao and Hsiao, 1989, 185). In a sense, the Taiwanese even followed the Japanese to the American markets, and recently, to invest in quasi-newly developing countries like China and the ASEANs.

1.16.2 *Japanese Technology*

We have seen that the bulk of Taiwanese traded goods was produced by SMEs, most of which were operated by the Taiwanese. Several historical coincidences between Japan and Taiwan may be noted.

First, when Taiwanese economic growth started to take off in the mid-1960s, Japanese multinationals expanded at the same time, especially after 1968. They have engulfed almost all industrial sectors in Japan (Ozawa, 1979, 74). In view of the geological proximity, cultural similarity, historical background, and the resemblance in the pattern of economic development (Hsiao and Hsiao, 1989, 158), the first stop for the infant Japanese multinationals was in Taiwan (and Korea). Thus Taiwanese economic development was paralleled by the growth of Japanese multinational activities, which in turn reflected Japanese economic development. As the Taiwanese economy advanced, Japanese direct investment in Taiwan was also upgraded. There has been a spill-over effect of Japanese economic growth on Taiwan and other Asian countries (Itaya, 1991, 68). By 1990, there were 706 Japanese firms in Taiwan. These firms consisted of 5.6 percent of the 12,522 Japanese multinationals overseas, ranking sixth in number (Toi and Morioka, 1992, 258).

Second, unlike large-scale American multinationals, by the end of 1975, 58.6 percent of Japanese multinationals in Taiwan were themselves SMEs in Japan, having employees of only 300 or less. Japanese multinationals preferred joint ventures and accepted minority ownership (Ozawa, 1979, 75) by seeking out their Taiwanese counterparts. Thus Taiwanese SMEs were able to maximize the benefits of imitation and learning.

Third, American multinationals are generally more capital-intensive and more oriented toward the markets of host countries, as well as having a uniform sectorial pattern in different countries and regions. In contrast, Japanese multinationals are generally more labor-intensive and export oriented, possessing investment patterns that differ from country to country and region to region (Kojima, 1985a, 33; 1985b, 4–10). Indeed, as we have seen, Taiwan benefitted from both types of multinationals in different industrial sectors. In the area of foreign trade and economic development in the later period, the Japanese multinationals probably contributed more to the vitality of the Taiwanese SMEs.[80]

[80]The difference of Japanese and American multinationals, as characterized by Kojima, the rise of SMEs, and the spill-over effect of Japanese economic growth probably explain at least partially the rapid Taiwanese and Korean economic growth as compared with Mexico and South American countries, which are under the predominant influence of American economy and American multinationals. Our study provides a new explanation of the difference (Winckler and Greenhalgh, 1988).

Fourth, the predominant influences of Japanese multinationals, imported Japanese intermediate materials, and capital equipment should be emphasized again.[81] Taiwanese entrepreneurs have been familiar with Japanese machines and equipment. They can read Japanese operational instructions and documents directly (Itaya, 1991, 64) without going through Chinese translations, which are generally poorly done. Even American and European manuals and documents are often available through the Japanese sources.

1.16.3 *High Social Mobility*

As is in Japan, there is high social upward mobility in Taiwan. Many farmers started as laborers. In small enterprises, employers and employees are more or less treated equally. Because of the smallness, employees could learn skills on the job quickly. After they did, and accumulated some savings, they would move out and, with the help of family members, become shop managers or factory owners in the neighborhoods and countryside. The possibility of fast upward mobility encouraged the establishment of many small enterprises in Taiwan. At the same time, the turnover rate of workers in small enterprises is very high in Taiwan.[82]

In general, SMEs are flexible in hiring workers, easy to adjust the working hours, simple to supervise, adaptable to suit the changes in clients' designs and orders, and have the advantage of face-to-face contact between the owners/managers and the clients. In short, the small-scale operation of SMEs may reduce the principal-agency problems. It may be noted that, although there may be an improvement in the living standards, it came with a great cost of long working hours, inferior working conditions, and income supplemented by family members, especially children. Furthermore, the employees of SMEs generally have no labor insurance for health and accidents, and inadequate or even no job protection by labor regulations (Arrigo, 1984, 14).

---

[81] But this should not be overemphasized. The Taiwanese SMEs bought Japanese textile machinery because the price was about 50 percent cheaper than the American or European counterparts (Itaya, 1991, 66).

[82] One reason for the high turnover rate is that labor organization is strictly controlled by the government. "Instead of striking, the workers 'vote with their feet', hopping from factory to factory for slightly better wages" (Arrigo, 1984, 11). Sumiya *et al.* (1992), 165–66 point out this may be another reason that antagonism between employers and employees are not strong in Taiwan.

1.16.4 *The Outward Looking SMEs*

In addition to the help from multinationals and imitating Japanese economic activities, there were several reasons for the Taiwanese SMEs to be outward looking (Sumiya *et al.*, 1992, 291–294). First, as we have discussed in Section 1.15.4 (also see Fig. 1.22), the domestic markets have been either dominated by the government enterprises or by the large private group enterprises, squeezing most of the SMEs out of the domestic markets. The monopolistic position of public and group enterprises and the government monopoly of the commercial banking system also prevented the SMEs from growing through mergers and combinations. Second, as we have seen earlier, the Taiwanese SMEs rely heavily on informal financial markets and the shop owners' own savings. Furthermore, because SMEs are constantly in shortage of working capital, exports can provide instant cash payment or cash advance through Letter of Credit (L/C), while the payment receivables from the domestic sales generally take half to one year.

Third, exporters can receive government tax rebates or even tax exemptions, adding to the normal three percent profit rate for the exporters. Relatively high and stable effective exchange rates against the dollar from 1958 to 1973 also favored exports over domestic markets (Liang and Liang, 1982, 230). Fourth, exporters can remit U.S. dollars overseas through price manipulation, even under the strict foreign exchange control (Sumiya *et al.*, 1992, 293). The implicit lack of confidence in Taiwan's political future also prompts outward foreign investment, foreign emigration, and capital flight. The possibility of remittance overseas added to the incentive to export.

Fifth, in other countries like Japan, France, and Belgium, large firms, rather than small ones, are more export-oriented due to economies of scale (Chou, 1992, 1078). For the Taiwanese SMEs, the scale effect is immaterial, since most Taiwanese SMEs use labor intensive technology, and transfer their marketing operations to Japanese general trading companies, multinationals, and foreign exporters (ibid., 1080).

1.16.5 *On the Role of Government*

What is the role of the government in helping these energetic and independent SMEs domestically and internationally? It has been minimal. First, the government not only failed to nurture and protect Taiwanese SMEs, it invited overseas Chinese investors to compete directly with them, reflecting again the character of the émigré regime. The much touted

1970 "Statute for Encouragement of Investment" has been applicable only to incorporated enterprises. As is shown in Table 1.10 (row 11), almost 85 percent of private enterprises in Taiwan are unincorporated. Banking laws and stock market regulations are also biased against SMEs (Sumiya *et al.*, 1992, 156; also see Section 1.7.3.7). Second, although there were small and medium enterprise loans provided by the U.S. aid program in the 1950s, the important role of SMEs was recognized only recently. The very definition of SMEs was not available until September 1967 (ibid., 1069). Third, even after 1967, government policies with respect to SMEs were at best fragmented and confusing, revealing a constant shift of responsibility and coordination among the government agencies.[83]

This confusion might reflect the problems of language and communication between the "central government" and the Taiwanese. Finally, in 1981, a specialized office of the "Medium and Small Business Administration" was set up under the Ministry of Economic Affairs (ibid., 1092; MOEA, 1991, 165). After ten long years of half-hearted discussions, the basic law, "Statute of Developing Medium and Small Business" was finally promulgated only in 1991 (MOEA, 1991, 165). According to the statute, the government established "Medium and Small Business Development Fund," with a budget of half billion U.S. dollars (ibid., 168), and published the annual "White Paper on Medium and Small Business"[84] for the first time.

Today, every country protects its own citizens and business interests through foreign embassies and official representatives. This is not the case for Taiwanese business people. In 1971, the Republic of China was replaced by the People's Republic of China in the United Nations. The KMT government's misguided "One China" policy after 1971 drove Taiwan to international isolation (Tien, 1989, 224). To be sure, before 1971, the KMT government still had diplomatic recognition by the international community. However, the "central government" was so engulfed with the "One China" policy, coupled with the language barrier, that it seldom if ever, represented Taiwanese business interests.

Japan and the United Kingdom severed diplomatic ties with Taiwan in 1972, and the United States in 1979. Almost every year, additional countries severed diplomatic ties with Taiwan (ibid., 221–224). By 1988, only 22 of

[83]Some important measures by the KMT government are listed in Chou (1992), 1092.
[84]This is in contrast with the "Statute for Investment by Foreign Nationals" published in 1954 and also one for the overseas Chinese in 1955. Incidentally, Japan promulgated the "Basic Law for Medium and Small Business" in 1963 (Kiyonari, 1970, 322).

the 160 countries in the world recognized the KMT government.[85] Trade with these 22 countries amounted to less than 10 percent of Taiwanese annual foreign trade (ibid., 222). Despite the political severance, Taiwan still maintains trade relations with over 140 nations. To compensate the loss of formal relations, the KMT government established the China External Trade Development Council (CETDC) with more than 48 offices throughout the world (ibid., 225). Nevertheless, the government is unable to protect Taiwanese businessmen. "In commercial dealings there is little recourse when a foreign country or business fails to honor commitments. Obstacles to negotiations over trade arrangements have evolved simply because of the lack of official involvement. Moreover, without diplomatic missions Taiwan's business community is hard-pressed to acquire needed trade information in many nations" (ibid., 227). In fact, a survey in the early 1970s revealed that 76 percent of firms received export information from foreign customers, 33 percent from representatives abroad, and 28 percent from foreign partners (Chou, 1988, 186). The government played only a very minor role. Despite all of these domestic and international handicaps, Taiwanese enterprises, especially those SMEs, still could achieve rapid economic growth through foreign trade. If there is a "miracle," this is indeed the one. It definitely deserves more attention and analysis.

1.16.6 *On Education, Confucianism, and the Spirit of Settlers*

In Taiwan, as in Japan, China, and Korea, and other Western countries, education is generally regarded as an important means for socioeconomic upward mobility. In Section 1.4, we already saw that, by the end of the Japanese regime, the percentage of school-aged children in primary schools already reached 81 percent for boys and 61 percent for girls. It reached 84 percent in 1952, and 99.79 percent in 1992 (TSDB, 1993, 268). In 1968, the compulsory primary education was extended from six years to nine years. At the same time the KMT government pepped up the vocational training program to meet the demands of industry for skilled workers. (Li, 1988, 87–91). By 1980, Taiwan had a high percentage of the senior high

[85]They are Costa Rica, the Dominican Republic, Dominica, El Salvador, Guatemala, Haiti, the Holy See, Honduras, Malawi, Nauru, Panama, Paraguay, St. Christopher and Nevis, St. Lucia, St. Vincent and the Grenadines, the Solomon Islands, Saudi Arabia, South Africa, South Korea, Swaziland, Tonga, and Tuvalu (Tien, 1989, 222). None of them is a major power. Even South Korea dropped her recognition in 1992.

and vocational graduates (21%), only second to Korea (22%), and the highest percentage of university graduates (11%) among the four Asian NICs (Fields, 1985, 350).

While human capital is considered one of the factors of economic growth, Taiwan's human capital, at least before 1980 after WWII, was formed during the Japanese period. After the postwar 1968 reform, one would expect a lag of fifteen to twenty years before the school graduates attained decision making positions. Thus, the effects of the post-war changes to Taiwan's educational system on its economic development, if there are any, will show only after mid-1980. In addition, one would expect those effects to occur concurrently with the rise of the political activities of the Taiwanese intelligentsia.

Closely related with the effects of education was the assertion that Confucianism, or a 20th century revision of Confucianism, played a role in Taiwanese economic development (Metzger and Myers, 1989, 302). In a separate paper (Ref. Chapter 6), we have pointed out that there are problems of the definition of Confucianism, and that the usual concepts such as family values, respect of elders, hard work, scholarship, are shared with other societies and ethnic groups. Furthermore, despite the government claim, Confucianism may not have reached the farmers and workers, as the carpetbagger Chinese officials speak a language which is not understood by the ordinary Taiwanese farmers and workers, at least during the early postwar period. Thus, we attribute hard working, strong family ties, competition, etc. to be endemic to the Taiwanese, similar to the spirit of the settlers and frontier people like the Pilgrims and other Europeans who separated from Europe and sailed to America[86] (Kato, 1967, 140–142).

1.17 A Review of Later Post War Economic Development — 1964 to Early 1990s

Taiwanese economic development after 1964 benefited mainly from three indispensable sources: the Japan-Taiwan-USA Trade Triangle, Japan-USA direct foreign investment, and Taiwanese SMEs. Section 1.9 presents an

[86]When Taiwan was ceded "in perpetuity" to Japan in 1895, only 4,500 people, or less than 0.2 percent of the total at that time, decided to return to China after two years of the grace period (Ng, 1870, 238). Thus, the Taiwanese who stayed in Taiwan were basically separatists. For a good discussion of pilgrims and Americanism, see Kato (1969), 140–142. The work ethic and national character of Koreans may have different cultural explanations, see Pae (1992), 68.

overview of Taiwanese economic development from 1952 to 1993 using some basic macroeconomic and foreign trade indicators in real terms, that is, discounting the effect of price inflation. All indexes clearly indicate an impressive performance of the Taiwanese economy since 1964, especially during the 1980s, contrary to the expectation of many critics.[87]

In Section 1.10, economic development after 1964 is divided into three stages: the Take-off and Export Promotion Period (1964–73); the Second Import Substitution Period (1974–1980); and the Accelerated Growth and High-Tech Industrialization Period (1980–) (Fig. 1.12). In each period, some salient features of government economic planning, political events, and international environments are considered briefly. A special attention has been given to the Ten Major Construction Projects of 1974 (Section 1.10.2.1) and the Six-Year National Development Plan of 1991 (Section 1.10.3.4).

The turning point of vigorous export promotion and rapid growth after 1964 is trade policy reform at the end of the 1950s. In Section 1.11, we have shown that, contrary to the general assertions, the reform was brought out by external influences. Sections 1.12 and 1.13 looked at the Taiwanese trade performance as well as her relations with its major trading partners, Japan and the United States. In exports, more than two dozens of Taiwanese exports can claim "Taiwan as Number One" in the world. The contents of exported commodities indeed advanced from agricultural goods and agricultural processed goods to low technology manufactured goods, and then to high technology manufactured goods. However, if imports are considered, the whole picture changes. Japan is Taiwan's largest source of imported goods, and the United States is the largest market for exports from Taiwan throughout these years. The three countries form a Pacific trade triangle. The Taiwanese firms generally imported from Japan intermediate materials and capital goods, especially machinery and electric and electronic parts and equipment, and exported finished products of these items to the United States. Through historical, geographical, and cultural ties, Taiwan was fortunate to seize the opportunities of the two markets. In the system of world trade, Taiwan played the role of intermediary between the two countries.

---

[87]Taiwan was not alone in achieving high growth rate in the 1980s. From 1980 to 1990, average growth rate of GDP for Taiwan was 7.7 percent, for Korea, 9.7 percent, Hong Kong, 7.1 percent, Singapore, 6.4 percent, Thailand, 7.6 percent, and Botswana 11.3 percent (TSDB, 1993, 311–312; WDR, 1993).

As we have seen, Section 1.14 relates Taiwanese economic development with direct foreign investment and technology transfer through multinational companies. The higher the foreign ownership of the firms, the more likely the firms adopt foreign technology. Again, Japanese technology played an important role in the process, as can be seen from the development of the television industry in Taiwan. To examine the sources of vitality of Taiwanese economic activities, Section 1.15 analyzes the dual industrial structure in Taiwan. Public enterprises and group enterprises monopolized the production of non-traded goods, squeezing out the small-and-medium size enterprises (SMEs), forcing them to produce traded goods for exports, helped by Japanese trading companies, multinationals, and foreign importers.

Being driven out of the international community, the KMT government has been powerless to protect Taiwanese business people in foreign countries. The true bearers and promoters of Taiwanese economic development are the silent majority of Taiwanese entrepreneurs of the small-and-medium sized enterprices, helped by the Taiwanese workers and farmers, all of whom rose to the challenge of foreign competition.

1.18 Conclusions

Taiwanese economic development, prior to 1963, benefitted from four sources. The Japanese colonialists built infrastructure and social capital in prewar period. The Americans contributed by financing and maintaining economic growth, supporting the armed forces, and advising on the development policies during the most crucial postwar period. The Chinese contributed in human capital and textile capital. They also ruled the island under a one-family oligarchy and maintained political stability at least on the surface. The Taiwanese were the silent majority of timid tillers and toilers, generally educated and hardworking, but leaderless and apolitical. With these four contributors, Taiwan's initial conditions for take-off in the mid-1960s were not exactly "underdeveloped." Its starting point seems already higher than most of the developing countries in that period (Table 1.4 and Fig. 1.6).

After 1964, the Taiwanese economy entered the phase of export expansion, in which local Taiwanese entrepreneurs as well as direct foreign investment by multinational corporations began to play a prominent role. Taiwanese small and medium enterprises were helped by the Japanese multinationals with technology and marketing so that they could operate efficiently. The true miracle is that they operated and grew under adverse environments domestically and internationally. In general, Taiwanese economic development before 1993 was filled with many unique characteristics that might not be shared with many other developing countries.

In recent years, the role of the state in economic development has been one of the major topics in the economic literature. The KMT government in Taiwan might fit into the successful model of "development dictatorship." Throughout the world, dictatorship, not democracy, has been the rule rather than exception until most of the 1980s, but only a few have succeeded in economic development. Thus the Taiwanese history is an exception in its success.

This unique success stems from an inheritance of a well-organized social structure and economic infrastructure from colonialism, along with a massive infusion of U.S. foreign aid and advisers in the initial fifteen critical years after the War. Furthermore, Taiwan had the new émigré regime which spoke a different language, both literally and figuratively, without any ties to the local society. This regime tried hard to overcome past failure and was determined to succeed in the future. These were unusual features which no other developing countries seem to have ever had.

We also feel that the major impact of the 2-28 Incident in 1947, the one-family oligarchy, martial law, and the KMT's language policy on Taiwanese economic development has been that the policy decision-making process has degenerated into a simpler one in which few problems of conflict resolution were encountered. As governmental policy success in a democratic country is a process of conflict resolution, the Taiwanese case does not seem to present much of an interesting case (Hsiao, 1989, 367). Furthermore, if one argues that this sequence of events was necessary for securing economic stability and progress, then in terms of social cost and, with the benefit of hindsight, more people probably would choose a more democratic society but less rapid economic growth. A case in point is that if the local Taiwanese people, not the carpetbagger bureaucrats, had had some inputs in economic planning and decision making some decades ago, the severe problems of pollution and environmental devastation in Taiwan (Bello and Rosenfeld, 1990, 131) today could have been mitigated or even alleviated.

On the Growth Path. To conclude our analysis, it may be relevant to ask whether the time path of Taiwanese development has been the best or optimal. Earlier, we stated that by the end of the 1920s, Taiwan already achieved the primary export-led growth, and the import substitution phase should have started in the early 1930s. Unfortunately, the war interrupted this phase in 1937 and Taiwan was plunged into the period of controlled wartime economy under national mobilization until 1945. After the war, the chaotic period followed and the economic recovery was slow and lasted until 1952. The import substitution period resumed only after 1953. The period from 1947 to 1963 was still a period of a rigidly controlled economy, similar to the wartime economy under national mobilization. Thus the Taiwanese economy was interrupted for almost thirty years before it resumed more or less normal growth in 1964. If Taiwanese development after 1964 is any indication of how fast an economy could grow, the loss of thirty years is indeed disastrous. If Taiwan were an independent country, she could have developed much earlier and much faster. As we have seen previously, Taiwanese economic development paralleled with Japanese economic development during the prewar period. If Taiwan had continued her development since the mid-1930s, she could have surpassed Japan,[88] or grew as fast as Switzerland, Norway, or Sweden. The historical lesson is that Taiwan can never gain by involving itself, or more accurately by being dragged into, the wars of aggression or civil wars in the neighboring countries.

In reality, Taiwan finally resumed its normal growth in 1964. Its economic performance has been very impressive since then, thanks to many unique factors on which we have expounded in this paper, especially, the vitality of the Taiwanese small and medium enterprises; and inward foreign direct investment helped by the foreign multinational companies, especially the Japanese. From 1965 to 1980, the average annual growth rate of Taiwan's GDP was 9.9 percent (TSDB, 1993, 311); superseded, among the 125 countries, only by Botswana (13.9%), Saudi Arabia (10.6%), Singapore (10.0%); and equal to that of South Korea (WDR, 1992, 220–221). From 1980 to 1990, although the growth rate dropped to 7.7 percent (TSDB, 1993, 311), her per capita real GNP increased 3.6 times in ten years (see Fig. 1.11). Note that Taiwan is not the only high achiever. During the same period, Korea achieved 9.7 percent, Hong Kong, 7.1 percent, Singapore, 6.4 percent, Thailand, 7.6 percent, China, 9.5 percent, and Botswana, 11.3 percent (ibid., 311–312; WDR, ibid.).

---

[88] For a discussion of catching up with Japan, see Hsiao and Hsiao (2004).

In 1982, to upgrade its industrial structure and promote high-tech industries, Taiwan's government designated electronic information and machinery as strategic industrial sectors (Duan, 1989). It opened Shinchu High Tech Industrial Park at the end of 1980. It also planned to attract Japanese capital and technology by establishing a large modern automobile factory, which in turn will stimulate machinery, iron and steel, rubber and plastics and other industries. In its initial stage, the High Tech Park does not seem to have much impact, and negotiations with Toyota to locate there failed (ibid.). By the end of the decade, Taiwan had to depend on Japan for more and more of its hi-tech parts and equipment. It still could not master the vital technology in the targeted computer production. In 1990 alone, the computer industry imported from Japan about US $87 million worth of LCDs, which amounted to 100 percent of Taiwan's total demand for LCDs; US$ 164 million of DRAM, 98 percent; US$ 227 million of floppy disk drive, 96 percent of Taiwan's demand for DRAM; US$ 477 million of color monitors, 75 percent of Taiwan's demand (Hsieh and Chang, 1992, 71).

On Chinese Technology and Market. Frustrated by the tardy and reluctant Japanese transfer of technology, the lack of understanding the Japanese language among the second generation Taiwanese (ibid., 68), fueled by consistently huge trade deficits with Japan, it was suggested that Taiwan cooperate with China to form a vertical division of labor (people could be jailed or executed for such a thinking as traitors just six years ago!). The scheme was to be that China do the research, and transfer technology to Taiwan for production and exports, on which Taiwan has extensive experience for forty years. Further it was argued that this is the best arrangement since both the Chinese and the Taiwanese speak the same languages; are the same race; the price of Chinese inputs was cheaper; and unlike the Japanese, the Chinese would transfer technology without reservations (ibid., 74). Here again, the language problem played an important part in the argument. Apparently, the second generation Taiwanese and the Chinese in Taiwan did not understand Japanese as well as their parents, and found it more appealing to ask for help from China.

On the other hand, the revaluation of New Taiwan dollar, shortage of labor, high wage cost, and the lure of investment incentives from abroad attracted Taiwanese SMEs to make massive outward direct foreign investment in South East Asia, like Malaysia, Indonesia, Thailand, and especially China (MOEA, 1991, 155). Just like Japanese DFI came to Taiwan because of geological proximity, cultural similarity, historical background, and the resemblance in economic development, Taiwanese DFI flocked to China by exactly the same reasons (ibid., 159). By the end of 1993, about 12,000 Taiwanese enterprises poured more than US $11 billion in China (Pun, 1993). As predicted by Kojima, the majority of the Taiwanese SME owned production facilities in China were textile and footwear factories enterprises (ibid., 156). Given the proclivities of the Taiwanese toward trade, these new businesses were also export oriented, helping China to "rake in huge foreign exchange earning" (ibid.).

In view of Japanese development experiences, the outward investment by Taiwanese SMEs in China and South East Asia seems a "natural" trend, that is, of history repeating itself. However, the argument for technical cooperation with China was simply a manifestation of the failure of government policy of heavy and high-tech industrialization after 1974. First, it failed to nurture strong and large private enterprises for research, development and marketing. After so many years of protection, the large government and private enterprises spent less in research than the SMEs. In 1989, R&D expenditure for large enterprises was 1.1 percent of operating revenues, while that of SMEs was 1.81 percent, the latter is almost twice as large (ibid., 91). Second, it failed to nurture and integrate universities and research institution with the industries. Thus to develop even a simple infrared heating procedure, Taiwan had to seek advice from China (Lin, 1992), not from its own many universities and research institutes.

The KMT bureaucrats have been boasting "growth with equity," which should not come as surprise in view of the numerous highly competitive SMEs and highly exploited small farmers in Taiwan, as we have seen in this paper. Meanwhile, Korea has successfully developed large private enterprises in the heavy and high-tech industries. The difference in results is staggering.

As of mid-1983, Hyundai and Samsung conglomerates in Korea showed annual sales of US$ 8 billion and US$ 5.9 billion and employed 137,000 and 97,384, respectively. Taiwan's largest privately-owned corporation, Formosa Plastics, posted annual sales of US$ 1.6 billion and employed 31,211. For the past ten years from 1966 to 1976, new Taiwanese firms increased 150 percent, while those in Korea only increased ten percent (Pae, 1992, 107).

Taking advantage of their economies of scale in heavy and high tech industries, Koreans have now successfully developed and exported, to name some of the most well-known high tech products, Goldstar VCR and Camcorders, Samsung semiconductor and DRAM, Leading Edge Computers, and the Hyundai model of automobiles. Taiwan has nothing in equivalence. The most well-known Taiwanese product probably Tatung electric fans.

Like the Taiwanese SMEs, the competition in the domestic markets among the large enterprises in Japan and Korea are fierce. In fact, the experience of fierce competition at home enable them to compete with American and European mammoth multinationals in international markets (Nakamura, 1961, 30). This fact has two policy implications to Taiwan.

First, to compete in the international markets, and prepare for the incoming liberalization and internationalization of the domestic markets, privatization of the public enterprises in Taiwan is imminent. However, like their failure in land reform in China a generation ago, the KMT bureaucrats have been entwined and engaged in so much collusion with the public enterprises resulting in sluggish progress. Despite all the talk, a single case of privatization is yet to be realized. Even if privatization is realized, comparing with the large enterprises in Japan and Korea, the time may be too short to compete internationally.

Second, in view of fierce competition among enterprises even within its own country, and China's avowed determination to "liberate" Taiwan even by force (Tien, 1989, 244), it is not clear why the Chinese are willing to share their technical know-how with the Taiwanese. It is also not clear why the Chinese would rely on Taiwan for marketing their products when they have already doing that successfully by themselves in recent years. Furthermore, the Taiwanese themselves have been relying heavily on the Japanese for marketing. From this second point, we may also state that the direct investment of the Taiwanese enterprises in China seems to be self-destructive, since they are in effect helping China to earn foreign exchange to buy arms.

In entering the twenty-first century, the Taiwanese economy is facing many problems: hallowing effects of outward direct foreign investment, increasing protectionism abroad, world recession, rising regionalism, and mounting competition from the new NICs. It is not clear whether Taiwan can grow out of her heavy dependency on Japanese technology and marketing, and grow into an economy as exemplified by Switzerland, Norway, or Sweden.

The first and foremost problem the Taiwanese are facing today is clarification of Taiwan's political relation with China. With Taiwan's ambiguous political status in the world community, it will be difficult for Taiwan to develop into a regional or even an international center of finance, technology, and industry as envisioned in the Six-Year National Development Plan. It is clear how international legitimacy as a British colony has contributed to the growth of Hong Kong into a regional and international financial center. Recently, Taiwan applied for membership to the United Nations but was hindered by opposition from China. Without Taiwan's independence protected by the UN Charter, Taiwan's position in the world is indeed precarious.

Acknowledgments

We are indebted to Professors Han-yu Chang, Chun-Shun Chen, Shih-Meng S. Chen, Kiyoshi Kojima, Hsiao-fong Lee, An-lob Lin, Ta-hou Lin, Motoaki Moriya, Ramon H. Myers, Chiao-Dong Ng (Sho-do Ko), Shinkei Liu (Nakayama), Masami Toi, Wen-hsing Wu, and Tzong-shian Yu for the generous sharing of their personal publications with us at various stages of writing this paper. Dr. Robert C.L. Lee helped in search of literature. Professor John P. Powelson and Mr. Shawn Hanna read the paper and gave valuable comments and suggestions. This paper was presented at the John King Fairbank Center of East Asian Research, Harvard University, January 1994, and distributed as the Center Working Paper, Number 9, in September 1994. Comments from Professor William C. Kirby and the seminar participants are greatly appreciated. Conversations with Ms. Megan Green, Professors Henry Y. Wan Jr., and L. Sophia Wang were inspiring. We also appreciate the editor, Professor John Kuark, for his unusual patience and help in completing this paper. In preparing this chapter for this volume, most of the tables and charts have been reformatted or revised. We are also indebted to Professor Michael Luzius for advising and editing part of the paper. All errors of omission and commission are naturally ours.

Appendix 1A: Trade Orientation of 43 Developing Countries

The data in Table 1A below were taken from a World Bank study (WDR, 1987), except those of Taiwan, which was added by the authors from TSDB. Column (1) classifies 43 developing countries, which accounted for over 66.5 percent of the total output of developing countries in 1985 (ibid., 82). They were placed in following categories: strongly and moderately outward

Table 1A: Population, Area, and Trade Orientation
1963–73 and 1973–85

	Country	Popu			Area			Dif		Country	Popu			Area			Dif
	Unit	Mid			1000km2						Mid			1000km2			
		1976	*Rk*			*Rk*					1976	*Rk*			*Rk*		
	(1)	(2)	*(3)*		(4)	*(5)*		(6)		(1)	(2)	*(3)*		(4)	*(5)*		(6)
	Outward Oriented (OO)																
	Strongly OO (Category 1)									Moderately OO (Category 2)							
1	Singapore	2.3	*2*	*	1	*1*	*	0	1	Israel	3.6	*6*	*	21	*3*	*	0
2	Hong Kong	4.5	*9*	*	1	*2*	*	0	2	Malaysia	12.7	*21*	*	330	*22*		0
3	Taiwan	**16.3**	***27***		**36**	***6***		**0**	3	Thailand	43.0	*34*		514	*24*		0
4	Korea Rep	36.0	*32*		99	*10*		0	4	Brazil	110.0	*40*		8512	*42*		0
									5	Costa Rica	2.0	*1*	*	51	*8*		-1
									6	Guatemala	6.5	*15*	*	109	*11*		-1
									7	Côte d'Ivoire	7.0	*16*	*	323	*21*		-1
									8	Cameroon	7.6	*17*	*	475	*23*		-1
									9	Colombia	24.2	*29*		1139	*34*		-1
									10	Indonesia	135.2	*41*		1904	*37*		-1
Sum of *				2			2						6				
	Inward Oriented (IO)																
	Moderately IO (Category 3)									Strongly IO (Category 4)							
1	Tunisia	5.7	*13*	*	164	*15*		1	1	**Uruguay**	2.8	*4*	*	178	*16*		2
2	Nicaragua	2.3	*3*	*	130	*13*		0	2	Chile	10.5	*20*	*	757	*28*		2
3	Honduras	3.0	*5*	*	112	*12*		0	3	Turkey	41.2	*33*		781	*29*		2
4	**El Salvador**	**4.1**	***8***	*****	**21**	***4***	*****	**0**	4	Sri Lanka	13.8	*22*	*	66	*9*		1
5	Senegal	5.1	*11*	*	196	*17*		0	5	Pakistan	71.3	*37*		804	*30*		1
6	Kenya	13.8	*23*	*	583	*25*		0	6	**Burundi**	**3.8**	***7***	*****	**28**	***5***	*****	**0**
7	Yugoslavia	21.5	*28*		256	*19*		0	7	Domin Rep	4.8	*10*	*	49	*7*		0
8	Philippines	43.3	*35*		300	*20*		0	8	Zambia	5.1	*12*	*	753	*27*		0
9	Mexico	62.0	*36*		1973	*38*		0	9	Ghana	10.1	*19*	*	239	*18*		0
10	Bolivia	5.8	*14*	*	1099	*33*		-1	10	Tanzania	15.1	*24*	*	945	*32*		0
11	Madagascar	9.1	*18*	*	587	*26*		-1	11	Peru	15.8	*25*	*	1285	*36*		0
12	Nigeria	77.1	*38*		924	*31*		-1	12	Sudan	15.9	*26*	*	2506	*39*		0
									13	Argentina	25.7	*30*		2767	*40*		0
									14	Ethiopia	28.7	*31*		1222	*35*		0
									15	Bangladesh	80.4	*39*		144	*14*		0
									16	India	620.4	*42*		3288	*41*		0
Sum of *				8			1						10				

Sources: WDR (1987), 83. * denotes a country which has population or area less than that of Taiwan.

oriented (OO) countries, and strongly and moderately inward oriented (IO) countries. The period of the study was from 1963 to 1985. We have assigned numbers from Categories 1 to 4 for each category, and the table is divided in four parts.

Column (2) shows the population of each country, in millions, in mid-1976. Column (4) is the area in 1000s of square kilometer. Columns (3) ranks the countries by population, and col. (5) ranks them by area in ascending order. The asterisks indicate those countries which have either smaller population or smaller land area than those of Taiwan. Column (6) present changes in the openness of trade strategy of a country during the second period, 1973–1985, versus the first period, 1963–1973. Here, 0 means no change, 1 or 2 means an advance from the previous category to one or two steps toward a more outward oriented strategy, and −1 means a regression from the previous category to one step more inward (or less outward) oriented strategy. The countries are arranged in terms of changes during the two periods.

From Table 1A, the following interesting observations emerge.

(a) If we exclude Singapore and Hong Kong as city states, then Taiwan and South Korea are the only two countries which maintained strongly outward oriented strategy throughout 1963 to 1985. Despite all the talk of the advantages of this strategy, no other country followed it through the 1960s and the 1980s. Hence, we may conclude that Taiwan and Korea economic strategy was the exception rather than the rule among developing countries.
(b) In terms of population, Taiwan is not a small country. She ranked above three fourths of the countries in the United Nations (Hsiao and Hsiao, 1883, 46). Even in Table 1A, Taiwanese population is at the 63rd percentile (27th) among the 43 countries (col. (3)). The lower part of Table 1A shows that 18 out of 42 countries, which have less population than that of Taiwan, took inward oriented strategy in 1963–1973. Almost two third of countries which took strongly inward oriented strategy in 1963–1973 have population less than that of Taiwan. Among them, Uruguay, Burundi, and Dominican Republic had populations that were equal to or less than one third of Taiwan's population.
(c) Three countries, Israel, El Salvador, Burundi, had smaller populations as well as smaller area than that of Taiwan. Note also that they are evenly spread among the four categories (cols. (4) and (5)). This

indicates that the size of population and area has no bearing on the category of trade reform a country takes.

(d) Note that Burundi and El Salvador have both population and area much smaller than those of Taiwan, and they took inward strategy throughout the three decades.

(e) The last col. ((6)) of Table 1A is more revealing. Six out of ten moderately *outward* oriented countries changed to moderately *inward* oriented strategy from 1963–73 to 1973–85 (the countries with −1 in category 2). Three out of 12 *moderately* inward oriented countries even changed to strongly inward oriented strategy (the countries with −1 in category (3). The rest of nine countries in Category 3, except Tunisia, did not change their trade orientation at all (the countries with 0). Only one country, Tunisia, changed from moderately inward orientation to moderately outward orientation.

(f) In category 4, only 5 out of 16 strongly inward oriented countries became more open and changed to either moderately inward or moderately outward oriented strategy (countries with 1 or 2). All 11 others still maintained strongly inward strategies during the next decade, again this happened in spite of all the evidence of the advantages of outward oriented strategies (ibid., Chapter 5).

Appendix 1B: Details of Major Exports and Imports during the Early 1990s

Table 1B below presents a detailed classification and comparison of exports and imports in 1990 for Electrical Machinery and Apparatus, Machinery, and Basic Metals and Articles Thereof. Note the same major categories of classification in exports and imports. The value of exports are mostly higher than the value of imports in each category. There are rather small exports surpluses for some items, and those items are mostly basic materials used in other manufacturing products. This also indicates the limited success, if not failure, of the government plan for second import substitution. Apparently, there were bottlenecks in technology which the Taiwanese industry and government failed to overcome, thus relying heavily on the imports of the commodities in the same categories and classification. Those imports came from Japan and the United States, the Taiwan's major trading partners (Section 1.12.2).

Table 1B: Details of Some Major Exports and Imports Items, 1990

(US$ billion)

Item	Exp	Imp	Diff
A. ELECTRICAL MACHINERY AND EQUIPMENT AND PARTS THEREOF	**11.8**	**9.0**	**2.8**
1 Transmission apparatus for radio-telephone, radio-telegraph, radio-broadcasting or TV	3.0	0.8	2.2
2 Thermionic, cold cathode or photo-cathode valves and tubes, diodes, transmitters, semiconductor electronic integrated circuits and microassemblies	2.4	4.0	−1.6
3 Electrical printed circuit, apparatus for switching, etc.	1.0	0.9	0.1
4 Electric motors and generators	1.0	0.8	0.2
5 Electrical apparatus for line telephone or line telegraphy	0.7	0.5	0.2
B. MACHINERY	**11.3**	**7.4**	**3.9**
1 Automatic data processing machines and units thereof	3.8	1.0	2.8
2 Office machinery, parts and accessories for typewriter and calculator	2.6	0.5	2.1
3 Machine tools for metal or metal carbides	0.6	—	0.6
4 Sewing machine	0.5	—	0.5
5 Machine and mechanical appliances not elsewhere specified	—	0.9	−0.9
C. BASIC METALS AND ARTICLES THEREOF	**5.2**	**6.0**	**−0.8**
1 Articles of iron and steel	1.8	0.5	1.3
2 Tools, cutlery, spoons and forks of base metal, parts thereof of base metal	0.8	—	0.8
3 Iron and steel	0.7	2.8	−2.1
4 Copper and articles thereof	0.7	1.0	−0.3
5 Aluminum and articles thereof	—	0.8	−0.8

Sources: Section A. MOEA (1991), 118, 199–201; 168, 262–264. Section B. ibid., 118, 197–199; 168, 260–262. Section C. ibid., 163–167.

Data Sources

CYB *China Yearbook* (CYB), 1972–1973, Taipei: China Publishing Co.

MESI *Monthly Statistics of Exports and Imports, Taiwan Area, Republic of China*, December 1990. The Department of statistics, Ministry of Finance, Vol. 256, February 20, 1991.

OS16 *Statistics Related to Taiwan*, in Historical Inquiries into Japanese Overseas Activities, Okurasho, Vol. 16, Taiwan, Subvol. 5.

SA *Statistical Abstract of the Republic of China*, Directorate-General of Budgets, Accounts, and Statistics, Executive Yuan, 1966, 1969.

TSDB *Taiwan Statistical Date Book*, 1975, 1986, 1992, 1993, Council for Economic Planning and Development, Executive Yuan, Republic of China.

TSS *Fifty-one Year Statistical Summary of Taiwan Province* (SS51)
(Taiwan Sheng-51 Nianlai Tongji Tiyao), Statistics Department, of Taiwan Province Governor-General, December, 1946
WDR *World Development Report*, 1992, World Bank, New York: Oxford University Press.
WT *World Table*, 1976, World Bank, Washington DC, 1976.

References

Adelman, I. and C.T. Morris (1967). *Society, Politics, and Economic Development: A Quantitative Approach.* Baltimore: The Johns Hopkins Press.

Agency for International Development (AID) (1967). *Proposed Foreign Aid Program, FY 1968.* Summary Presentation to the Congress.

Amsden, A.H. (1985). "The State and Taiwan's Economic Development." In P.B. Evans and D. Rueschemeyer (eds.), *Bringing the State Back In.* Cambridge: Cambridge University Press.

Aoki, T. (1985). *The Pacific Era and Japan* (in Japanese). Tokyo: Yuhi Kaku.

Arnold, W. (1985). "Japan and Taiwan: Community of Economic Interest Held Together by Paradiplomacy." In R.S. Ozaki and W. Arnold (eds.), *Japan's Foreign Relations* (Chapter II). Boulder, CO: Westview Press.

Arrigo, L.G. (1980). "The Industrial Work Force of Young Women in Taiwan." *Bulletin of Concerned Asian Scholars*, 12(2): 25–38.

______ (1984). "Economic and Political Control of Women Workers in Multinational Electronic Factories in Taiwan: Martial Law Coercion and World Market Uncertainty." *Bulletin of North America Taiwanese Professors' Association*, 4(2): 16–24.

Belden, Jack (1967). "Land Problem," "Stone Wall Village." In Franz Schurmann and Orville Schell (eds.), *Republican China, Nationalism, War, and the Rise of Communism, 1911–1949* (310–327). The China Reader 2. Vintage Books. NY: Random House.

Bello, W. and S. Rosenfeld (1990). "High-Speed Industrialization and Environmental Devastation in Taiwan." *The Ecologist* 20(4): 125–132.

Brooks, M.R. and A. Frances (1991). "Barriers to Exporting: An Exploratory Study of Latin American Companies." In F.H.R. Seringhaus and P.J. Rosson (eds.), *Export Development and Promotion: The Role of Public Organizations* (Chapter 5). Kluwer Academic Publishers, MA: Norwell.

Cartwell, B., D. Luce and L. Weinglass (1978). *Made in Taiwan: A Human Rights Investigation.* New York: Asian Center, An Independent Affiliate of Clergy and Laity Concerned.

Chang, F.R. (1986). "A Study of Television Manufacturing Industry in Taiwan Area" (in Chinese). *The Quarterly Journal of the Bank of Taiwan*, 37(2): 57–70.

Chang, Han Yu and Raymon H. Myers (1963). "Japanese Colonial Policy in Taiwan, 1895–1906." *Journal of Asian Studies*, 22: 433–50.

Chang, Han-yu (1974). *Economic Development and Economic Thoughts*, Collection of Writings of Dr. Chang Han-yu (in Chinese) (volumes I and II). Taipei: Sanmin Bookstore.

Chang, Kuowie (ed.) (1968). *Economic Development in Taiwan*. Taipei: Cheng Chung Book Company.

Chang, Tsong-han (1980). *Taiwan's Industrialization before the War* (in Chinese). Taipei: Lian Jin Publisher.

Chen, C.S. (1982). "Export-Oriented Industrialization and Economic Development in Taiwan" (in Japanese). The *Tsukuba Economic Review*, 9 (March): 69–99.

——— (1988). "Evolution of Heavy Industry and Economic Development in Taiwan" (in Chinese). *Quarterly Journal of Bank of Taiwan*, 39(2): 1–49.

Chen, Long-chi and W.M. Reisman (1974). "Who Owns Taiwan: A Search for International Title." *Yale Law Journal*, (March): 599–671.

Chen, Fang-min (ed.) (1991). *Selected Documents of Post-war Taiwanese History-A Special Collection on the 228 Incident* (in Chinese). Taipei: 228 Peace Day Promotion Association.

Chen, Cheng (1961). *Land Reform in Taiwan*. Taipei: China Publishing Co.

Chen, Ching-chih (1975). "The Japanese Adaptation of the Pao-chia System in Taiwan, 1895–1945." *Journal of Asian Studies*, 34: 391–416.

Chen, Mu-Tsai (1972a). "A Study of Financial Structure in Taiwanese Agriculture and Industry." *Quarterly Journal of Bank of Taiwan*, 23(4): 1–37.

——— (1972b). "A Study of Interest Rates in Taiwan." *Quarterly Journal of Bank of Taiwan*, 23(4): 38–70.

Chen, Shih-meng S., Chung-Cheng Lin, C.Y. Cyrus Chu, Ching-hsi Chang, Jun-ji Shih and Jin-Tian Liu (1991). *Disintegrating KMT-State Capitalism, A Closer Look at Revitalizing Taiwan's State-and Party-Owned Enterprises* (in Chinese). Taiwan: Taipei Society.

Chiang, Zhen-nan (1971). "Analysis of Changes in the Fiscal Structure in the Process of Taiwanese Economic Development" (in Chinese). In *Economic Essays, A Special Issue of Collection of Papers in Honor of the 80th Birthday of Ex-President Shi-Jieh Wang*. Academia Sinica, August.

Chinese Engineering Association (CEA) (1958). *A History of Taiwanese Industrial Recovery* (in Chinese). Taiwan: Taipei.

Chou, Tian Cheng (1988). "The Evolution of Market Structure in Taiwan." *Rivista Internationale di Scienu Economiche e Commerciali*, 35(2): 171–194.

——— (1992). "The Experience of SMEs Development in Taiwan: High Export-Contribution and Export-Intensity." *Rivista Internationale di Scienu Economiche e Commerciali*, 39(12): 1069–1084.

Clubb, O.E. (1964). *Twentieth Century China*. New York: Columbia University Press.

David, Randolf S. *et al.* (1981). *Transnational Corporations and the Philippine Banana Export Industry*. Manila: Third World Studies Center, University of Philippines.

Deyo, F.C. (1989). *Beneath the Miracle, Labor Subordination in the New Asian Industrialism.* Berkeley: University of California Press.

Du, T.V. (1986). "DFI and Technology Importing Policy in Northeast and Southeast Asian Countries" (in Japanese). In S. Sekiguchi and T.V. Du (eds.), *Direct Investment and Technological Transfer-Japan and Northeast/ Southeast Asia.* Tokyo: Center of Japanese Economic Studies.

Duan, Chen-pu (ed.) (1989). *The Post-War Taiwanese Economy* (in Chinese). Beijing: Chinese Social Science Publisher.

Eaton, L. (1991). *Taiwan, Mini Dragons TV Series.* Maryland Public Television and Film Australia.

Fairbank, J.K. (1967). *China, The People's Middle Kingdom and the U.S.A.* Cambridge: Harvard University Press.

______ (1971). *The United States and China* (3rd ed.). Cambridge: Harvard University Press.

Fei, J.C.H., K. Ohkawa and G. Ranis (1985). "Economic Development in Historical Perspective: Japan, Korea, and Taiwan." In K. Ohkawa and G. Ranis, with Meissner (ed.), *Japan and the Developing Countries, A Comparative Analysis* (Chapter 3). Oxford: Basil Blackwell.

Fields, G.S. (1985). "Industrialization and Employment in Hong Kong, Korea, Singapore, and Taiwan." In W. Galenson (ed.), *Foreign Trade and Investment, Economic Development of the Newly Industrializing Asian Countries* (Chapter 8). Madison, WI: The University of Wisconsin Press.

Gillis, M., D.H. Perkins, M. Roemer and D.R. Snodgrass (1992). *Economics of Development* (3rd ed.). New York: W.W. Norton & Co.

Gold, T.B. (1986). *State and Society in The Taiwan Miracle.* New York: M.E. Sharpe, Inc.

Gradjdanzev, A.J. (1942). *Formosa Today: An Analysis of Economic Development and Strategic Importance of Japan's Tropical Colony.* NY: Institute of Pacific Relations.

Higgins, B. (1968). *Economic Development, Principles, Problems, and Policies.* New York: W.W. Norton & Co.

Ho, S.P.S. (1978). *Economic Development of Taiwan, 1960–1970.* New Haven: Yale University Press.

Hsiao, F. Sheng-tieh (1960a). "An Analysis of the Burden of Interest Cost on Private Industry in Taiwan" (in Chinese). *Quarterly Journal of the Bank of Taiwan,* 11(1): 17–51.

______ (1960b). "On the Size of the Private Industry and Its Financial Problem in Taiwan" (in Chinese). *The Monthly Correspondence of the Bank of Huanan,* 113 (May): 1–5.

______ (1989). "Book Review, The Evolution of Policy Behind Taiwan's Development Success, by K.T. Li." *The Journal of Asian Studies,* 48(2): 367–368.

______ (1992). "Economic and Cultural Backgrounds of Taiwan's 2-28 Incident-An Application of Social Expectation Theory" (translated in Chinese). In Yong-hsing Chen (ed.), *Proceedings of 2-28 Academic Conference* (77–113). Taipei: 2-28 Citizens' Study Group, Taiwan-U.S. Cultural Exchange Fund.

Hsiao, F.S.T. and M.C.W. Hsiao (1981). "International Comparisons of the Taiwanese Economy." *Newsletter of North America Taiwanese Professors' Association*, 1(2,3): 5–9.

______ (1983). "Some Development Indicators of Taiwan: A Comparative Study." *Journal of Economic Development*, 8(1): 45–58.

______ (1984). "Direct Foreign Investment and Economic Development — The Taiwanese Experience." *Bulletin of North America Taiwanese Professors' Association*, 4(2): 7–15.

______ (1989). "Japanese Experience of Industrialization and Economic Performance of Korea and Taiwan-Test of Similarity." In S.C. Hu and C.F. Lee (eds.), *Advances in Financial Planning and Forecasting (Supplement I) Taiwan's Foreign Investment, Exports, and Financial Analysis* (157–190) (Ref. Chapter 11). Greenwich, CT: JAI Press.

______ (1993). "Gains from Policy Coordination between Taiwan and the United States — On the Games Governments Play." In M. Dutta (ed.), Research in Asian Economic Studies (volume 5), *Asia-Pacific Economies: 1990s and Beyond* (239–264). Greenwich, CT: JAI Press.

______ (2003). "'Miracle Growth' in the Twentieth Century — International Comparisons of East Asian Development." *World Development*, 31(2): 227–257.

______ (2005). "Colonialism, Learning and Convergence: A Comparison of India and Taiwan." *Journal of Asia Pacific Economy*, 10(2): 146–177.

Hsiao, Frank, S.T. and L.R. Sullivan (1979). "The Chinese Communist Party and the Status of Taiwan 1928–1943." *Pacific Affairs*, 52(3): 446–467.

Hsiao, Hsing-huang M. (1990). "Emerging Social Movement and the Rise of a Demanding Civil Society in Taiwan." *The Australian Journal of Chinese Affairs*, 24: 163–179.

Hsiao, Kuo-ho (1987). *The Rise and Fall of Taiwanese Agriculture* (in Chinese). A volume in Forty Years of Taiwanese Experience Series. Taipei: Tsuli Evening News.

Hsiao, Mei-Chu W. (1987). "Tests of Causality and Exogeneity between Exports and Economic Growth: The Case of Asian NICs." *Journal of Economic Development*, 12(2): 143–159.

______ (1992). "Direct Foreign Investment, Technology Transfer, and Industrial Development — The Case of Electronics Industry in Taiwan." In M. Dutta (ed.), Research in Asian Economic Studies (volume 4A), *Asian Economic Regime: An Adaptive Innovation Paradigm* (145–164). Greenwich, CT: JAI Press.

Hsieh, Ji-sheng and Min-De Chang (1992). "Some Practical Problems of Relying Chineses Technology by the Small and Medium Size Enterprises, Using an Example from Aquiring Infrared Drying Technology." In Tzong-Shian Yu and Li-eng Chen (eds.), *Evaluation of Exchange and Cooperation of Industrial Technology Across the Taiwan Straits* (61–78). Taipei: Chung-Hwa Insititute of Economic Research.

Hsing, Mo-huang (1971). *Taiwan, Industrialization and Trade Policy.* Paris: OECD/Oxford University Press.

Ishikawa, Shigeru (1967). *Economic Development in Asian Perspective.* Economic Research Series, No. 8, The Institute of Economic Research, Hitotsubashi University. Tokyo: Kinokuniya Bookstore.

______ (1972). "Taiwanese Agricultural Change under Japanese Occupation" (in Japanese). In M. Shinohara and S. Ishikawa (eds.), *Taiwanese Economic Growth* (Chapter 1). Tokyo: Aziya Keizai Kenkyujo.

Itaya, Shigeru (1991). "The Role of Japan-Made Textile Machinery in Asian Economic Development" (in Japanese). *Aziya Kenhyu* (Asian Studies), 37(4): 1–78.

Jacoby, N.H. (1966). *U.S. Aid to Taiwan, A Study of Foreign Aid, Self-help, and Development.* New York: Frederick A. Praeger.

Jiang, Jian-pin (1985). *A Concise Economic History of Modern China* (in Chinese). Beijing: Peking University Press.

Johnson, H.G. (1968). *Comparative Cost and Commercial Policy Theory for a Developing World Economy.* Wichsell Lecture. Baltimore: Johns Hopkins University Press.

Kanemaru, Y. (1993). "Electric Power Industry and The Golden Age of National Industries in China: A Comparative Study of Shanghai and Jiangsu, 1879–1924" (in Japanese). *Aziya Kenhyu* (Asian Studies), 39(4): 29–84.

Kato, Hidetoshi (1967). *The Americans — Their Culture and Human Formation* (Americajin — Sono Bunka to Ningen Keisei). Tokyo: Kodansha Co.

Kao, Si-chin (1969). "Development of Machinery Industry in Taiwan." *Industry of Free China,* (April): 2–111.

Kerr, G. (1965). *Formosa Betrayed.* Boston: Houghton Mifflin.

King, M.H. (1993). "Development of ROC's Steel Industry in Step with Its Economy." *Industry of Free China,* 80(4): 37–49.

Kirby, W.C. (1984). *Germany and Republican China.* Stanford, CA: Stanford University Press.

______ (1990). "Continuity and Change in Modern China: Economic Planning on the Mainland and on Taiwan, 1943–1958." *The Australian Journal of Chinese Affairs,* 24: 121–141.

Kiyonari, Tadao (1970). *Structural Changes of Japanese Medium and Small Enterprises* (in Japanese). Tokyo: Shin Hyoron.

Ko, Sho-do (1988). *Taiwan, Its Secret of Explosion, The Asian Monster Leads Korea by Ten Years* (in Japanese). Tokyo: Sho-den Sha.

Kojima, Kiyoshi (1985a). "U.S.-Japan Direct Investment in Taiwan-Comparison of the Japanese Type and the MNC Type" (in Japanese). *World Economic Review* (Sekai Keizai Hyoron), 29(3): 33–44.

______ (1985b). "Japanese and American Direct Investment in Asia: A Comparative Analysis." *Hitotsubashi Journal of Economics,* 26(1): 1–35.

Kuo, Shirly, W.Y. (1983). *The Taiwan Economy in Transition.* Boulder, CO: Westview Press.

______ (1993). "Evolution of the Taiwanese Economy-Current Situation and Prospects." *Industry of Free China,* 80(2): 1–8.

Kusui, Ryuzo (1944). *A Study of The War-time Taiwanese Economy* (in Japanese). Taihoku: Nampo Jimbun Kenkyu Sho.

Kwan, Chi-hung and Yuichi Kitamura (1988). "Emergence of the Asian NIEs and the Pacific Trade Triangle." In *Papers on the Western Rim of the Pacific* (Part II, 15–34). Tokyo: Nomura Research Institute.

Lai, T.H., R.H. Myers and W. Wei (1991). *A Tragic Beginning, The Taiwan Uprising of February 28, 1947.* Stanford, CA: Stanford University Press.

Lamley, H.J. (1968). "The 1895 Taiwan Republic." The *Journal of Asian Studies*, 27(4): 739–62.

Lee, Hsiao-fong (1985). *Civil Representatives during the Early Post-War Period of Taiwan* (in Chinese). Tsuli Collections, #25. Taipei: Tsuli Evening Post.

Lee, J.S. (1993). "Taiwan's Economy and Its International Role." *Industry of Free China*, 80(2): 29–40.

Lee, Tung-hui and Kuo-Shu Liang (1982). "Taiwan." In B. Balassa (ed.), *Development Strategies in Semi-industrial Economies* (Chapter 10). Baltimore: The Johns Hopkins University Press.

Li, Kuo-ting (1988). *The Evolution of Policy behind Taiwan's Development Success.* New Haven: Yale University Press.

______ and Wan-ang Yeh (1982). "Economic Planning in the Republic of China." In K.T. Li and T.S. Yu (eds.), *Experiences and Lessons of Economic Development in Taiwan* (103–130). Taipei, Taiwan: Academia Sinica.

Liang, Kuo-shu and Chin-ing H. Liang (1982). "Trade and Incentive Policy in Taiwan." In Kuo-ting Li and Tsong-hsian Yu (eds.), *Experiences and Lessons of Economic Development in Taiwan* (219–256). Taipei, Taiwan: Academia Sinica.

Lin, Ching-yuan (1968). "Industrial Development and Changes in the structure of Foreign Trade, The Experience of the Republic of China in Taiwan, 1946–66." *IMF Staff Papers*, 25(July): 290–321.

______ (1973). *Industrialization in Taiwan, 1946–72: Trade and Import-Substitution Policies for Developing Countries.* New York: Praeger.

Lin, Ta-hou and Ming-wen Hu (1992). "Development Strategies of Small and Medium Enterprises in Taiwan in Year 2000" (in Chinese). *Report to Small and Medium Enterprises Bureau*, Ministry of Economic Affairs. Taipei: Taiwan Institute of Economic Research, June.

Lin, Tang-yu (1992). "An Analysis of Production Structure, Position, and Effectiveness of Government Policy on Taiwanese Textile Industry." *Quarterly Journal of Bank of Taiwan*, 43(2): 134–167.

Liu, Shin-kei (1975). *Post-War Taiwanese Economic Analysis* (in Japanese). Tokyo: Tokyo University Press.

Liu, Tai-ying and Jin-chuang Jian (1983). "The Economic Effects of Japanese Business Investment in Taiwan" (in Chinese). *Report to the Committee on Research, Development, and Assessment*, the Executive Yuan, submitted by Taiwan Institute of Economic Research.

Metzger, T.A. and R.H. Myers (1989). "Understanding the Taiwan Experience: An Historical Perspective," *The Pacific Review*, 2(4): 297–311.

Ministry of Economic Affairs (MOEA) (1991). *White Paper on Small and Medium-Size Enterprises. Republic of China*, Small and Medium Enterprises Bureau, Ministry of Economic Affairs.
Mizoguchi, Toshiyuki (1975). *The Economic Growth of Taiwan and Korea* (in Japanese). Tokyo: Iwanami Shoten.
Mizoguchi, Toshiyuki and K. Nojima (1981). "Estimates of Gross Domestic Product and Aggregate Expenditure of Former Japanese Empire" (in Japanese). *Keizai Kenkyu*: 232–256.
Moody, P.R. Jr. (1992). *Political Change on Taiwan: A Study of Ruling Party Adaptability*. Praeger: New York.
Nakamura, Takatoshi (1961). *Japan's Large Enterprises* (in Japanese). Iwanami Shinsho, #436. Tokyo: Iwanami Shoten.
Newman, R.P. (1961). *Recognition of Communist China, A Study in Argument.* New York: Macmillan Co.
Ng, Chiao-dong (Ko Sho-do) (1970). *A Study on the Republic of Taiwan* (in Japanese). Tokyo: Tokyo University Press.
OECD (1979). *The Impact of the Newly Industrializing Countries, on Production and trade in Manufactures.* Paris: Report by the Secretary-General.
Oh, Ikutoku (1970). *Taiwan, Its History in Agony* (in Japanese). Tokyo: Kobunsha.
Okurasho (1949). *Taiwan's Industries.* Historical Inquiries into Japanese Overseas Activities. Volume on Taiwan.
Ozawa, T. (1979). "International Investment and Industrial Structure: New Theoretical Implications from the Japanese Experience." *Oxford Economic Paper*, 31(1): 72–92.
Pae, S.M. (1992). *Korea Leading Developing Nations: Economy, Democracy, and Welfare.* Maryland: University Press of America.
Pang, Pai-hsian and Shi-meng Chen (1993). "Assessing Taiwan's Economic Policy and Policy-Making: A Political-Economy Approach." Paper presented at the First Conference on Pacific Basin Business, Economics and Finance, Rutgers University, New Jersey.
People's University, Department of Political Economy (ed.) (1979). *Economic History of Modern China* (in Chinese) (volumes I and II). Beijing: People's Press.
Pepper, S. (1986). "The KMT-CCP Conflict, 1945–1949." In D. Twitchell and J.K. Fairbank (eds.), *The Cambridge History of China* (volume 13, Chapter 13), *Republican China 1912–1949*, Part 2.
Pun, A. (1993). "Taiwan Firms on Mainland 500 List." *The Free China Journal*, November 5.
Rafferty, K. (1992). "Taiwan." *The Asia and Pacific Review*, (1991/92): 214–217.
Ranis, G. (ed.) (1992). *Taiwan-From Developing to Mature Economy.* Boulder, CO: Westview Press.
Riedel, J. (1992). "International Trade in Taiwan's Transition from Developing to Mature Economy." In G. Ranis (ed.), *Taiwan-From Developing to Mature Economy* (Chapter 7). Boulder, CO: Westview Press.

Saito, S. (1981). "The Technology Transfer Problems between Japan and Taiwan" (in Japanese). *World Economic Review* (Sekai Keizai Hyoron), 25(5) (May).

Sasamoto, Takeharu and Shigeto Kawano (1968). *A Comprehensive Study of Taiwanese Economy* (in Japanese) (volumes I, II, III). Tokyo: Aziya Keizai Kenkyujo.

Schive, Chi (1983). "Direct Foreign Investment, Technology Transfer, and Industrial Development in Taiwan" (in Chinese) *Proceedings of Conference on Taiwanese Industrial Development*, 2 (March): 471–501.

______ and R. Yeh (1980). "Direct Foreign Investment and Taiwan's T.V. Industry." *Economic Essays*, the Graduate Institute of Economics, National Taiwan University (November): 261–291.

Schurmann, Franz and Orville Schell (ed. and annotated) (1967). *Republican China: Nationalism, War, and the Rise of Communism, 1911–1949.* Vintage Books Edition. NY: Random House.

Shi, Ji and Zheng-zhong Li (1978). "A Study of the Methods of Improving Trade Deficits and Imports between China and Japan" (in Chinese). *Research Report submitted to the Ministry of Economic Affairs, Taiwan.*

Shinohara, Miyohei (1972). "Industrialization and Trade" (in Japanese). In Miyohei Shinohara and Sigeru Ishikawa (eds.), *Taiwanese Economic Growth* (Chapter 2). Tokyo: Aziya Keizai Kenkyujo.

Steven, R. (1990). *Japan's New Imperialism.* Armonk, NY: M.E. Sharpe, Inc.

Su, Beng (1980). *Four Hundred-Year History of the Taiwanese People* (in Chinese). San Jose: Paradise Culture Association.

Sumiya, Mikio, Sin-kei Liu and Zhao-yen Tu (1992). *The Taiwanese Economy* (in Japanese). Tokyo: Tokyo University Press.

Szczepanik, E. (1958). *The Economic Growth of Hong Kong.* London: Oxford University Press.

Takahashi, Kamekichi (1937). *A Study of Modem Taiwanese Economy* (in Japanese). Tokyo: Chigura Shobo.

Thorbecke, E. (1979). "Agricultural Development." In W. Galenson (ed.), *Economic Growth and Structural Change in Taiwan: The Postwar Experience of The Republic of China* (Chapter 2). Ithaca: Cornell University Press.

Tien, Hung-mao (1989). *The Great Transition, Political and Social Change in the Republic of China.* Stanford, CA: Hoover Institution Press.

Toi, Masami and Koji Morioka (1992). *An Approach to Japanese Economy* (in Japanese). Tokyo: Mineruva Shobo.

Tsiang, Sho-chieh (1985). *Lessons from Economic Development of Taiwan* (in Chinese). Taipei: Commonwealth Publishing Co.

Tsurumi, Patricia E. (1977). *Japanese Colonial Education in Taiwan, 1895–1945.* Cambridge, MA: Harvard University Press.

Tsurumi, Yoshiyuki (1982). *Banana and the Japanese — Between the Filipino Plantation and the Dining Table* (in Japanese). Iwanami Shinsho, #199. Tokyo: Iwanami Shoten.

Vogel, E.F. (1979). *Japan As Number One: Lessons for America.* Cambridge, MA: Harvard University Press.

Wang, Jian-shen, Hsian-yun Ji and Yong-chiuan Chen (1984). *1947 Taiwan's 228 Revolution* (in Chinese). Los Angeles: Taiwanese Cultural Enterprise.

Wang, Tsuo-rong (1959). "The Path to Taiwanese Economic Development" (in Chinese). *The Chinese Economy*, 164: 1–15.

Winckler, E.A. and S. Greenhalgh (ed.) (1988). *Contending Approaches to the Political Economy of Taiwan*. New York: M.E. Sharpe, Inc.

Wu, Hui-lin and Tien-chen Chou (1988). "Small and Medium Enterprises and Economic Development in Taiwan." *Industry of Free China*, (March): 15–25.

Wu, Rong-yi, Chang-fu W. Lian, Tian-cheng Chow and Zhao-kao Li (1980). *The Effects of U.S. Investment on Taiwanese Economy* (in Chinese). Institute of American Culture. Taipei: Academia Sinica.

Wu, Ruo-yu (1992). *Political and Economic Analysis of Post-War Public Enterprises in Taiwan* (in Chinese). Institute for National Research. Taipei: Chang Yung-Fa Foundation.

Wu, Wen-hsing (1986). *A Study of Taiwanese Social Leadership Group during the Japanese Occupation Period* (in Chinese). National Taiwan Normal University, Institute of History, Doctoral Thesis, 1–360.

Xia, Chi-cheng (1951). "On Money Circulation, Prices and Production" (in Chinese). *Public Finance and Economic Monthly*, 1(8).

Yajima, K. (1986). *The Complete Scope on the Taiwanese Economy* (in Japanese). Tokyo: Nihon Keizai Tsusinsha.

Yeh, Rong-song (1980). "Development of the Taiwanese Television Industry as Seen from the International Product-Cycle" (in Chinese). *The Quarterly Journal of the Bank of Taiwan*, 31(March): 156–205.

Yeh, Wan-ang (1969). "Structure and Size of Manufacturing Industry in Taiwan." *Industry of Free China*, 31(4): 111–36.

Yu, Tsong-hsian and T.A. Chen (1982). "Fiscal Reforms and Economic Development." In Kuo-ting Li and Tsong-hsian Yu (eds.), *Experiences and Economic Development in Taiwan*. Taipei: Academia Sinica.

Zhang, Bun-jin (1969). "Report on Random Sample Analysis of Overseas Chinese and Foreign Investments." Mimeograph.

Chapter 2

Taiwan in the Global Economy — Past, Present, and Future

2.1 Introduction

The spirit of the 'child of Taiwan' reveals to us that even though Taiwan, Penghu, Kinmen and Matsu are tiny islands on the rim of the Pacific, the map of our dreams knows no limits. The map extends all the way to the horizon as long as our 23 million compatriots fear no hardship and move forward hand in hand. Long live freedom and democracy! Long live the people of Taiwan!

Thus concluded the inauguration speech of the newly elected Taiwanese President Chen Shui-bian on May 20, 2000. It culminated Taiwan's "double miracles" in politics and economy during the past century of hard work and struggle.

In this paper, we would like to show that Taiwan has come a long way.

The development of Taiwan's economic and political events are influenced and shaped by its geographical position as a relatively small island at the center of the northwest side of the Asia-Pacific region[1] (Fig. 2.1). With almost the same altitude as Hawaii, Taiwan is surrounded by several large countries in the world, "large" in one way or another (Table 2.1). To the west, there is China, the most populous country with the third largest landmass (although one of the lowest per capita GNP countries) in the world. Japan is in the northeast, the world's second largest country both in terms of its economic size (the GDP level) and its standard of living (the GNP per capita level). To the east beyond the Pacific Ocean, there is the United

[1]The distance is mainly taken from a website, "How far is it" http://indo.com/distance/. The original map was taken from Yano (1990), 685. Also see Klintworth (1995), 9. Ohsono (1998), 151 uses a similar diagram to show Hong Kong to be the center of East Asia.

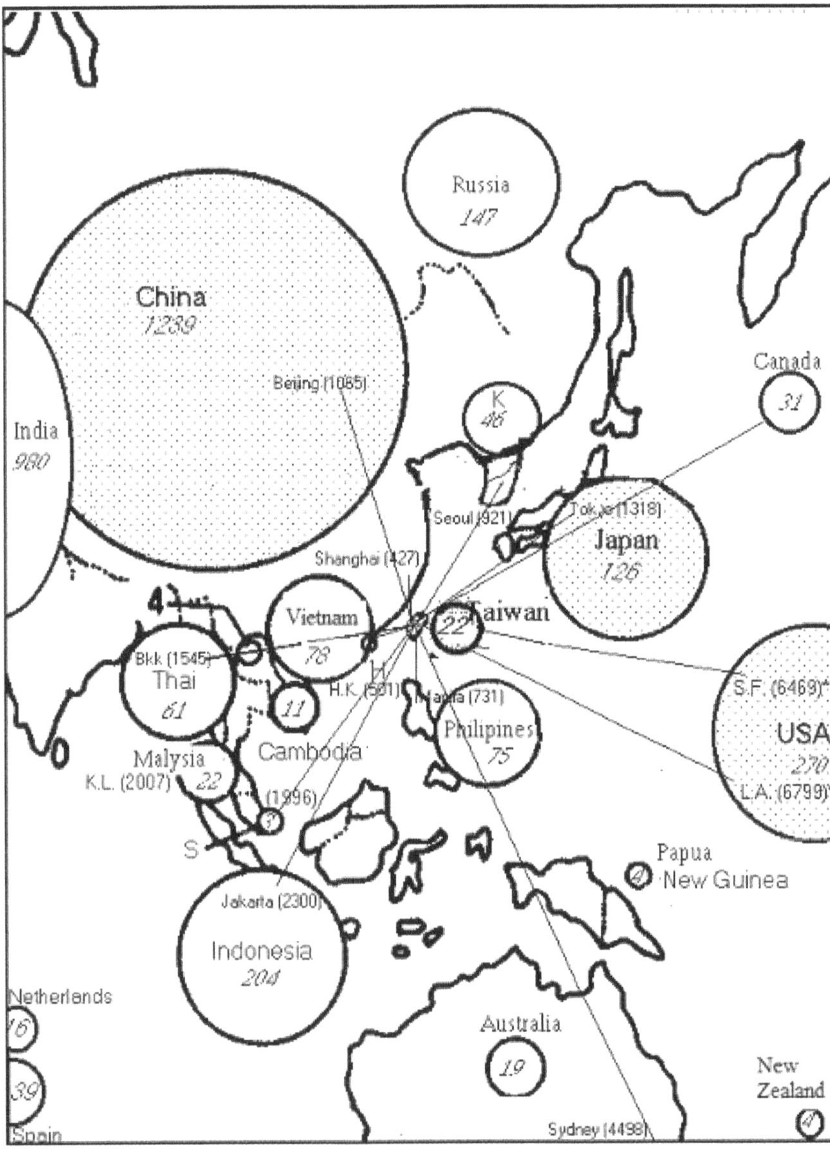

Figure 2.1: Taiwan as the Center of East Asia and Western Pacific

Sources: Population (in million) in the italic, taken from WDR, 1997. Distance (in miles) in parentheses. See Footnote 1 in the text.

Table 2.1: Taiwan in the World Economy

	Area			Pop			Pop Density			GDP			GNP per capita		
Unit	1000 km^2			millions mid-95			person/km^2			US$ billion			US$		
Country	1995	Rkg	%tle		Rkg	%tle	1995	Rkg	%tle	1995	Rkg	%tle	1995	Rkg	%tle
Taiwan	**36**	**113**	**16**	**21**	**39**	**71**	**589**	**4**	**97**	**260**	**19**	**86**	**12,396**	**25**	**81**
Singapore	1	133	1	3	114	15	3,000	2	99	84	37	72	26,730	8	94
H.K.	1	134	0	6	85	37	6,200	1	99	144	28	79	22,990	13	90
Korea, Rep	99	89	34	45	23	83	454	6	96	455	11	92	9,700	27	80
Malaysia	330	56	58	20	40	70	61	65	51	85	36	73	3,890	36	73
Thailand	513	42	69	58	17	87	113	37	72	167	25	81	2,740	52	61
Philippines	300	61	54	69	14	90	229	20	85	74	41	69	1,050	78	42
Indonesia	1,905	13	90	193	4	97	101	42	69	198	23	83	980	79	41
Japan	378	51	62	125	8	94	331	9	93	5,109	2	99	39,640	2	99
China	9,561	3	98	1,200	1	99	126	32	76	698	7	95	620	93	31
India	3,288	7	95	929	2	99	283	11	92	324	15	89	340	108	19
USA	9,364	4	97	263	3	98	28	96	28	6,952	1	99	26,980	6	96
Nethrlnds	37	112	16	16	48	64	419	7	95	396	12	91	24,000	11	92
Canada	9,976	2	99	30	29	78	3	129	4	569	9	93	19,380	15	89
Australia	7,713	6	96	18	43	68	2	131	2	349	13	90	18,720	17	87
U.K.	245	67	50	59	16	88	239	18	87	1,106	5	96	18,700	18	87
Spain	505	43	68	39	25	81	78	57	57	559	10	93	13,580	24	82
Portugal	92	91	32	10	66	51	108	40	70	102	33	75	9,740	26	81

Sources: Taiwan, from TSDB (1996). All other countries, from WDR (1997).
Boxed countries have values (or ranking, rkg, or percentile, %tle) equal to or smaller than Taiwan.

States, the largest economy with the third largest population, the fourth largest area, and the sixth highest GNP per capita country in the world. In addition to these three great Pacific powers, Indonesia is far down in the southwest, with the fourth largest population in the world. Sandwiched among these giants, those who inclined to the Chinese position of chauvinism and irredentist tend to consider Taiwan is too small to be a country.

Thus, in Section 2.2, we first address the question of whether Taiwan is "small" in the global economy. We have shown that either from the size of population, the GDP level, the GDP per capita level, or from the volume of production and export items, Taiwan ranks very high compared with other countries in the world. Taiwan's central position in the northeast side of the Asia-Pacific region lured the Europeans, the Chinese, the Japanese, and the Americans to the island. Thus, in Section 2.3 we review the Taiwanese history with the emphasis on the interactions among these peoples during the past four hundred years.

Section 2.4 then examines briefly Taiwan in the global economy before the 19th century. The Dutch as well as the Spanish formally colonized Taiwan from 1624 to 1662 to trade with China and Japan. The Kingdom of Cheng followed from 1662 to 1683, and traded with the Japanese, the English, and others, but not with China and Holland. Ch'ing conquered Taiwan in 1683 and held it until 1895. From 1683 to 1760, Taiwan was virtually under the autarky system, and from 1760 to 1860, Taiwan traded exclusively with China. Taiwan was reintroduced to international trade after 1860, only to be ceded to Japan in 1895.

The modernization of the Taiwanese economy and society came during the Japanese period after 1895. In Section 2.5, we show that Taiwanese agricultural production reached its apex and ranked very high in the world by the end of the 1930s, and massive industrialization started in earnest during that time with the help of resources imported from Japan, China, and Southeast Asia.

Section 2.6 then shows that, after a postwar interruption, Taiwanese industrialization continued, especially after the mid-1960 when the Pacific trade triangle among Taiwan, Japan, and the United States was formed. The trade triangle sustained the rapid Taiwanese economic growth. Rapid economic growth, as shown in Section 2.7, was also helped by the inward direct foreign investment from Japan and the United States, especially in the 1970s and the 1980s. In the 1990s, Taiwanese outward direct foreign investment rose rapidly, about half of which was invested in China. In Section 2.8, we first show that, despite severe setback in the international political arena, Taiwan's national competitiveness for the future has never been stronger. However, the military threat from China has overshadowed the Taiwan's bright future. Thus, we also analyze the economic and political relations between Taiwan and China and conclude with some final remarks.

Numerous papers have been written on Taiwanese economic development. The most recent and comprehensive reviews are contained in Thorbecke and Wan (1999), 3. To our knowledge, however, few works examine Taiwanese economic development from the historical, geographical, and comparative perspectives. Systematic studies of Taiwanese economy under Japanese colonialism and Japanese influence in the postwar period have not been written. Links between the prewar and postwar economic development, Taiwan-Japan-United States trade nexus, and the changes of inward and outward foreign direct investments after the lifting of Martial

Law in 1987, and its consequence of facing complicated relation with China economically and politically also are lacking. This paper brings these topics together with the benefit of our previous works, and provides some overviews of a new area of research. Thus, the paper could supplement the main features left out in Thorbecke and Wan (1999), and help in the future efforts at the new direction of long-run Taiwanese economic development and prediction.

2.2 Taiwan is a Large Country in the Global Economy

In fact, Taiwan is not a "small" country in many aspects as compared with other countries. Table 2.1 shows Taiwan's rankings of area, population, population density, the GDP level, and the GNP per capita level with other 133 countries listed in the 1997 *World Development Report* published by the World Bank. Although Taiwan's area is only 36,000 km^2, ranked 113rd, it is about the size of the Netherlands. Its population ranked 39th, at the 71 percentile, and its population density ranked 4th, at the 97th percentile, slightly larger than Malaysia and Australia, and about half of that of Spain and South Korea. Its GDP level ranked 19th, at the 86th percentile. Thus, its aggregate economic activities surpassed any of the ASEAN countries, Portugal, Mexico, Sweden, and Denmark, and are only slightly less than Belgium and Argentina. Few people are aware that Taiwan's economic size is as much as 80 percent of that of India, and 75 percent of that of Russia and Australia. Its GNP per capita ranked 25th, at 81st percentile, and is comparable with some OECD countries like Portugal and Spain. If 55 other "smaller" member countries of the United Nations, not listed in the *1997 World Development Report,* are considered, Taiwan's area and population percentiles will improve to the 40th and 79th percentiles, respectively, and its percentiles for the GDP level and the GNP per capita level will increase to a whopping 90th and 87th percentiles, respectively.

In the field of international trade, Taiwan's achievement is indeed more staggering. The Taiwanese economy advanced steadily from exporting agricultural goods and agricultural processed goods (rice, sugar, canned foods, etc.) to low technology manufactured goods (textile, metal manufactures, machinery), and then to high technology manufactured goods (electronic products, electrical machinery products, information and communication products, etc). In the 1960s, Taiwan was the number one country of exporting mushrooms and asparagus to the world market. In the 1980s, Taiwan could claim more than two dozen of exporting items as "Taiwan as Number One" in the world. In 1983, Taiwan exported 520 million pairs of plastic shoes, one pair for every nine persons in the world; 11 million dozen umbrella, one for every 40 persons in the world; and more than 6 million tennis rackets. In addition, it exported 3.16 million sets of sewing machines, having 80 percent of world sewing machine exporting market; 240 million units of mini-motor, having 70 percent of world mini-motor exporting market; 80 million bicycle tires, having 50 percent of world bicycle tire exporting market.[2]

By 1986, Taiwan produced the world's largest number of computer terminals, printed circuit boards, monitors, recreational boats, electronic calculators, telephones, etc. (MOEA, 1991, 239). In 1993, Taiwan supplied 76 percent of the world's exports of handheld scanners for personal computers, 62 percent of motherboards, 51 percent of monitors, and 25 percent of sewing machine, 29 percent of ABS fiber, 9 percent of bicycles. All ranked number one in the world. The achievement is indeed staggering. In that year, there were 10 items ranked number one, including those mentioned above, three items in number two (desktop scanner, PTA, machine mould), and five items in number three (PS petrochemical, personal computers, lighting diode, printed circuit board, and desk-top scanner) in the world export markets.

The most noteworthy achievements in the 1990s are in the area of personal computers and integrated circuits. In fact, in 1995 Taiwan produced more than 10 percent of world's personal computers, and its production of keyboards and motherboards ranked number one in the world (Nikkei, 1996). In 1998, the global production shares by volume of the scanner (85%), case (75%), motherboard (66%), SPS (66%), keyboard (65%), mouse (60%), monitors (58%), sound card (49%), video card (40%), notebook PC (39%), and graphics card (31%), all ranked number one in the world. There is no ranking of the world share of CD-ROMs (33%) and desktop PCs (16%), but its ranking should also be high. Taiwan in 1998 ranked "the number three producer of information technology world wide, only behind the United States and Japan."[3] Indeed, as we will explore

[2]Duan (1989), 313. No sources of data are given. Note that this is a Chinese text, which generally say nothing good about Taiwan.

[3]Underwood (1999), 22. Source: Institute for Information Industries, Market Intelligence Center, Taiwan. "Taiwan IT companies produced more than US$19 billion in hardware products in 1998. Adding offshore production, the total reached US$32 billion, an increase of 8.4 percent over 1997" (ibid.)

further later in this paper, Taiwan is certainly a very large country in the world in almost all categories except its land area.

2.3 An Overview of Early Taiwanese History from an International Perspective

Taiwan's geographical position also determines its historical relations with the surrounding countries. Before the 17th century, Taiwan was initially inhabited by nine ethnic groups[4] of Malay-Polynesian origin. While some claim that Chinese population on Taiwan may trace back to the third century[5] (230 A. D., the Period of Three Kingdom), a recent study indicates that a reliable Chinese account on Taiwan appeared[6] only in 1349. From the 16th century on, the Han people began arriving in the western part of Taiwan from the coastal area of southern China. They were fishermen, pirates, criminals, or tax evaders. So were Japanese pirates (Vertente *et al.*, 1991, 49). Most of them made no efforts to settle permanently, and the Ming government of the time never extended its rule on Taiwan (Vertente *et al.*, 1991, 34; See Fig.[7] 2.2a)). Thus, when the Dutch from the Dutch East India Company[8] in Batavia of Indonesia occupied and settled in the southern part of Taiwan (see Fig. 2.3) in 1624 as the base of entrepot trade with Japan (Su, 1980, 57) and monopolizing its trade with China

[4]There are several suggestions on classification. See Su (1980), 16–17.

[5]Wu (1958), 5. Most politically oriented Chinese adopt this point of view. For details, see Su (1980), 20–35.

[6]A book by Wang Ta-yuan, *Brief Account of the Island Barbarians*, 1349. Wang mentioned Penghu, Liu-chiu, and P'i-shi-yeh, "which probably refers to Taiwan." See Vertente *et al.* (1991), 26. Many old chronicles could not distinguish among Ryukyu Islands, Taiwan, and Penghu (Pescadores) islands, which are a group of tiny islands located between Taiwan and the mainland. Ibid., 39; also Su (1980), 21.

[7]Figure 2.2 is an extension and refinement of Fig. 1 in Klintworth (1995), 4. We use a solid line to denote the separation of the two countries, and a dotted line to show weak relations between Taiwan and China. Figure 2.2 reinforces the false of the Chinese claim that "Taiwan was part of 'the sacred territory of China since ancient times'" as quoted in Klintworth (1995), 5.

[8]The Dutch gained independence from Spain and established The Republic of Holland in 1579. They "allied themselves with England ... in an attempt to wrest hegemony over the European seas from Portugal and Spain, ... and sent warships to ... the Asian seas, occupying and plundering colonies." "For this purpose, the Dutch monarch established the Dutch East India Company in 1602. ... and ... establish(ed) a permanent residence in Batavia ..." (Su, 1986, 11).

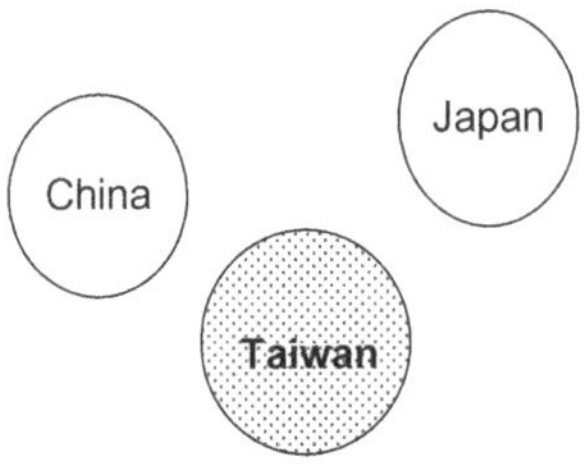

Figure 2.2a: Before 17th Century.

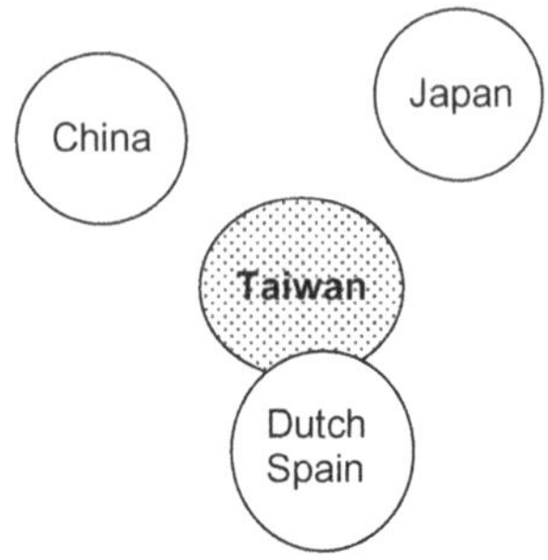

Figure 2.2b: The Dutch and Spanish Period (Dutch, 1624–1662; Spanish, 1626–1642).

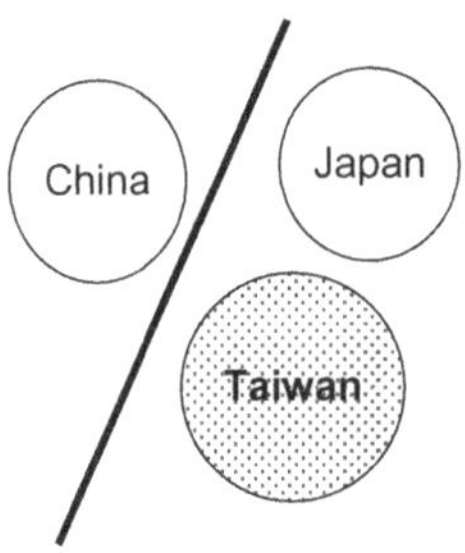

Figure 2.2c: The Cheng Period (1662–1683).

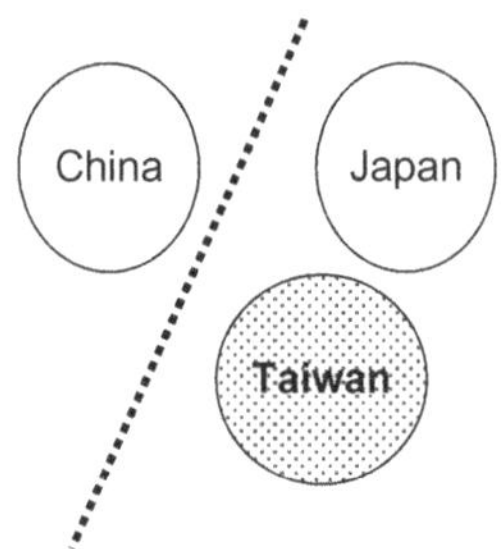

Figure 2.2d: The Ch'ing Period, I (1683–1760).

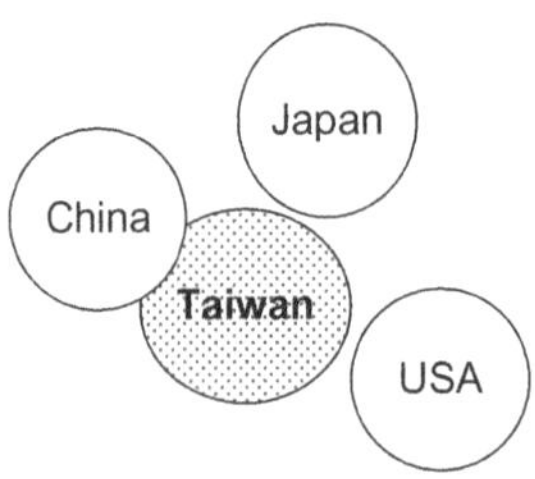

Figure 2.2e: The Ch'ing Period, II (1760–1895).

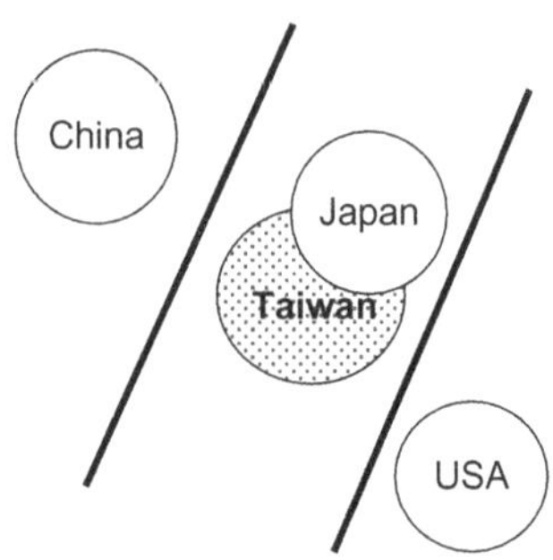

Figure 2.2f: The Japanese Period (1985–1945).

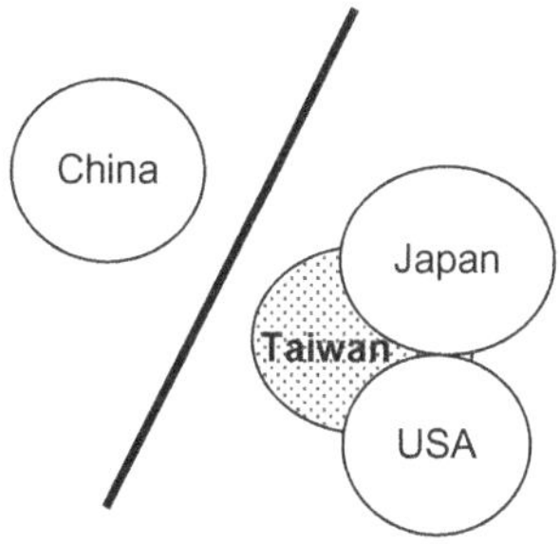

Figure 2.2g: The Cold War Period (1945–1991).

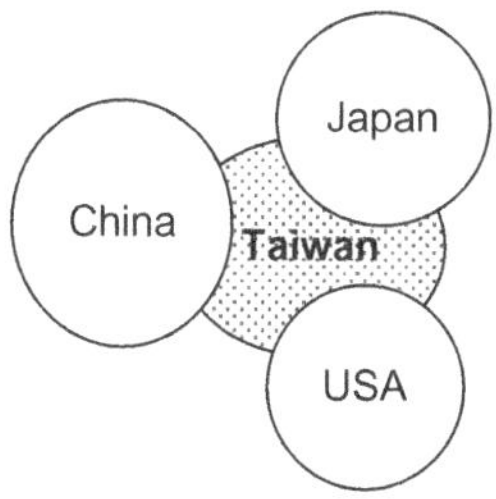

Figure 2.2h: Post Cold War Period (1991–).

(Vertente *et al.*, 1991, 69), the Ming government did not protest nor interfere.[9]

The Dutch built Fort Zeelandia in Tainan area and ruled Taiwan for 38 years from 1624 to 1662. They had shortage of labor and bought in "Han serfs" from China (Su, 1986, 13; 1980, 69–74). Meanwhile, the Spanish in the Philippines felt the threat of the Dutch and tried to expel them from Taiwan. They landed and settled in Santiago near Keelung (see Fig. 2.3) in 1626 (Su, 1980, 79). In the following year, the King of Spain declared that Formosa belonged to the Spanish crown (ibid., 80). However, the Dutch eventually expelled the Spanish from Taiwan in 1642 and controlled the northern and southern parts of the island (ibid., see Fig. 2.2b).

The shortest distance from Taiwan to China is only 110 miles, and so Taiwan has been often influenced by events in its neighbor. In 1661, the Manchus overthrew the Ming government, a foreign tribe that invaded China from the north and established the Ch'ing Dynasty. Ming's defeated general, Cheng Ch'eng-kung (Koxinga), fled to Taiwan and drove away the Dutch.[10] The family of Cheng ruled Taiwan and expanded its territory in the southern part of Taiwan (see Fig. 2.3), while fighting with the Manchus,

[9]It seems that the description about the events leading to the Dutch occupation of Taiwan is clearer in Su (1980), 58 than that in Vertente (1991), 58 or 74. Su wrote that after eight months of bloody battle with the Dutch, the Ming government agreed on two conditions for peace. If the Dutch retreat from Pescadores, which China considered its territory, the Ming will not interfere Dutch's occupation of Taiwan, and that the trade with China could be tacitly tolerated. In discussing why the Dutch came to the southern Taiwan instead of the northern part, Ang (1999), 58 did not mention the agreement specifically.

[10]Actually, an official peace treaty between Cheng and the Dutch was signed on February 1, 1662 (ibid., 104).

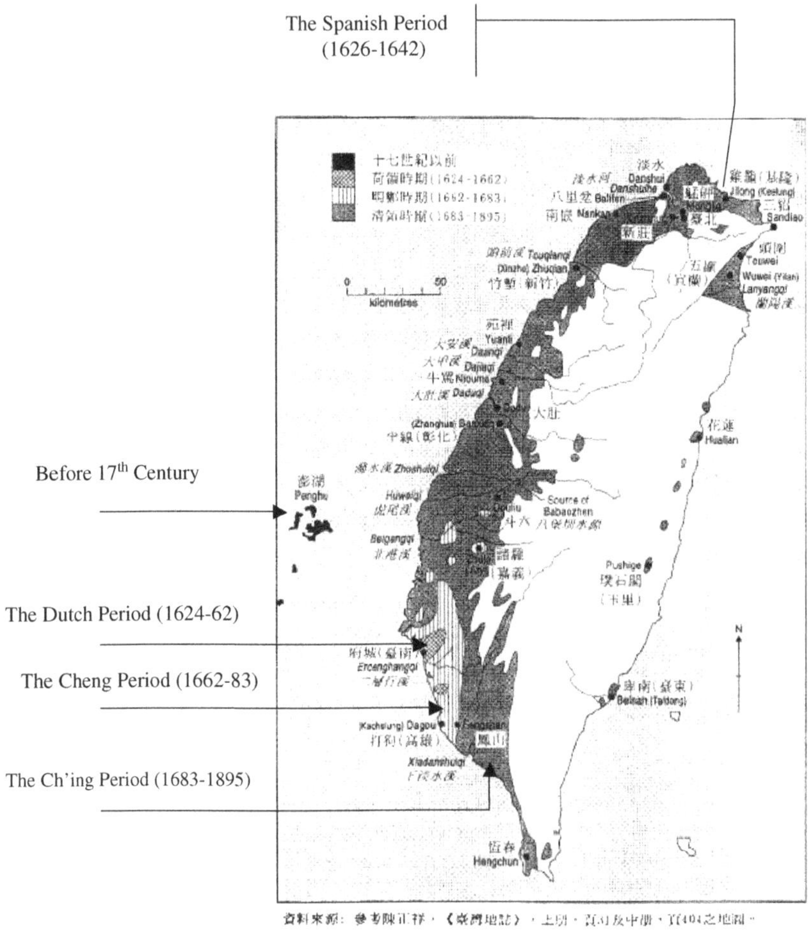

Figure 2.3: Han Settlement on Taiwan — A Historical Perspective

Sources: Taken from T. Liu (1995), 297, also in T. Liu (1998), 166. Originally taken from Chen (1959–60), vol. I, 31 and vol. II, 404.

for 23 years from 1662 to 1683 (Vertente *et al.*, 1991, Chapter 5). During this period, trade with other countries, except China, flourished (see Fig. 2.2c). Taiwan then came under the Ch'ing government, which lasted 212 years in Taiwan from 1683 to 1895.

The Ch'ing government ruled Taiwan with indifference and passivity (ibid., 130), and continued the discriminatory and prohibitive rule of the Dutch colonial system with added "decadent feudalism of China."

(Su, 1986, 23–24; 1980, 118–246). By the end of its rule, its territory had expanded to the coastal flatland area of western Taiwan (Fig. 2.3). The government controlled only major cities, and its rule did not extend to the vast mountain area and the eastern part of Taiwan (Fig. 2.3). Being keenly aware of its limitations, for almost one hundred years the Ch'ing government banned immigration and emigration between Taiwan and the mainland lest people should run into the mountains and revolt against its rule. Thus, Taiwan was isolated from China and other part of the world for 78 years from 1683 to 1760 (see Figs. 2.2d and 2.2e).

Despite the precaution, the settlers frequently rebelled against the Manchus.[11] The Taiwanese economy expanded only slowly and its trade was confined exclusively to China. Only after the mid-19th century when the English and France forced open the ports of Taiwan (Vertente *et al.*, 1991, 136–137), other European powers followed, and Taiwan re-entered the world trading system (Su, 1986, 34–35; Huang and Chen, 1995, 312, 321).

At the end of the first Sino-Japanese war, China ceded Taiwan and the Pescadores to Japan "in perpetuity" by the Treaty of Simonoseki in 1895.[12] After crashing the short-lived *Democratic Republic of Taiwan* established by the local people,[13] for the first seven years, the Japanese still had hard time eradicating the sporadic armed rebellion against its rule. Even by 1901, a Japanese government survey drew[14] along the center of Taiwan dividing east and west "the approximate boundary line separating savage district and territory under actual control of Japanese administration." In fact, it

---

[11] According to Hsu (2000), during a period of 212 years from 1683 to 1895, there were 107 rebellions against the Ch'ing government and at least 51 armed conflicts among the local ethnic groups. The Taiwanese were not known to be submissive to the government authorities.

[12] Article II of The Treaty of Peace between Japan and China in 1895 states that "China cedes to Japan in perpetuity and full sovereignty ... the island of Formosa, together with all the islands appertaining or belonging to said island of Formosa...." (Cohen and Teng, 1990, 103). However, in the so called "Cairo Declaration," November 22–26, 1943, attended by Roosevelt, Churchill, and Chiang, stated that "It is their purpose that ... all the territories Japan has stolen from the Chinese, such as Manchuria, Formosa, and the Pescadores, shall be restored to the Republic of China...." The word "stolen" is a wartime language, which does not reflect the fact. Furthermore, it is worth noting that the "Cairo Declaration" is merely a news release or bulletin of the State Department of the United States and was NOT signed by any of the attending heads of the state. Thus it does not have any legal binding. For a latest discussion, see Chiang (2000).

[13] Vertente *et al.* (1991), 154–156. It was the first republic in Asia. For details, see the doctorial thesis by Ng (1970), and also the Ph.D. thesis by Huang (1987).

[14] Vertente *et al.* (1991), 155. James W. Davidson compiled the map in 1901.

was only in 1930 that the Japanese administration, for the first time in the Taiwanese history, actually controlled and integrated the all of Taiwan with iron fists.[15] By the 1920s, Taiwan had been placed into the Japanese economic domain exclusively (see Fig. 2.2f) and was trading almost entirely with Japan. Ironically, under Japanese colonialism, Taiwan started modern economic and social development, building the foundations for rapid post-war economic growth.[16]

Japanese influence continued even after WWII. Similar to the Cheng Period in the 17th century, the Nationalist Republic of China was over-thrown by the communist People's Republic of China in 1949, and the defeated Generalissimo Chiang Kai-shek fled to Taiwan where he established the Republic of China on Taiwan (although he pretended that he was still the ruler of China). China was off-limit for the Taiwanese from 1949 up until the end of the cold war in the late 1980s (Klintworth, 1995, 28). At the same time, China itself was isolated economically and politically from the global economy.[17] As we will see in details below, during this cold-war period Taiwan was able to ally with Japan and the United States (Fig. 2.2g) and to form a trade triangle with these two powerful countries. Thus, it catapulted itself to rapid economic growth.[18]

After the death of Chiang, the authoritarian regime of Taiwan started to thaw, culminated in the lifting of 38-year-old martial law in 1987 (Hsiao and Hsiao, 2001) and the democratic election of the first president in 1996. The termination of the "Period of Mobilization for Suppression of the Communist Rebellion" in 1991 also ended almost the half-century old enmity with China. The event also coincided with China's reform and open-door period from 1989 until now (Ishida, 2000, 277–279). This stimulated the Taiwanese outward foreign direct investment in China and negotiation between the two countries. When the world experienced the end of the

[15]In 1930, when Japan started exploiting mountain resources, the aborigines revolted against the Japanese (the Wushe Incident). It was savagely suppressed, and new policy for the mountain regions and aborigines was put in effect. Vertente *et al.* (1991), 159. We submit that the incident was significant for Taiwan's national "unification." The fact belies the Chinese claim that "whole" Taiwan was part of China, as the local Chinese government never ruled the mountainous regions of Taiwan even during the Ch'ing period.

[16]Jacoby (1966), 71; Ho (1978), 90, 100–101; Klintworth (1995), Chapter 2. Hsiao and Hsiao (1996), 219–221, 234–235, 240–242.

[17]The years from 1949 to 1989 corresponds to China's self-reliance period (1949–1978) and economic adjustment period (1979–1989). See Ishida (2000), 274–276.

[18]Twu (1975); Hsiao and Hsiao (1996), 264–267, 273–276, 282–285; M. Hsiao (1992).

cold war in 1991, Taiwan entered the new era of internationalization and globalization (Fig. 2.2h).

2.4 The Taiwanese Economy before the 19th Century

We now examine briefly the position of Taiwan in the global economy before the 19th century. As we have seen in the previous section, while sporadic Han Chinese immigrants and the aborigines lived on the island before the 17th century, the Dutch, and, for a very short period, the Spanish in the northern Taiwan, formally colonized Taiwan in 1624. The modern Taiwanese economic history should start from the Dutch period.

2.4.1 *The Dutch Period — Global Trade in the 17th Century*

The original purpose of the Dutch and the Spanish in coming to Taiwan was to use it as the trade entrepot between China and Japan. Later, they found that they might also gain by colonizing Taiwan and trading native products with Japan and China. Thus, the Taiwanese economy was already export-oriented in the 17th century.[19]

As early as the second half of the 16th century, Europeans, Chinese, and Japanese were known to come to Taiwan for either transferring commodities to the third countries[20] or for trading with the Taiwanese aborigines with agate, cloth, salt, copper, etc. for buckskin (Nakayama, 1959, 24–25). In order to trade with China, the Dutch colonized the southern part of Taiwan in 1624. Its influence spread to the northern area like Keelung and Tamsui by the 1650s (Su, 1980, 74; Chang *et al.* 1996, 48). At the beginning, they traded the daily necessities for buckskin and venison supplied by aborigines. Later, they brought in Chinese agricultural laborers (Han serfs, as characterized by Su, 1986, 13), and encouraged Han immigrants and aborigines to cultivate sugar cane and rice paddy to be refined for exports (Chou, 1957).

The Dutch exported buckskin, venison, dried fish, and sugar to Japan in exchange for Japanese silver. From 1634 to 1661, the magnitude of the exports of buckskin was simply amazing: it ranged from the high of 151,400 pieces in 1638 to the low of 19,140 pieces in 1642. The Dutch

[19]The following three sections on the Dutch, Cheng, and Ch'ing periods are taken partly from Hsiao and Hsiao (1999), 481–489.

[20]Nakayama (1959), 25; Su (1980), 77–78. In a 1554 map by Portuguese, Taiwan was called Ilha Formosa (Chang *et al.*, 1996, 60).

then exported Japanese and European silver, along with venison, antlers, rice, sulfur, and dried fish, which were produced in Taiwan, to China in exchange for raw silk, silk and satin, herbal medicine, porcelain, and gold. These precious commodities, along with spices, which were purchased from Southeast Asia, were then shipped to Holland from Taiwan. Some of the raw silk and silk products were also re-exported to Japan (Su, 1980, 78–79; Chou, 1957, 61).

Another important trading partner under the Dutch regime was Persia. To Persia, Taiwan exported tea and much of its sugar output, along with camphor and copper, which were imported from Japan, and Ginseng, which was imported from China. As usual, Han immigrants and native aborigines produced buckskin, sugar, and rice; the Dutch collected the commodities, and monopolized the export business. During the Dutch occupation from 1624 to 1662, the trading activities in Taiwan were very lucrative. In accounting for the total profits in Asia in 1649, the Dutch reported once that, among the 19 trading posts in Asia, the trade with Taiwan alone earned 25.6 percent of the total Asian profits, only next to the trade with Japan (38.8%) (Su, 1980, 80).

2.4.2 *The Cheng Period — Continuation of Global Trade*

In 1662, after being defeated by the ascending Ch'ing dynasty, the Ming general Cheng Ch'eng-kung and his troop fled to Taiwan, drove away the Dutch, and established the Kingdom of Cheng (Chang *et al.*, 1996) or the Kingdom of Formosa, as was called by the British (ibid., 90). The Cheng government adopted the Dutch economic system. Its major concern was to "return to China," rather than developing Taiwan for the benefits of the Taiwanese. The government welcomed trading with all countries except China and Holland (Chou *et al.*, 1959). The Ch'ing government also closed and banned the coastal area for travel to and trade with Taiwan, although illegal trade relations between Taiwan and China persisted.

Trading with Japan continued to prosper. Every year, eight to fifteen Taiwanese ships sailed to Japan for trade. Taiwan exported sugar, buckskin, silk products, and herbal medicine to Japan, and on the return trip imported copper, lead, weapons, and other military materials (Chang *et al.*, 1996, 92).

The Cheng government also increased trade with Southeast Asian countries. Every year, one or two Taiwanese ships sailed to Luzon, Indochina, Cambodia, Thailand, Malacca, and Batavia. The British took the place of the Dutch in Taiwan's trade with the Europeans. From 1670 to 1680, the British and the Cheng government had three commerce treaties, and in 1671, the British established a trading house in Taiwan. However, until the end of the Cheng Kingdom in 1683, that business did not flourish (ibid.).

In general, during the Cheng period, Taiwan continued to trade with foreign countries. The government mainly conducted the trade, and the commodities imported were mainly military materials.

2.4.3 *The Ch'ing Period — from Autarky to the Bilateral Trade and Development of Taiwanese Capitalism*

The Ch'ing government conquered the Kingdom of Cheng in 1683. To avoid future insurgence against China using Taiwan as a base, it proclaimed a strict ban of immigration from the coastal cities in China to Taiwan. Trade between both sides of the Taiwan Strait was restricted and discouraged. The policy changed several times after 1732 and was revoked for good only in 1760 (Su, 1980, 128–129; Su, 1986, 26). As a result, Taiwan's economy was forced into an autarky system. It stagnated for a long period as it retreated from the global scene.

From 1760 to 1860, Taiwan traded almost exclusively with China, mostly with people in Fujian. Taiwan exported agricultural products like rice, sugar, jute, rattan, camphor wood to China, and imported manufactured products like cotton fabric and cloth, silk, paper, porcelain (Huang and Chen, 1995, 320), agricultural equipment, and wine. In one account, during 1741, Taiwan produced slightly more than 100 million dans[21] of rice, half of which was exported to China (Oh, 1970, 77).

After 1860, Tamsui and Anping in Taiwan were opened to the Europeans under the Peking Treaty between China and England. The Europeans came to trade with Taiwan, and Taiwan was reintroduced to the global economy.[22] As it might be expected, the openness of trade reduced the importance of China as Taiwan's trading partner, and restructured Taiwan's trade composition. Taiwanese rice lost its competitiveness to Southeast Asian rice in China, and with a rapid increase in Taiwanese population, rice export was greatly reduced (Huang and Chen, 322, 331). Furthermore, Taiwanese sugar was gradually replaced by local sugar in

[21] 1 dan = 1 hectoliter.

[22] For a specific aspect of globalization of Taiwanese trade through an English company during this period, see Huang (1999).

China, and more of it was, instead, exported to Hong Kong, Australia, the United States, Japan, etc.

Meanwhile, Taiwan's tea replaced sugar to become the largest export item. In 1895, more than 81 percent (16 million pounds) of Woolong tea was exported to the United States (ibid., 331), the rest went to Europe. Taiwan also became the world's largest producer of camphor. In 1868 (and 1895), Taiwan exported 1.6 (and 6.9) million pounds of camphor, 2.6 (and 2.3) times larger than the second largest exporter, Japan (ibid., 334). Coal was one of the new export items, mainly sold to China.

At that time, unfortunately, more than 50 percent of total imports were opium. Other imports consisted of manufactured goods, like cotton and its products, woolen fabrics, kerosene, metals (especially lead for sealing sugar boxes), matches (100% from Japan), and other miscellaneous goods, which increased importance over the years. However, like the other periods, there had been trade surpluses every year since 1872, and the surpluses increased until the end of the Ch'ing period (ibid., 337–339).

Before 1860, various Taiwanese export associations controlled most of Taiwan's trade with China (ibid., 354; Twu, 1975, 373). After 1860, they lost in competition to foreign traders, especially the British, who set up trading houses in Taiwan. The old-fashioned export associations simply could not compete with the Western management system. Although the profits in coastal trading were very high, about 30 percent per annum on average, due to political instability in China and market fluctuation, the trading was highly speculative and risky, and many ventures went bankrupt (Hao, 1986, 346 and Chapter 10).

As time went by, some Taiwanese merchants were able to learn management practices from the Europeans and started their own trading companies. Toward the end of the 1890s, some Taiwanese trading companies even excelled over the European trading houses.[23] In the tea trade, for an example, in 1874, the export volume of tea by Taiwanese traders exceeded two times of that by foreign traders. By 1881, about 90 percent of Taiwanese tea was exported by Taiwanese merchants (Huang and Chen, 1995, 361). They also dominated in exporting camphor and sugar, as well

[23] "The Chinese merchants by and large out competed Western traders because of their familiarity with local conditions, their ability to dispense with additional middlemen and their satisfactions with a relatively small profit margin" (Hao, 1986, 346). The relation and relative influence of local and foreign capital are still unclear, and more research is called for.

as importing opium and textiles (ibid., 361–364). In general, we submit that, before the Japanese occupation in 1895, Taiwan had experienced a Commercial Revolution,[24] which, in England, was considered to be a prelude to "Industrial Revolution."[25]

Like merchants in England, the sign of transition from the commercial revolution to the industrial revolution in Taiwan had already appeared before the Japanese occupation in 1895. Some Taiwanese merchants, like the Lin Pun-yuan family of Pangchiao, traded domestically and internationally, and even established local banks and money exchange houses to lend money to tea producers (Huang and Chen, 1995, 364; Su, 1980, 320). Some sugar traders also financed sugar producers (Twu, 1975, 380). In general, by the end of the 19th century the Taiwanese merchants were able to dominate the trade, and to accumulate wealth through the commercial relations with China, England, and the Netherlands. Eventually, the merchants also became moneylenders to the local producers.[26] It was reported that, by 1895, at least four Taiwanese families had wealth of 10 to 40 million taels, and there were 17 Taiwanese millionaire families.[27] Indeed, Taiwan had the makings of a classic "bourgeois-nationalist revolution."[28]

2.5 Taiwan in the Global Economy during the Japanese Period

The victory of Japan in the first Sino-Japanese war in 1895 over the Ch'ing government and over Taiwanese uprisings distorted the "natural"

[24]Commercial Revolution in the Middle Ages in Europe occurred in the period 950–1350 (Lopez, 1971), that in England, "from the English Restoration to American Independence," 1660–1776 (Davis, 1967, 3–4), and in China "along the coast from the 1820s to 1883" (Hao, 1986, 338).

[25]Davis (1967), 24. The importance of international trade continued even during the Industrial Revolution. See Hobsbawn (1968), 38.

[26]From the Marxists points of view, this process is important in the development of capitalism, see USSR (1955), Vol. I, 87–88; Vol. II, Chapter 12, "Commerce, credit, and Money Circulation."

[27]Twu (1975), 381. However, there are some conflicting observations on the Taiwanese economy before 1895. Yanaihara observed that until the very end of the Ch'ing period in Taiwan, "no single modern bank, modern corporation, modern factory existed... All the establishments of capitalist enterprises in Taiwan came only after Japanese occupation" (Yanaihara, 1929, 55). More research is needed.

[28]The Taiwanese Communist Party observed this point in 1928 on the development of Taiwanese capitalism. For detail, see Hsiao and Sullivan (1983), 278.

development along the path to full-blown Taiwanese capitalism.[29] Japanese capital flooded into Taiwan and suffocated, so to speak, the Taiwanese native capital from creation of large-scale modern banks and factories.[30]

As Japanese capitalism was still in the infant period, the new colonial government at first tolerated the existence of the local Taiwanese capitalists. Except sugar and those commodities under national monopoly (opium, salt, camphor, tobacco, etc.), few restrictions were imposed on the production and distribution of daily necessities (Twu, 1975, 397). At the same time, the government drove away the European and Chinese commercial capital by setting up a discriminatory tariff system, establishing the Bank of Taiwan (1899) to substitute foreign financial control, instituting monopoly system, and helping Japanese merchants to overtake the foreign monopoly of sugar trade (Yanaihara, 1929, 43–48; Azuma, 1941, 93–95; Su, 1980, 338).

By the 1920s, however, Japanese capital flooded into Taiwan, and the larger and modern Japanese-owned firms overshadowed the Taiwanese-owned firms. Led by the sugar companies, all the major, larger firms and banks were held by Japanese private capitalists.

However, small Taiwanese enterprises also flourished. In 1936, there were about 7,000 Taiwanese manufacturing firms.[31] At the end of 1938, some 310,000 to 410,000 Taiwanese farms and landlords produced and sold paddy rice, which was refined into rice by about 3,300 local Taiwanese

[29]This is also the argument presented in the 1928 Political Thesis of the short-lived Taiwanese Communist Party (1928–1931). For references, see Hslao and Sullivan (1983). We adopted their line of arguments for different reasons. The thesis is influenced by the political and economic principles of the Japanese Communist Party in the 1920s along the line of the Marx theory of capitalism, which emphasizes the internal (like domestic saving), rather than the external (like commercial), factors of capital accumulation. In Japan, it is known as the Ohtsuka Proposition (Ohtsuka Shigaku) (Kakuyama, 1980, 22–23), and was propagated in early post-war Taiwan by Chang (1974).

[30]Economic development under the Japanese regime may be divided into five periods (Hsiao and Hsiao, 1998; 1996, 215–221): The initial period (1895–1905); the intermediate period (1905–1931); the quasi-war-stage (1931–1937), which covers the period from the Manchurian Incident to the beginning of the Sino-Japanese War; the first war-stage (July 1937–1941), which covers the Sino-Japanese War and the beginning of World War II; and the second war-stage (1942–1945), which covers World War II until the end of the war. The first two periods are based on the classification of Sumiya *et al.* (1992), Chapter 1, and are rather well documented. The last three periods are given in Kusui (1944) and correspond to the period of Japanese militarism.

[31]Calculated from Table 1a in Hsiao and Hsiao (1999a), 495. The existence of small-and-medium size manufacturing enterprises in Taiwan is not at all a postwar phenomenon.

millers.[32] Among them, 732 firms bought rice for exports. In late 1930s, about 90 percent of rice exported to Japan were monopolized by four major trading companies (Kawano, 1968, 129). Taiwanese firms remained small and numerous. Similarly, from 1936 to 1937, 127,000 small farms cultivated sugar cane (about 30% of total farmers), which was sold to 49 Japanese sugar factories in Taiwan (ibid., 92). During the same period, four major sugar companies exported nearly 88% of sugar produced in Taiwan to Japan (ibid., 87–88). Thus, the production of sugar and the distribution of sugar and rice, and other exports and imports, were almost completely under the control of the Japanese. There was little room for the Taiwanese to engage in export businesses. Native development of commercial capitalism gave way to the Japanese.

2.5.1 *Taiwanese Agriculture in the World Production*

Under colonialism, Taiwanese were mostly farmers and toilers.[33] At least until the mid-1930s, the major emphasis in economic development was in agriculture. In fact, Taiwan developed agriculture with handicaps. It is not only small in land, as we have seen in the first section, but also not all of this small land is suited for developing agriculture. Only 31 percent of the area has an elevation below 100 meters. The rest has an elevation either between 100 and 1000 meters (37%), or above 1000 meters (31%) (Chen, 1963, 89). It is "one of the most mountainous islands in the world" (ibid., 87). "There are more than 20 peaks with an altitude of more than 3500 meters... This is very seldom found... in the whole world, considering the small size of the island" (ibid., 88). The arable area, mineral resources, and sites suitable for hydroelectric generation are severely limited. The island is exposed to monsoons, typhoons, earthquakes, and even droughts. Heat and rain washed away nutritive soil elements (like phosphorus and potash), leaving mostly acidic soil.[34] Furthermore, since Taiwan is located in a subtropical zone, plant diseases and bugs are prevalent (Ping, 1947, 64).

---

[32]Mizoguchi and Yamamoto (1984) counted that Taiwanese millers consisted of 94 percent in 1929 and 93 percent in 1939. We submit that this is an origin of the postwar Taiwanese small-and-medium enterprises (Hsiao and Hsiao, 1999a). Note that, in colonial Korea, unlike Taiwan, the Japanese dominated the rice milling business in 1939 (ibid.).
[33]This section is taken partly from Hsiao (1997).
[34]Chen (1963), 137; Ping (1947), 62–63; Detailed soil analyses for local area can be found in SS51, 517–520.

Despite these natural disadvantages, Taiwan's subtropical location enables it to produce quite different crops. It is this geographical advantage that made Taiwan unique in the Japanese Empire, and the Japanese saw the comparative advantage of developing agriculture in Taiwan (Hsiao, 1997). To cope with the natural disadvantages, the Japanese developed Taiwanese agriculture by intensive research and development,[35] and organized rural institutions (Ho, 1978, 57–65). They kept systematic and meticulous meteorological records since 1896 (Tang, 1947, 16; Chen, 1963, 121), conducted soil surveys and agricultural experimentation, invested heavily during the 1920s in extensive flood control and modern irrigation systems (Ho, 1978, 36–37), introduced or improved new breeds of plants and crops which withstood weather changes, diseases, and bugs (Tang, 1947, 12–14), used fertilizer extensively (Ishikawa, 1967, 102–105), and improved cultivation methods (Tang, 1947, 14–19).

By 1938, the utilization rate of the arable land in Taiwan was[36] 24 percent (59,000 hectares), higher than Korea (20%) and Japan proper (17%), but lower than major countries, like Denmark (62%), India (57%), Italy (49%), and England (46%), but much higher than that in any province in China (Tang, 1947, 1). The total area of cultivated land has remained almost constant between the prewar and the postwar periods (TSDB, 2000).

By 1944, 96 field crops were planted in Taiwan (Ping, 1947, 75). The six major crops were paddy rice (41.8% of the value of total agricultural production,[37] the same below), sugar cane (18.1%), sweet potatoes (6.7%), bananas (4.1%), pineapples (2.2%), and tea (1.9%) (ibid., 76). Rice, sugar cane, and sweet potatoes have been consistently the major agricultural produces of Taiwan during the prewar and early postwar periods.

The increase in Taiwan's agricultural productivity was remarkable. Between 1905 and 1909, per hectare output of Taiwan's agricultural production was only about a half of that of Japan, but it caught up to about 80 percent by the end of the prewar period, and reached the same amount between 1960 and 1964 (Shinohara and Ishikawa, 1972, 18). By another measure, however, output per farm family of agricultural products in Taiwan during 1935–39 was already about 50 percent higher than that

[35] Japanese studies and research on Taiwan started long before their occupation (Wu, 1995), followed by intensive "explorations" immediately after the occupation (Wu, 1997).
[36] The sources of data are not given. We think it is taken form TEY41, 120–124.
[37] From Ping (1947), 76, which is taken from 1944 Taiwan agricultural Yearbook. Note that the value of total agricultural products includes 9.7 percent of hog and 2.4 percent of chicken.

of Japan[38] (ibid., 19). Through irrigation and agricultural and biological innovation, Taiwan became the most advanced rice producing country in the whole of Asia during the 1930s and the 1950s (ibid., 19; Chang, 1957). Similar statements can be made for other crops.

Rice production increased steadily over the years. In 1938, the maximum amount of production reached six times that of 1900. Similarly, sugar cane production increased 31 times, sweet potatoes nine times, bananas 36 times, peanuts five times, tobacco 66 times, and pineapples 20 times. Note that all crops, except tea, increased steadily, and reached maximum production by the end of the 1930s. After 1940, agricultural production started to level off and decreased giving way to industrial production following Japan's plunge into the Pacific War.

The magnitude of agricultural production was staggering when we compare Taiwan's achievement with the world. From 1934 to 1938, Taiwan, on average, produced 1.3 million tons of rice per year. This is about 1 percent of the world rice production, compared with about 8 percent in Japan, and 34 percent in China, and ranked about 10th place in the world.[39] Although Taiwan's production was small if compared with these two large neighboring countries, if we consider the size of Taiwan's area and population, we will find immediately that Taiwan stands out. In 1940, Taiwan produced more than 50 times its fair share of rice in terms of its proportion of total world area, and 3.3 times of its share in total world population.[40]

The international statistics of two cash crops are available, and they are even more staggering. During 1934 to 1938, Taiwan on average produced 2.4 percent (0.04 million tons) of the world's tea and 2.2 percent of the world's banana per year. Taiwan's tea production was the sixth largest in

---

[38]Note that this is different from the comparison of per farm family disposable income (Ping, 1947). Hayami and Ruttan (1970) argues that in Japan, there was a rapid growth in agricultural output and productivity from 1886 to 1920, followed by a much slower growth in the 1920s and 1930s, due to the rice imports from Taiwan and Korea, and decline in technological progress.

[39]In addition to the 8 countries in Table 3, add Korea (3.6 million tons in 1937; YS43, 103). According to YS43, 101, Taiwan's rice production in 1937 was 1.8 million tons, and that of world production was 93.8 million tons. Hence, Taiwan's share was 1.9 percent of the world production.

[40]In 1940, Taiwan comprised an area of about 0.02 percent of the world area, and 0.27 percent (5.7 million) of the world population (Hsiao, 1997, 498). In other data, on average from 1937 to 1940, the percentage of Taiwan's rice production ranges up to 1.9 percent of the world rice production (93 million tons), ranked ninth in the world. See YS43, 101.

the world (next to India, Ceylon, Indonesia, Japan, and China, YS43, 140) and its banana production was the third largest in the world.[41] This means that Taiwan produced tea and bananas more than 120 times of its share in terms of its area and more than eight times its share of total world population!

Most of the output of rice, tea, and banana was exported. During 1934 to 1938, on average, about 51 percent (0.7 million tons) of rice per year, and about 62 percent of bananas was exported to Japan (Chou, 1958, 37, 48). In contrast, about 80 percent of tea was exported, mostly to countries other than Japan (TEY41, 144–146), and consisted of about 3 percent to 4 percent of Taiwan's total exports (SS51, Tables 324, 326). The amounts are awesome if we consider the world export market. Taiwan's exports of bananas (0.15 million tons, including exporting to Japan) constituted about 5.4 percent of the world exports in 1937 and 1938, competing for the first or second place in the world banana export market (YS43, 144). Taiwan's exports of tea (9.7 kilo tons) from 1936 to 1939 were, on average, about 2.2 percent of total world exports (447 kilo tons) during the same period, competing for the 6th largest tea exporting country in the world (YS43, 139). This pattern of exports continued long after the early postwar period (TSDB, 1985).

Sweet potato, used as a secondary food staple in villages, feeds for hogs, and raw material for producing alcohol, was the third important crop. During 1934–1938, Taiwan produced 1.7 million tons of sweet potatoes, a whopping 3.7 percent of world production, ranked fourth in the world, next to China, Japan, and the United States (1.8 million tons). Despite large production, most of them were used domestically. On average, only 2.6 percent of its production was exported to Japan (Chou, 1958, 46). Taiwan's Sugar production was indeed very impressive. From 1938 to 1940, Taiwan produced, on average, 1.2 million tons of sugar per year, which is almost 7 percent of the world sugar production during that period (17 million tons), ranked fourth among the sugar producing countries, only next to India (2.9 million tons, the same below), Cuba (2.7), and Indonesia (1.5) (YS43, 130).

We note that 70 percent to 80 percent of pineapple production in Taiwan was canned (Ping, 1947, 78) and, along with tea, exported to Japan and other countries. From 1936 to 1938, Taiwan produced, on average,

[41]No data are available for two other major producers, India and Ecuador, see Y91, 206. Thus Taiwan might be either 4th or 5th during 1934–38.

1.2 million boxes of canned pineapple per year, consisted of a whopping 7.5 percent of the world production (16 million boxes), ranked the third in the world, only next to Java (12 million boxes) and Malaya (2.6 million boxes). (YS43, 145).

During the Ch'ing and Japanese periods, salt production was monopoly of the government and was one of Taiwan's major products and exports. In 1938, Taiwan's salt production was about 0.241 million tons, which was about 0.5 percent of the world production (37 million tons), and ranked 13th in the world production. Its importance continued even after WWII. In fact, from 1951 to 1960, Taiwan produced on average 0.3 million tons of salt per year: 63 percent of the output was exported, with 85 percent exporting to Japan.

Before WWI, Taiwan and Japan were the only two countries in the world producing natural camphor (YS41, 365). From 1891 to 1895, the world annual camphor exports were about 31 kilo tons. Taiwan exported, on average, 56 percent of the world annual exports (Chen, 1963, 422). After WWI, Germany developed synthetic camphor and Taiwan's production fluctuated and decreased. By 1939, it was estimated that Taiwan still produced about 50 percent of natural camphor, or 30 percent of the world production (ibid., 428), although the importance of its value in Taiwan's total production and exports decreased considerably.

Thus, by the end of the 1930s, Taiwan already was the world's major producing country of bananas (3rd), canned pineapples (3rd), sugar (4th), sweet potatoes (4th), tea (6th), rice (10th), peanuts (10th), and salt (13th). Unlike many other colonies, Taiwan was by no means a "monoculture" country. To produce so many different agricultural products in so large quantities, the infrastructure of the society, like transportation, communication, and education, must have been built to accommodate such massive development. In the early 1940s, based on this agricultural accumulation and the basis of wealth,[42] the Japanese were able to develop industry in Taiwan quickly and massively, although it was too late.

When the war ended in 1945, Taiwan already had a highly advanced agricultural sector. The war damage to Taiwan's agriculture was minimal (slightly less than 50%) as compared with other industries, and it recovered quickly by 1950 (Kai and Chu, 1951, 61). After 1949, when about 2 million

[42]It has been said that industrialization in colonial Taiwan was not so much financed by the large capitalists from Japan proper, but much more by the local saving in Taiwan. TEY41, 81; Ho (1979), 84.

Chinese refugees and soldiers flooded Taiwan, every three Taiwanese farm laborers had to support one Chinese soldier, and every 1.1 farm laborer supported one non-producing Chinese soldier, refugee, or bureaucrat (Hsiao and Hsiao, 1996, 228). The Chinese civil war and refugees induced chaos and extreme poverty during the early postwar era. The misery had nothing to do with Japanese colonialism, although the Chinese contend otherwise. This real burden for the Taiwanese occurred when the Chinese came to Taiwan after WWII. Without prewar development of the agricultural sector as we have stated above, the Taiwanese economy would have collapsed. Elsewhere we have seen the upsurge in agricultural productivity during the early postwar period (Hsiao and Hsiao, 1996, 240–242). We submit that, unlike many other developing countries, the very foundation and potentiality of such a postwar take-off to higher productivity were laid in the prewar period.

2.5.2 *Industrial Development — Taiwan in the "Great East Asia Co-Prosperity Sphere"*

By the second half of the 1930s, Taiwanese agriculture had reached its limit: The arable land was exhausted. Agricultural technology and its research and development had also reached their ceilings. At the same time, rapid industrialization, militarization, and scarcity of resources in Japan proper also forced industrialization and a readjustment of Taiwan's economic structure (Kusui, 1941, 508; 1944, 159–170). It all started after the completion of the Sun-Moon Lake hydraulic power plant in 1934, tripling Taiwan's electricity output to 150,000 kw (Takahashi, 1937, 420). The power plant was followed by the development of an aluminum factory (1935), an iron alloy factory (1935), a shipping yard (in 1936), and other industries like pulp (in 1935), fertilizer (in 1937), and oil and fats (in 1935) (Kusui, 1944, 69–74).

From the mid-1937s on, as the Taiwanese economy entered the war-stage, the emphasis was on metal processing and refinery, machinery (including weapons, airplanes and automobiles), petroleum, chemical and pharmaceutical industries (Kusui, 1944, 158, 168). They are mostly defense-related industries. At the same time, light industries of daily necessities, such as light bulbs, glass, ink, pencils, porcelain, radios, leather, nail, and agricultural machinery, etc., were developed for war-time self sufficiency (Sumiya *et al.*, 1992, 21), independent of Japan proper. Thus, Taiwan entered the import-substitution phase of economic development, which continued after the war until the mid-1960s. By 1939, the value of industrial output exceeded that of agricultural output for the first time.[43] Taiwan was no long an agricultural society.

As we have seen, Taiwan is a natural resource-poor country. The most important mining product was coal (0.22% of world coal output in 1941), followed by a limited amount of gold (0.06% of world gold production in 1941), crude oil, and natural gas.[44] Only those industries producing soda, nitrogen, cement, carbide, glass could manage to use domestically produced industrial salt, limestone, and natural gas (shown in the callout box in Fig. 2.4). To develop heavy and chemical industries as well as machinery industry, Taiwan had to rely on foreign resources. Figure 2.4 shows the major sources of resource imports. The item in parentheses shows the product that was actually produced during 1939–1940 (Chang, 1980, 109–111), and the items in italic were planned sources of imports (TEY41, 518–19; also Kusui, 1944, 177–178). All of them could be imported "from the 'Japan-Manchuria-China bloc' and the Southeast Asian countries close to Taiwan" (TEY41, 519). The figure illustrates the strategic role and the regional position of Taiwan in Japan's prewar "Great East Asia Co-Prosperity Sphere." In fact, Japan's "southward movement policy" would have been inconceivable without Taiwan (Yano, 1975, 149). Taiwan was envisioned as having a lofty mission,[45] to exploit the rich resources of South China and South Seas (Nanshi Nanyo) for the prosperity of Japan and "all the previously oppressed people" living in the region.[46]

---

[43]Kusui (1944), 157; also see Sumiya *et al.* (1992), 21. In real terms, they came very close to each other (NT$ 435 million vs. NT$ 412 million) in that year. The proportion for the three industries, agriculture, manufacturing, and services, in real terms were 33 percent, 31 percent, and 36 percent, respectively, in 1939. Wu (1995), 635.

[44]See Hsiao (1997), 503–504.

[45]In addition, over 300,000 Taiwanese youth went overseas as volunteer workers or soldiers, or "industrial soldiers" (Lin, 1996, 225). The "lofty mission" or "calling" also manifested in the Taiwan's marching songs, like the songs of the Taiwanese Army (Taiwangun no Uta), The Honor of Taiwanese Volunteer Corps (Homare no Taiwan Shiganhei), Marching to the South (Nanshin no Uta), Marching of the Emperor's People (Komin Koshin Kyoku), etc. (Nampokensha, 1943?, 124–133. In the title of the book, the cherry flower is Japan's national flower). Part of the last song has been translated in English in Lai *et al.* (1991), 30–31.

[46]Kusui (1944), 287, and various literature published at that Time. The Taiwanese (and the Japanese) activities in Southeast Asia are coming out only recently, see Schneider (2000). As much as we oppose Chinese military threat on Taiwan, we do not condone any aggression of war. However, the historical facts about Taiwanese activities in the past should not be buried and unrecognized. Just like the Japanese, the Taiwanese have learned that military aggression does not pay. Both learned in the postwar period that without resorting to force, both countries and all people in South China and South Seas can achieve "co-prosperity" by trading, a lesson for China today.

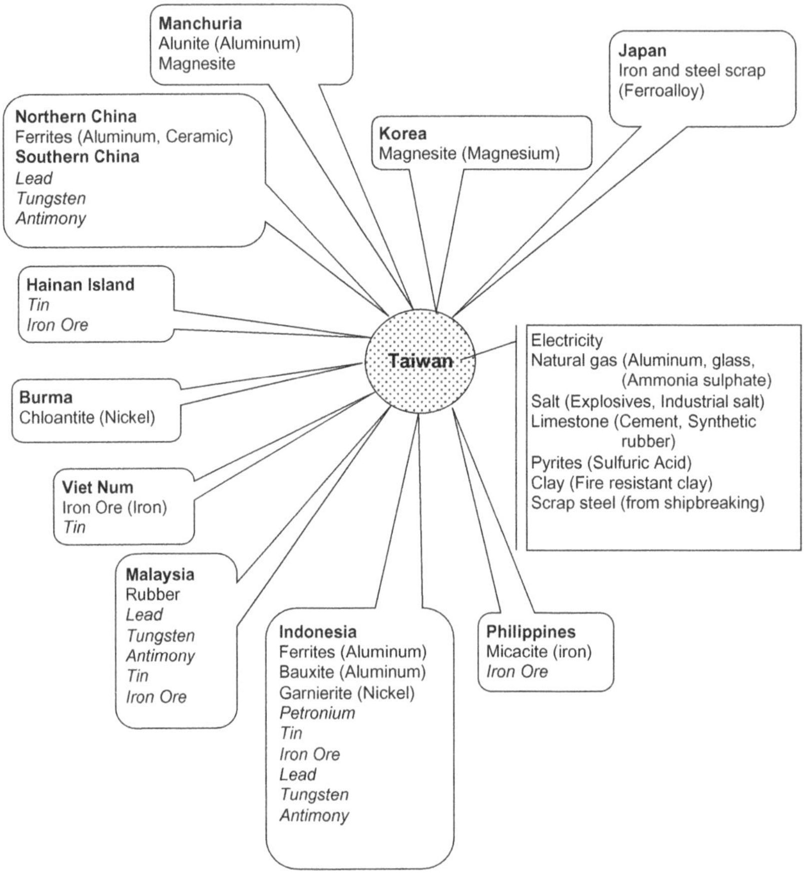

Figure 2.4: Taiwan's Prewar Industrialization and Resources

While Taiwan's prewar industrialization was too late and most industries were just burgeoning, a wide range of light and heavy industries, including all the basic industries for future industrialization, had been established on the island. They stabilized the postwar economy and paving the way for rapid postwar industrial development in the mid-1960s. Since the initial conditions before the economic take-off play an important role in the growth process, as often asserted by the new growth theory, Taiwan was probably one of the few countries that had the most favorable initial conditions among all the developing countries in the postwar period. In this sense, we submit that there is no "miracle" in Taiwanese economic development after the war.

2.6 Postwar Taiwan in the Global Economy

After WWII,[47] the Chinese Nationalist (Kuomintang, KMT) Government confiscated and combined Japanese-owned firms and banks, and converted them into 50 or so public enterprises.[48] Non-Taiwanese speaking Chinese bureaucrats and managers replaced non-Taiwanese speaking Japanese capitalists. Lacking resources and technical ability to engage in new industries, the government had to rely on the old industrial base left over by the Japanese. At the end of the war, the Japanese left behind basic metal, chemical, and other "heavy" industries, which were relatively capital intensive in those days. As we have seen in Fig. 2.4, most raw materials for these heavy industries had to be imported, and their finished products had a limited market in the war-torn Taiwanese economy. Thus immediately after the war, the KMT government had difficulty in deciding whether to spend scarce capital and precious foreign exchange to restore the war damage and to maintain these white-elephant industries (Lin, C., 1968, 296). However, internal and external political developments around 1949 and 1950 altered the picture virtually overnight. The civilian and military industries built by the Japanese in Taiwan to take advantage of resources in South China and the South Seas to fight the Allied Forces were now utilized by the KMT government to fight Chinese communists in the defense of Taiwan. Essentially the KMT perpetuated the Japanese-controlled wartime economy and industries (Hsiao and Hsiao, 2001; Twu, 1975, 499), though on a larger scale due to massive U.S. aid which supported the influx of Chinese refugees and 600,000 Chinese soldiers at that time (Hsiao and Hsiao, 1996).

Taiwanese firms remained small and fragmented, and "a broad movement from below upward" was also severely limited. Until the end of the 1970s, banks and financial institutions, insurance, stock exchange, education, transportation, communication, utilities, public media, etc. were either highly or completely restricted. Nowhere could Taiwanese small-and-medium size enterprises (SMEs) enter the businesses of even local transportation, newspapers, shipping, aviation, gas, electricity, etc.[49]

---

[47]This section is mainly based on Hsiao and Hsiao (1996), 262–268.

[48]Taiwan's postwar economic development may be divided in six stages (Hsiao and Hsiao, 1996): The Chaotic Period (August 1945–1949); The Transition Period (1950–1953); Recovery and Import Substitution Period (1953–1963); Take-off and Export Promotion Period (1964–1973); Second Import Substitution Period (1974–1980); Accelerated Growth and High-tech Industrialization Period (1980–).

[49]Chou (1992), 99. Private electric companies and factory owned private electric plants once thrived during the Japanese colonial period. See Lin (1997).

But there are important differences in the postwar period. The Japanese had exploited Taiwan's agricultural and industrial resources without Taiwanese initiative, and capital and technology were almost completely under their control.[50] Nevertheless, when the Japanese left Taiwan in 1945, they also left behind physical plants and the people who assisted them in managing and operating the plants. More importantly they left behind technical know-how, new skills, human capital, and a whole set of social and economic infrastructure. In addition to an extensive irrigation system, effective farm organizations, pervasive educational system, massive electric generating facilities, extensive transportation and communication network (Hsiao and Hsiao, 1996, 219–221), they also left behind the changes of customs and habits for modern industrial society,[51] such as appreciation of manual labor,[52] propensity

[50]Using these points the Chinese economists tend to "miniaturize" the economic and social development in Taiwan during the Japanese period, see e.g., Chang (1980), 112, 255; Chou (1958).

[51]Economists often ignore these points. Other customs and habits include the ban of foot binding for women, pig-tail hair dressing for man, cleanness, and maintenance of private and public hygiene (Wu, 1999). The last change includes "ventilation and lighting of a house, building of a lavatory inside the house, ...the habits of bathing, washing hands after relieving, a waste basket and waste disposal arrangement for every house, spittoons and garbage cans in public places, ...set a certain date for house cleanings and village cleanings, etc." See Wu (1999), 6. Also, Tsurumi (1977), 154–155. These cannot take for granted and need a vigorous enforcement. In considering modernization, Ishida (2000), 268 reports from his fieldwork in 1993 at Liaoning University, a major university in China, that "even at the Liaoning University, people spit on staircases and hallways, garbage are all over the place, the toilets are not hygienic, the smell floats in the air up to hallways and classrooms. The student dining room has few tables and chairs. Students eat rice and side dishes from one small enameled eating ware like a face-washing bowl, standing. I wonder whether this is really the place for research and education at the highest academic institute." The first author of this paper had similar experience in Beijing in the mid-1980s.

[52]The Confucian ethic of despising labor must be eradicated. As early as in 1907, in "the revised Common School Regulations, ...agriculture, commerce, and manual arts became compulsory in schools which offered them. The teaching of these subjects was designed to fight the deep-rooted repugnance literate Taiwanese felt toward manual labor" (Tsurumi, 1977, 50). In a confidential memo, the Japanese wrote that "The [upper class] Taiwanese...despised manual labor and had nothing but contempt for honest and useful occupations which required physical skill or exertion" (ibid., 51). Thus the teacher's responsibility was to "make the next generation of native leaders less prejudiced against agricultural, commercial, and manual occupations" (ibid.). Undoubtedly, this attitude toward labor and work ethics has contributed

to innovate,[53] the habit of keeping time and being on time, the concept of law and order,[54] respect for ruling by law and following instructions. In other words, the social, cultural, and psychological environments for economic take-off, despite some of them were undoubtedly coerced by the colonial government for the sake of the mother country and military purposes, were already created in the 1930s and the early 1940s. Using the modern terminology, Taiwan's "institutional reform" was completed long time before the end of WWII. The reform enabled the prewar rapid development of agriculture and industry, and also has been essential, but often ignored in the literature, to the postwar rapid economic growth.[55]

Other important differences are foreign influences and international markets. The U.S. advocacy of free market and free trade, and the U.S. influence on KMT government policies through the U.S. Aid Program, nurtured the Taiwanese small-and-medium enterprises (SMEs) (Hsiao and Hsiao, 1996, 238–239). The rapid rise of postwar Japanese capitalism ironically stimulated the Taiwanese entrepreneurs and helped the Taiwanese SMEs (ibid., 284–285). The postwar technological innovations of product-life-cycle commodities promoted Taiwanese enterprises. In terms of trading practices, however, there is an important similarity to the prewar situation. Until the early 1980s, foreigners, especially Japanese trading companies, have dominated the trading business.

tremendously to the growth of rural industry in Taiwan (Hsiao and Hsiao, 1999a, 512–513).

[53]As we have noted before (Hsiao and Hsiao, 1996, 240, Footnote 32), the ex-President T.H. Lee, then a member of Joint Committee of Rural Reconstruction (JCRR), an U.S. Aid organization, once remarked in 1959–1960 to a group of his graduate students at National Taiwan University that the Taiwanese farmers read Japanese magazines, even before the JCRR experts, to diversify and improve their farming methods. (About Japanese language in rural Taiwan, see Tsurumi, 1977, 154). This is in contrast with the report that, at the beginning of the Green Revolution (introduction of Ponlai rice) in Taiwan during the early 1920s, Japanese used police force to enforce the use of new seeds of rice among Taiwanese farmers.

[54]Tsurumi (1977), 156 gives an interesting episode: Around 1969, "a remark made... by a mainlander resident of Taiwan in his fifties: 'Those stupid Taiwanese. All they learned under the Japanese was to line up in queues.'"

[55]More elaborate and same argument can be found in Cho and Kim (1991), 6–7.

2.6.1 *Major Trading Partners*

Figures 2.5 and 2.6 are area diagrams that dramatically characterize major Taiwanese trading partners.[56] Both figures show that the United States and Japan are the two largest trading partners throughout the post-war period until the end of the 1980s. Figure 2.5 shows that Japan was the largest export market for Taiwan until 1966. Japan's share in total Taiwanese exports ranged from 60 percent in 1955 to a mere 8.4 percent in 1998. After 1967 the United States became Taiwan's largest export market. The U.S. share of total Taiwanese exports ranged from 49 percent in 1984 to 29 percent in 1992. Since 1990, Taiwanese exports to Hong Kong, as the

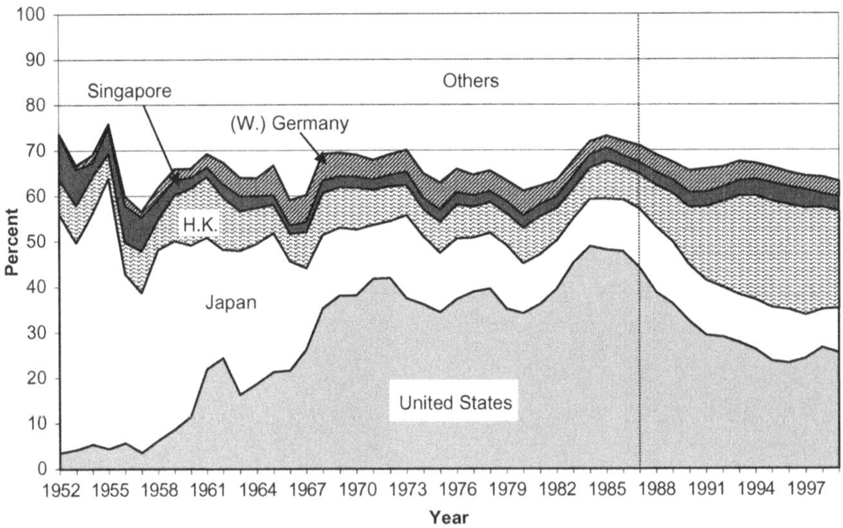

Figure 2.5: Direction of Taiwanese Exports
(Country Shares of Real Total Exports, 1986 = base year)

[56]Figures 2.5 and 2.6 are in real terms calculated from the nominal values in TSDB (1989), 210–212; (2000), 210–214, divided by the wholesale price index (WPI) in TSDB (2000), 179. The base year of the WPI published in TSDB (2000) is 1996. Thus, to compare with our previous calculation (Hsiao and Hsiao, 1996, 263–265, Figs. 8, 9, 10) we have converted the base year to 1986. The conversion to real values is important since when the dollars are exchanged in NT Dollars, we want the values of NT Dollars to have the same purchasing power over the years. Since Taiwan's WPI has been generally stable, especially in the 1990s, the general shape and trend of all figures in real values have similar shape and trend as those in nominal values.

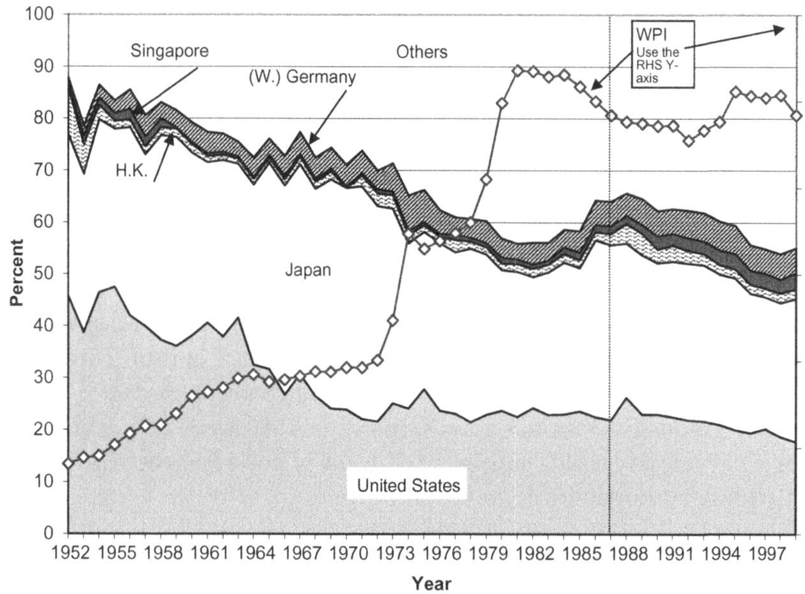

Figure 2.6: Direction of Taiwanese Imports
(Country Shares of Real Total Exports, 1986 = base year)

entrepot to China, have exceeded exports to Japan. In 1999, Hong Kong's share was 21 percent and Japan's share only 10 percent. Up to 60 percent of Taiwanese exports to Hong Kong was re-exported to China.[57] Like the United States, Taiwan has a hard time breaking into Japanese domestic markets. Despite Taiwanese efforts in attaining a diversification of trading partners, Fig. 2.5 shows that the relative export shares of Singapore, which is the entrepot to the ASEAN countries, and of West Germany, which is the gateway to Europe, and of others remain almost unchanged, although exports to these countries have accelerated since 1985 (TSDB, 2000). This means that trade with these countries has increased only at the same pace with the trade with Japan and the United States. Throughout the 1980s and the 1990s, Taiwan was one of the most active exporting counties in the world. The total exports in 1980 were about US$ 20 billion, ranking 20th

[57]Ishida (1999), 161. His data is based on *Monthly Economic Statistics of Two Sides of the Straits*, No. 71, July 1998, 19–20. However, his data on exports to and imports from Hong Kong do not match those in TSDB. Morrison and Cooper (1999), 120, even estimate up to 88 percent.

among the 133 countries listed in WDR,[58] and in 1995 were about US$ 112 billion, ranking 21st in the world.

The major importing partners, however, are just the reverse of the major exporting partners. Figure 2.6 shows that, prior to 1963, Taiwan imported primarily from the United States. Japan was busy with its economic reconstruction, and the United States was the only major partner helping Taiwan's reconstruction with the huge aid program. The roles of the United States and Japan were reversed in the mid-1960s when the U.S. economic aid program was terminated. After 1964, imports from Japan have become dominant. Japan's share in Taiwanese imports ranged from 45 percent in 1971 to 25 percent in 1982. The U.S. share in total Taiwanese imports ranged from 48 percent in 1955 to 18 percent in 1999. It has decreased gradually. Taiwan's total imports in 1980 were US$ 20 billion, ranking 21st in the world, and in 1995, total imports increased to about US$ 104 billion, ranking 15th in the world.[59]

Through the postwar era, imports from the United States and Japan alone ranged from 45 percent (1998) to 80 percent (1954) of total Taiwanese imports, while exports to these countries also ranged from 34 percent (1997) to 64 percent (1955). Here lies the dependency criticism of Taiwanese economic development.[60] Both Japan and the United States constantly played very important roles.

2.6.2 *Taiwan, Japan, and the United States Nexus*

Figure 2.7 dramatizes Taiwan's trade relationship with the United States and Japan.[61] The trade volume and the deficits with both countries from 1952 to 1974 becomes invisible when the scale is in billions of dollars. Thus we have plotted the data from 1952 to 1965 in the units of US$ 10 million (the left panel), and from 1966 to 1975 in the units of US$ 100 million (the middle panel), and after 1975, in the units of US$ billion dollars

[58] The calculation is based on WDR (1997), 242, and TSDB (2000), 210.

[59] Same as footnote above.

[60] However, Taiwan is not unique, and nothing to be alarmed, in one-sided trade relation with other countries. Even in 1998, 31 percent of the Japanese exports and 24 percent of Japanese imports were to and from the United States, while the corresponding figures for Taiwan were only 27 percent and 19 percent, and, for Korea were 17 percent and 22 percent, respectively. See EPA (2000), 314, 320.

[61] Calculation of Fig. 2.7 is the same as Figs. 2.5 and 2.6. Balance of trade (BOT) is commodity exports X (in heavy solid line) minus commodity imports M (in lighter solid line) in Fig. 2.7.

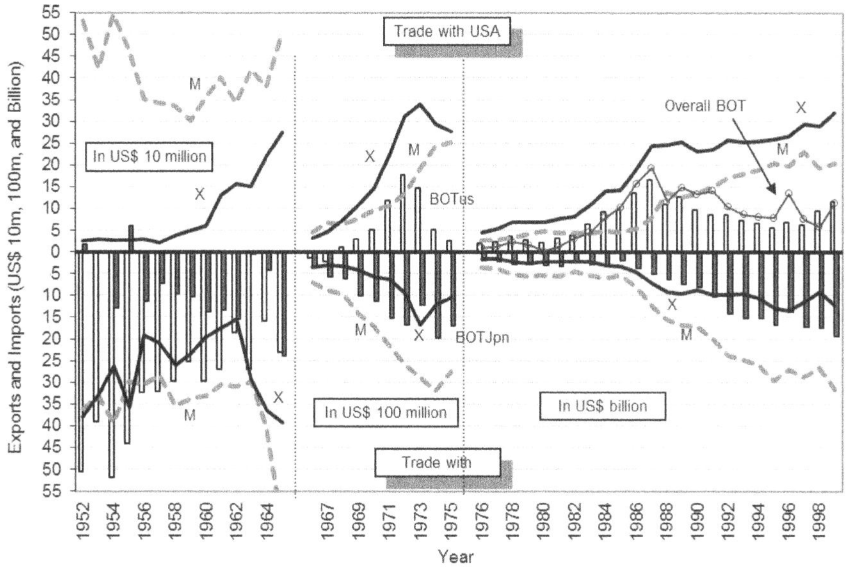

Figure 2.7: The Structure of the Pacific Trade Triangle
Real Exports, Imports, and Balance of Trade

(the right panel). As shown in the lower part of the diagram, from 1952 to 1999, Taiwan's real imports from Japan (M in the lower part) are consistently higher than Taiwan's real exports to Japan (X in the lower part). This means Taiwan consistently had a negative balance of trade with Japan since 1953 (except 1955). The dark solid bars in the lower part show this.

The situation is quite different with the United States. Before 1967, Taiwan also had trade deficits with the United States every year. After 1968, however, Taiwan's real imports from the United States (M in the upper part) have been consistently lower than its real exports to the United States (X in the upper part), bringing about real trade surpluses. The empty bars in the upper part of the figure show this.

After 1968, both deficits with Japan and surpluses with the United States have increased over time with the progress of Taiwan's industrialization. In Fig. 2.7, this is illustrated as an explosion to the two sides of the horizontal axis like a broom. After 1988, exports to the United States slowed down under the watchful eyes of the U.S. government under the Omnibus Trade Competitiveness Act passed in the U.S. Congress in 1988 (Hsiao and Hsiao, 1995). At the same time, imports from the United States increased considerably, narrowing down the bilateral trade surpluses. With devaluation of the U.S. dollar and upward revaluation of the Japanese yen, Taiwanese exports to Japan jumped up greatly between 1985 and 1988 but ran out of steam and flattened out afterward. Real commodity imports from Japan, however, continued to accelerate, indicating that the more Taiwan tries to increase its exports, whether to the United States or other countries, the more Taiwan has to rely on imports of materials and capital equipment from Japan. Despite almost desperate efforts by the KMT government,[62] Taiwan simply cannot elude its dependency on Japan!

Real trade surpluses with the United States peaked at US$ 17 billion in 1987 and then started to decline, while trade deficits with Japan continued to increase, although with a slower pace. The deficits with Japan reached an all-time high at US$ 19.3 billion (at the 1986 price) in 1999. However, Taiwan still has managed to achieve a huge surplus in its overall real balance of trade every year since 1976. For example, Taiwan had an overall surplus of US$ 11.3 billion in 1999. Figure 2.7 shows that Taiwan's real balance of trade, shown as the marked line with circles, tends to move closely with the real trade surpluses with the United States, implying that the latter are the main source of Taiwan's trade surplus.

2.6.3 *A Pacific Trade Triangle*

From the above discussions, we may derive several characteristics of the Taiwanese economy in the postwar period:

(a) Taiwanese trade relies very heavily on the United States and Japan. Taiwan relies more on the U.S. markets for exports, and on Japan for imports.
(b) In the 1980s, Taiwanese trade with both the United States and Japan bloomed significantly. Its increase in exports to the United States was paralleled by the increase in imports from Japan and, to a lesser degree, from the United States.
(c) After 1968, Taiwan has persistently had real trade surpluses with the United States and trade deficits with Japan, although the overall

[62]The following episode is illuminating. In February 1982, to reduce US$ 3.2 billion trade deficits with Japan, Taiwan surprised the world by unilaterally banning imports from Japan more than 1,500 commodities for an indefinite time, and heavy trucks and diesel engines for one year. Tokyo threatened to cancel Taiwan's preferential tariff and trade status. The ban inflicted serious damage to Taiwanese exports and its national economy. As Tokyo also could not wage a trade war simultaneously with the U.S. and the EEC, both sides reached a compromise and the ban on half of the goods were lifted by November that year. For details, see Arnold (1985), 194–196; Aoki (1985), 157.

trade balance with all traded partners is consistently positive since 1976. Despite many serious attempts to reverse the trade deficits with Japan,[63] the Taiwan government has never succeeded. Figure 2.7 illustrates this point. In real terms, the deficits with Japan have worsened greatly in recent years after the Taiwan government has emphasized the development of high-tech industries in the late 1980s.

(d) From Fig. 2.7, the following trade patterns emerge. Taiwan imports intermediate goods and raw materials mainly from Japan[64] and exports manufactured goods mainly to the United States. These triangular relations among Taiwan, Japan, and the United States are the backbone of the rapid growth of the Taiwanese economy.

Elsewhere (Hsiao and Hsiao, 1996, 258–262) we have shown that textile products in the 1960s and the 1970s, as well as machinery products and electrical products in the 1980s and in the 1990s, were the leading export items. Taiwan's industrialization also centered on these three leading commodities. There has been a huge expansion of exports in machinery products and electric equipment. Exports to the United States and imports from Japan are especially dramatic. A less dramatic increases in exports can also be observed for basic metals and articles, and Chemicals. The machinery products and electric equipment are significant in both exports and imports in the 1980s and the 1990s.

2.6.4 *On Sustained Growth*

Many economists contend that Taiwan was fortunate (meaning the government was wise enough) to adopt export-promotion policy in the mid-1960s, which pushed the economy to rapid growth. However, as we have shown in the Appendix, the export promotion policy itself does not ensure rapid growth. With risk of some repetitions, here is the answer to the important question how Taiwan's outward oriented strategy has been sustained. It is due to special geographical and historical circumstances.

(a) Taiwan was already an export-oriented country under the Japanese regime. The Taiwanese were very much accustomed to the notion of

[63]See reports by Shi and Li (1978); Liu and Jian (1983). In addition to the desire to be independent of Japan, anti-Japanese feeling of the Chinese officials also played in these attempts.

[64]Since Taiwan has perpetual trade deficits with Japan, the Taiwan government discourages importing consumer goods from Japan.

"production for exports" for living and profits. As soon as the Taiwanese economy recovered from war damages and the society recuperated from the terror[65] of the February 1947 Incident, Taiwan started exporting traditional agricultural products like sugar, rice, bananas, tea, and canned foods to Japan. When the KMT government started its export-promotion policy in the mid-1960s, the Taiwanese already had more than two generations of successful experience with exports as a modern business practice.

(b) In the early 1960s, textile products, lumber and timber products, plywood, electrical and machinery apparatus, chemicals, and basic metals were added to rice, sugar, and bananas for exports (TSDB, 1975, 190–191). The postwar rapid economic development is the continuation of the prewar agricultural and industrial development, which was interrupted by WWII and China's civil war (Hsiao and Hsiao, 1998; ibid., 2000). Much to the dismay of the Chinese bureaucrats in Taiwan (Shi and Li, 1978), the historical tie between Taiwan and Japan persisted and strengthened in the postwar era: First Japan as the number one export market for Taiwan, then as the number one country from which Taiwan imports intermediate goods and capital goods.

(c) One of the major hurdles of an export business is international marketing. A country may produce goods, but may not find a market in which to sell the products. We have seen that, except during the last part of the Ch'ing rule of Taiwan, Europeans and Japanese conducted most of the foreign trade. After WWII, even during the 1970s and the 1980s when the KMT government encouraged the establishment of local "large trading companies," 60 percent of total exports was handled by either foreign-owned, or foreign-and-Taiwanese-jointly-owned, trading companies. Furthermore, the majority of these foreigners were Japanese. The remaining exports were divided almost evenly: 20 percent by the manufacturers and traders and the government-owned Central Trust, and 20 percent by 36,000 Taiwanese small trading companies (Yajima, 1986, 107). It was also estimated in 1981 that the Japanese Shoshas[66] alone, directly or indirectly, handled 40 percent to 50 percent of Taiwanese foreign trade (Liu, 1996, 145). Another

[65] See for the effects of the 2–28 incidents, see Hsiao (1992); Lai *et al.* (1991); Hsiao and Hsiao (1996), 223–224.

[66] In addition to marketing, Sogo Shosha also helps in financing, foreign exchanges, organizing, and consulting (Steven, 1990, 70). There seems no study of their actual operations in Taiwan.

government survey in 1984 showed that 75 percent of total exports (in terms of value) was controlled by foreign businesses. Most of them were Japanese companies (ibid.). Through Japanese joint ventures and trading companies, Taiwanese firms were able to solve most of their marketing problems. The reason is simple. In addition to geographical proximity and historical ties in the early postwar period, many older Taiwanese entrepreneurs spoke and read Japanese. Japanese customs and habits were not completely alien to them. This undoubtedly removed major hurdles[67] of technological transfer and facilitated the trade between Taiwan and Japan after the war.[68]

This venue of marketing through foreign companies also proved successful for conducting trade with the United States and other countries. In 1973, Taiwan replaced Japan in the U.S. shoe market, and in 1976, Taiwan replaced Italy to become the world's largest exporter of shoes. By 1980, shoe manufacturing was Taiwan's third largest exporting industry, following only textiles and electronics (Skoggard, 1996, 55–56). However, ten or so foreign branch offices or agencies handles two-thirds of the shoe export business (Liu, 1996, 130).

(d) In a recent paper, Coe, Helpman, and Hoffmaister (1995) have shown that opening trade with industrial countries is effective in increasing the total factor productivity (TFP) of a developing countries. They also found that which country is selected is also important. "A developing country whose trade is more biased towards industrial countries that have large cumulative experiences in R&D has higher productivity." And among the developed countries, "The United States has by far the largest domestic capital stock,..., about five times as high as Japan, which is the country with the second largest effect." Thus, by historical coincidence and geographical proximity, as shown in Fig. 2.1, both Korea and Taiwan are indeed very fortunate to be associated with the

[67] According to a survey, barriers to exporting are cultural, language difference, special customs requirements, market information (particular markets, availability, usefulness, and awareness), product design and specification requirements, government policy, etc. (Brooks and Frances, 1991, 102).

[68] A Taiwanese president, age 46, of a sewing machine company stated that "About forty years ago, Singer set up an affiliate in Taichung. This firm encouraged and helped the local people to build factories to produce sewing-machine parts. In 1972, I started to run this business... Techniques from Japan and a bunch of brave young people are what made Taichung the sewing-machine capital of Taiwan. Although our technology... originated in Japan, we're now totally independent of it, thanks to our own R&D." Interview by Hwang *et al.* (1998), 30.

United States and Japan as their major trading partners, and as we have seen above, Taiwan's trade with both countries has been about 50 percent of total trade since 1952.

Factors other than the pacific trade triangle, such as availability of cheap labor, the rise of multinational companies, and international division of labor, the Vietnam War, long prosperity and growth in the world economy, especially in Japan and in the United States, and advocacy and encouragement of free trade and free markets by the world organizations like International Monetary Fund and the World Bank, government macroeconomic policy and planning, all helped make Taiwan's drive to export a great success. However, we consider that these amenities were of secondary importance since they were also available to all other countries. Thus, we submit that the outward-looking propensity of the Taiwanese people and the Chinese bureaucrats in Taiwan, along with the triangle relationship with Japan and the United States, spurred by the decreasing value of the New Taiwan dollar against the U.S. dollar, have sustained the outward-looking strategy of Taiwan, and made it a success even until today.

2.7 Direct Foreign Investment and Economic Growth

Japan and the United States are not only Taiwan's most important trading partners, but also their manufacturers also invested directly and heavily in Taiwan, supplementing Taiwan's domestic investment at the beginning of its industrialization and throughout the postwar period.

2.7.1 *An Overview of Inward DFI in Taiwan*

In the early 1950s,[69] when the newly independent former colonies, and semi-colonies such as China, were still recovering from the horror of exploitation and imperialism,[70] Taiwan was probably the only country in the world that invited much-suspected direct foreign investment (DFI) with open arms.[71] Seeing Taiwan's success, Korea followed suit, along with other developing countries, China and the ASEANs in the 1980s.

[69]This subsection is partly based on Hsiao and Hsiao (1996), 269–272.
[70]China's unequal treaties ended only in 1943, and Chiang Kai-shek published *China's Destiny* "to show the harm they had done to China" (Fairbank, 1967, 62).
[71]We reasoned that this was because the émigré regime of the Republic of China on Taiwan had no roots in Taiwan and wanted to break its isolationism internationally and domestically.

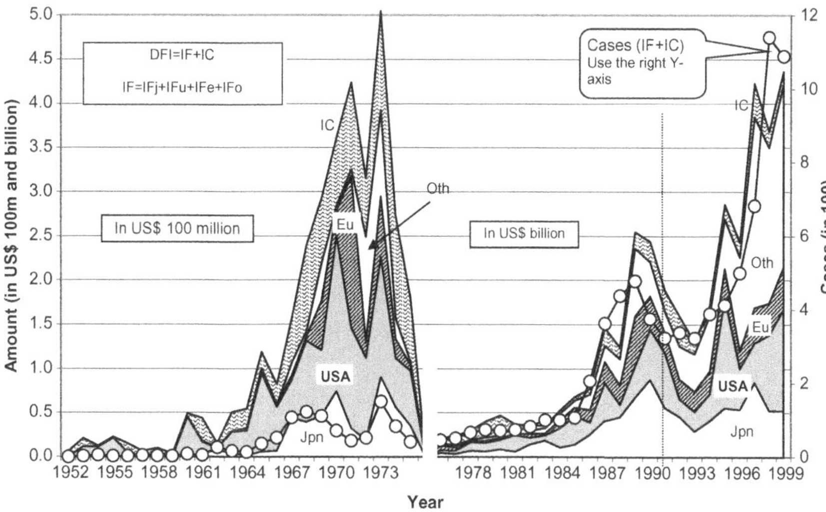

Figure 2.8: Real Direct Foreign Investment in Taiwan Cases and Amount Approved

Figure 2.8 shows the increase of the approved amount of DFI in Taiwan from 1952 to 1999. As in the case of trade statistics, we have converted the data into real terms,[72] using the 1986 wholesale price index as the base. Overseas Chinese investment (IC) is shown in the upper wave pattern in Fig. 2.8. The rest of the chart shows the (non-overseas Chinese) foreign investment (IF), consisting of investment from Japan (white area), the United States (grey area), Europe (dark upward diagonal area) and other countries (white area) (IF = IFj + IFu +IFe + IFo). IC consists of investment from those overseas Chinese mostly residing in Hong Kong and Japan. Before 1965, IC was an important source of DFI. However, the weight of IC in total DFI decreased after 1965, taken over by IF from the U.S.A. After 1982, IC's weight in total DFI decreased drastically, and became negligible after mid-1980s. IF from the U.S.A. started in 1953, and was superseded by investment from Japan most of the time after 1982 until 1995. In any case, as with trade relations, Japanese and American investments have dominated DFI in Taiwan from 1966 to 1995. While investment from Europe is also increasing, after 1995 "other sources" of foreign investment have exceeded all others.

[72]That is, all data are divided by Taiwan's WPI with 1986's wholesale price being taken as 100 (TSDB, 2000, 179, 258, 260).

The main areas in the "other sources" category are British territories in Central America,[73] which include Virgin Island, Bermuda, Belize, and British West Indies. The diagram shows two facts which indicate the resilience of Taiwan in the global economy: the two oil shocks in 1973–74 and 1979–80 eventually spurred, rather than depressed, DFI, and that Taiwan still can attract and even increase continuously the American and Japanese investments despite strong competition from China and elsewhere in recent years. In fact, as shown in Fig. 2.8, the record amount of DFI (IF+IC) was reached just recently in 1999 at US$ 4.23 billion in real value with 1,089 cases.[74] The Taiwanese economy has never been so strong.

Altogether, from 1952 to 1999, 11,111 cases (shown by the solid line with circles in Fig. 2.8) with the amount of US$ 37 billion (in nominal values[75]) of DFI were approved for IF and IC. Among IF, Japan is the largest contributor with 3,230 cases (US$ 8.3 billion, same below), followed closely by the U.S.A., accounting for 1,694 cases (8.7b), Europe, for 928 cases (4.1b). Other countries were responsible for 2,562 cases (12b). The bulk of FDI has occurred only recently (TSDB, 2000, 260).

In general, from 1952 to 1999, 26 percent of Taiwan's DFI has been in electronic and electric products, totaling US$ 9.4 billion in 1,544 cases. This is followed by other products, 13 percent, US$ 4.8 billion in 1,927 cases; banking and insurance, 13 percent, US$ 4.6 billion in 502 cases. None or very few DFI were in agriculture, fisheries and livestock, paper and paper products and construction (TSDB, 2000, 261). Among the foreign investment (IF), the lion's share goes to electronic and electric products (US$9.2 billion/1,339 cases, same below), followed by chemicals (3.7b/470 cases), services (3.2b/1,229 cases), foreign trade (2.5b/1,754 cases), and machinery, equipment and instrument (1.6b/431 cases) (ibid.). Indeed, through forward and backward linkages, foreign capital has helped build Taiwan as the kingdom of electronics and computer,[76]

[73]Investment Commission (2000), April. We suspect that these so called DFI may be Chinese (mainland) capital registered in Central America, and pose a grave security problem for Taiwan.
[74]In terms of nominal values, the maximum amount was reached two years earlier, in 1997, at US$ 4.27 billion (TSDB, 2000, 258).
[75]In real value of 1986 price, the total amount of FDI comes to US$ 40 billion.
[76]We have examined the effect of DFI on technology transfer, DFI and Taiwan's television industry in Hsiao and Hsiao (1996), 273–276, and Hsiao, M. (1992).

and had a significant positive effect on the real growth of Taiwan's GDP.[77]

2.7.2 *The Active Role of Taiwanese in the Global Economy — Outward Direct Foreign Investment*

As the Taiwanese economy matures, it has started investment in foreign countries. The spurt of outward investment occurred after the mid-1980s, mainly due to dollar depreciation against the New Taiwan dollar and yen, rising wage rates and labor shortage in Taiwan, and the lifting of martial law[78] in 1987 that was followed by acceleration of economic and political liberalization, which in turn invigorated environment protection activities and labor movements. Like Figs. 2.6 to 2.8, Fig. 2.9 shows Taiwanese outward investment in real values (1986 = base year) by area: American (grey area), Asian (white area), European and other regions (black area).

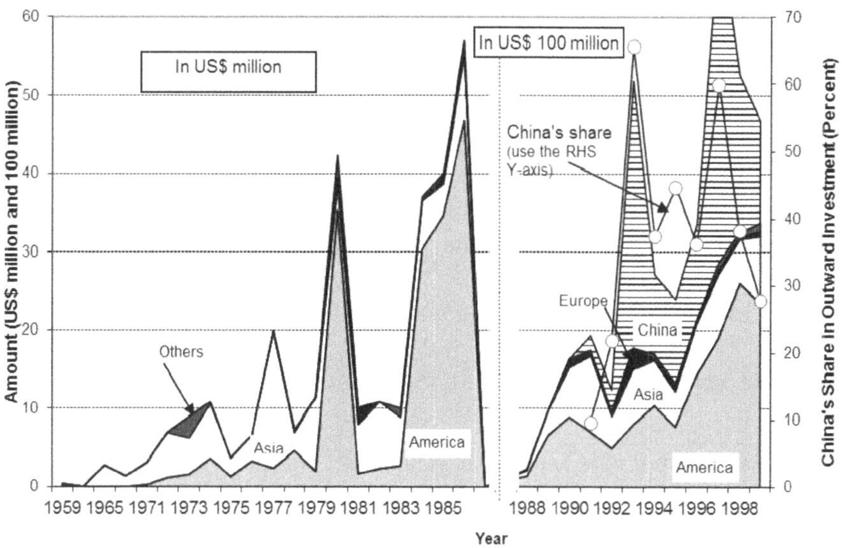

Figure 2.9: Taiwanese Outward Investment In Real Value (1986 = Base Year)

[77]In a previous paper (Hsiao, M., 1992, 151), it is shown that, using the 1967 to 1987 data set, when the real growth rate of DFI increases by 1 percent, it may generate a 0.11 percent increase in the growth rate of Taiwan's GDP.

[78]For the acceleration of economic and political liberalization after the lifting of martial law in 1987, see Hsiao and Hsiao (2001).

We also added Taiwan's investment in China (dark upward diagonal area), which will be explained in detail in the following section. Taiwan's outward investment (not including China, same below in this section) was rather irregular and small before 1987, and increased steadily and sharply from a mere US$ 0.1 billion with 45 cases in 1987 to US$ 3.4 billion with 774 cases in 1999, an amount that was the maximum yearly investment in real value (US$ 3.3 billion in nominal value). In 1999, Taiwan's outward investment (not including China) was about 80 percent of its inward direct foreign investment that year.[79]

In fact, Taiwan's outward investment practically started[80] only in 1965, and from 1952 to 1999, total outward investment amounted to US$ 21.9 billion in nominal value[81] with 5,426 cases (TSDB, 2000, 262). According to the Investment Committee (2000) report, two-thirds of total outward investment went to the American region (63%), followed by Asia (32%) and Europe (3.3%, mostly in Germany). Oceania (in Australia) and Africa (Liberia and South Africa) consisted of only 1.6 percent. As high as one-third (32%) of the total outward investment went to British Territories in Central America (US$6.9b/690 cases), followed by the United States (21%, 4.6b/2,075 cases), Malaysia (6.4%, 1.4b/239 cases), Singapore (5.4%, 1.2b/276 cases), and Hong Kong (4.9%, 1.1b/528 cases). We suspect that most of the larger Taiwanese investment in British territories transferred to China.[82] Investment in Japan is very disappointing, consisting of only 1.4 percent (0.4b/195 cases) of the total. Like exports to Japan, Japanese markets are very hard to break.

By industrial categories, 37 percent of Taiwanese outward investment goes to banking and insurance (8.1b/830 cases), followed by electronic and electric products (17%, 3.7b/1,484 cases), others (8%, 1.7b/712 cases),

---

[79]However, according to Se and Asamoto (1999), 175, if outward investment is measure from balanced of payment statistics instead of the approval base, outward investment already exceeded inward foreign investment every year since 1988. For the relation between inward and outward investment using Investment-Development Path analysis for Taiwan, see Van Hoesel (1996) and Se and Asamoto (1999).

[80]The total outward investment for 1952 to 1999 was US$ 21,879 million (TSDB, 2000, 262), and that for 1965 to 1999 was US$ 21,872 million, a difference of about US$ 7 million, which account for the outward investment from 1952 to 1964.

[81]In real value, it is US$ 22.4 billion. The difference is almost negligible.

[82]According to the "Principal Statistics of Approved Direct Mainland Investment via Third Countries," the total investment in China from 1991 to 1999 is US$ 14.5 billion, 22,134 cases (TSDB, 2000, 264). The difference in the number of cases seems to indicate that, for political and security reasons, most of Taiwan's private large investment go through the third countries in British Territories or Hong Kong (Ishida, 1999, 169).

foreign trade (7%, 1.6b/881 cases), and chemicals (6.1%, 1.3b/211 cases). "Electronic and electric products" was the largest item (26%) of inward direct foreign investment. It appears that the electronic and electric product industry has a dual structure in Taiwan: The high profit margin and high-end part of the industry stay in Taiwan, and the more labor intensive part of the industry moves out to China via British Territories, also to Malaysia, Singapore, and Hong Kong, circumventing the increase in wages in Taiwan.

2.7.3 *Trade and Investment in China*

As shown in Fig. 2.2g, the enmity between Taiwan and China separated both countries from 1949 to 1987, when the 38-year long martial law was lifted. While China started attracting trade and investment from Taiwan after its implementation of the reform program in 1979, the Taiwanese government lifted its strict restriction on travel to China only in 1987 (see the gap in Fig. 2.9). In 1988 Taiwan granted indirect imports of some 50 Chinese agricultural and industrial raw materials through third countries, and only after 1990 indirect exports and indirect investment were permitted.[83] Indirect contact with China made official statistical data hard to collect.[84]

The columns of the left-hand-side panel of Fig. 2.10 show Taiwanese data[85] on exports to China (X_t/2, the upward patterned columns) and imports from China (Mt/2, the empty columns), both figures are divided by 2 so that all the data may be presented in one diagram. The lines show the Chinese data on Taiwanese exports to China (X_c, the dotted line) and Taiwanese imports from China (M_c, lower solid line) for 1980 and 1990 to 1995. The Chinese data consistently underestimate export figures by more than 50 percent as compared with those of Taiwan, but the import estimates are almost 50 percent of that of Taiwan. In any case, both data show a very rapid increase in Taiwanese exports to China and a very slow

[83]Ishida (1999), 139–140, and Morrison and Cooper (1999). Yu (1996) divides the trade and investment relationship between Taiwan and China in four periods, the frozen period (1949–1978), the defrosting period (1979–1987), the warming-up period (1988–1995), and period after 1996. The Chinese data in Morrison and Cooper are based on those "supplied by the Chinese Embassy, Washington, D.C." and the Taiwanese data are from "Taiwan Ministry of Economic Affairs." We have tried to identify the data from published sources.
[84]There are some discrepancies in trade data and we are unable to make more useful analysis.
[85]Morrison and Cooper (1999), 123; Ishida (1999), 157. Ishida is based on *Monthly Economic Statistics of the Two Sides of Strait*, No. 71, July 1998. Morrison and Cooper's data, 1990–1995, are the same as Ishida.

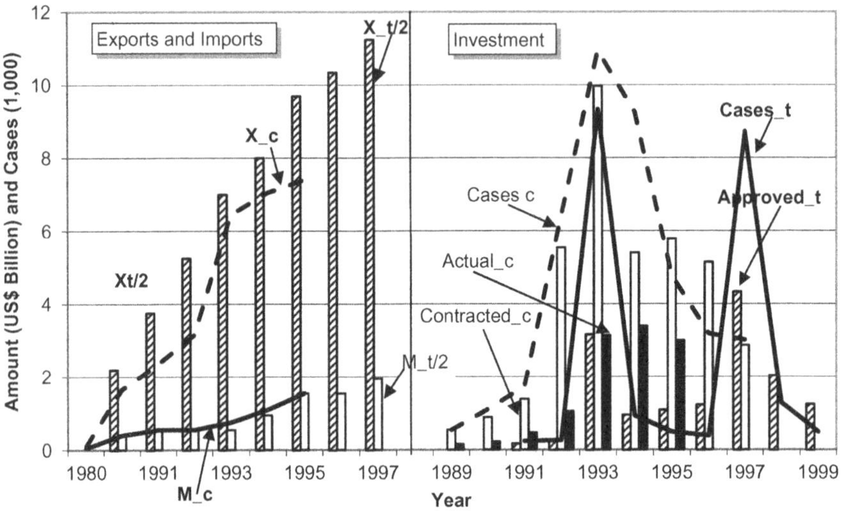

Figure 2.10: Taiwanese Trade and Investment in China
Comparison of Taiwanese (t) and Chinese (c) data (In Nominal Values)

increase in imports from China, resulting in a large trade surplus for Taiwan every year since 1981: The trade surplus in 1997 was US$ 18.5 billion, more than enough to offset Taiwan's total trade deficits of US$ 17.3 billion that year (TSDB, 2000, 210). Most of the items exported from Taiwan to China were fur and its products, pulp and papers, textiles, printings, chemicals and their products, etc. (Yu, 1996).

The right-hand-side panel of Fig. 2.10 presents Taiwan's investment in China. The solid line (Cases_t) and the upward patterned column (Approved_t) on the left side of the three-columns group show Taiwan's data on approved investment to China in nominal value.[86] We also show the approved investment in real value on the right-hand side of Fig. 2.10. The rather irregular trend of investment in China probably reflects the unpredictable political relation between the two countries, and the large bumps in both the amount approved and the cases in 1993 and 1997 are the results of passing two new laws in Taiwan that set the deadline for Taiwanese firms to register their China investment or face fines (Morrison and Cooper, 1999, 125; Ishida, 1999, 158).

[86] Morrison and Cooper (1999), 125, listed up to 1995. We extended the data to 1997 by TSDB (2000), 264. Both data are also the same as Ishida's (1999), 158, which is taken from Monthly Economic Statistics of Both Sides of Strait, ibid.

Aside from these two years, Fig. 2.9 also indicates that Taiwanese investment in China has been not only increasing alarmingly, but also becoming so large that it consists of almost one-third to more than one-half of the Taiwan's total outward investment in recent years (see the circled line in the right-hand-side panel, which is measured on the right Y-axis). In fact, the outward investment to China from 1991 to 1999, the period for which Taiwan government has data, consist of 44 percent of total outward investment from 1991 to 1999. It is more alarming in terms of cases: the approved cases (not shown in the charts) for investment in China from 1991 to 1999 is whopping 83 percent of the accumulated cases, which was 26,687 cases. More and more small-and-medium sized enterprises in Taiwan are investing in China, and there is a sign that larger enterprises are following suit. Most of the projects went to South China, in the categories of electronic and electric appliances, food and beverage processing, basic metals and metal products, and plastic products, etc. (TSDB, 2000, 264–265). It all started from low-end labor-intensive industries. However, in recent years, more and more capital intensive and high technology industries also move to China. For national security reasons, the Taiwan government has tried to limit and regulate China investment and to promote the "Southward Policy," that is, to invest in Southeast Asia.[87] Even so, in 1999, investment in China still amounted to 28 percent (US$ 1.3 billion, 499 cases) of the total outward investment that year.

To show the discrepancies in collecting the data, we also illustrate the Chinese data[88] on Taiwanese investment in China (the right-hand side of Fig. 2.10). The middle empty columns (Contracted_c) show the contracted investment, which is far larger than the actual investment (Actual_c in filled dark columns), indicating the potential problem of using "approved" investment statistics of Taiwan. The dotted line (Cases_c) shows the Chinese data on the (contracted?) cases. The Chinese data may be 1.2 times (1993) to 24 times (1992) greater than the Taiwanese data.[89] It is

[87]Indeed, history repeats for Taiwan. The problem with Taiwan today is that it has no institutes like Research Institute of People and Culture of the South (Nanpo Jinbun Kenkyujo), which belonged directly to the Governor-General of Taiwan to study Southeast Asia during the Japanese period.

[88]Morrison and Cooper (1999), 124; Ishida (1999), 158. Both data sets are consistent.

[89]The Taiwanese data tend to understate as firms may be reluctant to register to avoid government control, and the Chinese data tend to overstate as some foreign firms may register under a Taiwanese name to take advantage of the preferential treatment afforded to the Taiwanese firms in China. Morrison and Cooper (1999), 120.

not clear why the Chinese data also have a large bump in 1993, as the new Taiwanese laws should not affect Chinese statistics. This may cast the reliability problem of Chinese data.

2.8 Taiwan and the Global Economy in the 21st Century

During the past 100 years, the Taiwanese economy has followed the classical case of development: It developed from the traditional feudal society to modern agricultural development. It went through the typical stages of exports of agricultural and processed goods, and then industrial development through the phases of import substitution, export promotion, and high-tech industrialization.

One of the popular views about Taiwanese economic development is that it started after the war "from a state of extreme poverty and political and social backwardness" (Lai *et al.*, 1991, 1), implying that Taiwan's economic success is a case of the "rags to riches" dream in less than forty years. Even a chapter of a book is devoted to this title and theme (Chan and Clark, 1992). Similar views are abundant among many economists. However, according to Maddison's data (1995), the real GDP per capita of Taiwan measured in 1990 Geary-Khamis dollars reached the prewar highest level of $1,522 in 1942, and then plummeted to $693 in 1944, a year before the end of WWII. According to Maddison's data, the figure in 1944 was well below[90] the real GDP per capita in 1904 and 1905 ($712). The change can be perceived roughly from Fig. 2.11, which shows the ten-year moving average of real GDP per capita in 1990 Geary-Khamis dollars for Taiwan, South Korea, and some OECD countries in the logarithmic scale. Apparently, here are the "rags," as the Taiwanese standard of living plunged below its 1904 level! Even in 1952, the real GDP per capita ($1,020) is only comparable to that of 1924 ($1,034). The early postwar poverty, slow recovery, and the deprivation of the Taiwanese were the results of the civil war in China carrying over by the Chinese to Taiwan. It is not a consequence of colonialism. It was a temporary setback for the long-run

[90]Wu (1991) presents the real GDP per capita in New Taiwan dollars from 1920 to 1971, as measured in 1937 prices (Wu, 1991). It increased from NT$ 142 in 1920 to NT$ 213 in 1931, and reached the prewar maximum of NT$ 225 in 1939. It then started decreasing and plummeted to a mere NT$ 45 in 1945. The recovery was very slow. Wu's data also show that until the mid-1950s, it dipped even below the 1920 level. It recovered to a mere 56 percent of the prewar level in 1952, still way below the 1920 level.

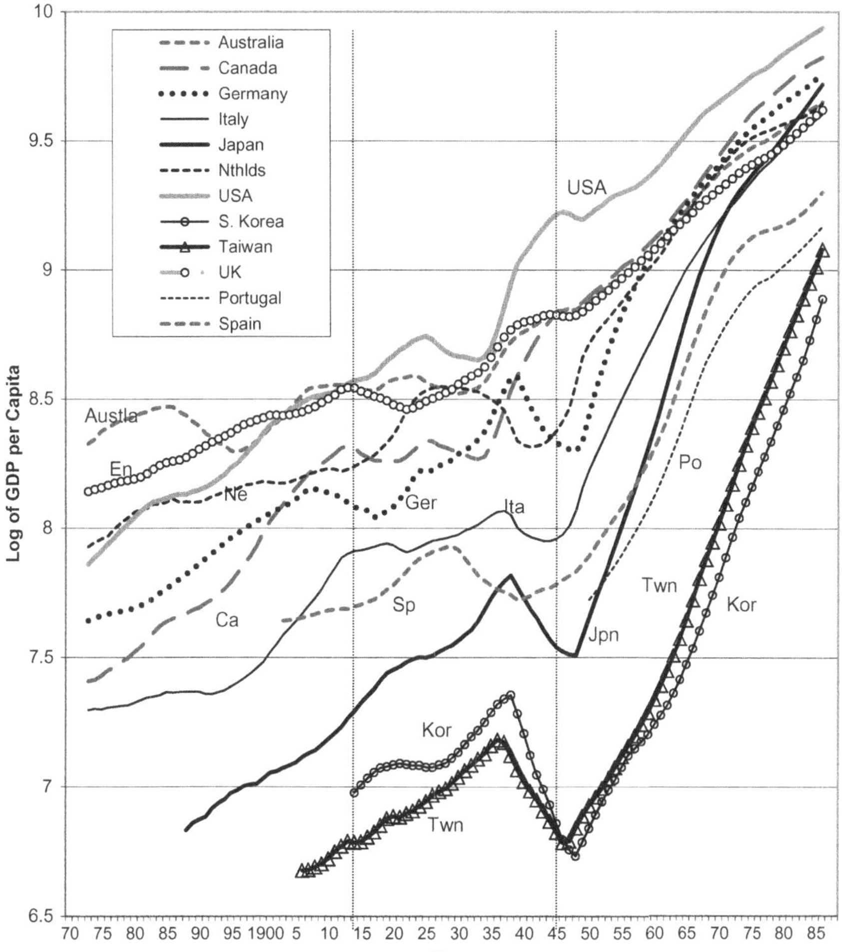

Figure 2.11: Real GDP per capita of Taiwan, Korea, and Some OECD Countries (Ten-Year Moving Average).

economic development,[91] which started in 1895 up to the early 1940s, and was interrupted for more than two decades and then continued only after the mid-1960s.

As we have elaborated in this paper and elsewhere, it is simply unreasonable, if not wrong, to ignore prewar development and consider

[91]Using the Perron tests of time-series analysis, we have shown that the plunge of GDP per capita in 1944 was indeed temporary (Hsiao and Hsiao, 1999b).

only the "miracle" of postwar Taiwanese economic development. In fact, according to the same Maddison's data, Taiwanese real GDP per capita growth rate (1.97%) ranked 3rd or 4th in the world during the prewar period, following Japan (2.64%) and Korea (2.03%), and almost tied with that of Norway (1.98%), as can be seen from the slope of the curves in Fig. 2.11. By the early 1940s, its real GDP per capita level was higher than other Asian countries, except Japan[92] and Korea. In fact, the "Taiwan miracle" already started in the prewar period (Hsiao and Hsiao, 2000b). Due to an influx of the Chinese refugees, government mismanagement of the economy, and wartime mobilization to fight against the Chinese communists, the Taiwanese real GDP per capita recovered to the prewar peak only in 1963 (at US$1,612).[93]

After the transition period, the economy took off to steady growth in the mid-1960s. It grew faster than any country in Asia including Japan, and even faster (the lines are steeper) than all of the advanced countries in the postwar period (Hsiao and Hsiao, 2001; 2000). Although, compared with Japan, its real GDP per capita decreased after the war until 1970, Taiwan started to catch up with Japan after 1970 (ibid.). In terms of real GDP per capita, as shown in Fig. 2.11, Australia and Canada, some of the former British colonies, already caught up with the United Kingdom by 1990. Likewise, by 1990, in terms of nominal GNP per capita, Taiwan came very close to Spain and Portugal, its former colonial powers. Eventually, Taiwan (at US$ 12,333, TSDB, 2000, 332) surpassed Portugal (US$ 10,690) and came very close to Spain (US$14,080) in 1998 (World Bank, 2000, 231). If Taiwan continues its current track of progress, it is not inconceivable that Taiwan may even surpass the Netherlands and Japan.[94]

2.8.1 *Competitiveness Indexes*

After the 1997–1999 Asian financial crisis, we are reasonably optimistic about the future of Taiwan. Figures 2.12 and 2.13 show its international competitiveness in global economy as evaluated by two international

[92]This is corroborated by actual observations at that time. In a report to the United States Congress, Conlon Associates (1959), 139 wrote that "Taiwan did not enter the post war era without advantages. Progress under Japan had been extensive. Prior to World War II, the Taiwanese had a standard of living second only to that of Japan itself in Asian. The people had acquired many industrial and agrarian skills. The years immediately after 1945, however, were years of chaos...."

[93]For the early postwar economic conditions of Taiwan, see Hsiao and Hsiao (1998).

[94]We have discussed this in Hsiao and Hsiao (1998, 1999b).

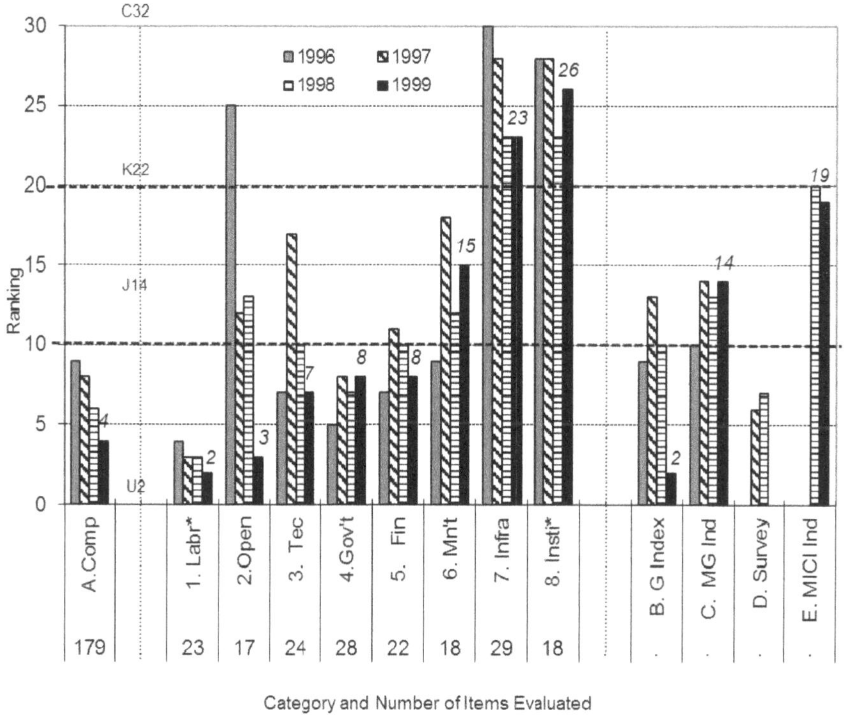

Figure 2.12: Taiwan's Competitiveness in the Global Economy WEF Data, 1996–1999

organizations: the World Economic Forum (WEF) and the International Institute for Management Development (IMD). WEF defines national competitiveness as the capability of maintaining high economic growth rate of a nation for the coming five to ten years. As shown in the lower row of the X-axis of Fig. 2.12, it consists of 179 variables (in 1998), which are classified into eight categories. They are then weighted to derive the national competitiveness index and ranking (Chang, 1998). In 1999, WEF evaluated 59 major trading countries. Taiwan ranked 4th, superseded only by Singapore, United States, and Hong Kong. Figure 2.12 also shows that Japan ranked 14th, Korea, 22nd, and China, 32nd, out of 59 countries (WEF, 1999, 11). The four columns in each category show the ranking of each index from 1996 (the grey column) to 1999 (the wide downward diagonal filled column). Taiwan's competitiveness ranking has been improving consistently since 1996 (from 9th, to 8th, to 6th, and to 4th).

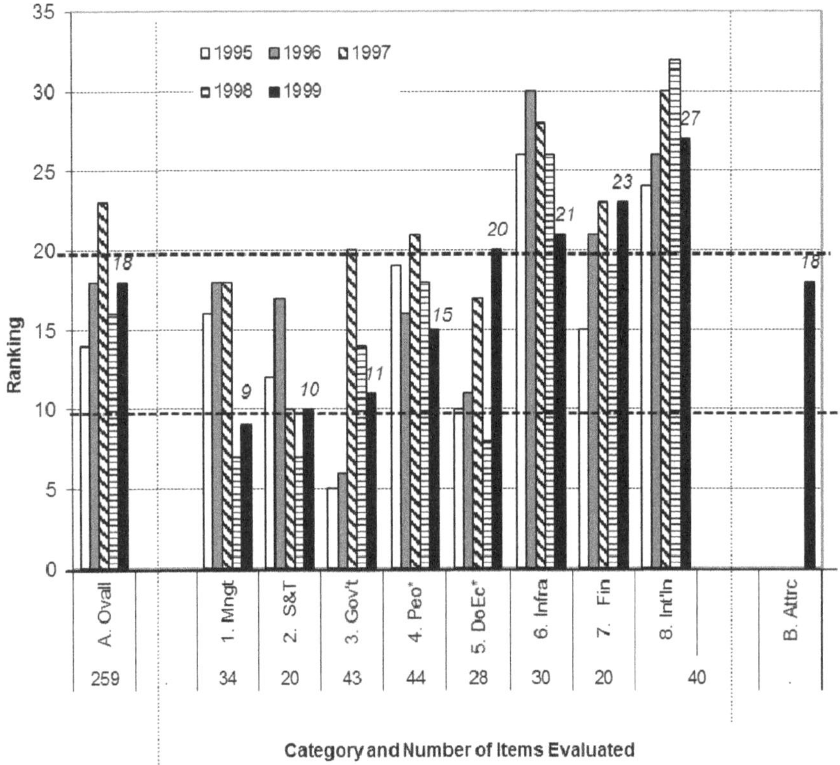

Figure 2.13: Taiwan's Competitiveness in the Global Economy IMD Data, 1995–1999

Taiwan's 1999 ranking in the eight categories are Labor, 2nd, Openness, 3rd, Technology, 7th, Government, 8th, Finance, 8th, Management, 15th, Infrastructure, 23rd, and Institution, 26th (ibid.). In response to the financial crisis from 1997 to 1998, Taiwan's openness improved considerably. So also did its finance sector, to some extent. Among the Asian countries, Taiwan is well-prepared for the next phase of the new economy of information technology (EPA, 2000, 105). Its computer hardware production in 1998 ranked third in the world, next only to the United States and Japan (ibid.). As much as 80 percent of families in Taiwan own cable TVs, even exceeding that of the United States (ibid.). Taiwan's labor performance is consistently the best among the 59 countries, including work ethic (4th), unemployment insurance (5th), social welfare system (6th), etc.

(WEF, 1999, 205). This may be the reason that Taiwan can still attract massive inward foreign direct investment even though its wage rate is higher.

Taiwan's "Institutions" have the worst performance. According to WEF's national competitiveness balance sheet (ibid., 205), the culprits are product liability (36th), judiciary independence (36th), organized crime (37th), legal corruption (37th), and litigation costs (41st). Although Taiwan's "Infrastructure" has been improving during the past years, it still ranked 23rd in 1999, mainly due to the lack of private investment in infrastructure (31st), road indicator (41st), and cellular telephones (42nd). Other liabilities include foreign access to capital markets (56th), government influence (58th), and insider trading (58th).

In addition, the WEF also adds four more aggregate indexes (the last four categories in Fig. 2.12). The "growth index (G)" predicts the average growth rates from year 2000 to 2008 based on the experience of the last eight years. In 1999 (the black column), Taiwan faired exceptionally well in this prediction: 4.29 percent, ranked 2nd, only second to Singapore, 5.02 percent, among the 59 active countries in the world. In terms of the "market growth index (MG)," which is the predicted growth rate times the size of the economy to measure each country's contribution to world economic growth, Taiwan ranked 14th. Instead of the competitive Survey of company CEOs, a new index, the "microeconomic competitive index (MECI)," which measures the microeconomic foundations of economic development, was substituted in 1998. For this, Taiwan ranked 19th in 1999. In general, the most important indexes are competitiveness and growth, both of which Taiwan ranked near the very top.

Taiwan's rankings in the IMD annual reports are somewhat inferior but still respectable. Like WEF indexes, IMD's Overall Competitiveness index "ranks nations' environments and analyzes their ability to provide an environment in which enterprises can compete" (IMD, 1999, 14). It has 288 variables, which are also grouped into eight Competitiveness Input Factors, as shown in Fig. 2.13. Six categories are similar to those of the WEF, and "Labor" and "Institutions" are substituted by "People" and "Domestic Economy," respectively. The IMD indexes seem to emphasize competitiveness of firms and so reflect more on short-term conditions of the economy. In the case of Taiwan, most of the indexes worsened during 1996 and 1997, and improved in 1999, which are shown by the dark filled columns with ranking on the tip.

In 1999, the IMD evaluated 47 industrialized and emerging countries. The overall competitiveness index for Taiwan in 1999 was 18th (the first group of columns in Fig. 2.13), still better than most of the active countries, although lower than Singapore (1st), the Netherlands (5th), Hong Kong (7th), Canada (10th), Australia (12th), Japan (16th), but much higher than all the other ASEAN countries and China (29th) and Korea (38th). Its ranking of the eight categories are Management, 9th, Science and Technology, 10th, Government, 11th, People, 15th, Domestic Economy, 20th, Infrastructure, 21st, Finance, 23rd, and Internationalization, 27th. Compared with the WEF rankings, both evaluations agree on high rankings in Technology and Government, a similar ranking in Finance, but quite different in five other categories. IMD also has an extensive list of strength and weakness of items in each category (IMD, 1999, 313). In addition, it has added three new Location Attractiveness Rankings in 1999 to "show which countries are the most attractive for locating or relocating Manufacturing, R&D, and Services and Management activities" (ibid.). In this, Taiwan ranked 18th overall (see the last category B in Fig. 2.13), which consists of Manufacturing, 9th, R&D, 19th, and Services and Management, 19th (ibid., 311). The high ranking on attractiveness of manufacturing activities again substantiates the recent increase of inward foreign direct investment that we have seen in Fig. 2.8.

2.8.2 *Economics and Politics with China — Some Concluding Remarks*

As we have stated in this paper, geography and history determine the economy and politics, and politics and economics are closely interwoven. Examples are trade frictions, tariff negotiations, regulations on inward and outward foreign investments, or even the gunboat diplomacy of yesteryears.[95] For the future of the Taiwanese economy, however, the most urgent problem it faces today is, unfortunately, the basic problem of nation-building, which other countries already experienced a long time ago, and the ensuing military threat from China for "unification."

We have seen the tremendous growth of Taiwan's trade and outward investment in China in the 1990s. Taiwanese firms are the second largest

[95] In fact, we have pointed out that the true "miracle" is that Taiwan achieved rapid economic growth without government protection in foreign economic relations. Hsiao and Hsiao (1996), 288. Ichimura (1995) discusses economics and politics of Japan extensively. His discussions and suggestions for Japan also apply to Taiwan.

foreign investors in China, next to Hong Kong, in the early 1990s,[96] and are probably the largest investors throughout the 1990s if Taiwanese indirect investment through Hong Kong is considered. The growth and magnitude up to now probably indicate complementarities of economic relations between the two countries. As the world competitiveness indexes have shown, while the future prospects of Taiwan in the global economy have been excellent and bright, they hinge greatly, if not crucially, on Taiwan's political relations with China. Any discussions of Taiwan in the global economy in the future cannot, and should not, avoid its problem with China. The basic problem is China's territorial claim on Taiwan and the threat of the use of military forces. But China's territorial claim is tenuous at best, and that both countries would be benefited by a peaceful resolution of the dispute in a civilized manner.

As we have seen in Sections 2.2 and 2.3, while it is true that some Han people from China visited Taiwan and some might have settled there, and there were some sporadic but vague records of Taiwan in old Chinese and Japanese literature, no nation claimed Taiwan as its territory until the early 17th century. Despite its proximity, the Ming Dynasty was relieved and content when the Dutch claimed Taiwan, instead of Pescadores, as its territory in 1624. It was the Dutch and the Spanish who introduced Taiwan to world trade as far away as with Southeast Asia and Europe in the 17th century, a prelude to Taiwan's global position in the 20th century after WWII. The Dutch were replaced by the Kingdom of Cheng, which continued global trade but imposed a trade ban on China. Taiwan then came under the Ch'ing regime after 1683, and became a formal Chinese province only in 1886. The history certainly belies the Chinese claim today that "Taiwan has been 'an inalienable part of China since ancient times dating back 1700 years.'"[97]

Ch'ing ruled Taiwan with disinterest and inefficiency. It considered that "Taiwan is a trifling place — taking it would add nothing, relinquishing it would not be a loss."[98] It ruled Taiwan loosely and its power had never extended to the vast mountainous region of Taiwan. The Japanese saw

---

[96] EPA (2000), 142. In 1998 and 1999, Taiwanese investment in China was exceeded by Hong Kong and the United States, and almost the same, or slightly less than, Japanese investment in China.

[97] As repeated in Klintworth (1995), 264.

[98] These are the words of the Ch'ing Emperor K'ang Hsi (1662–1722), as quoted in Vertente *et al.* (1991), 130.

the strategic position of Taiwan. Thus, Taiwan was ceded to Japan in the 1895 Treaty of Simonoseki after the first Sino-Japanese War.[99] Note that Taiwan was certainly not "stolen from China," as was claimed in the 1943 "Cairo Declaration." During the Chinese resistance against the Japanese invasion of China in the 1930s and early 1940s, the Chinese Communist Party and the KMT Government in China was aware of the treaty, and fully supported the independence of "the Taiwanese nationality," along with the Koreans, before WWII (Hsiao and Sullivan, 1979). The 1928 and 1931 Political Theses of the Taiwanese Communist Party[100] also proclaimed the "national liberation movement" and Taiwan independence, which were supported by the USSR's Comintern (Communist International), the Japanese Communist Party, and the Chinese Community Party (Hsiao and Sullivan, 1983).

Only after 1943, however, the KMT, and subsequently the People's Republic of China in 1949, has asserted that Taiwan be "returned" to China in accordance with the "Cairo Declaration" (ibid., 1979). The fact is, the "Cairo Declaration" was merely a news release of the United States Government that was not signed by any Allied leaders, and as such it does not provide the international legal base of the Chinese claim. The peace treaties between Japan and the Allies (1951), and even between Japan and the Republic of China (1952), which formally ended WWII, also did not specify the legal status of Taiwan. Since the People's Republic of China (PRC) has never governed Taiwan even for one moment, and since Taiwan has its own effective territory, government, army, and the people, Taiwan has never been an integral part of PRC,

---

[99] After the Treaty of Shimonoseki, through the interference of Russia, France, and Germany, China retained Liaodong Peninsula in southern Manchuria. Understandably, the Chinese side preferred to cede Taiwan to Japan, rather than to raise the question on Taiwan to reverse the Japanese decision to return Liaodong Peninsula to China. Faced with the alternate, the Chinese negotiators were so eager to cede Taiwan to Japan that they even advised the Japanese how to eradicate the Taiwanese rebels who rose against the secession (Ng, 1970, 25–26; Huang, 1987, 73). In addition to the three countries, England, Spain, and the United States were also interested in Taiwan but never interfered with Japan's acquisition of Taiwan (Ng, 1970, 36–39; Huang, 1987, 83–87).

[100] In keeping with "One Country, One Party" principle, Comintern recognition, as well as the Chinese and the Japanese Communist Parties' acceptance, of the "Taiwanese Communist Party" "as an independent communist party in 1931 also provided tacit backing for Taiwan's eventual political autonomy from China" (Hsiao and Sullivan, 1984, 286).

quite contrary to the Chinese claim.[101] In fact, as we have seen in this paper, Taiwan has thrived when Taiwan was, and is, politically independent from China.[102]

Historical facts aside, it is anachronistic and unacceptable to claim territory by foolishly contending ancestral kinship and geographical proximity.[103] Cooperation or unification between Taiwan and China, if there is any, must be based on the consensus of the people of Taiwan through peaceful and civilized negotiations between the two countries, not by finger wagging or bullying and the threat of force. As we have shown in this paper, while Taiwan may be small in terms of its land mass and population compared with those of China, it is large in many other respects, including its per capita and aggregate GNP, trading prowess, foreign exchange reserves, inward and outward foreign investments, and its national competitiveness, especially in the new-economy fields of information technology. The win-win situation for both Taiwan and China can be achieved only when China recognizes Taiwan as an independent country,[104] which is exemplary for China to achieve its own economic and political miracles in the new century. Whereas for China, as we have just

---

[101] Kintworth (1995), 14 observed that "Taiwan has been under the effective administrative control of a government in Beijing for no more than one of two decades in the last several centuries. Taiwan was China's for a few years in the 1660s and from 1887 to 1891. For most of the rest of its time in modern history, Taiwan was controlled by the Dutch, the Japanese, or the Americans, or largely neglected by the mainland Chinese." By the Chinese logic, since China was once a part of the Mongol Empire for 90 years (1279–1368), China should be "inalienable integral part" of the Mongolian People's Republic.

[102] Klintworth (1995), 8. Taiwan has been "lucky" by not falling into the fate of China's Hainan Island in the past 100 years (ibid., 55; Hsiao, 1987; Hsiao, 1997, 507, Footnote 36). "Agricultural Taiwan, Industrial China" was the future plan for Taiwan by the Nanking Nationalist (KMT) Government in 1946 (Hsiao, 1997, 507; also see Kirby, 1995).

[103] Even China's "leading scholar" on Taiwan, Li Jiaquan (the former Director of Institute of Taiwan Studies, Chinese Academy of Social Sciences) holds such a view, unable to give one good reason of unification. See the quotation in Klintworth (1995), 265. If "Socialist Theory of Market" is China's "philosophy of poverty," the dogma of territorial claim is the telltale of China's "poverty of philosophy." Its poverty was just recently demonstrated again fully in Wei (2000), in a vivid contrast to Chiang (2000), the leading article in the same issue of the journal. It is not coincident that China has to resort to force.

[104] This may be a dream, but so were the collapse of the "Great East Asia Co-Prosperity Sphere," German Nazi, the Soviet Union, and democratization of Taiwan during our life time. If Taiwanese are persistent, the dream will come true. The first sign of thawing and the test of civility should come by China's blessing of Taiwan's membership in the United Nations. When the day comes, its impact on the world economy and politics will far exceed the unification of the two Germanys or the two Koreas.

seen above, this recognition is not unprecedented, it will tremendously enhance the position of Taiwan and China in the global economy and politics.[105]

Appendix 2A: Export Promotion Policy May Not Be Sustainable

The general theme on the literature of Taiwanese economic development is that export-oriented policy works (for an example, see the latest papers in Thorbecke and Wan, 1999). This is not at all true, although the notion is so popular that many economists take it for granted. Here is a simple counter-example. Let the national income model be

$$Y = C + I + G + (X - M). \quad (1)$$

where, as usual, Y is national income, C, consumption, I, investment, G, government expenditure, X, exports, and M, imports. Let's assume the simplest economic behavior:

$$S = Y - C = sY,\ I = K',\ S = I,\ X' = gX,\ M = mY,\ N' = nN, \quad \text{and}$$
$$Y = AK^{a}N^{1-a},$$

where S is savings, K is capital, N is population, $X' = dX/dt$, etc., and s (saving rate), g (export growth rate), m (marginal propensity to imports), and n (population or labor growth rate) are positive constants. Then, the model reduces to per capita magnitude as

$$k' = (s + m)Ak^{a} - gh\,e^{(g-n)t} - nk$$

where $k \equiv K/N$, $h \equiv X(0)/N(0)$.

This is Solow's fundamental equation of economic growth if $g = m = 0$. The equation shows that, when t is sufficiently large, per capita capital *decreases* if the growth rate of exports, g, is larger than the growth rate of population, n ($g > n$). This condition is satisfied in most of the

---

[105] Just consider the fact that, in 1998, the foreign exchange reserves for Japan was US$ 212 billion, China, 141.1 billion, Hong Kong, 88.4 billion, and Taiwan, 84.4 billion, ranking 1st to 4th in Asia (Taiwan Briefs, 1999, 14). Twu (1997), 168 observes that "Taiwanese money" is the reason China wants "unification" with Taiwan under the cover of fanatic Chinese nationalism, and warned that it might rekindle the fear of "yellow peril" in the region.

developing countries, and certainly is the case for Taiwan, Korea, and Japan. Furthermore,

$$\partial k'/\partial g = -hg^2 e^{(g-n)t} < 0.$$

Thus, increase in the growth rate of exports (g) will decrease capital accumulation at any moment of time. Hence, in this model, export-oriented policy results in decumulation of per capita capital, quoad hoc, decrease in per capita GDP. It is by no means a "common sense" that exports necessarily promote growth.

After all, if that is indeed the case, every country may just do so to achieve economic development. In fact, in the late 1970s, OECD (1979) designated ten Newly Industrializing Countries (NICs) as the fast export expanding countries. In less than two decades, only the four Asian NICs have remained. There is nothing "fortunate" or "wise" about government policy changes in Taiwan (and Korea) in achieving rapid growth. Their economies may decline also.

Acknowledgments

We are indebted to Professors Teruo Asamoto, Shinichi Ichimura, Hiroshi Ishida, Chung H. Lee, Ts'ui-jung Liu, Yuzin Chiautong Ng, Eric D. Ramstetter, Jaw-yann Twu (Muraoka), Henry Wan, Jr., Wen-hsing Wu for generous sharing of their publications at various stages of writing this paper. Our special thanks go to Mr. Pao-Jui Chen for rushing a copy of new TSDB 2000, to Professor Hiroshi Setooka for sending valuable new data, and to Professor John P. Powelson for comments and making the paper more readable. We also appreciate the editor, Professor Peter C. Y. Chow, for his successful conference arrangement, patience, and encouragement. All errors of omission and commission are ours.

Statistical Data Sources

SS51 *Fifty-one Year Statistical Summary of Taiwan Province* (Taiwan Sheng-51 Nianlai Tongji Tiyao), Statistics Department of Taiwan Province Governor-General, December, 1946.

Investment Commission (2000), *Monthly Statistics on Overseas Chinese and Foreign Investment, Outward Investment, Outward Technical Cooperation, Indirect Mainland Investment, Guide of Mainland Industry Technology*, April. Ministry of Economic Affairs: Taipei, Taiwan.

TEY4x *Taiwan Economic Yearbook* (Taiwan Keizai Nempo), Vol. x, 194x (x denotes the year of publication). Taipei: Taiwan Keizai Kankokai.

TSDB *Taiwan Statistical Data Book*, 1975, 1985, 1993, 2000. Council for Economic Planning and Development, Republic of China.

Y91 Yano, I. (1991). *100 Years of Japan, Viewed by Numbers* (Suji de miru Nihon no Hyakunen), Tokyo: Kokuseisha.

YSxx Yano, K., & Shirazaki, K., *Illustration of Japanese National Achievements* (Nihon Kokusei Chosa), yearly since 1927 (xx denotes the year of publication).

References

Ang, Ka-im (1999). "Commerce, Trade, and Aborigines in the Northern Taiwan in Early Era" (in Chinese). In Huang and Ang (1999) in this References.

Aoki, T. (1985). *The Pacific Era and Japan* (in Japanese). Tokyo: Yuhi Kaku.

Arnold, W. (1985). "Japan and Taiwan: Community of Economic Interest Held Together by Paradiplomacy." In R.S. Ozaki and W. Arnold (eds.), *Japan's Foreign Relations* (Chapter 11). Boulder, CO: Westview Press.

Azuma, K. (1941). "Taiwanese Economy before the Economic Control" (in Japanese). In Chapter 3, TEY41, listed in the Statistical Data Sources above.

Brooks, M.R. and A. Frances (1991). "Barriers to Exporting: An Exploratory Study of Latin American Companies." In F.H.R. Seringhaus and P.J. Rosson (eds.), *Export Development and Promotion: The Role of Public Organizations* (Chapter 5). Norwell, MA: Kluwer Academic Publishers.

Chan, S. and C. Clark (1992). *Flexibility, Foresight, and Fortuna in Taiwan's Development: Navigating between Scylla and Charybdis.* London: Routledge.

Chang, Han-yu (1957). "Technical Development of Taiwan's Rice Agriculture During the Japanese Period" (in Chinese). *Quarterly Journal of the Bank of Taiwan*, 9(2) (September). Also in: *Collected Works of Dr. Chang Han-yu* (Vol. 1, 363–393). Taipei: San-min Bookstore, 1974.

______ (1974). *Economic Development and Economic Thoughts, Essays of Dr. Han-yu Chang* (in Chinese). Volume II. Taipei, Taiwan: Committee of Publishing Essays of Dr. Han-yu Chang.

Chang, Sheng-yen, Wu Wen-hsing, Wen Zheng-hua and Dai Bao-tsung (1996). *The Development of Taiwan* (in Chinese). Taipei: National Kong-Chung University.

Chang, Tsong-han (1980). *Prewar Taiwan's Industrialization* (in Chinese). Taipei, Taiwan: Lian-jin Publising Company.

Chang, Wen-po (1998). "The Meanings and Implications of National Competitiveness." *Industry of Free China*, 88(12) (December).

Chen, Cheng-hsiang (1963). *An Economic and Social Geography.* Taipei: Fu-min Geographical Institute of Economic Development.

______ (1959–1960). *A Geography of Taiwan* (Taiwan dizhi). Vol. I and II. Taipei: Fu-min Geographical Institute of Economic Development.

Chiang, Y. Frank (2000). "State, Sovereignty, and Taiwan." *Fordham International Law Journal*, 23(4) (April): 959–1004.

Cho, Lee-Jay and Yoon Hyung Kim (1991). "Political and Economic Antecedents to the 1960s." In Lee-Jay Cho and Yoon Hyung Kim (eds.), *Economic Development in the Republic of Korea.* Hawaii: University of Hawaii Press.

Chou, Hsian-wen (1957). "Exploitation Economy in Taiwan during the Dutch Period" (in Chinese). *Volumes on Taiwan Studies*, No. 40. Taipei: Bank of Taiwan.

——— (1958). *Taiwanese Economic History in the Japanese Occupation Period* (in Chinese). *Taiwan Studies*, No. 59. Taipei: Bank of Taiwan.

Chou Hsue-pu *et al.* (1959). "Historical Documents on Trade between Taiwan and England" (in Chinese). *Volumes on Taiwan Studies*, No. 57. Taipei: Bank of Taiwan.

Chou, Tian-Cheng (1992). "Small-and-Medium Enterprises on the Fringe of the Power" (in Chinese). In H. Hsiao *et al.* (1992) listed in this References section (Chapter 5).

Coe, D.T., E. Helpman and A.W. Hoffmaister (1995). "North-South R&D Spillovers." NBER Working Paper Series, No. 5048, March.

Cohen, Mark J. and Emma Teng (1990). *Let Taiwan be Taiwan, Documents on the International Status of Taiwan.* Washington, D.C.: Center for Taiwan International Relations.

Conlon Associates (1959). *United States Foreign Policy: Asia.* Studies No. 5. Prepared at the request of the Committee on Foreign Relation, United States Senate. Washington, D.C.: U.S. Government Printing Office.

Davis, Ralph (1967). *A Commercial Revolution, English Overseas Trade in the Seventeenth and Eighteenth Centuries.* London: The Historical Association.

Duan, Zheng-pu (ed.) (1989). *Postwar Taiwanese Economy.* Beijing: China Social Science Publishers.

Economic Planning Agency (ed.) (EPA) (2000). *Asian Economy 2000* (Ajia Keizai 2000). Tokyo: Ministry of Finance Press.

Fairbank, John K. (1967). *China, The People's Middle Kingdom and the U.S.A.* Cambridge, MA: Harvard University Press.

Hao, Yen-p'ing (1986). *The Commercial Revolution in Nineteenth-Century China, The Rise of Sino-Western Mercantile Capitalism.* Berkeley, CA: University of California Press.

Hayami, Y. and V.W. Ruttan (1970). "Korean Rice, Taiwanese Rice, and Japanese Agricultural Stagnation: An Economic Consequence of Colonialism." *Quarterly Journal of Economics*, 84 (November): 562–89.

Ho, Samuel P.S. (1978). *Economic Development of Taiwan, 1860–1970.* New Haven, CT: Yale University Press.

Hobsbawn, E.J. (1968). *Industry and Empire, An Economic History of Britain since 1750.* London: Weidenfeld and Nicolson.

Hsiao, Frank S.T. (1997). "Colonialism or Comparative Advantage? — On Agricultural Development in Colonial Taiwan." *Proceedings of the National Science Council, Part C: Humanities and Social Sciences*, 7(4), October, 497–513. (Ref. Chapter 4).

——— (1992). "The Economic and Cultural Backgrounds of Taiwanese 228 Civil Strife — An Application of Social Expectation Theory" (in Chinese). In

Proceedings of 1991 Conference on Research on 2-28 Civil Strife, Yong-hsing Chen (ed.). Taipei, Taiwan: the U.S.-Taiwan Cultural Exchange Foundation, 228 Citizen's Study Group, and Modern Research Foundation, 77–113. (Ref. Chapter 7).

______ (1987). "The Effects of Direct Foreign Investment — The Taiwanese Experience and Its Implication to China" (in Chinese). In *Proceedings of the Second International Conference on the Future of Taiwan.* Xiamen, China, August 1985, edited by Huan-qui Quo and Fu-san Zhao, cosponsored by the Institute of Taiwan Studies, Chinese Academy of Social Sciences, Simon Fraser University, and Institute of Taiwan Studies, Xiamen University. Beijing: China Friendship (Yuo-yi) Publication Co., 1987, 69–118.

Hsiao, Frank S.T. and Mei-Chu W. Hsiao (2001). "Economic Liberalization and Development — The Case of Lifting Martial Law in Taiwan." Forthcoming in *The Transformation of an Authoritarian Regime: Taiwan in the Post-Martial Law Era.* Taiwan Studies Promotion Committee, Academia Sinica, Taipei, Taiwan. December, 2000. University of Colorado, Department of Economics, Discussion Paper 99–29 (Ref. Chapter 12).

______ and ______ (2000). "International Comparison of Taiwanese Economic Growth-A Long Run Perspective." Working Paper, Department of Economics, University of Colorado.

______ and ______ (1999a). "The Historical Traditions of Taiwanese Small-and-Medium Enterprises" (with Mei-chu W. Hsiao). In Huang, Fu-San and Ka-im Ang (eds.) (1999) listed in this References section. 464–524. (Ref. Chapter 6).

______ and ______ (1999b). "Catching Up but Falling Behind in the Long Run — On Capitalistic Development of Taiwan and Korea." Working Paper No. 110, Economic Research Center, School of Economics, Nagoya University, Japan (Revised and published in *Review of Development Economics*, 8(2) (May 2004): 223 236).

______ and ______ (1998). "Colonial Linkages in Early Postwar Taiwanese Economic Development." In William C. Kirby and Michael S. Weiss (eds.), *Harvard Studies on Taiwan: Papers of the Taiwan Studies Workshop, Volume II* (Ref. Chapter 5). Harvard University: John King Fairbank Center for East Asian Research.

______ and ______ (1996). "Taiwanese Economic Development and Foreign Trade." In Kuark, J.T. (ed.), *Comparative Asian Economies*, in the *Contemporary Studies in Economic and Financial Analysis* (Vol. 77, Part B) (211–302), Greenwich, CT: JAI Press. Originally published in *Fairbank Center Discussion Paper* No. 9, 1994, Harvard University, and also in William Kirby and Megan Greene (eds.), *Harvard Studies on Taiwan: Papers of the Taiwan Studies Workshop, Volume I.* Harvard University: John King Fairbank Center for East Asian Research, 1995. (Ref. Chapter 1).

______ and ______ (1995). "Globalization of the Taiwanese Economy and U.S.-Taiwan Trade Relations." In Cheng Fu. Lee (ed.), *Advances in Pacific Basin Business, Economics, and Finance*, Vol. I (Ref. Chapter 10) (197–214). Greenwich, CT: JAI Press.

Hsiao, Frank S.T. and Lawrence R. Sullivan (1979). "The Chinese Communist Party and the Status of Taiwan, 1928–1943." *Pacific Affairs*, 53(3): 446–467.

______ and ______ (1983). "A Political History of the Taiwanese Communist Party, 1928–1931." *Journal of Asian Studies*, 52(2) (February): 269–289.

Hsiao, Hsin-huang, Yun-pong Chu, Jia-dong Hsu, Zhong-ji Wu, Tian-Cheng Chou, Ji-li Yan, Yun-han Chu and Zhong-chen Lin (1992). *Dissecting Taiwanese Economy: Monopoly and Exploitation under an Authoritarian Regime*. Taiwan Research Fund Series No. 2, Taipei, Taiwan: Taiwan Research Fund.

Hsiao, Mei-chu W. (1992). "Direct Foreign Investment, Technology Transfer, and Industrial Development — The Case of Electronic Industry in Taiwan." In M. Dutta (ed.), *Research in Asian Economic Studies* (Volume 4A) *Asian Economic Regime: An Adaptive Innovation Paradigm* (145–164) (Ref. Chapter 9). Greenwich, CT: JAI Press.

Hsu, Wen-hsiung (2000). *Social Organization and Disorder in Taiwan*. Taipei, Taiwan: Lien Ching Publishing Co. Summarized by Ching-shih Chen in *forum@natpa.org*, July 19, 2000.

Huang, Fu-san (1999). "The Change of Jardine, Matheson & Co. Trading Practice toward Taiwan When Taiwan Opened Ports." In Huang, Fu-san and Ka-im Ang (1999), listed in this References section, 83–105.

Huang, Fu-san and Ka-im Ang (eds.) (1999). *Taiwanese Commercial Traditions, Collected Papers* (*Taiwan Shangyeh Chuangtong Lunwenji*). The Preparatory Office of the Institute of Taiwanese History, Academia Sinica. Taipei, Taiwan.

Huang, Fu-san and Tsu-yu Chen (1995). "Business Development" (in Chinese). In Rong-Tsong Jian (ed.), *Modern History of Taiwan, Volume on Economy*, Taipei: Taiwansheng Wen Hsian Wei Yuan Hui.

Huang, Hsiu-zheng (1987). *Secession of Taiwan and 1895 Resistance against Japanese*. Ph.D. Thesis, Institute of History, National Taiwan Normal University, Taipei.

Hwang, Jim, Oscar Chung and Violet Chang (1998). "Voices from the Heartland." *Free China Review*, 48(1) (January).

Ichimura, Shinichi (1995). *Economic Development of Japan and Her External Economic Relations*. Translated in Chinese by Wen So *et al.* Beijing: Beijing University Press.

International Institute for Management Development (IMD) (1999). *The World Competitiveness Yearbook*. Lausanne, Switzerland.

Ishida, Hiroshi (2000). *The Strategies for Social and Economic Development in Rural China* (Chiukoku Noson no Kaihatsu Senryaku — Nohmin wa "Yutaka" ni Nattanoka). Economic and Political Studies #117, Osaka, Japan: Institute of Economic and Political Studies, Kansai University.

______ (1999). *The Structure of Taiwan Economy and Its Dynamics* (Taiwan Keizai no Kozo to Tenkai). Tokyo: Ohtsuki Shoten.

Ishikawa, Shigeru (1967). *Economic Development in Asian Perspective*. Economic Research Series, No. 8, The Institute of Economic Research, Hitotsubashi University. Tokyo: Kinokuniya Bookstore Co.

Jacoby, Neil H. (1966). *U.S. Aid to Taiwan, A Study of Foreign Aid, Self-help, and Development.* New York: Frederick A. Praeger.

Kai, Chang Kuo and D.B. Chu (August, 1951). "Compilation of Taiwan's Production Index and Survey of Taiwan's Production Trends" (in Chinese). *Finance and Economics Monthly* 1(9): 58–62.

Kakuyama, Sakae (ed.) (1980). *Studies on Western Economic History* (Koza: Seiyo Keizaishi). Volume I. Tokyo: Dobunkan.

Kawano, Shigeto (1968). *Taiwan's Rice Economy*, 1941. Translated into Chinese by Ying-yen Lin, Taiwan Studies No. 102, 1968. Taipei, Taiwan: The Bank of Taiwan.

Kirby, William C. (1995). "Planning Postwar Taiwan Industrial Policy and the Nationalist Takeover, 1943–1947." In William C. Kirby and J. Megan Greene (eds.), *Harvard Studies on Taiwan: Papers of the Taiwan Studies Workshop* (Vol. 1, 286–301). Fairbank Center for East Asian Research, Cambridge, MA: Harvard University.

Klintworth, Gary (1995). *New Taiwan, New China, Taiwan's Changing Role in the Asia-Pacific Region.* New York, NY: St. Martin's Press.

Kusui, Ryuzo (1944). *A Study of The War-time Taiwanese Economy* (Taiwan Senji Keizairon). Taihoku: Nampo Jimbun Kenkyujo.

______ (1941). "Problems in Taiwan's Industrialization" (Taiwan Kogyka no Shomondai). In TEY41.

Lai, Tse-han, Ramon H. Myers and Wou Wei (1991). *A Tragic Beginning: The Taiwan Uprising of February 28, 1947.* Stanford, CA: Stanford University Press.

Lin, Chi-yuan (1968). "Industrial Development and Changes in the Structure of Foreign Trade, The Experience of the Republic of China in Taiwan, 1946–66." *IMF Staff Papers*, 25 (July): 290–321.

Lin, Ji-wen (1996). *Studies of War Mobilization System during the Last Stage of Japanese Occupation Period (1930–1945)* (in Chinese). Taipei, Taiwan: Tao-Hsiang Publishing Co.

Lin, Ping-yan (1997). *The Beginning of Taiwanese Experience: The History of Taiwan Electric Power Inc.* (in Chinese). Taipei, Taiwan: The Resource Center of Taiwan Electric Power Inc.

Liu, Bang-li (1996). "The Structure of Post-war Taiwanese External Trade Network" (in Chinese). *Quarterly Journal of the Bank of Taiwan*, 47(1): 125–150.

Liu, Tai-ying and Jin-chaung Jian (1983). *The Economic Effects of Japanese Business Investment in Taiwan* (in Chinese). Report to the Committee on Research, Development, and Assessment, the Executive Yuan, submitted by Taiwan Economic Research Institute, Taipei, Taiwan.

Liu, Ts'ui-jung (1998). "Han Migration and the Settlement of Taiwan — The Onset of Environmental Change." In Mark Elvin and Liu Ts'ui-jung (eds.), *Sediments of Time, Environment and Society in Chinese History.* Cambridge, UK: Cambridge University Press. Also, reprint of the Chinese version, Taipei: Institute of Economics, Academia Sinica, 1995.

Lopez, Robert S. (1971). *The Commercial Revolution of the Middle Ages, 950–1350.* Upper Saddle River, NJ: Prentice-Hall.

Maddison, Angus (1995). *Monitoring the World Economy, 1820–1992.* Paris: Developing Center, OECD.

Ministry of Economic Affairs (MOEA) (1991). *White Paper on Small and Medium-Size Enterprises.* Taiwan: Small and Medium Enterprises Bureau, Ministry of Economic Affairs.

Mizoguchi, Toshiyuki and Y. Yamamoto (1984). "Capital Formation in Taiwan and Korea." In Myers, R.H. and M.R. Peattie (eds.), *The Japanese Colonial Empire, 1895–1945.* Princeton, NJ: Princeton University Press.

Morrison, Wayne M. and William Cooper (1999). "China-U.S.-Taiwan Economic Relations." In Frank Columbus (ed.), *Asian Economic and Political Issues,* Volume II. New York: Nova Science Publishers, Inc.

Nakayama, T. (1959). "Taiwan's Buckskin Production and Its Exports to Japan in the 17th Century" (translated into Chinese). *Volumes on Taiwan Studies,* No. 71. Taipei: Bank of Taiwan.

Nampokensha (1943?). *Military Songs for Young Cherry Flowers* (Wakasakura Gunkashu). Nampokensha: Taipei, Taiwan.

Ng, Yuzin Chiautong (Ko Sho-do) (1970). *A Study of the Republic of Formosa, 1895, A Chapter in the History of Taiwan Independence Movement.* Tokyo: The University of Tokyo Press.

Nikkei. *Nikei Sangyo Sinbun* (Japan Economic and Industry Daily), various issues.

Oh, Iku-toku (1970). *Taiwan, Its History in Agony* (Taiwan, Kumon suru sono Rekishi). Tokyo: Kobunsha.

Ohsono, Tomokazu (1998). *Maps for Seeing Asia, New Edition* (Shin, Ajia o Miru Chizu). Tokyo, Japan: Kodansha.

Organization for Economic Cooperation and Development (OECD) (1979). *The Impact of the Newly Industrializing Countries, on Production and Trade in Manufactures.* Report by the Secretary-General. Paris: OECD.

Ping, R. (1947). "Characteristics of Taiwanese Agriculture" (in Chinese). Taipei: *Journal of the Bank of Taiwan,* 1(1) (June): 55–86.

Rabb, Theodore K. (1967). *Enterprise and Empire, Merchant and Gentry Investment in The Expansion of England, 1575–1630.* Cambridge, MA: Harvard University Press.

Schneider, Adam (2000). "The Taiwan Development Company and Indochina: Subimperialism, Development, and Colonial Status." In *Taiwan Historical Research,* 5(2): 101–133. Taiwan: Academia Sinica.

Se, Akio and Teruo Asamoto (ed.) (1999). *Studies on Taiwanese Economy* (Taiwan Keizai Ron). Tokyo: Keiso Shobo.

Shi, Ji and Zheng-zhong Li (1978). *A Study of the Methods of Improving Trade Deficits and Imports between Taiwan and Japan* (in Chinese). Research Report submitted to the Ministry of Economic Affairs, Taipei, Taiwan.

Shinohara, Miyohei and Shigeru Ichikawa (1972). Taiwanese Economic Growth (Taiwan no Keizai Seicho). Tokyo: Aziya Keizai Kenkyujo.

Skoggard, I.A. (1996). *The Indigenous Dynamic in Taiwan's Postwar Development, The Religious and Historical Roots of Entrepreneurship.* Armonk, N.Y.: M.E. Sharp.

Steven, R. (1990). *Japan's New Imperialism.* Armonk, N.Y.: M.E. Sharp.

Su Bing (1980). *400-Year History of The Taiwanese People* (Taiwanren Subai-nien-shi). San Jose, CA: Paradise Culture Associates.

______ (1986). *Taiwan's 400-Year History, The Origins and Continuing Development of the Taiwanese Society and People.* Washington, D.C.: The Taiwanese Cultural Grass Roots Association.

Sumiya, Mikio, Shin-kei Liu and Chau-yen Tu (1992). *The Taiwanese Economy,* (in Japanese). Tokyo: Tokyo University Press.

Taiwan Briefs (1999). In *TOPICS, The Magazine of International Business in Taiwan.* Taipei: The American Chamber of Commerce in Taiwan, 28(10) (December 1998/January 1999).

Takahashi, Kamekichi (1937). *A Study of the Modern Taiwanese Economy* (Gendai Taiwan Keizairon). Tokyo: Chikura Shobo.

Tang, W.T. (1947). "Taiwan's Agriculture and its Research" (in Chinese). *Quarterly Journal of the Bank of Taiwan,* 1(3) (December): 1–19.

Thorbecke, Erik and Henry Wan Jr. (1999). *Taiwan's Development Experience: Lessons on Roles of government and Market.* Boston: Kluwer Academic Publishers.

Tsurumi, P.E. (1977). *Japanese Colonial Education in Taiwan, 1895–1945.* Cambridge, MA: Harvard University Press.

Twu, Jaw-yann (1975). *Taiwan under Japanese Imperialism* (Teikoku Shugika no Taiwan). Tokyo: Tokyo University Press.

______ (1997). *Hong Kong, Taiwan, and Greater China, Arrival of the New Century of Three China?* Tokyo: Jiji Tsushin Sha.

Underwood, Laurie (1999). "The Park that Chips Built." *TOPICS, The Magazine of International Business in Taiwan.* Taipei: The American Chamber of Commerce in Taiwan, 29(3) (April).

USSR Institute of Economics, Academy of Sciences (1955). *Textbook on Economics.* Translated into Japanese by the Association of Marxism-Leninism Dissemination. Vols. I and II. Tokyo: Gohdo Publishing Co.

Van Hoesel, Roger (1996). "Taiwan: Foreign Direct Investment and the Transformation of the Economy." In J.H. Dunning and R. Narula (eds.), *Foreign Investment and Governments: Catalysts for Economic Restructuring.* New York: Routledge.

Vertente, Christine, Hsueh-chi Hsu and Mi-cha Wu (1991). *The Authentic Story of Taiwan, An Illustrated History, based on Ancient Maps, Manuscripts and Prints.* Knokke, Belgium: Mappamundi Publishers, and also Taipei Taiwan: S.M.C. Publishing Inc.

Wei, Su (2000). "Some Reflections on the One-China Principle." *Fordham International Law Journal,* 23(4) (April): 1169–1178.

World Bank (1997, 2000). *World Development Report* (*WDR*). New York: Oxford University Press.

World Economic Forum (WEF) (1999). *The Global Competitiveness Report.* Cambridge, MA: Harvard Institute of International Development.

Wu, Chuang-da (1958). *Development of Taiwan* (Taiwan de Kaihua) (in Chinese). Beijing: Ke-Hsueh Publisher.

Wu, Tsong-min (1995). "Long-run Fluctuations in Aggregate Outputs of Taiwan and Changes in Economic Structure" (in Chinese). In Rong-Tsong Jian (ed.), *Modern History of Taiwan* (609–636). Taipei: Taiwan Sheng Wenshian Weiyuanhui.

Wu, Wen-hsing (1995). "Japan's Investigations and Studies on Taiwan before the Occupation" (in Chinese). In *The Proceedings of the First Academic Conference on Taiwanese Local Culture* (567–576). Taipei: Center of Education and Humanity Studies, National Taiwan Normal University.

______ (1997). "Tokyo Imperial University and the Evolution of 'Academic Explorations' of Taiwan" (in Chinese). In *100 Years of Taiwanese Historical Studies — Reviews and Studies* (1–28). Taipei: Institute of Taiwan History Preparation Office, Academia Sinica.

______ (1999). "Transformation of Taiwanese Society under Japanese Colonialism and its Historical Implications" (in Chinese). *The Proceedings of the Fourth Conference of East Asian History Education*, Society for the Comparative Study of History and History Education. Tokyo.

Yajima, Kinji (1986). *The Complete Scope on the Taiwanese Economy* (Taiwan Keizai no Subete). 2nd edition. Tokyo: Nihon Keizai Tsushinsha.

Yanaihara, Tadao (1929). *Taiwan under Imperialism* (in Japanese). Tokyo: Iwanami Shoten.

Yano, Tooru (1990). *A Cyclopedia of Asia/Pacific, New Regionalism and the Role of Japan* (Jiten, Azia Taiheiyo–Atarashii Chiekizoh to Nihon no Yakuwari). Tokyo: Chuo Keizai Sha.

______ (1975). *Genealogy of 'Southward Movement'* (Nanshin no "Keifu"). Chuko Shinsho, 412. Tokyo: Chuoh Koronsha.

Yu, Tzong-shian (1996). "Relations between Two Sides of the Strait and the Taiwanese Economy." *Industry of Free China*, 86(6) (December).

Chapter 3

Taiwan in the Global Economy — End of the "Miracle"?

Although geographically rather small, Taiwan is anything but insignificant in the global economy, especially Taiwanese people's contributions in the field of information and communication technology (ICT). This paper discusses Taiwan from the vantage point of the global economy, using some of Taiwan's macroeconomic and competitiveness indicators to compare and rank them with other countries and regions based on the data from world organizations. Time-series data of the past two decades suggest that the postwar Taiwanese economic miracle may have been over after the early 1990s. We conclude that Taiwan's economy is at a crossroads. The Ma government policy of further promoting closer ties with China, instead of attending to basic reforms, may not be the best path for the Taiwanese economy.

3.1 Taiwan's Economic Evolution: Agrarian to High-Tech

Taiwan's economic development has come a long way since the prewar period, advancing steadily from exporting agricultural goods and agricultural processed products to low technology manufactured and then to high technology manufacture.

By the latter part of the 1930s Taiwan was already the world's major producer of rice, sugar, sweet potatoes, tea, bananas, and canned pineapples, providing the foundation for Taiwan's early postwar economic development. In the 1960s, Taiwan was the number one country for exports of mushrooms and asparagus to world markets. In 1983, the island could claim more than two dozen products for which it was "Number One" in the world, for such items as plastic shoes, umbrellas, and tennis rackets.

In addition, it exported 3.16 million sets of sewing machines (80% of its world export market), 240 million units of mini-motors (70%), and 80 million bicycle tires (50%) (MOEA, 1991).

At the same time, Taiwan developed its electronics industry: transistor radios, tape recorders, black-and-white TVs, etc. in the 1960s; CRTs, color TVs, IC pilot production, electronic watches, etc. in the 1970s; IC, IBM PC/ AT, color monitors, 256K DRAM, etc. in the 1980s; motherboards, monitors, scanners, and mice in the 1990s. By 1986, Taiwan produced the world's largest number of computer terminals, printed circuit boards, monitors, recreational boats, electronic calculators, telephones, etc. Taiwan ranked as the second or third largest exporter of a number of other products as well. Taiwan as Number One in the world had been achieved in many areas. The achievements are indeed staggering.

Taiwan thus has a long and distinguished history of economic development, from the first economic miracle during the pre-World War II Japanese period to the second economic miracle after the war. Taiwan is an exemplary case of successful economic development in modern world history.

3.2 Taiwan's Domestic Economy

With an area of 36,000 km^2 and a population of 23.1 million[1] in 2012, Taiwan's population density is 717 persons per km^2, ranking at 16th out of 255 countries and regions (CIA-COW, 2012). Until recently, some Taiwan's macroeconomic indicators, like GDP (Gross Domestic Product), GDP per capita, foreign trade and reserves, competitiveness indexes, compare well with those of the world.

3.2.1 *GDP (in PPP)*

Taiwan's global position in GDP can be seen in Fig. 3.1, which shows that Taiwan's 2011 GDP level in purchasing power parity (PPP) was

[1]Taiwan's land area, 35,980 km^2 (date of info NA) and population 23,113,901 (July 2012, est.) are from CIA World Factbook (CIA-COW, 2012), It ranks Taiwan's land area and population as #139/250 (45th pctl, excluding NA) and #51/238 (79th pctl, excluding NA), respectively, among world's 250 and 238 countries and regions, respectively. In what follows, we have excluded the data on World, EU, and ocean regions as a whole from the CIA-COW (2012) rankings to obtain 255 countries and regions. To be consistent, unless noted otherwise, we take the data from CIA.

A summary statistics of Sections 3.2 to 3.4 are given in Appendix 3A.

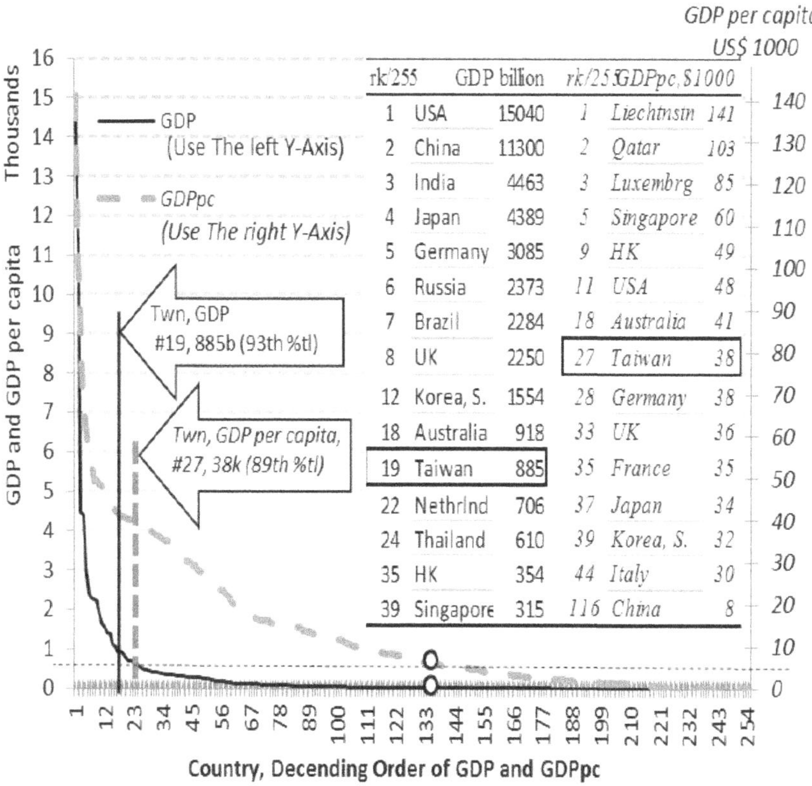

Figure 3.1: Taiwan's GDP and GDP per capita (in PPP) in the World Ranking

255 Countries/regions, 2011 (CIA-COW, 2012)

US$885 billion, same below, ranking Taiwan no. 19 (93rd pctl)[2] among the 255 countries and regions, almost the same as Australia (US$918b; #18, same below), more than two times higher than Hong Kong (354b, #35) and Singapore (315b, #39). China, with 58 times the population of Taiwan, had a GDP only 13 times greater. The 2011 median GDP (in PPP) for all countries was only US$19 billion (Nicaragua, #128), about 3.8 percent of Taiwan's GDP.

[2]Note that, for simplicity, in this chapter, we use # to denote the ranking number in descending order, b, billion, m, million, K, 1000, tr, trillion, and pctl, percentile, all in the parentheses.

3.2.2 *GDP (PPP) per capita*

Figure 3.1 also shows that Taiwan's GDP per capita (in PPP) in 2011 was $37,900, ranking it somewhat farther behind at 27th among the 255 countries and regions (90th pctl). See the right hand side of the Fig. 3.1 and the heavy dotted lines in the chart. From the table, we see that while Taiwan's GDP per capita (PPP) is below that of Singapore (60K, #5) and Hong Kong (49K, #9), it is the same or higher than that of some world powers: Germany (38K, #28), the United Kingdom (36K, #33), France (35K, #35), Japan (34K, #37), and South Korea (32K, #39). Taiwan's per capita GDP was about 4.5 times that of China ($8K; #116).[3]

Note that, like many other macroeconomic variables, the world distribution of both GDP and GDP per capita is extremely L-shaped. The median GDP per capita in PPP among the 255 countries and areas was a mere $7,300 (Namibia, #128), only 19 percent of Taiwan's number, showing Taiwan's high standard of living.

3.2.3 *GDP Growth Rate*

CIA data also give mostly 2011 estimates of annual GDP real growth rate for all countries (adjusted for inflation, in national currency of countries and areas). Taiwan's 2011 estimated annual growth rate is given as 5.2 percent, although TSDB (2012, Table 3-1) lists 4.0 percent for 2011, down from 10.7 percent in 2010, but up from −1.8 percent in 2009. In any case, at 5.2 percent, Taiwan ranks at #66th (74th pctl) among 255 countries and regions. It is much worse than other states such as India (7.8%, #12), China (9.5%, #6), and Mongolia (11.5%, #3) with their still youthful economies.

But Taiwan was still not as bad as all the Organization for Economic Cooperation and Development (OECD) countries such as South Korea (3.9%, #103), Germany (2.7%, #129), USA (1.5%; #174), and Japan (−0.5%; #202), due to the general world economic recession. The median GDP growth rate among the 255 countries was 2.8 percent (Brunei, #128).

[3]In addition to CIA-COW (2012) data, Hsiao (2012) has discussed and compared the estimations of GDP per capita in PPP by the IMF, the World Table of the University of Pennsylvania, and the Intelligence Unit of The Economist. Some postwar data and optimistic views on Taiwan are in Dutta (2006). For comparisons of long-run growth among Taiwan, South Korea, and Japan, see HH (2003).

3.2.4 *Unemployment Rate*

Taiwan's 2011 unemployment rate was estimated at 4.3 percent, ranking Taiwan no. 40 (84th pctl) among 255 CIA countries and regions. This rate is down from 5.85 percent in 2009, the historically highest for Taiwan since the data became available in 1952 (TSDB, 2012, 21), but still higher than any annual unemployment rate before 2000.

Although world recession was the main explanation, Taiwan's situation was worse than its near neighbors: Singapore (1.9%; #12), Hong Kong (3.3%; #28), South Korea (3.4%; #30), but better than China (6.5%; #67), and other OECD countries: Japan (4.8%; #44), Germany (6.0%; #59), the United Kingdom (7.9%; #93), United States (9.1%, #104). The 2011 world median was 12.3 percent (Jordan, #128).

3.3 Taiwan's External Economy

In the category of international trade, Taiwan's accomplishments are more impressive. As an island surrounded by ocean, Taiwan historically has been an outward-looking trade-oriented country since the end of the 19th century (HH, 1996, 2002).

3.3.1 *Exports*

According to the TSDB (2012), after the end of WWII, Japan was the largest export market for Taiwan (24% of Taiwan's 1966 total exports), but in 1967, it gave way to the USA (26.2% of its 1967 total exports); then, in 2000, to Hong Kong and China (24.4% of 2004 total exports), and in 2004, to China alone (19.9% of 2004 total exports).

Based on the CIA-COW (2012) estimate, in 2011, Taiwan exported US$325 billion, ranking no. 18 (93rd pctl) among 255 countries and regions. Despite its lack of natural resources, Taiwan's exports were almost the same as that of Spain (330b; #17), slightly higher than Switzerland ($308b, #19), India (($298b, #20), and Australia ($266b; #21), but lower than any other NIEs (Newly Industrializing Economies) in 2011: South Korea (558b; #7), Hong Kong (451b; #11), and Singapore (432b; #13). The 2011 export median of the 255 countries and regions was US$2.7 billion (Mauritius, #128), which was only 0.8 percent of Taiwan exports.

3.3.2 *Imports*

According to TSDB (2012), the U.S. was the main supplier to Taiwan before 1963, with 41.4 percent of total imports that year. But, since 1964 until today, Japan took over the role. The CIA-COW estimates the value of Taiwan's total imports in 2011 as US$299 billion, ranking #19 (93rd pctl) among 255 countries and regions. They were almost the same as Switzerland ($299b, #18), Russia ($310b, #17), and Australia ($236b; #20), but less than its fellow Asian NIEs: South Korea ($525b; #8), Hong Kong ($493; #10), and Singapore ($386b; #13). Like Fig. 1, both world exports and imports have strong L-shaped curves. The median of 2011 world imports of the 255 countries was US$4.6 billion (Virgin Islands, #128), only 1.5 percent of Taiwan's imports.

3.3.3 *Stock of Outward Foreign Direct Investment (OFDI)*

Taiwan's outward foreign direct investment (OFDI) started in earnest only after the mid-1980s, and has been directed overwhelmingly toward China.

According to CIA-COW (2012) data, Taiwan's estimated stock of OFDI up to the end of 2010 was US$162 billion, ranking at 22nd, or 75th pctl, among 85 reporting countries (or 91st pctl if all 255 countries and regions are included). A majority of countries and regions either have no data or do not engage in outward or inward FDI.

Taiwan's outward FDI stock is almost the same as Singapore (US$179b; #21) and South Korea ($139; #23), but less than that of Hong Kong ($988b, #6), Japan ($880; #8), and China ($374; #14). The 2011 median of the world OFDI stock of 85 countries is US$22.8 billion (Venezuela, #43), which is only 14 percent of Taiwan's figure.

3.3.4 *Stock of Inward Foreign Direct Investment (IFDI)*

Before 1962, the investment from overseas Chinese dominated Taiwan's inward foreign direct investment (IFDI) for many years. After 1963, especially after 2000, it dwindled to miniscule, and other foreign direct investment, mostly from the U.S. and Japan, has dominated.

According to CIA-COW (2012), Taiwan's IFDI at the end of 2011 was only US$65 billion, ranking no. 51 (45th pctl) among 91 reporting countries (or 80th pctl if all 255 countries and regions are included). Using the CIA-COW data, Taiwan's IFDI stock was lower than the median of $76 billion (Nigeria, #46), almost the same as a newly developing country such as Vietnam (68b; #50), about half that of historically conservative South Korea ($130b; #29), and only 6 percent of Hong Kong ($1,141b; #3), and 20 percent of Singapore ($318b; #18).

Despite the government efforts, Taiwan had the smallest IFDI stock among the NIEs; it is indeed a lackluster performance for a developed country. It appears that the inward FDI to Taiwan was substituted by that to China.

As in Fig. 3.1, the world distribution of both OFDI and IFDI are extremely skewed to the right (L-shaped).

3.4 Foreign Exchange and Global Competitiveness

One of the brightest spots for the Taiwanese economy in recent years has been its total foreign exchange reserves and its ranking in competitiveness indexes.

3.4.1 *Foreign Exchange*

Taiwan has had positive reserves (foreign exchange, gold, including Special Drawing Rights in IMF) every year since the mid-1970s and its reserves accelerated quickly in early 1980. By the end of 2011, Taiwan's reserves came to $418 billion (31 Dec. 2011 estimate), ranking no. 5 (97th pctl) among 175 reporting countries (or 98th pctl if all 255 countries and regions are included) (CIA-COW, 2012). Taiwan's reserves were superseded only by China ($3,316b; #1), Japan ($1,063; #2), Saudi Arabia ($556b; #3) and Russia (513b; #4), and were higher than that of South Korea ($320; #8), Singapore ($248.7b; #11), and Germany ($216.5; #12). Taiwan's large reserves are the result of past accumulation of trade surpluses.

The distribution of world foreign reserves is also strongly L-shaped. The end-of-2011 median reserves were $5 billion (Bahrain, #88), which were only 1.2 percent of those of Taiwan.

3.4.2 *Global Competitiveness Index*

The Global Competitiveness Index (GCI) is constructed annually by the World Economic Forum (WEF). It defines national competitiveness as the capability of maintaining a high economic growth rate of a nation for the coming five to ten years. For 2012–13, according to the WEF (2012), 13, Taiwan's index was 5.28 out of 7.00, ranking no. 13 (91st pctl) among 144 countries, unchanged for the second year, although still high, historically lower than Singapore (5.67; #2), closer to the United Kingdom (5.5.45; #8), Hong Kong (5.41; #9), and Japan (5.40; #10), but higher than that of South Korea (5.12; #19) and China (4.83; #29). The 2012–13 median score for 144 countries was 4.14 (Montenegro and Ukraine, #72 and #73).

In fact, Taiwan's overall index has been slipping continuously from no. 4/59 (93rd pctl) in 1998–99.[4] Among the sub-indexes, Taiwan's innovation and business sophistication factors index ranked at no. 14 (5.1, 90th pctl) out of 144 countries (WEF, 2012, 338), slipped greatly from no. 7/139 (5.2, pctl) during 2010–2011 (WEF, 2010, 316). Still, as we will see below, the Taiwanese contribution to the world's applied technology is indeed significant.

3.4.3 *World Competitiveness Index*

The other index is the World Competitiveness Index (WCI), published annually by the Institute of Management Development (IMD) in Switzerland. It ranks a nation's business environment and analyzes the ability to provide an environment in which enterprises can compete (IMD, 1999; HH, 2002, 203) Taiwan's WCI rating has fluctuated during the past decade. It improved from no. 18 (62nd pctl) out of 47 countries in 1999 to no. 6 (90th pctl) out of 58 countries in 2011, and then, with a score of 89.957, Taiwan ranked no. 7 (89th pctl) out of 59 countries in 2012 (IMD, 2012, 6), a slip of one rank from 2011.

Although still high, Taiwan's rate has been consistently behind that of Hong Kong (100.0; #1) and Singapore (95.923; #4), but higher than that of South Korea (76.747; #22), China (75.769; #23), and Japan (71.354; #27). The 2012 median WCI for the 59 countries was 69 (Thailand, #30), less than one-third of Taiwan's score.

3.5 The "Republic of Technology: Information and Communications"

By the end of the 1990s Taiwan ranked as "the number three producer of information technology worldwide, behind only the United States and Japan."[5] In a manner of speaking, one could say that Taiwan had become the "Republic of Technology in Information and Communications" (ROTIC).

3.5.1 *ROTIC in the Last Decade*

Various issues of the *Taiwan Statistical Data Book* (TSDB) since 2002 have shown the products for which Taiwan ranked as first, second, and

[4]See HH (2002), 200. In 1999, Taiwan was superseded only by Singapore, USA, and HK.
[5]Cited in HH (2002), 167. Original source: Institute for Information Industries, Market Intelligence Center, Taiwan.

third in world production, and most of them are related to information and communication technology, indicating that Taiwan is indeed a kind of "Republic of Technology" in this critical area of modern manufacturing.

Combining some items for the sake of discussion here, the production of three items — optical discs, IC Foundry, and IC Packaging — were consistently number one products of the world with production facilities in Taiwan. Three items — Mask ROM, IC testing, and Electro-deposited copper foil ("ED Cu") — became prominent in the mid-2000s; and by 2009 the first two items almost completely monopolized world markets (99% and 71%, respectively), which was still the case in 2012. These three items are still produced in Taiwan (TSDB, 2012, Table 4-b).

However, TSDB also reveals that the six items which were prominent (no. 1) in 2002 — motherboards (72% of 2002 world market share, same below), notebook PCs (56%), wireless LANs (30%), LCD Monitors (59%), xDSL CPE (45%), and Glass Fiber (31%) — moved to offshore production by 2009, presumably to China, with greatly increased world market shares, indicating expanded production in China. In fact, the title of "Republic of Technology" is gradually slipping away to the offshore production in China, as discussed below.

3.5.2 *Taiwan's Major Actors (IT Companies)*

Behind the faceless statistical numbers, there are known and unknown heroes. The major actors are, in addition to the hardworking, well-trained, well-disciplined Taiwanese workers, Taiwan's contract manufacturers such as Acer, Arima, ASUSTek, BenQ, Compal, Formosa Plastic, Foxconn, Hon Hai, HTC, Inventec, Media Tek, Quanta, TSMC, UMC, and Wistron.[6] TSMC and UMC are the world's leading semiconductor foundries. In mid-2011, the world's largest contract PC maker was Quanta, which made more than 50 million notebook computers in 2010, generating revenue of more than US$35 billion. The world's number two PC maker is Compal,[7] and the number 3 is Acer,[8] all of Taiwan. The *Financial Times* also reported

[6]The list is taken from DigiTimes and Einhorn *et al.* (2005). For the latest survey, see "Taiwan motherboard industry overview," "Taiwan DRAM module industry overview," "Notebook market overview," ICT reports, etc. in www.digitimes.com, downloaded in September, 2011. Also, see "List of electronics brand," Wikipedia.
[7]Kwong, Nuttall, and Hille (2011).
[8]Kwong and Dembosky (2011).

that Computex, in Taipei in May, 2011 was "the world's second-biggest consumer electronic trade fair."

"Taiwan's success is also China's," wrote *BusinessWeek* (Einhorn *et al.*, 2005). It estimated that 40 to 80 percent of China's ICT hardware exports were made in Taiwanese-owned factories. "All the manufacturing capacity in China is overlaid with the management and marketing expertise of the Taiwanese, along with all their contacts in the world."[9] In 2006, among the 20 top foreign direct investment companies in China, there were four from Taiwan, Hon Hai (with sales revenue of 125.6 billion RMB, same below in this section; #1), which far outpaced #2 US Motorola (73.6b), followed by Quanta (36.3b; #8), Inventec (35.7b; #9), and Foxconn (29.7b; #19). (WPC, 2008, Table 1-3-57).

The U.S. Council of Economic Advisors in the early 2000s estimated unofficially that "an interruption of Taiwan-supplied IT products would cut GDP by 0.7 percent (or $5.5 billion a month)" since the US computer-producing sector accounts for about 2.8 percent of US GDP (Osius, 2002). Taiwan's high-tech supply is as important as Mideast oil for the world economy (Einhorn *et al.*, 2005).

3.6 Taiwan's Economic Prospects

As noted above, all indexes show that Taiwan has done very well, except the GDP growth rate and inward FDI, ranking between the 74th to 98th percentiles in 2011 among the 255 or so countries and regions listed in the World Factbook. Taiwan's record is especially impressive in the area of foreign trade and reserves, innovation and ICT industries. From the 1980s to the 2000s, Taiwan played an important role in international economic activity, and as such, definitely is important today in the global economy, and especially for the U.S. and China.

As the world enters the second decade of the century, economic conditions in the developed world, especially the U.S. and the European Union, are grim with economic recession and sovereign debt problems. By contrast, the large developing countries, like Brazil, Russia, India and China (BRIC), are growing rapidly, thus dramatically and drastically changing the world economic environment. Where does Taiwan fit into this new global economy?

---

[9]See Einhorn *et al.* (2005). For the role of Taiwanese invested firm (TIF) in China, see HH (2006), 208–215. For an economic analysis of FDI and Taiwanese investment in China, see HH (2004, 2006).

Recently, Chevalerias (2010) declared that the postwar "Taiwanese economic miracle is over. Since at the end of the 1980s, changes in macroeconomic conditions forced Taiwanese industry to restructure." However, we should note first that industrial restructuring does not mean the end of the economic "miracle," and slowing down of economic growth may be due to economic maturing rather than the end of the "miracle." Nevertheless, in the following sections, we will discuss some of the economic problems facing Taiwan.

Taiwan's structural changes occurred internally and externally. Internally, the massive ICT industry developed in Taiwan had labor shortages, high wage rates and high land prices, plus tighter environmental regulations since the 1990s, all forcing Taiwanese traditional industries to move to China, followed by high-tech industries, resulting in a hollowing out of the Taiwanese economy.

At the same time, externally, despite the world-class inventiveness and dedication of the Taiwanese workers, the firms and the government flocked to ICT industry and failed to develop other fields like biochemical, pharmaceutical, precision instruments, and alternate energy industries. Even within the ITC industry, Taiwan has failed to develop crucial core technologies and relied heavily on imports from Japan, the U.S., and even South Korea.[10] They also failed to develop Taiwan's own brand names in the world consumer market, and remain largely as contract manufacturers. In fact, none of the more than fifteen Taiwanese ICT actors we have noticed above are known among world consumers, with the possible exception of Acer (computers), Asus (tablets), and HTC (Smartphones), a stark contrast with South Korean brands like Samsung, LG, and Daewoo, etc.

Thus, the profits of the Taiwanese firms are squeezed from below by high patent costs, and from above by being controlled by foreign patents and foreign retailers, such as HP, Dell, Sears, etc.[11] Furthermore, when the world ICT industry matured and started stagnating and even declining, no other star industries in Taiwan were ready for substitution.

---

[10]Some examples are given in Chevalerias (2010), 40.

[11]In technical terms, most of the Taiwanese firms stay at the original equipment manufacturers (OEM) stage. While some advanced to Original Design Manufacturing (ODM), very few advanced to Original Brand Manufacturing (OBM). The problem of double squeeze of the Taiwanese firms already occurred in the 1970s and the 1980s, for example, in the industrial sewing machine industry, see HH (1996), 282–283. For the problems of marketing, see ibid., 268. During the early period, the Taiwanese producers had to rely on Japanese Shoshas for marketing.

3.7 Deepening Relations with China

After the 2008 presidential election in Taiwan, President Ma Ying-jeou and his government tried to reinvigorate the economy by tying Taiwan even closer with China to take advantage of China's cheap labor and vast market, and to ride the coattails of China's rapid growth. In June 2010, Taiwan and China signed a controversial "Economic Cooperation Framework Agreement" (ECFA), which took effect[12] on September 12, 2010. The objectives of that agreement were to reduce tariffs and trade barriers for both countries, and for Taiwan, to increase exports, domestic investment, and inward FDI. Another important reason for the pact, according to the Ma government, was that Taiwan would be able to negotiate and conclude free trade agreements (FTA) with other major trading countries, even though China was strongly opposed to this prospect (HH, 2006). By June, 2011, the critics were pointing out that the Ma government "grossly exaggerated the benefits of ECFA" (Chen, 2011). According to Chen, the benefits of tariff reduction were only 1 percent of what Ma had proclaimed; the growth of Taiwan's exports to China was not only slower than that of other countries' exports to China, but also slower than Taiwan's exports to countries other than China.[13]

Even while Taiwan has been becoming more dependent on China, the opposite has been true for China, which has been expanding its ties with the rest of the world. China is now Taiwan's no. 1 export market, but Taiwan's ranking in China's total imports slipped from no. 2, 11.3 percent of China's 2000 total imports, to no. 3, only 8.3 percent of China's 2010 total imports, surpassed by Korea (no. 2, 9.9%).

The decline in Taiwan's trade competitiveness with all its major trading partners is alarming. While Taiwan's FDI to China increased at an alarming rate (84%), Taiwan's domestic investment and inward FDI decreased; on the other hand, China reiterated its strong opposition to Taiwan having FTAs with any other countries. Hence, so far it appears that none of the Ma government's expectations from the ECFA have been realized. The double squeeze, along with relatively high labor costs at home, geographic

[12]See the Wall Street Journal, 9/11/2011, and Wikipedia (2011a). For controversy surrounding the signing of ECFA, see Wikipedia (2011b); its economic effects, see Chevalerias (2010). For recent political development since Ma's election, see Bush (2011), Muyard (2010), and Hsiao (2012); for the signing of ECFA and its consequences on world economy, see Chen (2014) and Wu (2014).
[13]Also see Chen (2014).

proximity, cultural affinity, the new division of labor in the ICT industry, and globalization, have all caused Taiwanese firms to move to China en masse since the 1990s, and the trend accelerated in the 2000s. The following statistics from TSDB (2012) and comparison with some other countries reveal Taiwan's economic conditions and its growing dependence on China.

3.7.1 *Outward FDI*

Taiwan's outward foreign direct investment (OFDI, on approval base) to China has been increasing rapidly since 1991 when the data was first published. In 1999, 28 percent of OFDI went to China (TSDB, 2012, Tables 12-6 and 12-8a). It accelerated and doubled after 2002, and by 2010, a whopping 84 percent, US$14.6 billion out of 17.8 billion total OFDI (add about 2 percent if HK is included), was invested in China. Although the proportion reduced to 80 percent in 2011 (ibid.), Taiwan's OFDI relies almost exclusively on China. The rest of outward FDI are almost equally divided between Americas (mainly USA) and Asia.

3.7.2 *Inward FDI*

As the domestic industry loses foothold in Taiwan, the inward FDI also has stayed away from Taiwan and presumably moved to China. On the approval basis, the annual inward FDI reached the all-time high of US$15.3 billion in 2007, but it then reduced almost a half to $8.2 billion in 2008, another half to $4.8 billion in 2009, and down again to mere $3.8 billion in 2010, only 25 percent of its peak. Although it increased to US$4.9 billion in 2011 (ibid.), with the deepening economic and political dependence on China, coupled with Taiwan's increasing international isolation, the downward trend appears to continue. The future prospect of inward FDI is bleak.

3.7.3 *Exports to China*

In 2000, Taiwan's combined exports to China (2.9% of total exports, same below, US$4.4b) and Hong Kong (21.5%, US$32.7b) replaced its exports to the USA (23.4%, US$35.6b). However, in 2004, China alone (19.9%, US$36.3b) quickly replaced the USA (15.8%, US$28.8b), to become Taiwan's number one export market.

In 2010, Taiwan's export dependency on China reached 28 percent, US$77 billion out of 275 billion total exports (it would be 42%, US$115b, if Hong Kong was included), which was the highest since Taiwan has had a trade record with China starting in 1991. Although its China dependency reduced slightly to 27 percent, US$84 billion out of 308 billion (40%, US$124b, if Hong Kong was included) in 2011, Taiwan's reliance on Chinese market far outpaced that on the USA (11.8%, US$36b; #2) and Japan (5.9%, US$18b; #3).

In fact, in 2011, Taiwan's export dependency on China was highest among other countries that Taiwan trades with (CIA, 2012), such as Korea (24.4%), Japan (20%), USA (7%), Singapore (11.0%) and other ASEAN members.[14]

3.7.4 *Imports from China*

Despite government's import control from China, since 2006, China has replaced the USA (#2 since 1963) to become the second largest source of imports for Taiwan. In 2011, Taiwan's import dependency on China reached the highest level at 16 percent, US$44 billion out of 281 billion total imports, much higher than its dependency on the USA (9.2%, US$26b, #3), although slightly smaller than its dependency on Japan (19%, $52b, #1).

Compared with the neighboring countries (CIA, 2012), in 2011, Taiwan's import dependency on China (16%) was almost the same as that of Korea (16.5%), lower than that of Japan (21.5%), and USA (18.4%), but higher than that of Singapore (10.4%), and other ASEAN countries. Despite import controls, its imports from China keep increasing and those from USA and Japan keep decreasing. As in other advanced countries, after ECAFA, it is expected that cheap Chinese products will continue flooding the Taiwanese market.

3.8 Taiwan and Its Major Trading Partners

Externally, Taiwan's share of imports and exports with its two other major trading partners, the United States and Japan, are changing rapidly.

3.8.1 *United States*

Figure 3.2 shows U.S. imports from, exports to, and the balance of trade (BOT) with Taiwan (the first columns) for 1990, 2000, and 2010. We have

---

[14]Hong Kong's 2011 estimated exports dependency rate on China was 52 percent and that of import dependency rate was 45 percent. For the data, see CIA (2012).

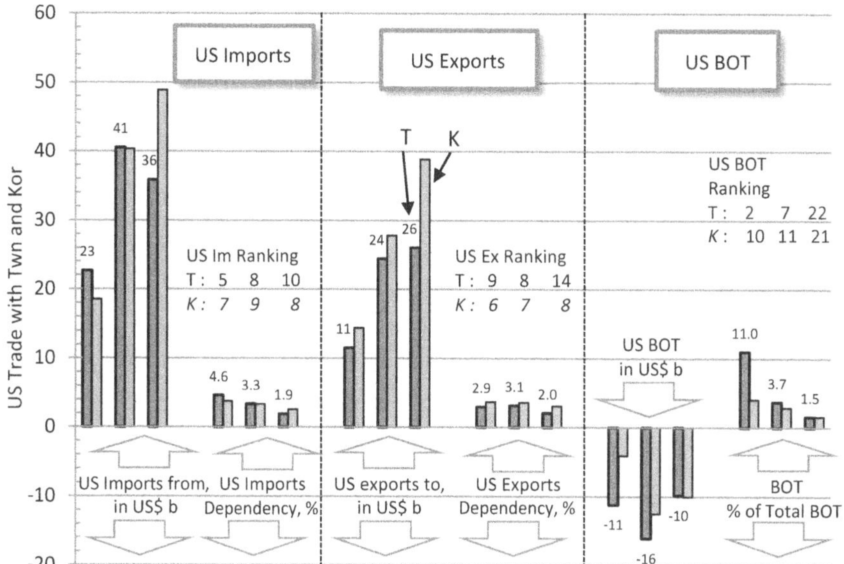

	'90	'00	'10	.	'90	'00	'10	'90	'00	'10	.	'90	'00	'10	'90	'00	'10	.	'90	'00	'10
Twn	23	41	36		4.6	3.3	1.9	11	24	26		2.9	3.1	2.0	-11	-16	-10		11.	3.7	1.5
Kor	18	40	49		3.7	3.3	2.6	14	28	39		3.7	3.6	3.0	-4	-12	-10		4.0	2.9	1.6

Figure 3.2: U.S. Imports from, Exports to, and BOT with Taiwan and Korea US$ billion, percentages, and ranking

added South Korea (the second columns) for comparison (SAUS, 2012, Table 1307).

Imports from Taiwan United States imports from Taiwan almost doubled from 1990 to 2000 (from US$23b to US$41b), but decreased to $36 billion in 2010. (See the first panel of Fig. 3.2). In terms of Taiwan's imports into the United States, total imports (US imports dependency on Taiwan), and its US imports rankings, Taiwan continued to slip, from 4.6 percent in 1990 to 3.3 percent in 2000 and to mere 1.9 percent in 2010. Its ranking slipped correspondingly from no. 5 to no. 8, and then to no. 10 in 2010, respectively. The importance of Taiwanese imports in the US market reduced considerably.

In a stark contrast, Korea's exports to USA (US$18b) were lower than that of Taiwan in 1990, but continued to increase, and almost caught up with Taiwan in 2000 (40b), then greatly surpassed Taiwan (49b) by 2010. In 2010, Korea's import share in the US import market was 2.6 percent, ranked #8, outpacing Taiwan's by 1.9 percent.

Exports to Taiwan United States exports to Taiwan more than doubled (US$11b to 24b) from 1990 to 2000 (see the middle panel of Fig. 3.2), but stagnated from 2000 to 2010 (US$24b to 26b). The ranking of the Taiwan market in US total exports has decreased from no. 8 to no. 14 during the last decade, and the US exports dependency of Taiwan changed from 3.1 percent to 2.1 percent. This is also in stark contrast to Korea: the US exports to Korea increased steadily, although the export share in US total exports and export ranking decreased slightly, but it still remained at #8 in 2010.

Balance of Trade The United States incurred negative balance of trade (BOT) with both countries during the last two decades (the last panel of Fig. 3.2). In 1990, Taiwan was the #2 deficit country of the US (with US$−11b), next only to Japan (US$−40b), but it has eased during the last two decades, and by 2010, Taiwan became #22 country with the BOT deficit of mere US$1.0 billion, about 1.5 percent of US total deficit (US$−635b) that year. Taiwan's importance in reducing US trade deficit has declined considerably. Korea's BOT has the same pattern of change as Taiwan, except that the change is not as drastic as that of Taiwan. In general Taiwan's trade relations with the USA indicate the declining role and reduced competitiveness of Taiwanese products in the U.S. economy.

3.8.2 *Japan*

The decline of Taiwan's import share and ranking in Japan is even more dramatic: In 2000, Taiwan was no. 3 (¥1.9 trillion yen), or 4.7 percent of Japan's total imports, just following China (#1, ¥5.9 tr) and South Korea (#2, ¥2.7 tr). However, by 2011, Taiwan had slipped to no. 11 (¥1.8 tr), or 2.7 percent of Japan's 2011 total imports (¥68 tr) (JSY, 2013).

Taiwan's role as Japan's exports has also been declining, from no. 2 (¥4 tr, 7.5%) of Japan's total exports (¥51.6 tr) in 2000, second only to the USA (¥15 tr), to no. 4 (¥4 tr, 6.2% of total imports of ¥65.5 tr) in 2011.

Another concern is that the value of Taiwan's imports from Japan, mostly essential high tech parts, remain almost the same, and at the same time, Taiwan's loss of the Japanese market has been staggering during the last decade.

3.8.3 *China*

Even in China, Taiwan's no. 1 exporting market, as already noted in Section 3.7.3, Taiwan's ranking in China's total imports slipped from no. 2

(US$25.5b), 11.3 percent of China's 2000 total imports, to no. 3 (US$116b), only 8.3 percent of China's 2010 total imports (US$1,396b) (CSY, 2001, 2012), surpassed by Korea (#2, 9.9%, US$138b).

3.9 Worsening Domestic Economy

Domestically, in addition to the worsening unemployment rate, Taiwan has been experiencing drastic slowing down in major economic indicators.

3.9.1 *Nominal and Real GDP in Local Currency*

In this section, we use the national currency (GDP at the current price), instead of PPP, since it is the one directly perceived by the local people. The left-hand side of Fig. 3.3 shows Taiwan's 10-year growth rate of nominal and real GDP in NT$ (TSDB, 2012, Table 3-1). The solid line shows the nominal growth rates in percentage (%). From 1952 to 1961, nominal GDP grew 305 percent. In the next decade, 1962 to 1971, it grew 239 percent, and then jumped to 467 percent during the next decade, 1972–1981. However,

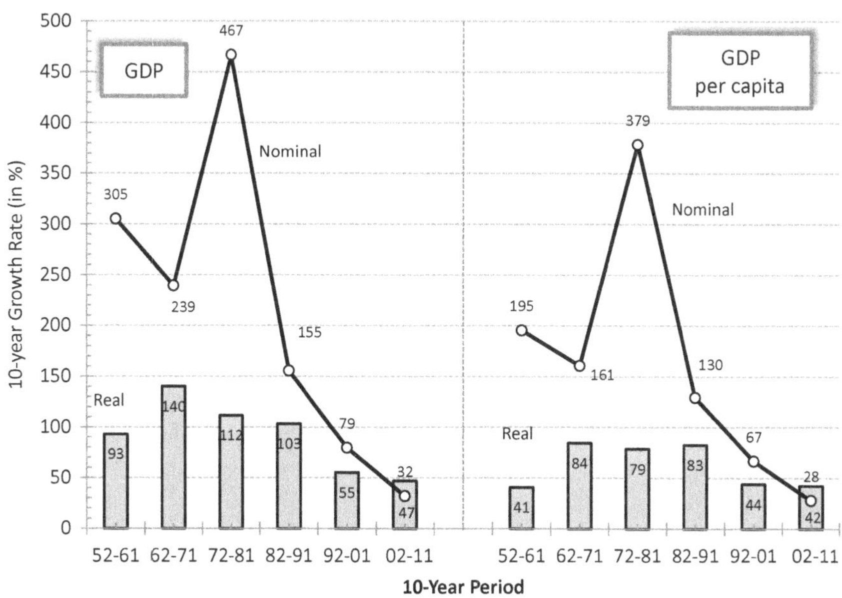

Figure 3.3: Nominal and real GDP
In NT$, 10-year Growth Rates

after 1982, the ten year growth rate slowed considerably: in 1992–2001 and 2002–2011, the growth rates were only 79 percent (NT$ 5.5 trillion to 9.9 trillion) and 32 percent (NT$ 10.4 tr to 13.7 tr), respectively.

Nominal GDP contains inflation rate. Thus, in terms of the ten-year growth rates of real GDP at 2006 prices, as shown by the columns on the left, it peaked earlier during 1962 to 1971 (at 140%), and it decreased continuously to mere 47 percent (NT$ 10.1 tr to 14.8 tr) during the last decade. The decrease in real terms is not as dramatic, but it has been decreasing continuously during the last two decades.

3.9.2 *Nominal and Real GDP per capita in Local Currency*

Local residences are more concerned with changes in GDP per capita. The 10-year growth rates of nominal and real GDP per capita[15] are shown on the right-hand side of Fig. 3.3. As can be expected, the pattern is the same as those of nominal and real GDP on the left. Like GDP, after more than doubling in the previous decades before 1981, during the last decade (2002 to 2011), GDP per capita increased a pitiful 28 percent in nominal terms (NT$ 443K to 592K) and 42 percent in real terms (NT$ 447K to 636K), feeding the growing discontent of the people.

3.9.3 *Monthly Earnings*

The decrease in GDP per capita is also reflected more seriously at the industrial level. Figure 3.4 shows that the average nominal monthly earnings of employees of manufacturing (the line with filled black circles) and service sectors (the line with white triangles) (TSDB, 2012, Table 2-12a) (these are mostly private enterprises) moved together. In terms of the growth rates, they grew about 134 percent and 127 percent, respectively, from 1982 to 1991, but only about 43 percent and 42 percent, respectively, from 1992 to 2001. Even worse, the average earnings remained almost flat, 13 percent (NT$ 38K to 44K) and 7 percent (NT$ 44K to 47K), respectively, from 2002 to 2011. Their earnings have been almost stagnant for the last two decades. If price inflation is considered, the average real monthly earnings have in fact decreased during these years.

Note that the nominal monthly earning of gas and electricity industry (mostly public enterprises, the line with white circle markers) consistently

[15]We divide nominal and real GDP by Taiwan's population (TSDB, 2012, Table 2-2). The results are slightly different from those given in Table 1-1a, TSDB (2012).

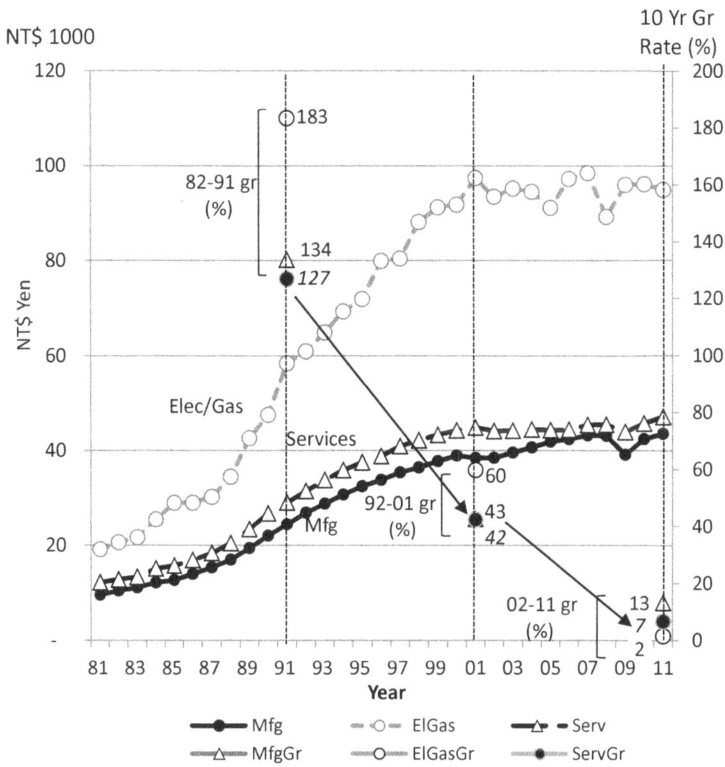

Figure 3.4: Taiwan's Average Monthly Earnings
Manufacturing, Services, Utility

earned more than twice that of the other two industries. However, its earnings also stagnated during the last two decades, and they increased mere 2 percent (NT$ 93K to 95K) from 2002 to 2011.

Thus, whether in the private or public sectors, the stagnation of wages and salaries fed into restlessness, misery, and malcontents of the Taiwanese in recent years.

3.9.4 *International Comparisons*

From an international perspective, Taiwan is one of the worst, if not the worst, countries among comparable countries. According to the US Bureau of Labor Statistics (BLS, 2011, Table 1), Taiwan's hourly compensation costs in manufacturing in 1997 were US$7.04, 31 percent of that of USA, but, after thirteen years, in 2010, it only increased to US$8.36, a mere 24 percent of USA's, showing the relative decrease in labor compensation in Taiwan as compared with that of the USA.

In contrast, the comparable South Korea data showed that the hourly compensation costs were US$9.36 (41% of the US level, same below) in 1997 and increased to US$16.62 (48%) in 2010; those of Japan were $22.28 (87%) in 1997, and also increased to $31.99 (92%), respectively, in 2010.

In other recent BLS data, in 2010, among the thirty six countries (BLS, 2012, Chart 3.1), Taiwan ranked 31st in hourly compensation costs (about US$8.00), showing Taiwan's unusual lag in hourly compensation in manufacturing.

In fact, from 2000 to 2007, Taiwan's average annual growth rate in manufacturing hourly compensation costs was one of the lowest (about 2.5%) among thirty four countries in the BLS chart, and it had the worst (no. 34) negative growth rate (about −1%) from 2007 to 2010 (ibid., Chart 3.4).

It appears that Taiwan's wage and salary levels are also lagging far behind the other countries. Surprisingly, despite the fact that Taiwan has become more competitive in terms of labor cost, it is not reflected in any comparative advantage of increasing exports or inward FDI.

3.9.5 *Persistent High Unemployment Rates*

In Section 3.2.4, we pointed out that Taiwan's unemployment rate in recent years has been worse than that of its near neighbors (cross section comparison). Here we would like to point out that, historically, as Fig. 3.5 shows, Taiwan's unemployment rate has been increasing from the low of 1.5 percent in 1994 to 5.9 percent in 2010, the highest unemployment rate since 1952 (time series comparison) (TSDB, 2012, Table 2-8b). Note that, despite the promise of "Golden Decade" by President Ma in 2008 election, the unemployment rate persists at high level.

3.9.6 *Inflation*

The upper line of Fig. 3.5 shows the consumer price index with the base at 2006 (ibid., Table 10-4). It has increased 7 percent from 2006 to 2011. Although the price also has an increasing tendency in recent years, it appears that up to now inflation is not a serious problem in Taiwan. An exception is the food price, which has increased 14 percent from 2006 to 2011 (ibid.), aggravating the misery of the general public.

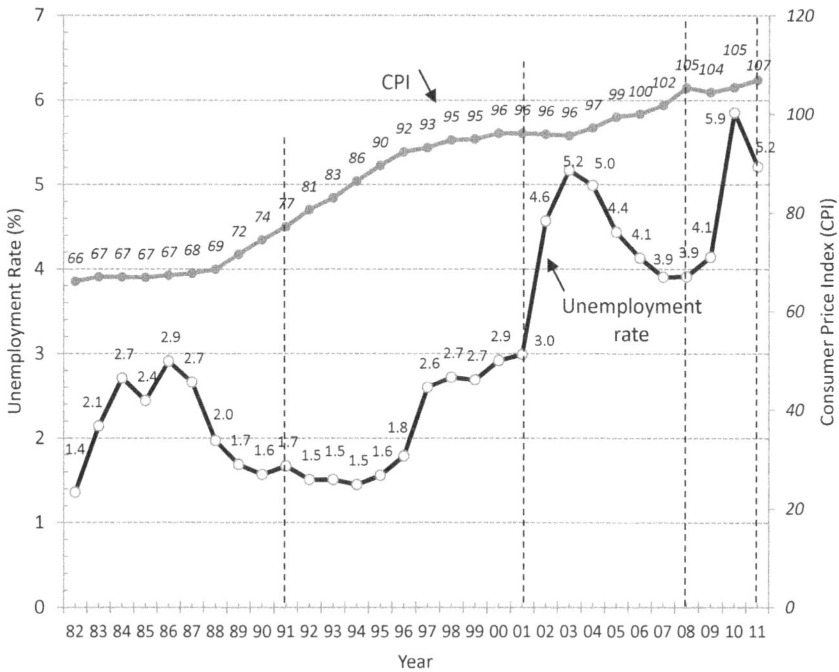

Figure 3.5: Taiwan's Unemployment Rate and CPI (CPI, 2006 = 100)

3.10 Conclusions — Taiwan's Economy at the Crossroads

Taiwan has come a long way in its development, from the prewar period to the postwar period, and finally, culminating with one of the most successful economies in the world. But now the island is at a critical crossroad.

3.10.1 *Political Risk and Policy Reform*

Despite its achievements, the Taiwanese economy today is showing signs of slowing down, while becoming more reliant on the Chinese market. This may be partly due to the maturity of the Taiwanese economy, but there are concerns that the rankings of Taiwanese economic performance in various macroeconomic indicators are slipping behind other countries, especially South Korea, in recent years. The Taiwanese ICT industry is experiencing a major structural change with many domestic companies moving production to China, hallowing out the Taiwanese economy. The overreliance of the Taiwanese economy on China may lead to the end of the miracle.[16]

While Taiwan has not yet seen benefits from the ECFA, it may wreak havoc on Taiwan's economy and national sovereignty. An influx of cheap Chinese goods, services, and large numbers of laborers and students in the coming ten years (the time limit set by WTO for opening up 95 percent of Taiwan's economy to free trade) threaten the already lack luster earning gain, and perhaps the survival of Taiwanese traditional small-and-medium enterprises, as already experienced by developed countries such as the U.S. and Japan.

Furthermore, with pervasive Chinese influence on the small island of Taiwan and China's territorial ambition, it may be difficult to maintain security and keep confidential materials of government and business from the Chinese. Even Taiwan's inventiveness, one of the island's inherent strengths, may be surpassed by China.

Politically, despite closer economic relations and the Ma government's friendly gestures, even to the degree of subordinations, China continues to block Taiwan's meaningful participation in international organizations, and steadily increases the missiles targeted at Taiwan. For China, it appears that the ECFA is merely a means to achieve its territorial claim on Taiwan.[17] Under such conditions, the detrimental effects. of the ECFA on Taiwan could be very serious, due to the huge difference between Taiwan and China in size and population, between free and authoritarian societies, and between Taiwan's Kuomintang (KMT) and Chinese Communist Party (CCP), with the legacy of historical enmity and distrust between them. Thus, the ECFA appears not to be the panacea that the Ma government hoped for.

---

[16]While the individual Taiwanese ICT companies and firms like Hon Hai and Foxconn are thriving and expanding through economic globalization, especially by moving to China, Taiwan's home economy and wages are stagnant and even shrinking, as we have seen in Section 3.9. Similar effects of globalization may also happen in Japan, Europe, and the United States. It appears that China as a "chaotic attractor of foreign direct investment" (HH, 2004) contributed dichotomy of richer companies and poorer countries and people.

[17]For China's territorial claim, see HH (2002), 203–205. The critics are concerned with Ma's hidden agenda of unification with China through closer economic relations. See Wikipedia (2011a,b) and Chevalerias (2010). In recent disclosure in Wikileaks: on May 31, 2007, Ma said to AIT Director Young that KMT's "'Taiwan-centered values' would not alter the party's original goal of 'national unification.'" Ma repeated the same line in June 1, 2007 (Mo, 2011).

3.10.2 *Restructuring and Reinventing the Taiwanese Economy*

The past two decades of relying on cheap Chinese labor, land, and market have not prevented the downward slide of Taiwan's economy from its peak. Taiwan must recognize the "China trap" of taking the easy way out and face its political dangers. Instead, Taiwan should diversify its industrial bases, develop core technology, and build its own trade brand names to compete in the global market. This is a long-term economic policy that will not necessarily achieve quick results. Patience is called for. In the meantime, as an independent member of WTO, Taiwan could aggressively negotiate with its other major trading partners, especially the USA, Japan, Singapore, and ASEAN (HH, 2006), to join regional free trade agreements as a countervailing policy against China and to avoid international isolation.

Taiwan should pay close attention to the US government's recent "rebalancing strategy" toward Asia, maintain a good relation with the United States and Japan, and prepare and play a positive role in the new US policy. The first step is increasing Taiwan's trade relations with the USA and participating in the Trans-Pacific Partnership (TPP), and aim to join the Free Trade Area of the Asian-Pacific (FTAAP) through APEC and the United States. Recent development shows that the new governments of Japan and Korea are considering joining TPP. Taiwan should not miss the opportunity. At the same time, the immediate objective should be to reinforce the Trade and Investment Framework Agreement (TIFA) with the USA, and eventually conclude a Taiwan-US Free Trade Agreement (FTA), which could make the China factor less potent (HH, 2006). In any event, Taiwan's economy and the island's sovereignty are clearly at a crossroads. Taiwan, *quo Vadis*?

3.10.3 *Where is Taiwan?*

The high rankings of the Taiwan's economic activities and performance in various arenas among the countries and the regions in the world show that Taiwan does matter in the international community. Taiwan has played an important role in the development of world economy through its productive and innovative activities in electric and electronic manufacturing, and investment in China and ASEANs, helped the rise of the Asian economy. Yet, the Taiwanese wonder why Taiwan is not recognized as a sovereign country by most other nations in the world, nor been admitted as a member of the United Nations. Furthermore, when it comes to the records of

Taiwan's economic and other achievements, most foreign and international documents list Taiwan by bogus names such as Taiwan Province of China (false); Taiwan, China (ambiguous); or Taipei, China (funny); or simply do not list it at all. On top of that is the obvious fact that Taiwan has been effectively excluded, due to pressure from China, from almost all of the world's important international organizations, as discussed in more detail in the essay by Wu Rong-i, and others, in Lee and Williams (2014). The world is unjust and unfair to the nation of 23 million hard working people.

Appendix 3A: Summary Table of Sections 3.2 to 3.4

Table 3A: Taiwan in the Global Economy

Summary of Domestic and External Indicators

Section in Chpt	Item	Value	Unit	Wold rank No.	Cntry/ reg No.	Percentile pctl*	year
	Area	36,000	km^2	139	250	45	2012
	Population	23.1	million	51	238	79	2012
	Pop density	717	km^2	16	255	94	2012
	Taiwan's Domestic Economy						
3.2.1	GDP (in PPP)	885	US$ b	19	255	93	2011
3.2.2	GDP(PPP) per capita	37,900	$	27	255	90	2011
3.2.3	GDP growth rate	5.2	%	66	255	74	2011
3.2.4	Unemployment rate	4.3	%	40	255	84	2011
	Taiwan's External Economy						
3.3.1	Exports	325	US$ b	18	255	93	2011
3.3.2	Imports	299	US$ b	19	255	93	2011
3.3.3	Outward FDI (Stock)	162	US$ b	22	85	75	2010
3.3.4	Inward FDI (Stock)	65	US$ b	51	91	45	2011
3.4.1	Foreign Exchange	418	US$ b	5	175	97	2011
3.4.2	Global comp. Index (WEF)	5.28	point	13	144	91	2013
3.4.3	World comp. Index (IMF)	89.96	point	7	59	89	2012

Notes: *(pctl at x) = (L + 0.5E)*100/n, where n is the sample size, L = n − x, is the number of values less than x, and E is the number of values equal to x. We take E = 1.

Acknowledgments

We owe our thanks to Drs. Shyu-tu Lee, Stan Yang, and Jack Williams for editing and shortening the paper. Figures 3.3 to 3.5, Appendix 3A, percentages and percentiles, in-text references have been added to this chapter for clarity. Sections 3.8.1 and 3.9.4 have been expanded. All errors of omission and commission are mine.

References

Bureau of Labor Statistics (BLS). U.S. Department of Labor (2011). "International Comparisons of Hourly Compensation in Manufacturing, 2010." *News Release* USDL-11-1778. Downloaded from www.bls.gov/ilc in November 2012.

Bureau of Labor Statistics (BLS). U.S. Department of Labor (2012). "Charting International Labor Comparisons. 2012 edition." Downloaded from www.bls.gov/ilc in November 2012.

Bush, Richard C. (2011). "Taiwan and East Asian Security." *Orbis*, 55(2) (Spring): 274–289.

Chen, Po-Chi (2011). "The Facts Prove That the Government Grossly Exaggerated the Benefits of ECFA" (in Chinese). August 24, 2011. Look (Kan) Magazine, #094. Downloaded in September 2011 from http://www.taiwanthinktank.org/chinese/page/3/26/2185/0.

——— (2014). "ECFA and China's Strategy to the World." In Shyu-tu Lee and Williams (eds.), 223–231, listed in this References section.

Chevalerias, Philippe (2010). "The Taiwanese Economy After the Miracle." *China Perspectives*, 2010(3), 35–44. Special Feature, *Taiwan: The Consolidation of a Democratic and Distinct Society.*

China Statistical Yearbook (CSY) (2001) (2011). Downloaded in September 2011 from http://chinadataonline.org.

Central Intelligence Agency (CIA) (2012). "Exports — Partners (%)." Downloaded in November 2012 from https://www.cia.gov/library/publications/the-world-factbook/fields/2050.html. Also, "Imports- Partners (%)." Downloaded in November 2012 from https://www.cia.gov/library/publications/the-world-factbook/fields/2061.html.

Central Intelligence Agency (CIA-COW) (2012). The World Factbook, as reproduced in *Countries of the World* (COW) (2012). Photius Coutsoukis, downloaded in October 2012 from http://www.photius.com/rankings/index.html.

Dutta, M. (2006). "Taiwan's Paradigm of Integrated Industrialization with Optimum Macroeconomic Parameters." *Journal of Asian Economics*, 17: 832–851.

Einhorn, Bruce *et al.* (2005). "Why Taiwan Matters." *Businessweek*, 3933: 76–81.

Hsiao, Frank S.T. (2012). "Showing the Upside of Bumbling." Taipei Time, December 20, 2012. Downloaded from http://www.taipeitimes.com/News/editorials/archives/2012/12/20/2003550557

——— and Mei-Chu W. Hsiao (HH) (1996). "Taiwanese Economic Development and Foreign Trade." In *Comparative Asian Economies*, John Y.T. Kuark (ed.), *Contemporary Studies in Economic and Financial Analysis 77* (Part B) (211–302). Greenwich, CT: JAI Press. Originally published in *Harvard Studies on Taiwan: Papers of the Taiwan Studies Workshop. 1.* (1995).

Cambridge, MA: The John K. Fairbank Center for East Asian Research, Harvard University (199–270) (Ref. Chapter 1).

______ and ______ (HH) (2002). "Taiwan in the Global Economy: Past, Present, and Future." In Peter C.Y. Chow (ed.), *Taiwan in the Global Economy, From an Agrarian Economy to an Exporter of High-Tech Products* (161–222) (Ref. Chapter 2). Westport, CT: Praeger.

______ and ______ (HH) (2003). "'Miracle Growth' in the Twentieth Century-International Comparisons of East Asian Development." *World Development*, 31(2): 227–257.

______ and ______ (HH) (2004). "The Chaotic Attractor of Foreign Direct Investment-Why China? A Panel Data Analysis." *Journal of Asian Economics*, 15(4): 641–670.

______ and ______ (HH) (2006). "Prospect of a US-Taiwan Free Trade Agreement: The China Factor and Critical Assessments." In Peter Chow (ed.), *Economic Integration, Democratization and National Security in East Asia: Shifting Paradigms in U.S., China, and Taiwan Relations* (191–239). Northampton, MA: Edward Elgar, 2007.

Japan Statistical Yearbook (JSY) (2013). Statistical Bureau, etc. Tokyo: Japan Statistical Association.

Institute of Management Development (IMD) (1999) (2012). *World Competitiveness Yearbook*, Stephane Garelli and IMD. Switzerland. "*Scoreboard*" retrieved in August 2011 from http://www.vi.is/files/IMD%202011%20-%20listar_831280280.pdf.

Kwong, Robin, Chris Nuttall and Kathrin Hille (2011). "PC Makers Step up Their Efforts to Combat Rise of Apples' iPad." *Financial Times*, May 31, 2011, 17.

______ and April Dembosky (2011). "Quanta's Search for Growth Takes It into Cloud Computing." *Financial Times*, May 31, 2011, 15.

Lee, Shyu-tu and Jack F. Williams (eds.) (2014). *Taiwan's Struggle: Voices of the Taiwanese*. NY: Rowman & Littlefield Publishers.

Ministry of Economic Affairs (MOEA) (1991). *White Paper on Small and Medium-Size Enterprises*. Republic of China: Small and Medium Enterprises Bureau. Taipei, Taiwan.

Mo, Yan-chih (2011). "WIKILEAKS: China Using ECFA to Push Unification." *Taipei Times*, September 9, 2011, 1. Retrieved in September 2011 from http://www.taipeitimes.com/News/front/archives/2011/09/09/2003512815.

Muyard, Frank (2010). "Mid-Term Analysis of the Ma Ying-jeou Administration, the Difficulty of Delivering the (Right) Goods." *China Perspectives*, 2010(3). Special Feature, Taiwan: The Consolidation of a Democratic and Distinct Society.

Osius, Ted (2002). *The U.S.-Japan Security Alliance, Why It Matters and How to Strengthen It*. The Center for Strategic and International Studies, Washington, D.C. Westport, CT: Praeger.

Statistical Abstract of the United States, 2012 (SAUS). Census Bureau, The United States Government, Washington, D.C.

Taiwan Statistical Data Book (TSDB) (2012). Council for Economic Planning and Development, Executive Yuan, Taiwan. Also available at www.cepd.gov.tw, retrieved in September 2011.

Tsusho Hakusho. *White Paper on Commerce* (WPC) (2008) (in Japanese). Tokyo: Ministry of Commerce and Trade, Government of Japan, Tokyo.

Wikipedia, the free encyclopedia (2011a). "Economic Cooperation Framework Agreement." Retrieved in September 2011.

_____ (2011b). "ECFA Debate." Retrieved in September 2011.

World Economic Forum (WEF) (2010) (2012). *The Global Competitiveness Report, 2010–2011 (2012–2013).* Klaus Schwab (ed.). Geneva: Switzerland.

Wu, Rong-I (2014). "Economic Integration in East Asia: The Perspective from Taiwan." In Lee and Williams (eds.), (215–222) (Chapter 18). Listed in this References section.

Part II

Japanese Colonial Linkages

Chapter 4

Colonialism or Comparative Advantage? — On Agricultural Development in Colonial Taiwan

4.1 Introduction

Under Japanese colonialism, Japanese capitalists invested heavily in developing Taiwanese agriculture, especially the production of rice and sugar. These were exported to Japan proper to satisfy Japanese demand. In return Taiwan became a market for Japanese industrial products, thus completing the usual pattern of colonialism (Ho, 1978, 29; Ranis, 1992, 208; Chou, 1958, 62). It has been often stated that, as colonists, the Japanese were reluctant to develop industries in Taiwan, and even when they tried to develop them, they promoted only those sectors which were not competitive with their home industries (Ho, 1984). Some examples are the textile industry, which is essential for people's well being, and the fertilizer industry, which is essential for growing rice and sugar in Taiwan. Chinese who came to Taiwan after the war often used the non-development of the textile industry (e.g., Chou, 1958, 87) and the fertilizer industry (e.g., Tang, 1958, 64) under the Japanese as glaring examples of the evil of Japanese colonialism.

The purpose of this paper is to show that, in the absence of multinationals and consumer products with life-cycle production processes that existed only in the postwar period, geographical and resource limitations, rather than the idea of colonialism, restricted Japan's choice of development pattern in Taiwan. It is true that the colonial Taiwanese economy was integrated into the Japanese economy, and its position in the Japanese economy changed to meet the needs of Japan's international position. While it was also true that Japan needed Taiwan's rice to supplement her own supplies and Taiwan's sugar to end the drain on her foreign exchange even if Japan had altered its policy to develop Taiwan's industries, Taiwan was in no way able to accommodate such a change. Thus, Japan developed agriculture on Taiwan not because Taiwan was its colony, but because Taiwan was one of the most natural resource poor countries in the world.

The process of Taiwanese agricultural development during the Japanese period is well known and has been studied extensively in the literature. However, most of these works emphasize either rice alone or organizational aspects (e.g., Chang, 1957; Myers and Ching, 1964) or give statistical estimations of agricultural input-output relations and growth rates (Ho, 1966; Ho, 1978, Chapter 4; Lee and Chen, 1983).

This paper takes a broader viewpoint and examines prewar Taiwanese agricultural development from an international perspective. We define "comparative advantage" in production loosely as the ability to or advantage of producing a product or a group of products as revealed in the high volume of output compared with other products domestically or internationally.[1] Hence, in arguing for a comparative advantage, we have shown the rapid growth of some Taiwan's major crop outputs and compared their outputs with those of other countries. We were able to ascertain that, by the end of the 1930s, Taiwan was the world's major producer of rice, sugar, sweet potatoes, tea, bananas, canned pineapples, and peanuts. We also show that Taiwan's agricultural sector was much more well developed than those of other colonies inside the Japanese Empire. We submit that very few countries in the world were so well endowed in agricultural products after WWII. Undoubtedly, the highly-developed Taiwanese agricultural sector was one of the factors which sustained the Taiwanese economy in the face of a massive influx of Chinese refugees in the 1950s, and catapulted it to rapid growth in the 1960s and 1970s. In view of a recent resurgence of interest in the revaluation of colonialism and postwar development (Tripathi, 1996), and also in the role of agricultural

[1]This "ability" or "advantage" may be a result of protective government policies, like high tariffs and import restrictions. As pointed out by a referee, Taiwan's sugar industry, especially during the early years of development, was unable to compete with Japanese or Cuban sugar. Incidentally, since a high volume of outputs necessarily ends up in exports, there is a relationship between our definition of comparative advantage in production and the more rigorous definition of "revealed comparative advantages" in international trade theory.

development in industrialization (Meller, 1995), international comparisons of Taiwanese agriculture during the prewar period may provide valuable insight on how countries could achieve rapid growth during the postwar period.

In Section 4.2, we describe the geographical features of Taiwan. We then show in Section 4.3 how the Japanese used modern science and technology to cope with geographical adversity and develop Taiwanese agriculture. The results of development are shown by comparing agricultural production in 1900 with that in 1940 for some major commodities in Section 4.4, and by comparing outputs in the late 1930s with international statistics in Section 4.5. Section 4.6 summarizes the output of other primary industries, including mining, forestry, livestock, and fishing. This is continued in Section 4.7, where we go a step further and show that Taiwan's comparative advantage had been revealed in its development of the agricultural products by comparing its agricultural sector and other sectors with those of other colonies in the Japanese Empire. Lastly, Section 4.8 concludes with the observation that comparative advantages of the Taiwanese economy, rather than colonialism, motivated the Japanese to develop Taiwanese agriculture.

4.2 Natural Environments

Although Taiwan has been known for its production and export of rice, sugar and a large variety of special crops and fruits, the natural environment of the island is not suited for massive agricultural development.

Table 4.1 shows that Taiwan comprises an area of about 0.02 percent of the world, smaller than most other countries. The countries chosen in Table 4.1 correspond to the countries in Table 4.3. Taiwan's population is relatively large, 5.7 million in 1940, which was 0.27 percent of the world population. A small area with a relatively large population made Taiwan one of the most heavily populated countries in the world, as shown in the last column of Table 4.1. Its population density in 1940 was 158 persons per km,[2] slightly lower than Japan, but higher than most other countries. This situation remains true today.

[2]Chen (1963), 137; Ping (1947), 62–63; Detailed soil analyses of local area can be found in SS51, 517–520.

Table 4.1: Area and Population of Some Countries.

	Area		Pop.		
Unit	1000 km^2	%	mil.	%	
Year	1939[1]		1940[2]		Pop. per km^2
World	146,300	100.00	2,145.2	100.00	15
Taiwan	36	0.02	5.7	0.27	158
Japan	383	0.26	71.9	3.35	188
China	11,103[4]	7.59	440.0[5]	20.51	40
India	4,079	2.79	316.0[3]	14.73	77
Bangladesh			70.3[6]	3.28	
Ceylon	66	0.05	5.9[8]	0.28	89
Indonesia	1,904	1.30	70.5	3.29	37
Thailand	583	0.40	16.1[8]	0.75	28
Burma	605	0.41	16.0[7]	0.75	26
Brazil	8,511	5.82	44.1	2.06	5
Philippines	296	0.20	16.5	0.77	56
U.S.A.	7,839	5.36	132.6	6.18	17

1. Based on YS43, 2–12. Changes in territories have been adjusted.
2. Based on YS91, 50, the data in YS91 have been adjusted for changes in territories.
3. In (a) it is listed as 356.9, which probably includes Bangladesh.
4. Based on YS33, 6, including Manchuria.
5. The author's estimation, YS43, 5, listed as 439.6 not including Manchuria and Mongolia.
6. Includes Pakistan.
7. From YS43, 5.
8. 1939 population, taken from YS43, 2.

Not all of this small area is suited for developing agriculture. Only 31 percent of Taiwan's land area has an elevation below 100 meters. The rest has an elevation either between 100 and 1000 meters (37%), or above 1000 meters (31%) (Chen, 1963, 89). It is "one of the most mountainous islands in the world" (Chen, 1963, 87). "There are more than 20 peaks with an altitude of more than 3500 meters... This is very seldom found... in the whole world, considering the small size of the island" (ibid., 88). The arable land, mineral resources, and sites suitable for hydroelectric generation are severely limited. The island is exposed to monsoons, typhoons, earthquakes, and even droughts. Heat and rain have washed away nutritive soil elements (like phosphorus and potash), leaving mostly acidic soils. Furthermore, since Taiwan is located in the subtropical zone, plant diseases and pests are prevalent (Ping, 1947, 64). However, Taiwan's subtropical location also enables her to produce many different varieties of crops.

4.3 Agricultural Development

It is in this context of natural adversity[3] that the Japanese developed Taiwanese agriculture by intensive research and development[4] and new rural institutions (Ho, 1978, 57–65). They kept systematic and meticulous meteorological records since 1896 (Tang, 1947, 16; Chen, 1963, 121), conducted soil surveys and agricultural experimentation, invested heavily during the 1920s in extensive flood control and modern irrigation systems (Ho, 1978, 36–37), introduced or improved breeds of plants and crops capable of withstanding weather changes, diseases, and bugs (Tang, 1947, 12–14), extensively used fertilizers (Ishikawa, 1967, 102–105), and improved cultivation methods (Tang, 1947, 14–19).

In developing Taiwanese agriculture, it is not surprising that the Japanese introduced their farming methods to Taiwan. In the prewar period, Japan's per hectare agricultural output and per hectare application of fertilizer were highest in the world[5] (YS43, 177). Hence, they also initiated the use of home-prepared fertilizer as well as chemical fertilizer in Taiwan. The per hectare application of fertilizer in Taiwan increased from 2,796 kg in 1912 to 10,782 kg for home-prepared fertilizer (green manure and compost) in 1940, and from 81 kg in 1912 to 660 kg in 1940 for purchased (chemical) fertilizers.[6] This practice of intensive use of fertilizers by Taiwanese farmers continued after the war. During 1952 to 1963, Taiwan's per hectare application of commercial fertilizer was only second to Japan among the Asian countries (Ishikawa, 1967, 106).

Taiwan already had an extensive rice irrigation system before the Japanese occupation (TEY91, 179). In 1903, 28 percent of total cultivated

---

[3]Also see Chen (1963), 182–183, on the influence of geological setting on water resource development.

[4]Japanese studies and research on Taiwan started long before their occupation (Wu, 1995), and were followed by intensive "explorations" immediately after the occupation (Wu, 1997).

[5]In this paper, international comparisons are based on Yano and Shirazaki (YSxx), various issues, and Yano (1991). We use their data since they are readily available; the former has been continuously published annually from 1927 up to recent years, and the data have been adjusted for the changes in territories after WWII. Their original data are based on country statistics, statistical data of the pre-war League of Nations and the post-war United Nations.

[6]Ishikawa (1967), 103. The comparable figures for home-made fertilizers in Japan are 104 (and 13) kg in 1883 and of 196 (and 224) in 1958 (ibid., 99), and for Korea almost nothing (and 1) in 1910, 6,447 (and 164.1) in 1940 (ibid., 104). The numbers in parentheses shows purchased fertilizers.

land on Taiwan was irrigated and drained. This was increased to 41 percent in 1920 and 62 percent in 1940 (Chen, 1963, 57). The most famous and largest Japanese-built irrigation system was the Kanan Irrigation System, which was started in 1920 and completed in 1930 at the cost of US$21 million, 50 percent of which was financed by the government (Chen, 1963, 165–166). This project transformed 150,000 hectares of bare land into sugarcane-producing fields[7] (Tang, 1947, 15).

Various agricultural organizations were established. As early as 1908, the government promulgated the Taiwan Public Irrigation Canal Act, and organized irrigation commissions (Chen, 1963, 165) and farmers' associations in rural areas. These played an important role in promoting cooperation among farmers and facilitating communication between farmers and the government. By 1940, there were 63 irrigation commissions, and 10,997 public and private irrigation canals irrigated 550,000 hectares of land (Tang, 1947, 15). At their peak, there were 5,511 agricultural organizations in 1939 (SS51, 515). These organizations were preserved and strengthened after the war (Ho, 1978, 63).

By 1938, the utilization rate of arable land in Taiwan was[8] 24 percent (59,000 hectares), which is higher than Korea (20%) and Japan proper (17%), lower than major countries such as Denmark (62%), India (57%), Italy (49%), England (46%), but much higher than in any province of China (Tang, 1947, 1). The total area of cultivated land has remained almost constant between the prewar and postwar periods (TSDB, 1995).

By 1944, 96 field crops were planted in Taiwan (Ping, 1947, 75). The six major crops were paddy rice (41.8% of the value of total agricultural production,[9] the same below), sugarcane (18.1%), sweet potatoes (6.7%),

[7]This consisted of one-third of the total irrigated area, and one-sixth of all cultivated land in Taiwan. The chief engineer of the project, Yoichi Hatta, died in 1942 on an assignment in the Philippines. His wife committed suicide by throwing herself into the reservoir. The local people erected a bronze statue of him in 1946, and pay a tribute to his memory every year (Yamamoto, 1983).

[8]Tang (1947), 1, wrote "According to the 1941 data, the total value of agricultural production already reached 568,904,937 Japanese yen, . . . the utilization rate of the arable land in Taiwan was 45.12 percent, behind only Denmark, India, Italy, England, and much higher than that in China (Tang, 1947, 1). As usual in most of the Chinese papers, the sources of data are not given. We think it is based on TEY41, 120–124.

[9]From Ping (1947), 76, which is taken from 1944 Taiwan Agricultural Yearbook. Note that the total value of agricultural products includes 9.7 percent from hogs and 2.4 percent from chicken.

bananas (4.1%), pineapples (2.2%) and tea leaves (1.9%) (ibid., 76). Rice, sugarcane, and sweet potatoes have consistently been the major agricultural products of Taiwan during the prewar and postwar periods.

To increase efficiency of land utilization, the Japanese developed a very complex rotation cycle for paddy fields as well as dry fields, rotating rice production with other field crops in one to three year cycles.[10] A unique "muddy-in" planting method[11] and a rotating method for sugarcane and other major crops were also developed. When the limit of the expansion of arable land was reached in 1917 (20% of all land), these methods increased per hectare yields.[12] According to one account, these methods were unique in the world, reflecting advanced intensive cultivation (Tang, 1947, 14–15).

The increase in Taiwan's agricultural productivity was quite remarkable. Around 1905–1909, per hectare output of Taiwan's agricultural land was only about a half of that of Japan, but it caught up to about 80 percent by the end of the prewar period, and reached equal output between 1960 and 1964 (Shinohara and Ishikawa, 1972, 18). By another measure, however, the per farm family output of agricultural products in Taiwan during 1935–39 was already about 50 percent higher than that of Japan[13] (ibid., 19). Through irrigation and agricultural and biological innovation, Taiwan became the most advanced rice-producing country in the whole of Asia (ibid., 19; Chang, 1957). Similar statements can be made for other crops.

[10]See Tang (1947), 14. The 30 popular rotations and their cycles are listed in Chen (1963), 238–240, without, as usual throughout the book, proper credit to the Japanese. Also see Chou (1958), 33–35.

[11]In Taiwanese, it is called "ko-ah" or in Mandarin, "Hu-tze," planting method (see Tang, 1947, 14). It is "an unusual farm practice extensively adopted in Taiwan," "a practice of planting a crop in the field a few weeks before the harvest of the previous crop. For instance, the fall Hu-tze sugarcane is planted in late September before the harvest of the second crop of paddy rice" (Chen, 1963, 244). From the description alone, both Tang (1947), 14–15 and especially Chen (1963), 245 are ambiguous about whether the method is a prewar Japanese innovation.

[12]The cultivated area fluctuated between 20 percent and 24 percent (which was reached in 1938) from 1915 to 1994. SS51, 516, and TSDB (1995).

[13]Note that this is different from the comparison of per farm family disposable income (ibid.). Hayami and Ruttan (1970) argued that in Japan, there was rapid growth in agricultural productivity from 1886 to 1920, followed by much slower growth in the 1920s and 1930s, despite rice imports from Taiwan and Korea, and decline in technological progress.

4.4 Agricultural Growth

The first part of Table 4.2 shows production changes in primary industries using the 1900 output[14] as 1. The number in braces shows the percentage of the value of the selected major items in the value of the total output in

Table 4.2: Production of Some Major Products in Taiwan.

Item	Unit	1900	1910	1920	1930	1940	Max	Year
AGRICULTURE {the first 6 items include 84% of total agricultural value}								
Rice	mil.t	0.3	0.6	0.7	10.5	11.3	14.0	1938
		(1)	(2)	(2)	(3)	(4)	(6)	
Sugarcane	mil.t	0.4 [a]	2.2	2.6	7.0	10.0	12.8	1939
		(1)	(5)	(6)	(17)	(24)	(31)	
Sweet potatoes	mil.t	0.2	0.6	0.8	13.3	15.1	18.0	1937
		(1)	(3)	(4)	(6)	(7)	(9)	
Tea	mil.kg	10.4	13.7	9.0	10.4	11.6	17.2	1918
		(1)	(1)	(1)	(1)	(2)		
Bananas	mil.t	0.6 [b]	0.7	0.4	1.3	1.7	2.2	1937
		(1)	(1)	(6)	(20)	(27)	(36)	
Pineapples	mil.t		7 [c]	6	69	129	146	1937
			(1)	(1)	(10)	(18)	(20)	
Peanuts	mil.kg	6.1	9.6	14.8	23.4	28.7	31.7	1937
		(1)	(2)	(2)	(4)	(5)	(5)	
Tobacco	mil.kg	0.4	0.8	1.0	1.5	5.9	9.8	1942
		(1)	(2)	(3)	(4)	(16)	(66)	
MINING {4 items, 56%}								
Coal	mil.t	0.04	0.2	1.1	1.6	2.8	2.9	1941
		(1)	(5)	(28)	(40)	(70)	(72)	
Gold	tons	0.3	1.6	0.5	0.5	0.8	1.6	1915
		(1)	(5)	(2)	(2)	(3)	(5)	
Grude oil	1000 kl	0.007	0.6	1.2	0.8	6.0	22.8	1927
		(1)	(85)	(171)	(114)	(857)	(3257)	
Natural gas	mil.m^3	NA	NA	NA	21 [e]	25	30	1937
			*		(1)	(1.1)	(1.4)	
FORESTRY {1 items, 45%}								
Timber	mil.m^3	NA	NA	0.2 [d]	0.2	0.4	09	1942
				(1)	(1)	(2)	(5)	

(*Continued*)

[14]The base year 1900 was used consistently in Chou (1958). It is a poor choice since the data in 1900 were unreliable, if not erroneous (Myers and Ching, 1964). However, the base year in Table 4.2 can be easily changed to 1910 or 1920 without affecting the conclusions.

Table 4.2: (*Continued*)

Item	Unit	1900	1910	1920	1930	1940	Max	Year
LIVESTOCK {2 items, 93%}								
Cattle	1000	NA	63	41	32	21	63	1910
			(1)	(0.7)	(0.5)	(0.3)	(1)	
Hog	mil	NA	0.6	0.8	1.4	1.1	1.5	1935
			(1)	(1.3)	(2.3)	(1.8)	(2.5)	
FISHERIES {1 item, 64%}								
Fish [f]	mil Kg	5	10	16	54	106	106	1940
		(1)	(2)	(3)	(11)	(21)	(21)	
Salt [g]	kilot	47	104	58	305	176	513	1942
		(1)	(2)	(1)	(6)	(4)	(11)	

mil = million, t = ton, kg = Kilogram, m^3 = cubic meter; 1900 = 1.
A number in ( ) is the multiple of the number in 1900 or the first number available.
A number in { } shows the percentage of the value of all selected products in each category of the total value of all products in each category, during 1937–1939. See Kai and Chu (1951).
(a) Figure for 1902–1903. (b)1909 figure. No data before 1909. (c) 1913 figure. The original unit is pieces.
We take 1 piece = 1 Kg. See Kai (1952). (d) 1922 figure. (e) 1932 figure. (f) Include pond fisheries. Chou (1985), 261; Kai (1952). (g) Government purchases, SS51, 1023.
Sources: SS51; Chou (1958); Kai (1952).

each category. The last two columns show the greatest prewar output and the year in which it occurred.

Thus, the value of the output of the first six items in the agricultural category consists of 84 percent of the total agricultural output[15] during 1937–1939. The other agricultural products, including tobacco, citrus, soybeans, corn, etc. consist of miscellaneous items. We included tobacco in the table to show the accelerated production during the 1940s. From Table 4.2 we see that the output of major agricultural products increased at least five times, and in some cases even up to 66 times, during the 40-year period. The only exception in the table is tea, which maintained more or less the same level of production during the Japanese period.

Rice production increased steadily over the years, and the maximum output in 1938 was six times that of 1900. Similarly, sugarcane output

[15]The first three items continued to be major crops in Taiwan in 1960. In terms of value, 1960 rank of crops was paddy rice (56.3%), sweet potato (11.1%), sugarcane (6.9%), peanuts (4.0%), soybean (2.0%), tobacco (1.7%), tea (1.5%), pineapple (1.2%), banana (1.2%), see Chen, 203. Note that the output of soybeans and tobacco has increased.

increased 31 times, sweet potatoes 9 times, bananas 36 times, peanuts five times, tobacco 66 times, and pineapples 20 times. Note that all crops, except tea, increased steadily, and increased more quickly toward the end of the prewar period. Most crops reached maximum production by the end of the 1930s. By the end of war, Japanese efforts in developing Taiwanese agriculture again began to reap large payoffs. However, agricultural production started to level off and decrease, giving way to industrial production, following Japan's plunge into the Pacific War.

In addition to traditional crops, new varieties of crops were introduced. One way to observe this is to determine the year in which the name of a crop appears in statistical data books. The crop may be a traditional product which gained importance over the years, or a new variety of crop introduced through agricultural research by cross-breeding or foreign import. According to the *Fifty-one Year Statistical Summary of Taiwan Province* (SS51), production data for soybeans appeared in 1913, white grapefruits and mangoes in 1916, arrowroots (for making starch) in 1919, betel nuts and papayas in 1921, corn, barley, guavas, grapes, and loquats in 1928, cassava in 1931, cotton in 1935, coffee and sorghum in 1937, and several kinds of vegetables at different times. Several new products appeared almost every two to three years, and culminated by the end of the 1920s.

It is well known that in the 1960s, Taiwan was once the world's largest exporter of asparagus and white mushrooms introduced in the mid-1960s (Hsiao and Hsiao, 1995, 221). Few people know that successful cultivation of asparagus and white mushroom in Taiwan was performed by the Japanese in 1935. However, research and development begun in 1935 was halted due to the war (Chen, 1969, 209; Hu, 1969, 178). These crops, and others except cotton, were considered nonessential commodities under the Japanese militarism during that period. Research was resumed vigorously after the war,[16] and had eventually succeeded in the commercialization of the new products.

[16]It is not clear how postwar success was related to prewar research. Chen (1969), 209, only stated that "The cultivation of Asparagus already started in 1935.... At that time Taipei Agricultural Improvement Station introduced the Palmetto variety from Japan for cultivation, but didn't reach the stage of mass production...." Hu (1969), 178, states that "As early as 1935, a Japanese, Sakurai, introduced white mushroom fungi, and successfully cultivated them. The results were formally published. However, due to the war, the research was halted short of mass production. After the war, in 1953, the author introduced a white mushroom variety from University of Pennsylvania in the United States,...". In a personal conversation, Professor Ping-li Tsai, a horticulturist at National Taiwan University, told the author that, in biological science, initiative in

Japan's textile industry relied almost completely on imported cotton (YS43, 153). In earlier years of their occupation, the Japanese tried to plant cotton in Taiwan, but failed due to tropical diseases and bugs. After introducing new varieties and new cultivation methods, they achieved success in 1931 (Ping, 1947, 82), and in 1935 Taiwan produced 0.1 million tons of cotton (SS51, 555). The planting area, however, competed with rice cultivation, and the Japanese tried to transfer successful varieties to South East Asia.[17] Cotton output in Taiwan reached a peak of a mere 1.1 million tons (valued at 0.6 million yen) and declined thereafter (ibid.).

Taiwan's textile industry started after WWI. Power looms were introduced in 1919. By 1933, there were 33 weaving firms, but these had merged into 10 firms in 1941, mainly using recycled cotton cloth (Chou, 1958, 87). Cotton weaving was introduced in Taiwan only in 1941, as part of self-sufficient wartime economic mobilization plan, transferring "surplus" looms and spindles from Japan, and production started in 1942 (ibid.). Thus, the Japanese did attempt to develop a textile industry in Taiwan after 1931, but because of a limited supply of cotton due to wartime shipping disruption, combined with the intensifying war effort, it was too little and too late.[18] It should be noted that the postwar development of the textile industry[19] in Taiwan benefitted from three sources: turnkey plant importation of textile mills from China when the Nationalist Government

research is always important because, "even if it failed, the failure is a prelude to future success."

[17]See Cheng (1952b), 10. According to Cheng's interpretation of the literature, the Japanese tried to plant cotton in Taiwan after they occupied North China since they were not so sure about mobilizing the Chinese farmers to plant cotton (ibid.).

[18]As a referee pointed out, the question is why development did not occur earlier. When Japan acquired Taiwan in 1895, Japan had just completed the import substitution phase for cotton yarn. Exports of yarns exceeded imports in 1897, mostly to China, including Manchuria. The textile industry continued to grow, using imported cotton from China and India (Ishii and Matsumoto, 1960, 35, 42–43, 46). "In the period 1900–1940 ... production of cotton yarn [increased] four times and cloth ... six times ... cotton yarn and cloth accounted for 51–68 per cent of all commodity exports" (Minami, 1986, 132–135). Prewar Japan was constantly uneasy about importing cotton, and tried cotton cultivation in its colonies (ibid., 40). WWI brought the prosperity of the textile industry, followed by deep depression and excessive capacity. To avoid being at a disadvantage after China's tariff reforms, the industry moved to invest in China in 1919 to secure the market. Clearly, among the Japanese colonies, unlike the sugar industry, Taiwan has no comparative advantages in developing a textile industry.

[19]This was advocated by the government economists but opposed and ridiculed by academic economists represented in the Finance and Economics Monthly. See Cheng (1952a, 1952b).

fled to Taiwan, the acquisition of surplus American cotton through U.S. aid programs, and heavy government protection (Hsiao and Hsiao, 1995, 217). Note an interesting similarity: In the prewar period, Taiwan acquired "surplus" textile machines from Japanese capitalists as Japan reallocated resources to build its Greater East Asia Co-Prosperity Sphere, and in the postwar period, Taiwan again acquired used Chinese textile machines from fleeing Chinese capitalists.

4.5 International Comparisons

We have seen that Taiwanese agriculture developed tremendously from 1900 to 1940. What was Taiwan's position among the major producing countries? Column (a) of Table 4.3 shows that, from 1934 to 1938, Taiwan on average produced 1.3 million tons of rice. This is about 1 percent of world rice production, compared with about 8 percent in Japan, and 34 percent in China, etc., and ranked about 10th in the world.[20] Although Taiwan's production was small if compared with these two large neighboring countries, if we consider the size of Taiwan's area and population, we will find immediately that Taiwan stands out. Comparing Table 4.1 and Table 4.3, we see that, in 1940, Taiwan produced more than 50 times its fair share of rice in terms of its proportion to total world area, and 3.3 times its fair share in terms of population.[21]

International statistics on two cash crops are available, and they are even more striking. Table 4.3 shows that, from 1934 to 1938, Taiwan on average produced 2.4 percent (11 kilo tons) of the world's tea and 2.5 percent (0.2 million tons) of the world's banana. Taiwan's tea production was sixth largest in the world (next to India, Ceylon, Indonesia, Japan, and China) (YS43, 140) and banana production was the third largest in the world.[22] This means that Taiwan produced more than 120 times its fair share of tea and bananas in terms of its area and more than eight times its share in terms of population!

---

[20]In addition to the 8 countries in Table 4.3, add Korea (3.6 million tons in YS43, 1937, 103). According to YS43, 101, Taiwan's rice production in 1937 was 1.8 million tons, and that of world production was 93.8 million tons. Hence, Taiwan's share was 1.9 percent of the world production.

[21]In other data, on average from 1937 to 1940, the percentage of Taiwanese rice production ranges up to 1.9 percent of the world rice production (93 million tons), and Taiwan ranked ninth in the world. See YS43, 101.

[22]No data are available for two other major producers, India and Ecuador, see Y91, 206. Thus Taiwan might be either 4th or 5th during 1934–38.

Table 4.3: International Comparison of Agricultural Outputs of Some Major Producing Countries

Product	Rice		Sugar		Sweet			Tea		Banana		Pinaple		Peanuts		Salt	
Note	(a)		(b)		Potato(c)			(d)		(e)		Canned (f)		(g)		(h)	
Unit	mil.t		mil.t		mil.t			kilo t		mil.t		mil.boxes		mil.t		mil.t	
Yr	'34-38	%	'38-40	%		%	Year	'38	%	'34-38	%	'36-38	%	'37-38	%	1938	%
Col. 1	2	3	4	5	6	7	8	9	10	11	12	13	14	15	16	17	18
[Rkg]		[10]		[4]		[4]			[6]		[3]		[3]		[10]		[13]
World	151.5	100	17.3	100	46.4	100	'34-38	463	100	8.1	100	16	100	8.8	100	37	100
Taiwan	**1.3**	**0.9**	**1.2**	**6.9**	**1.7**	**3.7**	**34-38**	**11**	**2.4**	**0.2**	**2.5**	**1.2**	**7.4**	**0.05**	**0.6**	**0.2**	**0.5**
Japan	11.5	7.6			3.5	7.5	1940	54	12					0.01	0.1	0.5	1.4
China	50.7	34			18.1	39	'34-38	41	8.9					2.8	32	4.8	4.8
India	32.3	21	2.9	17				195	42					3.4	39	1.9	5.1
Banglsh	11.2	7.4															
Ceylon								97	21							0.04	0.1
Indonsia	6.1	4	1.5	8.7				75	16					0.3	3.4	0.08	0.2
Thailand	4.4	2.9												0.2	0.5		
Burma	7	4.6												0.2	2.3	0.05	0.1
Brazil			1.1	6.4						1.5	19						
Philipp	2.4		1.0	5.8	0.2	0.4	1937			0.9	11			0.01	0.1	0.05	0.1
Java			0.8	4.6	1.2	2.6	1938					12	71				

Notes:
(a) Taiwan's figures are from Chou (1958), 37. Others from Y91, 205. Philippines' figures are from Y43, 101.
(b) YS43, 130.
(c) Data for the World and China are from Y91. Taiwan's data are calculated from SSSI (also in Chou, 1958, 46). Others items and the ranking are from YS43, 124, for single year as noted in the right column.
(d) YS43, 140. Including the estimate for China.
(e) From Y91, 206. Y91's data is based on the FAO Production Yearbook.
(f) Y43, 145. The second largest producer was Malaya (2.4 million boxes).
(g) YS43, 116. China includes Manchuria and Kwantung.
(h) YS43, 214.

Most of the output of these three crops was exported. From 1934 to 1938, on average, about 51 percent (0.7 million tons) of rice, and about 62 percent of bananas were exported to Japan (Chou, 1958, 37, 48). In contrast, about 80 percent of tea was exported, mostly to countries other than Japan (TEY41, 144–146), and comprised about 3 to 4 percent of Taiwan's total exports (SS51, Tables 324, 326). These amounts are awesome if we consider the world export markets for these commodities. Taiwan's exports of bananas (0.15 million tons, including those to Japan) constituted about 5.4 percent of total world exports in 1937 and 1938, taking the first or second place in the world banana export market (YS43, 144). Exports of tea (9.7 kilotons) from 1936 to 1939 were, on average, about 2.2 percent of total world exports (447 kilotons) during the same period, ranking the 6th largest tea exporter in the world (YS43, 139). This pattern of export "colonialism" continued long after the early postwar period (TSDB, various issues).

Sweet potato, used as a secondary staple food, a feed for hogs, and raw material for producing alcohol, was the third most important crop. Table 4.3 shows that, during 1934–1938, Taiwan produced 1.7 million tons of sweet potatoes, a whopping 3.7 percent of world production, and ranked fourth in the world, next to China, Japan, and the United States (1.8 million tons, not shown). Despite this large output, most sweet potatoes were used domestically. On average, only 2.6 percent of production was exported to Japan (Chou, 1958, 46).

We could not locate world outputs for sugarcane and pineapples. However, since these are used solely in the food processing industry to produce sugar and canned pineapple, respectively, we may indirectly estimate their production from the final output. Taiwan's sugar production was very impressive. From 1938 to 1940, Taiwan produced on average 1.2 million tons of sugar, which is almost 7 percent of world production during that period (17 million tons), and ranked fourth among sugar producing countries, behind only India (2.9 million tons), Cuba (2.7), and Indonesia (1.5) (YS43, 130).

We note that 70 percent to 80 percent of pineapples produced in Taiwan were canned (Ping, 1947, 78) and exported to Japan and other countries. From 1936 to 1938, Taiwan produced on average 1.2 million boxes of canned pineapple, which was a whopping 7.4 percent of the world production (16 million boxes), and ranked third in the world, behind only Java (12 million boxes) and Malaya (2.6, not shown in the table) (YS43, 145). The second to the last column of Table 4.3 shows that average peanut production in 1937–38 was 54.5 kilotons (or 0.05 million tons) which was only about 0.6 percent of world production, but still enabled Taiwan to rank 10th among the peanut producing countries of the world. Other agricultural outputs were oranges, 0.4 percent of world production (7.8 million tons) in 1937 (YS43, 144), and jute, 1 percent of world production (4.6 million tons) from 1937 to 1939 (ibid., 172).

Thus, by the later part of the 1930s, Taiwan was already the world's major producer of rice, sugar, sweet potatoes, tea, bananas, canned pineapples and peanuts. Unlike many other colonies in the world, Taiwan was by no means a "monocultural" country. To produce so many different products in such large quantities, the social infrastructure, including transportation, communication, and education, had to accommodate such massive development (Hsiao and Hsiao, 1995, 205). In the early 1940s, building on this agricultural accumulation and basis of wealth,[23] the Japanese were able to develop industry quickly and massively, although it was too late. Elsewhere we have shown that due to mismanagement of the economy and continued hostility with Communist China, Taiwan's economic development was disrupted until the mid-1960s (Hsiao and Hsiao, 1996).

When the war ended, Taiwan already had a highly advanced agricultural sector. War damage to Taiwan's agriculture was minimal (slightly less than 50%), and it had recovered by 1950 (Kai and Chu, 1951, 61). Elsewhere we have seen the upsurge in agricultural productivity during the early postwar period in Taiwan[24] (Hsiao and Hsiao, 1995, 219). We submit that, unlike many other developing countries, the foundation and potential for such a postwar takeoff to higher productivity were laid in the prewar period (ibid., 20).

An increase in productivity indeed sustained Chinese refugees after the war. About 2.4 million Chinese refugees moved to Taiwan from 1945 to 1951, bloating the Taiwanese population to 8.5 million. On average, every Taiwanese farm labor had to support approximately one Chinese refugee (ibid., 210). Without the prewar development of agriculture, the Taiwanese economy probably would have collapsed.

4.6 Other Primary Industries

The second part of Table 4.2 shows the output of some representative products in mining, forestry, livestock, and fisheries.

---

[23]It has been said that industrialization in colonial Taiwan was not so much due to the large capital from Japan proper, but much more to local capital in Taiwan. TEY41, 81. More study is called for on this point.

[24]In Hsiao and Hsiao (1995), 219, we erred in stating that Taiwan has been blessed with "fertile land" and a variety of crops (ibid., 220). Most people will be misled when they travel along the North–South railway or highway in Taiwan and enjoy the scenery of green agricultural fields stretching to the infinite horizon.

The four items in the mining category comprise 56 percent of the total value of mining outputs during 1937–1939. The most important mineral output in Taiwan has been coal. Coal fields increased in number from 20 in 1897 to 353 in 1940, and output increased about 72 times during the Japanese period, with the maximum output of 2.9 million tons attained in 1941. Gold, crude oil, and natural gas also increased tremendously, indicating the efforts of the Japanese to explore Taiwan's mineral resources.

Even when coal output was at its peak, however, Taiwan's total output consisted of only 0.22 percent of the world output (1321 million tons) (Y91, 156). Gold and crude oil production reached their maximum prewar outputs in 1915 and 1927, respectively. The available statistics show that the 1940 gold production was only 0.06 percent of world gold production (1276 tons) (YS43, 241). Natural gas production started in 1932, and it did not increase much despite great demand during the war period. The erratic production pattern indicates meager underground reserves of these minerals.

Other minerals include silver, electrolytic copper, pyrites, sulphur, and dolomite, etc. (Chen, 1963, 512; Chou, 1958, 164–196). Their outputs and underground reserves are negligible (ibid., 482; ibid., 169). Conspicuously absent in Taiwan is iron ore, which is often considered one of the basic materials for industrialization.

There are two basic kinds of chemical fertilizers, phosphate and nitrogenous. The first kind uses rock phosphate, which Taiwan produces but its quality is low and so had to be imported, while the second uses limestone,[25] which Taiwan produced after 1942. The Japanese established a fertilizer company (two plants, one in the north, one in the south) in 1920 to produce the former and another company (two plants in the north) in 1935 to produce the latter. In 1937 Taiwan produced 25 kilotons of the former and 6 kilotons of the latter (Tang, 1958, 64), and about 200 kilotons of ammonium sulphate[26] was imported. After the war, these two companies

[25]Tang (1947), 30. Before 1942, limestone used in the cement, sugar, and fertilizer industries was imported from Japan. In early 1950s, the Taiwan Fertilizer Company used 130 kilo was tons of limestone produced at its own mine. Rock phosphate was imported from the United States and the northern Philippines. However, after 1950, the company was able to use low quality rock phosphate for production. Tang (1958), 68.

[26]From 1935 to 1939, Taiwan's imports of ammonium sulphate were, on average, about 170 kilotons from Japan (YS43, 178) and 29 kilotons from other countries (ibid., 182). According to SS51, 957, 961, in 1937 the costs of Taiwan's fertilizer imports were 38 and 16 million yen from Japan and other countries, respectively. In 1938, Japan produced 493 million yen and imported 155 million yen of fertilizers. YS43, 178.

were confiscated and reorganized as the Taiwan Fertilizer Company (TFC). Despite the complaints by the Chinese about the underdevelopment of the fertilizer industry in Taiwan, TFC was the only fully operative fertilizer company in the whole of China before 1948.[27]

About two million hectares, or 55 percent, of Taiwan's land area is forest land, of which only 67 percent, or about one third of the total land area, is accessible for logging (Chen, 1963, 397, 414). During the Japanese period, Taiwan's supply of timber was consistently below demand, and, since 1926, Taiwan had imported more than half of its needs from abroad, almost exclusively from Japan (Chou, 1958, 213–215).

Cattle and hogs are important to Taiwanese farmers. Their excrement serves as manure for maintaining farm productivity. Cattle are used for transportation and tillage, and hogs are a major source of meat and side-income (Chen, 1963, Chapter 12). The Japanese introduced livestock of better breeds to withstand tropical diseases and pests (Chou, 1958, 226–237). However, due to limited land area and weather (high humidity and temperature), the variety of livestock and their numbers were limited. Thus, livestock raising in Taiwan has been very self-sufficient, as shown in Table 4.2. The ratio of principal livestock in 1939 was roughly as follows (Chen, 1963, 466):

> One head of yellow cattle: 6.2 (4.2) water buffaloes: 41 (42) hogs, 1.6 (1.7) goats: 166 (97) chickens: 48 (49) ducks: 9.7 (19) geese.

The figures in parentheses are for 1959. Note that there is not much change in the numbers over the 20-year period, except that the number of chickens was cut in half and that of geese doubled. Further analysis is needed to determine whether these figures indicate the same standard of living in farm households at the two times.

As Taiwan is surrounded by the sea, it has a relatively abundant output of marine and aquatic products. The Japanese introduced modern fishing methods, marine science and schools, pond aquaculture, and fishermen's unions (Chou, 1958, Chapter 9). Table 4.2 shows that output of fisheries

[27]There were only two chemical fertilizer companies in China in 1947. TFC was jointly owned by the National Resources Committee (NRC) (60%) and the Provincial Government of Taiwan (40%). It was the only publicly owned (large) fully operative fertilizer company in China at that time. The other one was privately owned, but was damaged during the war, and "had not recovered the prewar peak production of 45,000 tons." Kuoshiguan (1984), 314. For a summary of the postwar development of the fertilizer industry in Taiwan, see Hsiao and Hsiao (1995), 215–216.

products increased 21 times during the Japanese period. However, although there were some exports of fisheries products, a portion of domestic consumption had to rely on imports from 1918 until the end of WWII. In 1938, the total catch was 69 kilotons, which was only 1.9 percent of the Japanese catch (3,690 kilotons), and 0.33 percent of the total world catch (21,100 kilotons) (Y91, 232).

Long before the Japanese occupation, salt production was a Ch'ing Government monopoly and was one of Taiwan's major products and exports, as shown by the relatively large amount (47 kilotons) of government purchases in 1900. The Japanese maintained this monopoly, and expanded salt fields and increased salt workers as industrial and military demand for salt increased. This is reflected in a 11-fold increase to 1942. About half of the production was exported to Japan (YS43, 212). The last two columns of Table 4.3 shows that, in 1938, Taiwan's salt production was about 0.241 million tons, which was about 0.5 percent of world production (37 million tons), but still ranked 13th in world production.[28] Thus, salt production was an important industry in Taiwan, and its role continued even after the war. In fact, from 1951 to 1960, Taiwan produced on average 0.3 million tons of salt per year: 63 percent was exported, with 85 percent of exports going to Japan. This "colonial" relationship continued even after the war.

Before WWI, Taiwan and Japan were the only two countries in the world producing natural camphor (YS41, 365). From 1891 to 1895, Taiwan exported on average 56 percent of the world's camphor exports (31 kilotons) (Chen, 1963, 422). After WWI, Germany developed synthetic camphor and Taiwan's production fluctuated and decreased. By 1939, the production of natural camphor was estimated at 6 kilotons, and that of synthetic camphor, 4 kilotons (YS41, 366). However, it can be estimated that Taiwan still produced about 50 percent of the natural camphor, or 30 percent of the world production of camphor (ibid.; Chen, 1963, 428), although its importance in Taiwan's total output and exports had decreased considerably.

4.7 Development in Other Japanese Colonies

We have seen that Taiwan's agricultural resources are much greater than mineral and other industrial resources, both in terms of development

[28]In addition to the countries listed in col. 17 of Table 4.3, others include some developed countries, indicating the importance of salt production: USA (8.4 million tons), USSR (4.0), Germany (4.7), England (3.1), France (2.3), etc. YS43, 214.

potentials and in comparison with other similar agricultural countries. If the conventional view that colonialism is to acquire colonies to serve as "appendages" supplying agriculture products and industrial raw materials, and at the same time as markets for industrial commodities produced by the master country[29] (Ho, 1984, 347–351), then we would expect that the Japanese also did the same in other prewar colonies. However, the data does not seem to support this popular theory.

Figure 4.1 consists of five panels for five Japanese colonies in 1938. They were Taiwan (1895–1945), Korea (1910–1945), Kwantung (1905–1945), South Sakhalin (1905–1045), and Nanyang (1919–1945). Among them, Korea, Taiwan, and Sakhalin are larger, having about 60 percent, 10 percent and 10 percent of the area of Japan proper. In contrast, the areas of Kwantung and Nanyang are less than 1 percent of that of Japan (Mizoguchi and Umemura, 1988, 3–5). Industries are divided into five

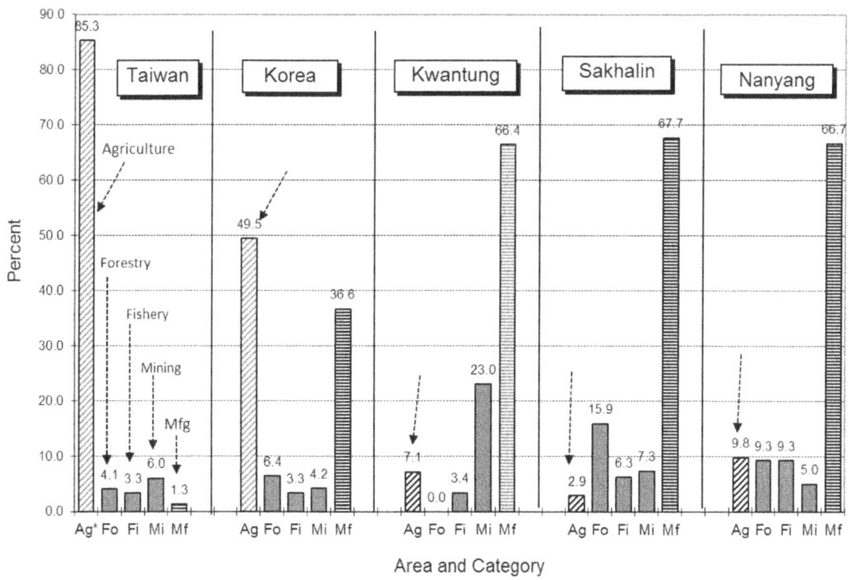

Figure 4.1: Composition of Industries in Japanese Colonies 1938

Note: Category items in each area add to 100 percent.

[29]This pattern of colonialism is a "well-known model of colonial development ... based upon the European colonial experiences in Asia and Africa" (Ho, 1984, 380–383).

categories: agricultural (Ag), forestry (Fo), fisheries (Fi), mining (Mi), and manufacturing (Mf). These are shown on the X-axis.[30] The percentage of the output value of each sector in each panel is shown on the vertical axis. All industrial outputs in each country/area should add up to 100 percent. The height of the bars shows clearly that Taiwan was an exception. In 1938, its agricultural sector consisted of a whopping 85 percent, the mining sector was only 6 percent, and other industries were negligible. Korea was similar, but the weight of the agricultural sector was only about 50 percent, and its manufacturing sector had 37 percent. The conditions in other three colonies are clearly reversed. All had a dominant manufacturing sector and very small agricultural and mining sectors, contrary to the conventional view. This again reveals in retrospect that the Japanese developed agriculture in Taiwan because Taiwan had an advantage in developing agriculture compared with other Japanese colonies.

Even if Taiwan had a comparative advantage in developing agriculture, Japan could still develop textile and fertilizer industries in Taiwan. Why did it not do so? Was it because Taiwan's markets were reserved for Japanese industries? Securing markets might have been the case in an earlier period, but seems not to be the main concern in the 1930s. Figure 4.2 shows the composition of the industrial sector in Taiwan, Korea, Kwantung, and Manchuria for each different period.[31] The importance of the food industry (Fo) seems to be proportional to the agricultural sector in each colony. The textile industry (Te) in Taiwan was small and was not increasing in size, but those in Korea and Kwantung were relatively large and expanding over the years, probably due to the ready availability of raw cotton. Apparently, Korea and Kwantung had a comparative advantage in developing the textile industry.

---

[30]The data are taken from Ichii (1941), 176–177.

[31]The data for Taiwan, Korea, and Kwantung are taken from Ho (1984), Table 4, for Manchuria are taken from Chao (1982), 81, Table H-5. Manchuria is included since Manchuria, as well as the northern and central parts of China, may be regarded as the area under the "informal empire of Japan" (Mizoguchi and Umemura, 1988, 4). In Chao, machinery (Ma) includes transport equipment. "Others" (Ot) in Fig. 4.2 includes printing, building materials, and miscellaneous in Chao. The Manchurian data are available only for 1936 and 1939, as noted in Fig. 4.2. In Ho's data, the first two periods are the same for all three countries. The third period differs in length: In Taiwan 1938–40, in Korea 1936–40, and in Kwantung 1934–36. The figures represent average percentage distribution of gross output during the period shown. H = Heavy Industry = Ch + Me + Ma.

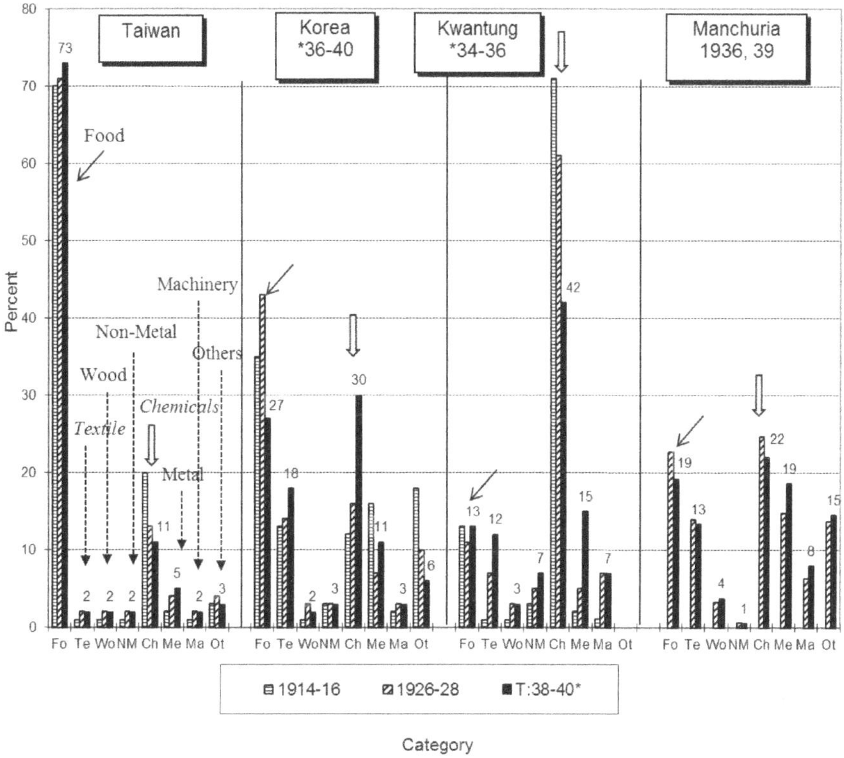

Figure 4.2: Composition of Manufacturing in Japanese Colonies 1914–16, 1926–28, 1938–40

Note: Category items for each period in each area add to 100 percent.

Similarly, the importance of chemical industry (Ch), which includes the fertilizer industry, in Taiwan decreased over the years, while that of Korea (mostly fertilizer industry) almost doubled in size,[32] so much so that its proportion even exceeded that of the food industry during the latter part of the 1930s. Unlike Taiwan's food industry, the proportion of the chemical industry of Kwantung (mainly vegetable oil production) decreased considerably, giving way to metal (Me), textile, and non-metalic

[32]Korea's industrialization started around the mid-1930s; industries included ammonium sulphate and other chemical products (YS41, 439). In 1938, Korea produced 1 million tons of ammonium sulphate, as compared with Japan's 1.1 million tons (YS43, 179). In 1936, she produced 0.2 million tons of iron and 0.09 million tons of steel, as compared with Japan's 2.0 and 5.2 million tons, respectively (YS41, 234).

mineral industries, probably due to easier access to the resources of newly established Manchukuo. Except for wood (Wo) and non-metalic mineral (NM) industries, the industrial development of natural resource rich Manchuria was much more balanced. While Manchuria produced soybeans, wheat, barley, corn, etc., most of the Japanese investment went to producing coal, iron, steel, transportation equipment (automobiles, locomotives, and airplanes) and other manufactured goods (Manshikai, 1964, 354–374). Thus, contray to the conventional view, the Japanese developed light industries, and even heavy industries, in their colonies.[33]

Although the data in Fig. 4.2 do not include it, we may point out that the Japanese also invested heavily in the textile industry in north and central China during the prewar period. Japanese investment in China started in 1902 in Shanghai (Yamaguchi, 1968, 224). After WWI, due to the increase in wage rates in Japan and the increase in textile tariffs in China, and to take advantage of cheaper labor costs and the ready accessibility of raw cotton, the Japanese textile industry started building factories in China, especially after 1921 (ibid., 229). By the early 1940s, Japan had invested in 2.2 million spindles and 34,000 looms in the Shanghai, Qingdao, and Tianjing areas, and operated 0.5 million spindles and 9,000 looms in Manchuria and Kwantung (YS43, 160). Clearly, inside the prewar Japanese Empire, apart from the sugar industry, Taiwan had no comparative advantage to attract massive Japanese investment in industry.[34]

---

[33]In fact, the purpose of "East Asia Comprehensive Plan" (Tooa Kokudo Keikaku, national planning, Raumordnung) was to make a rational allocation of natural resources between the countries and regions inside the Japanese Empire, and "to improve the welfare of each country" in the Japan-Manchuria-China bloc. Its basic principle is industrialization in accordance with the comparative advantages of each country while paying attention to the welfare of the whole bloc (Ichii, 1941). This point has been emphasized in a Chinese economic history textbook (Chiang, 1985, 279): "In October 1940, the Japanese Cabinet passed the 'Summary of Establishing Comprehensive Planning' and proposed what is called the 'Principle of Proper Place/Proper Production'(shi-ti shi-chan chu-yi), and determined a 'proper division of labor among Japan, Manchuria, and China'. It was decided that Japan should develop the military industry, machinery industry, and precision instrument industry; Manchuria should emphasize electric industry, mining industry, and part of machinery industry and light industry; North China should emphasize mining and salt industries; Central China would be allowed some light industry" (ibid.).

[34]Here we see the factors which may lead to the development of a textile industry: Protection of the infant industry by the government (through tariffs), cheap labor, and easy access to raw materials. As pointed out by a referee, thanks to U.S. aid and the establishment of a sovereign government in Taiwan, which was separate from Japan and China, Taiwan's textile industry took off after the war.

In general, it did not seen to matter to the Japanese whether colonial development took the form of agriculture, light manufacturing industry, or heavy industry, as may be seen from the fact that Japanese capital developed heavy industries in Manchuria (Manshikai, 1964) where coal and iron are abundant and developed a fertilizer industry in prewar Korea. Another interesting observation is that a large Korean-owned textile mill, the Kyongsong Spinning and Weaving Company, not only survived the onslaught of Japanese capital and government interference, but even grew and expanded throughout the entire period of Japanese occupation (Eckert, 1991).

"Agricultural Taiwan" would also have continued to be an accurate description if Taiwan were not separated from the Chinese mainland after WWII. According to a report prepared by National Resources Commission (NRC) in February 1946, Taiwanese industry was expected to develop "in harmony" with its natural resources and raw material supply, and Taiwan's economic development was to "synchronize" with that of China.[35] In effect, this means Taiwan would have played a very minor supporting role in China's planned self-sufficient "national defense industry." In the "First Five-year Program for China's Postwar Economic Reconstruction" prepared by the NRC and Central Planning Bureau in January 1946, "Taiwan was part of the 'Southern region' with the provinces of Guangdong, Guangxi, and Fujian. Its anticipated economic strategy favored the development of agricultural exports and light industry,... the southern region as a whole was to receive only 9.8 percent of the total state allocations in the plan" (Kirby, 1995, 293). Thus, industrialization on Taiwan was simply not a part of this program. It is not difficult to imagine that the postwar economic condition of Taiwan under China's rule would probably have been worse than its prewar position under Japan's rule.[36]

The Chinese who came to Taiwan after the war were awed by the scale and productivity of Taiwan's sugar industry. An NRC agent reported that "this Commission never had the experience of large scale production[37]

---

[35]Kirby (1995), 293–294. While denouncing Japanese colonialism, the same theme of "synchronization" and "economic considerations" are abundant in almost all Chinese writings; see Chen, Chou, Ping, W. Tang, Y. Tang, and Wan listed in the References section.

[36]We need not look beyond Hainan Island under the People's Republic of China. Hainan's climate is more favorable for sugarcane production (NRCS, 67). For detailed analysis and comparison with Taiwan, see TEY43, 217–234.

[37]The fact is that there was no other operating sugar company under the control of NRC, although there were two companies (one in Sichuan, one in Guangdong) under

of sugar during the war against Japan." He also saw the economic advantages of sugar production. "When the Japanese managed the sugar industry, ... peak production reached 1.4 million tons per year, and sugarcane acreage expanded to 16,700 hectares..." In contrast, "China's sugar production in the past was about 0.3 million tons per year, but she needed a total of 0.9 million tons. Thus, if Taiwan's sugar industry could recover and produce one million tons per year, ... then it can save and earn foreign exchange." This was precisely the same conclusion that the Japanese arrived at when they came to Taiwan.[38] Here again we may envision a postwar "Agricultural Taiwan, Industrial China." Thus, in short, so far as the prewar Taiwanese economy was concerned, colonialism did not necessarily manifest itself in a so-called "Agricultural Taiwan, Industrial Japan."

4.8 Some Concluding Remarks

We have documented the development of Taiwanese primary industry in detail. To recapitulate, by the end of the 1930s, Taiwan's agricultural production of bananas and canned pineapples ranked third in the world, sugar and sweet potatoes ranked fourth, tea, sixth, rice and peanuts, 10th, and salt 13th. Indeed we submit that few countries in the world were endowed with so many kinds of products in such large quantities.

---

preparation (choupei) in 1948. Kuoshiguan (1984), 255–258. The closest such experience they ever had was investment in China Sugar Company to produce molasses for alcohol. NRCS (1947), 66.

[38]Cheng (1952a), 11, quotes K. Takabashi, "after 1897 until a year before the Russo-Japanese War (1903 to 04), the trade deficit was 301 million yen, with sugar imports alone reaching 161.3 million yen, that is on average, 23 million yen a year." Thus, the Japanese began developing Taiwan's sugar industry, as sugar had been Taiwan's major export commodity before the Japanese took over Taiwan in 1895. This conventional view has recently been challenged by Wu (1996). Wu shows that the immediate purpose of developing the sugar industry was to help the colonial government attain fiscal independence from the Central Government. In fact, according to Yanaihara (1929), 10, during the first several years of occupation, Japan subsidized Taiwan with 7 million yen every year, a heavy burden. Thus there was an argument in some quarters of Japan that Japan should sell Taiwan either to a foreign country or China for 100 million yen. The 1897–98 subsidies were cut to 4 million yen. To make up the loss, the Kodama-Goto administration in Taiwan wanted to pursue capitalistic development of the Taiwanese economy. As one of such projects, based on five year feasibility studies of industrial resources of Taiwan (Davidson, 1972, 312; Wu, 1996, 6), they finally came up with the suggestion to establish a modern sugar company, which was realized at the end of 1900 (Yanaihara, 1929, 11). Taiwan gained fiscal independence from Japan proper after 1905 (Mizoguchi and Umemura, 1988, 29). However, Taiwan's sugar helped Japan eliminate its trade deficit in sugar only after 1919 (Takahashi, 1937, 204).

In other categories of primary industries, such as mining, forestry, livestock, and fisheries, growth was, although equally impressive, not important in terms of quantity or quality. Some of these items even had to be imported to satisfy domestic demand. Many people, especially Chinese writers (see, for example, Chou, 1958), faulted the Japanese for developing only agriculture and not "industry" in Taiwan, and for pursuing a prototypical "colonial relationship." We have shown clearly that, under existing resource constraints, it was only natural that the Japanese government first developed Taiwan's agriculture through intensive and extensive research and development, and then pursued an industrialization program of developing industries closely related to agriculture, rather than focusing on mineral and other resource development.

We have also shown that the Japanese did invest in textile and fertilizer industries in Taiwan, but failed to develop them into large scale industrial projects. Major industries were under almost complete control by Japanese capitalists,[39] who were fiercely competitive among themselves and ruthlessly profit-seeking. Thus only explanation for the lack of industrial development is that Taiwan was not suited for such development at that time. This may be seen from the fact that Japanese capital did invest heavily in these industries in Korea and China. Natural resource endowment and the relationship of Taiwan's economy to that of Japan comprised comparative advantages which Japan capitalized on in focusing on agricultural development in Taiwan. Thus, it was comparative advantage, rather than colonialism, which guided the Japanese in formulating their development policy for Taiwan. Naturally, as we will show elsewhere, our arguments here do not deny that a colonial relationship existed in Japanese exploitation of Taiwan's resources without Taiwanese initiative and participation.[40]

In the process of arguing our point, we have compared Taiwanese agricultural production with world production, and we have seen that, by the late 1930s, prewar colonial Taiwan was already among the most

[39]See Cheng (1952c). 21, Japanese Zaibatsu invested in Taiwan, with about 102 companies headquartered in Taiwan, investing 194 million yen, and 23 companies headquartered in Japan, investing 26 million yen, one half of which was invested by Mitsubishi. Tu (1975), 354.

[40]Did the Taiwanese benefit from such tremendous agricultural progress? Using total value of production (including industrial production), an early Chinese estimate shows that per capita output was about 25 yen in 1902, and about 255 yen in 1937, an increase of more than 10 times. Even accounting for inflation, this is an increase of three times. See Wan (1947), 88–89. This is a difficult problem and will be a topic of another paper.

advanced agricultural countries. Unfortunately, these achievements were obscured behind the facade of the Great Japanese Empire (Dai Nippon Teikoku). While no development program can be completed without the efforts of farmers and workers, Taiwan and Taiwanese farmers and laborers have seldom been recognized and credited with any part of this success.[41] In a sense, our research is a tribute to the Taiwanese tillers and toilers, who made such achievements possible while suffering humiliation and deprivation under an authoritarian colonial regime.

Acknowledgments

This paper was written while the first author was a visiting scholar at the Fairbank Center for East Asian Studies at Harvard University. His thanks go to Center staff and faculty members, especially Professors William C. Kirby and Erza Vogel, for providing him an excellent research environment. The original paper was presented at the Taiwan Studies Workshop at the Fairbank Center, at a seminar at National Taiwan University, and also at the Taiwan Studies Conference on "The Japanese Legacy in Post Colonial Taiwan," Washington University and University of Missouri, St. Louis, all in 1996. Comments and suggestions from Professors Joseph Allen, Meng-Mau Lee, Ping-li Tsai, Robert Weller, Tsong-min Wu, and other participants of the workshop, the seminar, and the conference are greatly appreciated. David Pietz of Washington University and James Thomas of the Korea Institute of Harvard University made useful suggestions. Mr. John Yung-hsiang Lai of Harvard-Yenching Library and Prof. James M. Chen and Prof. Song-Ken Hsu helped with references. The paper also benefitted greatly from very helpful comments and suggestions of a referee of this journal. As usual, all errors of omission and commission are the author's.

Statistical Data Sources

Fifty-one Year Statistical Summary of Taiwan Province (SS51) (Taiwan Sheng-51 Nianlai Tongji Tiyao). Statistics Department of Taiwan Province Governor-General, December, 1946.

Taiwan Economic Yearbook (TEY4x) (Taiwan Keizai Nempo). Vol. x, 194x (x denotes the year of publication).

---

[41] There was an exception. In pointing out the high technical level of Taiwan's sugar industry as compared with those in other sugar producing countries, the author of one article finally attributed it to the high quality of Taiwanese workers as a result of many years of "Japanization (Kominka)." See TEY43, 96–99, 101.

Taiwan Statistical Data Book (TSDB). Council for Economic Planning and Development, Republic of China, annual, since 1966.

Yano, K. and K. Shirazaki. *Illustration of Japanese National Achievements* (YSxx) (Nihon Kokusei Chosa), annual, since 1927 (xx denotes the year of publication).

Yano, I. (1991). *100 Years of Japan, Viewed by Numbers* (Y91) (Suji de miru Nihon no Hyakunen). Tokyo: Kokuseisha.

References

Chang, H.Y. (1957). Technical development of Taiwan's rice agriculture during the Japanese period (in Chinese). *Quarterly Journal of the Bank of Taiwan*, 9(2) (September). Also in Collected Works of Dr. Chang Han-yu, Vol. I. Taipei, Taiwan: San-min Bookstore, 1974.

Chao, K. (1982). *The Economic Development of Manchuria: The Rise of A Frontier Economy.* Center for Chinese Studies, Ann Arbor, MI: The University of Michigan.

Chen, C.S. (1963). *Taiwan: An Economic and Social Geography.* Taipei, Taiwan: Fu-min Geographical Institute of Economic Development.

Chen, C.R. (1969). Taiwan's Asparagus (in Chinese). In *Taiwan's Newly Developed Industries* (Taiwan zhi Hsinhsing Kongye), Taiwan Studies Series, No. 100, Economic Research Section, the Bank of Taiwan, 209–244.

Cheng, H.C. (1952a). Lessons from Taiwanese Industrialization before Japan's Surrender (in Chinese). *Finance and Economics Monthly*, 2(10) (September): 8–14.

——— (1952b). Lessons from Taiwanese Industrialization before Japan's Surrender, Part II (in Chinese). *Finance and Economics Monthly*, 2(11) (October): 8–14.

——— (1952c). Japanese Zaibatsu and Taiwan's Industry (in-Chinese). *Finance and Economics Monthly*, 2(12) (November): 8–12.

Chiang, J.P. (1985). *Concise History of the Modern Chinese Economy* (in Chinese). Peking, China: University of Peking Press.

Chou, H.W. (1958). *Economic History of Taiwan during the Japanese Occupation* (in Chinese). Vols. 1 and 2, Economic Research Section, the Bank of Taiwan, Taipei.

Davidson, J.W. (1972). *The Island of Formosa, Past and Present*, originally published in 1903, New York, Macmillan, translated into Chinese by Chi-hong Tsai, the Bank of Taiwan, Taiwan Study Series, No. 107, Taipei, Taiwan.

Eckert, C.J. (1991). *Offspring of Empire, the Kochang Kims and the Colonial Origin of Korean Capitalism*, 1876–1945. Seattle, WA: University of Washington Press.

Hayami, Y. and Ruttan, V.W. (1970). "Korean Rice, Taiwanese Rice, and Japanese Agricultural Stagnation: An Economic Consequence of Colonialism." *Quarterly Journal of Economics*, 84 (November): 562–89.

Ho, S.P.S. (1978). *Economic Development of Taiwan, 1860–1970.* New Haven, CT: Yale University Press.

_____ (1984). Colonialism and Development: Korea, Taiwan, and Kwantung. In R.H. Myers and M.R. Peattie (eds.), *The Japanese Colonial Empire, 1895–1945* (Chapter 9). NJ: Princeton University Press.

Ho, Y.M. (1966). *Agricultural Development of Taiwan, 1903–1960.* Nashville, TN: Vanderbilt University Press.

Hsiao, F.S.T. and M.C.W. Hsiao (1995). "Taiwanese Economic Development and Foreign Trade." In W.C. Kirby and J.M. Greene (eds.), *Harvard Studies on Taiwan: Papers of the Taiwan Studies Workshop* (Vol. 1, 199–270). Fairbank Center for East Asian Research, Harvard University. Originally published as Fairbank Center Discussion Paper, Number 9, 1994, Harvard University. Also in: John Y.T. Kuark (ed.) (1996), *Comparative Asian Economies, in the Contemporary Studies in Economic and Financial Analysis* (Vol. 77, Part B, 211–302, Refer Chapter 1). Greenwich, CT: JAI Press.

_____ and _____ (1996). Colonial Linkages in Early Postwar Taiwanese Economic Development. Paper presented at the Taiwan Studies Workshop, the Fairbank Center for East Asian Research, Harvard University, and at the Taiwan Studies Conference on *The Japanese Legacy in Post Colonial Taiwan*, the Joint Center for East Asian Studies, Washington University and University of Missouri, St. Louis.

Hu, K. R. (1969). "Taiwan's Mushrooms (in Chinese)." In *Taiwan's Newly Developed Industries* (Taiwan zhi Hsinhsing Kongye), Taiwan Studies Series, No. 100, Economic Research Section, the Bank of Taiwan, 177–208.

Ichii O. (1941). East Asia Comprehensive Plan (Tooa Kokudo Keikaku) (in Japanese). Tokyo: Dobunsha.

Ishii, K. and M. Matsumoto (1960). *Formation and Development of the Japanese Textile Industry* (in Japanese). In Lectures on Modern Japanese Industries. Vol. VII, Textile Industry. Tokyo: Iwanami Shoten.

Ishikawa, S. (1967). *Economic Development in Asian Perspective.* Economic Research Series, No. 8, The Institute of Economic Research, Hitotsubashi University. Tokyo: Kinokuniya Bookstore Co.

Kai, C.K. and D.B. Chu (1951). Compilation of Taiwan's Production Index and Survey of Taiwan's Production Trends (in Chinese). *Finance and Economics Monthly*, 1(9) (August): 58–62.

Kirby, W.C. (1995). "Planning Postwar Taiwan Industrial Policy and the Nationalist Takeover, 1943–1947." In W.C. Kirby and J.M. Greene (eds.), *Harvard Studies on Taiwan: Papers of the Taiwan Studies Workshop* (Vol. 1, 286–301). Cambridge, MA: Fairbank Center for East Asian Research, Harvard University.

Kuoshiguan (1984) (ed.). *First Compilation of the Historical Documents of the National Resources Commission* (Ziyuan Weiyuanhei Dangang Shiliau Chupian). Vol. 1, Taipei: Kuoshiguan (National Historical Archive).

Lee, T.H. and Y.E. Chen (1983). "Agricultural Growth in Taiwan, 1911–1972." In Y. Hayami, V.W. Ruttan and H.M. Southworth (eds.), *Agricultural Growth in Japan, Taiwan, Korea, and the Philippines* (Chapter 3). Honolulu, HI: East-West Center, The University Press of Hawaii.

Manshikai (1964). *Forty-Year History of Manchurian Development*, Vol. II (in Japanese). Tokyo: Manshu Kaihatsu Yonjunenshi Kankokai.

Meller, J.W. (1995) (ed.). *Agriculture on the Road to Industrialization*. Baltimore, MD: The Johns Hopkins University Press.

Minami, R. (1986). *The Economic Development of Japan, A Quantitative Study*. London: The Macmillan Press, Ltd.

Mizoguchi, T. and M. Umemura (eds.) (1988). *Basic Economic Statistics of Former Japanese Colonies, 1895–1938, Estimates and Findings*. Tokyo: Toyo Keizai Shimposha.

Myers, R.H. and A. Ching (1964). Agricultural Development in Taiwan under Japanese Colonial Rule. *Journal of Asian Studies*, 23 (August): 555–570.

National Resources Commission Secretariat (NRCS) (1947). Report of the First NRC Meeting (in Chinese). *Bulletin of National Resources Commission* (Ziyuan Weiyuanhei Gongbao), 13(2) (August): 58.

Ping, R. (1947). Characteristics of Taiwanese Agriculture (in Chinese). *Journal of the Bank of Taiwan*, 1(1) (June): 55–86.

Ranis, G. (1992).*Taiwan — From Developing to Mature Economy*. Boulder, CO: Westview Press.

Shinohara, M. and S. Ishikawa (1972). *Taiwan's Economic Growth* (SI) (in Japanese). Tokyo: Ajia Keizai Kenkyujo.

Takabashi, K. (1937). *A Study of the Modern Taiwanese Economy* (in Japanese). Tokyo: Chikura Shobo.

Tang, W.T. (1947). Taiwan's Agriculture and its Research (in Chinese). *Quarterly Journal of the Bank of Taiwan*, 1(3) (December).

Tang, Y.J. (1958). "Fertilizer Industry in Taiwan (in Chinese)." In *Essays on the Industry of Taiwan* (Taiwan Kongye Lunji), Vol. II, Taiwan Studies Series, No. 66, Economic Research Section, the Bank of Taiwan, 61–76.

Tripathi, D. (1996). Colonialism and Technological Choices in India: A Historical Overview. *The Developing Economies*, 34(1) (March): 80–97.

Wan, S. (1947). Characteristics of Taiwan's Industry (in Chinese). *Quarterly Journal of the Bank of Taiwan*, 1(1) (June): 87–110.

Wu, W. H. (1995). "Japan's Investigations and Studies on Taiwan before the Occupation" (in Chinese). *The Proceedings of the First Academic Conference on Taiwanese Local Culture*, Taipei, Taiwan, 567–576.

______ (1996). The Prelude to Sugar Industry Reform in Taiwan During the Japanese Period (in Chinese). *Kaohsiong History and Culture*, Vol. 3, 1–11.

______ (1997). "Tokyo Imperial University and the Evolution of "Academic Explorations" of Taiwan" (in Chinese). In *100 Years of Taiwanese Historical Studies — Reviews and Studies*. Taipei, Taiwan, 11–28.

Yamaguchi, K. (1968). *Economic History of Japan* (in Japanese). Tokyo: Tsukuma Shobo.

Yamamoto, R. (ed.) (1983). *A Bridge to Taiwan* (in Japanese). Vol. II. Osaka: TP Publishing Co, 88–92.

Yanaihara, T. (1929). *Taiwan Under Imperialism* (in Japanese). Tokyo: Iwanami Shoten.

Chapter 5

Colonial Linkages in Early Postwar Taiwanese Economic Development

This paper measures quantitatively, and presents diagrammatically, the degree of linkages between prewar and early postwar Taiwanese economic development. After a brief introduction of the Taiwanese economy in both periods, we examine long-run time series data of real GDP in the NT dollar and the U.S. dollar, the production structure, the labor composition, the trade structure. In general, the existing data seem to suggest that the postwar recovery to prewar peaks was not completed in the 1950s, and not even until the mid-1960s.

5.1 Introduction

One of the popular views about Taiwanese economic development is that Taiwan started forty years ago "from a state of extreme poverty and political and social backwardness" (Lai, Myers, and Wei, 1991, 1), implying that Taiwan's economic success is a case of the "rags to riches" dream in less than forty years. Even a chapter of a book is devoted to this title and theme (Chan and Clark, 1992). Others, while recognizing Taiwan's Japanese heritage of economic development and industrialization, argue either that industrialization during the last ten years of the Japanese occupation had only limited impact beyond infrastructures (Amsden, 1985, 346–348), or that the industrial sector at the beginning of the early 1950s was "small, both absolutely and relative to the rest of the economy," suggesting that the general conclusion of the "rags to riches" story still holds even if we consider Taiwan's prewar background (Ranis, 1979, 207–209).

While indeed there may have been a "miracle" of Taiwanese economic development in later years, as we have recognized elsewhere (Hsiao and Hsiao, 1996), the early postwar Taiwanese economic development came from neither "rags" nor a "miracle." This paper reevaluates the myth of "rags" in the Taiwanese economic development.

Since the 38-year long martial law imposed by the KMT (Kuomintang) government was lifted in 1987, some younger economists in Taiwan have begun to reexamine Taiwanese economic development impartially and objectively.[1] One of their achievements is the construction of long-term economic time series, without which the prewar and postwar economic development of Taiwan is very difficult, if not impossible, to evaluate objectively. Our purpose here is to take advantage of the recent completion of the time series, to measure quantitatively, and show diagrammatically, the degree of linkages between the two periods. The quantitative measures we use are simple ones, borrowed from psychology and education statistics. We believe that our work is the first attempt to deal with these two areas statistically, although our analysis may give rise to more questions than answers.

In recent years, the "Taiwan model" stands out as an exemplary case of successful economic development. Many developing countries have sought to "learn" from the model. Understanding Taiwan's colonial linkages and initial conditions will place the "miracle" in proper historical and international perspectives. If the "Taiwan model" is of any use in making policies for other developing countries, it cannot be built on unsubstantiated assertions.

It should be noted that the purpose of this paper is limited to analyzing the linkages between prewar and postwar Taiwanese economic development, and thereby highlighting the initial economic conditions at the time of Taiwan's take-off in the mid-1960s. How important these initial conditions are in subsequent Taiwanese development, and what roles these conditions have played during the ensuing years are the subject of another examination.[2]

The paper is arranged as follows. In Section 5.2, we present briefly some background on early postwar Taiwanese economic development, which may provide some bases for the findings presented in subsequent sections. Section 5.3 is devoted to the timing of prewar peaks, and recovery to these peaks in the postwar period. We show that the postwar recovery to prewar peaks was not completed until the mid-1960s. Section 5.4 then examines the linkages in terms of three economic structures: industrial production, labor composition of industries, and foreign trade. The degree of linkages is shown by Spearman's rank correlation coefficients. Some concluding remarks are given in Section 5.5.

---

[1]To insure objectivity, the group even called the period of 1895–1945 "the Japanese period," instead of "the Japanese occupation period," as being used by the KMT Government.

[2]The importance of the initial conditions and "a theory on why these initial conditions mattered as much" has been investigated by Rodrik (1995) and Sachs and Warner (1996).

5.2 A Brief Account of Taiwanese Economic Development

Under the Ch'ing government before 1895, Taiwan was a traditional agricultural society. She exported rice and sugar, her main staples, across the Formosa Straits to China and imported other daily necessities and equipment from China.

Following Taiwan's secession to Japan from China in 1895 after the first Sino-Japanese War (1894–1895), economic development under the Japanese regime may be divided into five periods: The initial period (1895–1905); the intermediate period (1905–1931); the quasi-war-stage (1931–1937), which covers the period from the Manchurian Incident to the beginning of the Sino-Japanese War; the first war-stage (July 1937–1941), which covers the Sino-Japanese War and the beginning of World War II; and the second war-stage (1942–1945), which covers World War II until the end of the war. The first two periods are based on the classification of Sumiya *et al.* (1992), Chapter 1, and are rather well documented. The last three periods are given in Kusunoi (1944) and correspond to the period of Japanese militarism.[3] The last period is still shrouded in war time secrecy and confusion. More in-depth studies of this period are called for (Hsiao and Hsiao, 1996; Twu, 1975; Chang, 1980; and Kobayashi, 1973). The classification of the period is important: first, it corresponds to the gradual industrialization of the Taiwanese economy in this period, and second, it highlights the problems in studying the Taiwanese economy during the war periods.

Following Taiwan's transfer to China and designation as a province in August 1945, Taiwan's postwar economic development may be divided in six stages (Hsiao and Hsiao, 1996): The Chaotic Period (August 1945–1949); The Transition Period (1950–1953); Recovery and Import Substitution Period (1953–1963); Take-off and Export Promotion Period (1964–1973); Second Import Substitution Period (1974–1980); Accelerated Growth and High-tech Industrialization Period (1980–).

Thus, the Taiwanese economy has experienced many different stages of transition. For the purpose of this paper, however, we may roughly divide the economy in four stages during the past 100 years. During the Japanese period, the economy before 1937 was the primary export-led economy, and the period after 1937 to the end of the war was the wartime controlled economy. After WWII until the mid-1960s, we had the recovering period,

[3]Kusunoi (1944), 40–42. It may also be divided as the pre-quasi-war period (before 1931), the quasi-war period (1931–37), and the war period (after 1938), see Okurasho (1947), 209.

and after 1964 until today, we have sustained growth period. In this paper, we are interested in the linkages between the economic conditions of the two middle periods.

In the Chaotic Period after the war, the Taiwanese economy was mostly in ruin due to Allied air raids, and inflation was rampant. The Chinese officials and army who took over Taiwan were incompetent and corrupt. Thus in February 28, 1947, the Taiwanese revolted (Lai, Myers, and Wei, 1991, Hsiao, 1992), which was cruelly suppressed within a month with government terror continued until early 1950. While the Taiwanese were recuperating from the February 1947 incident, the Nationalist Government of China was defeated by the Communists on the mainland and reestablished itself on Taiwan in 1949. In the following year, the Korean War broke out and the United States resumed economic and military aid to Taiwan. U.S. economic aid lasted 15 years until 1965, averaging approximately US$ 100 million a year (Jacoby, 1966, 38), about 6 percent of Taiwanese GNP during this period (Chang, 1974, 81). The Taiwanese economy entered into a new stage of development.

Economic recovery began in the early 1950s following the chaotic period. Before World War II, the advanced agricultural sector completed the phase of primary-export-led growth, while the industrial sector was already in the stage of import substitution, during which an economic policy of self-sufficiency was adopted. The island was productive, thanks to agricultural development during the colonial period (Hsiao, 1997), and the Taiwanese people were well disciplined, educated, and diligent. Basic social and economic infrastructures, like modern transportation (highways, railroads, and harbors), communication (telephones and telegraphs), schools for all levels, irrigation and flood control, and electric power generating facilities were already in place at the end the war (Ho, 1978; Lin, 1973). They saved the KMT government considerable investment in infrastructures at the beginning of the postwar economic recovery period (Chang, 1974, 79).

However, the available infrastructure was overused due to the sudden influx of Chinese refugees from the mainland and the high rate of natural increases in the Taiwanese population immediately after the war. This can be seen from the fact that, while the infrastructure was built before the war, every eight to nine Taiwanese had to share the same facilities with one Chinese refugee (Hsiao and Hsiao, 1996, Table 1.3). Furthermore, despite the U.S. advice recommending reduction in military expenditure (Jacoby, 1966, 122), the KMT government maintained 600,000 soldiers during and after the period of U.S. aid. Military personnel consisted of 6.7 percent of the total population in 1953, one of the largest ratios of military forces in the world (Jacoby, 1966, 118). "During 1951-65, military expenditures averaged 9 to 11 percent of the GNP, even more than in the rich and advanced economy of the United States. They consistently formed about 85 percent of the outlays of the national government, and around 50 percent of the combined outlays of government at all levels" (Jacoby, 1966, 118). The government had huge deficit spending (Chiang, 1971, 2) and the future appeared bleak.

Under these postwar conditions, the natural approach for survival was to return to the phase of primary-export-led growth completed in the first two stages of the colonial period. This entailed the earning of foreign exchanges by exporting traditional products of sugar and rice while also developing existing industries and encouraging and protecting old import-substituting industries, which sprouted during the last several years of self-sufficiency and self-reliance before the end of the war (Kobayashi, 1973). There were some new import-substituting industries, such as synthetic fiber and electronics, to save precious foreign exchanges.[4] Domestically, with U.S. aid on one hand and firm KMT rule on the other, the government implemented schemes which taxed consumers heavily and extracted contributions from (or exploited) Taiwanese farmers and laborers (Hsiao and Hsiao, 1996; Liu, 1975). As we will see below, due to increased population and military forces, for the first ten to fifteen years after the war the Chinese regime in Taiwan was forced to play the catch up game of restoring prewar peaks achieved during the Japanese period. Lacking resources and technical ability to engage in new industries, the government had to rely on the old industries base left over by the Japanese.

At the end of the war, the Japanese left basic metal, chemical, and other "heavy" industries, which were relatively capital intensive in those days. Some raw materials for these industries, such as aluminum, magnesium, and petroleum had to be imported, and their finished products had a limited market in the war-torn Taiwanese economy. Thus immediately after the war, the KMT government had difficulty in deciding whether to spend scarce capital and precious foreign exchanges to restore the war damages and maintain these white elephant industries (Lin, 1968, 296). However, internal and external political developments around 1949 and 1950 altered the picture virtually overnight. The civilian and military

[4]Other new industries include electric equipment, automobile, petroleum chemistry, plastics, pharmacy, chemical seasoning, mushrooms, asparagus, and milk, see BOT (1969).

industries built by the Japanese in Taiwan to take advantage of resources in South China and the South Sea to fight the Allied Forces were now utilized by the KMT government to fight Chinese communists in the defense of Taiwan. Essentially, the KMT perpetuated the Japanese controlled wartime economy (Twu, 1975, 499), though on a larger scale due to U.S. aid which supported an increased population and 600,000 soldiers.

In the following section, we will show that, similar to the decline of the Taiwanese economy during the last stage of the war period, the early postwar controlled economy under militarism also suffered a toll which delayed the economic recovery until the mid-1960s.

5.3 Prewar Peak and Postwar Recovery

During the Japanese period, industrialization proceeded gradually but steadily, as shown in Fig. 5.1. The heavy solid line of Fig. 5.1 traces Taiwan's real GDP (RGDP) from 1920 to 1969, measured in billion New Taiwan (NT) dollars in 1937 prices using the second Y-axis on the right. Figure 5.1 also shows the production composition[5] of real GDP: the primary industry (Prim, the dotted line), the secondary industry (2nd, the light solid line) and the tertiary industry (Ter, the dashed line). These compositions are measured from the left Y-axis. The real GDP is the sum of these three industrial outputs (measured from the second Y-axis on the right).

From Fig. 5.1, the prewar real GDP peaked in 1939 at NT$ 1327.64 million. Frantic war efforts increased prices and reduced real GDP. By the end of the war, intensive air raids by the Allied Forces decreased RGDP to a mere NT$ 314.61 million in 1945. The following year RGDP began a smooth and steady recovery. But the prewar peak was regained only in 1954. In 1952, the year in which Taiwan's statistics began to be recorded systematically (TSDB, each year), and the reference year of most of the development studies of Taiwan, the GDP measured in New Taiwan dollars was still only about 85 percent of the prewar peak.

[5]The statistical methodology of the Wu estimates from 1920 to 1951 is given in Appendix of Wu (1991), in which he also discusses the Mizoguchi-Umemura estimates (Mizoguchi and Umemura, 1988) and the Lee estimates. The complete data from 1910 to 1990 are given in Wu (1995).

Lee's estimates of real Net Domestic Product (NDP) and its composition are available in the Appendix of Ho (1978), Table A1. The primary industry includes agriculture, forestry, and fishery, the secondary industry includes mining, manufacturing, construction, and utilities, the tertiary industry includes communication and transportation, government services, and storage.

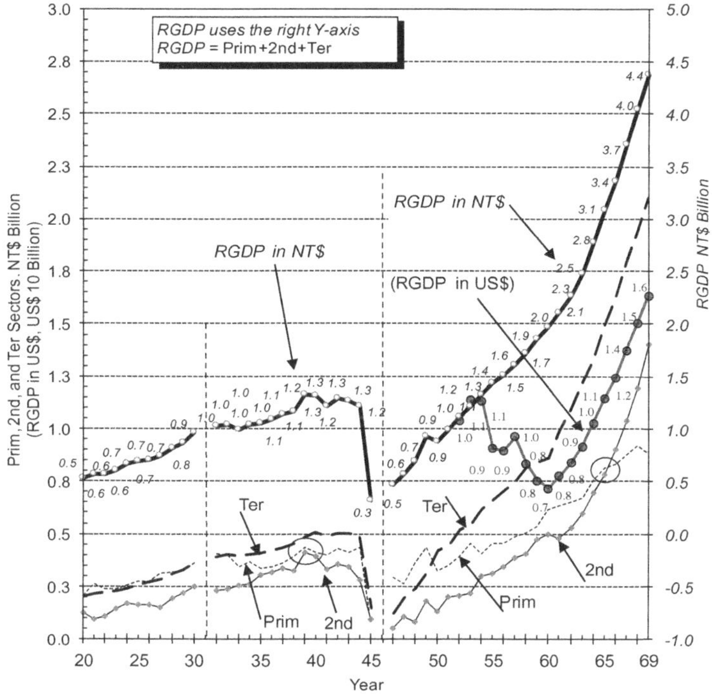

Figure 5.1: RGDP and its Distribution, 1920–1969, in 1937 Prices

A similar pattern appears in the three components of real GDP. Figure 5.1 shows that the agricultural sector recovered to the prewar peak first in 1949, but dipped again until 1953 when it reached full recovery and growth. The war damage to the industrial sector was most severe. In 1945, output was less than a quarter of the 1939 prewar peak (412.21, in million NT$, the same below), and dipped even lower in 1946, a year after the war. It did not fully recover until 1958 (401.40) and 1959 (471.87). The service sector fared better. It reached prewar peak in 1940 (505.73), dipped to about 30 percent of the peak at the end of the war (148.17), and recovered completely in 1952 (516.99).

In nominal terms, the value of industrial output exceeded that of agricultural output for the first time in 1939 (Kusunoi, 1944, 157; also see Sumiya *et al.*, 1992, 21). In real terms, they came very close to each other in Fig. 5.1 (435.14 and 412.21) in that year (circled in Fig. 5.1). The proportion for the three industries: primary (agriculture), secondary (manufacturing), and tertiary (services), in real terms were 33 percent,

31 percent, and 36 percent, respectively, in 1939. The Taiwanese economy seemed to enter a new phase of economic growth. However, it failed to sustain itself. The industrial output continued to be below the agricultural output after 1941. This lasted during the whole period of the 1950s and up to 1966 (the second circle in Fig. 5.1). Only after 1966, we see the sustained transformation of the Taiwanese economy. Note from the diagram how close the industrial output came to the agricultural output during the second half of the 1930s as compared with the large difference of the two sectors in the 1950s and beyond until 1963. If production structure is any indication of the degree of industrialization, this seems to be another manifestation that, despite all the efforts of the KMT government, the Taiwanese economy was relatively more industrialized in the late 1930s than in the immediate postwar period extending to the mid-1960s.

International comparison of national income is generally made in U.S. dollars. The heavy dotted line on the right side of Fig. 5.1 shows real GDP in U.S. dollars. The data after 1952 are readily available from government publications (e.g., TSDB and SAROC). The Taiwanese data source on GDP is given at 1986 prices (that is, real GDP) in New Taiwan dollars (TSDB, 1993, 25). We have converted it to U.S. dollars by dividing it by the U.S. exchange rate (ibid., 152), taking the average of buying and selling rates. This is what we call RGDP/US$ in Fig. 5.1, shown as a line with black circles, which is measured from the left Y-axis in US$ 10 billion. Starting from real GDP of US$ 10.39 billion in 1952, it increased and then decreased precipitously and fluctuated slightly due to severe devaluation of the New Taiwan dollar and possibly the inflationary pressure.[6] It recovered to the 1952–53 level only in 1964–65 and grew steadily thereafter. As we have observed up to now, if we can assume that by 1952 the Taiwanese economy was still not quite recovered to prewar peaks, this line indicates that, when

[6]The US$ exchange rate increased 156 percent, from NT$ 15.6 in 1952 to NT$ 40 in 1960, and was fixed at NT$ 40 from 1960 to 1972. The wholesale price index (WPI) increased 96 percent from 16.15 in 1952 to 31.64 in 1960, using 1986 prices = 100. The inflation rate subsided afterward until 1972. From 1960 to 1965, the WPI increased only 11 percent, from 31.64 to 35.01. It increased to only 38.43 in 1970. See Hsiao and Hsiao (1996) (in Ref. Chapter 1, Fig. 1.11). Note that, in the early postwar period, the exchange rates were tightly controlled by the government, and might not reflect the "market rates." Note also that in 1969, Wu's RGDP in 1937 price gives NT$ 4,328.8 million, but TSDB's RGDB in 1986 price gives NT$ 654,682 million. Dividing the latter by US exchange rate, NT$ 40.05, we have US$ 16,346 million, or about US$ 16 billion, as shown in Fig. 5.1. The same applies for other years. We take the data as they are given.

measured in U.S. dollars, it did not recover to the prewar peak until the mid-1960s or somewhat later.[7]

This is rather surprising. In spite of all the efforts and talk of government bureaucrats and scholars about postwar industrialization and government policies for economic growth, the Taiwanese economy did not recover during the 1950s.

Since economic welfare is generally measured in per capita income, the solid heavy line in Fig. 5.2 presents real GDP per capita in New Taiwan dollars from 1920 to 1971, as measured in 1937 prices (Wu, 1991). The real per capita GDP (RGDPpc) increased from NT$ 142 in 1920 to NT$ 213 in 1931, flattened out during most of the 1930s, and reached the prewar maximum of NT$ 225 in 1939. It then started decreasing and plummeted to a mere NT$45 in 1945. Probably due to a combination of sudden influx of Chinese refugees around 1949 and the natural increase in Taiwanese population, the recovery of per capita real GDP is much slower than that of real GDP shown in Fig. 5.1. Until the mid-1950s, it dipped even below the 1920 level. Apparently, here are the "rags," as the Taiwanese standard of living plunged far below its 1920 level! It recovered to a mere 56 percent of the prewar level in 1952, still well below the 1920 level. As we have observed in the previous section, the wartime controlled economy and the government policy priority[8] of "recovering the mainland" during this period kept the standard of living from complete recovery until mid-1960s.

The heavy dotted line in Fig. 5.2 shows per capita real GNP in U.S. dollars after 1952. It is derived by dividing real GNP per capita[9] in New Taiwan dollars at 1986 prices (taken from TSDB, 1993, 30) by U.S. dollar exchange rates. The numbers are divided again by 10 to fit into the scale of the left Y-axis (shown as RGNPpc/10 in the parentheses to correspond to the parentheses in the label of the left Y-axis). The real GNP per capita in U.S. dollars tells a quite different story. In real terms (using 1986 prices),

---

[7]There seems no study of US$ exchange rates in the early postwar period. Ho (1978, 106) states that "In the early 1950s inflation kept the NT$ (New Taiwan dollar) overvalued..." If this is the case, decrease in real GDP *in terms of the US dollar*, as shown in Fig. 5.1, will be more pronounced. More research is called for on this point.

[8]"Central government expenditures on economic development were mere one percent until 1960, two percent in 1965, and 7 percent in 1970," and "maintained about 20 percent from 1975 to 1990" (Hsiao and Hsiao, 1996, in Ref. Chapter 1, Table 1.6), consistent with the government policy priority.

[9]Here we use per capita GNP (at 1986 prices before adjustment of terms of trade), instead of per capita GDP, to take advantage of the readily available official data (TSDB, 1993, 30).

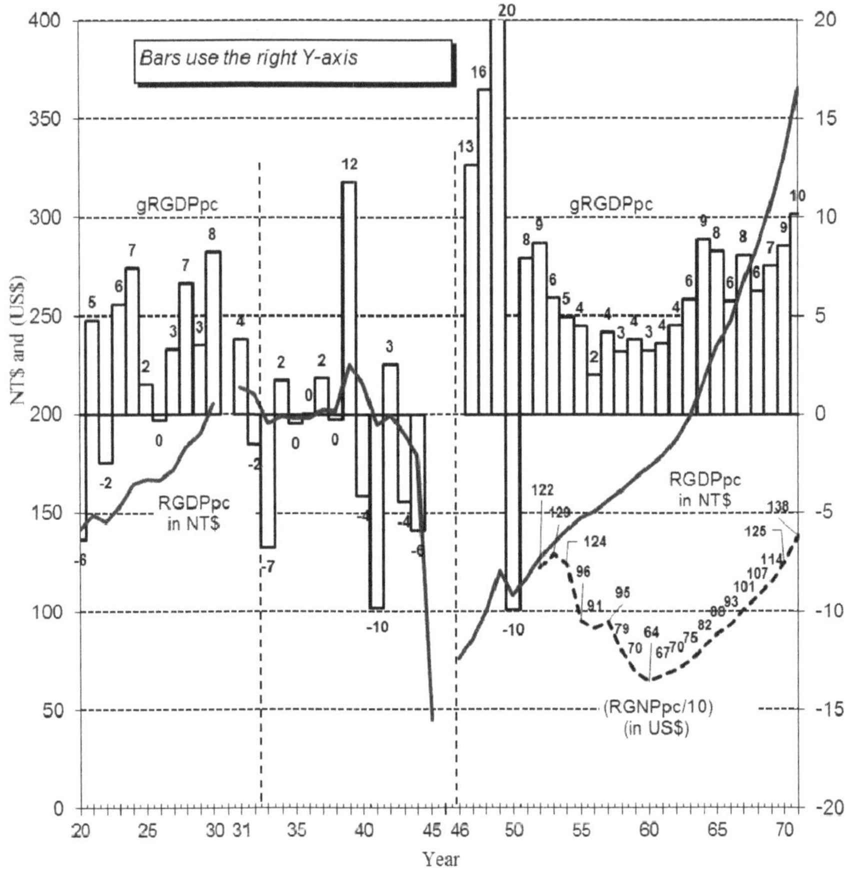

Figure 5.2: Per Capita RGDP and RGNP
In 1937 Prices (NT$), 1986 Prices (US$)

Taiwanese per capita GNP in 1952 already reached US$ 1,216 (121.6 in Fig. 5.2), more than six times larger than per capita GNP in nominal value (ibid., 30), thanks to Taiwan's overvaluation of the New Taiwan dollar. It increased to US$ 1,287 (or 128.7 in Fig. 5.2) in the following year, and then started decreasing to a bottom of US$ 642 (shown at 64.2) in 1960, mainly due to continuous devaluation of the New Taiwan dollar. It surpassed the 1952–53 record only in 1969–70.[10] Considering the very slow recovery,

[10]After 1971, real GNP per capita took off and increased steadily to US$ 8,630 in 1992, which is about 85 percent of the nominal GNP per capita. See Hsiao and Hsiao (1996) (Ref. Chapter 1, Fig. 1.11).

or even stagnation, of real standard of living, the above observation of real GNP per capita seems to be consistent with the earlier findings that Taiwan's real consumption expenditure surpassed prewar levels around 1960 (Mizoguchi, 1975, 23, 28).

The above observations are also reflected in growth rates of these series. The gray bars in Fig. 5.2 show the growth rates of per capita real GDP measured from the right Y-axis. There were considerable fluctuations before the end of the war, and they were generally positive after the war, as evidenced by the steady growth of the heavy solid line.

In general, we have observed two important events in this section. First, Taiwan's postwar per capita income grew steadily from a bottom of about NT$ 100 or so around 1952, the year from which the government began publishing economic statistics systematically and regularly, to NT$ 300 or so in 1970. The 1952 per capita GDP is only about half that of 1920. This is the source of the so called "Taiwan miracle," and the view of the "rags," a "state of extreme poverty" forty years ago. While it is true that there was "extreme poverty" immediate after the war, poverty was due mainly to the war and mismanagement of the economy. The economic and social foundations of the economy built by the Japanese were still intact. Thus Taiwan's situation was quite different from that of other developing countries when it comes to the initial conditions of economic development. Second, if the peaks of the Japanese period are considered, the Taiwanese economy already had achieved considerable development during the prewar period.[11] The postwar Taiwanese economy did not manage to recover to prewar levels during the 1950s, and the Taiwanese standard of living did not match the prewar peak until the mid-1960s or perhaps not until 1970. Indeed, contrary to the literature on Taiwanese economic development, the postwar Taiwanese economic performance before 1970 was hardly[12] "miraculous," and certainly not a story of "rags to riches." In fact, it had

[11]By the later part of the 1930s, Taiwan already was world's major producing country of bananas (3), canned pineapples (3), sugar (4), sweet potatoes (4), tea (6), rice (10), and peanuts (10). The number in the parentheses is Taiwan's world ranking. Hsiao (1997) (in Ref. Chapter 4, Table 4.3).

[12]According to Wu's estimates (1995), the average real GDP growth rate in period 1938–1970 is 4.59 percent, in period 1911–1939 is 4.18 percent. They are hardly differentiable. The rate for period 1952–1970 is 8.76 percent, which is almost twice higher than that between 1938–1970. Similarly, the average per capita real GDP growth rate in period 1938–1970 is 1.57 percent, much *lower* than that in period 1911–1939, which is 2.12 percent. The rate for period 1952–1970 is 5.66 percent, which is 3.6 times higher than that between 1938–1970. Once again, a "miracle" occurs if we ignore the pre-war statistics.

a long period of recovery, and the takeoff started slowly and painfully. However, after it recovered to prewar peaks in the mid-1960s, it accelerated in the 1980s.[13]

5.4 Linkages between the Two Periods

In the previous section, we have shown the linkages of aggregate outputs between the two periods. This section examines prewar and postwar linkages in terms of three economic structures: industrial production, labor composition of industries, and foreign trade. They are presented in Figs. 5.3 to 5.6. The legends and some notes regarding these figures are given in Appendix. We have chosen these three structures mainly because they are some of the more important measures of industrialization, and also because their data are readily accessible to us. Admittedly, other indicators, such as investment, urbanization, human resources, the tax system, etc., might also be used for comparison. Unfortunately, consistent and systematic estimates of long-term statistics for these items are still not available.

At a less aggregated level, the linkages in some major individual industries in Taiwan during the early postwar period, such as the electric power industry, the fertilizer industry, the sugar industry, the cement industry, have been explored in Hsiao and Hsiao (1996) and also in Sasamoto and Kawano (1968).

5.4.1 *The Production Structure*

Figure 5.3 presents indexes of production from 1936 to 1958 for comparable groups of commodities based on the calculations given by Ho (1978), 365–368. The data before the end of the war (1936 to 1946) use 1937 as the base year, and those of the postwar period (1946 to 1958) take 1954 as the base year. The data for the two periods are measured in different monetary units, and shown in the form of indexes, hence the two periods are not comparable in terms of absolute values. However, we submit that the diagram, if used with caution along with the findings in Figs. 5.1 and 5.2, will provide interesting contrasts between the prewar and early postwar industrial structure in Taiwan. The "General" index (the patterned bars on the left-hand side) includes mining, manufacturing,

[13]Elsewhere we have discussed the Japanese legacy, The Taiwan-Japan-USA nexus, the rise of small and medium size Taiwanese enterprises, etc. as the sources of Taiwanese economic growth (Hsiao and Hsiao, 1996, in Ref. Chapter 1).

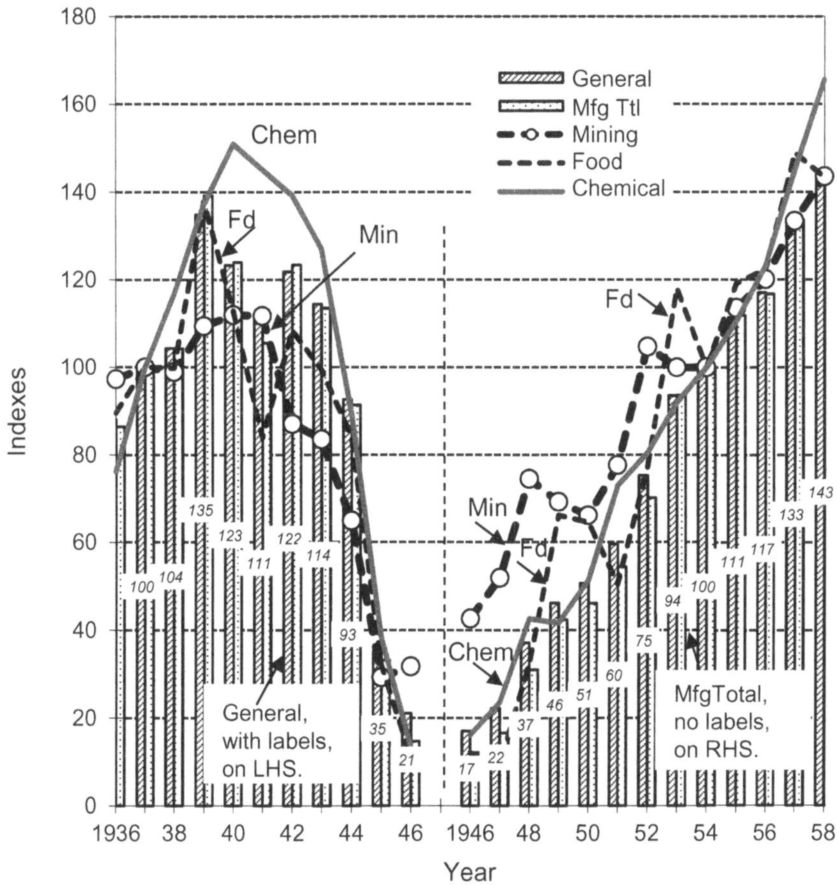

Figure 5.3: Indexes of Industrial Production 1936–46 (1937 = 100), 1946–58 (1954 = 100)

and electricity; the "manufacture total" (the empty bars on the right-hand side) includes food, chemicals, nonmetallic mineral, textile, metal, and monopoly (tobacco, liquor, etc.). In 1946, the indexes for Chemicals, Food, the Manufacturing Total, and the "General" items were more or less at the same level in Fig. 5.3. This suggests the similarity of the percentage proportions of the production structure for these groups between the base periods, 1937 and 1954.

In Fig. 5.3, food production (the lighter dotted line) decreased more than the general production index from 1936 to 1946, while increasing faster

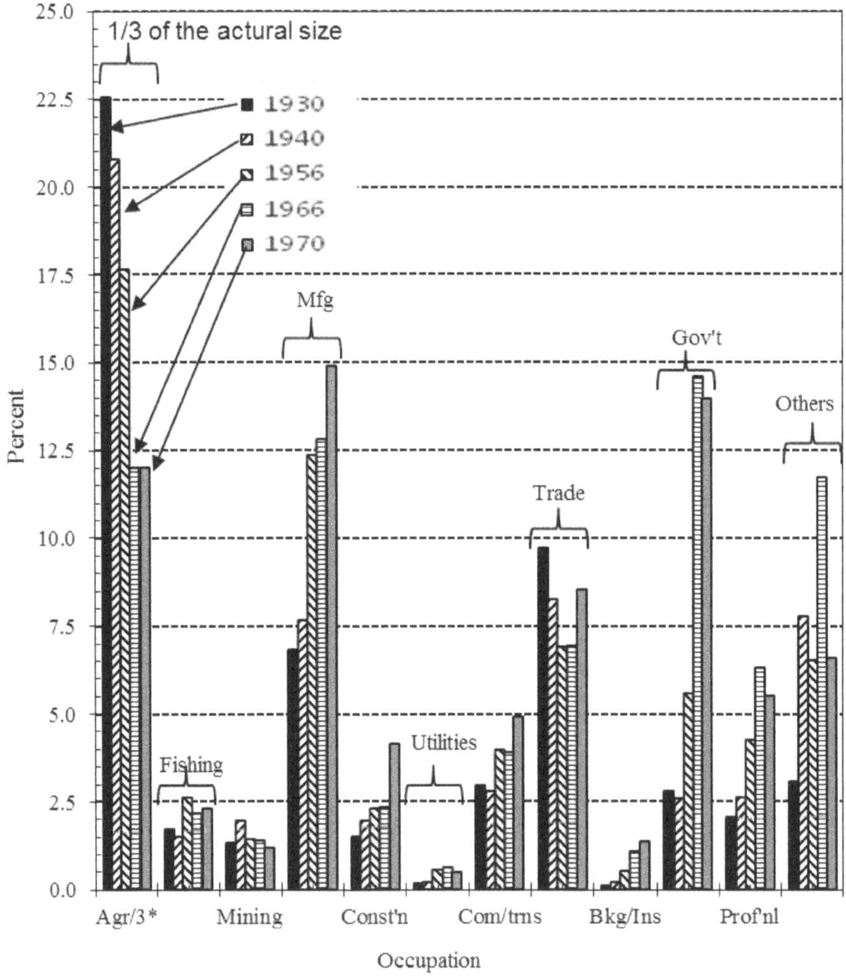

Figure 5.4: Composition of Labor by Industry
Census Years: 1940, 1956, 1966, 1970

after 1946. This seems to indicate again the effect of war under the Japanese regime, in which agricultural production yielded to industrial production, and the need of accelerated food production to feed the increased population shortly following the end of the war. In terms of indexes, the General and Manufacturing Total recovered to the prewar period in about 1958. Similar trends can be observed for electric power, metal, monopoly, and nonmetallic mineral products and other industrial products.

5.4.2 *The Labor Composition*

Figure 5.4 shows the composition of the labor force by industry for each census year of 1930, 1940, 1956, 1966, and 1970. Employment in the agricultural sector was so large that we have represented it by one-third of its actual proportional size (denoted as 1/3 at the top in the diagram). For each year, all the bars of the same pattern, say, the first black bars, must sum to 100 percent over all 12 commodity groups shown on the horizontal axis. The similarity in the proportion of labor employed, as shown by the ups and downs of the bars in each industry before and after the end of the war is obvious. The bars have almost the *same* relative heights for each commodity group, especially between 1940 and 1956 (the second and the third bars in each group. They are filled with wide slanted upward and downward patterns for easy comparison). This suggests that, in general, the industrial structure between 1940 and 1956 was very similar.

Despite similarity, conspicuous differences can be found in the proportion of government employees in 1966 and 1970 on the one hand, and employees in the manufacturing and "other" industries in 1966 on the other. The former may probably be due to a bloated bureaucracy, or overlapping government structures, that is, the "Central" and the "Taiwan Provincial" governments overlap, resulting in over-employment in the government sector.[14] Increase in employees in government and the manufacturing industry was more or less compensated for by the decrease in agricultural employment. The proportion of employment in the manufacturing industry also shows the difference between the prewar and postwar periods. Its proportion clearly doubled in the postwar period, although it was still less than 15 percent of the total employment.

Our observations on the composition of labor are confirmed by computing the Spearman rank correlation coefficient,[15] r. Table 5.1 presents the rank correlation coefficients. The number in parentheses shows the sum of the squares of differences in ranks. Table 5.1 shows the correlation coefficients for labor composition between 1930 and 1940 being 0.96,

[14] Government employees in 1940 and 1956 exclude military personnel living on military bases. Ho (1978), 326. Hence, part of drastic increase in 1966 and 1970 government employees may be due to including military personnel on military bases.

[15] Rank correlation is calculated from $r = 1 - (6\Sigma(d^2))/(n(n^2 - 1))$ where d is the difference between the ranks and n is the size of sample. See Tate (1955), 243–246. In case of ties, we assign the mean of the tied ranks to all the ranks of the tied scores (Tate, 1955, 245). The method of hypothesis testing when $n < 20$ is explained in Yamane (1973), 498–503.

Table 5.1: Rank Correlation Coefficients

		Composition of Labor (from Fig. 5.4)			
		1940	1956	1966	1970
1	1930	0.96 (12)	0.97 (8)	0.88 (34)	0.90 (28)
2	1940		0.92 (22)	0.85 (42)	0.87 (38)
3	1956			0.94 (18)	0.95 (14)
4	1966				0.98 (6)

Note: The number in the parentheses is the sum of squared differences.
Source: Calculated from the data in Ho (1978), 326.

between 1930 and 1956 being 0.97, etc. The coefficients are generally very high. For all entries in Table 5.1, the null hypothesis that any two series are uncorrelated could be rejected at the 5 percent level of significance. The coefficients between the years before the end of the war and the years after the war tend to decrease as the period becomes longer (rows 1 and 2). The coefficients of the two nearby years, that is, between prewar 1930 and 1940 (row 1), between postwar 1956 and 1966 (row 3), and between 1966 and 1970 (row 4), have generally higher values than others. Our statistics show that the labor structures between two nearby years are closer than those between two distant years, as expected. Hence, we may conclude that, in terms of industrial structure expressed in percentage distribution, they are even similar between 1940 and 1970. This observation is consistent with our previous findings on the composition of RGDP in Fig. 5.1.

5.4.3 *The Trade Structure*

It is natural to expect that the immediate years following the war, developing countries after independence maintained close economic ties with their former colonial rulers. In the case of Taiwan, this tendency was reinforced by Taiwan's separation from China after 1949. As in the colonial period, during the 1950s and the early 1960s, Taiwan exported sugar, and to a lesser degree, rice, mainly to Japan to earn necessary foreign exchange, and imported, with U.S. aid, industrial materials and capital goods from the United States to build up the existing industries and infrastructures left by the Japanese. We now compare the structure of exports, imports, and the balance of trade (BOT, 1969).

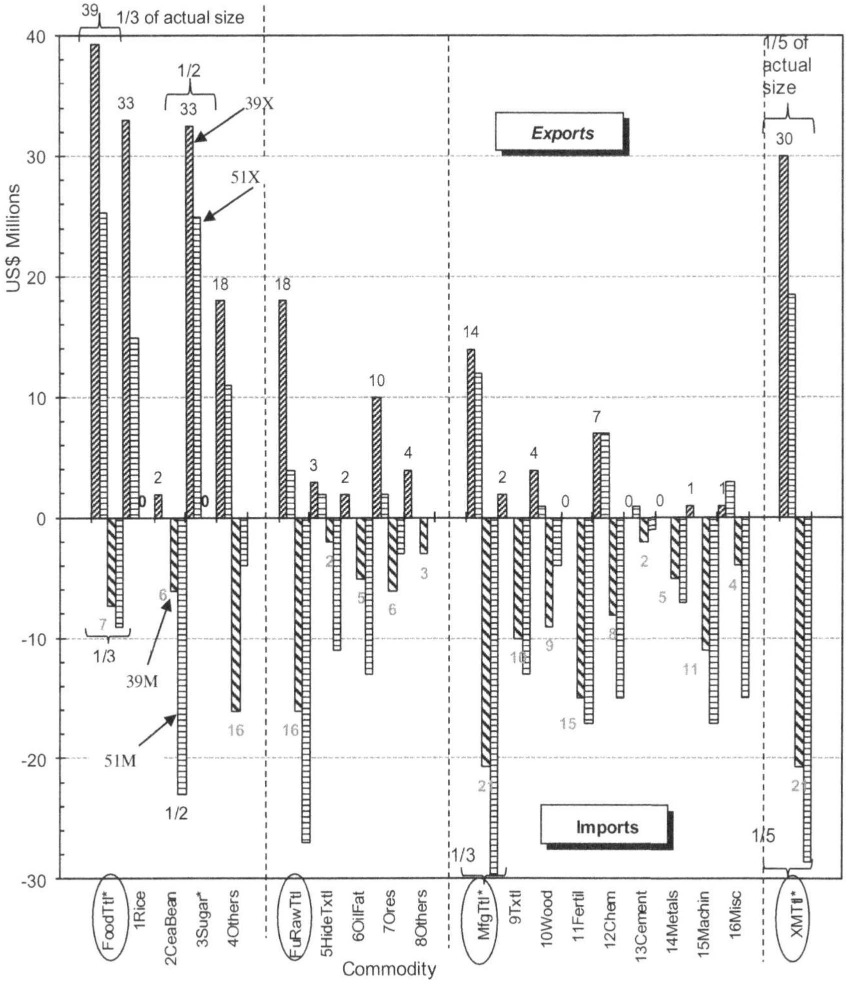

Figure 5.5: Taiwan's Exports and Imports

Selected Commodity Group, 1939, 1951

Figure 5.5 shows the trade structure between 1939 and 1951 in million U.S. dollars.[16] Exports are given by upward bars, and imports are drawn as downward bars. For both exports and imports, the slanted bars show 1939 values, and the parallel patterned bars show 1951 values. Each commodity

[16]The data in 1939 Japanese yen are converted to U.S. dollars by 3.96 yen per dollar. The 1951 data are in current U.S. dollars. See Lin (1973), 42, Footnote b.

category has four years: two years for exports (upward bars), and two years of imports (downward bars). To make the graphing of the diagram more manageable, we have reduced the data on foodstuff (FoodTtl, circled) and manufactures (MfgTtl, circled) to 1/3, and Sugar (item 3) to 1/2, of the original data for both years. We also reduced the total exports and imports (XMTtl) to 1/5 of the original data. These are indicated in the plot area of the chart as well as by an asterisk at the end of the commodity label along the X-axis.

In both 1939 and 1951, a huge quantity of foodstuffs, rice (item 1) and sugar (item 3), was exported, while a large quantity of manufactures, like textiles and apparel (item 9), fertilizer (item 11), and machinery, electric supplies, transportation equipment and instruments (item 15), were imported,[17] indicating the primary export-led economy in both years. It is interesting to note that, in 1939, Taiwan even had slight ability to export textiles and apparel (item 9), but in 1951 they had to be imported in large quantities, probably due to increase in population. Apparently, the import substitution phase in the textile industry still had not yet taken place in 1951. Comparing 1939 and 1951, Taiwan exported less rice and sugar, and imported more fuels and raw materials, and significantly more manufactured goods, reflecting once again the effects of increased population and the presence of large military forces.

The slanted bars in Fig. 5.6 show the 1939, and the parallel patterned bars, the 1951, balance of trade for each commodity group and its total trade (circled). Clearly, even six years after the end of the war, Taiwan still continued exporting large quantities of agricultural products (mainly to Japan) and importing increasingly more manufactured goods (from both Japan and the United States). If we ignore U.S. aid and assistance, we can say Taiwan continued her so called "a colonial pattern" of foreign trade.[18] In fact, such a pattern continued until the mid-1960s (see Figs. 1.15 and 1.16 of Ref. Chapter 1). Figure 5.6 also shows that, Taiwan had trade surpluses of about US$ 50 million in 1939, but, had about the same amount of trade deficits in 1951 (see the "Total" column). Despite these differences, both

---

[17]Some imports from U.S. Aid, especially from military assistance programs, were not included.

[18]Clearly, this "pattern" is due to the early stage of economic development. Elsewhere, we have shown that, even under the Japanese colonialism, the so called "Industrial Japan, Agricultural Taiwan," a favorite theme of the Chinese in postwar Taiwan, was in fact based on comparative advantage of Taiwan in producing and exporting agricultural products, rather than colonialism. See Hsiao (1997).

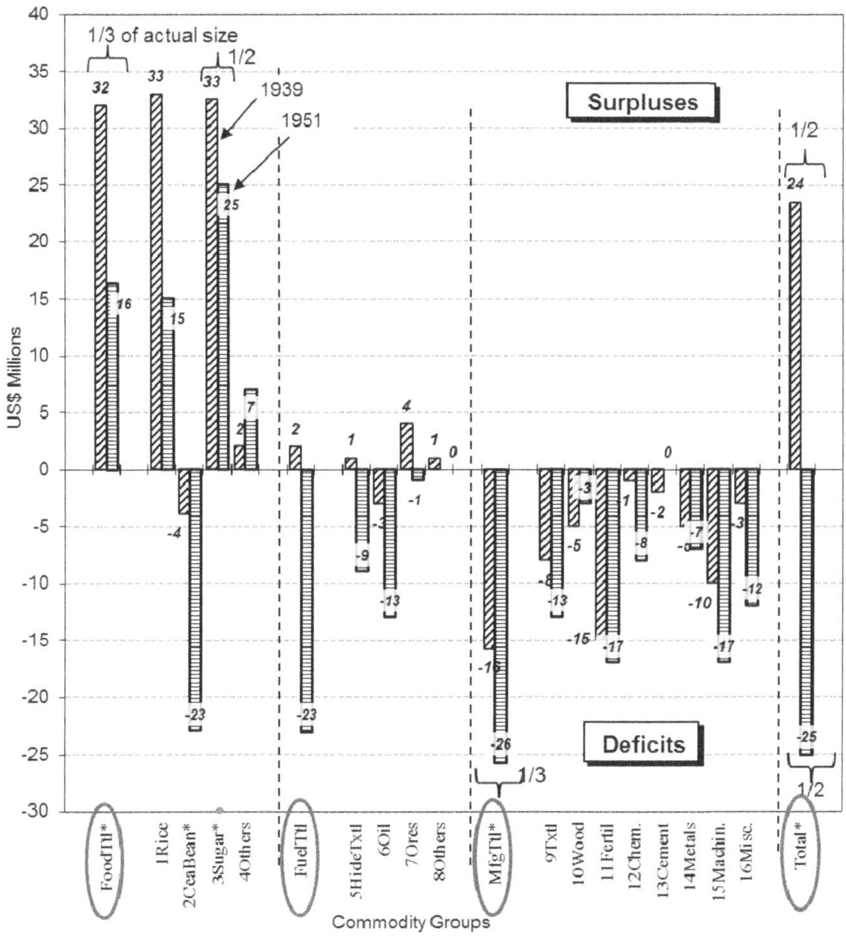

Figure 5.6: Taiwan's Balance of Trade
Selected Commodity Groups, 1939, 1951

Figs. 5.5 and 5.6 show clearly that trade structure, as shown by relative ups and downs, was generally similar in these two years.

In terms of proportion, the similarity of the composition of trade structure even extends to, surprisingly, as far apart as between years 1935, 1955, and 1965, especially in the export sector, as shown in Fig. 5.7. Note the similarity of the trade structures between 1935 (black bars for exports and slant patterned bars for imports) and 1955 (gray bars). The 1965 structure is shown by empty bars. Clearly, by 1965, the landscape of the bars changed considerably from 1935 and 1955. This means that the basic trade structure, and so the underlining basic production and consumption structures in Taiwan, during the twenty-year period between 1935 and 1955 had not been changed much, despite the change in regimes and the interruption of the war. The Chinese claim of differences and progress notwithstanding, strong linkages and similarities of the economies exist between these two periods. The two economies were basically the same, but the societies were different, as the postwar Taiwanese society was, among other things, overburdened by the Chinese refugees and armed forces (Hsiao and Hsiao, 1996, 210–211). Clearly, the real change in economic structure comes only in the mid-1960s, as we have shown previously.

The drawing of Fig. 5.7 is the same as that of Fig. 5.5. The difference here is that the entire 17 commodity groups of exports (or imports) listed in the horizontal axis in each year must add up to 100 percent, and each category has six-year data, three for exports as upward bars and three for imports as downward bars. The upper part of Fig. 5.7 shows exports. Except oil and wax (item 5) and pharmaceuticals (item 6), all other commodity groups had very similar proportions, indicating again a consistent export structure between 1935 and 1955. Exports of cereals, starch, seeds (item 2) are unusually large, 30 percent in 1935 and 24 percent in 1955. They are shown in Fig. 5.7 as only 1/5th of the actual magnitude for both years, and denoted as 1/5 in the upper part of the diagram. So were exports of foodstuffs, beverages, and tobacco (item 3), 55 percent in 1935 and 66 percent in 1955. They are shown in Fig. 5.7 as only $1/10^{\text{th}}$ of the actual magnitude for both years (denoted as 1/10 in the upper part of the diagram). These two items indicate that the Taiwanese economy in the years before the war and the postwar transition period was basically in the same phase of primary-export-led economic growth.

The lower part of Fig. 5.7 shows that there are more differences in import structure. In 1955, the middle gray bars show that the proportion of imports of 2Cereals, starch, seeds, 5Oil and fat, wax, and its products, 6Pharmaceutical, 8Fibers, ropes, and their materials, 16Clock, instruments, wheels, machinery increased greatly. This indicates the results of population increase and the need to import raw materials and capital goods for industrial use. On the other hand, the proportion of imports of 3Foodstuffs, beverages, and tobacco, 9Cloths and products, 17Miscellaneous (including woods) all decreased considerably. The decrease in cloth imports and increase in fibers suggests that the Taiwanese economy was also in the process of import substitution during the later period. Since there is not

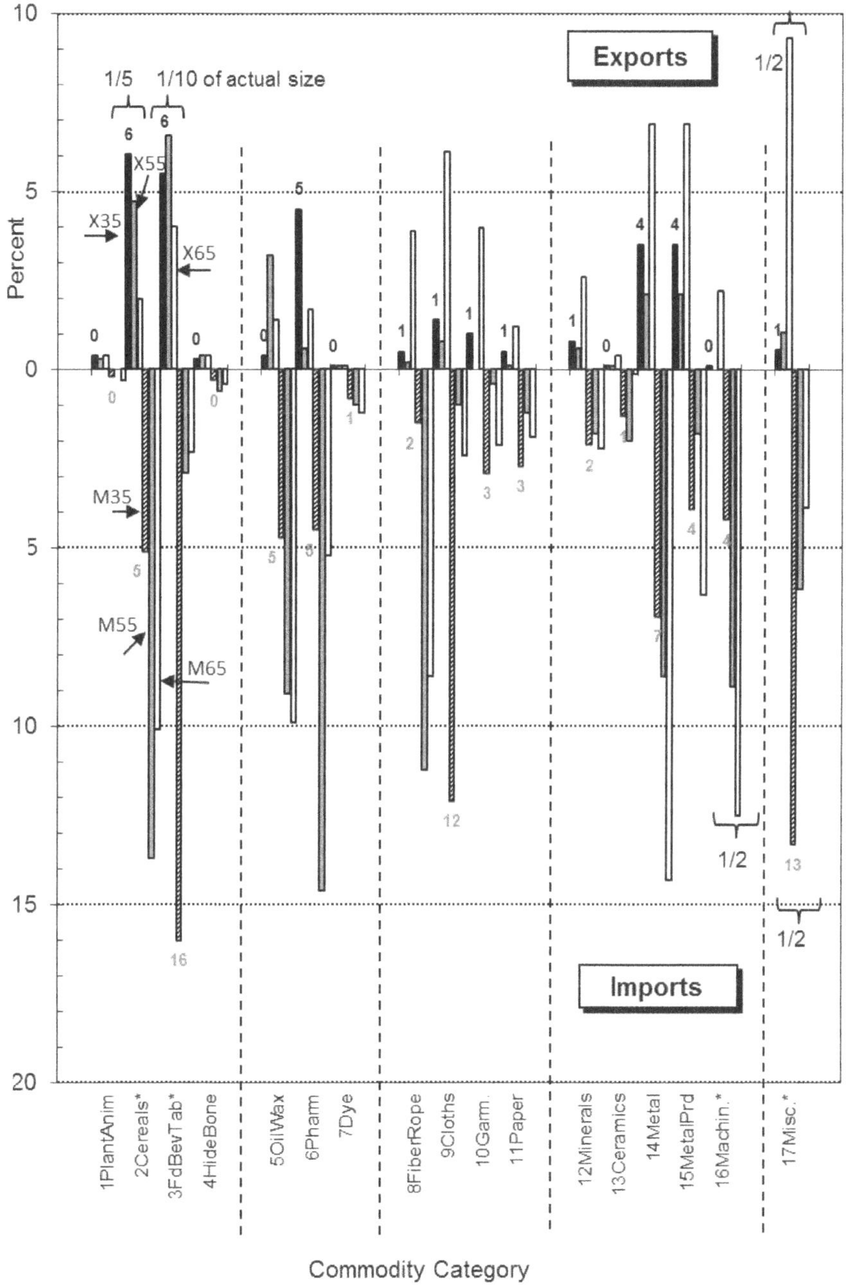

Figure 5.7: Composition of Taiwan's Exports and Imports
Comparison of 1935, 1955, and 1965

Table 5.2: Rank Correlation Coefficients

	Structure of Trade			
	Exports		Imports	BOT
	In US$ (from Figs. 5.5 and 5.6)[a]			
	1939/51		1939/51	1939/51
1	0.72		0.58	0.80
	(189)		(283)	(139)
	In percentage (from Fig. 5.7)[b]			
	1934/55	1935/65	1934/55	1935/65
2	0.70	0.76	0.57	0.69
	(246)	(193)	(348)	(250)

Sources: (a) Based on the data in Lin (1973), 42. (b) Based on the data in Mizoguchi (1975), 67. Other specifications are the same as Table 5.1.

much change in export structure, the difference between export and import structures seems to indicate that, although the basic structures are the same, more vigorous import substitution was taking place in the postwar period due to a much larger population.

Our observations on trade structure are again confirmed by Spearman rank correlation coefficients in Table 5.2. For Fig. 5.5, which compare the trade values in U.S. dollars between 1939 and 1951, the coefficients are 0.72 for exports and 0.58 for imports (row 1). The coefficient for the balance of trade (BOT, 1969) in Fig. 5.6 is at a higher rate of 0.80. For Fig. 5.7, which compares the percentage share of each items in total exports or imports, the coefficients (in row 2) are similar for the two years between 1935 and 1955, and also between 1935 and 1965, with coefficients in exports being much higher than those in imports. For the coefficients for exports, the null hypothesis that there is no correlation between the two series could be rejected at the 5 percent level of significance, and for those of imports, the null hypothesis could be rejected at the 10 percent level of significance.

In summary, Figs. 5.2 to 5.7 show that, up to the mid-1950s, Taiwanese industrialization was an expansion and extension of the industrial base already established under Japanese occupation. Considering that the first ten to fifteen years of the postwar Taiwanese economy were basically the period of an extension of the Japanese war-time controlled economy, it is not surprising that we obtain a strong correlation and broad similarity between the years before the end of the war and early postwar Taiwanese economy. Postwar Taiwanese economic development did not start from scratch, as is often asserted. In addition to taking advantage of the existing agricultural and industrial structures left by the Japanese, how did the government manage to support the population increase, military spending, and even the launching of a new phase of economic development? As we have noted elsewhere, the effects of monetary reform, land reform, U.S. aid, martial law, and the protection of the textile industry started to play important roles in ensuing periods (Hsiao and Hsiao, 1996).

5.5 Some Concluding Remarks

Our analysis points to the historical continuity of Taiwanese economic development between the prewar and postwar periods. We have also shown that, contrary to existing literature, early postwar Taiwanese economic development during the 1950s and up to the mid-1960s was primarily a "catching-up" phase, catching up to the prewar peaks of the Japanese period.

The "rags to riches" story is a myth, if this simply meant that Taiwan began from scratch as most developing countries face today. By measuring the degree of linkages between the prewar and the early postwar economic performance, this paper has shown that the "rags" are illusory. Taiwanese industries immediately after WWII had significant endowments from the colonial period, and that the initial conditions of economic development were already more conducive than most other developing countries.

As we have mentioned in the Introduction, our objective is very modest — to measure the degree of linkages between the prewar and postwar periods and the position of Taiwan in the 1950s. Space does not permit us to examine the important relationship between the initial conditions and the take-off phase which subsequently occurred after the mid-1960s. After all, a few countries with better initial conditions than Taiwan did not subsequently take off into sustained growth. To certain extent, we have done this elsewhere (Hsiao and Hsiao, 1996). We plan to continue our study on this subject.

The prevailing dichotomy which states that the Japanese developed Taiwan's agriculture, while the Chinese developed Taiwan's industries is too simplistic and inaccurate. The myth is due to neglecting the lines on the left-hand side (before 1945) of Figs. 5.1 to 5.3 and examining only the increasing curves on the right-hand side (the graphs after 1946). Our study even points to the possibility that if the KMT government were more committed to Taiwanese economic and social development immediately following the war, instead of steadfastly intent on "recovering the mainland," the rate of Taiwanese economic development could have been even quicker. In fact, Szczepanick (1958), 5, comparing the *slow* economic growth of Taiwan in the 1950s with that of Hong Kong, ably observed that the Chinese who were "the newcomers to Taiwan ... had difficulty in merging with the predominantly Fukienese indigenous population, speaking different language and thinking in different political terms ... the refugees who went to Taiwan were ... a group ready to rule or fight but not to work."

In concluding this paper, it should be emphasized that this paper is an attempt to utilize historical facts without postwar political distortion. It is not the purpose of this paper to advocate, as might be construed by some "rags to riches" advocates, that the Taiwanese people would have been better off under continued Japanese colonial rule. In view of the discrimination, humiliation, and persecution suffered under the Japanese regime before the war (Ho, 1984, 371–386), and fierce Taiwanese resistance to the colonial regime (Hsiao and Sullivan, 1979), continual Japanese rule on Taiwan was clearly out of the question (and for that matter, also for the Koreans and the Chinese in Kwantung. Ho, ibid.). We submit that this has never been a viable option for the future of Taiwan.

Appendix for Chapter 5 Sources and Explanations for Figures

5A. Figures 5.1 and 5.2

From Wu (1991, 1995) and TSDB (1993), 30.

5B. Figures 5.3 and 5.4

From Table A49 and Table A50 in Ho (1978), 366, 368. Private manufacturing, Total food, Chemicals in Table 49A are taken as comparable to Manufacturing (including sugar), Food (including sugar), Chemical and chemical products, respectively, in Table A50.

Figure 5.4 is based on the data in Table A22 of Ho (1978), 326.

5C. Figures 5.5 and 5.6

From Table 3-1 of Lin (1973), 42.

FoodTtl = Foodstuffs, beverages, and tobacco.
1Rice.
2CeaBean = Other cereals, beans.
3Sugar.
4Others = Other foodstuff, beverages, tobacco.

FuRawTtl = Fuels and raw materials.
5HideTxt = Hides, textiles, fibers, etc.
6OilFat = Oil and fats, petroleum.
7Ores = Ores and nonferrous metals.
8Others = Other minerals.

MfgTtl = Manufactures, n.e.s.
9Txtl = Textiles and apparel.
10Wood = Wood and wood products.
11Fertil = Fertilizer.
12Chem = Other chemical and rubber products.
13Cement = Cement, glass, and clay products.
14Metals = Iron, steel, and other metal manufactures.
15Machin = Machinery, electrical supplies, transportation equipment, and instruments.
16Misc = Miscellaneous manufactures.

XMTtl = Total of above groups.

5D. Figure 5.7

From Table 2.13 in Mizoguchi (1975), 67.

1PlantAnim = Plants, animals.
2Cereals = Cereals, starch, seeds.
3FdBevTab = Foodstuffs, beverages, and tobacco.
4HideBone = Hides, bones, shells, and their products.
5OilWax = Oil, wax, and its products.
6Pharm = Pharmaceutical.
7Dye = Dye, paints.
8FiberRope = Fibers, ropes, and their materials.
9Cloths = Cloths and products.
10Garm = Garments, their products.

11Paper = Paper, pulp, books.
12Minerals = Minerals, their products.
13Ceramics = Ceramics, glass, their products.
14Metal = Metal.

Acknowledgments

We are indebted to Tsong-min Wu of National Taiwan University for providing his data files and publications, to Keith Maskus for comments on the early draft, to Gary McClelland for consultation, to the McGuire Center of International Studies of the University of Colorado at Boulder for providing a research assistant. The original paper was revised and presented at the Taiwan Studies Workshop in Spring 1996 while the first author was a visiting scholar at the Fairbank Center for East Asian Research at Harvard University. It was presented at a seminar at National Taiwan University and also at the Taiwan Studies Conference on "The Japanese Legacy in Post-Colonial Taiwan," Washington University and University of Missouri, St. Louis, all in 1996. Comments and suggestions from Professors Joseph Allen, Meng-Mau Lee, David Pietz, James Thomas, Ping-li Tsai, Robert Weller, Tsong-min Wu, and other workshop and seminar participants are greatly appreciated. Mr. John Yunghsiang Lai of Harvard-Yenching Library helped with references. The original charts of the paper which were drawn using Quattro Pro have been redrawn using Microsoft Excel program. All errors of omission and commission are the authors'.

References

Amsden, A.H. (1985). "The State and Taiwan's Economic development." In P.B. Evans, D. Rueschemeyer and T. Skocpol (eds.), *Bringing the State Back* (Chapter 3). NY: Cambridge University Press.

Bank of Taiwan (BOT) (1969). *Taiwan's Newly Developing Industries.* Economic Research Section (ed.). Taipei: Bank of Taiwan.

Chan, S. and C. Clark (1992). *Flexibility, Foresight, and Fortuna in Taiwan's Development: Navigating between Scylla and Carybdis.* London: Routledge.

Chang, Han-yu (1974). *Economic Development and Economic Thoughts, Collection of Writings of Dr. Chang Han-yu* (in Chinese). Volume II, Taipei: Sanmin Bookstore.

Chang, Tsong-han (1980). *Pre-War Taiwanese Industrialization* (in Chinese). Taipei: Lien-Jing Book Company.

Chiang, Zhen-nan (1971). "Analysis of Changes in the Fiscal Structure in the Process of Taiwanese Economic Development" (in Chinese). In *Economic*

Essays, A Special Issue of Collection of Papers in Honor of the 80th Birthday of ex-President Shi-Jieh Wang, August. Taipei: Academia Sinica.

Ho, S.P.S. (1978). *Economic Development of Taiwan, 1960–1970.* New Haven: Yale University Press.

______ (1984). "Colonialism and Development: Korea, Taiwan, and Kwantung." In R.H. Myers and M.R. Peattie (eds.), *The Japanese Colonial Empire, 1895–1945.* NJ: Princeton University Press.

Hsiao, F.S.T. (1992). "Economic and Cultural Backgrounds of Taiwan's 2-28 Incident — An Application of Social Expectation Theory" (in Chinese). In Yong-hsing Chen (ed.), *Proceedings of 2-28 Academic Conference* (1991) (77–113). (Ref. Chapter 7). Taipei: 2-28 Citizens' Study Group, Taiwan-U.S. Cultural Exchange Fund, etc.

______ (1997). "Colonialism or Economic Advantage? -On Agricultural Development in Colonial Taiwan." Paper presented at the Taiwan Studies Workshop, Fairbank Center for East Asian Research, Harvard University, and National Taiwan University, 1996. *Proceedings of the National Science Council, Part C: Humanities and Social Sciences*, Taipei, Taiwan, 7(4) (October): 497–513. (Ref. Chapter 4).

______ and L.R. Sullivan (1979). "A Political History of The Taiwanese Communist Party, 1928–31." *Journal of Asian Studies*, 42(2): 269–289.

______ and M.C.W. Hsiao (1996). "Taiwanese Economic Development and Foreign Trade." In W.C. Kirby and J.M. Greene (eds.), *Harvard Studies on Taiwan: Papers of the Taiwan Study Workshop.* Cambridege, MA: John King Fairbank Center of East Asian Research, Harvard University, 1995. Reprinted in John Y.T. Kuark (ed.), *Comparative Asian Economies.* JAI Press, 1996. (Ref. Chapter 1).

Jacoby, N.H. (1966). *U.S. Aid to Taiwan, A Study of Foreign Aid, Self-help, and Development.* New York: Frederick A. Praeger.

Kobayashi, Hideo (1973). "On Taiwan's 'Industrialization' Policy after mid-1930s" (in Japanese). *Tochi Seido Shigaku* (Journal of History of Land System), 16(1) (October): 21–42.

Kusunoi, Ryuzo (1944). *A Study of The War-time Taiwanese Economy* (in Japanese). Taihoku: Nampo Jimbun Kenkyu Sho.

Lai, T.H., R.H. Myers and W. Wei (1991). *A Tragic Beginning, The Taiwan Uprising of February 28, 1947.* Stanford: Stanford University Press.

Lin, C.Y. (1968). "Industrial Development and Changes in the Structure of Foreign Trade, The Experience of the Republic of China in Taiwan, 1946–66." *IMF Staff Papers*, 25 (July): 290–321.

______ (1973). *Industrialization in Taiwan, 1946–72: Trade and Import-Substitution Policies for Developing Countries.* New York: Praeger.

Liu, Shin-kei (1975). *Post-War Taiwanese Economic Analysis* (in Japanese). Tokyo: Tokyo University Press.

Mizoguchi, Toshiyuki (1975). *The Economic Growth of Taiwan and Korea* (in Japanese). Tokyo: Iwanami Shoten.

______ and Umemura, Mataji (ed.) (1988). *Economic Statistics of Prewar Japanese Colonies* (in Japanese). Tokyo: Toyo Keizai Shimpo Sha.

Okurasho (1947). *Taiwan's Industries, Historical Inquiries into Japanese Oversees Activities* (in Japanese). Vol. 13, Taiwan, 2(4).

Ranis, G. (ed.) (1979). "Industrial Development." In W. Galenson (ed.), *Economic Growth and Structural Change in Taiwan, The Postwar experience of the Republic of China.* Ithaca, NY: Cornell University Press.

Rodrik, D. (1995). "Getting Intervention Right: How South Korea and Taiwan Grew Rich." *AEJ: Economic Policy* (April).

Sachs, J.D. and A.M. Warner (1996). "Achieving Rapid Growth in the Transition Economies of Central Europe." HDID Development Discussion Papers, #544, July, 64 pp. Cambridge, MA: Harvard Institute for International Development.

Sasamoto, Takeharu and Shigeto Kawano (1968). *A Comprehensive Study of Taiwanese Economy* (in Japanese). Vols. I, II, III. Tokyo: Aziya Keizai Kenkyujo.

Statistical Abstract of the Republic of China (SAROC) (1966) (1969). Directorate-General of Budgets, Accounts, and Statistics. Taipei: Executive Yuan.

Sumiya, Mikio, Shin-kei Liu and Jaw-yann Twu (1992). *The Taiwanese Economy* (in Japanese). Tokyo: Tokyo University Press.

Szczepanik, E. (1958). *The Economic Growth of Hong Kong.* London: Oxford University Press.

Taiwan Statistical Data Book (TSDB) (1993). Council for Economic Planning and Development, Executive Yuan, the Republic of China.

Tate, M.W. (1955). *Statistics in Education.* NY: Macmillan.

Twu, Jaw-yann (1975). *Taiwan under Japanese Imperialism* (in Japanese). Tokyo: Tokyo University Press.

Yamane, T. (1973). *Statistics, An Introductory Analysis*, 3rd ed. NY: Harper and Row, Publishers.

Wu, Tsong-min (1991). "An estimation of Taiwan's Gross Domestic Product: 1910–1950." (in Chinese). *Taiwan Economic Review*, 19(2) (June): 127–175.

______ (1995). "Fluctuations in Aggregate Output and Changes in Economic Structure" (in Chinese). In Fu-san Huang (ed.), *Modern History of Taiwan, the Volume on Economy* (609–639). Taipei: Taiwan Wenshian Weiyuanhui.

Chapter 6

The Historical Traditions of Taiwanese Small-and-Medium Enterprises — Origins of Taiwanese Capitalism

6.1 Introduction

Until a decade ago, few studies of Taiwanese economic development examined the existence and contribution of the small-and-medium enterprises (SMEs) in Taiwan's industrialization and trade. Most macroeconomic analyses merely exhibit some aggregate statistics, such as exports, imports, GNP or GDP, investment and savings, government policies, etc. Many studies tend to arrive at a conclusion as if Taiwan's KMT government were the only government in the world that knew how to manage the economy through tariffs and subsidies for rapid growth. The hard-working people who are the building blocks of these statistics, the Taiwanese SMEs, are often being overlooked.

The purpose of this paper is to examine the historical origin of Taiwanese SMEs. We first review the current dual industrial structures in Section 6.2. The difference between private and public enterprises in their number of firms, size of employees, and the value of outputs are examined. Section 6.3 finds the characteristics and significance of the SMEs in the Taiwanese economy. We show the patterns of the SMEs in Taiwan since the end of WWII. Section 6.4 describes the basic picture of the Taiwanese industry and trade that Taiwanese SMEs are export-oriented firms. The government enterprises made little, or only indirect, contributions to exports in the 1970s and the 1980s. Thus, the vanguard of exports expansion and economic growth are the Taiwanese SMEs. Section 6.5 presents a consistent comparison of the Taiwanese SMEs over the last three decades.

We then examine two areas of foreign trade for the past 400 years of the Taiwanese history. One is the direction and composition of trade, and another is the merchant of foreign trade. These are in Section 6.6, where we review the Taiwanese trade under the Dutch regime, the Cheng regime, and the Ch'ing regime. As a transit port between Japan, China, and Southeast Asia, the Taiwanese economy has been strongly trade oriented since its development 400 years ago. Sections 6.7 and 6.8 show the development of Taiwanese economy during the later years of the Ch'ing dynasty. By the end of the Ch'ing regime, the Taiwanese economy experienced a commercial revolution, and like the English economy before the Industrial Revolution, Taiwan had the makings of a classic "bourgeois-national revolution." We then argue that Taiwanese capital under the Japanese regime was distorted along the path to full-blown Taiwanese capitalism.

Section 6.9 shows that, despite the difficulties under the Japanese regime, Taiwanese SMEs made a steady growth. We then study in Section 6.10 the existence of the Taiwanese SMEs after the war. We argue that the government-owned public enterprises, which were confiscated and transformed from the large Japanese firms, along with large private enterprises, generally have dominated the production of non-traded goods, and are either monopolistic or monopolized the domestic markets. This, like the SMEs in the previous period, has limited the opportunities for the Taiwanese SMEs to grow to large enterprises, and at the same time, forced them to seek international markets. We then discuss the historical origin of today's Taiwanese SMEs. The main point here is that, contrary to the existing literature, the Taiwanese SMEs are not the product of postwar phenomenon. In Sections 6.11 and 6.12 we continue to examine the historical traditions of SMEs in the last 100 years, first by connecting the available data using several different estimation methods, and then by examining anecdotally some fieldwork by a sociologist and an anthropologist to corroborate the connection. In Section 6.13 we examine the roles of education, and suggest that the spirit of settlers and pioneers, rather than Confucianism, would better explain the vitality of the Taiwanese SMEs. Some concluding remarks are given in the last section.

6.2 The Dual Industrial Structures in Taiwan

The Taiwanese industry consists of two parts. On the one hand, there are huge public enterprises, which were confiscated from the Japanese government and various private Japanese capitalists after WWII. They were reorganized into 50 or so mammoth public enterprises. They have been mainly the enclaves for Chinese refugees who came to Taiwan with the KMT government after the war, and were run mostly by retired Chinese bureaucrats and generals with little knowledge of modern management (Tien, 1989, 136). On the other hand, there are numerous small private enterprises, which are mostly operated by the Taiwanese.

In the 1950s, electric power, sugar, and to a large extent fertilizer industries, were the major monopolies of the KMT government (Hsiao and Hsiao, 1996, Section 1.7.2). Even until the late 1980s, the government still either monopolized or controlled three major sectors of the Taiwanese economy: production, distribution, and finance (Liu, 1975, 108–135), especially in the banking sector. Since then, the weights of the government control in production and foreign trade have decreased over the years. The public enterprises had about 50 percent share of industrial output in the 1950s. It showed decreasing during the 1960s, but persistently maintained about 20 percent shares of industrial output since 1971 (Hsiao and Hsiao, 1996, Fig. 1.7). Even in the early 1990s, the total assets of the public enterprises were eight times larger than the total assets of the top 500 private companies in Taiwan (ibid., 236; Chen *et al.*, 1991).

The extreme dual structures of public and private enterprises in the manufacturing industry have not changed much since the 1950s.[1] In 1966, there were only 43 public enterprises (0.16% of the total establishments in the manufacturing sector). On average, each one had assets of NT$ 613 million, employed 1,854 persons, with sales of NT$ 433 million, and value-added of NT$ 149 million. In a vivid contrast, there were 27,666 private enterprises (99.84%). On average, each firm had assets of mere NT$ 2 million, employed 18 persons, with sales of NT$ 1.8 million, and value-added of NT$ 0.6 million. Public enterprises were, on average, about 300 times larger in assets, 100 times larger in work force, 240 times larger in both sales and value-added than the corresponding categories in the private industry. Among private enterprises, in the same year, only 15 percent of them were incorporated. The other 85 percent were unincorporated, and employed on average only seven persons (Hsiao and Hsiao, 1996, Table 1.10).

[1]The rest of this section is taken from Hsiao and Hsiao (1996), Section 1.15.1.1. This paper has been expanded and collected in this book as Chapter 1.

In 1976, after ten years of economic development, the basic dual industrial structures still remained the same. The number of public enterprises had more than doubled (from 43 to 89), the average value of assets per firm increased more than five times, and average sales had more than tripled. However, employment in public enterprises fell by 20 percent. The growth of private enterprises was more dramatic. The number of private enterprises increased more than 2.5 times (to 69,428 firms), and both the average value of assets and average sales per firm increased more than five times. The number of employees per firm increased about 40 percent, to 25 persons per enterprise, showing an increase in the scale of operation (ibid.). However, they are still far behind the public enterprises.

6.3 Characteristics and Significance of Taiwanese SMEs

Although the U.S. Aid "Small" Industrial Loan Fund was set up in 1954 (Hsiao, 1960a; Hsiao and Hsiao, 1996, Table 1.8), the statistical definition, which was the base of consistent government policy, on "small-and-medium scale enterprises" did not exist until September 1967. In that year, an SME was defined as "a manufacturing enterprise having total assets of less than NT$ 5,000,000 with not more than 100 persons regularly employed; or a commercial firm having an annual turnover of not more than NT$ 5,000,000 with less than 50 persons regularly employed" (Chou, 1992a, 1069). Since then, the definition changed five times (in 1973, 77, 79, 82, 91). For manufacturing, in 1973, the maximum assets in the definition increased four times to NT$ 20 million, and in 1977, the maximum assets and employees increased three times to NT$ 60 million and 300 persons. In 1982, the total assets limit increased again to NT$ 120 million for "manufacturing, processing, and handicrafts," and to NT$ 40 million for "commercial, transportation, and other services" (ibid., 1070; MOEA, 1991, 12). The major changes and the current definition at the year shown are summarized at the lower part of Fig. 6.1 along the X-axis. The frequent changes of definition make the time series comparison of the numbers of establishments, employees, the values of outputs very difficult.[2]

[2]As the formal definition of SMEs was not given until 1967, the exact definitions in 1961 and 1966 are unknown. The 1982 and 1991 definitions only specifies maximum total assets, and did not specify the number of employees, leaving the time series analysis even more difficult. At the bottom of Fig. 6.1, we assume that the definition in terms of the number of workers remains unchanged after 1981.

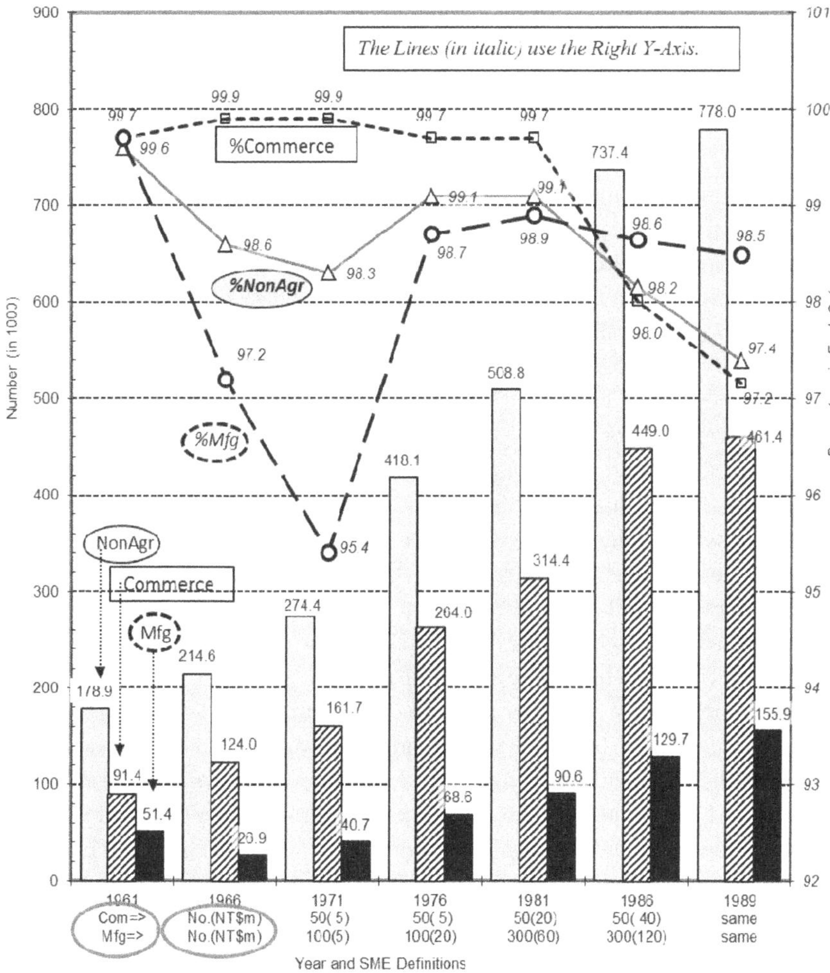

Figure 6.1: Number of Firms in Taiwanese SMEs

Non-Agriculture, Commerce, and Manufacturing Sectors

Notes: Definition of SME of Commerce and Mfg is given as No.(NT$m): No. = maximum number of employees; (NT$m) = maximum asset in NT$ million. See Section 6.3 for more details on definitions.

Figures 6.1 to 6.3 characterize[3] the Taiwanese SMEs over the past three decades. In Fig. 6.1, the three bars in each year present the trend of Taiwanese SMEs in three categories: the first gray bar shows the

[3]Data in Figs. 6.1 and 6.2 are taken from Tables 7 to 9 in Lin and Hu (1992).

non-agricultural field[4]; the second upward diagonal patterned bar is for commerce; and the third black bar is for manufacturing (Mfg) industry. On the top of each bar, we show the number of establishments in the unit of 1,000. The line graphs, which use the right-hand-side Y-axis, show the percentages of SMEs in each of the three categories according with the definitions given along the X-axis: the solid line is for non-agricultural field, the dotted line for commerce, and the heavy dashed line for manufacturing.

Since the definition of SMEs has changed frequently, they are not exactly comparable. The trend only shows the society's relative perception of SMEs in each of the five-year periods. In general, however, we see that the numbers of SMEs have been increasing rapidly in all three categories, and has maintained consistently between 95 percent and near 100 percent in each category. For example, in the manufacturing industry (the black bars), the SMEs had increased (compounded) about 4.0 percent per year on average from 1961 to 1989. From 51,400 firms in 1961, the SMEs in the manufacturing industry grew three times to 155,900 firms in 1989. In terms of percentages (measured from the right-hand-side Y-axis), except 95.4 percent in 1971 and 97.2 percent in 1966, the number of SMEs in the manufacturing sector (the heavy dashed line) was consistently close to 99 percent (ranging from 98.5% to 99.6%).

The numbers of SMEs in the non-agricultural field[5] (NonAgr, shown as grey bars in Fig. 6.1) had much higher growth rates than those of the SMEs in the manufacturing industry. In 1961, the non-agricultural SMEs counted at 178,900, about 99.6 percent of total non-agricultural enterprises. They increased steadily with the increase of population, and in 1989, they grew more than four times to 778,000 firms, 97.39 percent of total non-agricultural enterprises, manifesting again the vitality of Taiwanese economic activities. It should be noted that, since the definition of SMEs broadened considerably in 1982 and afterward, the scale of SMEs in 1986 and 1989 in terms of assets and employees are, on average, about three times larger than those in 1961. Furthermore, the decrease in its share of

[4]In addition to commerce and manufacturing, "non-agricultural field" includes mining and quarry, electric/water/gas industries, construction, transportation and communication industries, insurance and financial services, and other profit organizations in social, agricultural, fishing, pastoral industries (Lin and Hu, 1992).

[5]The data include 1. Mining and quarrying, 2. Manufacturing, 3. Electricity, gas and water, 4. Construction, 5. Commerce, 6. Transportation, storage, and communications, 7. Financing, real estate, and business services, 8. Other profit organizations (Wu and Chou, 1988, Table 2).

total SMEs, about 3 percent, indicates the relative growth of larger private firms in non-agricultural field during the 1980s. Their average compound growth rate from 1961 to 1989 was about 5.2 percent. The majority of SMEs were in the commerce sector (shown as the middle patterned bars). Over the years, the SMEs in the commerce sector (patterned bars) were generally three to four times more than those in the manufacturing sector.

Figure 6.2 consists of three different panels.[6] For the convenience of comparison, the levels (columns) use the Y-axis on the left-hand-side with different units of measurement, which are shown in the shadowed boxes at the upper part of the diagram. As in Fig. 6.1, the line graphs (in italic) show the percentages in each category and are measured by the right-hand-side Y-axis. For convenience, the average (denoted as Avg) of the four years is also given in the diagram.

SME Workers The first panel from the left shows the number of workers in SMEs in 1966, 1976, 1986, and 1989. There is no data for non-agricultural field in 1966. From 1976 to 1989, the SME employment in the non-agricultural field (the patterned columns) was stable, maintaining about 2.4 million workers, consisting of about 65 percent of total employment in the non-agricultural field (the empty triangle above Avg bars). There were about 0.5 million workers employed in commerce, consisting of about 84 percent of total employment in the SMEs in the commerce sector (the empty square above Avg bars). About 1.1 million workers were employed in the SMEs in manufacturing, which was about 60 percent of total manufacturing employment (the empty circle above the Avg bars).

SME Output The second panel shows the contribution of SMEs to production. Except commerce, the value of non-agricultural as well as manufacturing outputs increased about four times from 1976 to 1989. The SMEs in the non-agricultural field contributed, on average, about NT$ 1.6 trillion (the three-year average of the amount shown in the figure, the same below), which was about 45 percent of the total non-agricultural output (the white triangle above the Avg column). Among them, NT$ 0.2 trillion came from commerce, consisting of about 77 percent of total commerce output (the square above the Avg column), and NT$ 1.0 trillion from manufacturing, consisting of about 42 percent of total manufacturing output (the white circle above the Avg column). Note that all levels of the three categories in the second panel (see the bars) are increasing, especially

[6]The data are taken from Lin and Hu (1992), Tables 6, 8, and 9, respectively.

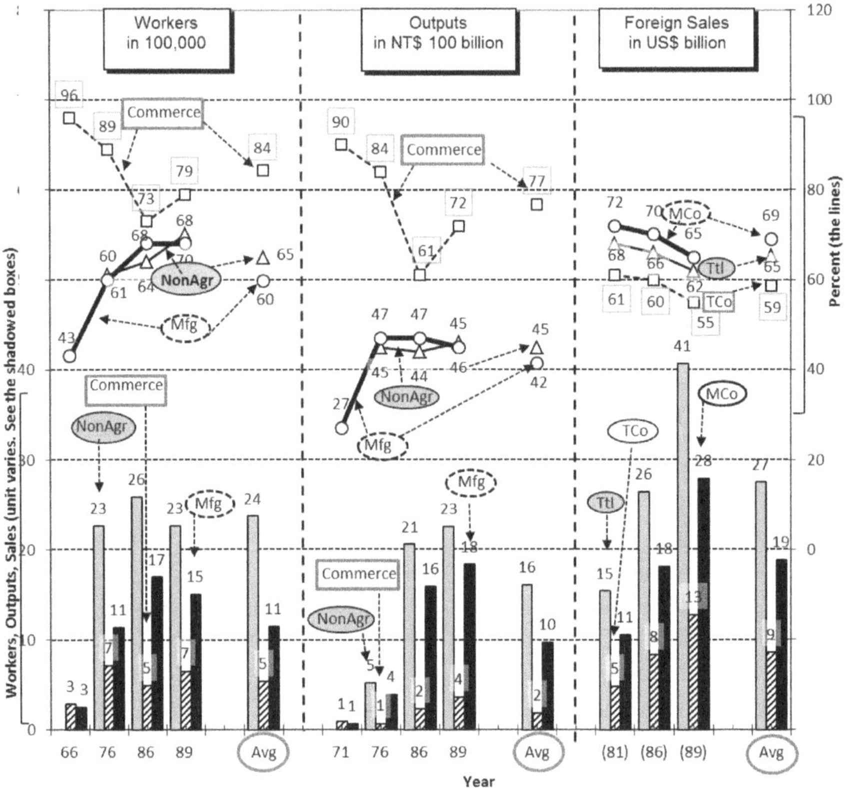

Figure 6.2: Contribution of Taiwan's SMEs
Employment, Value of Outputs, and Foreign Sales

Notes: (Year) shows that Panel 3 is different from the other two. Ttl = Tco + Mco. Ttl = Total Foreign Sales, Tco = Indirect Sales by Trading Companies, Mco = Direct Sales by Manufacturing Companies.

from 1976 to 1986. Since the numbers of employees during this period did not change much (as shown in the first panel), the figure shows that the labor productivity of the SMEs was increasing rapidly from the mid-1970s to the 1980s.

6.4 Contribution of the SMEs to Exports

Taiwan is known for its export-oriented economic growth. Who are the bearers of the export activities? If the top 100 exporters were taken, then, in 1981, the export share of public enterprise was only 3.2 percent of total exports, that of the share of the large private enterprise was 8.3 percent, and that of the foreign enterprise was 8.5 percent. Here we see that, despite their mammoth size in assets, employment, and sales, as we have seen in Section 6.2, the public enterprises contributed only 3.2 percent to exports in 1981! Among the public enterprise exports, 0.6 percent came from sugar and 0.1 percent from rice (Chou, 1988, 182–184). Exports by public enterprises have declined along with the sugar industry. By 1986, none of the public enterprises was listed in the top 100 exporters. Among the top 100 exporters, there were 67 private enterprises, contributing mere 8.3 percent of total exports, and 37 foreign enterprises, with 8.5 percent of the export share.[7] Together, these three kinds of enterprises within the top 100 exporters only took up about 18 percent to 20 percent of the total Taiwanese exports in 1981 and 1986. This means that the bulk, more than 80 percent of exports was done by SMEs during the 1980s.

We now extend our observations to top 500 exporting enterprises and top 500 general enterprises. From 1976 to 1980, the export share of the top 500 exporters was, on average, only about 13 percent, and that of the top 500 general enterprises was only about 26 percent of total exports (Chou, 1988, 183). This also indicates that the Taiwanese exporters are generally small-and-medium enterprises. Here again we see the relatively small contribution of these large private exporters and enterprises to Taiwanese total exports. Indeed, the SMEs are the backbones of Taiwanese exports and economic growth.[8]

SME Foreign Sales We have seen that, unlike Japan, Korea and many other countries, the major exporters in Taiwan are the SMEs. The third panel of Fig. 6.2 shows the value of foreign sales of SMEs. The year in parentheses denotes that Panel 3 is different from other two panels. Since the 1976 data are not available, we use 1981 data, as denoted in the diagram. In 1981, the figure shows that 68 percent of total exports (denoted by a triangle above the (81) bars) was contributed by the SMEs at the value of US$ 15 billion (see the "Ttl" grey bar).[9] The share fluctuates. It decreased to 66 percent in 1986 and to 62 percent in 1989. However, the absolute value increased more than two times during the 1980s: From US$ 15 billion

[7]The data on exports and exporters are given in Sumiya, Liu, and Twu (1992), 141. The value of total exports, NT$ 1,507,044 million, is taken from TSDB (1995), 192. Also see Hsiao and Hsiao (1996), Table 1.10.

[8]For Taiwanese SMEs in action, Japanese multinationals, the effects of the 2-28 Incident, and the difference between the first and the second generation mainlanders, etc., see a documentary film directed by Eaton (1991).

[9]Lin and Hu (1992), Table 5.

in 1981 to US$ 41 billion in 1989 (the grey columns). Percentage-wise, it generally maintained about 65 percent of total exports during the 1980s (see the triangle above the Avg columns). Here again, the data show the overwhelming importance of the SMEs in total foreign sales.

The total SME foreign sales in the third panel (Ttl) are calculated from the sum of two parts, indirect sales by the SME trading companies (TCo) and direct sales by the SME manufacturing companies (MCo) (Lin and Hu, 1992, Table 5). As can be seen from panel 3, the value of direct sales by SME manufacturers (MCo, the black columns) is generally twice larger than those by the SME trading companies (TCo, the patterned columns). In terms of percentage, the direct sales of the SMEs consist of about 69 percent of the total direct sales by the manufacturing industry (see the circle in the Avg group), and the indirect sales of the SME trading companies are about 59 percent of the total sales of the trading companies (see the square in the Avg group). For the SMEs, which operate on shoestring, direct sales are a way to cutting intermediate costs.

In any case, we have a basic picture of postwar Taiwanese industry and trade. The Taiwanese private SMEs are very much export-oriented. The public enterprises made almost no direct contribution to exports in the 1970s and the 1980s. Public enterprises and large private enterprises generally dominated the production of non-traded goods and domestic markets, and are monopolistic or simply monopolize the domestic markets (Chou, 1988, 181). The vanguard of export expansion and economic growth is the Taiwanese SMEs, mostly supported by imports of intermediate goods, raw materials, or capital equipment from foreign countries, and strengthened by technology transfer from direct foreign investment (Hsiao, 1992). They were helped by their own direct sales to foreign buyers and foreign trading companies, and by indirect sales through domestic trading companies.

6.5 A Consistent Comparison of the SMEs over Time

As we have stated in the previous sections, the definition of SMEs changed five times since 1967, indicating fragmented and confusing government policies toward SMEs (Hsiao and Hsiao, 1996, Section 1.15.2). It also made time series comparison impossible. Kajiwara (1995), 99 recompiled the data from the industrial census of the Taiwanese manufacturing industry for 1961, 1966, 1976, and 1986. He divided all the enterprises consistently into four categories in accordance with the number of employees: 1 to 9, 10 to 99, 100 to 499, and 500 or more. The results, as well as the new data

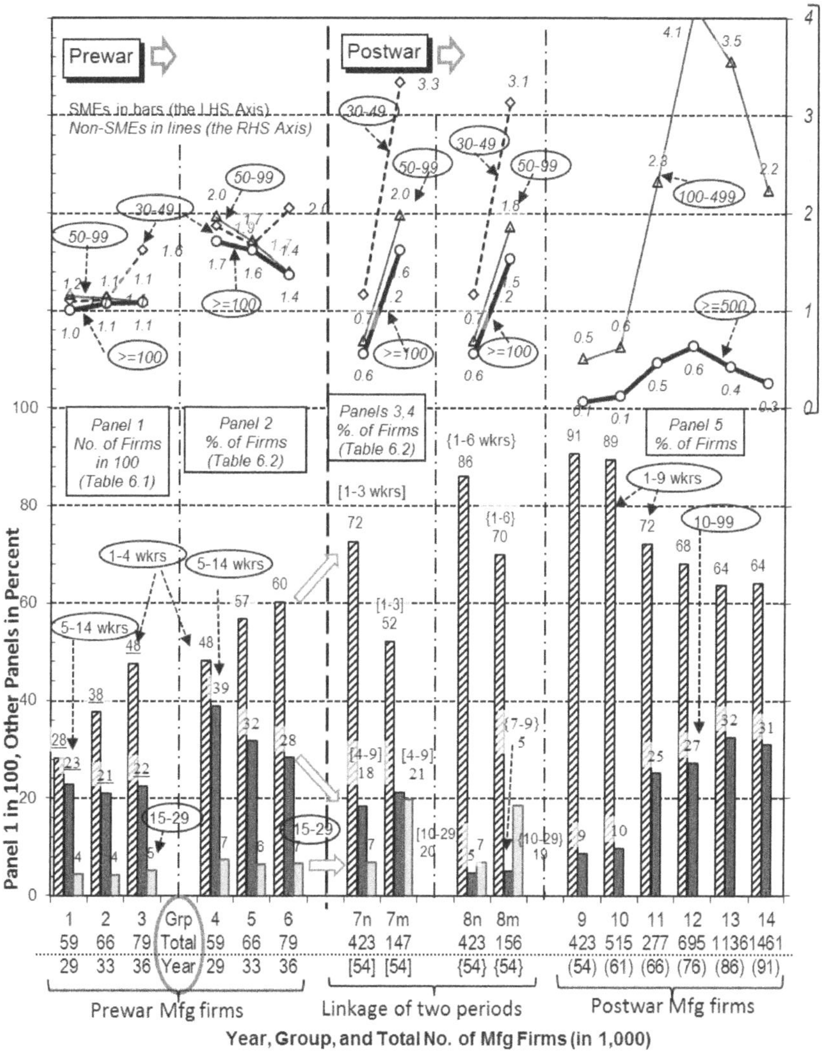

Figure 6.3: Number and Percentage of Manufacturing Firms

Employment, Value of Outputs, and Foreign Sales

Note: The first row of the X-axis corresponds to the "Group #" in Tables 6.1 and 6.2. The data are taken from these two tables.

in 1991, are shown by groups 9 to 14 in the last panel[10] of Fig. 6.3 (the first four panels will be explained in Sections 6.9 and 6.10). As in Fig. 6.2,

[10]The 1954 data are taken from Hsiao (1960b).

the year in parentheses, brackets, or braces indicates that this last panel is different from the other four panels. In Fig. 6.3, the first row of the X-axis designates the group number of the diagram as defined in Tables 6.1 and 6.2, the second row (Total), the total number of firms in the unit of a thousand, and the third row (Year), the year of the census.

The patterned bars show the percentage of firms which employed less than 10 workers and may be called small enterprises. The filled dark bar shows the percentage of firms which have workers from 10 to 99. We may regard the firms with workers less than 100 as the SMEs in this case. The percentage of firms with workers 100 to 499 is shown by the solid line with triangle markers, and that with 500 or more workers is denoted by the heavy black line with circle markers. Since percentages of the last two categories are very small, we use the right-hand-side Y-axis to move the origin upward and enlarge the scale. From panel 5, we see clearly that, from the late 1950s to the mid-1980s, the percentages of the firms with less than 10 workers (the patterned bars) decreased, while those of the firms with 10 to 99 workers (the black bars) and firms with 100 to 499 workers (the light solid line) increased. This probably is a consequence of rapid economic growth.

It may be interesting to note from this last panel of Fig. 6.3 that the percentage of the number of the firms with less than 100 workers from 1961 to 1986 is fairly stable. This is shown by the sum of the two bars which maintained between 99 percent in 1961 to 96 percent in 1986, as the decrease in the percentage of the firms with workers less than 10 is more or less compensated by the increase in the percentage of firms with workers between 10 and 99 (also see the last part of Table 6.2).

Figure 6.4 corresponds to the first two panels of Fig. 6.2 for the manufacturing industry. The left panel shows the percentage of workers employed in each category in each year. The percentages of workers employed in firms with less than 10 workers (the patterned bars) have reduced considerably from 31 percent in 1961 to only 10 percent in 1986. At the same time, the percentages of the workers employed in firms with 10 to 99 workers (the dark bars) as well as 100 to 499 workers (the solid line) have increased over time. This is consistent with the same trend in the number of firms shown in the last panel of Fig. 6.3. Note that the percentages of workers employed in the huge firms (with 500 or more workers) decreased consistently since 1966, corresponding to the decrease in the weight of public enterprises in Taiwan during that period. Overall, however, the employment in SMEs has maintained about 50 percent of

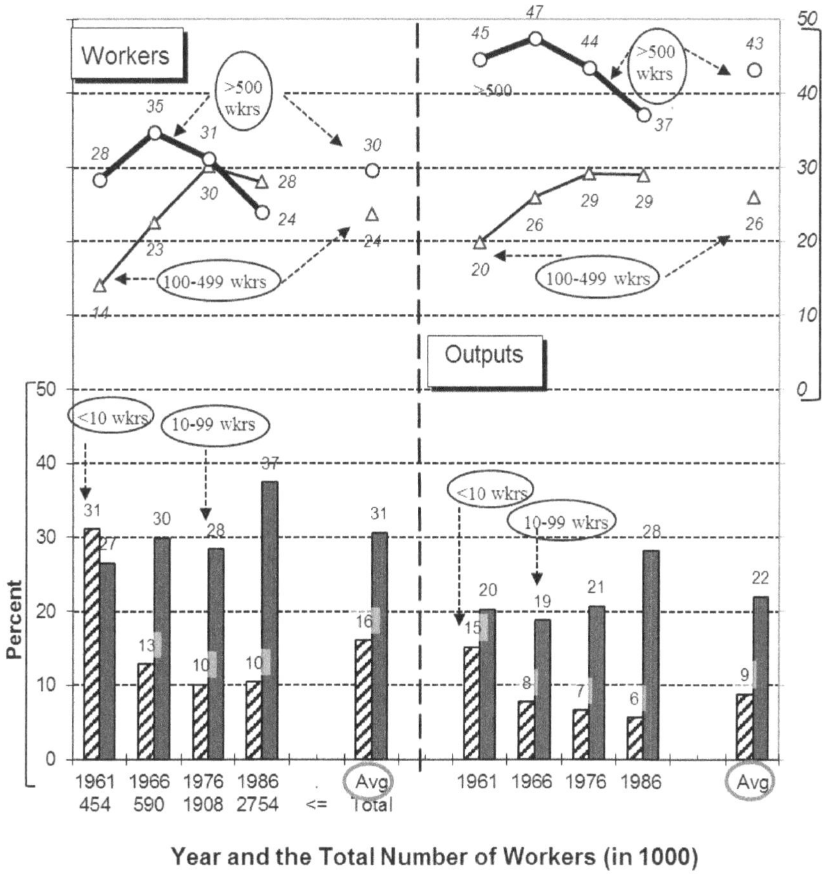

Figure 6.4: Number of Workers and Value of Outputs In Manufacturing Industry

total manufacturing employment (the sum of the two bars in each year) during the last three decades. This figure is less than the 60 percent figure obtained by various definitions of the SMEs used in the first panel of Fig. 6.2.

The right panel in Fig. 6.4 shows the percentage of the value of outputs in each category in each year. The percentage of output value decreased for the firms with less than 10 workers and also for the firms with 500 or more workers, and it increased for the firms with 10 to 99 workers and also those with 100 to 499 workers. Overall, it shows clearly that the SMEs have maintained about one-third of the total manufactured outputs (the sum of the two bars in each year) and the rest was produced by large enterprises.

In general, from Figs. 6.3 and 6.4, if we classify postwar Taiwanese manufacturing industry according to small (less than 10 workers), medium (from 10 to 99 workers), large (from 100 to 499 workers), and huge (500 to or more workers), then our diagrams illustrate the following interesting general propositions about the Taiwanese industrial structure.

A. Since the mid-1950s to the late 1980s, in terms of percentages, the small and huge firms (the patterned bars and the heavy black lines), the two extreme categories, decreased in the number of establishments, employees, and value of outputs.
B. the medium and large firms (the black bars and the solid lines), the two middle categories, increased in all three aspects. Thus, there is a tendency of convergence of the small firms to the middle categories of firms in these three aspects, which, in turn, are growing over time, while the relative importance of the huge firms has decreased.
C. Despite the different directions of changes, the SMEs in manufacturing industry taken as a whole maintained remarkably stable relations with large and huge enterprises, namely, about 97 percent, 50 percent, and 33 percent of total establishments, employees, and the value of outputs, respectively, in manufacturing during the past three decades.
D. Some exceptions to these general trends have appeared in the latter part of the 1980s, and it is worthwhile to watch carefully about the changes in the 1990s and beyond.

Combining the results of Figs. 6.1 to 6.4, we may conclude that Taiwan is indeed a kingdom of small-and-medium enterprises either in the relative or the absolute terms. How does this finding fit into Taiwanese business historical pattern? We would like to examine two areas of foreign trade for the past 400 years of the Taiwanese history. One is the direction and composition of trade, and another is the merchant of foreign trade.

6.6 The Taiwanese Trade in the 17th Century

In Section 6.4, we have shown that Taiwanese SMEs in the postwar period are very much export-oriented. In fact, the Taiwanese economy was already export-oriented in the 17th century. As early as the second half of the 16th century, the Europeans, Chinese, and Japanese were known to come to Taiwan for either transferring the commodity to the third countries[11] or trading with the Taiwanese aborigines for buckskin with agate, cloth, salt, copper, etc. (Nakayama, 1959, 24–25). In order to trade with China, the Dutch colonized the southern part of Taiwan in 1624. Its influence spread to the northern areas like Keelung and Tamsui by the 1650s (Su, 1980, 74; Chang, 1996, 48). At the beginning, they traded the daily necessities for buckskin and venison supplied by aborigines. Later, they brought in Chinese agricultural laborers (Han serfs, as characterized by Su, 1986, 13) to Taiwan, and encouraged Han immigrants and aborigines to cultivate sugar cane and rice paddy to be refined for exports (Chou, 1957).

The Dutch exported buckskin, venison, dried fish, and sugar to Japan in exchange for Japanese silver. From 1634 to 1661, the exports of buckskin ranged from the high of 151,400 pieces in 1638 to the low of 19,140 pieces in 1642. The Dutch then exported Japanese and European silver, along with venison, antlers, rice, sulfur, and dried fish, which were produced in Taiwan, to China in exchange for raw silk, silk and satin, herbal medicine, porcelain, and gold. These precious commodities, along with spices, which were purchased from the Southeast Asia, were then shipped to Holland from Taiwan. Some of the raw silk and silk products were also re-exported to Japan (Su, 1980, 78–79; Chou, 1957, 61).

Another important trading partner under the Dutch regime was Persia. To Persia, Taiwan exported tea and much of its sugar output, along with camphor and copper, which were imported from Japan, and Ginseng, which was imported from China.

As usual, buckskin, sugar, and rice were produced by Han immigrants and native aborigines, the Dutch collected the commodities, and monopolized the export business. During the Dutch occupation from 1624 to 1661, the trading activities in Taiwan were very lucrative. In accounting for the total profits in Asia in 1649, the Dutch reported once that, among the 19 trading posts in Asia, the trade with Taiwan alone earned 25.6 percent of the total Asian profits, only next to the trade with Japan (38.8%) (Su, 1980, 80).

In 1661, after being defeated by the ascending Ch'ing dynasty, Cheng Ch'eng-kung and his troop fled to Taiwan, drove away the Dutch, and established the *Kingdom of Cheng* (Chang, 1996) or the *Kingdom of Formosa*, as was called by the British (ibid., 90). The Cheng government adopted the Dutch economic system. Its major concern was to "return to

[11] Nakayama (1959), 25; Su (1980), 77–78. In a 1554 map by Portuguese, Taiwan was called Iha Formosa (Chang, 1996, 60).

China," rather than developing Taiwan for the benefits of the Taiwanese. The government welcomed trading with all countries except China and Holland (Chou *et al.*, 1959). The Ch'ing government also closed and banned the coastal area for travel and trade with Taiwan, although illegal trade relations between Taiwan and China persisted. The trade with Japan continued to prosper. Every year, eight to fifteen Taiwanese ships sailed to Japan for trade. Taiwan exported sugar, buckskin, silk products, herbal medicine to Japan, and on the return trip, imported copper, lead, weapons, and other military materials (Chang, 1996, 92).

The Cheng government also increased the trade with the Southeast Asian countries. Every year, one or two Taiwanese ships sailed to Luzon, Indochina, Cambodia, Thailand, Malacca, and Batavia. The British took the place of the Dutch in Taiwan's trade with the Europeans. From 1670 to 1680, the British and the Cheng government had three commerce treaties, and in 1671, the British established a trading house in Taiwan. However, until the end of the Cheng Kingdom in 1683, the business did not flourish between the two countries (ibid.).

In general, during the Cheng period, Taiwan continued to trade with foreign countries. The trade was mainly conducted by the government, and the commodities imported were mainly military materials.

6.7 Development of Taiwanese Capitalism

The Ch'ing government conquered Taiwan in 1683. To avoid future insurgents against China using Taiwan as a base, it proclaimed a strict ban of immigration from the coastal cities in China to Taiwan. The trade between both sides of the Taiwan Strait was restricted and discouraged. The policy changed several times after 1732, and was revoked for good only in 1760 (Su, 1980, 128–129; Su, 1986, 26). As a result, Taiwan's economy stagnated for a long period of time.

Before the formal opening of the Tamsui and Anping harbors under the Peking Treaty in 1860, Taiwan traded mainly with China, mostly with people in Fujian. Taiwan exported agricultural products like rice, sugar, jute, rattan, and camphor wood to China, and imported manufactured products like cotton fabric and cloth, silk, paper, porcelain (Huang and Chen, 1995, 320), agricultural equipment, and wine. In one estimate, during 1741, Taiwan produced slightly more than 100 million dans[12] of rice, half

[12] 1 dan = 1 hectoliter.

of which was exported to China (Oh, 1970, 77). Thus, a "colonial-type economic relation" between Fujian and Taiwan was formed during this period.[13] Import substitution of industrial goods did not take place, simply because the Chinese dumped imports on Taiwan (ibid., 76). Taiwan's import substitution industries, like porcelain, bricks, shoes and socks, started gradually only in the early 19th century (Huang and Chen, 1995, 326). Small shops prevailed in Taiwan.

After 1860, the Europeans came to trade with Taiwan, and as it might be expected, the openness of trade reduced the importance of China as Taiwan's trading partner, and restructured Taiwan's trade composition. Taiwanese rice lost its competitiveness to Southeast Asian rice in China, and with a rapid increase in Taiwanese population, rice export was greatly reduced (ibid., 322, 331). Furthermore, Taiwanese sugar was gradually substituted by local sugar in China, and more of it was, instead, exported to Hong Kong, Australia, the United States, Japan, etc.

After 1860, Taiwan's tea substituted sugar to become the largest export item. In 1895, more than 81 percent (16 million pounds) of Woolong tea was exported to the United States (ibid., 331), the rest went to Europe. Taiwan also became the world's largest producer of camphor. In 1868 (and 1895), Taiwan exported 1.6 (and 6.9) million pounds of camphor, 2.6 (and 2.3) times larger than the second largest exporter, Japan (ibid., 334). Coal was one of the new export items, mainly sold to China.

At that time, unfortunately, more than 50 percent of total imports were opium. Other imports consisted of manufactured goods, like cotton and its products, woolen fabrics, kerosene, metals (especially lead, for sealing sugar boxes), matches (100% from Japan), and other miscellaneous goods, which increased importance over the years. However, like the other periods in the Taiwanese history, there had been trade surpluses every year since 1872, and the surpluses increased until the end of the Ch'ing period (ibid., 337–339).

Before 1860, Taiwan's trade with China was mainly controlled by various Taiwanese export associations (ibid., 354; Twu, 1975, 373). After

[13]Ibid. A similar view is also given in Wakabayashi *et al.* (1993), 46. As aptly pointed out by a referee, the relationship was based on the "law of comparative advantages," rather than the coerced relationship between "metropolis and colony." Lin (1994), 73 calls it "regional division of labor." Elsewhere (Hsiao, 1997), the first author has shown that this law of comparative advantage, rather than blunt colonialism, even extended to Taiwanese economic development under the Japanese colonialism.

1860, they lost competition to the foreign traders, especially to the British, who set up trading houses in Taiwan. The old-fashioned export associations simply could not compete with the Western management system. Although the profits in coastal trading were very high, about 30 percent per annum on average, due to political instability in China and market fluctuation, the trading was highly speculative and risky, and many ventures went bankrupt (Hao, 1986, 346, Chapter 10).

As time went by, some Taiwanese merchants were able to learn the system from the Europeans and started their own trading companies.[14] Toward the end of the 1890s, some Taiwanese trading companies even superseded the European trading houses.[15] The Taiwanese/Chinese merchants "by and large out competed Western traders because of their familiarity with local conditions, their ability of dispense with additional middlemen and their satisfactions with a relatively small profit margin" (Hao, 1986, 346). In the tea trade, for an example, in 1874, the export volume of tea by Taiwanese traders even exceeded two times that by foreign traders. By 1881, almost 90 percent of Taiwanese tea was exported by Taiwanese merchants (Huang and Chen, 1995, 361). They also dominated in exporting camphor

[14]An interesting comparison of old and modern business practices in China and the fall and rise of companies was given in Chan (undated).

[15]The relation and relative influence of local and foreign capital are still unclear, and more research is called for. The following two contending views emphasize the dominant role of foreign capital. "It is British and American commercial capital, instead of local commercial capital which had developed during the Ch'ing period, had gradually transformed Taiwan from feudalistic economy to capitalistic economy before the Japanese occupation." Hayashi, (1943), 349. According to Ohyama (1942), 351–353, it is not that the Taiwanese national commercial capital failed to transform into industrial capital, it is foreign commerce capital and the feudalistic obstacles that prevented the development of full scale capitalism before 1895. "Before the Japanese occupation, although politically Taiwan was Ch'ing's territory, economically, it had the colonial characteristics of British and American capitalism.... while the feudalistic local commerce capital once organized craft guild ("zunft") type "Jiao" along the coastal area and controlled agriculture and mine production of the interior plain, the invasion of foreign capital dissolved Jiao, reduced local capital to comprador, an exclusive intermediate commercial organization of foreign capital. Foreign capital thus firmly dominated the local markets. This can be seen from the fact that important trading goods were under the hand of foreign commerce capital." The era of Taiwan's modern capitalism had to wait until Japanese colonial government to drive away the foreign capital, to modernize transportation, communication, land and banking system, and to attract Japanese capital from Japan. Also see Yanaihara (1929), 43–50. Pan (1947), 30–36 and Chang (1947), 111–113 have more detailed description along this line.

and sugar, as well as importing opium and textiles (ibid., 361–364). In general, we submit that, before the Japanese occupation in 1995, Taiwan had experienced a Commercial Revolution,[16] which, in England, was a prelude to "Industrial Revolution."[17]

Admittedly, there are many factors which gave rise to the Industrial Revolution.[18] One of the important factors is commercial revolution. It not only expanded the commodity markets through domestic and international trade, but also supplied capital for industrialization. Studies in economic history of England show that the most, if not the only, important source of external capital during the Industrial Revolution "came from commerce, especially from merchants who invested large sums in the industries producing the goods they sold" (Crouzet, 1972, 173). Among the merchants were bankers who engaged in the colonial slavery trade and tobacco lords.[19] Even if rich merchants invested in land and became landed "gentlemen," they also invested in industry, especial in railroads and canals.[20] Like merchants in England, the sign of transition from the commercial revolution to the industrial revolution in Taiwan had already appeared before the Japanese occupation in 1895. Some Taiwanese merchants, like the Lin Pun-yuan family of Pangchiao, traded domestically and internationally, and even established local banks and money exchange houses to lend money to tea producers (Huang and Chen, 1995, 364; Su, 1980, 320). Some sugar traders also financed sugar producers (Twu, 1975, 380). In general, by the end of the nineteenth century, the Taiwanese merchants were able to dominate the trade, and to accumulate wealth through the commercial relations with China, England, and the Netherlands. Eventually, the merchants also became money lenders to the local producers. It was reported that, by 1895, at least four Taiwanese families had wealth of 10 to 40 million taels, and there were

---

[16]Commercial Revolution in the Middle Ages in Europe occurred in the period 950–1350 (Lopez, 1971), that in England, from the English Restoration to American Independence, 1660–1776 (Davis, 1967, 3–4), and in China along the coast from the 1820s to 1883" (Hao, 1986, 338).

[17]Davis (1967), 24. The importance of international trade continued even during the Industrial Revolution. See Hobsbawm (1968), 38.

[18]For an extensive review, see five volume studies in Kakuyama (ed.) (1980).

[19]Williams (1994), Chapter 5. Some more supporting evidence is needed for these points, see Crouzet (1972), 175, and a new introduction by C.A. Palmer in Williams (1994).

[20]Kakuyama *et al.* (1980). 71, 91. Also see Rabb (1967), 68.

17 Taiwanese millionaire families.[21] Indeed, Taiwan had the makings of a classic "bourgeois-nationalist revolution."[22]

6.8 Taiwanese Capital under the Japanese Government

The victory of the Japanese in the first Sino-Japanese war in 1895 over the Ch'ing government and over Taiwanese uprisings distorted the "natural" development along the path to full-blown Taiwanese capitalism.[23] Unlike England, Japanese capital flooded into Taiwan and suffocated, so to speak, the Taiwanese native capital from creation of large scale modern banks and factories. We submit that this is the first source of Taiwanese SMEs.

As the Japanese capitalism was still in the infant period, the new colonial government at first tolerated the existence of the local Taiwanese capitalists. Except sugar and those commodities under national monopoly system (opium, salt, camphor, tobacco, etc.), few restrictions were imposed on the production and distribution of daily necessities (Twu, 1975, 397). At the same time the government drove away the European and Chinese commercial capital by setting up a discriminatory tariff system, establishing the Bank of Taiwan (1899) to substitute foreign financial control, instituting monopoly system, and helping Japanese merchants to overtake foreign monopoly of sugar trade (Yanaihara, 1929, 43–48; Su, 1980, 338).

A land survey was initiated in 1898 and completed in 1903. The forest and field survey was conducted from 1910 to 1914. The land reform in 1905 only affected large absentee land owners. They were paid by public

---

[21]Twu (1975), 381. However, there are some conflicting observations on the Taiwanese economy before 1895. Yanaihara (1929), 55, observed that "until the very end of the Ching period in Taiwan, no single modern bank, modern cooperation, modern factory existed... All the establishment of capitalist enterprises in Taiwan came only after Japanese occupation." More research is needed.

[22]This point was observed by the Taiwanese Communist Party in 1928 on the development of Taiwanese capitalism. For detail, see Hsiao and Sullivan (1983), 278.

[23]This is also the argument presented in the 1928 Political Thesis of the short-lived Taiwanese Communist Party (1928–1931). For references, see Hsiao and Sullivan (1983). We adopted their line of arguments for different reasons. The thesis is influenced by the political and economic principles of the Japanese Communist Party in the 1920s along the line of the Marx's theory of capitalism, which emphasizes the internal (like domestic saving), rather than the external (like commercial), factors of capital accumulation. In Japan, it is known as the Ohtsuka Proposition (Ohtsuka Shigaku) (Kakuyama, 1980, 22–23), and was propagated in early post-war Taiwan by Professor Chang (1974).

bonds and some of them were invested in banking or modern manufacturing industries. Some well-known examples are the establishment of Shoka Bank, Kagi Bank, and Taiwan Hemp Weaving Cooperation (Twu, 1975, 394; Su, 1980, 309). On the other hand, land was divided among the tenants, and each tenant had a piece of smaller land to cultivate. The need of secondary employment by the small land owner created many small businesses and individually managed factories (Twu, 1975, 394–95). Native capital, including the five collaborator-entrepreneur families,[24] flourished. By the 1920s, however, Japanese capital flooded into Taiwan, and the Taiwanese-owned firms were overshadowed by the larger and modern Japanese-owned firms in Taiwan. Led by the sugar companies, all the major, larger firms and banks were held by Japanese private capitalists.

Under colonial restrictions, the majority of Taiwanese firms consisted of fragmented numerous farmers and workers, and the scales of their shops and factories were small. It is shown that, in 1941, if incorporated companies were classified with paid-in capital according to three categories: less than 200,000 yen, between 200,000 yen to 500,000 yen, and over 500,000 yen, then, Taiwanese capital consisted of only 8.3 percent, 27.3 percent, and 2.8 percent in each category, respectively (Sumiya, Liu, and Twu, 1992, 24). Most of the Taiwanese companies took the form of partnership (instead of incorporation).

In reviewing the decline of five Taiwanese collaborator-entrepreneurs by the end of the Japanese period, Twu (1975), Chapter 5, suggests several reasons, which may also apply to the other Taiwanese firms as well. The first and foremost reason is the patently discriminatory measures against the Taiwanese firms. In 1912, seeing the rapid rise of Taiwanese national firms, the Governor-General of Taiwan proclaimed that "An organization which consists only of the Taiwanese, Chinese, or Taiwanese and Chinese, cannot use the word 'corporation' (Kaisha) in its commercial name." This decree was made to ensure the participation and control of the Japanese in Taiwanese companies.[25]

---

[24]They are the clans of Ku, two Lins, Yen, and Chen. See Twu (1975), 403–405, 412–464; Su (1980), 317–330. A summary can be found in Gold (1988).

[25]See Yanaihara (1929), 135–36, for detail. Also Twu (1975), 402. Officially, the reason for this decree was, however, to help Taiwanese in modern management, and at the same time to prevent the establishment of "undesirable" and "unsound" companies to protect Taiwanese investors.

The decree was rescinded in 1923, and substituted by the civil law and the commercial law of Japan proper. The new laws, however, were inconsistent with the Taiwanese inheritance custom of creating common estate among the offspring (called Saiki Kogyo[26]), which had the indirect effect of concentrating the family capital for investment. The new laws, instead, encouraged another aspect of Taiwanese inheritance custom, namely, dividing the estate equally among the children. By dividing the family capital thinly, the laws eventually weakened the influence of Taiwanese landlords and capitalists (ibid., 426). They hindered the growth of the Taiwanese companies.

The colonial government was eager to induce investment by the Taiwanese and the local Japanese. However, the Taiwanese always ended up with mere investors, and the real power of operating the company fell to the Japanese (Yanaihara, 1929, 59). The Taiwanese companies were advised and even forced directly and indirectly by the Bank of Taiwan or the colonial government to increase capital stock, or to merge, or to reorganize, in order to accommodate Japanese investment. The Bank then sent Japanese observers or retired officials to advise or supervise the operations of Taiwanese companies. There were some native companies that consisted of only the Taiwanese, but they then constantly received harassment from Japanese companies and even colonial officials.[27]

Thus, the chances for Taiwanese to advance to large independent capitalists were severely limited by conspicuously discriminatory practice by the Japanese colonists.[28] Toward the end of the Japanese period, when the colonial government wanted to mobilize Taiwanese labor and capital for the war efforts for the "Greater East Asian Prosperity Sphere," Hayashi (1943, 356) lamented that, in 1941, 67.6 percent of total paid-in capital (532 million yen) of Taiwan's industrial companies with 200,000 yen or more paid-in capital came from Japan proper, 23.5 percent from the Japanese

---

[26]See the personal experience of "jisigongye" in Skoggard (1996), 26–27.

[27]Twu (1975), 425, 445; Yanaihara (1929), 58, 134; Su (1980), 326, 329. Yanaihara gave in detail the experience of the Daito Trust Company as an example of harassment, ibid., 124, 136.

[28]This being said, it should be noted that, Yanaihara, a liberal economist who was sympathetic to the Taiwanese, wrote that one of the reasons for the rapid rise of modern capitalism in Taiwan after the Japanese occupation was due to the fact that the (retired) government officials and the CEO of other large enterprises were sent to new Taiwanese enterprises to "assist" their operations, despite the fact that there were many problems associated with it.

in Taiwan,[29] and only 8.3 percent came from the Taiwanese.[30] Most of the Taiwanese investment was in the areas of handicraft industry and agricultural processing industry like canning and textile, etc. (ibid., 359). The per capita investment in securities was about 342 yen for the local Japanese and mere seven yen for the Taiwanese, and the per capita popular post office saving deposits were 149 yen vs. 2 yen. The reasons for such large differences "should be found in non-economic factors." Hayashi (1943), 360, reasoned that Taiwanese were unfamiliar with the corporate organization and the stock market, and that the Taiwanese companies had bad management styles and squandered company funds through high dividends and high salaries, preventing the accumulation of company capital. In a special issue of "Taiwan's Industrialization and Mobilization of Taiwanese Capital," a Taiwanese economist Chin (1943) proposed[31] to use government tax policy and set up the upper limit of land price to prevent the Taiwanese to invest in land, and promote the tenant farmers so to mobilize farmers for industrial investment.[32] He also suggested that the financial institutions should accept the local stocks, securities, and land, especially for collateral borrowing, and establish Taiwan stock exchange. From these suggestions, we may see the difficulty of the Taiwanese enterprises under the colonial regime.

[29] 359 million yen from Japan proper, 125 million yen from local Japanese, a total of 484 million yen. This figure is closer to 455 million yen of total "stock investment" of the Japanese in Taiwan. See Hsi (1955), 129–145, which is summarized in Twu (1975), 354. There were 23 Japanese companies, which were headquartered in Japan, invested 261 million yen in Taiwan, and consisted of about 60 percent of the Japanese total investment in Taiwan. The rest of the Japanese investment, about 194 million yen, came from 102 local Japanese companies. The three Zaibatsu, Mitsubishi (28%), Nissan (19%), and Mitsui (17%) controlled most of the investment in Taiwan.

[30] The data came from the Finance Department, Public Finance Bureau, Taiwan Government-General, see Chin (1943), 19. Hayashi was the head of this department. The local Japanese investment was overstated, since it included investment by financial institutions and companies held by the local Japanese. Hayashi (1943), 360; Chin (1943), 19.

[31] Chin (1993) and three other authors (all are in Japanese names) in the same issue never mentioned the racial problem or racial discrimination, as did in Yanaihara (1929). One interpretation is that the society was presumably already integrated. In fact, after 1940, the major concern of the Japanese was how to mobilize Taiwanese labor and capital effectively and "fairly" to win the "sacred war." Another is that the war-time political and thought controls were so tight that such concerns were not appropriate, or dangerous, as the Taiwanese had experienced in the postwar "white terror" period. More research is needed in this area.

[32] His argument here is not clear, and apparently the same theme was stated elsewhere. Other authors seem to be more optimistic than Hayashi or Chin about capital mobilization, see Murai (1942).

6.9 Prewar Growth of Taiwanese SMEs

Despite all the difficulties for the Taiwanese firms to grow, the Taiwanese SMEs increased over time with population. The first two panels (from left) of Fig. 6.3 show the distribution of number of firms (groups 1 to 3) and percentages (groups 4 to 6) of manufacturing firms classified by the number of workers during the Japanese period. They are based on the data in Table 6.1. From 1929 to 1936, the total number of firms increased 2011 (from 5870 to 7881, see the X-axis of Panel 1), or 34 percent. The increase over the seven-year period came mostly from the steady increase of the firms with less than 5 workers and use power,[33] which increased 1925 firms

Table 6.1: Number of Manufacturing Firms

Prewar

Prewar Period — *The Number of Firms* Classified by the Number of Workers

Year	Firms Total No.	Group # listed in the first row of the X-axis of Fig. 6.3	<5@	5–14	15–29	*<30*	30–49	50–99	>=*100*	% *<30*	
1929	5870	*1*	2826	2285	435	*5546*	109	115	*100*	*94.48*	a
1930	6128		3276	2164	377	*5817*	102	127	*82*	*94.92*	
1931	6094		3369	2064	359	*5792*	91	124	*87*	*95.04*	
1932	6295		3609	1980	394	*5983*	100	115	*97*	*95.04*	
1933	6618	*2*	3756	2102	429	*6287*	111	113	*107*	*95.00*	
1934	6776		3901	2076	430	*6407*	146	114	*109*	*94.55*	
1935	7032		4166	2094	444	*6704*	128	96	*104*	*95.34*	
1936	7881	*3*	4751	2232	520	*7503*	161	109	*108*	*95.20*	

Proportion (%) of Taiwanese Owned Manufacturing Firms

in each category classified by size (workers)

Catetgory	5–49	50–99	100–199	>=200	
1929	85.6	57.6	17.0	14.8	b
1939	84.9	54.0	38.2	3.5	

Notes: <5@ = Less than 5 workers and using power (motors).
a. TCIS (1936). Also see Hori (1944), 185–186.
b. Mizoguchi and Umemura (1988), 77, based on Taiwan Kojo Meibo.

[33] This can be seen from the following calculation. From 1929 to 1936, the simple regression line for the total firms is $y = 249.6t + 5463.6$, with $R^2 = 0.8833$ (see Fig. 6A in the Appendix). During the same period, the simple regression line for the firms with less than 5 workers is $y = 234.14t + 2653.8$, with $R^2 = 0.949$. Hence both equations almost have the same slopes. This means that the two groups had more or less the same increments each year during the seven-year period, as may be seen directly from Table 6.1.

(from 2826 to 4751), that is, from 48 percent to 60 percent of the total firms, showing the vitality of the Taiwanese economic activities even under the adverse conditions.[34]

The firms with 5 to 14 workers decreased slightly, from 2285 to 2232, while larger firms, with 50 to 99 workers and those more than 100 workers, maintained more or less at the same numbers (around 100 or so firms) in each category. Since the total number of firms increased, the percentage of large firms decreased slightly. The medium-size firms, with workers from 15 to 29 and from 30 to 49, stayed at the same level from 1929 to 1933, but accelerated in 1936.

The above figures include the firms owned by the Japanese, who left Taiwan after the war. Thus, we have to estimate the number of firms owned by the Taiwanese. According to Table 6.1, in 1934, there were 260 firms with 30 to 99 workers and 109 firms with 100 or more workers, a total of 369 firms. From another source of the data, we also know that there were 331 incorporated companies in 1934, among them, 164 firms were owned by the Japanese.[35] Thus, we may assume that there were at least about an equal number (167) of Taiwanese firms which were incorporated at that time. If all the incorporated firms were large (with 30 workers or more), then, since there were 38 firms unaccounted for by above calculation, we may conclude that there were about 200 Taiwanese firms which employed at least 30 workers in mid-1930s.

Naturally, there were some Japanese firms which were not incorporated and smaller in size, as quoted in Fix (1996) in the case of the machinery industry in 1938.[36] However, we may assume that most of the firms,

---

[34]According to TCIS (1936), the firms with workers less than 5 only include those firms which use power. The total number of firms was 7881. Also see Hori (1944), 185. However, according to PBAS (1946), Table 265, in 1936, the number of firms which used power is mere 6150, and those which did not use was 1731, a total of 7881. There is a great discrepancy in statistics.

[35]See Chou (1958), 74. The number of the corporations owned by the Japanese Zaibatsu was counted as 125 in 1945. The number was reduced probably due to mergers and combinations under the war-time economic mobilization plan.

[36]Fix (1996) quotes Yamada's finding (1994) that, based on Taiwan Kojo Meibo (Factory Directory), there were 116, 33, and 16 small (1–14 workers), medium (15–49), and large (50+) factories, respectively, in machinery industry in Taiwan at the end of 1938. Among them, Japanese factories consisted of 31 percent, 58 percent, and 75 percent, respectively. On average, the Japanese held 41 percent out of a total of 165 machinery factories. According to PBAS (1946), Table 264, however, the total number of "machinery and instrument" factories in 1938 was 295. No explanation of the discrepancy was given. Note that most Japanese workers and firms were concentrated relatively high skill

90 percent or over, were Taiwanese firms, and mostly individual-operated[37] small firms with less than 5 workers. In fact, we may state this more precisely. The last two rows in Table 6.1 show the Taiwanese owned firms in terms of the number of workers in 1929 and 1939. As expected, it shows that the larger the size of the firms, the less possibility that they were owned by the Taiwanese. Note that, in 1929, 17.0 percent of firms with 100 to 199 workers were owned by the Taiwanese, so were 14.8 percent of the largest firms with 200 or more workers. By 1939, however, it appears that the former increased considerably and the latter decreased. It is not clear whether this was due to the fact that the Taiwanese firms of size 100–199 workers grew rapidly during the ten-year period, and the growth of largest firms was severely hindered by the Colonial Government.

Other parts of the economy also flourished with small enterprises. At the end of 1938, some 310,000 to 410,000 Taiwanese farms and landlords produced and sold rice paddy, which was refined into rice by about 3,300 local Taiwanese millers.[38] Among them, 732 firms bought rice for exports. In late 1930s, about 90 percent of rice exported to Japan was monopolized by four major trading companies (Kawano, 1969, 129). Taiwanese firms were destined to remain small and numerous. Similarly, in 1936 to 1937, 127,000 small farms cultivated sugar cane (about 30% of total farmers), which was sold to 49 Japanese sugar factories in Taiwan to make sugar (ibid., 92). During the same period, nearly 88 percent of sugar produced in Taiwan was exported to Japan by four major sugar companies (ibid., 87–88). Thus, production of sugar and distribution of sugar and rice, and other exports and imports, was completely under the control of the Japanese. There was almost no room for the Taiwanese to engage in export business.

6.10 Taiwanese Enterprises after the War

After WWII, the KMT government confiscated and combined the Japanese-owned firms and banks, and converted them into 50 or so public enterprises. Non-Taiwanese speaking Japanese capitalists were substituted by non-Taiwanese speaking Chinese bureaucrats and managers. In analyzing the source of numerous Taiwanese SMEs after the war, a Chinese economist

industries, like machinery, metal, and chemicals (Okurasho, 1954a, 169). Thus, the above percentages may not apply to industry as a whole.

[37] 6,065, or 90 percent, of a total of 6750 firms in 1934, see Chou (1958), 74.

[38] Mizoguchi and Yamamoto (1984) counted that Taiwanese millers consisted of 94 percent in 1929 and 93 percent in 1939. Note that, in colonial Korea, unlike Taiwan, the Japanese dominated the rice milling business in 1939 (ibid.).

ably pointed out in 1952 that official public capital crowded out local Taiwanese capital, and that the persistence of SMEs was originated from the Japanese period. He observed that, in the Japanese period, although the economy was dominated by Japanese private capital, it represented a special power of the colonial rulers, and was equivalent to postwar public capital, hampering the growth of local capital (Lin, 1952, 14).

Thus, even after the war, Taiwanese firms remained small and fragmented, and "a broad movement from below upward" was also severely limited. Like the colonial period, generally speaking, the SMEs concentrated in service and commercial sectors. However, the KMT government controls these sectors most tightly. Banks and financial institutions, insurance, stock exchange, education, transportation, communication, utilities, public media, etc. were either highly or completely restricted. Nowhere can the SMEs enter the businesses of even local transportation, newspapers, shipping, aviation, gas, electricity, etc.[39] Especially in early postwar years, "the Taiwanese were excluded from access to local bank credit through the centralized and discriminatory banking practices of the time" (Gates, 1996, 229). Ethnic stereotypes were not unheard of (ibid.).

But there are important differences in the postwar period. There were foreign influences and international markets. The U.S. advocacy of free market and free trade, and the U.S. influence on the KMT government policies through U.S. Aid Program, nurtured the Taiwanese SMEs (Hsiao and Hsiao, 1996, Section 1.5.2.3). The rapid rise of postwar Japanese capitalism ironically stimulated the Taiwanese entrepreneurs and helped the Taiwanese SMEs (ibid., Section 1.6.1). The postwar technological innovations of product-life-cycle commodities fostered the Taiwanese SMEs. In terms of trading practice, however, there is an important similarity. Until the early 1980s, the trading business has been dominated by the foreigners, especially the Japanese trading companies.

From our historical perspectives as reviewed above, the historical traditions of Taiwanese SMEs after WWII may be explained briefly as follows.

(a) As we have seen in the previous sections, Taiwan was already an export-oriented country since the 17th century, especially under the systematic colonial management of the Japanese regime. The traded goods before

[39] Chou, (1992b), 99. Private electric companies and factory owned private electric plants once thrived during the Japanese colonial period. See Lin (1997).

WWII were primarily agricultural and processed agricultural products, and the majority of workers were farmers. Thus, the Taiwanese were very much accustomed to the notion of "production for exports" for living and profits. It is definitely not a postwar phenomenon, as often implied in the postwar literature. As soon as the Taiwanese economy recovered from the war damages and the society recuperated from the political terror of February 1947, Taiwan started exporting traditional goods like sugar, rice, bananas, tea, and canned foods to Japan. When the KMT government started its export-promotion policy after the mid-1960s, the Taiwanese people already had more than 400 years of export experience, which was intensified and modernized under the Japanese colonial regime.

(b) In the early 1960s, textile products, wood and timber products, plywood, electrical and machinery apparatus, chemicals, and basic metals were added to rice, sugar, and bananas for exports (TSDB, 1975, 190–91). Much to the dismay of the Chinese bureaucrats in Taiwan (Shi and Li, 1978; Liu and Jian, 1983), the historical tie between Taiwan and Japan persisted and strengthened: First Japan as the number one export market for Taiwan until the mid-1960s, then later as the number one country from which Taiwan imports intermediate goods and capital goods (Hsiao and Hsiao, 1996, Fig. 1.17).

(c) One of the major hurdles of the export business is international marketing. A country may produce goods, but may not find a market in which to sell them. We have seen that, except during the last part of the Ch'ing rule of Taiwan, most of the foreign trade was conducted by the Europeans and the Japanese. After WWII, even during the 1970s and the 1980s when the KMT government encouraged the establishment of local "large trading companies," 60 percent of total exports were handled by either foreign-owned, or foreigners and Taiwanese jointly owned, trading companies. Furthermore, the majority of these foreigners were Japanese. The remaining exports were divided almost evenly: 20 percent by the manufacturers and traders and the government-owned Central Trust, and 20 percent by the 36,000 small Taiwanese trading companies (Yajima, 1986, 107). It was also estimated in 1981 that the Japanese Shoshas[40] alone, directly or indirectly,

[40]In addition to marketing, Sogo Shosha also helps in financing, foreign exchanges, organizing, and consulting (Steven, 1990, 70). There seems no study of their actual operations in Taiwan.

handled 40 percent to 50 percent of Taiwanese foreign trade (Liu, 1996, 145). Another government survey in 1984 showed that 75 percent of the total exports (in terms of value) were controlled by foreign businesses. Most of them were Japanese companies (ibid.). Through Japanese joint ventures and trading companies, Taiwanese firms were able to solve most of their marketing problems. The reason is simple. In addition to geographical proximity and historical ties in the early postwar period, many older Taiwanese entrepreneurs spoke and read Japanese. Japanese customs and habits were not completely alien to them. This undoubtedly removed major hurdles[41] of technological transfer and facilitated the trade between Taiwan and Japan after the war.[42]

This venue of marketing through foreign companies also proved successful for conducting trade with the United States and other countries. In 1973, Taiwan replaced Japan in the U.S. shoe market, and in 1976, Taiwan replaced Italy to become the world's largest exporter of shoes. By 1980, shoe manufacturing was Taiwan's third largest exporting industry, following only textiles and electronics (Skoggard, 1996, 55–56). However, two-thirds of the shoe export business was handled by ten or so foreign branch offices or agencies (Liu, 1996, 130).

6.11 Colonial Linkages of SMEs

In recent years, there have been several studies on the major Taiwanese entrepreneur elite during the prewar and postwar periods (e.g. Numazaki, 1993). As it becomes clear about the important role played by the SMEs in postwar Taiwanese economic development, one of the interesting questions is the origin of these Taiwanese SMEs.[43] The conventional wisdom is that

[41]According to a survey, barriers to exporting are cultural, language difference, special customs requirements, market information (particular markets, availability, usefulness, and awareness), product design and specification requirements, government policy, etc. Brooks and Frances (1991), 102.

[42]The president, 46, of a sewing machine company stated that "About forty years ago, Singer set up an affiliate in Taichung. This firm encouraged and helped the local people to build factories to produce sewing-machine parts. In 1972, I started to run this business... Techniques from Japan and a bunch of brave young people are what made Taichung the sewing-machine capital of Taiwan. Although our technology... originated in Japan, were now totally independent of it, thanks to our own R&D." Interview by Hwang *et al.* (1998), 30.

[43]Fix (1996) has surveyed some of the recent studies on both Taiwanese business elite and SMEs. This paper, in fact, tries to answer some of his questions.

the Taiwanese SMEs are the product of postwar development, as we have no data and studies linking the prewar and the postwar periods. Clearly this is not the case. The third and fourth panels in Fig. 6.3 try to connect the prewar (panels 1 and 2) and postwar (panels 3 and 4) firms using the 1954 Industry and Commerce Census data.[44]

Since the classification of the data is different, we have to make two adjustments.

First, the 1954 survey data classify the number of "production units" in the interval of firms with workers 1–3, 4–6, 7–9, 10–19, 20–29, 30–39, ... (see Table 6A in the Appendix), which is not consistent with the prewar data classification of 1–4, 5–14, 15–29, 30–49, ... as shown in Table 6.1 and Table 6.2. In order to see the linkage between the prewar and postwar periods, we regrouped the postwar data in two ways, as shown in the third and the fourth panels of Fig. 6.3. In groups 7n and 7m of Fig. 6.3 (also see Table 6.2, and col. (5) of Table 6A, of the Appendix), we have classified the data by 1 to 3 workers (the patterned bars), 4 to 9 workers (the black bars), 10 to 29 workers (the grey bars), 30 to 49 workers (the dotted line with diamonds), 50 to 99 workers (the solid line with triangles), and workers with 100 or more (the heavy dash line with circles). In groups 8n and 8m of Fig. 6.3 (also see Table 6.2, and cols. (10) and (11) of Table 6A), we have classified the data by 1 to 6 workers (patterned bars), 7 to 9 workers (black bars) (also see Table 6.2 and Table 6A in the Appendix). Other classifications are the same as groups 7n and 7m.

Second, the prewar data on firms with less than 5 workers include only those which use power motors.[45] Hence, we have to adjust the postwar data as in 7m and 8m in Fig. 6.3, which are adjusted for motor users only. This is done as follows. In 1954 survey data, there were 14,371 (34%) production units using motors, and 27,917 (64%) not using them (Hsiao, 1960b). There is no information on how these are distributed among various classes. In order to make the number close to 14,371 firms so that the data are comparable to prewar data, we arbitrarily multiply 0.25 to the number in the 1–3 class interval (that is a quarter of the firms in the class used power motors), and 0.4 to the number in the 4-9 class interval in group 7m (m for "motorized"), and keeping other classes the same as 7n (n for not

[44]ICCT (1954). Hsiao (1960b) has summarized some of its findings.

[45]The data are available only from 1929 to 1936 in TCIS, each table denotes clearly that the firms with less than 5 workers include only those using power (like motors). Also see Hori (1944).

Table 6.2: Number of Manufacturing Firms
Prewar and Postwar Periods

Year	Firms Total No.	Row sum	Group # listed in the first row of the X-axis of Fig. 6.3								Number Total	
Prewar Period				*Percentage of Manufacturing Firms Classified by the Number of Workers*								
				<5@	5–14	15–29	*<30*	30–49	50–99	*>=100*	<30	
1929		100.00	*4*	48.14	38.93	7.41	*94.48*	1.86	1.96	*1.70*	5546	
1933		100.00	*5*	56.75	31.76	6.48	*95.00*	1.68	1.71	*1.62*	6287	
1936		100.00	*6*	60.28	28.32	6.60	*95.20*	2.04	1.38	*1.37*	7503	
Postwar Period												
				1–3	4–9	10–29	*<30*	30–49	50–99	*>=100*	<30	
1954	[42288]	100.00	*7n*	72.47	18.27	6.87	*97.60*	1.15	0.68	*0.56*	41273	c
1954	[14670]	100.00	*7m*	52.22	21.06	19.80	*93.08*	3.33	1.97	*1.62*	13655	
				1–6	7–9	10–29	*<30*	30-49	50–99	*>=100*	<30	
1954	{42288}	100.00	*8n*	86.08	4.65	6.87	*97.60*	1.15	0.68	*0.56*	41273	c
1954	{15627}	100.00	*8m*	69.88	5.04	18.58	*93.50*	3.12	1.85	*1.52*	14612	
				1–9	10–99		*>=100*	100–499		*>=500*	<100	
1954	42288	100.00	*9*	90.73	8.70		*0.56*		0.50	*0.07*	42050	c
1961	51567	100.00	*10*	89.49	9.76		*0.75*		0.62	*0.13*	51180	d
1966	27709	100.00	*11*	72.12	25.10		*2.78*		2.31	*0.47*	26939	d
1976	69517	100.00	*12*	68.12	27.13		*4.75*		4.11	*0.64*	66215	d
1986	113639	100.00	*13*	63.60	32.43		*3.97*		3.54	*0.43*	109128	d
1991	146086	100.00	*14*	64.08	30.95		*2.48*		2.23	*0.26*	142365	e

Notes:
c. Hsiao (1960b), based on ICCT (1954). See the Appendix of this chapter for the derivation of 7n, 7m, 8n, and 8m, where m denote that the data is adjusted for firms using motors, n, not adjusted.
d. Kajiwara (1995), 99, based on ICCTF (1962, 1968, 1978, and 1988).
e. ICCFT, Table 43 (December 1993).

adjusted for power). We obtain 14,670 firms, which is close to 14,371 firms (see the sum row of col. (8), Table 6A). Similarly, we multiply 0.3 (instead of 0.25, as the class interval is larger than that in group 7m) to the number in 1–6 class interval and 0.4 to the number in the 7–9 interval in group 8m, and keep other classes the same as 8n. We obtain 15,627 firms (see the sum row of col. (13), Table 6A), which is also relatively close to 14,371 firms.

After these manipulations, we now compare panel two (groups 4 to 6) with panels three and four (groups 7 and 8) in Fig. 6.3. So far as percentages are concerned, generally speaking, the 1954 figures not adjusted for power users have an increasing trend among firms with less than 5 workers (1 to 3 or 1 to 6 class, the patterned columns of groups 7n and 8n, of workers in 1954) throughout the prewar and postwar period. It also appears that there is a decreasing trend for firms with 5 to 14 workers (black bars in panels 2, 3, and 4) during the two periods. This shows the continuity of the SMEs with less than 15 workers. There are some problems in the continuity of the firms with 15–29 workers in panels 2 and 3 when 1954 data are adjusted for power users (the grey columns). This is due to the fact that the lower limit of this 10–29 class interval for 1954 census was extended to 10 workers (instead of 15 workers), so the number of firms in the extended class interval increased considerably, resulting in large increase in the percentages (overflow to 19.8% and 18.6%, respectively, in groups 7m and 8m). Excluding this particular group, we see that by comparing the upper part of panels 2, 3 and 4, measured from the right Y-axis, the last three classes, 30–49, 50–99, and ≥100, of firms seem to be more or less consistent (in terms of the clustering pattern) in percentage distribution between the prewar and the postwar periods.

A much stable pattern between prewar and postwar periods appears if we classify the firms in only three categories, those with workers less than 30, between 30 and 99, and 100 or more. This can be seen from the enclosed columns in Table 6.2. From 1929 to 1954, the firms with less than 30 workers consistently ranged from 93 percent to 98 percent, and those equal to or greater than 100 workers ranged from 0.56 percent to 1.70 percent. Groups 9 to 14 of Table 6.2 and the last panel of Fig. 6.3 show that the real changes in the industrial structure occurred from 1966, when Taiwanese economy started to take off. Almost all of the changes came from the increase in the number of firms with 10 to 99 workers and 100 to 499 workers at the expense of firms less than ten workers (the weight of 100–499 class decreased by 1.9%, this may be due to changes in the definition of SME. See the X-axis of Fig. 6.1).

In addition to visual appeal, we have fitted the data with a regression line and an exponential function. The last column, except groups 9 to 14, of Table 6.2 gives the number of firms with workers less than 30 in each year. This is also illustrated in Fig. 6.5. We have two estimates due to different methods of adjusting the 1954 data for motor using firms. Estimate 7m uses the result of 7m, which gives the total motor using firms of 13655 in 1954 (col. (8) of Table 6A), and plotted as the 7m line with filled circle

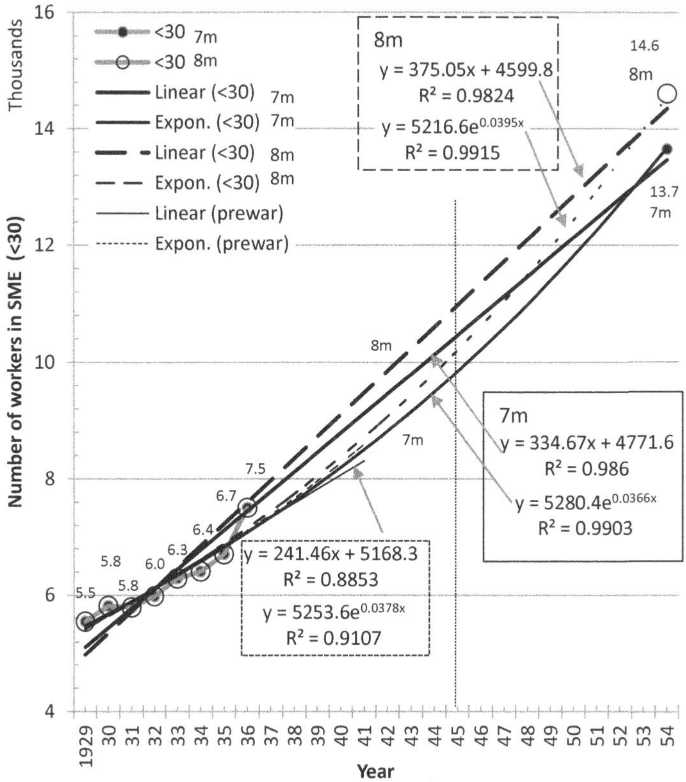

Figure 6.5: Linkage between Prewar and Postwar SMEs

markers. Estimate 8m uses the result of 8m, which gives the total motor using firms of 14612 in 1954 (col. (13) of Table 6A). It is plotted as the 8m line with large empty circle markers. The prewar data for both estimates are the same, that is, the filled circle markers and the empty circle markers overlap each other from 1929 to 1936. We also estimated the linear and exponential curves for the prewar data. They are summarized in the three boxes in Fig. 6.5 as follows:[46]

Prewar estimate of the equations. The dotted box on the lower part of Fig. 6.5 shows the estimation of linear and exponential equations. The variable x in the equations is the time (year). The exponential equation

[46]All the equations are estimated by using Microsoft Excel program.

shows that, from 1929 to 1936, the SMEs increased at a continuously compounded rate of 3.78 percent per year. Both fittings appear to be excellent.

Estimation 7m. The solid box in the middle of Fig. 6.5 shows the two equations for the 7m data set. It shows that from 1929 to 1954, the SMEs grew at 3.66 percent per year, almost the same as the prewar growth of 3.78 percent per year. In 1954, the estimated equations gives 13,473 firms for linear estimate and 13,675 firms for exponential estimate, both are almost the same as our originally estimated number of 13655. This shows the perfect connection between the prewar and postwar SMEs.

Estimation 8m. The dashed box at the upper corner of Fig. 6.5 shows the equations for 8m. It shows the SMEs grew at 3.95 percent per year from 1929 to 1954, almost the same as the prewar growth rate of SMEs. In 1954, the forecast values for both equations are 14,351 and 14,568 firms, respectively, only slightly less than the estimated 1954 estimated number of 14,612 firms, showing a perfect fit of the equations. This means that, despite the regime change, the trend of the prewar development of SMEs continued even after the postwar period. In turn, it shows the resilience, adaptability, perseverance, and ingenuity of the Taiwanese SMEs.

In any case, we have shown that there is continuity of the prewar and postwar Taiwanese SMEs for firms hiring workers less than 30. In fact, we also found that the continuity extends to the whole manufacturing industry for all firms using motors. We have noted that the 1954 industrial census showed that there were 14,371 firms using motors, and our reclassification of class interval of 1954 data shows that either 14,670 (7m) or 15,627 firms (8m) were using motors (see Table 6A). If we take these two numbers and the number of prewar manufacturing firms without considering their size (col. 2 of Table 6.1) and run the regression line and quadratic equation, we also obtain an almost perfect continuity[47] between the prewar and postwar industrial evolution in terms of number of the firms. This indicates that, when we discuss Taiwanese SMEs, or for that matter, the development

[47]In this case, the prewar regression line is given as $y = 364.25x + 4975.6$, $R^2 = 0.9844$, and the quadratic equation is $y = 5544.1\exp(0.0374x)$, $R^2 = 0.9908$. On the other hand, for case 7m, we obtain $y = 364.25x + 4975.6$, $R^2 = 0.9844$, and $y = 5544.1\exp(0.0374x)$, $R^2 = 0.9908$, and for case 8m, we have $y = 404.63x + 4803.8$, $R^2 = 0.9807$, and $y = 5481.5\exp(0{,}0401x)$, $R^2 = 0.9914$. The fitting appears to be as good, if not better.

of the Taiwanese industry as a whole, we should not ignore their prewar development.[48]

6.12 The Origin of SMEs

We have discussed the statistical linkage of Taiwanese SMEs between the prewar and postwar periods. Who are the people behind the numbers? Two field studies by social anthropologists are illuminating. In Section 6.10, we have found that, by 1980, Taiwan was the world's largest exporter of shoes. In 1980, Taiwan exported 413 million pairs of shoes and earned US $1.4 billion. There were 582 factories and 110,955 employees in the shoe industry. The highest record was achieved in 1986 with 843 million pairs at the value of US $3.2 billion, produced by 1,190 factories and 159,617 employees that year. The average employment per factory was 134 workers.[49]

The origin of the shoe industry was, however, in the grass hat industry which started in 1897 in central Taiwan using locally grown rushes as raw material.[50] As early as in 1916, there were 1,011 male workers and 21,305 female workers in the hat industry. In 1918, the workers increased to 66,152. Most of them were women, earning "extremely low" wages.[51] The record year of hat production was 1934, the industry produced 15.3 million hats, valued at 5.0 million yen (PBAS, 1946, Table 284),[52] and most of the hats were exported to the United States and other countries (Okurasho, 1952, 183). In general, the various sideline productions (handicrafts) in rural area, especially by female workers, were already prevalent in Taiwan in the prewar

[48]According to PBAS (1946) the total number of factories for 1937, 1938, 1939, 1940, 1941, was 8,025, 8,491, 8,623, 8,940, and 8,683, respectively. Even if we use these slightly different data, the results are the same. Note that, Lin (1952), 15 asserts that during the Japanese period, "the number of firms had reached more than 8,000,. . . after the war, these private industries only left about 6,000 or so, mostly with 3 to 5 workers, very seldom 300 or more than 300 workers." His 1952 estimate is only one seventh of the 1954 ICCT result. No explanation was given.

[49]Skoggard (1996), 55, 60. Another interesting example is Taiwan's bicycle production and exports, research done by researchers in Institute of Developing Economies (IDE) of Japan.

[50]Ibid., 54. Skoggard does not explain the process of transformation from the hat industry to the shoe industry.

[51]Okurasho (1954a), 168. The handicrafts were more popular in places where the agricultural productivity was lower, indicating the necessity of these sideline jobs to supplement low income (ibid.). On the poor conditions of the rural area in the 1930s, see Pan (1947), 46.

[52]It amounted to 15 percent of the world's grass hat production (Skoggard, 1996, 54). Okurasho (1954b), 113, however, shows that the highest value from 1936 to 1941 was reached in 1940, at 5.8 million yen.

period. In 1936, the registered sideline workers counted for 88,732, among them 74,227 workers were women, and 41% of them (mostly producing hats) were in Hsinchu area. Due to the informal nature of sideline jobs, the actual number of workers could be much larger (Okurasho, 1954a, 166–167). The spirit of massive and systematic production for exports in rural area was encouraged and developed by the Japanese colonial government. Here is the root of Taiwanese rural industry and a source of the Taiwanese SMEs in the postwar era.

At more personal level, Hu (1983) accounted the emergence of small-scale industry in Liu Ts'o, a small village of 789 people located in the Nan T'un district near Taichung in central Taiwan. In the 1930s, the industries in Taichung area were "food processing, timber, textiles, and the assembly of sewing machines." In Nan T'un districts, there were 12 factories in 1932, most of them were food processing factories, including rice processing, bamboo processing, soy sauce, peanut oil, incense, and paper. A Japanese cassava processing factory was built in Liu Ts'o around 1936, employed 30 to 40 temporary workers. "During the agricultural slack season, many Liu Ts'o villagers engaged in traditional handicrafts, such as the weaving of straw hats, straw mats, and baskets" (ibid., 390) to supplement meager agricultural income.

After the war in 1956, 24 years later, Nan-T'un's factories were slightly more than doubled to 26 factories, 21 of them were food-processing, and others were kiln, textile, and machinery manufacturers. In Liu Ts'o, the cassava factory was closed in 1945 when the Japanese left Taiwan. From 1945 to 1970, for a long 25-year period, only two small factories, one sewing machine assembly plant (in late 1950s?), and one sewing machine painting factory (in 1957) appeared in the village.[53] In the 1970s, machinery,

[53]Hu (1983), 391. Hu does not explain the gap between 1945 to 1970. We submit that the gap may be explained, at least partially, by the language problem. The Chinese who replaced the Japanese do not speak Taiwanese, and "The Taiwanese became the silent majority. The language problem eased gradually only after the next generation of the Taiwanese, who were educated under the Chinese system, started being socially active in the mid-1970s" (Hsiao and Hsiao, 1996, Section 1.5.1). In a small village like Liu Ts'o, the communication problem seemed to be intimidating and confusing, and prevented the prewar generation from transforming from agriculture to industry. Hu observed in the late 1970s that "all small-scale factories in Liu Ts'o are family based enterprises. In two-thirds of the total, the older generation in the family provides capital and facilities, whereas the younger generation contributes labor and skill" (Hu, 1983, 404). The gap also corroborates our assertion that Taiwanese economy could have grown much faster, see Hsiao and Hsiao (1996), Section 1.18.

chemical, and metal plants sprouted in Nan T'un, and "some young villagers who were sent to the city to learn industrial skills returned home and established auxiliary processing factories right in or next to their farm houses." Dramatic changes also occurred in Liu Ts'o. "Since 1970 approximately 20 small-scale factories have emerged. Thirteen of them were machinery-processing plants. The remaining ones were dedicated to wood product manufacturing, electroplating, vacuum-modeling and sealing, electronics assembly, and hat and bag manufacturing" (ibid., 392). From the various personal interviews reported in the paper, we can perceive the transformation of land capital into industrial capital, the risk-taking venture, the source of venture capital, and transfer of technology in a small Taiwanese village.[54]

Hu concludes that "unlike industrial zones, Liu Ts'o's small-scale industries emerged spontaneously and without government planning. Auxiliaries have been related to the expansion of export-oriented, labor-intensive manufacturing" (ibid., 401). "Most of them do not have licenses from the Bureau of Industry... Their workers do not participate in government-sponsored health and accident insurance. They also work overtime..." (ibid., 403). In short, "...the government has not given these rural factories encouragement and instruction" (ibid., 405). Thus, the business traditions of these Taiwanese rural industries could only be traced back to the Japanese period.

6.13 On Education, Confucianism, and the Spirit of Settlers

We have elaborated to show that the activity of the Taiwanese SMEs is not a postwar phenomenon, they have been deeply rooted in the prewar period, and survived the onslaught of discrimination and harassment by foreign businesses and governments. In a previous paper (Hsiao and Hsiao, 1996), we have studied the sources of Taiwanese vitality. We also observed the vitality of Taiwanese SMEs in export activities, which have been unprecedented in the four hundred years of the Taiwanese economic and business history. We pointed out that, like the agricultural sector, the vitality of the Taiwanese SMEs was, ironically, inherited from the

[54]These findings are contrary to some Chinese officials' stereotype of Taiwanese (SME) entrepreneurs in the early postwar era. See the quotation and discussions in Gates (1996), 228.

Japanese educational system, helped by the postwar Japanese technology and marketing network. The Taiwanese SMEs are very much on their own in business finance, and rely heavily on the informal financial markets.[55] Their upward movements are hindered by the government monopoly of upstream and midstream industries and the control of the banking system, and they found niches in export activities.

In Taiwan, as in Japan, China, Korea, and other western industrial countries, education is generally regarded as an important means for socioeconomic upward mobility. In 1944, a year before Japan was defeated in WWII, the percentage of school age children enrolled in primary schools already reached 81 percent for boys and 60 percent for girls, an average of 71 percent (Tsurumi, 1977, 148; Okurasho, 1952, 17). It reached 84 percent in 1952, and 99.79 percent in 1992 (TSDB, 1993, 268). Thus, the foundation of the modern educational system and the possibility of continuous improvement were firmly laid during the colonial period. In 1968, the compulsory primary education was extended from six years to nine years. At the same time, the KMT government pepped up the vocational training programs to meet the industrial demands (Li, 1988, 87–91). By 1980, in terms of employment by educational attainment of workers, Taiwan had a high percentage of the senior high school and vocational school graduates (21%), only second to Korea (22%), and also had the highest percentage of university graduates (11%) among the four Asian NICs (Fields, 1985, 350). While there may have some validity on the popular assertion that postwar educational system helped Taiwan's economic development, the immediate effects of the educational system probably contributed more to employees, especially the female employees in export processing zones, than to the employers of the SMEs.

Before the 1968 reform, the educational system in Taiwan was shabby and substandard, focused on rote learning, and centered on anti-communism political rhetoric and self-righteousness of the KMT government. After the reform, it probably will take another fifteen to twenty-year

[55]Gates (1996), 228–236 has interesting accounts of "financing petty capitalism" and "folk ritual," repudiating one of the most conspicuous postwar ethnic stereotypes of Taiwanese folk religion: that "extravagant festivals and construction of pompous ancestral shrines, temples, villas, and tombs... seriously curtails the accumulation of capital for productive purpose" (ibid., 228). Schak (1996) is also understanding. While acknowledging that "business entertainment... is found all over the world, Taiwanese have their own particular style of interaction in such venues...." For the SMEs in Taiwan, the venues are temples and local religion (Skoggard, 1996, 21–41).

social and work experiences for a graduate to attain a decision making position in the SMEs. Thus, the effects of postwar educational system on Taiwanese economic development may present, if there are any, only after the mid-1980s, concurrent with the rise of political activities of the Taiwanese intelligentsia. In any case, the effects of education on economic development need more careful examination. After all, recent two-digit rapid economic growth of China as well as the ASEANs during the past several years seems to be achieved without much educational reform.

Closely related to the effects of education is the assertion that Confucianism, or the revised one, played a role in Taiwanese economic development (Metzger and Myers, 1989, 302). The problem is that there is no clear definition of Confucianism, not to speak of the "revised" one. "Family cohesion, hard work, a propensity to be frugal and save, respect for authority, respect for education, the desire to compete for wealth and position, familiarity with the marketplace and the bureaucracy, and a tendency to take the educated elite as a reference group, open to their advice about say, crops or family planning" are vaguely suggested as the manifestation of Confucianism (ibid.). We submit that these traits are the same for all successful business people in any country in any generation and in any profession.

To be more specific, Skoggard (1996), 113, in doing fieldwork on Taiwan's shoe industry in a rural area in Taichung, found that Taiwanese "entrepreneurs practice a limited Confucianism: They honor and value the family, loyalty, human relations, but they oppose principles of hierarchy, ritualized behavior, respect for central authority, and rote learning. Also they believe in heterodox notions of magical power and transformation, brotherhood, and rebellion (Lam, Paltiel, and Shannon, 1994). Although they rightly fear its power, they have little love for the state." As we have observed above, the first part on family and loyalty is hardly the monopoly of Confucianism. Strong family ties are present in any society. Confucianism, if there is one, is not "the" Taiwanese culture.[56]

[56]While we agree that "Confucianism Is Not 'the' Chinese Culture" (Lam *et al.*, 206), we strongly disagree with argument by Lam *et al.* that violation of intellectual property rights were done by heterodoxy of "small-scale Taiwan enterprises" (ibid., 210). No statistics or sources of statistics and no field studies are given in the paper. It is not clear whether the prevalence of piracy of video and audio tapes, to name a few, by small businesses in the United States is also due to "non-Confucian heterodoxy." The problem of intellectual property rights in Taiwan ceased quickly after the KMT government tightened up the law. Apparently, the problem was legal, not cultural.

It is undeniable that the Taiwanese people have the virtues described above. So far as the Taiwanese are concerned, the "respect for authority," or better, the "fear of authority," and "little love for the state" (Skoggard, 1996, 113) are "learned behavior, not a cultural trait." It is learned under relentlessly oppressive authoritarian states of the past 100 years. As for being hard working, it has been reported that "the Taiwanese female workers are probably about 10 percent more efficient than the corresponding Japanese female workers" (Yamazaki, 1982, 33). The hard working nature of hat weaving Taiwanese women was observed by a Japanese journalist even in 1921 (Kataoka, 1921, 161). The Taiwanese themselves also admit that they are hardworking people (Skoggard, 1996, 122–123, 130, 150). But again this is hardly exclusive to Confucianism.

When we shop in Taipei, we are often impressed by the fact that almost every Taiwanese shop has an altar either to the God of Wealth or the Goddess of Kuan-im, along with family ancestors. In the rural area of Cautun in central Taiwan, where Skoggard did his fieldwork on the shoe industry, "production occurred in one large room in the back. Over the entrance to the main work space was an altar to the earth god, Tudi Gong.[57]" This is a common scenery in rural Taiwan. In Taiwanese villages, "The temple system creates a space and a medium for an endless cycle of transactions and conversation. Unlike Confucian state, the local gods deemed commerce an honorable and reputable activity, conferring on merchants the necessary symbolic power to carry out their business over as broad an area as possible. While town temples may include a shrine to Confucius and Mencius, the main altar is usually occupied by the principal god Guandi, the god of war and merchants" (ibid., 37).

In the loosely defined cast system of Confucianism, the order of social classes is scholars, peasants, craftsmen, and merchants (Shi, Nong, Kong, Shang in Chinese). Scholars and bureaucrats use "mind," so they govern, peasants and craftsmen use "hands," so they are governed. The merchants, including capitalists and entrepreneurs, belong to the lowest class since they make profits on other people's hard work and exploit consumers. Obviously, Confucianism has difficulty explaining capitalism.

In fact, the Japanese colonists knew better. As early as in 1907, in "the revised Common School Regulations, . . . agriculture, commerce, and manual arts became compulsory in schools which offered them. The teaching of

[57]Ibid., 97. Tudi Gong or other gods of the family's choice.

these subjects was designed to fight the deep-rooted repugnance literate Taiwanese felt toward manual labor" (Tsurumi, 1977, 50). In a confidential memo, the Japanese wrote that "The [upper class] Taiwanese... despised manual labor and had nothing but contempt for honest and useful occupations which required physical skill or exertion" (ibid., 51). Thus the teacher's responsibility was to "make the next generation of native leaders less prejudiced against agricultural, commercial, and manual occupations" (ibid.). Undoubtedly, this new attitude toward labor and work ethics has contributed tremendously to the growth of rural industry in Taiwan. Here we can see that the educational system during the early years of this century also alludes to the business tradition of postwar Taiwanese SMEs.[58]

Hard work, brotherhood, strong family ties, competition, worship of local gods, the temple system, etc. are the virtues inherited from the Han Taiwanese ancestors who escaped famine, purgation and cruelty in China and sought for a new world and settled in the wild virgin island infested with furious plagues and pirates four hundred years ago. Thanks to these virtues, the Han Taiwanese ancestors broke fresh ground and worked out their own destiny. As new settlers, the Han Taiwanese ancestors were also flexible in ideas, practical in daily life, and adaptable to new technology. All five kinds of Schumpeter's "new combination entrepreneurship" can be found in the Taiwanese shoe industry (Skoggard, 1996, 113). These virtues are the spirit of settlers and frontier explorers shared by the Pilgrims and other Europeans who sailed to America (Kato, 1968, 140–142), and also shared by other first generation Chinese who immigrated to Southeast Asian countries. These are also the virtues which propelled the Taiwanese, overseas Chinese (including people in Singapore and Southeast Asia), and the Americans to wealth and welfare.[59]

6.14 Some Conclusions

Since 1967, the official definitions of Taiwanese SMEs have changed five times. While the changes show the flexibility and relative social perception of the SMEs over time, they cause long-run time series analysis, and for that matter, the international comparison, very difficult. Thus, it is not

[58]The first author remembers that, in 1961, the leading government newspaper (Central Daily) had an editorial column advocating the need of vocational schools in Taiwan "since not every student is good enough and intellectual enough to enter regular high schools."

[59]The Koreans may have different cultural explanations, see Pae (1992), 68.

surprising that Taiwan can claim the dubious distinction of the Kingdom of Small-and-Medium Enterprises, as the number of SMEs has consistently exceeded 95 percent (generally closer to 99%) of the total enterprises in any category of industry. In this paper, we have tried to examine the characteristics of SMEs by classifying them with the size of workers employed in a firm in the manufacturing industry before and after WWII. This way, we may compare the changes of the number of SMEs in each category over time and among the nations. Only when we compare the numbers with other nations, we can really claim the distinction, and truly characterize the Taiwanese SMEs. This paper is a first step toward this direction. However, the main purpose of this paper is restricted only to the discussions of business historical traditions of the Taiwanese SMEs.

The problem is that different periods have different methods of defining SMEs. Thus, to have some definite idea of the changes, we have tried our best to estimate the number in each category to facilitate the comparison. The diagrams helped us visualize the trends over time. We have found the linkage between prewar and postwar periods in terms of growth rates and levels (numbers). The former implies that the prewar and early postwar industrial structures are basically the same,[60] as they grew at the same rates, at least until the mid-1960s. The latter shows the resilience, adaptability, and ingenuity of the Taiwanese SMEs.

To supplement our statistical analysis, we have examined anecdotally the rise of the shoe industry and the process of industrial development in a small village in central Taiwan. In both cases, we can trace the origin of the enterprises back to the day of the Japanese period. Despite many difficulties, like limitations of domestic markets due to government monopoly and oligopoly, restrictions of banking and loan markets, both before and after the war, the Taiwanese SMEs have grown steadily, and their scale of operation also increased after mid-1960s. We have also argued that the spirit of settlers, hardly Confucianism, alludes to their growth. Finally, in reviewing the past 400 years of Taiwanese business history, we have found that the commerce of foreign trade has been, with a few exceptions, consistently dominated by the foreigners. How to strengthen the international marketing is a basic problem for Taiwanese economic development in the future.

---

[60]Other similarities are explored in Hsiao and Hsiao (1996, 1998).

Appendix to Section 6.11: Colonial Linkages of SMEs

This Appendix gives the original data of 1954 ICCT (1956), as listed in Hsiao (1960b), which we used in the derivation of 7m and 8m in Table 6.2. Construction of Table 6A is explained in the Notes to Table 6A.

Table 6A: Estimation of the Postwar Firms Using Power (1954)

(1)	(2)	(3)	(4)	(5)	(6)	*(7)*	*(8)*	*(9)*	(10)	(11)	(12)	*(13)*	*(14)*
ICCT original range				New		*7n*	7m	*7m*	New		*8n*	8m	*8m*
Frm	To	no.	%	Rnge	ICCT	%	Level	%	Range	ICCT	%	Level	%
1	3	30645	72.47	1-3	30645	*72.47*	7661	*52.22*					
4	6	5756	13.61						1-6	36402	*86.08*	10920	*69.88*
7	9	1968	4.65	4-9	7724	*18.27*	3090	*21.06*	7-9	1966	*4.65*	787	*5.03*
10	19	2180	5.16										
20	29	724	1.71	10-29	2904	*6.87*	2904	*19.80*	10-29	2905	*6.87*	2905	*18.59*
30	39	324	0.77										
40	49	164	0.39	30-49	488	*1.15*	488	*3.33*	30-49	488	*1.15*	488	*3.12*
50	99	289	0.68	50-99	289	*0.68*	289	*1.97*	50-99	289	*0.68*	289	*1.85*
100	199	98	0.23										
150	199	48	0.11										
200	299	41	0.10										
300	399	18	0.04										
400	499	5	0.01										
500	999	14	0.03										
over 1000		14	0.03	>=100	238	*0.56*	238	*1.62*	>=100	238	*0.56*	238	*1.52*
Sum		42288	100		42288	*100*	14670	100		42288	*100*	15627	*100*
Sum	<30						13655	93.08				14612	93.50

Notes: Methods of reclassification of ICCT data and calculation.
Columns (1)–(3): Hsiao (1960b), based on ICCT (1954).
Columns (6), (11): Reclassified using col. (3).
Columns (7), (12): % distribution after reclassification. Data not adjusted for motorized firms.
They are reproduced as 7n and 8n in Table 6.2 and Fig. 6.3.
Columns (8), (13): Estimation of the number of firms using motors.
(a) = 30645*0.25; (b) = 7724*0.4; (c) = 36402*0.3; (d) = 1966*0.4.
Columns (9), (14): % distribution of firms using motors (shaded columns). They are reproduced as 7m and 8m in Table 6.2 and also Fig. 6.3.

Acknowledgments

The revised version of this paper has benefited from the participants of the Conference of Commercial Traditions of Taiwan, held at the Institute of

Taiwanese History, Preparatory Office, Academia Sinica, Taipei, Taiwan, in December 1996. We thank the Preparatory Office, especially, Professor Fu-san Huang and Mr. Kaim Ang, for their hospitality, and Professors Douglas Fix, Song-ken Hsu, Ta-hou Lin, Wen-hsing Wu, Miss Yi-san Chi, and the Starr East Asian Library of Columbia University for help in search of some references. Critical comments of a referee led to the addition of the commercial revolution in Section 6.7. In preparing for this chapter, the charts, tables, and Section 6.11 are redone using Microsoft Excel program. The Appendix and Fig. 6.5 are added for clarity. All errors of omission and commission are naturally ours.

References

Brooks, M.R. and A. Frances (1991). "Barriers to Exporting: An Exploratory Study of Latin American Companies." In F.H.R. Seringhaus and P.J. Rosson (eds.), *Export Development and Promotion: The Role of Public Organizations* (Chapter 5). Norwell, M.A.: Kluwer Academic Publishers.

Chan, Wellington, K.K. (undated). "Chinese Business Organization and Management: Its Traditional Form and the Beginning of Modern Reform." Working paper. Publisher unknown.

Chang, Han-yu (1974). "Economic Development and Economic Thoughts." *Essays of Dr. Hay-yu Chang*, Volume II. Committee of Publishing Essays of Dr. Han-yu Chang. Taipei: Sanmin Bookstore.

Chang, Sheng-yen *et al.* (1996). *The Development of Taiwan* (in Chinese). Taipei: National Kong-Chung University.

Chang, Yong-wu (1947). "The Characteristics of Commerce in Taiwan." *The Quarterly Journal of the Bank of Taiwan*, 1(1) (June).

Chen, Shih-meng S., Chung-Cheng Lin, C.Y. Cyrus Chu, Ching-hsi Chang, Jun-ji Shih and Jin-Tian Liu (1991). *Disintegrating KMT-State Capitalism: A Closer Look at Revitalizing Taiwan's State-and Party-Owned Enterprises* (in Chinese). Taiwan: Taipei Society.

Chin, Ho-gen (1943). "Taiwan's Industrialization and Mobilization of Taiwanese Capital" (in Japanese). *Taiwan Jiho*, 19–26 (March).

Chou, Hsian-wen (1957). "Exploitation Economy in Taiwan during the Dutch Period." *Volumes on Taiwan Studies*, no. 40. Taipei: The Bank of Taiwan.

——— (1958). *Economic History of Taiwan during the Japanese Occupation Period* (in Chinese). *Taiwan Studies*, no. 59. Taipei: The Bank of Taiwan.

Chou, Hsue-pu *et al.* (1959). "Historical Document on Trade between Taiwan and England." *Volumes on Taiwan Studies*, no. 57. Taipei: The Bank of Taiwan.

Chou, T.C. (1988). "The Evolution of Market Structure in Taiwan." *Rivista Internationale di Scienze Economiche e Commerciali*, 35(2): 171–194.

——— (1992a). "The Experience of SMEs Development in Taiwan: High Export-Contribution and Export-Intensity." *Rivista Internationale di Scienze Economiche e Commerciali*, 39(12): 1069–1084.

——— (1992b). "Small and Medium Enterprises in Power Peripheral." In Hsing-Huang Hsiao *et al.* (eds.), *Anatomy of Taiwanese Economy, Monopoly and Exploitation under Authoritarian System* (in Chinese) (Chapter 5). Taiwan Research Fund Series #2. Taipei, Taiwan: Chianwei Publisher.

Crouzet, Francois (1972). *Capital Formation in the Industrial Revolution.* London: Methuen and Co. Ltd.

Davis, Ralph (1967). *A Commercial Revolution, English Overseas Trade in the Seventeenth and Eighteenth Centuries.* London: The Historical Association.

Eaton, L. (1991). *Taiwan.* Mini-Dragon TV Series, Maryland Public Television and Film Australia.

Fields, G.S. (1985). "Industrialization and Employment in Hong Kong, Korea, Singapore, and Taiwan." In W. Galenson (ed.), *Foreign Trade and Investment, Economic Development of the Newly Industrializing Asian Countries* (Chapter 8). Madison: The University of Wisconsin Press.

Fix, Douglas (1996). "Late Colonial-era Taiwanese Small-scale Industrial Enterprises: A Conceptual Discussion." Paper presented at the Conference on Commercial Traditions of Taiwan, Academia Sinica, Taipei, Taiwan, December.

Gates, Hill (1996). *China Motor, A Thousand Years of Petty Capitalism.* Ithaca and London: Cornell University Press.

Gold, Thomas B. (1088). "Colonial Origins of Taiwanese Capitalism." In Edwin A. Winckler and Susan Greenhalgh (eds.), *Contending Approaches to the Political Economy of Taiwan* (Chapter 5). New York: M.E. Sharpe, Inc.

Hao, Yen-p'ing (1986). *The Commercial Revolution in Nineteenth-Century China, The Rise of Sino Western Mercantile Capitalism. Berkeley.* CA: University of California Press.

Hayashi, Masuo (1943). "Taiwan's Industrialization and Capital Mobilization." (in Japanese). In *Taiwan Keizai Nempo* (Taihoku) (Chapter 5, 384–400).

Hobsbawn, E.J. (1968). Industry and Empire, An Economic History of Britain since 1750. London: Weidenfeld and Nicolson.

Hori, Tsuneo (1944). *A Study of the Economy of Exterior Territories* (in Japanese). Tokyo: Ganshodo Shoten.

Hsi, Yi (1955). "Investment of the Japanese Zaibatsu in Taiwan" (in Chinese). *Taiwanese Economic History Series,* Vol. 2. Taipei: The Bank of Taiwan.

Hsiao, F. Sheng-Tieh (1960a). "An Analysis of the Burden of Interest Cost on Private Industry in Taiwan" (in Chinese). *Quarterly Journal of the Bank of Taiwan,* 11(1): 17–51. Reprinted in Chiu, C.H. (ed.), *Readings in Economic Development of Taiwan,* V: *Readings in Taiwan's Money and Finance* (Chapter 15). Taipei, Taiwan: Lianjing Publishing Co., 1975, 325–374.

——— (1960b). "On the Size of the Private Industry and Its Financial Problem in Taiwan" (in Chinese). *The Monthly Correspondence of the Bank of Huanan,* no. 113 (May).

Hsiao, Frank S.T. (1997). "Colonialism or Comparative Advantage? — On Agricultural Development in Colonial Taiwan." *Proceedings of the National Science Council, Part C: Humanities and Social Sciences,* 7(4), 497–513. Ref. Chapter 4.

______ and Mei-Chu W. Hsiao (1996). "Taiwanese Economic Development and Foreign Trade." In John T. Kuark (ed.), *Comparative Asian Economies.* Greenwich, CT: JAI Press. Originally published in *Fairbank Center Discussion Paper* No. 9, 1994, Harvard University, and *Harvard Studies on Taiwan: Papers of the Taiwan Studies Workshop*, Volume 1. Fairbank Center for East Asian Research, Harvard University, 1995. Ref. Chapter 1.

______ and ______ (1998). "Colonial Linkages in Early Postwar Taiwanese Economic development." Paper presented at Taiwan Studies Workshop, The Fairbank Center for East Asian Research, Harvard University, and at the Taiwan Studies Conference on The Japanese Legacy in Post-Colonial Taiwan, the Joint Center for East Asian Studies, Washington University and University of Missouri, St. Louis. Published in William C. Kirby and Michael S. Weiss (eds.), *Harvard Studies on Taiwan*, Volume II, *Papers of the Taiwan Studies Workshop* (Chapter 5, 91–117). John King Fairbank Center for East Asian Research, Harvard University, 1998.

______ and L.R. Sullivan (1983). "A Political History of the Taiwanese Communist Party, 1928–1931." *Journal of Asian Studies*, 52(2) (February): 269–289.

Hsiao, Mei-Chu W. (1992). "Direct Foreign Investment, Technology Transfer, and Industrial Development — The Case of Electronics Industry in Taiwan." In M. Jan Dutta (ed.), *Research in Asian Economic Studies* (Volume 4A) *Asian Economic Regimes: An Adaptive Innovation Paradigm* (145–164). Greenwich, CT: JAI Press. Ref. Chapter 9.

Hu, Tai-li (1983). "The Emergence of Small-scale Industry in a Taiwanese Rural Community." In June Nash and Maria P.E. Kelly (eds.), *Women, Men, and the International Division of Labor.* Albany: State University of New York Press.

Huang, Fu-san and Tsu-yu Chen (1995). "Business Development" (in Chinese). In Rong-Tsong Jian (ed.), *Modern History of Taiwan, Volume on Economy.* Taipei, Taiwan: Taiwansheng Wen Hsian Wei Yuan Hui.

Hwang, Jim, Oscar Chung, and Violet Chang (1998). "Voices from the Heartland." *Free China Review*, 48(1).

Industrial and Commercial Censuses of Taiwan Province 1954 (ICCT) (1954 Taiwansheng Kongshangye Pucha Zongpaokao) (1956). General Report. Taipei: Taiwansheng Kong Shang Pucha Zhishing Hsiaotsu, Taiwan, 1956.

Industrial and Commercial Censuses of Taiwan and Fukien Area (ICCTF), General Report. Taipei: The Committee on Industrial and Commercial Censuses of Taiwan and Fukien Area, Executive Yuan, Republic of China, 1983, and various issues.

Kajiwara, Hirokazu (1995). *Asia's Development Strategies*, (in Japanese). Tokyo: Toyo Keizai Shimposha.

Kakuyama, Sakae (ed.) (1980). *Studies in Western Economic History* (Koza, Seiyo Keizaishi). Volume I. Tokyo: Dobunkan.

Kataoka, Iwao (1921). *Taiwanese Manners and Customs.* Taiwan Nichinichi Shinbunsha, Taipei, Taiwan.

Kato, Toshiaki (1968). *The Americans, Their Culture and Personality*, (in Japanese). Tokyo: Kodansha.

Kawano, Shigeto (1941). *Taiwan's Rice Economy.* Translated into Chinese by Ying-yen Lin. Taiwan Studies No. 102, The Bank of Taiwan, Taipei, Taiwan, 1969.

Lam, D., J.T. Paltiel, and J.H. Shannon (1994), "The Confucian Entrepreneur? Chinese Culture, Industrial Organization, and Intellectual Property Piracy in Taiwan." *Asian Affairs* 20(4) (Winter).

Li, K.T. (1988). *The Evolution of Policy behind Taiwan's Development Success.* New Haven: Yale University Press.

Lin, Man-hong (1994). *Four Hundred Years of Splits and Connections along the Taiwan Strait — A Review of Economic and Trade History* (in Chinese). Taipei: Tze-li Evening News Publisher.

Lin, Ta-hou and Ming-wen Hu (1992). "Development Strategies of Small and Medium Enterprises in Taiwan in Year 2000" (in Chinese). Report to Small and Medium Enterprises Bureau, Ministry of Economic Affairs, submitted by Taiwan Economic Research Institute, June.

Lin, Yi-hsin (1952). "The Characteristics of Industry and Agriculture in Taiwan, Part II" (in Chinese). *Finance and Economics Monthly*, 2(12) (February): 14–17.

Lin, Ping-yan (1997). *The Beginning of Taiwanese Experience: The History of Taiwan Electric Power Inc.* Taipei: The Resource Center of Taiwan Electric Power Inc.

Liu, Bang-li (1996). "The Structure of Post-war Taiwanese External Trade Network" (in Chinese). *Quarterly Journal of the Bank of Taiwan*, 47(1): 125–150.

Liu, Shin-kei (1975). *Post-War Taiwanese Economic Analysis* (in Japanese). Tokyo: Tokyo University Press.

Liu, Tai-ying and Jin-chaung Jian (1983). *The Economic Effects of Japanese Business Investment in Taiwan* (in Chinese). Report to the Committee on Research, Development, and Assessment, the Executive Yuan, submitted by Taiwan Economic Research Institute.

Lopez, Roberts (1971). *The Commercial Revolution of the Middle Ages, 950–1350.* NJ: Prentice-Hall.

Metzger, T.A. and R.H. Myers (1989). "Understanding the Taiwan Experience: An Historical Perspective." *The Pacific Review*, 2(4): 297–311.

Ministry of Economic Affairs (MOEA) (1991). *White Paper on Small-and-Medium-Size Enterprises.* Small-and-Medium Enterprises Bureau, Ministry of Economic Affairs, Taipei, Taiwan.

Mizoguchi, Toshiyuki and Matazi Umemura (eds.) (1988). *Basic Economic Statistics of Former Japanese Colonies, 1895–1938, Estimates and Findings.* Tokyo: Toyo Keizai Shimposha.

Mizoguchi, T. and Y. Yamamoto (1984). "Capital Formation in Taiwan and Korea." In R.H. Myers and M.R. Peattie (eds.), *The Japanese Colonial Empire, 1895–1945.* NJ: Princeton University Press.

Murai, Ohzo (1942). "Aspects of the Problem of Taiwanese Industrialization" (in Japanese). *Takao Keizai Joho*, 5(2): 43–70. Taiwan: Takao Shokoh Kaigisho.

Nakayama, T. (1959). "Taiwan's Buckskin Production and Its Exports to Japan in the 17th Century." *Volumes on Taiwan Studies*, no. 71. Taipei: The Bank of Taiwan.

Numazaki, lchiro (1993). "The Tainanbang: The Rise and Growth of a Banana-bunch-shaped Business Group in Taiwan." *The Developing Economies*, 31(4).

Oh, Ikutoku (1970). *Taiwan, Its History in Agony*, (in Japanese). Tokyo: Kobunsha, rev. ed.

Ohyama, Tsunatake (1942). "The Activities of Zaibatsu in Taiwan" (in Japanese). In Taiwan Keizai Kankokai (ed.), *Taiwan Keizai Nempo* (Chapter 2). Tokyo: Kokusai Nihon Kyokai.

Okurasho, Control Bureau (1952). *Taiwan's Industries, Historical Inquiries into Japanese Overseas Activities* (in Japanese). Vol. 13, Taiwan, Part 2, no. 4. Tokyo: Ministry of Finance.

______ (1954a). *Taiwan's Economy, Vol. I, Historical Inquiries into Japanese Overseas Activities*. Vol. 14, Taiwan, Part 4 (1954a). Tokyo: Ministry of Finance.

______ (1954b). *Statistics Related to Taiwan, Historical Inquiries into Japanese Overseas Activities*. Vol. 16, Taiwan, Part 5. Tokyo: Ministry of Finance.

Pae, S.M. (1992). *Korea Leading Developing Nations: Economy, Democracy, and Welfare*. Maryland: University Press of America.

Pan, Zhi-chi (1947). "Social Economy of Taiwan." *The Quarterly Journal of the Bank of Taiwan*, 1(1) (June).

Provincial Bureau of Accounting and Statistics (PBAS) (1946). *Taiwan Province: Statistical Summary of the Past 51 Years*. Taipei, Taiwan.

Rabb, Theodore K. (1967). *Enterprise and Empire, Merchant and Gentry Investment in the Expansion of England, 1575–1630*. Cambridge, MA: Harvard University Press.

Schak, David C. (1996). "Taiwanese Management Culture: How Best to Explain It." Paper presented at the Conference on Commercial Traditions of Taiwan, Academia Sinica, Taipei, Taiwan, December. Published in Fu-san Huang and Ka-im Ang (eds.), *Taiwan's Commercial Traditions Collected Papers*. Institute of Taiwan Studies, Academia Sinica, Taipei, Taiwan, May 1999. 525–555.

Shi, Ji and Zheng-zhong Li (1978). *A Study of the Methods of Improving Trade Deficits and Imports between China and Japan* (in Chinese). Research Report submitted to the Ministry of Economic Affairs, Taipei, Taiwan.

Skoggard, I.A. (1996). *The Indigenous Dynamic in Taiwan's Postwar Development, The Religious and Historical Roots of Entrepreneurship*. Armonk N.Y.: M.E. Sharp.

Steven, R. (1990). *Japan's New Imperialism*. Armonk. N.Y.: M.E. Sharp.

Su, Bing (1980). *Four Hundred-Year History of the Taiwanese People* (in Chinese). San Jose: Paradise Culture Association.

______ (1986). *Taiwan's 400 Year History, The Origins and Continuing Development of the Taiwanese Society and People*. Washington D.C.: The Taiwanese Cultural Grass Root Association.

Sumiya, Mikio, Shin-kei Liu and Chau-yen Twu (1992). *The Taiwanese Economy*, (in Japanese). Tokyo: Tokyo University Press.

Taiwan Commercial and Industrial Statistics (TCIS) (Taiwan Shoko Tokei), 1921 to 1940, Annual. Taipei: Taiwan Sotokufu.

Taiwan Statistical Data Book (TSDB) (1993). Council for Economic Planning and Development, Republic of China, Taipei, Taiwan. 1993 and various issues.

Tien, Hung-mao (1989). *The Great Transition, Political and Social Change in the Republic of China*. Stanford, CA: Hoover Institution Press.

Tsurumi, P.E. (1977). *Japanese Colonial Education in Taiwan, 1895–1945*. Cambridge, MA: Harvard University Press.

Twu, Chau-yen (1975). *Taiwan under Japanese Imperialism* (in Japanese). Tokyo: Tokyo University Press.

Wakabayashi, Masatake, Sin Kei Liu and M. Matsunaga (1993). *Encyclopedia on Taiwan* (in Japanese). Tokyo: Nihon Taishukan. Translated in Chinese. Taipei: Ke-ning Book Store.

Williams, Eric (1994). *Capitalism and Slavery*. With a New Introduction by Colin A. Palmer. Chapel. Hill, NC: The University of North Carolina Press.

Wu, Hui-lin and Tien-chen Chou (1988). "Small and Medium Enterprises and Economic Development in Taiwan." *Industry of Free China* (March): 15–25.

Yajima, K. (1986). *The Complete Scope on the Taiwanese Economy* (in Japanese). Tokyo: Nihon Keizai Tsusinsha.

Yamada, Atsushi (1994). "Taiwanese Enterprises in Taiwan in the 1930s" (in Japanese). *Kyoto University Jimbun Gakuho* (March): 67–94.

Yamazaki, Kiyoshi (1982). "Upgrading of Industrial Structure in Middle Industrializing Countries and Multinationals" (in Japanese). *Sekai Keizai Hyoron*, 26(4): 28–38.

Yanaihara, Tadao (1929). *Taiwan under Imperialism* (in Japanese). Tokyo: Iwanami Shoten.

Chapter 7

Economic and Cultural Backgrounds of the 228 Incident in Taiwan — An Application of Social Expectation Theory

7.1 Introduction

It is commonly held that under Japanese colonialism, Taiwan was to benefit Japan by developing agriculture, especially rice and sugar, and in return Taiwan became the market for Japanese industrial products, thus completing the usual pattern of colonialism (Ho, 1978, 29; Ranis, 1979, 208). Furthermore, it has been argued that the Taiwanese were discriminated against by the Japanese politically and economically, although their economic condition improved in general (Ho, 1978, 91–102; Grajdanzev, 1942). These overall views are generally correct, at least through the mid-1930s.

The purpose of this project is to show that the situation changed considerably after the Sino-Japanese War in 1937, especially after the outbreak of the Pacific War in 1941, until the end of the war. During this last period, Taiwan was no longer considered a colony which supplied only foodstuffs to Japan, but was treated almost as part of Japan Proper, as far as Japan's newly acquired territories in South China and the South Seas (that is South and Southeast Asia) were concerned. Taiwan was to be fully industrialized with heavy industry and serve as Japan's "unmovable carrier" in the Pacific.

In what follows, Taiwan's industrial progress in the earlier period is described briefly in Section 7.2 from 1931 to the end of the WWII. Section 7.3 describes the Japanization of the Taiwanese people which started in earnest after the Manchurian Incident in 1931. We then show in Section 7.4 how the accelerated social expectations of the Taiwanese people was abruptly terminated by the unthoughtful and inefficient Chinese administration. The 1947 civil strife eventually broke out. In Section 7.5, based on the historical development explained in the last three sections, we construct the "social achievement" as the average of the economic achievement index and the educational/cultural achievement index. We then estimate the "social expectation index" (Feierabend and Feierabend, 1972) by fitting a non-linear regression curve to the "social achievement index." The 2-28 Incident of 1947 is then explained by the discrepancy between these two social indices. Some concluding remarks are given in Section 7.6.

The effects of industrialization and Japanization in the later Japanese period on the Taiwanese people and economy have never been studied systematically nor evaluated critically in the literature. In the post-war period, scholars and writers tend to downplay the implication of the 1947 uprising in Taiwan, which they consider to be simply a short-term deprivation resulting from the brutality and misadministration of the first Chinese governor (Newsman, 1961, 270). This argument is clearly inconsistent with the modern theory of revolution (Davies, 1962) and civil strife (Gurr, 1968), which holds that "the actual state of socioeconomic development is less significant than the expectations that past progress, now blocked, can and must continue in the future" (Davies, 1971, 136). Our study will show how such expectations were fostered under the Japanese regime and provides the missing link between the pre-war and the post-war periods.

Our study will also show that considerable industrial development was already underway in the later pre-war period. This will dispute the usual contention that the Japanese developed Taiwan's agriculture for exploitation only and it was the Chinese who developed Taiwan's industries.

Finally, we propose a new interpretation of the 1947 incident based on the economic factor and also the educational/cultural factor. The introduction of the educational/cultural factor in this paper is unique in the literature of the 2-28 Incident, and our interpretation appears to be consistent with the psychological and institutional approaches of the general theories of political violence (Goldstone, 1986, 1–18).

7.2 Industrialization under the Japanese Regime

Taiwan's industrialization under the Japanese regime may be divided into four periods: Earlier Period, the Quasi War-Stage, the First War-Stage, and the Second War-Stage. The first two periods are rather well documented (Ho, 1977). Our emphasis will be on the last two periods.

7.2.1 *Industrialization in the Earlier Period*

Taiwan's industrialization started with the sugar industry by introducing modern refinery methods. Like Japan, the outbreak of WWI in 1914 stimulated the development of sugar and other related industries. The value of industrial products increased from 79.8 million yen in 1914 to 382.5 million yen in 1929, an increase of more than 500 percent in fifteen years (Shinohara, 1972, Table 13). However, the industrial composition in the total gross value of production only increased from 34.0 percent to 41.3 percent, since other industries such as agriculture, fishing, forestry, and mining also increased at more or less the same magnitude during the same period (Grajdanzev, 1942, 91). There are two qualifications to such rapid growth. First, the bulk of the industrial output, 70 to 75 percent, consisted of foodstuffs, especially sugar (Shinohara, 1972, Table 17). Second, the other products such as chemicals, machinery, and textiles, are also related to the sugar processing industry, like alcohol, sugar refinery machines, machine repairing, and hemp and jute bags as containers for sugar and rice. The rest of the industrial products were produced by small scale firms for local use, like cement, bricks, buckets, etc. (Takahaski, 1937, 423 430).

It should be noted that the Japanese did try to industrialize Taiwan long before the Manchurian Incident in 1931. As early as 1917, they planned to develop 100,000 KW electricity from Sun-Moon Lake, despite the fact that the total electricity consumption at that time was less than 10,000 KW per year. The plan was aborted because of the repression after WWI and because the Japanese were busy developing their own industries in Japan (Takahaski, 1937, 7, 423–24).

The second half of the 1920s and early 1930s was a rather exciting period of resistance by the Taiwanese nationalist or leftist political organizations, characterized by disputes and strikes by numerous industrial and agricultural unions (Hsiao and Sullivan, 1983). Such political resistance and union activities came to end eventually when the Japanese colonial government tightened its political and economic grip on Taiwan as Sino-Japanese tensions escalated in the mid-1930s, while at the same time Taiwan's industrialization program gradually took shape. This program may be divided into three stages: The Quasi War-Stage, from the Manchurian Incident in September 1931 to the outbreak of the second Sino-Japanese War in July 1937; the First War-Stage, from the Sino-Japanese War to the beginning of the Pacific War in December 1941; and the Second War-Stage, which coincided with the period of the Pacific War (Kusui, 1944, 40–43). Each stage is described briefly in the following sections.

7.2.2 *The Quasi War-Stage of Industrialization (1931–1937)*

This stage started rather slowly. The blueprints of industrialization during this stage can be seen from the reports of two study groups sponsored by the Taiwan Government-General: the Ad Hoc Study Board of Industries (Rinji Sangyo Chosa Kai) in November 1930, and the Study Board of Tropical Industries (Nettai Sangyo Chosa Kai) in May 1935. The purpose of the first board was to improve the island's industries to meet international competition imposed on Japan. The recommended program of this board was still heavily biased toward the production of sugar and rice, and emphasized exporting processing industries for sugar, tea, fruits, canned pineapples, etc., although it also recommended developing cement and coal mining (Kusui, 1944, 50–53). By 1935, the only large modern industries other than sugar processing were camphor, opium and alcohol, all of which were monopolized by the government (ibid., 65–66). The recommendation of the second board was more exciting. It proposed to import iron ore, bauxite and rubber from the West Indies and Malaysia, and to develop the island's industries in accordance with the comparative advantages between Taiwan and these areas. This was the starting point of Taiwan's Industrialization (ibid., 64). However, the only result from this recommendation was the establishment of a semi-official Taiwan Colonial Development Corporation (Taiwan Takushoku Kaisha) in November 1936. Its objective was to develop Taiwan as well as Japan to render "economic help" to South China and South Seas (Grajdanzev, 1942, 187).

The major development in this period was the completion of the Sun-Moon Lake hydraulic power plant in 1934, which stimulated the development of an aluminum factory in Kaoshiong (1935) and an iron alloy industry in Keelung (1935). Cheap electricity also stimulated other new industries in this period: shipping (1936), pulp (1935), fertilizer (1937), and oil and fats (1935) (Kusui, 1944, 69–74).

7.2.3 *The First War-Stage of Industrialization (July 1937 to December 1941)*

From mid-1937, the three basic slogans in Taiwan were "industrialization" (Kogyoka), "Japanization" (Kominka), and "Southward Advancement" (Nanshinka) (ibid., 85). The last reflects the adjustment of the Taiwanese economy and politics in response to Japan's interests in South China and the South Seas. The basic industrial policy was stated in the Five-Year Plan of Productivity Expansion (Seisanryoku Kakuju Go-Kanen Keikaku), which was implemented in 1938. The plan was broadly based on Japan's Southward Policy and the Japan-Manchukuo Consolidated Economic Construction Plan (Nichi-Man Sogo Keizai Kensetsu). The emphasis was on Taiwan's as well as Japan's needs, like metal processing and refinery, machinery (including weapons, airplanes and automobiles), chemical and pharmaceutical industries (ibid., 158, 168). On the other hand, partly due to increases in rice productivity in Japan and accessibility of sugar cane in the South Seas, Taiwan's agriculture was forced to reorganize and to place more emphasis on special crops, like cotton, hemp and jute, castor oil, sweet potatoes, etc.

With a vigorous promotion of the program the value of industrial output almost doubled from 363.8 million yen in 1937 to 659.8 million yen in 1941, while the agricultural output increased about 40 percent to 568.9 million yen in 1941. For the first time in the history of Taiwan, the value of industrial output exceeded that of agricultural output in 1939 and afterward[1] (ibid., 157). The weight of the food processing industry steadily decreased from 72 percent to 60 percent, while the proportion of the machinery and metals industries to total output almost doubled.

7.2.4 *The Second War-Stage of Industrialization (January 1942 to August 1945)*

The industrial policy after the outbreak of the Pacific War was to achieve Taiwan's economic independence from Japan proper. Because of difficulty in shipping and also the intensifying war effort in Japan itself, Taiwan was now supposed to build a self-sufficient economy, with the emphasis on

[1]This point is not known in the post-war literature. The feat was repeated only in 1963 and later (Ranis, 1979, 242). In the theory of economic development, this is considered one of the milestones, if not the milestone, of industrialization.

metal and machinery industries. Some miscellaneous goods, like candies, soy sauce, milk products, pencils, leathers, batteries, etc., were now also to be produced on the island (ibid., 379, 381). The greatest achievement in this period was the beginning of construction of the Daikokei River Power Plant and the Takken Dam in western Taiwan, the scale of which was reported to be several times larger than the Sun-Moon Lake Power Plant. There were expansions in the cement industry and merging of the iron and steel factories as steps toward establishment of heavy industry in Taiwan (ibid., 383–387).

Due to the secrecy of the total war, statistical data are not available. However, the highest industrial activities were reached in 1943. Even in 1944, although industrial production started slightly declining due to bottlenecks under the war efforts, production of petroleum, iron products, mica, asbestos, and alcohol exceeded the production targets by more than 60 percent on average, while food stuff and textile industries had been sacrificed (Kaneko, 1947, 100). After 1944, because many plants (like the three new cement plants) were constructed by moving the old facilities from Japan to Taiwan and the difficulty of shipping capital equipment and materials during the second part of the war, accompanied by intensive air raids by the Allied Forces in 1945, the industrialization program eventually came to a halt. Production plummeted. Columns (1) to (4) of Table 7.2 shows national income per capita, net domestic product per capita, and industrial and mining output estimates of Taiwan from 1911 to 1944. This table is explained in detail in Section 7.5.

7.3 Japanization Programs and Southward Advancement

The Japanization program (Kohminka Undo) started in earnest after 1931. The second more intensified program, called the "Public Service Movement of the Emperor's Subjects" (Kohmin Hohkoh Undo) started in 1941. The second stage can be subdivided into three periods: Organization, Adjustment, and Reorganization. The emphasis of this paper is on the second stage of Japanization.

7.3.1 *The First Stage of Japanization — The National Language Movement*

Since the Japanese occupation of Taiwan in 1895, the conflicting policy of assimilating Taiwanese and maintaining Japanese primacy has varied with domestic situations and international environment. With the outbreak of the Manchurian Incident in September 1931, however, the public opinion swung to the right and the Japanese government started suppressing Taiwanese nationalistic movements. In this year, it eliminated the Taiwanese Popular Party (Taiwan Minshuto) and broke up the Taiwanese Cultural Association (Taiwan Bunka Kyokai).[2] In April 1935, it announced the Taiwan Local Self-Government System (Chiho Jichi Sei) which allowed half of the District Assembly members to be elected by popular vote and the other half to be appointed by the Provincial Governors (Wu, 1983, 59–60; Kusui, 1944, 273–278; Kerr, 1974, 161–168.).

In April 1937, anticipating deepening of the Sino-Japanese War and Southward Movement, the Taiwan government advocated "Japanization" (or Assimilation Programs, called Kohminka Undo) and entered into wartime mobilization (August 1937). The ultimate ideals of Japanization are "Oneness between Japanese and Taiwanese" (Naitai Ichi Nyo) and "Taiwan as One Family" (Taiwan Ikka) (Kusui, 1944, 274). The first and foremost measure for attaining this goal is deemed to be popularizing the Japanese language among Taiwanese "as the Japanese spirit rests in the Japanese language..." (Tsurumi, 1977, 133): forbidding them to speak the native Taiwanese language, urging them to think and act like Japanese, even believe in the Japanese God (Shinto; see Kerr, 1974, 168).

Thus, in 1938, within one year, the number of Japanese language training schools (Kokugo Kohshujo and Kan-i Kokugo Kohshujo) increased 40 percent, from 4,369 to 7,306, and the number of students increased by 80 percent, from 263,372 to 472,042 (Wu, 1986, 325). See col. (2) of Table 7.3. The number of language training schools and students doubled the next year to 15,126 and 924,204, respectively (Wu, 1980, 325). Almost every village in Taiwan had an average of about three such language training schools (Wu, 1986, 326), This was done in addition to the accelerated increase (from 2% to 3%) in the percentage of Taiwanese school-aged children enrolled in elementary schools (Ko Gakko). See cols. (1) and (2) of Table 7.3.

Thus, by the end of 1944, 71 percent of six million Taiwanese people could speak and write Japanese. This is a rather unusual achievement considering that, only 15 years before in 1930, slightly more than 12 percent of the Taiwanese spoke Japanese (Oh, 1970, 133). Japanese were much less successful in changing the Taiwanese names and religion. From the

[2]For the earlier activities of these two organizations, see Hsiao and Sullivan (1983); Tsurumi (1977), 192–193.

announcement of "the name-change" campaign in August 1940 to the end of 1943 only 126,101 Taiwanese changed their family name (Lai *et al.*, 1987, Footnote 32, Chapter 4). This represented only 2 percent of the Taiwanese population at the end of 1943. Similarly, by the end of 1941, only 18,020 Taiwanese changed to Shinto, 10.3 percent of the Taiwanese population, and 35,116 changed to Japanese Sect Buddhism, 10.6 percent of the Taiwanese population. This is in great contrast with the Korean case, where the Japanese Colonial Government announced the "name-change" campaign in August 1940. 80 percent of 25 million Koreans changed their name within 6 months (from February to August 1940) (See Ko, 1981, 167–168).

7.3.2 *The Second Stage of Japanization — The Public Service Movement of the Emperor's Subjects*

The spread of language training schools in the later years was apparently aided by the second, more intensified, stage of the Japanization program called "Public Service Movement of the Emperor's Subjects" (Kohmin Hohkoh Undo). It was conceived in April 1941 as Taiwan's counterpart to the Imperial Rule Assistance Movement (Taisei Yokusan Undo) in Japan proper, which was initiated in the previous year. This movement in Taiwan was a form of national mobilization similar to the well-known Chinese people's commune system. The group of the movement was called the "Public Service Association of Emperor's Subjects (Kohmin Hohkoh Kai, KHK), the organization of which is the same as the government organization, that is, the Association and the Government becomes a Two-In-One System (Ni-i Ittai Sei). Thus, the President of KHK was the Governor-General of Taiwan, and the local branches were headed by district governors and local administrators. The lowest echelon was called the Public Service Squad (Hohkoh Han), which coincided with the Ko of the Hoko System (a Ko consists of about 10 families) (Nakai, 1944, 268).

The main promoter of the movement was the Public Service Prime-Aged Brigade (Hoh Koh Soh-nen Dan), to which Japanese veterans and reserved officers were encouraged to participate. Thus, it was a paramilitary organization. The other was called Kikyo Club, which was organized for the purpose of mobilizing unmarried Japanese and Taiwanese women for social services and production. The KHK had three slogans: Training, Production Promotion, and Home-front Maintenance (Kunren, Zohsan, Jugo no Seibi) aiming at leadership and youth training, production for the war effort, and unifying Taiwanese and Japanese under "Taiwan as one family (Taiwan Ikka) (ibid., 273). The resulting New-Japanese-Nationality (Shin Nihon Minzoku) was to play the leadership role among other nationalities in the Greater East Asia Co-Prosperity Sphere (Dai-toa Kyoeiken) (Kusui, 1944, 287).

The development of the KHK may be divided in three periods: organization, adjustment, and reorganization (Nakai, 1944, 272–287).

The organization period: April 1941 to July 1942. During this period the KHK organized 235,089 families into 13,969 Public Service Squads all over Taiwan (the larger squads in the cities ranged from 22 to 98 families).

The adjustment period: July 1942 to December 1943. The KHK either absorbed or created under its control the Public Service Association (Hohkoh Kai) of Buddhism, Theatrical Arts, Literature, Fine Arts, Music, and other cultural organizations. It also created the Public Service Association of Taiwan Industries (Sangyo Hohkoh Kai), of Agriculture, and of Commerce. The Taiwan Youth Brigade (Taiwan Seishohnen Dan) was also transferred to the KHK from the control of the Governor-General of Taiwan. In this period the KHK promoted the New Life Movement (Shin Seikatsu Undo), the National Health Movement (Kenmin Undo), the Common-Use-of-National-Language Movement (Kokugo Johyoh Undo), the Saving-for-Victory Movement (Hissho Chochiku Undo), and the Metal-Collection Movement (Kinzoku Kaishu Undo), etc.

During this period, Industrialization, Japanization and Southward Advancement are considerably strengthened. The local Taiwanese or Chinese culture and religious belief and worship were then despised, suppressed, or destroyed for the sake of carrying out the war, hand in hand with the Japanese (Ko, 1981, 176, 178). This is particularly important since the Special Volunteer Army System (Rikugun Tokubetsu Shiganhei Seido) was put in effect in April 1942 and the Special Volunteer Navy System (Kaigun Tokubetsu Shiganhei Seido) in July 1943. A total of 17,000 Taiwanese "Special Volunteer Soldiers," aged 17 to 30, were drafted by the end of the War (ibid., 185–187).

The reorganization period: December 1943 until the end of War. As the war efforts intensified, the Japanese government published "Taiwan's Decisive-War Readiness Strengthening Measures" (Taiwan Kessen Taisei Kyoka Hohsaku) in October 1943. The major point of reorganization is to add considerably more Taiwanese in the leading position of the KHK

Association. At the same time, as Japan became deeply involved in the War, it mobilized the Taiwanese further by introducing the conscription system in Taiwan (September 1944). With great fanfare, it was touted at the time that Taiwanese were now completely the same as, and equal to, the Japanese. They were "entrusted to fight along with Japanese soldiers" and to "lead the people in South China and the South Seas." They marched to the war front singing "Marching Song[3] of the Emperor's Subject." To the end of the War 207,183 Taiwanese were sent to the front: 80,433 as soldiers, 126,750 either as military laborers or paramilitary servicemen (Gunpu or Gunzoku) (ibid., 187, 265). The paramilitary servicemen were sent to South China and the South Seas as interpreters, agricultural specialists, health workers, and laborers (Kusui, 1944, 316; Grajdanzev, 1942, 192–193).

7.3.3 *Political Gain and Educational Advancement of Taiwanese Leaders*

In the political arena, in order to enlist Taiwanese further support, the Japanese Central Government abolished the Ministry of Colonial Affairs (Takumusho) in September 1942. The Taiwan government was then directly administered by the Ministry of Internal Affairs (Naimusho) of Japan. It was touted at the time that Taiwan was now "promoted" from the colony to the position of "the second Japan Proper" (Daini no Naichi) or "Quasi-overseas" (Jun Gai-chi), as opposed to Japan's newly acquired territories in South China and the South Seas, which were now under the administration of the Ministry of the Great East Asia (Daito-a Sho) (ibid., 206–207; Kusui, 1944, 410). The salaries of Taiwanese bureaucrats were then increased 30 percent to be more or less equal to their Japanese counterparts who drew 40 percent to 60 percent more than their regular salary to serve in the "colony."

After the introduction of conscription in Taiwan in March 1945, the Election Law for the Members of the House of Representatives (Shugi-in Gi-in Senkyo Ho) was revised so that Taiwanese (and Koreans in Korea) candidates could be elected to participate in the national government policy making. Five Taiwanese were to be elected from the five election districts in Taiwan (Ko, 1981, 189–190). At the same time, the Ordinance of the House

[3]This song summarizes what we have described in this section. The complete translation can be found in Lai, Mayer, and Wei (1987), Chapter 4.

of Peers (Kizoku-in Rei) was also revised in March 1945. Three renowned Taiwanese were then selected by the Emperor to represent the Taiwanese in the House of Peers.

In conclusion, we have constructed block by block how the Taiwanese economic, social, and political positions have improved over the 15 years before the end of the War. It started from the language movement, increase in the elementary school enrollment, and as the war intensified, the Taiwanese status was further improved by serving in the Public Service Association, or by becoming Army and Navy Volunteers and eventually as conscripted soldiers. At the same time, the Central Government had also grudgingly conceded to the colonial people by first granting local elections and eventually accepting national representatives in both Houses in Japan Proper. All such improvements in status was, however, apparently the by-product of Japan's national mobilization of the War. We may consider this as a passive upward movement.

On the other hand, as the Japanese language was popularized, as the elementary school enrollments increased, as the economic condition of the island improved, and finally, as the Taiwanese social and political status improved, more and more Taiwanese families would, and could afford to, send their children for higher education. Thus, enrollment in high school and colleges increased. This active upward movement is shown in col. (3) of Table 7.3. Paradoxically, the Japanese in Taiwan were well aware of the fact that higher education for Taiwanese meant a collapse of Japanese primacy. Thus, they used various means to restrict and discriminate against Taiwanese youth from receiving higher education. The frustrated youth from mostly wealthy Taiwanese families went to Japan Proper (Nai-chi) for a college and even a high school education (Wu, 1981, 420; Tsurumi, 1977, Chapter 5; Ko, 1981, 249, 254 258). This active upward trend in the Taiwanese society is shown in column (4) of Table 7.3. The number of overseas students increased steadily, and accelerated after the introduction of the Japanization program.

As the Taiwanese received higher education, the structure of the educational backgrounds of the Taiwanese leadership class also changed dramatically. See Table 7.1 for the composition of the Taiwanese leadership class in terms of schools (Wu, 1983, 210–220). The Taiwanese leaders were selected from various Who's Who in Taiwan published in 1916, 1929, 1934, and 1943, respectively. In the 1910's, there was less than 5 percent Taiwanese leaders who received higher education (middle schools, professional colleges, and overseas education). The proportion increased to

Table 7.1: School Background of Taiwanese Elite

Schooling	1910s	1930s	1940s
Taiwanese (a)	48.3	23.9	4.1
Common (b)	10.9	10.3	12.9
Middle (a)	4.0	12.2	16.5
Normal	4.0	8.9	9.6
Medical	22.5	0.3	1.5
College	0.0	13.4	15.9
Oversee (d)	1.3	18.2	26.9
Unknown	8.9	12.8	12.6
Sum	99.9	100.0	100.0
Total persons	302	1017	1557

Notes: (a) Old style Taiwanese schools in which Chinese Classics were taught in Taiwanese.
(b) Ko Gakko (elementary schools) tor Taiwanese (schools for the Japanese were called Shoh Gakko).
(c) Include graduates from middle schools in Taiwan only.
(d) Include those studied in middle schools in Japan.

almost 50 percent in 1940's (Wu, 1983, 210–220). About half of them studied overseas, mostly in Japan Proper.

7.4 Implications to the Post-war Period — The 2-28 Incident

7.4.1 *Increased Expectations*

We have seen that Taiwan's industries grew rapidly and its economy had improved considerably during the war period. Although in many respects its achievements still trailed behind Japan Proper (Grajdanzev, 1942; Chen, 1955), the Taiwanese were well aware that they were catching up. In fact, in 1938, per capita real Gross Domestic Expenditure (GDE) in Taiwan was merely about 57 percent of that in Japan Proper (Mizoguchi and Nozima, 1981, Tables 3B and 4B), probably the highest relative ratio to Japan the Taiwanese ever enjoyed.[4]

As the Allied bombing on Taiwan intensified after 1944, the Taiwanese also saw that the arrogant Japanese were isolated and discouraged in

[4]This may be compared with 1983 per capital income of Taiwan, which was only 30 percent of that of Japan (US$8,478.6) (TSDB, 1986, 317). In 1977, the figure was only 18 percent! (see Hsiao and Hsiao, 1983, 52.)

the segregated areas of the city without access to food, which was abundant in the farms and villages. The official recognition of the Taiwanese ability through the "Japanization" movement to enlist their support of industrialization and the general war effort, which finally afforded them the status of the "Second Japan Proper" (which might not be appreciated by the islanders), probably enhanced Taiwanese expectations of continued ability to improve their economic and political status. On the other hand, many Taiwanese elite who received better education were still implicitly and explicitly discriminated against.[5] Many even could not find appropriate jobs (Ko, 1981, 249–251). Their pride was hurt. Thus,

> "Conservative or radical, Taiwan's anti-colonialism was a product of Japanese education. Modern Japan no longer held mysteries for the Taiwanese.... They soon discovered that they, who in competition had proved themselves capable of first-class performance, were treated as second-class citizens." (Tsurumi, 1997, 211).

This discovery turned many intellectuals into anti-colonialists.

> "...Taiwanese anti-colonialism was largely a movement of intellectuals...both wings were led by highly educated, Japanese trained islanders." (ibid.).

The defeat of the Japanese in August 1945 was naively conceived by the Taiwanese, especially the Taiwanese intellectuals, as the end of discrimination and a better life. They indulged themselves in being called "brethren" (Tongbau) by the Chinese. After all, for six million Han-Taiwanese, China had been their motherland although she was remote and sometimes forgotten and abused.

The ardent expectations of equalitarian and felicitous life were shortly broken by the Chinese, who were formally substituted the position of the Japanese in Taiwan on October 25, 1945 and acted as foreign conquerors (Su 1980, 701–702; Kerr, 1985, 52, Newsman, 1961, 191, 270; Su, 1986,

---

[5]Among the 6.1 million people in Taiwan in the early 1940s, only 5.5 percent (335,000) were Japanese (Kusui, 1944, 301). Most of them lived in a segregated portion of the cities (Barclay, 1954, 121–124), and occupied all the high governmental positions and professional jobs (45% in 1930) . They also grabbed the important implemental positions in manufacturing, commerce and transportation (Barclay, 1954, 67; Grajdanzev, 1942, 32–33).

59–60). As George Kerr witnessed:

> In the early months of 1946, there was a general pattern of looting. China's coastal cities were war-starved, Taiwan was comparatively rich. Busy gangs sent back their plunder to the continent as fast as possible. They made no distinction between Japanese and Formosan shops and properties, looting... especially feed stocks. At the lowest level in this scavenging period, the National garrison troops–a tattered lot–ill clothed, ill-fed, and poorly disciplined, simply wandered about, sometimes far into the countryside, picking up what they wanted. (Kerr, 1965, 53).

This personal account is corroborated by the repeated issuance of military discipline regulations by the Chinese government (12/17/45, 1/15/46, 7/26/46) and use of military police to maintain law and order on the streets (6/3/46) (The above dates in parentheses are from the chronology in Sasamoto and Kawano, 1968, the same below). Thus, in less than one and a half years under the Chinese administration, the Taiwanese revolted on February 28, 1947. Ten to twenty thousand civilians were massacred[6] (Kerr, 1965; Newsman, 1961, 43, 67, 270).

7.4.2 *Economic, Political and Cultural Deprivation*

Unlike the last several years of the Japanese period, which was shrouded with war time secrecy and confusion, and was a taboo for both post-war Taiwanese and Chinese, the tragedy of the Incident and its aftermath has been rather well-documented, especially by overseas Taiwanese (Kerr, 1965; Lai *et al.*, 1987; Su, 1980, 699–798; Lin, 1984; Wang *et al.*, 1984). For our analysis of social achievement and social expectation, however, the following five points which induced the civil strife may be emphasized:

(1) The economy experienced an unprecedented hyperinflation. The price of rice per catty was 3.6 yen in October 1945; it increased to 16.8 yen in February 1946 and to 80.0 in January 1947 — an increase of over 22-fold (Su, 1980, 737). Despite the Taiwanese objection, Governor Chen Yi established the Taiwan Provincial Trade Bureau (Taiwan-shen Maoyiju) in November 20, 1945, and announced the continuation of the notorious Monopoly Bureau (Zhuang-mai ju) on December 17, 1945. The Trade Bureau managed the confiscated Japanese assets and monopolized

[6]Some estimate as high as 30,000 to 40,000. See Lin (1984), 172; Lai *et al.* (1991), 180, estimates it as 8,000.

all the external trade of Taiwan. The Monopoly Bureau monopolized the supply of basic commodities. These two bureaus became the source of major mismanagement, corruption, and plunder (Lin, 1984, 22–25).

According to an eyewitness at that time,

> "The price of materials controlled by the government increased much faster than the privately supplied materials. For example, the prices of private rice and coal increased 420-fold and 430-fold since year after the War. However, the government controlled sugar increased 790-fold; salt, 1600 fold; cement, 2570-fold; matches, 1000-fold..." (quoted from Zhuang, 1949, 89; Su, 1980, 738).

In addition, in a short time period, the government-operated railroad fare increased five-fold (1/26/46); bus fare, 1.5-fold (4/1/46); and electricity, two-fold (2/8/47). Production activities plunged under inflation, corruption, and plunder. Previously, under the Japanese regime, full-employment was maintained during the War Period. Under the new Chinese regime, despite the departure of 335,000 Japanese (Kusui, 1944, 301), Taiwanese were unemployed and under-employed (Oh, 1870, 140). It is estimated that unemployment reached 800,000 workers (Su, 1980, 738). When another 100,000 young repatriated Taiwanese soldiers and militia from overseas were added, the unemployment reached almost 15 percent of the population.[7] Run-away inflation and massive unemployment were unheard of under the Japanese regime.

(2) It may be argued that inflation in Taiwan was not as severe as that in China, and was influenced by Chinese inflation. This argument is not convincing. Taiwan had a different monetary system from that of China. Foreign exchange between Taiwan and China was prohibited except remittance by the government officials (Kaneko, 1947, 134). Thus, the source of inflation must be sought within Taiwan itself. Since the source of hyperinflation was the increase in the money supply determined by the lending policy of the Bank of Taiwan, which was influenced by government revenue and expenditure, one major reason of increase in the Bank lending was ably observed by Zhuang:

> "The Chen-I government seized 150,000 tons of white sugar from the Taiwan Sugar Company and transferred it without compensation to the

[7]Lai *et al.* (1987), footnote 46, Chapter 5, wrote that "According to an official estimate, unemployment in 1946 came to 8 percent of the workers, a figure probably far lower than the actual number out of work."

> Chinese mainland. The administration's such unreasonable way deprived the Taiwan Sugar Company of working capital. In order to rebuild the company, the Bank of Taiwan had to increase additional 4 billion Taiwan dollars to help finance reconstruction" (Zhuang, 1949, 90, quoted from Lin, 1984, 24).

In addition to the official "plundering" of foodstuff (4/16/46, 8/21/46, 9/17/46), smuggling of sugar, rice, and machinery out of Taiwan was also rampant, as the government tried repeatedly to stop contrabandist (11/30/45, 1/14/46, 3/13/46, 4/11/46, 5/25/46, 12/12/46, 12/15/46). Shortage of foodstuff resulted in famine in the southern part of Taiwan (1/15/46) and an off-shore island (6/12/46). Again, to the Taiwanese, large scale smuggling and famine were unheard of under the Japanese administration.

(3) Within four months after the Chen-I government took over the Japanese regime, Japanese books and magazines were restricted (2/12/46), movie films were censored (7/1/46). Japanese records were banned (8/7/46), and all the unlicensed magazines and newspapers, which were mostly printed in Japanese, were ordered to close (8/24/46). Finally, uses of Japanese in high schools were prohibited (9/14/46). Only a year after the Chinese took over, the Japanese edition of newspapers were eliminated. Since the Japanese and native Taiwanese languages are different from the Chinese language, these and other measures terminated the tool of effective communication among the Taiwanese and between the Taiwanese and the Chinese. Under the pretense of "returning to the motherland," few Taiwanese intellectuals protested.[8]

(4) The upholding of the Chinese language as the official language gave the Chinese government a convenient excuse to fill the higher and more responsible government positions with "Ah Sua," the Chinese "carpetbaggers" (Kerr, 1965, 52) and "Bua Sua" ("half carpetbaggers," who are "Sinicized Taiwanese," who went to China during the war). For example, when Governor Chen-I appointed the new Head Administrators of the eight prefectures in Taiwan, 6 of them were Chinese, 2 were "Bua-Sua", none of them were local Taiwanese (12/27/45). All the mayors, all the division heads of the provincial government, all the managers of government

---

[8]Only after 40 years, an overseas Taiwanese, L.F. Hsieh (1987) was able to criticize the Taiwanese intellectuals at that time for accepting such a dire experience. Interestingly, Hsieh's argument was "gravely protested" by some of the older Taiwanese intellectuals who are still upholding the vision of the "great motherland" (Chen, 1987).

enterprises were filled by Chinese, with one or two exceptions in which "Bua-Sua" were appointed. None were given to the local Taiwanese (Wang, etc., 1984, 40–42), despite the fact that, as we have seen in Section 7.3, Taiwanese leaders were generally more well-educated. The Chinese simply replaced the Japanese in this newly acquired old "territory," and established a colonial government. It has been pointed out that under such émigré regime, people tend to revolt (Welch, 1980).

(5) Two other incidents disappointed the Taiwanese intellectuals during this period:

(a) repeated delay in receiving monthly salaries for school teachers and staff members (5/23/46) . Salaries were even delayed up to three months in Taipei Prefecture (8/10/46);
(b) due to traffic with the Chinese continent after the War, and the mismanagement of the health organization, we saw the prevalence of epidemic diseases (Kaneko, 1947, 33). The black plague was first imported from Fuzhou, on the opposite side of the Taiwan Strait (6/17/46). Over 300 died of cholera in the southern part of Taiwan (7/1/46). It spreaded north to I-Ran (7/19/46) and eventually to Taipei (8/17/46, 11/13/46) and to Taitong (Eastern Taiwan) (1/20/47). Epidemic outbreaks of smallpox were reported in the middle and the southern regions of Taiwan (1/9/47, 1/16/47). Other dreadful, but long subdued diseases like typhoid fever, para typhoid, amoebic dysentery, and epidemic encephalitis were also reported to be in epidemic proportions (5/19/47, see Kaneko, 1947, 35).

7.4.3 *The Incident (Summary)*

Like the Great Russian Revolution, and many other revolutions, the incident started from seemingly routine confrontations between a civilian and a policeman. On February 27, 1947, several investigators from the Taiwan Monopoly Bureau seized contraband foreign cigarettes from a stall woman. When she resisted, she was knocked down on the street. The crowd gathered, and the policeman panicked and fled, shooting one man to death. This ignited the civil strife in Taipei, and spread immediately to the southern part of Taiwan. The Taiwanese almost seized the whole island, but negotiated with the corrupt government. Before long, the Chinese army landed from China, the violence ended with massacre of the Taiwanese people, especially the students and intellectuals in the cities, the villages seemed to be relatively calm. We refer the details to Lai *et al.* (1991), Kerr (1965), Su (1980), and Oh (1970), etc.

7.5 Estimation of Social Achievement and Expectations

In the previous section, we have described how the steadily increasing social achievement and social expectation was suddenly terminated by the Chinese "recovery" of Taiwan. In this section, we construct a model of civil strife which explains the outbreak of the 2-28 Incident. In this paper, the "social achievement" is defined as the average of the economic achievement index (see Section 7.5.1) and the social/cultural achievement index (Section 7.5.2). "Social expectations" are then defined as non-linear regression curve of the social achievement (Section 7.5.3).

Briefly, the social expectation theory (Feierabend *et al.*, 1972, 111) is also called the J-curve model of revolution (Kimmel, 1990, 76), and is part of more general relative deprivation theory (Rule, 1988, 200–223). In Psychology, it is called frustration-aggression hypothesis, namely, frustration nurtures aggression. In Sociology, the frustration of a social group is called systematic frustration, the basic tenant is that systematic frustration leads to violent political action. Social change is a special factor, like other social phenomena, gives rise to systematic frustration. The systematic frustration at any point of time is a function of the gap between the social expectations and social achievement (Feierabend *et al.*, 1972, 111). When social welfare increases over a long time, and plunged suddenly, then revolution occurs. Such a plunge, like the upside-down J letter, increases the gap between expectations and achievement up to the unbearable degree, and incurs political violence.

Gurr (1968) provides some statistical analysis, and found that the long run deprivation (like economic and political discriminations, national separatism, etc.) has greater influence on domestic unrest. However, the most important factors are the combination of three factors: long-run deprivation, short-run deprivation (measured by exports and imports values, inflation, the growth rate of gross domestic product, etc.), and the number of past political conflicts. Our analysis of Taiwan's 2-28 Incident follows these lines of arguments.

In defining and constructing these indices, we have faced a great difficulty in collecting the data immediately before and after the WWII. Thus, we have to make some statistical extrapolation based on the data in the previous years and supplement them with the actual situation prevailed in that period.

7.5.1 *Construction of the Economic Achievement Index*

Since we are interested in the welfare aspects of the Taiwanese people, we have examined some economic data on national income and industrial output in per capita magnitude, which is generally considered as an important measure of social welfare. In Table 7.2, col. (1) presents Hsing's estimate of national income (NI) in 1935–37 prices, col. (2) shows Lee's estimate of Net Domestic Product (NDP) in 1937 prices. Both are taken from Ho (1978), 285, and are converted to per capita magnitude. Columns (3) and (4) list, respectively, Taiwan's industrial and mining output in 1934–36 period. Both are taken from Shinohara (1973), 65. They are listed here for reference, showing the steadily increasing trend of Taiwan's industrialization. The year-end population is given in Ho (1978), 313. To make the four indices comparable, they are converted to pure numbers by taking the 1936 magnitude as the base. They show the growth or decline of the economic variables and are calculated in cols. (5) to (8) of Table 7.2 and graphed in Fig. 7.1. Note that, in order to avoid crowding in the diagram, cols. (7) and (8) are plotted by taking the half of the original indices, measured from the right-hand axis. Thus, in Fig. 7.1, the 1936 index is taken as 50 instead of 100, or equivalently, in the chart, the left axis is measured from 0 to 110 and the right-hand axis is measured from 0 to 240.

From Fig. 7.1, we see that the overlapping part of Hsing's estimate of the (5)NIpc index (the solid light heavy line) and Lee's estimates of the (6)NDPpc index (black heavy dotted line), from 1929 to 1939, have very similar patterns of fluctuations. The per capita industrial output index (7) has larger fluctuations. However, it seems to have more or less similar pattern as the national income estimate in col. (6). Thus, as the economic achievement index (EcAI), which is shown in col. (9), we take the numbers in col. (6) from 1911 to 1928, and take the average of cols. (5) and (6) from 1929 to 1939. The missing data from 1945 to 1946 for the NIpc index (5), and from 1940 to 1946 for the NDPpc index (6) are constructed by extrapolation as explained below. Then the EcAI from 1940 to 1946 are taken as the average of the two estimated indexes (9)EcAI, as shown by the narrow dark line in the middle.

Table 7.2: Construction of Prewar Taiwan's Economic Achievement Index.

	(1)	(2)	(3)	(4)	(5)	(6)	(7)	(8)	(9)
	Real per capita output, OT$				Index, 1936 = 100			((5) + (6))/2	
	NIpc	NDPpc	Indust	Mining	NIpc	NDPpc	InduI	MinI	EcAI
1911		88.54				56.24			56.24
1912		92.28	37.55	2.24		58.62	46.42	45.44	58.62
1913		80.24	28.55	1.87		50.97	35.30	37.93	50.97
1914		76.92	35.11	2.11		48.87	43.40	42.80	50.13
1915		81.66	40.06	2.43		51.87	49.52	49.29	51.87
1916		92.02	50.89	2.48		58.45	62.91	50.30	58.45
1917		97.93	60.61	2.73		62.21	74.92	55.37	62.21
1918		81.45	51.78	2.13		51.74	64.01	43.20	51.74
1919		99.28	45.22	2.51		63.07	55.91	50.91	63.07
1920		86.99	39.92	2.42		55.26	49.35	49.09	55.26
1921		88.35	39.37	2.48		56.13	48.67	50.30	56.13
1922		83.21	48.92	2.84		52.86	60.47	57.61	52.86
1923		95.77	49.80	2.68		60.84	61.56	54.36	60.84
1924		112.18	58.14	2.79		71.26	71.88	56.58	71.26
1925		120.03	60.76	2.99		76.25	75.11	60.65	76.25
1926		116.93	85.81	3.40		74.28	106.09	68.97	74.28
1927		114.13	55.34	3.51		72.51	68.41	71.20	72.51
1928		126.72	67.37	2.92		80.50	83.29	59.23	80.50
1929	117.59	134.52	81.12	3.33	83.40	85.46	100.29	67.55	84.43
1930	121.14	135.82	76.94	3.57	85.91	86.28	95.12	72.41	86.10
1931	114.49	127.46	74.52	3.68	81.20	80.97	92.13	74.65	81.08
1932	124.54	145.58	84.58	3.72	88.33	92.48	104.56	75.46	90.41
1933	119.20	129.95	63.04	3.63	84.54	82.55	77.93	73.63	83.55
1934	119.96	138.17	64.68	4.02	85.08	87.78	79.96	81.54	86.43
1935	138.29	155.33	83.34	4.30	98.08	98.68	103.03	87.22	98.38
1936	141.00	157.41	80.89	4.93	100.00	100.00	100.00	100.00	100.00
1937	128.40	134.62	83.61		91.06	85.52	103.37		88.29
1938	117.31	142.01	86.13		83.20	90.21	106.48		86.71
1939	125.14	126.97	116.35		88.75	80.66	143.84		84.71
1940	120.91		102.02		85.75	77.41	126.12		81.58
1941	129.42				91.79	70.45			81.12
1942	135.10				95.82	62.18			79.00
1943	89.89				63.75	52.59			58.17
1944	60.09				42.62	41.68			42.15
1945					36.26	29.46			32.86
1946					17.95	15.92			16.94

Notes: Population figures are from Ho (1978), 313.
The boxed numbers are estimated figurers. See the text.
Col. (1) Hsing's estimates of national income (NI) in 1935–37 prices (Ho, 1978, 284).
Col. (2) Lee's estimates of Net Domestic Product in 1913 prices (Ho, 1978, 284).
Col. (3) Value of Industrial Output in 1934–36 prices. Shinohara and Ishikawa (ed.) (1972), 65.
Col. (4) Value of Mining Output in 1934–36 price. See ibid.

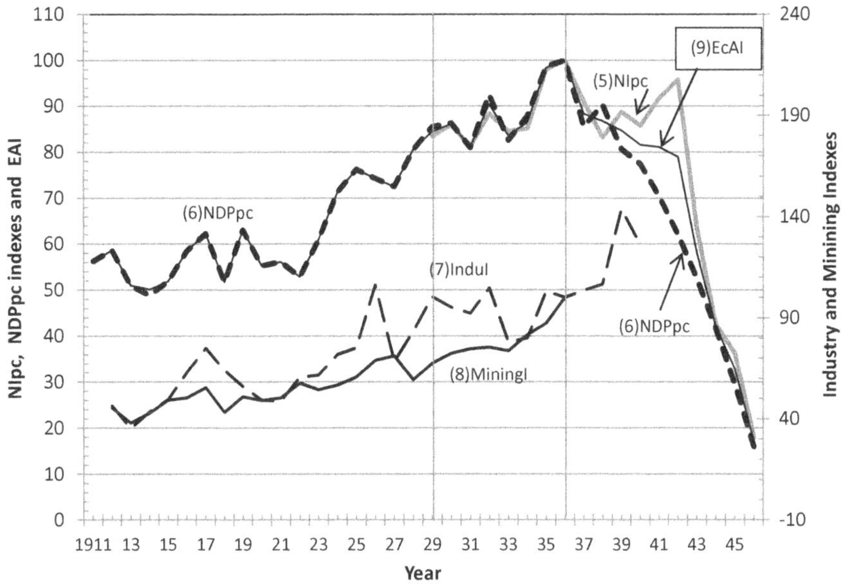

Figure 7.1: Taiwan's Economic Achievement Index (EcAI) 1911–1945, 1936 = 100

We first extrapolate col. (5) to 1945 and 1946 by the following quadratic formula[9]:

$$y = -1.236t^2 + 7.640t + 83.46, \quad R^2 = 0.8939 \tag{7.1}$$

which is estimated by data from 1936 ($t = 1$) to 1944 ($t = 8$) for $n = 8$. The period from 1936 to 1944 are taken to accommodate the declining trend of real income at the end of the War. The estimated values of 1945 and 1946 are obtained by entering $t = 9$ and $t = 10$.

The NDPpc index in col. (6) from 1940 to 1946 was made by extrapolating the up and down trends of NDPpc in col. (6) starting from 1932 and ending at 1939. The forecasting quadratic equation is:

$$y = -0.658t^2 + 5.542t + 80.823, \quad R^2 = 0.964 \tag{7.2}$$

[9]The formulas in this chapter are re-estimated using the graphs of Excel 2013. We tried to fit the quadratic curve such that the per capita values of IN and NDP in 1946 do not become negative.

where the coefficients are estimated by data from 1932 ($t = 1$) to 1939 ($t = 8$) for $n = 8$, which covers the Quasi War-Stage and the first part of the First War-Stage of industrialization. In estimating (7.2) for the NDPpc index (6) to fill the missing data after 1940, we take notice of the steeply declining trend of NIpc index (5) from 1936 to 1944. The estimated values are obtained by entering $t = 9$ to 15.

The economic achievement index from 1940 to 1945 is the average of the corresponding estimated indices of cols. (6) and (7). It is shown in col. (9) and drawn as the dark narrow line (9) EcAI from 1911 to 1946.

7.5.2 *Construction of the Educational/Cultural Achievement Index*

Based on the discussion in Section 7.3, we have chosen the student enrollment in various levels of schools in Taiwan as the surrogate index for educational and cultural achievement of the Taiwanese. Naturally, the choice is also based on the fact that the time-series data on education are readily available. Column (1) (CmSchl) of Table 7.3 shows the percentage of Taiwanese school-aged children enrolled in common (that is, elementary) schools.[10] Note that the percentage increased slowly but steadily, and accelerated slightly in the last several years (Tsurumi, 1977, 148). Column (2) (JLSchl) shows the increase in the enrollment in Japanese language training schools (Wu, 1986, 325). It increased steadily from 1931 to 1939 and declined afterwards. Column (3) (prfnl, the professionals) is the number of the Taiwanese graduates from medical, normal, vocational (including agricultural and forest, commercial, and industrial), and the Imperial Taihoku University (Wu, 1981, 416–418). The number fluctuated wildly, seemingly reflecting the ambivalent Japanese attitude toward the ideals of assimilation and the "Japanese primacy." It may also reflect a high dropout rate of dismayed Taiwanese students. Note that the number does not include high school graduates, and will be much larger if the data were available. Column (4) (In Jpn) shows the number of Taiwanese students enrolled in Japan Proper attending high schools, vocational schools, colleges, and universities (Wu, 1981, 4; Tsurumi, 1977, 128). The number increases steadily and accelerates rapidly after 1931.

Columns (1) to (4) are recalculated as percentages relative to the number in 1936 in cols. (5) to (8), and are plotted in Fig. 7.2. Note

[10]We do not have the original numbers. For the actual enrollment numbers from 1932 to 1941, the pattern of percentage change in enrollment with 1936 as the basis is the same as those shown in col. (5) for the same period.

Table 7.3: Construction of Prewar Taiwan's Educational/Cultural Achievement Indexes

Year	(1)	(2)	(3)	(4)	(5)	(6)	(7)	(8)	(9)	**(10)**	**(11)**
	%	Prsn	prsn	prsn	Index, 1936 = 100, %				((5)+(8))/2	**Social**	**Social**
	CmSchl	JLSchl	Prof	InJpn	Cmschl	JLSchl	Profnl	InJpn	EdCuAl	**Achv**	**Exptn**
1911	6.06		113	132	13.84		68.48	5.60	9.72	32.98	36.03
1912	6.63		127	176	15.14		76.97	7.47	11.30	34.96	36.11
1913	8.32		171	264	19.00		103.64	11.20	15.10	33.04	36.42
1914	9.09		189	315	20.76		114.55	13.36	17.06	33.60	36.96
1915	9.63		183	325	21.99		110.91	13.79	11.89	34.88	37.73
1916	11.06		183	327	25.26		110.91	13.87	19.57	39.01	38.72
1917	13.14		223	415	30.01		135.15	17.61	23.81	43.01	39.94
1918	15.71		200	482	35.88		121.21	20.45	28.16	39.95	41.39
1919	20.69		293	493	47.25		177.58	20.92	34.09	48.58	43.07
1920	25.11		282	564	57.34		170.91	23.93	40.64	47.94	44.98
1921	27.22		534	649	62.16		323.64	27.54	44.85	50.49	47.11
1922	28.82		599	757	65.81		363.03	32.12	48.97	50.91	49.47
1923	28.60		640	862	65.31		387.88	36.57	50.94	55.89	52.06
1924	28.69		684	850	65.52		414.55	36.06	50.79	61.02	54.88
1925	29.51		506	828	67.39		306.67	35.13	51.26	63.15	57.93
1926	28.42		247	886	64.90		149.70	37.59	51.25	62.76	61.20
1927	29.18		412	1240	66.64		249.70	52.61	59.63	66.06	64.71
1928	29.79		447	1405	68.03		270.91	59.61	63.82	72.16	68.44
1929	31.11		292	1449	71.04		176.97	61.48	66.26	75.34	72.39
1930	33.11		315	1317	75.61		190.91	55.88	65.75	75.92	76.58
1931	34.20	35649	153	1501	78.10	17.37	92.73	63.68	70.89	75.99	81.00
1932	35.87	38594	176	1627	81.91	18.81	106.67	69.03	75.47	82.94	85.64
1933	37.44	52059	197	1520	85.50	25.37	119.39	64.49	75.00	79.27	90.51
1934	39.33	98658	196	1971	89.82	48.08	118.79	83.62	86.72	86.64	95.61
1935	41.47	131148	170	2185	94.70	63.91	103.03	92.70	93.70	96.04	100.93
1936	43.79	205214	165	2357	100.00	100.00	100.00	100.00	100.00	100.00	106.49
1937	46.69	263372	162	2812	106.62	128.34	98.18	119.30	112.96	100.63	112.27
1938	49.82	472042	147	4123	113.77	230.02	89.09	174.93	144.35	115.53	118.28
1939	53.15	924204	163	5407	121.37	450.36	98.79	229.40	175.39	130.05	124.52
1940	57.56	763263	223	6015	131.45	371.94	135.15	255.20	193.32	142.24	130.98
1941	61.60	692469	336	6676	140.67	337.44	203.64	283.24	211.96	153.47	137.68
1942	61.56	531745	200	7091	140.58	259.12	121.21	300.85	220.72	159.27	144.60
1943	65.82				150.31			353.00	251.65	156.89	151.75
1944	71.31				162.85			388.96	275.90	161.72	159.13
1945					167.90			424.91	296.41	166.46	166.74
1946									0.00	23.51	36.18

Notes: Estimated numbers are enclosed in a box. See the text.

Column (1) Percentage of Taiwanese school-aged children enrolled in common elementary schools (CmSchl), 1907–44, from Tsuruai (1977), 148.

Column (2) Enrollment in all kinds of Japanese language training schools (JLSchl). Wu (1986), 325.

Column (3) Graduates of normal, medical, and vocational schools, and Imperial Taihoku University, the professionals (Prof). Wu (1981), 416–418.

Column (4) Enrollment of Taiwanese in high schools, colleges, and universities in Japan (inJpn). Wu, (1981), 420; Tsurumi (1977), 128.

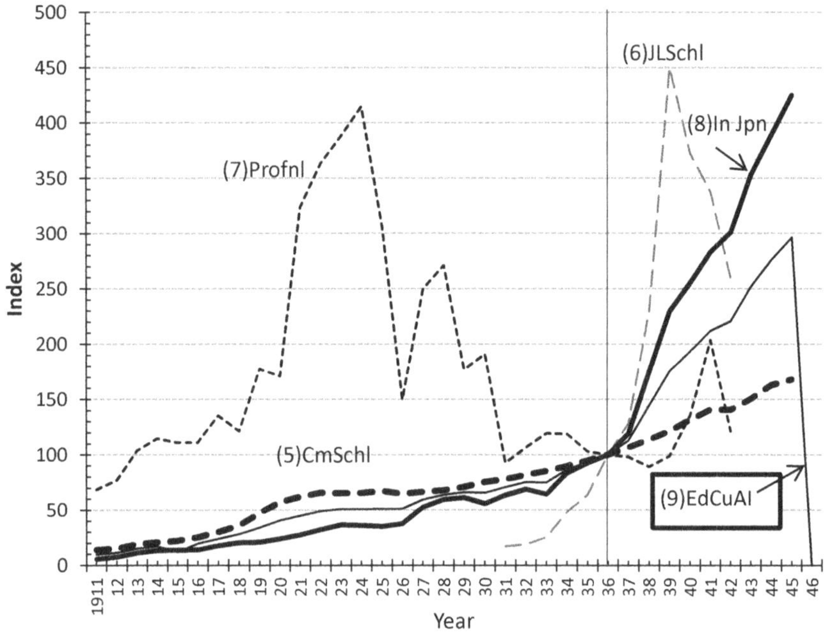

Figure 7.2: Taiwan's Educational/Cultural Achievement Index (EdCuAI) 1911–1945, 1936 = 100

that col. (5) should be interpreted as the change in the percentage of the Taiwanese elementary school enrollment relative to that percentage in 1936. It shows the steady increase in the percentage of enrollment. Since col. (5) (or (1)) and (8) (or (4)) show steady changes, and col. (8) shows the accelerated change after 1936, which coincide with the Taiwanese achievements described in Section 7.3, the average of these two series is taken to be the Educational/Cultural Achievement index (EdCuAI), shown in col. (9).

Column (5) is extrapolated linearly[11] to 1945 from 1944 using the following formula:

$$y = \underset{(59.395)}{106.65} + \underset{(17.837)}{7.66t}, \quad R^2 = 0.9815 \tag{7.3}$$

[11]From the shape of the curves, we extrapolated the missing values with linear equations in this section. We prefer linear equations since the t-values for the coefficients can be calculated. In (7.3) and (7.4), the t-values show the coefficients are (very) significant under the null hypothesis that the true coefficients are zero.

where t (for time) ranges from 1937 (=0) to 1944 (=7) for n = 8. The t-value is in the parentheses (same below). Similarly, col. (8) is extrapolated to 1945 from 1943 by

$$y = \underset{(11.422)}{137.26} + \underset{(9.059)}{35.97t}, \quad R^2 = 0.9535 \tag{7.4}$$

where t ranges from 1937 (=0) to 1942 (=5) for n = 6. The education/cultural achievement index (EdCuAI) in col. (9) is defined to be the simple average of cols. (5) and (8).

7.5.3 *Estimation of Social Achievement and Expectations*

The Social Achievement is defined simply as the average of the economic achievement index (EcAI) of col. (9), Table 7.2, and Educational/Cultural achievement index (EdCuAI) of col. (9), Table 7.3. This is shown in col. (10) of Table 7.3 and graphed in Fig. 7.3 as the curve with a zig-zag pattern. The curve abruptly turned down in 1946 because of the denial of the use of Japanese language and publications, negating all the past educational and cultural achievement. Thus, zero is entered at the end of col. (9). In fact, in 1946, the only one left is the economic achievement index, which is also reduced to a very low level due to the aftermath of the war, mismanagement of the economy and society, and the corruption of the

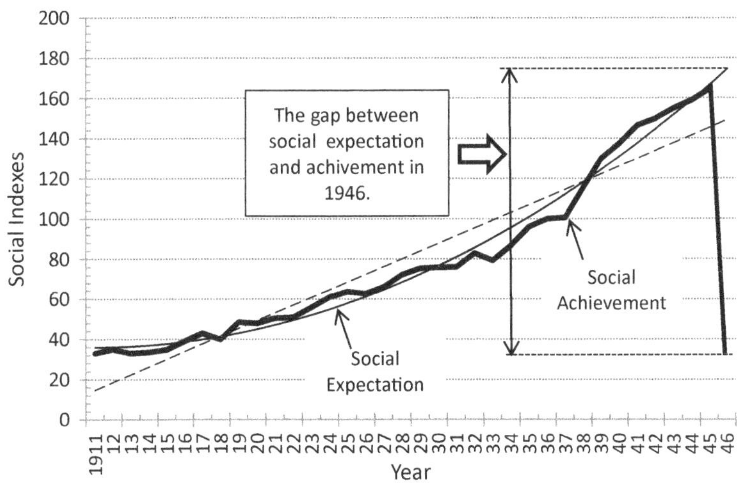

Figure 7.3: Social Achievement and Social Expectations
Taiwan 1911–1946

Chinese bureaucrats. We then fit a linear and quadratic regression curve to this social achievement curve by estimating the coefficients of a linear equation as:

$$y = \underset{(2.6562)}{10.875} + \underset{(19.3729)}{3.843t}, \quad R^2 = 0.9192 \tag{7.5}$$

for 1911 to 1945 (n = 35). A slightly better result can be obtained if we fit a quadratic equation,

$$y = 0.114t^2 - 0.2597t + 36.175, \quad R^2 = 0.985 \tag{7.6}$$

as shown in col. (11) of Table 7.3 from 1911 (t = 1) to 1946 (t = 36), and drawn as the light black curve in Fig. 7.3. We also draw the linear estimation (7.5), the slashed line in Fig. 7.3, for comparison.

Note that, by extrapolation, the social expectation curve continues to increase in 1946, leaving a huge gap between social expectation and social achievement, resulting in one of the most tragic incidents of civil strife in Taiwanese history.

7.6 Some Concluding Remarks

The 2-28 Incident (Gee Gee Patt Su-kia, as commonly called by the Taiwanese) is probably the first political violence which occurred in various developing countries during the first two decades since the end of the WWII. Unlike many similar incidents, a new nation did not emerge from this tragedy. Nevertheless, the analysis of this paper indicates that the Incident provides a classical case study of the general theories of political violence (Goldstone, 1986, 1–18).

7.6.1 *On Applicability of Three General Theories of Political Violence*

The applicability of the Davies-Gurr psychological approach to this case is obvious: "when people expect a better life, and have their expectations frustrated, are they likely to develop feelings of aggression and resentment." (Goldstone, 1986, 5). This paper has explained in details how the expectations were formed and how the frustrations set in before and up to the Incident. We go a step further and constructed the expectation curves which explain clearly the occurrence of the violence.

The second general theory of political violence is the social institution approach. In our case, this approach may be interpreted broadly as the change of the Japanese value system, which represented a modern civilized society, to the Chinese value system, which was a semi-feudalistic underdeveloped society (Su, 1980, 691–693, 739–742). This view may be summarized in a remark by a Chinese in his fifties in 1969 (Tsurumi, 1977, 156):

> "Those stupid Taiwanese, all they learned under the Japanese was to line up in queues."

The "cultural shock" of the two value systems resulted in an imbalance in the Taiwanese intellectual class and made the society unstable.

The third general theory is the resource mobilization approach. It asserts that "political violence is likely to occur only when aggrieved parties have the means to make such violence count–namely when they have the resources and the organization to take significant actions." We do not think this theory can explain the occurrence of the 2-28 Incident, as it was instantaneous, and there was no specific class or party to really take advantage of the general social discontent and led to a revolution. However, it seems to us that this theory does explain why the 2-28 Incident failed.

7.6.2 *On Some What-if Questions*

Our social achievement index consists of economic and educational/cultural indices, and we explained that the second index reduced to zero due to the Chinese government's ban on the use of the Japanese language in 1946, depriving the Taiwanese effective means of communication. A question may be asked that, from cols. (10) and (11), whether the political violence might be avoided if the Chinese government acted more considerately and tolerated the use of the Japanese language, thus reducing the gap between the social achievement and social expectation.

Our answer is affirmative. Since from our analysis, this will imply that no excuse for discrimination against what the Chinese called the "Taiwanese brethren", based on the language difference, and the Taiwanese leaders would have been appointed to Taiwan government's policy making positions. One only need imagine that if the well-respected and well-educated Lim Hian-dong were appointed as the Governor-General of Taiwan instead of General Chen Yi! However, considering the semi-feudalistic characters of Chinese leadership and society at that time, this is simply impossible. (Chen Yi, like Chiang Kai-sek, had been associated with Shanghai's notorious "Green Gang" in the days before Chiang's rise to power (Su, 1980; Kerr, 1965, 49)).

Thus, the tragedy could not have been avoided short of Taiwanese independence or American occupation of Taiwan. However, the Americans gave up the opportunity when they had decided to land on Okinawa just before the War ended (Kerr, 1965). On the other hand, while, at least up to October 1942, the Chinese treated Taiwan as an independent country (see Hsiao and Sullivan, 1979, 464), most Taiwanese considered China as their motherland, and were proud of having Chinese origin, as shown by the unusual resistant of the Taiwanese to change their family names to the Japanese names. From this and also by the fact that, even today, those Taiwanese intellectuals who resisted the Japanese in the early days still cannot distinguish between having a Chinese-origin and being a Chinese citizen (as revealed in Chen, 1987), we feel that independence at that time was simply out of the question.

Thus, the Taiwanese were doomed. The tragedy of the Incident was probably deeply seated in the nature of Chinese culture. It has been argued that "peoples whose politics link to Chinese culture were severed and, as in Taiwan's case, replaced by an alternative cultural tradition, transmitted through instruction in the Japanese language, ceased to be an integral part of the Chinese nation and emerged as a different "nationality," yet without losing all of their Chinese qualities" (Hsiao and Sullivan, 1979, 460). Since Taiwan was then "returned" to China, instead of being granted independence, it is not surprising when the first Chinese general who arrived in Taiwan remarked in his public address that (Kerr, 1985, 49):

> "Taiwan is a 'degraded territory' and the Formosans a 'degraded people.' The island was beyond the passes (Kuan wai), beyond the pale of true Chinese civilization."

As Kerr had aptly observed, this address "sets the tone for the subsequent Chinese occupation of Formosa." (Kerr, op. cit.)

7.6.3 *Implications for Post-Incident Development*

Two years after the Incident, in 1949, the new Chinese government in Taiwan started land reform which was completed in 1953. It has been reported to be a great success (Chen, 1961). We submit that the "success" is not very surprising since, like the similar reform in China after a successful revolution, it was paid at the bloody cost of the unsuccessful uprising in 1949. In both cases, all the potential opposition was totally annihilated in the process of civil strife in the previous years. Our analysis also reveals that the catch-up mentality of the Taiwanese people, as we have mentioned in Section 7.4.1, may have played an important role in the post-war economic development of Taiwan. In this connection our observation also seems to point to another question. Although the rapid post-war development of Taiwan was touted as a "miracle," the Taiwanese development was far less miraculous compared to post-war Japan. Hence, the relevant and more meaningful question that should be asked is why the post-war economic development of Taiwan has been so slow.

Acknowledgments

I am grateful to Professor Gail Bernstein, University of Arizona, former Chairman of the North East Asia Council of the Association of Asian Studies, for a travel grant in 1983 to the Hoover Institution for collecting data. I am also indebted to Drs. Ramon H. Myers, Fu-mei Chang Chen, both of the Hoover Institution, Professors Ted R. Gurr, Thomas F. Mayer, and Messrs. Seon Jai Kim and David G. Shaw, all of the University of Colorado at Boulder, for help at various stages of development of this paper. This paper has been translated in Chinese by Dr. Yi-Hsiong Lin of Colorado Department of Statistics and was published in Hsiao (1992). In preparing for this chapter, all charts and tables have been redrawn using Microsoft Excel program. All errors of omission and commission are the author's.

References

Barclay, George (1954). *Colonial Development and Population in Taiwan.* NJ: Princeton University Press.

Chen, Chen (1961). *Land Reform in Taiwan.* Taiwan: China Publishing Co.

Chen, Chi-Chang and others (1987). "A Letter to Minjinbao from former People's Party leading members." No. 9. Taipei: Minjinbao Weekly, April 30, 1987.

Chen, S.H. (1955). "Political Growth and Social Change in Taiwan." *Bulletin of the Department of Archeology and Anthropology*, National Taiwan University, No. 5, 76–103.

Davies, J.C. (1971). "Toward a Theory of Revolution." *The American Sociological Review*, 6(1): 5–19, February 1962. Collected in *When Men and Why*, ed. by J.C. Davies, New York: Free Press.

Feierabend, I.K. and R.L. Feierabend (1972). "Systematic Conditions of Political Aggression: An application of frustration-Aggression Theory." In I.K. Feierabend, R.L. Feierabend and T. Gurr (eds.), *Anger, Violence, and Politics, Theory and Research* (Chapter 9). Engelwood Cliffs, NJ: Prentice-Hall, Inc.

______, ______, and B.A. Nesvold (1972). "Social Change and Political Violence: Cross-National Patterns." In I.K. Feierabend, R.L. Feierabend and T. Gurr (eds.), *Anger, Violence, and Politics, Theory and Research* (Chapter 7). Engelwood Cliffs, NJ: Prentice-Hall, Inc., 1972.

Grajdanzev, A.J. (1942). *Formosa Today*. New York: Institute of Pacific Relation.

Goldstone, J.A. (ed.) (1986). *Revolution: Theoretical, Comparative and Historical Studies*. Belmont, CA: Wadworth/Thompson.

Gurr, T. (1968). "A Causal Model of Civil Strife: A Comparative Analysis Using New Indices." The *American Political Science Review*, 1104–1124. Collected in *When Men Revolt and Why*, J.C. Davies (ed.), New York: Free Press, 1971.

Ho, S.P.S. (1978). *Economic Development of Taiwan, 1860–1970*. New Haven: Yale University Press.

Hsiao, F.S.T. (1992). "Economic and Cultural Backgrounds of the 228 Incident in Taiwan — An Application of Social Expectation Theory" (in Chinese). Originally written in English under the title "Industrialization, Japanization, and Social expectations — An analysis of the 1947 Civil Strife in Taiwan." Was translated into Chinese by Dr. Yi-Hsiong Lin, and published in Yong-hsing Chen (ed.), *Proceedings of 1991 Conference on Research on the 228 Incident* (77–113). Taipei: the U.S.-Taiwan Cultural Exchange Foundation, 228 Citizen's Study Group, and Modern Research Foundation.

Hsiao, F.S.T. and M.C.W. Hsiao (1983). "Some Development Indicators of Taiwan: A Comparative Study." *Journal of Economic Development*, 8(1) (July): 45–58.

______ and L.R. Sullivan (1983). "A Political History of the Taiwanese Communist Party: 1928–1931." *Journal of Asian Studies*, 42(2): 269–289.

______ and ______ (1979). "The Chinese Communist Party and the Status of Taiwan, 1928–1943." *Pacific Affairs*, 52(3) (Fall): 446–467.

Hsieh, Li-Fa (1987). "Chong Er-er-ba" Shijian Kan Taiwan Zhishi Funzi de Lash Mandan (From 2-28 Incident to see the blind spot of the Taiwanese Intellectuals), *Minjinbao* (*Journal of Democratic Progressive Party*) No. 2, Reproduced in *Taiwan Tribune*, March 2.

Kaneko, Shigeo (ed.) (1947). *Furoku: Shuhsen Zengo no Taiwan ni Kansuru Shiryo* (*Appendix: Materials on Taiwan Before and After the End of the War*). Vol. 17, Taiwan, No. 3 of Part 6, in *Ohkrasho* (Ministry of Finance), *Nihonjin no Kaigai Katsudo ni Kansuru Lekishiteki Chosa* (*Historical Survey of Japanese Overseas Activities*).

Kerr, G.H. (1965). *Formosa Betrayed*. Boston: Houghton Mifflin Co.

______ (1974). *Formosa Licensed Revolution and the Home Rule Movement, 1895–1945*. Honolulu: The University of Hawaii Press.

______ (1985). *The Taiwan Confrontation Crisis*. Washington, D.C.: Formosan Association of Public Affairs, 1985.

Kimmel, M.S. (1990). *Revolution, A sociological Interpretation*. Philadelphia: Temple University Press.

Ko, Sho-do (Ng, Chiao-dong) (1981). *Taiwan Sotokufu* (*Taiwan Governor-General Building*). Tokyo: Kyoikusha Lekishi Shinsho.

Kusui, Ryuzo (1944). *Senji Taiwan Keizai Ron* (*Studies on the War-time Taiwanese Economy*). Taihoku: Nanpo Jinbun Kenkyujo.

Kuznets, S. (1979). "Growth in Structural Shifts." In W. Galenson (ed.), *Economic Growth and Structural Change in Taiwan* (Chapter 1). Ithaca: Cornell University Press.

Lai, J., R.H. Myers and W. Wei (1987). *Fourteen Days and Forty Years: A Study of the February 28, 1947 Incident in Taiwan*. Stanford, CA: Stanford University Press.

Lin, Qi-Xu (1984). "Taiwan Er-er-ba Shi Jian Zonghe Yanjiu" (A Comprehensive Study of the 228 Incident). *Taiwan Tribune*, California, February.

Mizoguchi, Toshiyuki and K. Nozima (1981). "Kyu Nihon Teikoku no Kokunai Sohseisan to Sohshishutsu no Suikei" (Estimation of Gross Domestic Product and Gross Domestic Expenditure of Previous Japanese Empire." *Keizai Kenkyu* (July): 232–256.

Nakai, J. (1944). "Kohmin Hohkoh Undo no Shinten (Progress of the Public Service Association of Emperor's Subjects)." In *Taiwan Keizai Nenpoh* (*Taiwan Economic Year Book*). Taihoku: Taiwan Keizai Kanko Kai.

Newsman, R.P. (1961). *Recognition of Communist China, A Study in Argument*. New York: Macmillan Co.

Oh, Iku Toku (1970). *Taiwan, Kumon suru sono Rekishi* (*Taiwan: Its History in Agony*). Tokyo: Kobundo.

Ranis, G. (1979). "Industrial Development." In W. Galenson (ed.), *Economic Growth and Structural Change in Taiwan*. (Chapter 3, 206–262). Ithaca: Cornell University Press.

Rule, J.B. (1988). *The Theory of Civil Violence*. Berkley: University of California Press.

Sasamoto, T. and S. Kawano (eds.) (1968). *Taiwan Keizai Sohgoh Kenkyu-Shiryo Hen* (*A Comprehensive Studies of Taiwanese Economy-Collection of Data*). Tokyo: Azia Keizai Kenkyujo (Institute of Developing Economies).

Su, Bing (1980). *Taiwanren Sibainian Shi* (*Four Hundred Years of the Taiwanese People*). San Jose: Paradise Culture Association.

______ (1986). *Taiwan's Four Hundred Year History, The Origin and Continuing Development of the Taiwanese Society and People*. Washington, D.C.: Taiwanese Cultural Grassroots Association.

Shinohara, Miyohei (1972). "Industrialization and Trade" (in Japanese). In Miyohei Shinohara and Sigeru Ichikawa (eds.) cited in this References.

Shinohara, Miyohei and S. Ishikawa (eds.) (1972). *Taiwan no Keizai Seichoh* (*Economic Growth of Taiwan*). Tokyo: Ajia Keizai Kenkyujo (Institute of Developing Economies)

Taiwan Statistical Data Book (TSDB) (1986). Council for Economic Planning and Development, Republic of China.

Takahashi, Kamekichi (1937). *Gendai Taiwan Keizairon* (*Studies in the Modern Taiwanese Economy*). Tokyo: Chigura Shabo.

Tsurumi, Patricia E. (1977). *Japanese Colonial Education in Taiwan, 1895–1945*. Cambridge, MA: Harvard University Press.

Wang, Jian Sheng, Hsian Yi Ji and Yong Chuan Chen (1984). *1947 Taiwan Er-Er-Ba Kemin* (*1947 Taiwan 228 Revolution*). Los Angeles: Taiwan Arts and Publishing, Inc.

Welch, C.E. Jr. (1980). *Anatomy of Rebellion*. Albany: State University of New York.

Wu, Wen Hsing (1983). *Riju Shichi Taiwan Shufan Jiaoyu Chi Yanjiu* (*A Study of Normal Education in Taiwan During the Japanese Occupation Period*). Taipei: Research Institute of History, National Taiwan Normal University.

______ (1986). Riju Shichi Taiwan Shehuei Lindao Jiecheng Chi Yanjiu (A Study of the Taiwanese Social Leadership Class during the Japanese Occupation Period). Doctoral Thesis. Taipei: National Taiwan Normal University, Research Institute of History.

______ (1981). *Riju Shichli Taiwan de Jiaoyu yu Shehuei Lindao Jiechenq zhi Suchao* (*Education in Taiwan and Portrayals of Social Leadership Class during the Japanese Occupation Period*). *Proceedings of Conference on History and Chinese Social Changes*. Taipei: Institute of Three People's Principles, Academia Sinica.

Zhuang, Jia-nong (1949). *Fen-nu de Taiwan* (*Indignant Taiwan*). Hong Kong: Zhiyuan Shuju.

Part III

Early Postwar Economic Development

Chapter 8

Product Life-Cycle and Diffusion of Technology — The Taiwanese Case

8.1 Introduction

Apart from contributions to the growth of national income, employment, capital formation, and exports, direct foreign investment is considered as a major channel to bring technological know-how to the host country, creating backward and forward linkages, which stimulate local development of industries (Lall, 1978; Hsiao, 1992; Sekiguchi and Du, 1986). The purpose of this paper is to examine empirically the validity of the product life-cycle theory as applied to the relation between multinational direct foreign investment (DFI) and technology transfer of the television industry in Taiwan. The applicability of the product life-cycle theory has been pointed out by Yeh (1980). In this paper, we use nonlinear regression analysis to verify the life-cycle theory for the television industry in Taiwan, and also measure the rate of technology diffusion in the case of the black and white television industry.

The paper is organized as follows. Section 8.2 discusses the relationship between DFI and product life-cycle theory, using the production of black and white television receivers in the United States, Japan, and Taiwan as an example. After televisions were introduced in Taiwan in 1962, we saw the rise of a television industry in Taiwan, and Taiwan has since become one of the largest exporting countries of televisions, computer terminals and monitors in the world (Yeh, 1980; Hsiao, 1992). In Section 8.3, we discuss the pattern of production of this product, and in Section 8.4, we discuss the pattern of entry and exit of new television producing firms in the Taiwanese electronics industry from 1962 to 1978. Finally, in Section 8.5, we measure the rate of diffusion of television production. Some concluding remarks are given in the last section.

8.2 DFI and Product Life-Cycle Theory

The product life-cycle model introduces elements of long-run industrial development and industrial location into international trade theory. It considers that many industrial products go through a life-cycle of three stages consisting of new, maturing, and standardized product periods, respectively. The location of industries and the direction of trade change with the product life-cycle. The theory as described by Vernon (1966) and Tilton (1971) may be summarized as in Fig. 8.1. In what follows, the years of events and international trade data for Taiwan, Japan, and the United States are taken from Yeh (1980), which is based on various U.N. *Yearbooks of Production Statistics* and *Japan Electronic Industry Yearbooks*, etc.

From the empirical observations, inventions generally occur in advanced countries like the United States, which provides easier access to the scientific knowledge and has higher income and higher wage rates. New products and their input specifications are usually unstandardized. The products have low price elasticity of demand. The market dimension, rivals, etc. are uncertain. All these factors prompt new products to be produced and consumed in the United States. Later, with a "demand lag," new products are exported to other advanced countries in Western Europe, which have more or less similar demand and production structures as the United States.

In terms of Fig. 8.1, production of a certain product, in this case the Black and White television receivers (BWTV), actually started in the United States in 1939. This is shown by the Q + M curve in Panel (a). The Product life-cycle theory predicts that, after a "demand lag", exports to other advanced countries, in this example, say Japan, will take place sometime around Year a. This is shown by the dotted curve (X) in Panel (a). Thus the difference between the Q + M curve and the dotted (X) curve is the domestic consumption (C). The dotted and slashed curves with X and M in parentheses in the figures show the "theoretical" curves, and the solid curves shows the actual occurrence of the events, at least for the starting points of the curves. Now if the "advanced countries" solely consists of Japan, according to the theory, Japan should have imported BWTV in Year a, as shown by the dotted curve (M) in Panel (b).

In the maturing stage, as standardization in inputs and also in products start taking place with product differentiation, economies of scale set in, and

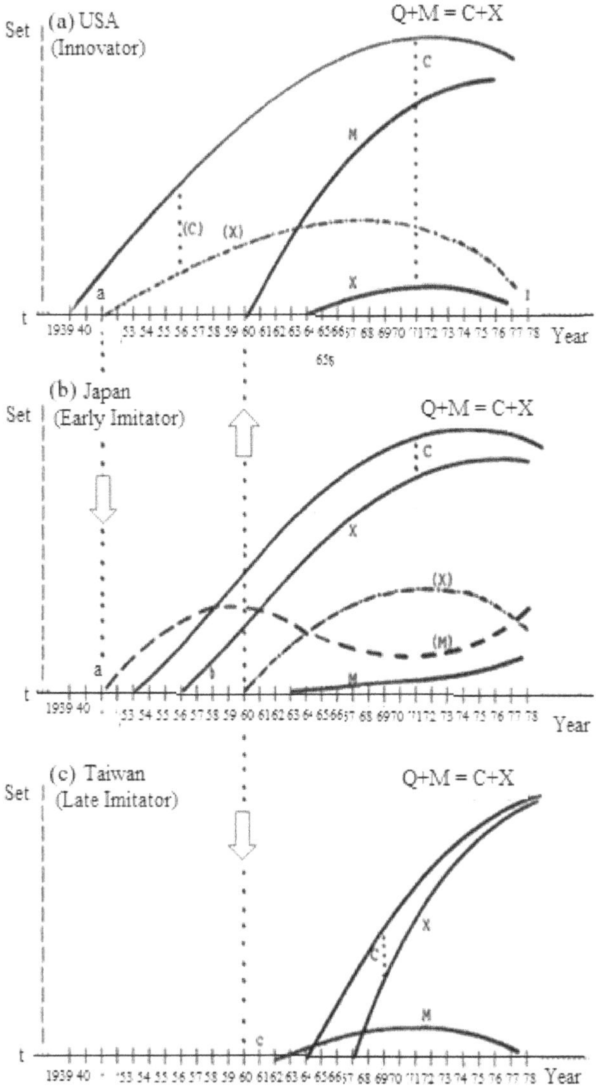

Figure 8.1: The Product Life-cycle of BWTV Receivers
The Taiwanese Case

the production cost consideration becomes important. This development induces the U.S. producers as well as the native Japanese firms to produce the product locally for the domestic market. In Panel (b) of Fig. 8.1, the theory predicts that this should have occurred somewhere around 1958 at point b in Japan. From then on, Japan's domestic supply of the BWTV consists of domestic production and imports, Q + M, in Panel (b). The difference between the Q + M curve and the "(M) curve" represents the domestic output of the BWTV. At first, the local products served as import substitutes from Year b to 1960, and all the local products were consumed domestically.

At this stage, it "may prove wise for the international firms to begin serving third-country markets from the new location. And if labor cost differences are large enough to offset transport costs, then exports back to the United States may become a possibility as well" (Vernon, 1966, 198–200). Thus theoretically, after Japan started production at Year b, Japan could export TV in, say, 1960 (see the dotted curve (X) in Panel (b)) to the third-country, in this case, Taiwan (see the "M curve" in Panel (c)), and also to the innovating country, the United States (see the M curve in Panel (a)). Hence, after 1960, Japan could have started the export promotion policy.

In the standardized stage, the above process more or less repeats itself, with further advancement in standardization of inputs, production processes, and products. At this stage, the products can be produced by unskilled labor. They tend to be high value items, to have high price elasticity of demand for individual firms, and to rely less on external economies provided by the advanced countries. Economies of scale and labor cost become some of the most important considerations in choosing the production location. Thus the less-developed countries offer competitive advantages (Vernon, 1966, 202.).

In our Fig. 8.1, the multinationals theoretically will start production in Taiwan sometime at point c. The theoretical curve is not shown here). However, the actual production started at 1964. At first, the local products in Taiwan served as import substitutes (from 1964 to 1967), and would be consumed by the domestic market. Thus the imports of the BWTV would start decreasing. As the local market saturated, export promotion policy would take place. As a matter of fact, after 1967 Taiwan started exporting the BWTV to the United States and later to Japan, as shown by the X curve in Panel (c) of Fig. 8.1. The Taiwanese BWTV were so competitive that both the US and the Japanese imports from Taiwan soared, especially to the United States (see the M curve in Panel (a) and in Panel (b)), while both country's TV exports decreased in the late 1970s (the (X) curve in Panels (a) and (b)).

The above statement is the scenario depicted by product life-cycle theory. It has many conceptual ambiguities (Taylor, 1987). Rigorous theoretical analysis is still wanting in the literature, and there seems no satisfactory method to test the hypotheses of the theory (Deardorf, 1984). Nevertheless, the theory has its intuitive appeal and we offer the following observations when it comes to the case of the BWTV development in the United States, Japan, and Taiwan. The actual occurrence of production, imports, and exports in these three countries are shown by the solid smooth curves in the three panels in Fig. 8.1.

(a) The three stages of the product life-cycle seem to be valid in all three countries, whether it is applied to production (Q) only, or to both production and imports (Q + M).
(b) The relation between imports and exports are, however, reversed in two cases. In the United States, exports of the BWTV started late in 1964, and it remained relatively insignificant as shown by the solid curve X in Panel (a). This may be due to the large, almost insatiable, consumer markets in the United States. On the other hand, in Japan, as shown in Panel (b), production (1953) preceded exports (1956) by three years, and exports (1963) preceded imports by seven years.
In the Taiwanese case, as shown in Panel (c), imports (1962) preceded domestic production (1964) by two years. This precedence is predicted by the theory. However, in Taiwan, imports have never played any significant role. Exports (1967) of the BWTV immediately followed by its production within three years. The period of import substitution was very short. Thus, unlike the common beliefs, so far as the BWTV is concerned, there was no period of import substitution in Japan, and the period of import substitution was minimal in Taiwan. The explanation is simple. In the early 1950s and 1960s, faced with seemingly everlasting shortage of foreign exchanges, both countries could not afford to import "luxury" goods like television receivers. Through tariffs and other restrictions, imports were kept at minimum. When the firms were allowed to produce, the output was almost solely aimed at foreign markets to earn the valuable foreign exchanges. Such mentality exists even today, causing trade imbalance and friction among Taiwan, Japan, and the United States.
(c) There is a difference in the transfer of TV technology from the U.S.A. to Taiwan and to Japan. Engineering/production technology may be transferred in four ways: through imitation, licensing and royalty, free information, and direct foreign investment (Johnson, 1980). The Japanese depended mostly on the first three methods (Park and

Table 8.1: Sales and Exports of TV's in Taiwan, 1976

Units: %

Firms	Ownership by frgn national	BWTV Sales	BWTV Expts	BWTV Xi/X	COTV Sales	COTV Expts	COTV Xi/X
	(1)	(2)	(3)	(4)	(5)	(6)	(7)
Foreign		58.71	100.0	65.93	21.13	100.00	92.91
USA	100	51.55	100.0	57.90	4.99	100.00	21.95
Nethrlnd	100	0.24	100.0	0.27	0	0.00	0
Japan	100	6.92	100.0	7.76	16.14	100.00	70.96
Joint	25	19.46	55.4	12.09	54.92	2.24	5.46
National	0	21.83	79.5	21.98	23.95	1.32	1.63
Total		100.00		100.00	100.00		100.00

Sources: Yeh (1980), 186–87. X = total exports of BW or COTV.

Moritani, 1982, 139), while the Taiwanese relied heavily on direct foreign investment (Hsiao, 1992). Table 8.1 shows that, in 1976, the market share of the foreign owned firms in Taiwan was almost 60 percent (col. (2)). A full 100 percent of their BWTV were exported (col. (3)), and their exports constituted 66 percent of the total Taiwanese BWTV exports that year (col. (4)). This means that the multinationals not only introduced the production/engineering technology into Taiwan, they also brought in sales/management technology. The Taiwanese were the producers. This probably is the reason that the Taiwanese were able to achieve "rapid growth" in television production and exports in such a short period. This is shown by steeper X curve in Panel (c) of Fig. 8.1.

The exports and production of the color television (COTV) have the same pattern as BWTV, except that export dependency of the foreign firms is as high as 93 percent, as compared with 66 percent for BWTV.

In general, although there are some important variations in our findings of the product life-cycle model, the basic reasoning underlining the model seems to be able to explain the relationship between direct foreign investment and the international transfer of technology.

8.3 DFI and Diffusion of Technology

In the previous section, we have seen the international transfer of TV technology from the U.S.A. to Japan and then to Taiwan. After the new technology is transferred to a country, it must be adopted by the native firms and spread to the local industries and economy. In this section, we study domestic inter-firm technology transfer through foreign and national firms in Taiwan.

The degree of technology diffusion may be seen from either the level of production using the specific technology or the number of firms which adopt new technology. New technology may be regarded as being imbedded in new product which is produced by using that technology. Thus, diffusion of technology may be seen from the trend of production.

Figures 8.2 and 8.3 estimate the trend of production (Q+M), exports, and imports of the Taiwanese BWTV and color television (COTV) receivers. In both figures, we have regressed the variable on time using the following polynomial function:

$$X(t) = a + bx + cx^2 + \cdots + gx^6$$

or $X(t) = \sum_{i=0}^{i=6} a_i x^i$. In order to fit the data with a simplest equation for all dependent variables, we have tried all the degrees of i from 1 to 6. The case

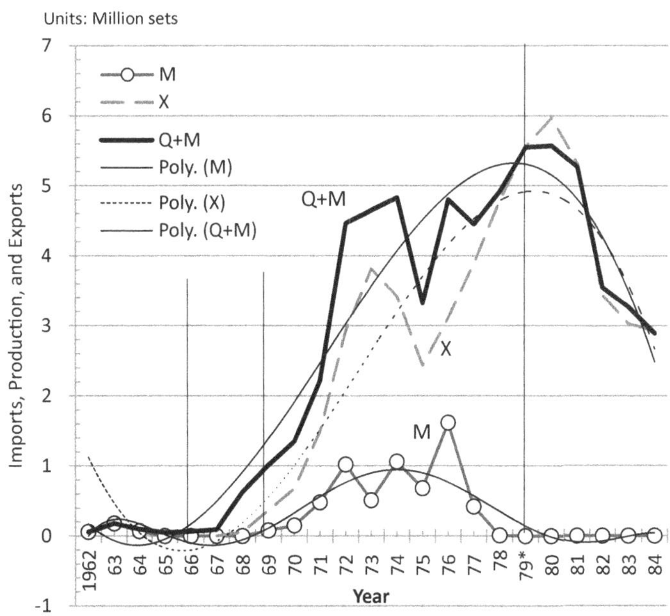

Figure 8.2: Imports, Production, and Exports of BWTV
The case of Taiwan, 1962–1984

with the largest R^2, and with higher t-values, is chosen for each dependent variable. The estimated curves are also drawn in Figs. 8.2 and 8.3. In both figures, because the values of imports are very small, we have to magnify them 10 times in order to see them in the graphs. Thus imports may be ignored in both charts.

Taiwan's imports (M), production and imports (Q+M), and exports (X) data in million sets for BWTV are shown in Fig. 8.2. We fitted the three data sets from 1962 to 1984 with polynomial equations as follows. The Q+M data are fitted with

$$y = -0.3478x^3 + 10.672x^2 - 53.294x + 60.107, \quad R^2 = 0.9188$$

where x denotes year ranging from 1962 to 1984. Similarly, the exports (X) data are fitted with

$$y = -0.4064x^3 + 14.015x^2 - 104.62x + 203.35, \quad R^2 = 0.8542$$

and the imports (M) date with

$$y = -0.0003x^6 + 0.0215x^5 - 0.6225x^4 + 8.34x^3 - 51.165x^2 + 127.37x - 83.933, \quad R^2 = 0.7004$$

Since negative values do not make sense, they may be ignored. The fitted curves show that imports (M) started in 1962, but decreased until 1968, due to the government protection of the infant industry. The policy relaxed in 1969, but imports remained low. Production (Q) started in 1962 and accelerated from 1967 up to 1978, exports (X) started in 1967 and accelerated in 1969 up to 1978. Clearly the trend of the three curves follows the prediction of the life-cycle theory quite well, at least up to 1978, consistent with the theoretical model[1] in Part (c) of Fig. 8.1.

Our data shows a step further and depicts what will happen after the end of the theory. By the end of 1970, the production of BWTV reached its maximum. It appears that the domestic market was saturated after 1980, and all the BWTV produced in Taiwan were exported. Both production and exports of BWTV decreased, probably due to the progress of the color television (technological progress). The fitted curve of Q + M slightly presents the S shape, but the point of inflection occurred very early, in 1967–68, after production started in 1962.

[1]In 1980, exports (X) exceeded production. This may be the case if inventory of overproduction in the previous years is considered.

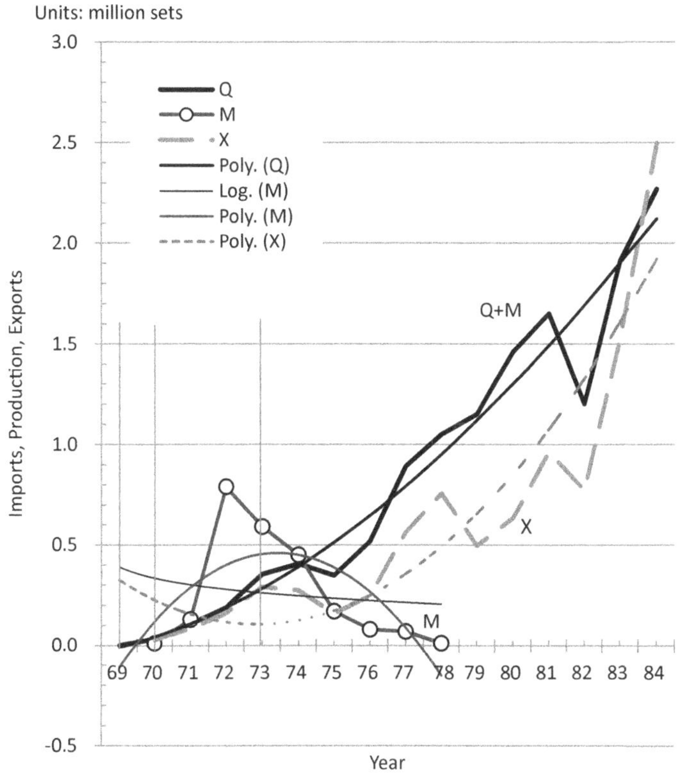

Figure 8.3: Imports, Production, and Exports of COTV
The case of Taiwan, 1969–1984

Figure 8.3 shows imports (M), production plus imports (Q+M), and exports (X) of color television receivers (COTV) in Taiwan from 1969 to 1984. The production-imports curve (Q+M) is fitted with a cubic equation,

$$y = -0.007x^3 + 0.790x^2 + 2.791x - 4.459 \quad R^2 = 0.9493$$

where x is the year from 1969 to 1984. Similarly, the exports curve (X) is fitted with a quadratic function,

$$y = -2.9089x^2 + 31.55x - 39.615 \quad R^2 = 0.5101$$

The imports curve is given as

$$y = 1.4652x^2 - 14.262x + 45.286 \quad R^2 = 0.84$$

Both production Q + M and export curves present an upward trend. It appears there was a strong domestic demand for COTV in the 1970s, but in the early 1980s, a strong foreign demand caught up. In 1983 and 1984, the data show that exports exceeded production and imports. During these two years, part of exports might come from inventory reduction. Although, unlike the theoretical model of the life cycle model in Fig. 8.1, the pattern of fitted output and exports curves is convex to the X-axis, it may be the case that the COTV industry in Taiwan was in the early stage of the life-cycle model in the 1980s, as compared with the BWTV, and the pattern would eventually turn to concave functions, conforming with the theoretical model, as in the case of BWTV in Fig. 8.2. The import curve (M) peaked in 1974 and decreased to minimal after 1978 as the local COTV saturated the domestic market and the government discouraged its imports.

8.4 Entry and Exit in the Television Industry

Table 8.2 presents the diffusion of technology by the number of production firms which adopted new technology, in this case, the technology of producing BWTV and COTV receivers. According to the data, from 1962 to 1978, 39 firms entered the market to produce the BWTV: 8 foreign firms, 27 national (Taiwanese) firms, and 4 joint ventures (col. (1)). Note the vitality of the national firms. The technical transfer was achieved through four joint ventures in the first three years (1 in 1963, 3 in 1964). It is also interesting to note that, among the 39 firms entered from 1962 to 1978, 17 failed or retreated: they are 16 national firms and one foreign firm (col. (3)). Apparently, the national firms have a very high casual rate. By the end of 1978, only 22 firms existed (col. (5)).

Column (6) shows the entry of firms in the production of color television receivers (COTV). Since many BWTV producers also started producing COTVs simultaneously, the data were not clearly separated. Column (8) gives the number of firms which produced television receivers in various years. The cumulative sum of firms in cols. (2) and (4), along with their difference in col. (5) for the existing BWTV firms are graphed in Fig. 8.4.

8.5 Rate of Diffusion of Television Production

From Table 8.2, the existing producing firms of BWTV in each year (col. (5)), the new entry firms (col. (1)), and the exiting BWTV television producing firms (col. (4)) are graphed in Fig. 8.4. The number in the parentheses corresponds to the column number in Table 8.2.

Table 8.2: Sales and Exports of TV's in Taiwan, 1976

	BWTV					COTV		TV
	(1) Entry	(2) cum	(3) Exit	(4) cum	(5) BW	(6) Entry	(7) CO	(8) Total
1962	n	1		0	1			1
63	vn	3		0	3			3
64	3v2n	8		0	8			8
65	f	9	2n	2	7			7
66		9		2	7			7
67	3n	12		2	10			10
68	2fn	15	n	3	12			12
69	n	16		3	13	2vn	3	16
70	f7n	24	2n	5	19	2nf	6	25
71	fn	26		5	21	2nf	9	30
72	f3n	30	3n	8	22	f	10	32
73	2n	32	3n	11	21		10	31
74		32	2n	13	19	n	11	30
75	f	33	nf	15	18		11	29
76	2n	35		15	20	nn	13	33
77	f	36		15	21	nf	15	36
78	3n	39	2n	17	22	2f	17	39
Total	39 =8f27n4v		17 f16n			17 =5f8n4v		

Notes: f = foreign owned firm, n = national (Taiwanese) firms, v = joint venture. 2fn means 2 foreign owned firms and 1 Taiwanese owned national firm. 1 in 1n or 1f is omitted.
Source: Schive and Yeh (1980).

The existing BWTV firms in col. (5) of Table 8.2 are fitted to a logistic curve of the following form (Thirtle and Ruttan, 1987, 82):

$$\ln [p(t)/(1 - p(t))] = \alpha + \beta t$$

where $p(t) = n(t)/N$, $n(t)$ is the total number of new technology adopters at time t, and N is the number of potential adopters. Thus $p(t)$ is the probability that a firm has adopted new technology at time t, and $p(t)/(1 - p(t))$ is the conditional probability that a non-adopting firm will adopt new technology at time t, given the previous adoption. Here β is called *the rate of diffusion of innovation*, and α is a constant (of integration).

Since the number N of potential adopters is unknown, it is estimated by the following approximation of the differential equation (Johnston, 1984,

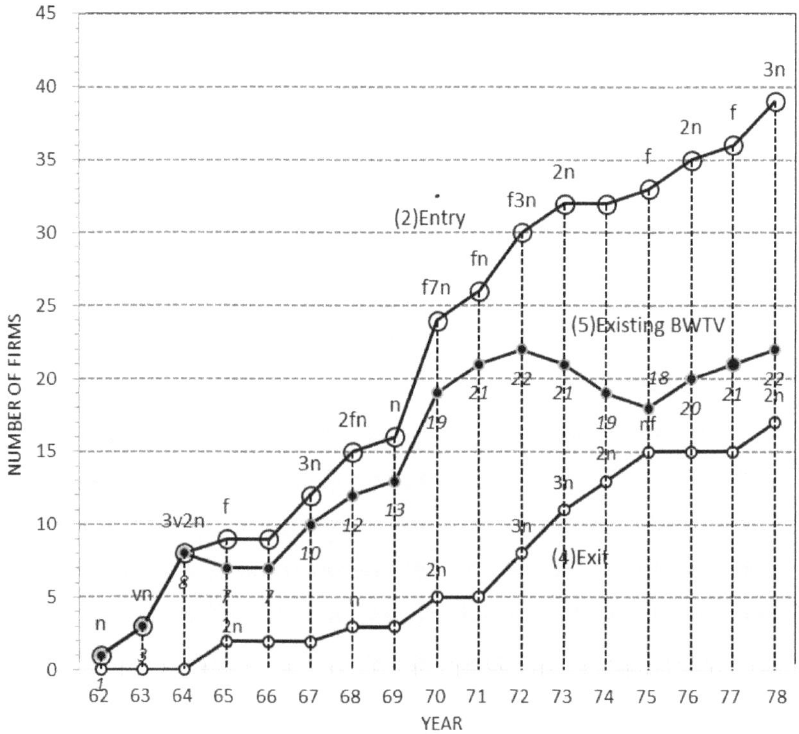

Figure 8.4: Entry and Exit of BWTV Firms

Taiwan, 1962–78

Note: Number in the parentheses shows the column number of Table 8.2.

73), which is the original equation that yielded the logistic curve above:

$$(n(t{+}1) - n(t))/n(t) = a + bn(t)$$

where n(t) is defined above, $a = \beta$ and $b = -\beta/N$, or $N = -\beta/b$. From col. (5) of Table 8.2, the least squares estimate of N is 21. Since the largest number in col. (5) of Table 8.2 is 22, we take N = 23. Substituting N = 23 in equation, and using the least squares method again, we obtain[2]

$$\ln[\hat{p}(t)/(1-\hat{p}(t))] = -1.830 + \underset{(7.816)}{0.320t}, \quad R^2 = 0.8039$$

[2]Let $\hat{p}_t = (2)_t/N$, where $(2)_t$ is the entry of column (2) at time t, t = 1962 to 1978. Then, regress $\ln(\hat{p}_t/((1-\hat{p}_t))$ on t, t = 0, 1, 2, ..., 16, we have the regression results.

where the t-ratio is in the parentheses. The result shows that, in Taiwan, the bandwagon effect of prior adopters on the remaining potential adopters is so large that, in any given year, one out of three potential firms will imitate the prior adopters and use new technology.

We have also tried to use different number N of potential firms. For $N = 100$, the rate of diffusion reduces, as may be expected, to 0.153. However, for $N = 500$ and 1000, the rates stay at 0.140. Thus, the value of the rate of diffusion is not very sensitive to the estimated number N of potential adopters which is estimated at the beginning of the period.

The value of the rate of diffusion obtained here differs from a Taiwanese study (0.165), which uses an unpublished in-house survey data (Wu and Chen, 1988, 82). However, our result seems to be comparable with other empirical studies on the diffusion processes in electronics industry (Wu and Chen, 1988, 83). The point of inflection of the estimated logistic curve is at $t = -\alpha/\beta = 5.72$. Thus the cumulative probability of firms adopting the new technology changes from acceleration (increasing at an increasing rate) to deceleration (increasing at a decreasing rate) in about six years.

8.6 Some Concluding Remarks

From the tables and figures, the following important variations to product life-cycle theory may be observed.

(a) From Table 8.2 and Fig. 8.4, unlike the prediction by theory, the innovator in the case of the Taiwanese TV industry is a national firm established in 1962, followed immediately by three more Taiwanese firms and four joint ventures. The 100 percent foreign owned multinational corporation entered into the market only in 1965, and not by a U.S. company, but by a Dutch company, Phillco (Schive and Yeh, 1980).

(b) The first three joint ventures were associated with Japanese firms: Sanyo, Matsushita, and Sharp. They were imitators of the U.S. technology, not the innovators as the theory might predict. Apparently, the cultural and geological proximity played an important role in the industrial entry game.

(c) As shown by Table 8.1, all foreign owned firms are multinationals from the U.S., Japan, or Europe. They entered the Taiwanese market not to take advantage of the closeness to the domestic market, but solely for low labor cost and for exporting the goods produced there (col. (3) of Table 8.1). The domestic market was left to the Taiwanese firms and joint ventures.

(d) The national firms actively participated in the technology diffusion process. 27 out of 39 firms which entered the Taiwanese TV market were national firms (col. (1), Table 8.2). However, the casualty of the national firms was also extremely high, 16 out of the 17 firms failed by 1978 were Taiwanese national firms (col. (3), Table 8.2).

(e) According to the theory of innovation and diffusion processes, the cumulative number of adopters as expressed by the logistic curve should take the S-shaped curve (Mahajan and Peterson, 1985, 8–11; Thirtle and Ruttan, 1987, 81). Here the turning point is estimated at six years. However, if the cumulative adopters are drawn simply against the time axis, this is not the case in the Taiwanese TV industry. Both the (2) Entry curve and (5) Existing BWTV curves in Fig. 8.4 do not seem to show that the BWTV diffusion curve over time are S-shaped diffusion process. Similarly, it can be shown that the COTV diffusion curve has a reversed S-curve.

In conclusion, we have shown in this paper that, for the Taiwanese TV industry, the product-life cycle theory may be used to interpret international transfer of technology and direct foreign investment in Taiwan. Once technology was transferred to Taiwan, the diffusion process took the familiar form. Although there are some variations to the theory, we consider that the Taiwanese development pattern in terms of technology transfer and diffusion of technology generally followed the prediction of the life-cycle theory.

Acknowledgments

In collecting data for this research, the authors are grateful for help from Professors Po-chih Chen, Chi Schive, and Rong I. Wu. This paper was presented to the North American Economics and Finance Association (NAEFA): The Fifth International Congress, July 1989, at the University of Colorado at Boulder. Helpful comments by two discussants, Professors Joseph Horton and Walton T. Wilford, are also appreciated. The original tables and charts of the paper which were drawn using Lotus 1-2-3, have been redrawn and re-estimated using Microsoft Excel program. Naturally, all errors of omission and commission are the authors'.

References

Deardorf, A.V. (1984). "Testing Trade Theories and Predicting Trade Flows." In R.W. Jones and P.B. Kenen (eds.), *Handbook of International Economics*, Vol. I (Chapter 10). New York: North Holland.

Hsiao, M.C.W. (1992). "Direct Foreign Investment, Technology Transfer, and Industrial Development — The Case of Electronics Industry in Taiwan." In M. Jan Dutta (ed.), *Asian Economic Regimes: An Adaptive Innovation Paradigm*, Monograph in *Research in Asian Economic Studies*, Greenwich, Connecticut: JAI Press (Ref. Chapter 9 in this book).

Johnson, H.G. (1980). *Comparative Cost and Commercial Policy Theory for a Developing World Economy.* Wicksell Lecture, 1968. Baltimore: John Hopkins University Press, 1980.

Johnston, J. (1984). *Econometric Methods*, 3rd ed. New York: McGraw-Hill, 1984.

Lall, S. (1978). "Transnationals, Domestic Enterprises, and Industrial Structure in Host LDCs: A Survey." *Oxford Economic Papers*, 30(2) (July): 217–248.

Mahajan, V. and R.A. Peterson (1985). *Models for Innovation Diffusion.* A Sage University Series, No. 07-048. London: Sage Publications.

Park, U.H. and M. Moritani (1982). *Economics of Technology Absorption*, (in Japanese). Tokyo: Toyo Keizai Shimpo Sha.

Schive, C. and R. Yeh (1980). "Direct Foreign Investment and Taiwan's T.V. Industry." *Economic Essays*, the Graduate Institute of Economics, National Taiwan University, Taiwan, November, 261–291.

Sekiguchi, S. and T.V. Du (1986). *Direct Investment and Technology Transfer-Japan and Northeast/Southeast Asia* (in Japanese). Tokyo: Center of Japanese Economic Studies.

Taylor, M. (1987). "Enterprise and Product-Cycle Model: Conceptual Ambiguities." In F.E. Hamilton (ed.), *Industrial Change in Advanced Economies* (Chapter 5). Wolfeboro, N.H.: Croom Helm.

Thirtle, C.G. and V.W. Ruttan (1987). *The Role of Demand and Supply in the Generation and Diffusion of Technical Change.* New York: Harwood Academic Publishers.

Tilton, J.E. (1971). *International Diffusion of Technology: The Case of Semiconductors.* Washington, D.C.: The Brookings Institution. 73.

Vernon, R. (1966). "International Investment and International Trade in the Product Cycle." *Quarterly Journal of Economics*, 80: 190–207.

Wu, R.I. and Y.H. Chen (1988). *Effects of American Investment on Trade and Technology Transfer* (in Chinese). Taipei: The Institute of American Culture, Academia Sinica.

Yeh, R. (1980). "Development of the Taiwanese Television Industry as Seen from International Product Cycle" (in Chinese). *Quarterly Journal of the Bank of Taiwan*, 31(2) (June).

Chapter 9

Direct Foreign Investment, Technology Transfer, and Industrial Development — The Case of Electronics Industry in Taiwan

Direct foreign investment (DFI) contributes to the growth of economic activities in the host country. More important, direct foreign investment is considered as a major channel to bring technological know-how to the host country, creating backward and forward linkages which stimulate local development of industry (Lall, 1978; Sekiguchi, 1979; Hsiao and Hsiao, 1984). In this paper, we will first survey the general features of DFI in Taiwan in Section 9.1, followed by measuring the effect of DFI on the Taiwanese economy in Section 9.2. We will also study the difference of the effects of the American DFI and the Japanese DFI in Taiwan.

In Section 9.3, we examine the technology transfer through DFI in Taiwan using the survey data of national and foreign firms in 1973 and 1978. To be more specific, our study concentrates on the relationship between DFI and technology transfer in the electronics industry, especially the television industry in Taiwan, as Taiwan is a large exporter of televisions, computer terminals and monitors, and calculators in the world. We then, in Section 9.4, illustrate with statistical data how Taiwan's television industry goes through the process of imports to import substitution, and then to export promotion. Some concluding remarks are given in the last section.

9.1 Overview of the DFI in Taiwan

The DFI in Taiwan started around 1953 (Hsiao and Hsiao, 1984). In this section, we review briefly the DFI situation in Taiwan and describe the statistical data. In 1953, the Taiwanese government approved U.S. $1.65 million (in 12 cases) of investment by overseas Chinese (DFIOC) and U.S. $2.04 million (in 2 cases) of investment by foreign nationals (DFIFN).[1] In July 1954, the government announced the "Statute for Investment by Foreign Nationals," which was followed in November 1955 by the announcement of the "Statute for Investment by Overseas Chinese." Ten years later, in 1966, U.S. $8.38 million (in 51 cases) of DFIOC and U.S. $20.9 million (in 52 cases) of DFIFN were approved. Subsequently, in December 1970, a more attractive and comprehensive "Statute for Encouragement of Investment" was announced. The major encouraging part of this statute for foreign firms was the "five-year tax holiday" and a maximum of 25 percent corporate income tax after five years. These foreign investment statutes were amended several times since their publications. These special treatments combined with other economic and social factors have attracted a massive inflow of investment in Taiwan from foreigners and overseas Chinese.

Figure 9.1 depicts the amounts of DFIFN, DFIOC, and their sum, total DFI, in Taiwan. From 1953 to 1987, a total of U.S. $7.35 billion of DFI was approved. Among them, DFIFN consisted of U.S. $5.91 billion and DFIOC was U.S. $1.43 billion. Figure 9.1 also shows that, especially since 1967, the DFIFN increased rapidly while the DFIOC grew slowly. In 1987, the approved DFIFN (U.S. $1.22 billion) was more than six times that of the DFIOC (U.S. $195.73 million). The DFIFN has constantly played a greater role than DFIOC in the growth of the Taiwanese economy. Before 1967, almost all the DFI in Taiwan came from the United States and Japan. After 1967, some European countries started to join the United States and Japan to invest in Taiwan.

Figure 9.2 shows the amount of DFIFN in Taiwan by country. Over the past 21 years (1967–87), a total of U.S. $2.14 billion from the United States, U.S. $1.77 billion from Japan, U.S. $0.94 billion from Europe, and U.S. $0.91 billion from other countries were invested in Taiwan. In 1967, the distribution of DFIFN was: the United States, 40.6 percent (U.S. $15.71 million); Japan, 41.2 percent (U.S. $15.95 million); Europe, 4.8 percent (U.S.

[1]Since the data of actual DFI in Taiwan are not available, the approved cases and amounts of DFI published by Taiwan's government were used in this paper. As a matter of fact, both DFI by overseas Chinese (DFIOC) and DFI by foreign nationals (DFIFN) may be classified as foreign investment.

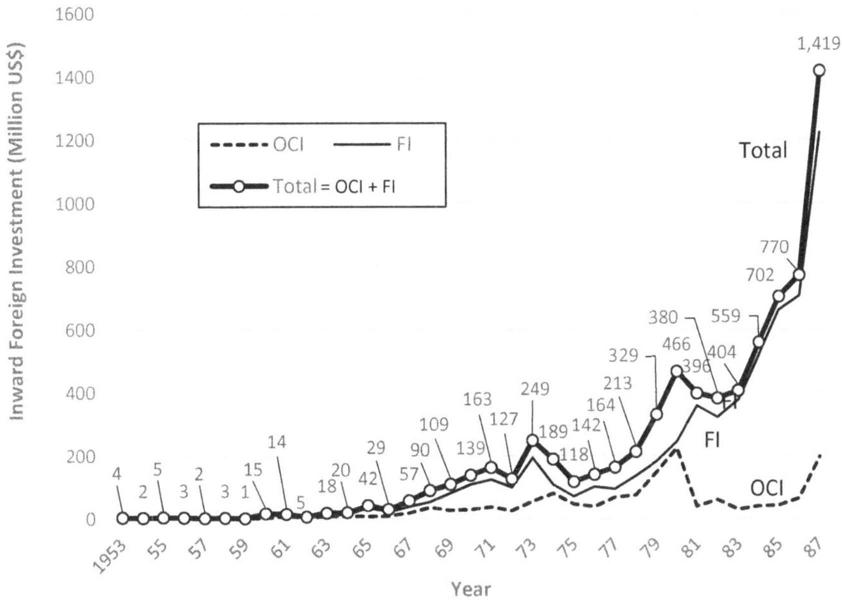

Figure 9.1: Direct Foreign Investment in Taiwan, 1953–1987
Source: Council for Economic Planning and Development of Taiwan, *TSDB* (1988).

$1.87 million); and other countries, 13.3 percent (U.S. $5.13 million). In 1987, the distribution changed to: the United States, 33.9 percent (U.S. $414.06 million); Japan, 32.6 percent (U.S. $399.24 million); Europe, 18.3 percent (U.S. $224.05 million), and other countries, 15.2 percent (U.S. $185.71 million). The shares from the United States and Japan decreased nearly 15 percent, while the shares from European countries increased nearly 14 percent. This is one of the evidences which shows that, in the past 20 years, Taiwan had increased its trade activities with more partners around the world, especially with the European countries.

In terms of investment cases, there are differences between DFIFN and DFIOC. From 1953 to 1987, 4,232 cases of DFI were approved. In 1967, 107 cases of DFIFN and 105 cases of DFIOC were approved. Twenty years later, in 1987, the DFIFN had more than tripled to 363 cases, while the DFIOC had remained about the same level at only 117 cases. Due to the geographical proximity and the 51 years of Japanese occupation in Taiwan before World War II, the Japanese businessmen are more familiar with the Taiwanese economic and cultural environments. There is no surprise that

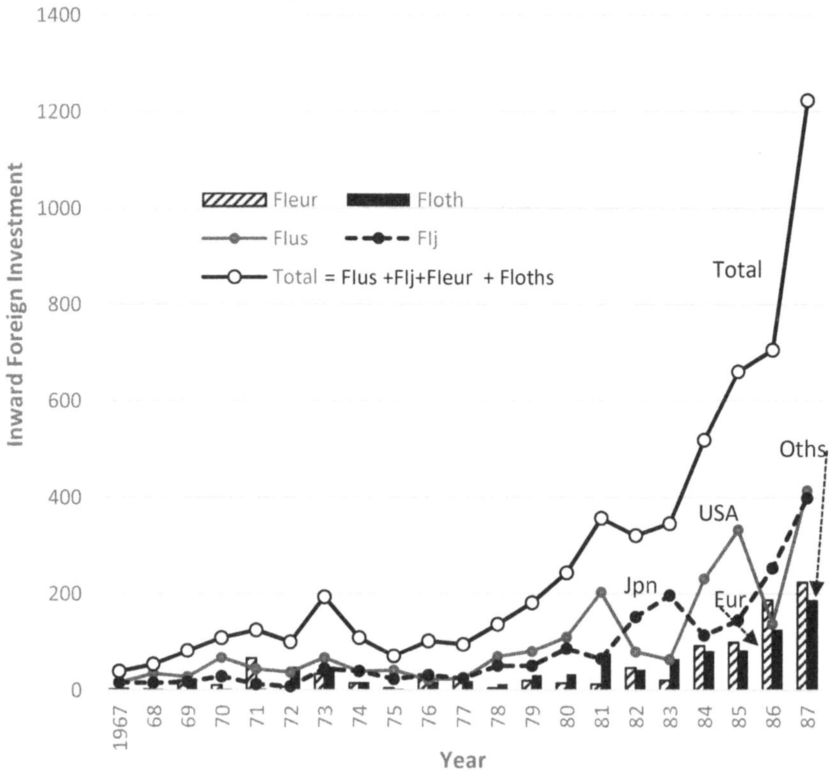

Figure 9.2: Amount of DFIFN in Taiwan by Country, 1967–1987
Source: Council for Economic Planning and Development of Taiwan, *TSDB* (1988).

more cases of DFI in Taiwan were from Japan than from other countries: in 1967, 76 cases were from Japan and 18 cases were from the United States; in 1987, 207 cases were from Japan and 74 cases were from the United States. In general, the DFI in Taiwan from the United States has larger amounts with less cases, while the DFI in Taiwan from Japan has smaller amounts with more cases.[2]

Table 9.1 presents the aggregate amount of DFI in Taiwan by industry from 1952 to 1987. The foreign nationals concentrated their investment (Column DFIFN) in electronic and electric products (35%), chemicals

[2]See the Council for Economic Planning and Development of Taiwan, TSDB (1988).

Table 9.1: Inward Direct Foreign Investment in Taiwan by Industry: 1952–1987

	Industry	DFIFN US$ mi	DFIFN %	DFIOC US$ mi	DFIOC %	DFI (Total) US$ mi	DFI (Total) %
1	Agriculture & Forestry	0.729	*0.01*	3.432	*0.24*	4.161	*0.06*
2	Food & Beverages	167.357	*2.83*	55.235	*3.85*	222.592	*3.03*
3	Electronic & Electric Products	2081.121	*35.19*	48.810	*3.40*	2129.931	*28.98*
4	Fisheries & Livestock	6.856	*0.12*	16.897	*1.18*	23.753	*0.32*
5	Textiles	76.392	*1.29*	117.139	*8.16*	193.531	*2.63*
6	Paper & Paper Products	17.651	*0.30*	23.188	*1.62*	40.839	*0.56*
7	Chemicals	1225.010	*20.71*	106.238	*7.40*	1331.248	*18.11*
8	Non-metallic Mineral Products	129.809	*2.19*	289.227	*20.15*	419.036	*5.70*
9	Metal Products	478.394	*8.09*	38.267	*2.67*	516.661	*7.03*
10	Machinery, Equip., & Instrmnts	655.663	*11.09*	33.483	*2.33*	689.146	*9.38*
11	Transportation	92.353	*1.56*	56.911	*3.97*	149.264	*2.03*
12	Construction of Buildings	14.749	*0.25*	94.498	*6.59*	109.247	*1.49*
13	Banking & Insurance	228.228	*3.86*	100.048	*6.97*	328.276	*4.47*
14	Foreign Trade	41.690	*0.70*	27.892	*1.94*	69.582	*0.95*
15	Services	595.896	*10.08*	356.111	*24.82*	952.007	*12.95*
16	Others	102.097	*1.73*	67.640	*4.71*	169.737	*2.31*
	Total	5913.995	*100*	1435.02	*100*	7349.011	*100*

Source: TSDB (1988).

(21%), machinery, equipment, and instruments (11%), services (10%), and metal products (8%). On the other hand, the overseas Chinese were in favor of the investment (col. DFIOC) in services (25%), non-metallic mineral products (20%), and textiles (8%). Adding DFIFN and DFIOC together, the total DFI activities were concentrated on electronic and electric products (29%), chemicals (18%), and services (13%). The inflow of direct foreign investment in Taiwan's electronic and electric products industry had contributed to Taiwanese capital formation and technology transfer simultaneously. In Sections 9.3 and 9.4, we will look into the effects of DFI and technology transfer on the growth of Taiwan's television industry, which shows clearly how an industry goes through the process of imports to import substitution, and then to exports. This process was enhanced by technical cooperation through DFI.

9.2 The Effect of DFI on Taiwan's GDP

For a developing country like Taiwan, the major objective of inducing direct foreign investment is to increase the nation's economic activities. Our purpose here is to use an econometric method to examine whether there is a significant effect on the growth of Taiwan's GDP from the growth of DFI and its subcategories: DFI from foreign nationals and DFI from overseas Chinese. We will also investigate the effect based on disaggregate DFI from the United States and Japan, the two most important countries that have supplied DFI to Taiwan.

In our regression analysis, we used the data from 1967 to 1987. All variables were in terms of their real growth rates.[3] We first apply the ordinary least-squares method to estimate the regression equations. However, the Durbin-Watson *d*-test indicates the existence of positive first-order autoregressive errors in all cases (Judge *et al.*, 1988, 394). This is the same problem encountered by Kojima (1985b, 36; also see 1985a, 296). In our case, to improve the estimation, we apply the Cochrane-Orcutt iterative procedure, which is an appropriate method of correcting autocorrelation problem, to estimate first-order autoregressive errors model for all equations (Judge *et al.*, 1988, 384–399). The estimated results are presented in Table 9.2.

The estimated Equation (1) shows that the growth of DFI has a significant and positive effect on the growth of Taiwan's GDP. When the current growth rate of DFI increases by 1 percent, it may generate a 0.11 percent increase in the growth rate of Taiwan's GDP. This also implies that, with the hard-working and high quality labor, the various incentive policies for foreign investment in Taiwan from the 1960s to the 1980s have made a significant contribution to the growth of the Taiwanese economy.

When we disaggregate the DFI into DFIFN and DFIOC, Equation (2) shows that the DFI by foreign nationals (slope coefficient = 0.087) has a greater effect than the DFI by overseas Chinese (slope coefficient = 0.043) on the growth of Taiwan's GDP. This finding agrees with the fact reported in the previous section that the DFI by foreign nationals has larger amounts with a concentration of investment in high-tech and heavy industries, which generated more economic activities for the Taiwanese economy. On the other hand, the DFI by overseas Chinese has smaller amounts with an

[3]The real values of all variables are based on the 1981 constant price. The U.S. producer price index for industrial commodities is used to calculate the real values of all DFI series. The time-series of the growth rates of a variable is obtained by taking the first difference of natural-log values of the variable, for example, the growth rates of GDP $(t) = \ln\text{GDP}(t) - \ln\text{GDP}(t-1)$.

Table 9.2: Relationships between the Growth Rates of GDP and DFI in Taiwan, 1967–1987

1. $GDP(t) = 0.117 + 0.109DFI(t) - 0.032DFI(t-1)$
   (1.95) (2.1)** (0.62)
   $R^{**2} = 0.425$ $d = 2.024$ $Rho = 0.668$

2. $GDP(t) = 0.118 + 0.087DFIFN(t) - 0.060DFIFN(t-1) + 0.043DFIOC(t)$
   (2.03) (2.0)** (1.28) (1.52)*
   $+ 0.030DFIOC(t-1)$
   (1.19)
   $R^{**2} = 0.591$ $d = 2.234$ $Rho = 0.667$

Notes:
1. All variables in the above regression equations were in terms of their real growth rates:

   $GDP(t)$ = the growth rate of GDP at time t,
   $DFI(t)$ = the growth rate of DFI at time t,
   $DFIFN(t)$ = the growth rate of DFI by foreign nationals at time t,
   $DFIOC(t)$ = the growth rate of DFI by overseas Chinese at time t,

2. All regressin equations were first-order autoregressive errors models estimated by the Cochrane-Orcutt iterative procedure.
3. The number in the parentheses is the absolute value of t-ratio for the coefficient.
4. R^{**2} = coefficient of determination.
5. d = Durbin-Watson d-statistic.
6. Rho = first-order autocorrelation coefficient.
7. ** = the slope coefficient is significant at 5 percent level.
8. * = the slope coefficient is significant at 10 percent level.

emphasis of investment in the service industry, which may not have a strong and lasting effect on Taiwan's economy.[4]

We found that none of the lagged variables of DFI had a significant effect on GDP. This may imply that most of the DFI in Taiwan were short-term high-tech industries rather than long-term heavy industries. We also noticed that the coefficients of determination (R^{**2}) were not high. One reason for this may be the omission of some variables, such as the growth

[4]We also estimated the regression relationship using DFI from the United States, DFI from Japan, and their lagged values as independent variables. The estimated results show that these country DFI variables are not significant at 5 percent level, and so the results are omitted from this paper. In addition, we have taken the suggestion of a referee to estimate GDP as a function of the share of DFI in gross domestic investment (we use the data of gross capital formation). The estimated t-statistic for the DFI share variable is only 0.426. Apparently, the DFI share is not a significant variable to explain GDP in this case.

rates of labor, domestic investment, and exports in regression equations. Naturally, we may formulate and estimate some sophisticated econometric models for forecasting the relationship between GDP, DFI, and other economic variables. However, forecasting is not our purpose in this paper.

9.3 DFI and Technology Transfer

There are two kinds of technology: engineering/production technology and management/marketing technology. Both are relevant and important to developing countries. They may be transferred in four ways: through imitation, direct foreign investment, royalty and licensing, and free information (Johnson, 1980). In this paper, our emphasis is on technology transfer through DFI.

Table 9.3 and Fig. 9.3 show the close relationship between the DFI in Taiwan and technology transfer. In 1973 Survey of the five industries,

Table 9.3: DFI and Technology Transfer

Firms	Total firms No.	Adptd (%)	New products (%)	Total firms No.	Adptd (%)	New prod (%)	New prod (%)	New prod (%)
	5 Industries			Electronics				
	(1)	(2)		(3)	(4)			
1973*								
National(0)	185	7.57		17	23.53			
Foreign	126	85.71		45	95.56			
minority(1)	23	60.87		7	71.43			
majority(2)	103	91.26		38	100.00			
Total	311	39.23		62	75.81			
	8 Industries			Electronics			8 Industries	
	(5)	(6)	(7)	(8)	(9)	(10)	(11)	(12)
1978**								
National	131	21.37	(67.86)	30	13.33	(50.00)	41.98	30.00
Foreign	68	70.59	(62.50)	24	95.83	(60.87)	54.41	62.50
Total	199	38.19	(64.47)	54	50	(59.26)	46.23	44.44

Notes: *1973 survey includes five industries: (1) textile, (2) clothing, (3) plastic and plastic products, (4) metal and its product, and (5) electronic and elctric products.
**The 1978 survey includes 8 industries: in addition to the five mentioned in the 1973 Survey, (6) automobiles and parts, (7) chemicals, and (8) machinery.
Sources: Compiled from the survey reports in Schive (1983), Tables 2, 3, and 4.

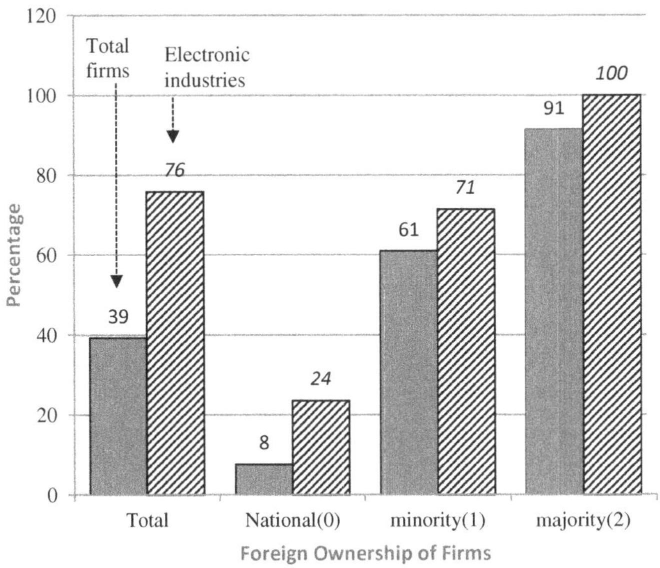

Figure 9.3: The Slanted Structure: Technology Transfer in Taiwan 1973 Survey

39 percent of the 311 firms in the survey reported that they adopted foreign technology either through technical cooperation or royalty and licensing agreements. These firms were fast growing exporters with at least one million dollars of annual exports, and 80 percent to 90 percent of their outputs were exported (Schive, 1983, 477). We have shown in Table 9.1 that the electronic and electric products industry has the highest concentration of foreign investment. Among all firms surveyed, 39 percent of them adopted foreign technology. However, in the case of electronic and electric products, which has high concentration of DFI, the percentage was almost doubled: 76 percent of the 62 firms using foreign technology (see the last row of cols. 3 and 4 of Table 9.3).

If the firms are divided into three categories according to the degree of foreign involvement, a clear pattern appears (this was also noted in Schive, 1983, 479). We divide the firms into "national firms" which are completely owned by the Taiwanese, the "minority owned foreign firms" which foreigners own less than 50 percent of the stocks, and the "majority owned foreign firms" in which more than 50 percent of the stocks are owned by the foreigners. Then the proportions of the firms which adopted foreign technology became 7.6 percent, 60.9 percent, and 91.2 percent, respectively, for the five industries (col. 2), and the proportions increased to 23.5 percent, 71.4 percent, and 100 percent, respectively, for the electronic and electric products industry (col. 4). This "slanted structure," as we may call it, is shown clearly in Fig. 9.3, where we denote national firms as 0, minority owned foreign firms as 1, and majority owned foreign firms as 2, to show the step-wise increase in the foreign capital and technology.

The pattern is the same in the 1978 Survey, in which some major products were selected first and then one or two major producers of the products were chosen for surveying. The firm was asked whether its major product is the first product introduced in Taiwan (Schive, 1983, 479). Among the 199 major producers selected, 38 percent adopted foreign technology. In particular, among the 54 major electronic and electric firms selected, 50 percent reported using foreign technology. If the firms are divided into two different ownerships, the proportions of adopting foreign technology among the national firms and the foreign firms were 21.4 percent and 70.6 percent, respectively, for the eight industries (col. 6). The proportions were 13.3 percent and 95.8 percent, respectively, for the electronic and electric products industry (col. 9). Thus, among the 199 major firms in Taiwan, foreign firms have at least three times higher tendency than the national firms to adopt foreign technology. From the pattern that we obtained using the above two surveys, it shows clearly that, in general, the higher the DFI in a firm or an industry, the higher the possibility that the firm or the industry adopts foreign technology. Thus the empirical rules suggest that technology transfer is an increasing function of DFI.

The last two columns of Table 9.3 show the percentages of national and foreign firms which produced new products. Although the "new products" may be "mature commodities" using "mature technology" in advanced countries, so far as the Taiwanese industries are concerned, they represent new technology and technology transfer from foreign countries. Thus, in terms of innovative activities of introducing new products, foreign firms are in general slightly more active than the national firms (col. 11), and twice more active in electronic and electric products industry (col. 12).

It may be interesting to note that, among the firms which did adopt foreign technology, about 60 percent of them used it to produce new products, rather than improve the existing technology. Generally speaking, there seems no major differences in the innovative activities between the national and foreign firms which adopted foreign technology (cols. 7 and 10). This seems to indicate that so far as product innovation is concerned, the native firms are as innovative as the foreign firms. There may be two interpretations of this situation. To be competitive on the horizontal aspect, the native firms should be as innovative as the foreign firms. On the other hand, on the vertical competition aspect, it is conceivable that the new products introduced by the foreign firms may be more sophisticated final products like transistor radios, black-and-white or color television receivers. The native firms may produce new products which are used as parts in the local foreign firms, and the product design and specifications may be given and assisted by foreign firms (Saito, 1981, 49). In any case, we submit that technology transfer did occur through DFI and this, in turn, has undoubtedly contributed to the Taiwanese exports and economic development.

The most effective way of transferring technology is probably through foreign personnel employed in the foreign firms. Table 9.4 shows the number of such employees in Taiwan. In 1982, about 1,765 foreign citizens worked in the foreign firms in Taiwan. About half of them were in the area of general administration and the other half worked as technicians. They made up about 2 percent of the total administrators and technicians of the foreign firms (see the last row of Table 9.4). About 35 percent to 40 percent of the foreign personnel were working in the electronic and electric products industry as either administrators or technicians (cols. 3 and 6). None of the foreign personnel worked as laborers. Undoubtedly, through personal contacts with the local administrators and technicians, this large influx of foreign personnel induced by DFI has played an important role in transferring engineering/production technology as well as management/marketing technology.

Table 9.5 shows the number of technical cooperation in some Asian countries. From 1952 to 1983, there were 1,871 cases of technical cooperation in Taiwan (col. 1). Japan is the principal supplier of technology

Table 9.4: Employment in Foreign Firms in Taiwan, 1982

Including Oversea Chinese Firms

	Administrators			Technicians			Workers		
Citizenship	All ind. (1)	Electro (2)	% (3)	All ind. (4)	Electro (5)	% (6)	All ind. (7)	Electro (8)	% (9)
Total Employee	49124	17870	36.4	39252	19008	48.4	237285	90553	38.2
Foreigners	916	360	39.3	849	300	35.3			
%	1.9	2.0		2.2	1.6				

Sources: Ministry of Economic Affairs (1982), 81, Tables 4 and 5.

Table 9.5: Sources of Technology Transfer in Some Asian Countries

Unit: %

	Receivers					
	Taiwan *1952–83*	S. Korea *1962–85*	Sing. *1983*	Malay *1960–81*	Thai *1981*	Phil *1978–79*
Suppliers	(1)	(2)	(3)	(4)	(5)	(6)
Japan	65.5	54.6	25.0	30.5	36.3	20.7
USA	21.4	23.2	24.4	14.7	18.8	46.0
UK	0.0	3.8	9.4	13.5	7.7	6.7
Other Adv. Countries	13.1	18.3	41.2	25.9	25.5	22.7
Developing Countries	0.0	0.0	0.0	15.5	11.6	4.0
Total(cases)	1871	3397	541	348	388	150

Source: Mostly based on the data from Institute of Developing Economies, as shown in Du (1986), 155.

(65.5%), followed by the United States (21.4%), and other advanced countries, mainly from Europe (13.1%). In terms of industrial distribution, 25.2 percent is in electronic and electric products, 20.0 percent in chemicals, 15.5 percent in machinery, equipment and instruments, and 13.4 percent in metal products (Schive, 1985). This distribution has not changed much since 1974 (Hsiao and Hsiao, 1984, Table 9.2).

Table 9.5 also shows that the previous colonial relationship between suppliers and receivers of technology has some effects on determining the direction of technology transfer. In general, Japan is a larger supplier, followed by the United States and the United Kingdom. In Taiwan and South Korea, most of the older natives understand, and even speak, Japanese. This historical background may explain the unusually high proportion of technology transfer from Japan to these two countries (65.5% and 54.6%, respectively, see cols. 1 and 2). The 11 percent difference between Taiwan and South Korea probably reflects the general attitude toward the Japanese in the two countries. On the other hand, the Philippines had 46 percent of the technical cooperation from the United States. This may be due to the close relationship between the Philippines and the United States before, during, and after World War II.

Most technical cooperation takes the form of intra-firm transactions (Du, 1986, 154). For example, it is found that among the major 75 firms in Thailand which received technical assistance, 53 of them are foreign firms related to multinationals. In the case of Malaysia, 80 percent of technology receiving firms are also foreign firms, and 7.7 percent of these firms are completely owned by multinationals (Du, 1986, 155). Thus, as in the Taiwanese case, DFI is also an important channel in transferring technology from advanced countries to the other Asian developing countries.

It may be of interest to note that there is technology transfer from the developing countries, presumably from the Asian Newly Industrializing Countries (Asian NICs), Taiwan, South Korea, Hong Kong, and Singapore, to the ASEAN countries (see the row of Developing Countries in Table 9.5). Clearly, technology is transferred internationally because some countries possess relative, rather than absolute, technological superiority. Technology, like water, simply flows toward the lower land. Technology which is recently established in Asian NICs probably is more "appropriate" and easy for adaptation in the less developed countries.

9.4 Technology Transfer in the Television Industry

We have seen that DFI in Taiwan has concentrated on the electronic and electric products industry, which is the largest employers among the foreign firms. In particular, the production and exports of black-and-white televisions, followed by color televisions, have been so dramatic that it prompted a series of related studies in Taiwan (see Yeh, 1980; Schive and Yeh 1980; Chu, 1975; Chen, 1985; Chang, 1986). Based on these studies and government's published data, we focus our study on technology transfer and the growth of the Taiwanese television industry.

The first black-and-white television broadcasting station in Taiwan appeared in 1962 with help from Japan's NHK. At that time, Taiwan's domestic demands for televisions depended completely on imports. Taiwan imported 6,000 units and 18,000 units of black-and-white televisions in 1962 and 1963, respectively. The production of the black-and-white televisions started in 1964. In that year, the production level were about 30,000 units. The firms were mostly joint ventures with the Japanese firms and their initial purpose was to sell in Taiwan's domestic market. The exports of black-and-white televisions started in 1967 with 2,000 units. In the next year, 1968, the production was boosted up to 630,000 units and the exports increased to 56,000 units, when RCA and Admiral of the United States joined in the production in Taiwan for the sole purpose of exports (see Yeh, 1980). From then on until 1980, the black-and-white television industry in Taiwan grew with amazing speed. In 1980, the production reached the peak level of 5.58 million units, and almost all of them were exported to the world market. After 1980, the production and export of black-and-white televisions started to decline because of its substitution by the demand for color televisions. By 1988, Taiwan produced and exported only about 1.3 million units of black-and-white televisions.

The technological know-how to produce black-and-white televisions soon induced the technology of producing color televisions in Taiwan (the forward linkage). The first color television broadcasting in Taiwan started in 1969. In that year, 113 units of color televisions were produced and another 1,000 units were imported for consumption. From then on, the production of color television increased with more amazing speed than that of the black-and-white televisions. The output was about 20,000 units in 1970, and it increased to 1.46 million units in 1980 and 4.45 million units in 1987. The exports of color television started in 1970, and the export-output ratio was about 77 percent and 87 percent for 1971 and 1987, respectively. From 1970 to 1984, the average growth rate of the color television production and exports has been about 60 percent per year, which was higher than that of the black-and-white television (about 50% per year).

With the development of the television industry, its parts industry has also sprouted (the backward linkage). In late 1960s, the imported black-and-white television picture tubes were gradually substituted by domestic production. By 1973, the exports of black-and-white television picture tubes exceeded its imports which dwindled to a very small amount by 1978. The process of change from imports to import substitution, and then to exports also occurred in the production of television tuners. In this case, the exports of tuners exceeded its imports in 1975. Color television picture tubes are more difficult to build. Up until 1978, Taiwan still imported large quantity of color television picture tubes. It was reported that Taiwan RCA and Taiwan Admiral have 150 subcontractors, and Zenith has more than 50 local firms supplying television parts. These local subcontractors received technical assistance from the parent companies in the United States (Saito, 1981, 49).

To visualize the effects of technical assistance on the productions of television and its parts in Taiwan, the technical assistance agreements and the technology providing countries are reported in Table 9.6. There were 66 cases of television related technical cooperation between 1965 and 1977 (col. 7). Japan provided slightly more than half (39 cases), followed by the United States (21 cases), and then Netherlands (5 cases), and one case from another country (col. 8).

Table 9.6: Technology Transfer of Television Industry in Taiwan

	T.V.		Parts				Total tech Coop	
Year	BW TV (1)	Color TV (2)	Picture Tube (3)	Tuner etc. (4)	Transformer etc. (5)	Other parts (6)	Cases (7)	Country (8)
1965			j				1	j
1966								
1967								
1968	u	u		u		u	4	4u
1969		3j	2d	2u	j	2jud	11	5j3u3d
1970	u	8ju	3j			juo	16	12j3uo
1971		ju	2u	u		j	6	2j4u
1972	u	u	u			ju	5	j4u
1973					j	2j2u	4	2j2u
1974		j			u		2	ju
1975		5j	4j		j	2j	12	12j
1976		j				j	2	2j
1977	jd		d				3	j2d
1978								
Total	5	23	14	4	4	16	66	
	j3ud	19j4u	8j3u3d	4u	3ju	8j6udo		39j21u5do

Notes: BW TV = Black and White Television
CO TV = Color Telesvion
Other Parts = Technical assistance related to flight back transformers, yoke coils, and others
j = with Japanese firms
u = with U.S.firms
d = with Dutch firms
o = with firms from other countries
(3ju means cooperation with three Japanese and one U.S. firms. 1u = u, 1 is omitted)
Source: Schive and Yeh (1980) and Yeh (1980).

Before 1968, there was only one case of technical assistance on picture tubes production (col. 3). Thus the production of television before 1968 seems to be merely a complete knocked-down parts assembly. The effects of technology transfer on Taiwan's television production and exports were shown after 1968 in the table. The difficulty of building color television receivers is shown by the fact that before the large quantity production and exports in 1970s, the industry received 13 cases of technical assistance (including 11 cases from Japan and 2 cases from the United States; see col. 2). From 1971 to 1976, the color television industry received additional 11 cases of technical assistance (including 8 cases from Japan and 2 cases from the United States; see col. 2). After these technical assistance, the data show that the production of color television increased from 0.9 million units in 1977 to 1.8 million units in 1978. It seems that production doubled after solving some technical problems. This is in contrast to the case of black-and-white television, which required only five cases of technical assistance from 1968 to 1977 (col. 1) before the production reached the highest level in 1980.

Other obvious examples of the relation between technical assistance and exports are provided by the exports of television picture tubes and tuners. After receiving 9 technical assistance related to picture tubes productions (including 4 cases from Japan, 3 cases from the United States, and 2 cases from Holland; see col. 4, 1965–1972), the exports of both black-and-white and color picture tubes increased significantly during the mid-1970s. "The tuner is perhaps the most critical assembly in a television receiver" (Skinner and Rogers, 1968, 103). The production and exports of television tuners, in the early 1970s, were spurred by the four cases of technical assistance from the United States (col. 4).

In summary, Table 9.6 presents an overview of the foreign technology transfer in Taiwan's television industry. From these evidences, we may state that, without these technology transfers through DFI, the Taiwanese television industry probably would have grown slower, if it grew at all, and it might also miss the opportunity of export expansion as other developing countries also started producing televisions shortly afterward.

9.5 Conclusion

In this paper we have shown that DFI has effects on the growth of Taiwan's GDP. We have also shown that foreign technology may be transferred by DFI through technical cooperation and foreign employees in the foreign firms in Taiwan. It is found that the higher the foreign ownership of the firms, the more likely that the firms adopt foreign technology and become more innovative.

However, product innovation is found to be almost the same between native firms and foreign firms. This may reflect the vitality and progressiveness of the Taiwanese people and the society. These factors are, we conjecture, the most important source of the rapid economic growth experienced by the Taiwanese economy.

The same vitality and progressiveness are shown in our examples of the Taiwanese television industry. It is clearly demonstrated that the Taiwanese were able to absorb foreign technology for production and exports, which in turn improved their standard of living. From the production of simple black-and-white televisions, the Taiwanese advanced to produce technically more sophisticated color televisions. This shows that they can meet the changing demand of the domestic and world markets. Taiwan also started developing the parts industry to support the local production. Although they had difficulty in producing color television picture tubes at the beginning, they finally mastered the technology which is now applied to build computer terminals and microcomputer monitors (Chang, 1986).

In the television industry, Taiwan is a late comer. The success of technology transfer may be seen from a 1978 survey of 65 representative Japanese firms of machinery makers. The survey reported that by 1978, Taiwan's television and radio production technology already caught up with that of Japan, while the Philippines' television production technology still lagged that of Japan by five to ten years (Watanabe, 1981, 47). Taiwan's television industry started in 1962. However, according to the United Nations statistics (Yeh, 1980, 165), by 1976, the Taiwanese share of the world television production was 7.1 percent (out of the world production of 45.82 million sets). It ranked fourth in the world, only after Japan (30%), the United States (13.8%), and the USSR (13.3%). The Philippines started producing television in 1956, Mexico and Brazil in 1955. Nevertheless, their world shares remained almost constant at about 0.2 percent, 1.3 percent, and 2.9 percent, respectively, during the same period. Despite Taiwan's limited natural resources, small land area, and some problems related to DFI, the rise of Taiwan to a giant in world television production is truly extraordinary. What are the sources of such vitality and progressiveness of the Taiwanese? We have barely touched these interesting topics in this paper.

Acknowledgments

The second author wishes to express her sincere appreciation to Professors M. Jan Dutta, Kiyoshi Kojima, Anthony M. Tang, and James T.H. Tsao for their helpful comments. The author also greatly appreciates the detailed comments and suggestions from the referees. Thanks also go to Professor Frank S.T. Hsiao for his valuable suggestions. Nevertheless, all errors are naturally the author's. In preparing for this chapter, we used the Microsoft Excel Program to redo the charts and tables.

References

Chang, F.R. (1986). "A Study of Television Manufacturing Industry in Taiwan Area" (in Chinese). *The Quarterly Journal of the Bank of Taiwan*, 37(June): 57–70.

Chen, C.N. (1989). "The Entry, Exit and Growth of Electronic Firms in Taiwan Area" (in Chinese). *Academia Economic Papers*, The Institute of Economics Academia Sinica, Taipei, Taiwan, 13(March): 47–90.

Chu, J.H. (1975). "Electronics Industry in Taiwan" (in Chinese). The Quarterly Journal of the Bank of Taiwan, 26(March): 112–130.

Council for Economic Planning and Development of Taiwan (1988). *Taiwan Statistical Data Book (TSDB), 1988.* Council for Economic Planning and Development, Taiwan.

Du, T.V. (1986). "DFI and Technology Importing Policy in Northeast and Southeast Asian Countries." In S. Sekiguchi and T.V. Du (eds.), *Direct Investment and Technological Transfer-Japan and Northeast/Southeast Asia* (in Japanese). Tokyo: Center of Japanese Economic Studies.

Hsiao, F.S.T. and M.C.W. Hsiao (1984). "Direct Foreign Investment and Economic Development — The Taiwanese Experience." *Bulletin of North America Taiwanese Professors' Association*, 4(December): 7–15.

Johnson, H.G. (1980). *Comparative Cost and Commercial Policy Theory for a Developing World Economy: Wicksell Lecture, 1968.* Baltimore, MD: The Johns Hopkins University Press.

Judge, G.G., W.E. Griffiths, R.C. Hill, H. Lutkepohl and T. Lee (1988). *Introduction to the Theory and Practice of Econometrics.* 2nd ed. New York: Wiley.

Kojima, K. (1985a). *Japan's Direct Foreign Investment* (in Japanese). Tokyo: Bunshindo.

______(1985b). "U.S.-Japan Direct Investment in Taiwan-Comparison of the Japanese Type and the MNC Type" (in Japanese). *World Economic Review* (Sekai Keizai Hyoron), 29(March): 33–44.

Lall, S. (1978). "Transnationals, Domestic Enterprises, and Industrial Structure in Host LDCs: A Survey." *Oxford Economic Papers*, 30(July): 217–248.

Ministry of Economic Affairs, Taiwan (1982). *Survey of Foreign Enterprises, Its Operations, and Its Contributions to the Taiwanese Economic Development.* Taipei, Taiwan.

Saito, S. (1981). The Technology Transfer Problems between Japan and Taiwan" (in Japanese). *World Economic Review (Sekai Keizai Hyoron)*, 25(May).

Schive, C. (1985). "A Study of Technology Transfer Channels in Taiwan" (in Chinese). *Economic Papers No. 76.* Chung-Hua Institution for Economic Research, Taipei, Taiwan, September.

______(1983). "Direct Foreign Investment, Technology Transfer, and Industrial Development in Taiwan" (in Chinese). In *Proceedings of Conference on Taiwanese Industrial Development* Vol. 2, 471–501. Taipei, Taiwan: The Institute of Economics Academia Sinica, March.

Schive, C. and R.S. Yeh (1980). "Direct Foreign Investment and Taiwan's T.V. Industry." In *Economic Essays*, 261–291. The Graduate Institute of Economics, National Taiwan University, November.

Sekiguchi, S. (1979). *Japanese Direct Foreign Investment.* Montclair: Allanheld, Osman, & Co.

Skinner, W. and D. Rogers (1968). *Manufacturing Policy in the Electronics Industry*, 3rd ed. Homewood, IL: Irwin.

Watanabe, T. (1981). Economic Development of the NICs and the Benefits of the Late-Comers: Examples from Korea." *Sekai Keizai Hyoron (World Economic Review)*, 25(August): 45–50.

Yeh, R.S. (1980). "Development of the Taiwanese Television Industry as Seen from the International Product-Cycle" (in Chinese). *The Quarterly Journal of the Bank of Taiwan*, 31(March): 156–205.

Chapter 10

Globalization of the Taiwanese Economy and U.S.-Taiwan Trade Relations

10.1 Introduction

The globalization of an economy is distinguished from internationalization. Globalization is characterized as an economy that is actively participating in external economic activities, such as promotion of foreign trade and outward foreign investment, and contribution to international organizations. Internationalization is characterized as an economy that is easing government controls of foreign exchanges and opening up a country's domestic market for foreign imports and investment.[1] Thus internationalization includes what we usually call the trade liberalization movement (Hsiao, 1989).

The purpose of this paper is to present some important measures of globalization of the Taiwanese economy, and study the impacts of globalization on the U.S.-Taiwan trade relation. Since the problem of the U.S.-Taiwan trade relations is only one of many facets of the world economy, our discussions will be imbedded into broader problems of imbalance and adjustment of the world economy. The second section uses various indices of the international trade structure as indicators of globalization. Next,

---

[1]There may be different definitions of internationalization. It may also be referred differently as "restructuring" of an economy, or "the shift from an export-led to a domestic demand-led growth." See Higashi and Lauter (1987), Footnote 5, 32, and xi. In the *1989 Economic White Paper of Japan*, one chapter was devoted to globalization of the Japanese economy. It has four characteristics: first, increases in bidirectional international relations through trade and capital movement; second, global strategies of corporations through direct foreign investment; third, taking an active international role corresponding to Japan's position in the world; fourth, increases in tourists abroad and direct foreign purchases. This paper follows the same approach (EPA, 1989, 163–164).

we introduce other indicators, including direct foreign investment and some socioeconomic indices. The fourth section discusses the U.S.-Taiwan trade relation in the face of persistent U.S. trade deficits. Here we show that globalization leads to internationalization in Taiwan and other Asian countries. The fifth section analyzes the market shares and growth rates of Japan, Taiwan, and South Korea in the U.S. import markets in major manufacturing categories. In the next section, we give some thoughts on the effects of short-run and long-run adjustment policies. The last section concludes the paper.

10.2 The Taiwanese Trade Structure as an Indicator of Globalization

In the controversies between trade as an engine or handmaiden of growth, we have shown that the causality runs both ways for the Asian Newly Industrializing Countries (NICs) and Japan (Hsiao and Hsiao, 1989; Hsiao, M., 1987). Globalization of the Taiwanese economy as well as the economies of Japan and other Asian countries has been achieved through actively engaging in international trade. For Taiwan, globalization started in the mid-1960s after the end of the U.S. aid program. In fact, internationalization and globalization proceeded more or less at the same time under the strict control of an authoritarian regime. The Taiwanese, faced with the termination of the U.S. aid and the growing threat of Chinese invasion, embarked on vigorous efforts of economic development by attracting direct foreign investment and promoting exports. The literature on the process of Taiwanese economic development is abundant (e.g., Galenson, 1979; Gold, 1986; Liang and Hou, 1988), and we also have made some observations elsewhere (Hsiao and Hsiao, 1983, 1989, 1990; Hsiao, 1992). Here, we would like to emphasize recent globalization of the Taiwanese economy.

Figures 10.1 and 10.2 characterize the globalization process in Taiwan from 1970 to 1988 in terms of the expansion in external trade, the changes in outward and inward direct foreign investment in Taiwan, the increase in the number of foreign visitors and the Taiwanese travelers, increase in the passenger traffic of international airlines, and the number of Taiwanese students returned from studying abroad. In both diagrams, the data in 1980 are taken as the basis for comparison and are taken as one. It is shown as the solid horizontal line across the diagram. The figures for 1988 are plotted as the solid gray columns, and those for 1988, as the patterned columns.

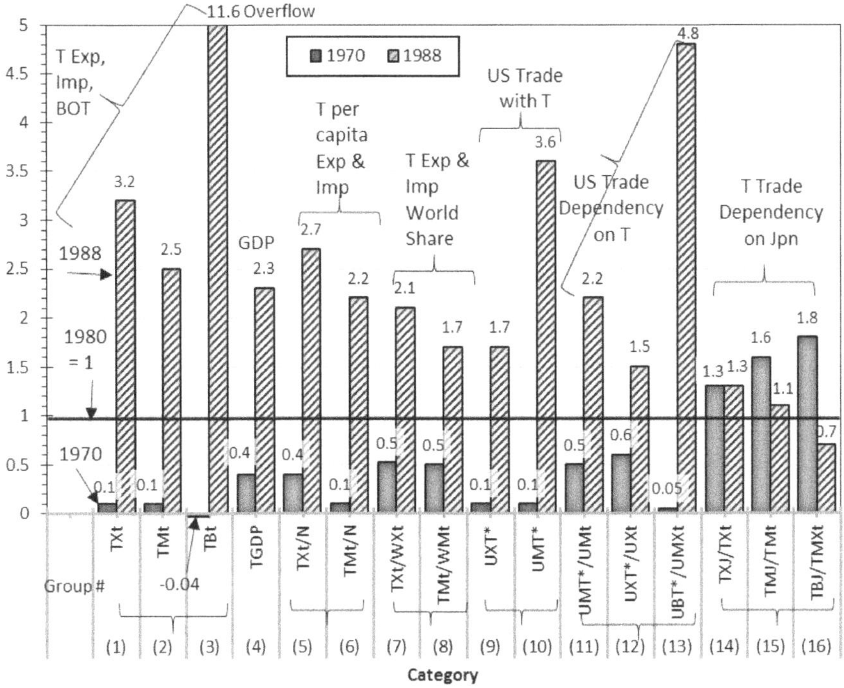

Figure 10.1: Some Economic Indicators of Taiwan

Comparison of 1970, 1980, and 1988

Notes: B = BoT, J = Japan, M = Imports, MX = imports + exports, N = population, T = Taiwan, t = total, U = USA, W = World, X = Exports.

In many instances, the 1970 figures are very small, often 10 percent, or 0 percent of the 1980 after rounding. In this case, the gray column is almost invisible.

Such comparison of two decades of data is meaningful since almost all the data we used have shown a steady increase over the period under review. Generally speaking, to show the process of economic expansion and globalization, the three bars in each group should start from a gray bar in 1970 which is less than the unit line in the middle, and the patterned bar for 1988 should be higher than the unit line. Figures 10.1 and 10.2 show that this is indeed the case most of the time. They show that the patterned bars are generally much longer than the unit line, indicating that the globalization of the Taiwanese economy proceeded more than twice as fast in 1980. We now explain the diagrams. The number in parentheses below corresponds to the group number along the X-axis in the figures.

(1), (2) Total Exports and Imports. The left hand side of Fig. 10.1 starts from Taiwan's total exports (TXt, the capital T for Taiwan, the small t for total) and total imports (TMt). In 1970, both TXt and TMt are only about 10 percent of the 1980 figures. They grew steadily about ten times in current U.S. dollars from 1970 to 1980. From 1980 to 1988, exports grew more than three times, and imports 2.5 times.

(3) Balanced of Trade. Taiwan's export promotion policy has been proved to be tremendously "profitable." Before 1970, Taiwan had trade deficits every year (except 1964). In 1970, it recorded a deficit of $43 million. That year turned out to be the year of transition. From 1971 to the present, Taiwan earned trade surplus every year except 1974 and 1975 during the first oil crisis. The surplus in 1980 was $78 million. This was clearly erratic, possibly due to the second oil shock. Taiwan earned $1,329 million in 1979 and $1,411 million in 1981, and the trade surpluses have been steadily increasing afterward. Thus for a fair estimation, we have taken the three-year average of 1979 to 1981, $939.3 million, as the 1980 base year figure. Since the trade surplus in 1988 was $10.93 billion, we obtain the figure that Taiwan's trade surplus increased 11.6 times in eight years from 1980 to 1988, as shown in Group (3). In fact, in 1987, Taiwan's trade surplus reached a record high at $18.6 billion. Thus the simple comparison of trade surplus in 1988 with that of 1980 still underestimates the vitality of the Taiwanese economy.

(4) Gross Domestic Product (GDP). Through "trade as an engine of growth" argument, we expect GDP of Taiwan to increase proportionally with its trading activities. The change in Taiwan's GDP (TGDP) is not as dramatic, but it is still admirable. Group (4) in Fig. 10.1 shows that TGDP increased 2.5 times from 1970 to 1980, and increased 2.3 times from 1980 to 1988.

(5), (6) Per Capita Imports and Exports. The next four groups present the dramatic increase of the Taiwanese trade activities in relative perspective. They show that from 1970 to 1980 the per capita exports (TXt/N in (5)) more than doubled, and the per capita imports (TMt/N in (6)) increased about 10 times (to $1,123 and $1,119, respectively). From 1980 to 1988, the per capita exports increased 2.7 times to $3,062, and the per capita imports increased 2.2 times to $2,509.

(7), (8) World Share of Exports and Imports. Another measure of Taiwan's globalization is reflected by the shares of the Taiwanese exports and imports in the world exports and imports (TXt/WXt and TMt/WMt). Both have doubled during the 1970s (from about 0.52% in 1970 to 1.05%

in 1980). From 1980 to 1988, the Taiwanese export share in the world increased 2.1 times (to 2.25%) and that of import share increased 1.7 times (to 1.78%). Thus, as a measure of the speed of globalization, we may say that the Taiwanese trade activities grew almost four times faster than the world average during the past 20 years. By 1987, Taiwan is the eleventh largest exporter and the seventeenth largest importer in the world (Hsiao, F., 1989, Table 2).

(9), (10) U.S. Exports and Imports from Taiwan. The next statistics show the impact of globalization of the Taiwanese economy from the American point of view. From 1970 to 1980, both the U.S. exports to, and imports from, Taiwan (UXT* and UMT*, where * denotes the figure for 1987) increased 10 times. However, from 1980 to 1987, the U.S. exports to Taiwan increased only 1.7 times (from $4.3 billion to $7.4 billion), while U.S. imports from Taiwan increased 3.6 times (from $6.8 billion to $24.6 billion), during the same seven-year period. The change is less dramatic in terms of the Taiwanese shares in total U.S. imports and exports (UMT*/UMt in Group (11) and UXT*/UXt in Group (12)). From 1980 to 1987, the share of Taiwanese imports in total U.S. imports increased 2.2 times, but U.S. exports to Taiwan in the total U.S. exports, only 1.5 times.

In any case, the discrepancy in imports and exports left the United States with a relatively large trade deficit with Taiwan. The deficit increased from $22 million in 1970 to $2.5 billion in 1980, and then to $17.2 billion in 1987. In relative terms, the ratio of the U.S. trade deficit with Taiwan to the U.S. total trade (imports plus exports, UBT*/UMXt in Group (13)) increased 20 times from 1970 to 1980, and 4.8 times from 1980 to 1987. Similar changes also appeared in the U.S. trade relations with Japan and other Asian NICs: South Korea, Hong Kong, and Singapore. The large trade deficits inevitably led to trade frictions between the United States on the one hand and Japan and the Asian NICs on the other.

(14), (15) Taiwan's Trade with Japan. Taiwan's trade relations with Japan are different from those with the United States. From 1970 to 1980, Taiwan's export dependency ratio with Japan (TXJ/TXt in (14)) decreased 30 percent (from 1.3 to 1.0), and then in 1988 it increased 1.3 times again (from 14.5% to 11% and then to 14.5%). Taiwan's import dependency ratio with Japan (TMJ/TMt in (15)) decreased 60 percent (from 1.6 to 1.0) from 1970 to 1980, and went up slightly by 10 percent in 1988 (from 43% in 1970 to 27% in 1980, and then to 30% in 1988).

In fact, in absolute terms, Taiwan's trade with Japan, like that with the United States, also increased about ten times during the 1970s. That is, exports increased from $0.2 billion in 1970 to $2 billion in 1980, and imports increased from $0.6 billion in 1970 to $5.4 billion in 1980 (TSDB, 1989, 215). The imports then increased 2.8 times to $14.8 billion and exports 4 times, to $8.8 billion, in 1988.

(16) Trade Balance with Japan. Taiwan's trade deficit with Japan has been chronic; it has had deficits every year since 1956. In 1988, the deficit with Japan was $6 billion, in contrast to Taiwan's surplus of $10.5 billion with the United States that year (TSDB, 1989, 215). Although Taiwan's trade deficit with Japan is increasing every year, the increasing rate does not seem to be alarming, as its ratio with total trade (TBJ/TMXt) has been decreasing. During the 1970s, the ratio decreased 80 percent (from 14.5% to 8.0%), and from 1980 to 1988, it decreased further to about 70 percent of the 1980 ratio (from 8.0% to 5.5%). This again is in a sharp contrast with that of the United States. The ratio of the U.S. trade deficit with Taiwan relative to the total U.S. trade with Taiwan (UBT/UMXT in (13)) increased drastically during the last decade.

In general, the higher the Taiwanese exports to the United States, the higher the Taiwanese imports from Japan, with a certain time lag. This indicates Taiwan's dependence on Japanese capital goods and intermediate products, and also on the American consumer markets.

10.3 Other Indicators of Globalization

Figure 10.2 shows other nine indicators of globalization of the Taiwanese economy. The numbers along the X-axis correspond to the group number in the text.

(1) Outward Investment Ratio. One of them is the ratio of Taiwan's outward investment to GDP (OIt/TGDP in (1)). Before 1970, due to the shortage in investment funds, direct outward foreign investment was not approved. In 1980, according to the government record, the approved outward investment was $42 million, 17 cases, in 1980. In 1988, it increased to $218 million, 109 cases (TSOC, 1988, 48). Thus, from 1980 to 1988, the outward investment increased 5.2 times. Since, from Fig. 10.1, we know that the Taiwanese GDP increased 2.3 times, the amount of outward investment over GDP increased about 2.3 times (=5.2/2.3) during the eight-year period.

(2) Outward Investment to the United States. Slightly more than half of the outward investment went to the United States. An example is the Taiwanese bid in December 1989 on Wyse Technology Inc., a former

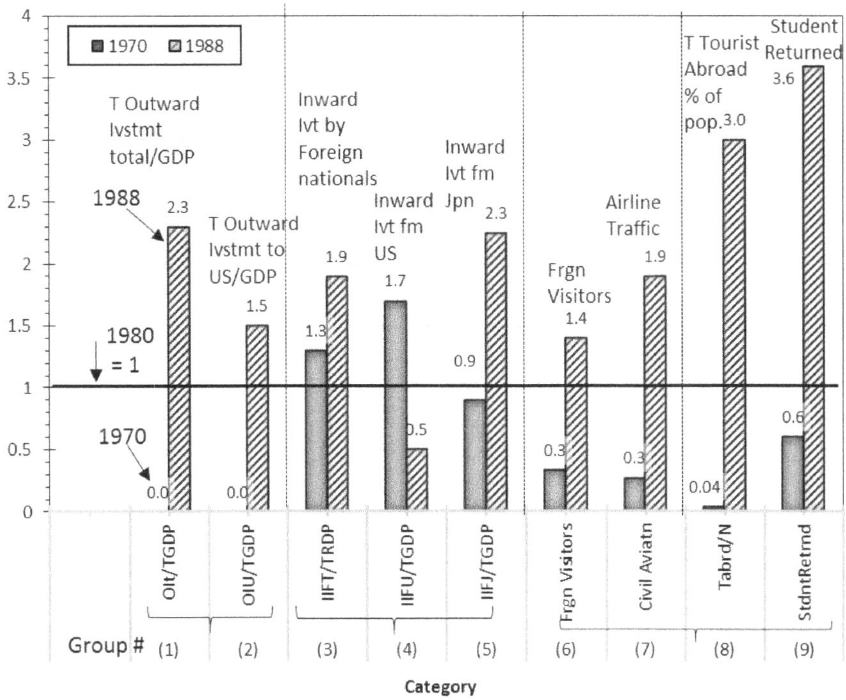

Figure 10.2: Some Socioeconomic Indicators of Taiwan Comparison of 1970, 1980, and 1988

Notes: OI = Outward Investment, II = Inward Inv't, F = For = Foreign, N = population, T = Taiwan, t = total, U = USA.

Silicon Valley superstar. However, in recent years, it also went to some Southeast Asian countries, like the Philippines (8%), Thailand (5.5%), Indonesia (5%), and Malaysia (2.7%) (TSOC, 1988, 53–56).[2] Thus, the ratio of the Taiwanese outward investment to the United States over Taiwan's GDP (OIU/TGDP in (2)) only increased 1.5 times in recent years. In 1988, the industries that the Taiwanese invested in overseas were electronic and electronic appliances (29%), services (22%), and chemicals (14%).

(3) Inward Foreign Investment. Another indicator of globalization is direct investment by the "foreign nationals" and by the "overseas Chinese," although they are in fact foreigners. The ratio of the officially

[2]For some details of the Taiwanese direct foreign investment in Thailand, see Ramstetter (1988).

approved direct foreign investment by the foreign nationals to Taiwan's GDP (IIFt/TGDP in (3)) decreased 30 percent in 1980 compared to the figure in 1970 (6.6% to 5.3%). It then almost doubled from 1980 to 1988 (to 10.0%). Figure 10.2 shows the changes by comparing three years using 1980 data as 1.

(4) The U.S. Investment in Taiwan. The dollar amount of U.S. direct investment in Taiwan increased over time. It was $67.8 million, $110.1 million, and $134.7 million for 1970, 1980, and 1988, respectively. However, its ratio over Taiwan's GDP (IIFU/TGDP in (4)) decreased steadily: in 1980, it had only 70 percent of 1970 level (from 0.41% to 0.24%), and it reduced about 50 percent again from 1980 to 1988 (to 0.13%). In Fig. 10.2, Group (4) shows that relative to 1980 data, 1970 data is 1.7 times larger than that of 1980, and 1988 data is only one half of 1980 data.

(5) Japanese Investment in Taiwan. On the other hand, the Japanese investment in Taiwan shows a reversed picture. In the dollar amount, the Japanese investment increased from $28.5 million in 1970 to $86.1 million in 1980 (TSOC, 1988, 22). The IIFJ/TGDP ratio in Group (5) shows that the ratio increased almost at the same pace as TGDP from 1970 to 1980. It then more than doubled and grew faster than TGDP from 1980 to 1988 (to $431 million). Historically, the cumulative investment in Taiwan from the United States (34%) is only slightly higher than that from Japan (32%) (TSOC, 1988, 21–22).

The last three indicators are socioeconomic indices.

(6) Foreign Visitors. From 1970 to 1980, foreign visitors to Taiwan tripled from 0.5 million to 1.4 million (TSDB, 1989, 135). In 1988, it increased another 40 percent to 1.9 million. Here the visitors include what the government calls the "overseas Chinese," who range from 10 percent to 15 percent of the total visitors in recent years.

(7) Airline Traffic. The passenger traffic, including the foreigners and the Taiwanese, of international airlines also increased at a fast pace. Group (7) of Fig. 10.2 shows the percentage change. From 1970 to 1980, the passenger traffic was up almost 4 times from 1 million to 3.7 million persons (TSDB, 1989, 129), and in 1988 it almost doubled, to 7.1 million persons.

(8) Tourists Abroad. The last two groups show the proportion of Taiwanese tourists abroad in the population and the Taiwanese students returned from studying abroad. The tourists abroad were 0.017 million persons (TSA, 1974, 816), 0.5 million persons (TRTS, 1980, 47), and 1.6 million persons (TRTS, 1988) in 1970, 1980, and 1988, respectively.

In terms of its ratio over population, it was only 0.12 percent in 1970, and 2.72 percent in 1980. The ratio tripled to 8 percent of the 1988 population.

In terms of Group (8) in Fig. 10.2, using 1980 as the base year, the ratio in 1970 was only 4 percent of the 1980 ratio, and in 1988 the ratio tripled. This means that, twenty years ago, only about one out of 1,000 people went abroad as tourists. By 1988, 80 persons out of 1,000 people in Taiwan went abroad. The increase in tourist traffic greatly broadened contact between the Taiwanese and foreign countries, and helped the advancement of internationalization of the Taiwanese Society.

(9) Students Returned. As Taiwan has advanced to one of the developed countries, a more dramatic change has occurred recently in the number of students returned from studying abroad. Figure 10.2 shows that the rate of students returned from abroad in 1970 (407 persons) was about 64 percent of the 1980 level (640 persons) (TSDB, 1989, 296). The change in that ten-year period is very limited. However in 1988, 2,296 students returned, 3.6 times that of 1980. This may be compared with the students leaving Taiwan to study abroad (not shown in Fig. 10.2). From 1970 to 1980, the number of students studying abroad increased almost 3 times, from 2,056 students to 5,933 students (TSDB, 294). But from 1980 to 1988, it increased only about 20 percent, to 7,122 students. One interpretation is that, as the globalization of the Taiwanese economy proceeds, the college graduates find more domestic and foreign employment opportunities within Taiwan. More young people choose to stay in Taiwan after graduation. At the same time an increasing number of the Taiwanese students studying abroad find attractive employment opportunities in the home country.

10.4 Impacts of Globalization and U.S.-Taiwan Trade Relations

As shown elsewhere (Hsiao, F., 1989), economic globalization has been led by the Japanese since the early 1960s, and followed closely by the four Asian NICs. The people in the Asian NICs constitute only 1.5 percent of the world population (Japan has 2.6%).They are crowded in 0.1 percent (0.4% for Japan) of the world land area (WDR, 1989). However, in 1987, the value of exports from Japan ranked third in the world, next only to what was formerly West Germany and the United States. The exports from Taiwan, South Korea, Hong Kong, and Singapore ranked eleventh, thirteenth, twelfth, and eighteenth, respectively, in 1987 (GATT). Their import activities ranked somewhat behind, fifth for Japan, seventeenth, fifteenth, thirteenth, and nineteenth, respectively, for the Asian NICs in the order mentioned.

There is a peculiar pattern of trade structures among the Asian NICs, especially in Taiwan and Korea. Both countries import industrial materials, parts, and equipment from Japan, and export finished manufactures, like household electronics and appliances, and machinery, to the United States. Their trade balances with Japan have been negative and those with the United States have been positive (Hsiao and Hsiao, 1989; Hsiao, F., 1989). As shown in Fig. 10.3, this pattern has repeated year after year for Taiwan since 1968 (TSDB, 1988, 215), and for South Korea since 1976 except the three years from 1979 to 1981 (KESY, 1989, 218–221).[3] The two

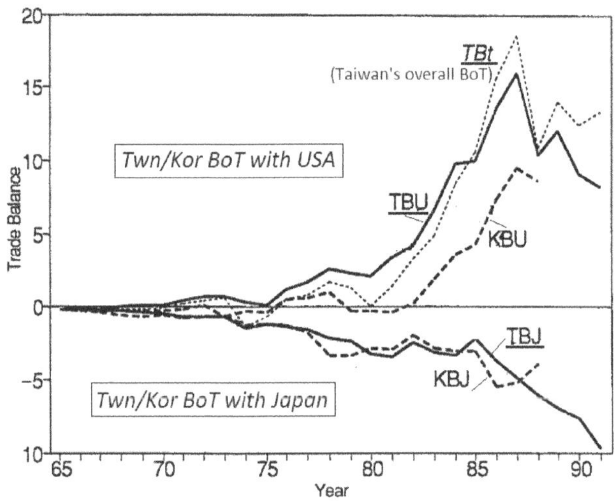

Figure 10.3: Trade Balances of Taiwan and Korea With Japan and the United States, in US$) Billion

Notes: B = BoT, J = Japan, K = South Korea, T = Taiwan, t = total, U = USA.

[3]In February 1982, to reduce a US$3.2 billion trade deficit with Japan, Taiwan surprised the world by unilaterally banning imports from Japan on more than 1,500 consumer goods for an indefinite time, and heavy trucks and diesel engines for one year. Tokyo threatened to cancel Taiwan's preferential tariffs and trade status. The ban inflicted serious damage to Taiwanese exports and its national economy. As Tokyo could not wage a trade war simultaneously with the United States and the EEC, both sides reached a compromise and the ban on half of the goods were lifted by November of that year. For details, see Arnold (1985), 194–196; Aoki (1985), 157.

countries' trade surpluses with the United States, however, are only a recent phenomenon. Before 1968 for Taiwan and before 1976 for South Korea, both countries incurred small deficits every year with Japan and also with the United States.

Despite trade surpluses with the United States since 1968, the overall trade balances of Taiwan and South Korea were consistently negative for a long period. The turning point came for Taiwan in 1971 (TSDB, 1988, 215) and for South Korea only in 1986 (KMSKE, 1989, 203). Since then, Taiwan (except 1974 and 1975) and South Korea have been enjoying overall trade surpluses. In 1985, Taiwan's total foreign exchange reserves (with gold) were US$23.4 billion (same below). They were more than tripled to $79.4 billion in 1988, second only to Japan ($98 billion), and surpassing (West) Germany ($56 billion, TFS, 1989; IFS, 1989) and the United States ($48 billion, IFS, 1989). South Korea's total foreign exchange reserves also increased from $2.8 billion in 1985 to $12.3 billion in 1988. The increase in foreign exchange reserves also occurred in Hong Kong and Singapore. The arduous export activities and increasing trade surpluses have changed the global economic position of the Asian NICs. At the same time, the persistent global economic imbalances present a serious threat to the prosperity of the world economy (Fase, 1989).

In 1987, the U.S. trade deficit with the four Asian NICs reached around $38 billion, that is, about 22 percent of the total U.S. deficit. It was only reasonable that the United States removed the four Asian NICs from the Generalized System of Preferences (GSP) program in January 1988. Thus, they are no longer eligible for the GSP duty-free privilege for certain products (IER, March 1988, 4).

Frustrated by the persistent and huge trade deficits in general, and with Japan in particular, and the slow pace of negotiation with Japan and in a lesser degree with South Korea and Taiwan (NYT, May 2, 1988, D2; October 25, 1988, P1), the U.S. Congress passed the Omnibus Trade and Competitiveness Act in August 1988. The Act requires the U.S. Trade Representative to publish annual reports on foreign trade barriers of the U.S. exports, make investigations, negotiations, and even retaliation by provoking the so-called *Super 301 provision.*

Not surprisingly, the first report in April 1989 singled out Japan, Taiwan, and South Korea, along with the EEC, Brazil and India as alleged offenders. After a month of intensive negotiations, Taiwan was dropped from the list by agreeing to appreciate its currency sharply against the dollar. South Korea was also excluded from the list by agreeing to dismantle half of its 140 restrictions on agricultural imports, and to make increased access to the domestic market by foreign firms (FOF, June 2, 1989, 397). The Taiwanese government also proposed to cut tariffs on "4,800 agricultural, consumer and industrial products to open Taiwan's market wider to foreign traders" (TFCJ, March 20, 1989).

The American pressure on Taiwan has accelerated since then. In July 1989, the Taiwanese banking law was revised to attract more foreign and domestic banks, and abandoned the official control of interest rates (FOF, 1989, 616–17). In August, in order to avoid trade sanctions, the Taiwanese government agreed to allow American observers to monitor drift net salmon fishing which was killing marine animals in the North Pacific (NYT, August 26, 1989, A29). By November, the United States "eased a threat of trade sanctions against Taiwan and South Korea as they began cracking down on piracy of American products in their countries" (NYT, November 2, 1989, D1). Although some problems, like more liberalization, currency evaluation, and rice exports from Taiwan, still remain, "the U.S. has reaped positive results from the pressure it put on its trading partners.... most have moved toward reforms" (NYT, May 13, 1989, A33). Along with the globalization of their economies through trade, the internationalization of domestic markets of the Asian NICs is also in progress at a fast pace.

In 1988, the U.S. exports to Japan increased 34 percent, and her trade deficits, with Japan in particular and with the rest of the world in general, have decreased for the first time in more than ten years. As the currencies of the Asian NICs, especially the New Taiwan Dollar and the Korean Won, were loosely tied to the U.S. dollar, devaluation of the U.S. dollar and evaluation of the Japanese yen initially benefited the Asian NICs by increasing exports to Japan, as well as to the United States by filling the U.S. import market vacated by the Japanese. Low-priced products from the Asian NICs have flooded the Japanese markets since 1986. The Taiwanese exports to Japan literally jumped 32 percent in 1986, 53 percent in 1987, and 26 percent in 1988, while its imports from Japan also increased more or less at the same pace at 49 percent, 43 percent, and 25 percent, respectively (TSDB, 1989; NYT, April 25, 1988, D8). There seems a possibility that the Taiwanese and the Korean markets can be integrated with the Japanese markets. This is one basis of our assertion that these three countries as a group are now ready for forming the Asian Economic Community (Hsiao, F., 1989). However, recent reports indicate that the run on the imports from the Asian NICs in Japanese markets subsided in early 1989

(JTBT, March 1989, 36–39).[4] The future of the imports from the Asian NICs in the Japanese markets is still in doubt.

In the U.S. market, both Taiwan and South Korea performed less dramatically under the watchful eyes of the U.S. Government. From 1986 to 1988, Taiwan's exports to the United States increased at 29 percent, 25 percent, and −1 percent, respectively. At the same time, Taiwan's imports from the United States shot up to 14 percent, 41 percent, and 70 percent, respectively. South Korea also increased two-side trade with the United States. Both Taiwan and South Korea had expanded trade with the United States and Japan faster than they had expected. Therefore, as shown in Fig. 10.3, both countries accumulated more trade surpluses with the United States at a faster pace, and at the same time, continued to incur trade deficits with Japan. Recent reports indicate that the U.S. trade deficits with Taiwan, South Korea, and Japan have been fluctuating in a decreasing trend. There is a hope that trade imbalance among them may eventually be corrected. However, the solution to the basic problem of structural imbalances in the world economy seems still far away.

10.5 The Taiwanese Exports in the U.S. Market

Taiwan's import dependency ratio with Japan for 1970, 1980, and 1988 was 43 percent, 27 percent, and 30 percent, respectively. At the same time, its export dependency ratio with Japan was 15 percent, 11 percent, and 14 percent, respectively. On the other hand, Taiwan's import dependency ratio with the United States for 1970, 1980, and 1988 was 23.9 percent, 23.7 percent, and 26.6 percent, respectively. Its export dependency ratio was 38.1 percent, 34.1 percent, and 38.7 percent, respectively. Thus, the United States and Japan are the most important trading partners for Taiwan since the end of the World War II. With nearly 40 percent of the exports going to the United States, the globalization of the Taiwanese economy indeed depends heavily on the U.S. market.

Table 10.1 shows the U.S. imports from Japan, Taiwan, and South Korea. The changes in manufacturing imports over the four-year period from 1984 to 1987 are also given. The first column shows the total amount of manufacturing commodities that the United States imported in 1987.

[4]The Asian NICs product boom in Japan subsided by early 1989 due to consumers' demand for higher quality products and the problem of providing after-service. See JTBT (March 1989), 36–39.

Table 10.1: The U.S. Import Market Shares of Japan, Taiwan and Korea (1987)

	(Units: US$ million, %)	USImp Total	3 Shares Subtotal	The import share (%) of Japan	Taiwan	Korea
	General Imports Total	405901	126184	84575	24622	16987
	Import share	100.0	31.1	20.8	6.1	4.2
(1)	Manufactured goods	53356	22.9	12.3	6.9	3.7
2	Paper, paperboard	6595	4.1	2.2	1.1	0.8
3	Iron and steel	8490	33.3	26.1	1.4	5.8*
4	Nonferrous metals	7991	6.2	5.6	0.4	0.2
(5)	Machinery	99433	48.6	36.0	7.7	4.9
6	Power generating	10860	23.1	22.0	0.7	0.5
7	General industrial	11111	37.5	28.4	6.7*	2.4
8	Telecommunications	20821	72.3*	51.1*	11.4*	9.9*
9	Electrical	24428	42.5	27.0	8.7	6.7*
10	Office machinery and data processing equipment	18462	62.6*	48.0*	10.4*	4.2
(11)	Transport equipment	78376	43.6	39.8	1.0	2.8
12	Automobiles, buses, trucks	57024	49.3	45.7*	0.0	3.6
13	New passenger cars	47858	48.8	44.5*	0.0	4.3
14	Motor vehicles parts	13740	30.2	28.1	1.4	0.6
(15)	Clothing	20490	31.0	1.8	14.3*	14.8*
(16)	Footwear	7237	57.6*	0.1	33.3*	24.2*

Sources: SAUS (1986), 809, and (1989), 787. * indicates important items. General Imports Total includes agricultural goods.

The second column is the sum of market shares of each commodity for Japan, Taiwan, and South Korea. On the average, they have a 31 percent share ($126 billion) of the total U.S. manufacturing imports. Among them, Japan's share is 21 percent ($85 billion), Taiwan, 6 percent ($25 billion), and Korea, 4 percent ($17 billion). In the three subcategories, namely, telecommunications, office machinery and data processing equipment, and footwear, the three countries have dominated over 50 percent of the U.S. import market. They also dominate nearly half of the American import markets in new passenger cars, other automobiles, buses, and trucks. In fact, in November 1989, AT&T complained to the U.S. International Trade Commission that "the Asian phone manufacturers' slice of the (telephone) market had grown to 60 percent in 1989 from 40 percent in 1986 as a result of below market pricing" (FOF, 1989, 906).

Among the three countries, Japan dominates in all fields except clothing and footwear. In 1987, Taiwan had relatively large shares in footwear (33%, \$2.4 billion), clothing (14%, \$2.9 billion), telecommunications (11%, \$2.4 billion), office machinery and data processing equipment (10%, \$1.9 billion), and general industrial machinery. Similarly, South Korea has advantages in footwear (24%, \$1.8 billion), clothing (14%, \$3 billion), telecommunications (10%, \$2.1 billion), electrical machinery (7%, \$1.6 million), iron and steel manufactured goods (6%, \$0.5 billion). They are denoted with asterisks in Table 10.1.

From 1984 to 1987, the U.S. imports grew 75 percent from \$326 billion to \$406 billion. Figure 10.4 shows that during these four years, most of the

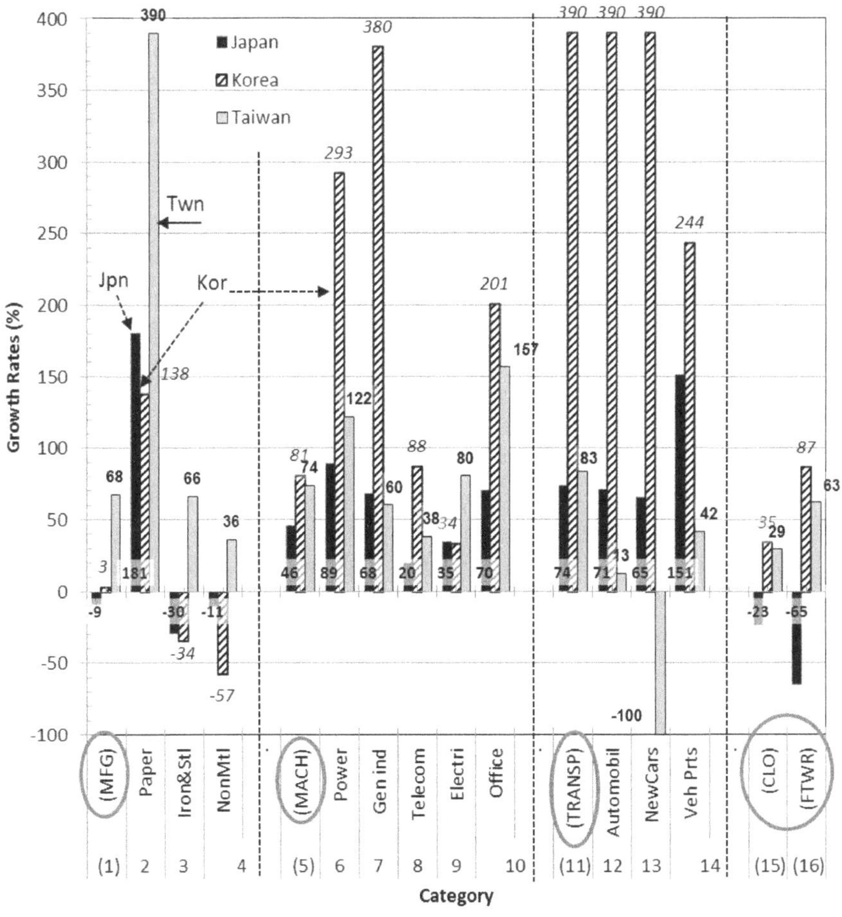

Figure 10.4: Growth Rates of U.S. Industrial Imports

Four-year rates, 1984–87, in percent

import categories from these three countries (Japan, Taiwan, and South Korea) also increased. For each group, the first black bar shows the four year growth rate of Japan, the second patterned bar, of Korea, and the third gray bar, of Taiwan. The numbers above the solid bars are the actual four-year growth rates of each country. The labels of large category are enclosed with parentheses along the X-axis. They correspond to the first two title columns of Table 10.1. There are several exceptions to the general trend of increases. Japan and Korea decreased their exports of iron and steel and nonferrous metals (2) to the U.S. markets, but Taiwanese exports in these categories increased. In the U.S. import markets, Japanese imports of clothing (15) and footwear (16) are declining, while Taiwanese and Korean imports in these two categories were increasing. It appears that the Japanese are advancing to relatively high technology products like paper and paperboard (2) and motor vehicle parts (14), leaving a huge room in clothing and footwear for the Taiwanese and Koreans.

However, the Taiwanese are catching up with the Japanese in paper and paperboard (2) which increased from a mere \$1 million in 1984 to \$72 million in 1987. Koreans are also catching up in new passenger cars (13), which increased from \$5 million in 1984 to \$2.1 billion in 1987. Reflecting their growth in the heavy machinery industry, the Koreans also increased exports of power generating machinery (6) (from \$14 million to \$55 million), general industrial machinery (7) (from \$56 million to \$269 million), and motor vehicles parts (14) (from \$25 million to \$86 million). Being squeezed between the Japanese and the Koreans, the Taiwanese apparently gave up the new passenger car market completely (the last significant value was \$7 million in 1984). With the high growth rates of the Korean exports in many categories, especially in "new passenger cars (13)," "automobile, buses, trucks (12)," and "general industrial goods (7)," all increased almost 400 percent in short four-year period, it is expected that the Korean exports will catch up with the Taiwanese exports in the U.S. markets in a few years.

10.6 Some Thoughts on the U.S.-Taiwan Trade Adjustments

From our analysis, so far as the Taiwanese economy is concerned, there are two problems of trade imbalance: One with the United States, and another with Japan. Both problems are chronic and defy any easy short-term solutions. Taiwan's problem of trade imbalance with the United States is a problem shared with Japan, South Korea, and Hong Kong. It is also a problem of the economic structure of the United States. Taiwan alone probably will not be able to solve this trade imbalance problem. In fact, the United States is Japan's largest exporting country and Japan is the United States' largest importing country. The United States has had about a $50 to $60 billion trade deficit annually with Japan in recent years. Thus, if the United States can solve the trade imbalance problem with Japan, the deficits with Taiwan and other Asian NICs probably will not be so important and prominent.

Historically, deficits in merchandise trade (and also the current account) of the United States appeared in 1971 for the first time in recent years (SAUS, 1989, 773). It became persistent and deepened after the two oil price shocks. Recent data show that the U.S. trade deficit in 1988 was $138 billion, which is lower than that of 1987 (the current account deficit in 1988 was $135 billion) (IFS, August 1989, 546). On the other hand, Japan and (West) Germany accumulated trade surpluses continuously. In 1988, Japan still had an over-all trade surplus of $77 billion, and (West) Germany, $73 billion (IFS, August 1989, 312, 242). Thus the fundamental problem seems to lie in the basic structure of the world economy, rather than the regional problem between the United States and Taiwan or South Korea.

We have seen that the cause of trade deficits in the United States was the increase in its demand for imports. The U.S. imports certainly helped recover and maintain world economic prosperity, especially, in the East Asian countries. At the same time, the maintenance of appreciated dollar in the 1970s and the early 1980s promoted low price imports, and helped the United Sates maintain high growth rates and high employment without experiencing severe inflation. Relatively high domestic interest rates also helped the United States induce large amounts of capital inflow to finance the current account deficits without serious financial crises.

To curb the persistent trade deficits of the U.S. and the trade surpluses of Japan and (West) Germany, the Ministers of Finance of the three countries, with ministers from France and Canada, met in September 1985 at the Plaza Hotel in New York City and agreed on the need of international policy coordination to maintain an orderly devaluation of the U.S. dollar (the Plaza agreement). The value of the dollar started falling, and it stabilized in the early 1990s to about 150 to 160 yen and around 27 New Taiwan dollars per U.S. dollar. The basic problem seems whether the U.S. dollar may be depreciated further to promote more U.S. exports and discourage imports, whether the U.S. interest rates may be lowered to encourage domestic investment, enhance productivity and efficiency, without hurting the foreign capital inflow.

Furthermore, it has been asserted that in the United States, the income elasticity of imports from the Asian NICs and Japan are high (Park, 1989). The price elasticity of the imports from the Asian NICs is also high and generally higher than that from Japan. This is so since the bulk of the Taiwanese and Korean exports to the United States consists of low-tech items like clothing and footwear, as we have seen in Table 10.1. On the other hand, in Japan, both the income elasticity and the price elasticity of the imports from the Asian NICs are low. Thus a one-percent decrease in the growth rate of the United States national income, or a one-percent depreciation of the U.S. dollar as compared with the New Taiwan dollar or the South Korean Won, will hurt the Taiwanese or Korean economies, without their being able to compensate their losses by penetrating much into the Japanese market. The Japanese probably would finally come out as the winner and may step up their exports to the United States. The problem of trade imbalance may be solved between the United States and the Asian NICs, but it may aggravate between the United States and Japan. Thus, the price mechanism does not seem to work effectively to correct the trade imbalance problem of the United States' current account. It is a long-run structural problem that defies any short-run drastic changes in exchange rates and interest rates.

10.7 Conclusions

We may summarize the results of this paper and some conclusions derived thereof as follows. Globalization and internationalization of the Taiwanese economy started in the mid-1960s and proceeded in a fast pace though foreign trade. The Taiwanese economy relies heavily on exports to the United States and imports from Japan. As a result of vigorous export promotion policy and closed domestic market, trade friction between Taiwan and the United States becomes a serious problem. However, we emphasize that the trade imbalance between Taiwan and the United States is not a regional problem. It is only part of trade imbalances in the world economy.

The Taiwanese economy, as well as the economies of the other Asian NICs, depends very much on the Japanese and the American markets. In 1987, Taiwan's share in the United States total imports was 6 percent ($25 billion), while Korea's was 4 percent ($17 billion), and Japan's

21 percent ($85 billion). These three countries compete with each other in the United States and have 31 percent of the U.S. import market. The problems of trade imbalances between Taiwan and the United States in particular, and in the world economy in general, are long-run problems that seem to defy short-run solutions. Japan, (West) Germany, and the United States, in turn, face their own problems of trade imbalances. Unless the economic problems among the powers are solved, it is questionable that Taiwan alone can do much about the world trade imbalances. Even if Taiwan and South Korea internationalize their domestic markets and open up their markets without any reservations, as their domestic markets are limited, the United States probably will not be able to export sufficient amounts of goods and services to these two countries and balance the U.S. trade. On the other hand, if the larger trade imbalance problems of the world economy can be solved, the problems between the United States and Taiwan either may be solved automatically, or may become not important, although annoying, issues.

Meanwhile, the Taiwanese may want to internationalize their domestic market further and expand the trade ties with the Southeast Asian and European countries. They may also take advantage of their new immense financial power and economic position. The world is watching the Taiwanese with admiration and respect. With almost $80 billion of exchange reserves, Taiwan, along with Japan and (West) Germany, may play an important role in reducing the third world debts. Taiwan should break her political isolation (NYT, January 19, 1989, Al3) and, as a *developed* country, should engage in the activities of interregional and international economic and political organizations.

Acknowledgments

We are indebted to Professor Tsong-min Wu for help in collecting a set of data, to Professor Bong Yong Kim for discussions. All errors of omission and commission are the authors'. In preparing for this chapter, the Microsoft Excel program has been used in some charts and tables.

References

Aoki, T. (1985). *Taiheiyo no Seiki to Nihon (The Pacific era and Japan).* Tokyo: Yuhi Kaku.

Arnold, W. (1985). "Japan and Taiwan: Community of economic interest held together by paradiplomacy." In R.S. Ozaki and W. Arnold (eds.), *Japan's foreign relations* (Chapter 11). Boulder, CO: Westview Press.

Fase, M.M. (1989). "Reflections on world economic imbalances." In D.E. Fair and C. de Boissieu (eds.), *The international adjustment process, new perspectives, recent experience and future challenges for the financial system* (243–260). Boston: Kluwer Academic Publisher.

FOF *Facts on File* (1988, 1989). Various issues. NY: Berkery, Noyes & Co.

Galenson, W. (ed.) (1979). *Economic growth and structural change in Taiwan.* Ithaca, NY: Cornell University Press.

GATT *International Trade* (1988–1989). Volumes 1 and 2. Geneva: GATT Secretariat.

Gold, T.B. (1986). *State and society in the Taiwan miracle.* Armonk, NY: M.E. Sharpe, Inc.

Higashi, C. and G.P. Lauter (1987). *The internationalization of the Japanese economy.* Boston: Kluwer Academic Publishers.

Hsiao, F.S.T. (1989). "Globalization of the Japanese economy and the Asian NICs-Toward the Asian economic community." Paper presented at the *International Symposium on Globalization of the Japanese Economy*, Komazawa University, Tokyo, Japan. November 25–26. Published in *The Globalization of Japanese Economy*, International Symposium, The 40th Anniversary of Economics Faculty, Komazawa University, 1990.

Hsiao, F.S.T. and M.C.W. Hsiao (1983). "Some development indicators of Taiwan: A comparative study". *Journal of Economic Development*, 8(1) (July): 45–58.

——— and ——— (1989). "Japanese experience of industrialization and economic performance of Korea and Taiwan-Tests of similarity." In S.C. Hu and C.F. Lee (eds.), Advances in financial planning and forecasting, Supplement I, *Taiwan's foreign investment, exports and financial analysis*, 157–190). Greenwich, CT: JAI Press. (Ref. Chapter 11).

——— and ——— (1990). "Causality and cointegration in a Pacific trade triangle." Paper presented at the sixth International Conference, the North American Economics and Finance Association, Mexico City, Mexico, August.

Hsiao, M.C.W. (1987). Tests of causality and exogeneity between exports and economic growth: The case of Asian NICs." *Journal of Economic Development*, 12(2): 143–159.

——— (1992). "Direct foreign investment, technology transfer, and industrial development: The case of electronics industry in Taiwan." In M. Jan Dutta (ed.), *Research in Asian economic studies* (Volume 4A), *Asian economic regimes: An adaptive innovation paradigm* (145–164). Greenwich, CT: JAI Press. (Ref. Chapter 9).

IER *International Economic Review.* A monthly publication of the Department of Commerce, U.S.A., various months.

JFS *International Financial Statistics.* International Monetary Fund, various years.

JTBT *Tokyo Business Today.* A monthly magazine of Japan's business and finance. Tokyo, various months.

KESY *Economic Statistics Yearbook* (1989). The Bank of Korea.

KMSKE *Major Statistics of Korean Economy* (1989). National Bureau of Statistics, Economic Planning Board. Republic of Korea.

Liang, K.S. and C.I. Hou (1988). "Taiwan in the 1980s: Policies and prospects." In M. Jan Dutta (ed.), *Research in Asian economic studies* (*Volume* I, Part A), *Asian industrialization: Changing economic structures.* Greenwich, CT: JAI Press.

NYT. *The New York Times.* Various issues. NYC: The New York Times.

Park, Y.C. (1989). "The little dragons and structural change in Pacific Asia." *The World Economy*, 12(2) (June): 125–161.

Ramstetter, E.R. (1988). "Taiwan's direct foreign investment in Thailand: The potential for technology transfer." *Development and South-South Cooperation*, 4(7) (December): 113–127.

SAUS *Statistical Abstract of the United States* (1989). Washington, D.C.: Bureau of Census, Department of Commerce.

TFCJ *Free China Journal.* Various issues. Taipei, Taiwan.

TFS *Financial Statistics*, Taiwan District [compiled in accordance with the JFS format] (1984, April; 1989). The Central Bank of China, Taiwan.

TSDB *Taiwan Statistical Data Book* (1980, 1988). Council for Economic Planning and Development, Republic of China, Taiwan.

TSOC *Statistics on Overseas Chinese and Foreign Investment, Technical Cooperation, Outward Investment, Outward Technical Cooperation, The Republic of China* (1988). The Investment Commission, Ministry of Economic Affairs. December. Taipei, Taiwan.

TSA *Statistical Abstract of the ROC* (1974). DGBAS, Executive Yuan, Republic of China, Taiwan.

TRTS *Report of Tourism Statistics* (1980, 1988). The ROC Tourism Bureau. Taipei, Taiwan.

WDR *World Development Report* (1989). The World Bank. NY: Oxford University Press.

Chapter 11

Japanese Experience of Industrialization and Economic Performance of Korea and Taiwan — Tests of Similarity

11.1 Introduction

Since the end of World War II (WWII), the economic performance of four Asian newly industrializing countries (NICs), Taiwan, South Korea, Hong Kong, and Singapore, has been regarded as "miraculous." This is a sharp contrast to some other stagnating or even declining developing countries in Africa, South America, and many socialist countries. Due to geographical proximity, the colonial relationship before the War, and close economic interaction after the War, Taiwan and South Korea (Korea hereafter), two of the largest countries among the Asian NICs, are often considered typologically in the same family as Japan, compared with, and distinguished from, other countries. All three countries share Confucian philosophy and a respect for learning. They have the same "initial conditions" of economic development, "with a labor surplus, limited natural resources, extensive human resources, and fairly equally distributed land area" (Ohkawa and Ranis, 1985, 5). In the course of development, they also had successful land reform and large defense expenditure.

Thus, many observers, while recognizing the differences of each country even in this family, have pointed out that Taiwan and Korea have "learned" from the Japanese historical experience, which is a "miracle" in itself. The "Japanese model" can indeed be "learned" by some, if not all, of the developing countries. The purpose of this chapter is to test econometrically how Taiwan and Korea have "learned" from Japan.

The term "learning" here is interpreted as "similarity" in outward-looking development strategies and change in economic structures. After all, "similarity" becomes the appearance of "learning" when one country in the group developed one step earlier than the others. To be more specific about "similarity," in terms of macroeconomic indicators, there are some specific characteristics common to all three countries. The change in economic condition is shown in the rapid growth in gross domestic product (GDP) and exports. In more disaggregated aspects, changes in society and economy are manifested in rapid industrialization through shifts in the sectorial composition of GDP, accompanied by even faster changes in commodity composition in exports and imports. Another interesting characteristic among these three countries is the area concentration in the direction of trade. These three structural changes are discussed in detail in Section 11.3.

Before we discuss the structural changes, the period of comparison has to be determined, so the comparison can be made for an approximately equivalent stage of development. This is done in Section 11.2. Section 11.4 defines similarity among the three countries by the patterns of growth rates of real GDP and real exports, and presents econometric methods of testing what we call the "similarity of the first kind" and the "similarity of the third kind." Some concluding remarks are given in Section 11.5.

11.2 Transition Growth of the Three Countries

Modern economic growth of Japan started around 1870 after the Matsukata Deflation (Yamazawa and Hirata, 1978, 183) and that of Korea and Taiwan started around 1950. Therefore, there is a problem in comparing equivalent development stages among these countries. According to a recent study, what Japan took more than 60 years to achieve before the War has been attained (or "telescoped") by Taiwan and Korea into about 30 years after the War (Fei *et al.*, 1985, Table 3.1, 37). As shown in Fig. 11.1, this period may be divided into five phases (ibid.). The first four phases between 1870 and 1940 for Japan, and from the early 1950s to 1982 for Korea and Taiwan, are described briefly in this section. In addition to the major economic events, some important historical events in Japan (Hall, 1970; Inoue, 1966), Korea (Kojima *et al.*, 1980; KDI, 1975), and Taiwan (Oh, 1970) are also taken into consideration.

11.2.1 *Phase 0*

This is the "isolated period" of Japan before 1870, and "traditional export expansion period" for Korea (before 1953) and Taiwan (before 1950). It

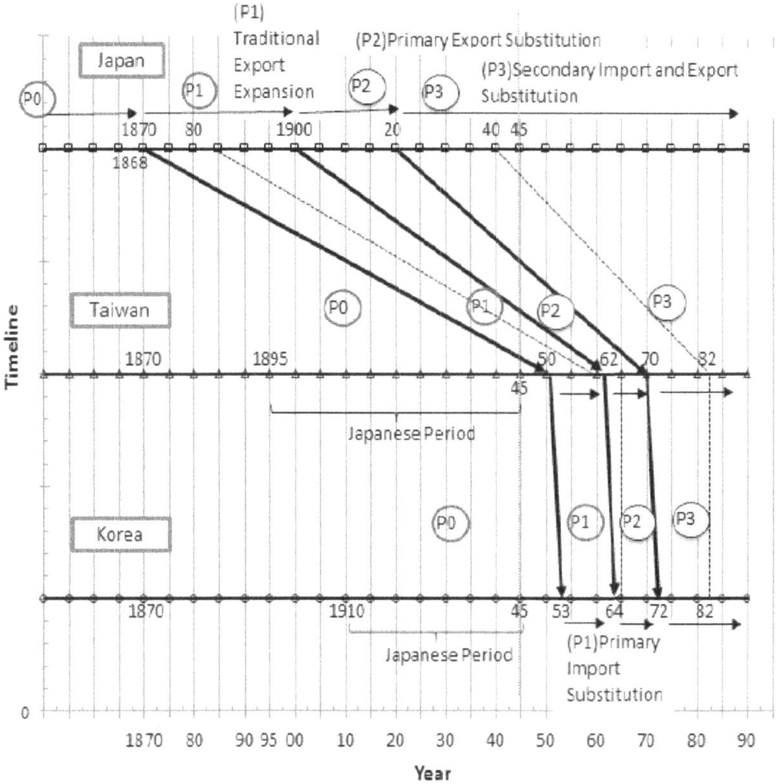

Figure 11.1: Transition Growth of Japan, Taiwan, and Korea

should be noted that in Japan, the Meiji Restoration took place in 1868, a land reform was completed between 1873 and 1880. In Korea, the Republic of Korea was established in 1948 and land reform was almost completed by 1950, just before the Korean War in June that year. The Korean War destroyed most of the industries and the arable land. The Panmunjom Peace Treaty was signed in July 1953. In Taiwan, the Taiwanese were recuperating from the February 28 massacre by the Nationalist Government troops and mass arrests of 1947. A land reform in Taiwan started in 1949 and was completed by the end of 1953.

11.2.2 *Phase 1*

For Japan, Phase 1 covers the period from 1870 to 1900. This is the "traditional export expansion period coupled with mild primary import substitution," for commodities like raw silk, tea, and then matches, cotton and silk textiles, glass, and other cotton products (Kanamori, 1964, 12). During this period, the Sino-Japanese War occurred in 1894, resulting in cession of Taiwan to Japan in the following year.

Phase 1 is the "primary import substitution" period for Korea (1953–1964) and Taiwan (1950–1962). With massive U.S. aid, both countries recovered rapidly. Production of textile and other consumer goods for the domestic markets began. At the end of the period, both countries were able to export light consumer goods.

11.2.3 *Phase 2*

This is the period of "the primary export substitution" for Japan (1900–1920), Korea (1964–1972), and Taiwan (1962–1970). During this period all countries exported intensive manufactured products" (Fei *et al.*, 1985, 45), instead of land intensive "traditional primary-product exports." During this phase, Japan emerged as a dominant power in Asia, won the Russo–Japanese War in 1905, annexed Korea in 1910, and eventually shed off the last unequal tariff treaties from the World Powers in 1911. Japan pressed Twenty-one Demands on China in 1915, expanded exports, and the economy bounced up while the World Powers were busy engaging in WWI.

In Korea and Taiwan, the economy took off to modern economic growth 1966 and 1963, respectively (Tsiang and Wu, 1985, 321–322). The U.S. aid to Taiwan and Korea was discontinued in 1965 and 1972, respectively. Both countries also benefited from Vietnam's "special procurement" boom.

11.2.4 *Phase 3*

This is the "secondary import and export substitution" period for all three countries: Japan for the period after 1920, Korea, after 1972, and Taiwan, after 1970. In all three countries, the expansion of the production of consumer goods induced the "backward linkage effects" on domestic production of producer goods. During this phase, Japan came out of the 1929 world recession. Similarly, both Korea and Taiwan successfully rode out the two oil shocks (1973–1974 and 1979–1980). Japan then joined the World Powers, built up heavy and chemical industries, and instigated the "Manchurian Incident" in 1931, the Second Sino-Japanese War in 1937, and plunged into WWII in 1941.

In 1970, Korea passed the "Law of Fostering Iron and Steel Industry" and, 1973, published the "Heavy and Chemical Industry Construction Plan." Taiwan, "Ten Basic Construction Projects" was announced in 1973, followed by "Twelve Construction Projects" in 1977 (Yajima, 1986).

We have seen that, despite the difference in time span, there are similarities in the phases of economic development between Japan on the one hand and Korea and Taiwan on the other. Their experiences are not only similar in economic events, but also in social and political environment and changes. However, the differences in their experiences may also be noted as follows (Yamazawa and Hirata, 1978, 182–183).

First, in the initial phase, the science and technological gap in the late nineteenth century between Japan and the developed Western World was probably much smaller than the gap faced by Korea and Taiwan after WWII. Thus, in the case of Korea and Taiwan, higher educational level of workers and foreign direct investment were needed to assist their rapid development. They also borrowed technology heavily from Japan (Hsiao and Hsiao, 1984).

Second, in international markets, Japan was able to export goods to both developed and underdeveloped countries. On the other hand, Korea and Taiwan, faced with stiff competition from other developing countries, can export only to the developed countries, especially to the United States. They stepped into the markets that were vacated by the Japanese who had advanced to a higher segment of the markets (Kojima *et al.*, 1980).

Third, although Japan had to spend about 40 years since the Meiji Restoration to recover extraterritoriality concession in 1899 and tariff autonomy in 1911, it never was under colonial rule. In contrast, Korea and Taiwan suffered from Japanese colonialism for 36 and 51 years, respectively. Naturally, their unfortunate-experiences also contributed to the common features of the society and economy among these three countries.

In addition to similarities and differences between Japan on the one hand and Korea and Taiwan on the other, there are also similarities and differences between Korean and Taiwan (Scitovsky, 1986). The major similarities have been shared with Japan and have been described. Some important differences since the end of WWII may be delineated as follows.

First, Taiwanese firms are more numerous and smaller than Korean firms, that is, the Industrial concentration rate is much higher in Korea than in Taiwan. As a consequence income distribution in Taiwan is more equitable than that in Korea (ibid., 143). Second, Korea has amassed large foreign loans, but none in Taiwan (ibid., 144). Third, Korea had a higher inflation rate and in general adopted low Interest rate policy, while Taiwan went in the opposite direction (Tsiang and Wu, 1985). Fourth, Korea's labor productivity and personal saving ratios are generally lower than those in Taiwan (Scitovsky, 1986, 158, 170).

These and other differences are, however, mostly due to the differences in economic policy rather than in the more fundamental social, cultural, and natural environments, which are usually taken as exogenous factors in the sense of Schumpeter. Thus, we feel that the similarities dominate the differences in all these three countries, and that grouping them together as one family may be justified.

11.3 Output and Trade Structures

As shown in the previous section, Japan, Korea, and Taiwan achieved rapid economic growth through an export-oriented policy. In this section, we examine the similarity of these countries in terms of the changes in output structure, trade composition, and trade orientation.

11.3.1 *Industrial Origin of Output*

Table 11.1 presents the industrial origin of net domestic product (NDP) at current market prices. Because data for NDP are not available for Korea, closest measure of NDP, gross national product (GNP), is used. Since what we are interested in here is the percentage distribution of the industrial origin of NDP or GNP, rather than the absolute amount, the Korean data should be comparable with those obtained from the other two countries.

Following Clark (1957) and Kuznets (1966), the economy's industries are classified into three categories, agricultural (primary), manufacturing (secondary), and service (tertiary) industries. They found that in the course of economic development, the share of agricultural output decreases while that of manufacturing output increases. All three countries shared this general tendency during the period being studied.

In Table 11.1, Japan's agricultural output decreased from 43 percent in 1885 to 18 percent in 1940, while manufacturing output increased from 16 percent to 53 percent in the same period. The reversal of the relative weight occurred around 1910, which is in phase 2 of the transition (also see Fig. 11C1 in Appendix 11C).

Table 11.1: Industrial Origin of NDP at Current Market Price (%)

	Year	Agr	Mfg	Services
JAPAN	1885	43.0	16.2	40.8
P1	1890	46.1	16.5	37.4
P2	(1900)	37.7	24.1	38.2
	1910	30.8	31.1	38.1
P3	(1920)	29.5	36.2	34.2
	1930	16.6	42.0	41.4
	1940	18.3	52.9	28.8
	std	*11.4*	*13.57*	*4.32*
	avg	*31.7*	*31.30*	*36.99*
	V	*36.0*	*43.36*	*11.69*
KOREA	1953	47.3	12.7	40.0
P1	1955	44.8	15.8	39.4
	1960	36.9	19.8	43.3
P2	(1964)	46.0	21.3	32.7
	1965	38.7	24.2	37.1
	1970	28.4	29.0	42.6
P3	(1972)	26.4	29.3	44.3
	1975	24.7	33.6	41.7
	1980	14.4	40.7	44.9
	−1984e	13.9	40.9	45.2
	std	*11.3*	*8.89*	*3.89*
	avg	*34.2*	*25.16*	*40.67*
	V	*33.2*	*35.33*	*9.57*
TAIWAN	1952	35.9	18.0	46.1
P1	1955	32.9	21.1	46.0
	1960	32.8	24.9	42.3
P2	(1962)	29.2	25.7	45.1
	1965	27.3	28.6	44.1
P3	(1970)	17.9	34.7	47.4
	1975	14.9	39.2	45.9
	1980	9.3	45.0	45.7
	−1985e	7.0	44.8	48.2
	std	*9.7*	*9.26*	*1.54*
	avg	*25.0*	*29.65*	*45.33*
	V	*38.9*	*31.24*	*3.39*

Sources: **Japan**, Ohkawa *et al.* (1974), 202. Services include imputed house rents. **Korea**, BOK (1971), 15; (1985), 249, for Gross National Product (GNP). Mfg includes mining, construction utilities. All others, except agriculture, forestry, and fishing, are included in Services. **Taiwan**, TSDB (1986), 39. Services include "Transportation and Communication," "Commerce", and "Others."

e, estimate.

−1984 −sign before the year means the data of the year was not included in the calculation of std, avg, and *V*. Same in Tables 11.2 and 11.3.

Compared with Japan, the "initial condition" of the Korean economy is more heavily agriculture-oriented and less manufacture-oriented, while that of Taiwan is just the opposite. During the 1980s, which is roughly comparable to the 1940s in Japan, the weight of agricultural output in Taiwan was less than 10 percent and that of manufacturing output was 45 percent, while the agricultural weights in Korea and Japan still were 14 percent and 18 percent, respectively, and the manufacturing weights were 41 percent and 53 percent, respectively. The heavy emphasis on manufacturing in Japan came at the expense of reduction in service sector output. This may reflect Japan's war efforts in the Second Sino-Japanese War and just before Japan plunged into WWII. The relative importance of agricultural and manufacturing output shares in Korea changed around 1970 while that of Taiwan changed around 1965 (also see Myers, 1986, 19–20). Like Japan, both turn around years were in phase 2 (also see Fig. 11C1 in Appendix 11C).

Note that the weight of services in all three countries remained more or less constant, hovering between 51 percent and 47 percent throughout the whole period. The only exception is the early 1940s during which Japan was plunging into WWII. This observation is also consistent with those by Kuznets (1966), Chapter 3, and others.

To facilitate the comparison of the data at the beginning of the second and the third phases of development, the years are enclosed in parentheses in Table 11.1 and subsequent tables. The similarity in magnitude and change may be noted.

Sample standard deviation (std), mean (avg), and the coefficient of variation (V), defined as 100 × std/avg, are also calculated for each country. These summary statistics are calculated for the years listed in the table, from 1885 (or 1870 if the data are available) to 1940 for Japan, from 1953 to 1980 for Korea, and from 1952 to 1980 for Taiwan, respectively. The negative sign before the year shows that the data for that year are excluded from the calculation of summary statistics.

We note that the values of V for each industry are close in all three countries. For examples, the agricultural shares in all three countries have V values between Korea's 33 percent and Taiwan's 39 percent, showing more or less the similar magnitude of variation compared to the mean in the agricultural sector. In the service sector the V values in all countries range between Taiwan's 3 percent and Japan's 12 percent, showing a rather stable tendency of output shares in the service sector.

11.3.2 *Commodity Composition of Trade*

As the countries become industrialized, the commodity composition of exports and imports also changes. This is shown in Table 11.2. The similarity in the export composition between Korea and Taiwan is striking. In the mid-1950s, the composition of exports in both countries was about 90 percent agricultural goods and about 10 percent manufactured goods. The situation was completely reversed in 1980: about 10 percent agricultural goods and about 90 percent manufactured goods. In this respect, the changes in Japan's composition were much milder. It started at about 65 percent in agriculture and about 35 percent in manufacturing in 1870, and, in 1940, it reached only about 20 percent and 80 percent proportions. Only in 1950, 5 years after the end of WWII, did Japan reach 10 percent and 90 percent commodity compositions in exports (see Table 11.2). This time difference in changes in the export composition probably is a reflection of the difference in resources and population endowments. Korea and Taiwan are much smaller than Japan in both respects (Hsiao and Hsiao, 1983). The lower change is also reflected in a smaller value of V for Japan than those for Korea and Taiwan (also see Fig. 11C2 in Appendix 11C).

Similarity in the overall exports structure and its changes, however, does not imply that the contents and changes in major export commodities are the same for all these countries. For Korea, the change is a shift from exports of silk, fish, coal, tungsten, and iron ore, to steel products, machinery, and petrochemicals (KDI, 1975, 276–278), and, more recently, to apparel and clothing, ships, and passenger cars (BOK, 1987, 204–207). For Taiwan, the change is from exports of rice, sugar, and canned foods to textiles, metals, and machinery (Ho, 1978, 133–135), and, more recently, to plastic articles and electric and electronic equipment (TSDB, 1986, 221–223). This is in contrast with Japan, whose major export commodities changed from silk, tea, and fish products to cotton thread, cotton and silk fabrics, chemicals, and metals by the end of the 1930s (Yamaguchi, 1968, 188–190; Ohyama, 1967). In fact, fibers and textiles were still Japan's major exports (30%) even during 1950–1955. Their share started to decrease only after 1955, and machinery became the dominant export item (35%) (Kanamori, 1968, 311).

If we compare the export composition of the three countries, in the beginning of phase 2, both Korea and Taiwan had almost the same

Table 11.2: Commodity Composition of Trade (%)

		Exports		Imports		
	Year	Agr	Mfg	Food	Raw	Mfg
JAPAN	1870	65.5	34.5	59.2	2.6	38.2
P1	1880	51.4	45.6	16.7	4.4	78.9
	1890	41.6	58.3	31.2	8.3	60.5
P2	(1900)	28.3	71.6	19.6	28.0	52.3
	1910	21.0	79.1	10.3	49.8	40.0
P3	(1920)	15.8	84.2	10.2	53.9	35.9
	1930	17.4	82.7	14.7	53.6	31.8
	1940	17.5	82.5	13.6	42.8	39.1
	–1950	10.0	90.0	33.6	42.0	24.4
	–1960	9.8	90.2	14.1	58.5	27.4
	std	*18.56*	*19.05*	*16.48*	*22.56*	*15.91*
	avg	*32.31*	*67.31*	*21.94*	*30.43*	*47.09*
	V	*57.43*	*28.29*	*75.15*	*74.16*	*33.78*
		Agr	Mfg	Consump	Raw	Capital
KOREA	1955	90.7	9.1	8.3	68.0	23.5
P1	1960	85.8	14.2	9.6	66.0	14.0
P2	(1964)	50.9	49.0	16.9	64.3	18.5
	1965	38.9	61.0	13.7	69.0	17.3
	1970	22.6	77.4	16.2	51.7	32.1
P3	(1972)	15.7	84.2	14.5	52.1	33.3
	1975	18.2	81.6	13.2	57.9	28.8
	1980	9.5	90.2	8.4	65.8	25.4
	–1985	8.2	91.7	4.7	56.9	38.2
	std	*31.77*	*31.74*	*3.41*	*6.97*	*7.11*
	avg	*41.53*	*58.34*	*12.60*	*61.84*	*24.12*
	V	*76.49*	*54.40*	*27.04*	*11.26*	*29.47*
TAIWAN	1952	91.9	8.1	19.9	66.8	13.3
P1	1955	89.6	10.4	8.8	74.7	16.5
	1960	67.7	32.3	8.2	64.0	27.8
P2	(1962)	49.5	50.5	8.3	68.3	23.4
	1965	54.0	46.0	5.1	65.6	29.3
P3	(1970)	21.4	78.6	4.9	62.8	32.3
	1975	16.4	83.6	6.8	62.6	30.6
	1980	9.2	90.8	5.8	70.8	23.4
	–1985	6.2	93.8	8.5	67.7	23.8
	std	*32.22*	*32.22*	*4.85*	*4.20*	*6.80*
	avg	*49.96*	*50.04*	*8.48*	*66.95*	*24.58*
	V	*64.48*	*64.38*	*57.26*	*6.27*	*27.68*

(*Continued*)

Table 11.2: (*Continued*)

Sources: **Japan**. Kanamori (1964), 5–6. Agr includes "Raw materials" and "Miscellaneous items." Mfg includes "Completed and half completed manufactured goods." Food includes "Miscellaneous items." **Korea**, BOK (1962), 222; (1971), 279; (1987), 203. Exports or imports do not add to 100 percent due to "Not elsewhere unclassified" term. SITC codes in Agr = 0, 1, 2, 3, 4; Mfg = 5, 6, 7, 8; Capital Goods = 7, 8; Raw Materials = 2, 3, 4, 5, 6; Consumption Goods = 0, 1. **Taiwan**, TSDB (1986), 207–208. Agr includes "Processed Agricultural Products."; Mfg = "Industrial Products."; Raw = "Agricultural and Industrial Raw Materials."

50 percent distribution of agricultural goods and manufactured goods. Japan in 1900 had a much higher proportion, 72 percent, of exporting manufactured goods. However, at the beginning of phase 3, Japan in 1920, Korea in 1972, and Taiwan in 1970, they had almost the same structure. The share of the agricultural good exports was about 15–20 percent, and that of manufactured good exports was about 80–85 percent (also see Fig. 11C2 in Appendix 11C).

From Table 11.2, the dominance of the manufactured good exports started in the 1890s for Japan, around 1965 for Korea, and around 1962 for Taiwan. In all cases, the dominance occurred about several years before the turning point for the agricultural output share and the manufactured output share (see Table 11.1). Thus, one may conjecture that international trade might have acted as an engine, rather than handmaiden, of economic growth (see Kavoussi, 1985, for some related references) in all these three countries. In other words, foreign demands for manufactured goods may first induce expansion of the domestic manufacturing industry, stimulating production of manufacturing goods relative to the agricultural goods, prompting the former share to exceed the latter, thus promoting economic growth at home. We will discuss this problem in the next section.

The import side of the commodity composition in Table 11.2 reflects the process of industrialization for the resource-poor countries. Due to the difference in the method of collecting data 100 years ago, the commodity composition for Japan is classified as food, raw materials, and manufactured goods (Kanamori, 1964, 6) while that of Korea and Taiwan is classified as consumption goods, raw materials, and capital goods. Since we do not have direct access to the original Japanese and Taiwanese custom office records, the exact contents of each category are unknown. However, it may be safe to assume that "food" corresponds to "consumption goods," and "manufactured goods" corresponds to "capital goods."

Table 11.3: Direction of Trade[a] (%)

Country		Exports					Imports				
		Asia	Eur	NAmer	SAmer	Oths	Asia	Eur	NAm	SAm	Oths
JAPAN											
P1	1873	22.1	51.9	19.5	0.0	6.5	35.2	58.5	3.6	0.0	2.7
	1880	23.1	31.7	42.4	0.0	2.8	20.8	71.7	7.3	0.0	0.2
	1890	28.3	27.9	37.7	0.0	6.1	31.7	51.1	8.9	0.0	8.3
P2	(1900)	46.6	21.1	27.4	0.0	4.9	31.3	44.0	22.0	0.0	2.7
	1910	38.0	24.8	33.7	0.0	3.5	47.6	36.2	12.3	0.4	3.5
P3	(1920)	48.2	10.7	32.3	2.1	6.7	34.8	14.3	41.2	1.5	8.2
	1930	45.6	9.2	39.2	1.2	4.8	35.9	19.7	34.4	0.5	9.5
	1940	62.1	6.5	20.7	4.3	6.4	42.7	5.7	39.2	5.9	6.5
	–1950	46.4	12.0	25.4	3.7	12.5	32.4	4.0	48.0	4.1	11.5
	–1960	36.0	13.2	33.2	4.4	13.2	30.4	10.9	42.8	3.2	12.7
	std	*14.0*	*14.9*	*8.4*	*1.6*	*1.5*	*8.0*	*23.0*	*15.3*	*2.0*	*3.4*
	avg	*39.3*	*23.0*	*31.6*	*1.0*	*5.2*	*35.0*	*37.7*	*21.1*	*1.0*	*5.2*
	V	*35.7*	*64.9*	*26.7*	*165*	*28.2*	*22.8*	*61.1*	*72.3*	*196*	*64.7*
KOREA											
P1	1952	66.8	0.1	33.1	0.0	0.0	8.8	0.1	1.1	0.0	90.0
	1955	51.5	7.4	41.0	0.0	0.0	12.4	10.1	23.4	1.0	53.1
	1960	75.0	13.5	11.5	0.0	0.0	29.7	24.4	42.3	1.3	2.4
P2	(1964)	55.5	13.2	30.2	0.3	0.8	36.2	9.7	50.6	0.4	3.1
	1965	49.0	12.2	36.8	0.1	1.9	49.2	8.8	39.9	0.2	1.8
	1970	37.8	9.1	50.1	0.1	2.9	56.9	11.0	30.7	0.2	1.1
P3	(1972)	36.4	10.2	50.9	0.2	2.3	58.5	11.1	27.2	0.2	3.0
	1975	40.4	18.4	34.7	0.4	6.1	59.2	8.3	28.4	0.2	3.8
	1980a	38.0	15.1	28.3	0.8	17.8	57.0	7.1	23.6	0.2	12.1
	–1985a	32.1	11.7	39.6	2.5	14.2	39.9	10.3	22.9	1.7	25.2
	std	*13.7*	*5.3*	*12.0*	*0.3*	*5.7*	*20.1*	*6.3*	*14.2*	*0.4*	*31.4*
	avg	*50.0*	*11.0*	*35.2*	*0.2*	*3.5*	*40.9*	*10.1*	*29.7*	*0.4*	*18.9*
	V	*27.5*	*47.7*	*34.0*	*124*	*161*	*49.0*	*62.8*	*47.6*	*105*	*166*
TAIWAN											
P1	1955	89.0	5.4	4.5	0.3	0.8	42.2	7.0	49.0	0.1	1.8
	1960	79.1	6.0	12.3	0.0	2.6	47.4	11.2	38.8	0.0	2.6
P2	(1962)	63.3	8.7	25.5	0.3	2.1	47.7	8.3	39.0	0.5	4.5
	1965	61.0	10.3	23.3	0.1	5.3	51.1	8.5	33.0	1.2	6.2
P3	(1970)	39.1	10.1	41.5	0.5	8.7	57.6	9.7	25.0	2.5	5.2
	1975	36.2	15.0	37.8	0.7	10.3	51.7	12.7	28.6	0.4	6.6
	1980	34.4	15.8	36.4	2.0	11.4	58.4	0.9	24.9	0.8	14.9
	–1985	30.9	9.7	51.2	0.5	7.7	52.2	12.2	25.4	2.2	8.0
	std	*21.7*	*4.0*	*13.8*	*0.7*	*4.3*	*5.8*	*3.8*	*8.8*	*0.8*	*4.3*
	avg	*57.5*	*10.2*	*25.9*	*0.6*	*5.9*	*50.9*	*8.3*	*34.0*	*0.8*	*6.0*
	V	*37.8*	*39.4*	*53.4*	*118*	*72.5*	*11.4*	*45.3*	*25.9*	*106*	*72.0*

a = Some major trading partners in each area only, not inclusive.
Sources: **Japan** Kanamori, (1964), 7–8. **Korea** BOK (1960), 326–327. (1966), 235; (1971), 282–287; (1974), 232–239; (1987), 212–215. **Taiwan** TSDB, (1986), 218–219. Exports as well as imports sum up to 100 percent for each year for each country.

If this is the case, the similarity between Korea and Taiwan is again striking. Both countries had maintained very high levels, about 60 percent, of imported raw materials, and about 25 percent of the capital goods. The coefficient of variation in these two categories is also rather small and similar in both countries. In contrast, the Japanese food imports decreased steadily, except the years immediately after WWII, and imports of raw materials increased from 3 percent in 1870 to 43 percent in 1940, and increased to almost 60 percent in 1960. The Japanese difference with Korea and Taiwan may again reflect the different in land area, population, and natural resource endowments (also see Fig. 11C3 in Appendix 11C).

As industrialization in Korea and Taiwan progressed, the contents of raw materials in imports also changed. For Korea, the import contents of raw materials shifted from cotton, cotton thread, chemical fertilizer, and chemicals, to petroleum oils, organic chemicals, and coal (BOK, 1962, 1976, 1987). Similarly, for Taiwan, the changes were from cotton and chemical fertilizer to crude oil, chemicals, and iron and steel (TSDB, 1975, 1986). The capital goods imports consisted mainly of machinery, electrical and machinery apparatus, etc. (TSDB, 1986, 234–235). In contrast, Japan imported cotton and fur fabrics, cotton thread, sugar, and iron in the early stage of development. Later, the contents of imports changed to cotton, wool, iron, and machinery (Yamaguchi, 1968, 143–144, 189–190).

As in the case of the commodity composition of exports, comparison of the composition of raw materials, and manufactured and capital goods imported at the beginning of phase 2 for Japan vis-a-vis Korea and Taiwan seems to show that Japan heavily imported manufactured goods (52%) while Taiwan and Korea heavily imported raw materials (over 64%). However, at the beginning of phase 3, 52–63 percent of imports were raw materials and 32–36 percent were manufactured and capital goods in all three countries. Here again the similarities are overwhelming. With regards to the coefficients of variation of imports, there seem no special patterns among the three countries.

11.3.3 *Direction of Trade*

Another useful aspect of the trade structure is direction of trade. In order to achieve comparability, the direction of trade in Table 11.3 is classified into five categories: trade with Asian, European, North American, South American, and other countries. As mentioned in the previous section, prewar Japan had the advantage of trading with both the developing

Asian countries and the developed European and North American countries. Thus, in the early Japanese development, the European markets dominated both exports and imports. The dominance shifted to the North American markets, especially to the United States as the latter gradually emerged as an industrial power and became markets for Japanese products and for source of her capital goods imports. The export share of the North American markets surpassed that of European markets in 1880, and the latter became almost negligible by 1940. The import share of the North American markets surpassed that of the European markets only around 1920, reflecting a long history of Japanese reliance on European technology through imports.

The data on Japanese trade with the Asian countries shown in Table 11.3 do not include trade with Korea and Taiwan, which were Japanese colonies during their phase 2 and phase 3 prewar development. Thus, if trade with Korea and Taiwan during this period were included in the data, the share of Asian countries in the direction of trade would have been much higher among the country composition of trade. It might have gone up to more than 60 percent (Kanamori, 1964, 5). After 1890, about half of exports to Asian countries were directed to China, which provided markets for Japanese cotton thread, fabrics, and fish products. On the import side, 30–50 percent of Japanese imports from Asian markets were from India, which supplied Japan's much needed cotton (Yamaguchi, 1968, 190–191).

To the advanced countries in Europe and the United States, Japan exported raw silk, porcelain, and cotton products and, in return, imported machinery, steel, and iron from them, mainly from England, France, Germany and Italy. Imports of cotton combined with low wages during that period helped Japan develop her textile industry, the product of which was then exported to the Asian countries (Kanamori, 1964, 19–23). Here lies the difference between Japan vis-a-vis postwar Korea and Taiwan. Japan was able to export her light manufacturing goods, cotton products, soap, matches, paper, etc. to Asian countries and also to import raw materials, like rice, rubber, sugar, and cotton from them. On the other hand, in postwar Korea and Taiwan, both countries were deprived of the opportunity to sell light industrial goods to the other Asian developing countries. This is the case since all other developing countries had also started their own industries, especially textile. It is generally accepted that Japan's early expansion of the cotton textile industry was followed by the heavy and chemical industries. The latter were fortuitously helped by the vacuum in the world export market created by WWI (ibid., 19).

Japan's trade with South American countries, and also other countries, mostly Australia, increased rapidly after phase 3 development. However, as Korea and Taiwan, the share was still less than 10 percent in the country composition of the trade during the period concerned. For all three countries, the trade with South America had very high coefficients of variation, all exceeding 100 percent.

For a long time after WWII, the trading partners of Korea and Taiwan had been confined almost exclusively to Asian and North American markets, predominantly with Japan and the United States. European markets never played any significant role as they once did with Japan, although the situation started to change in recent years. For Korea, trading with Japan constantly dominated both import and export markets.

Both Korea and Taiwan relied on Asian countries, mainly Japan, as their major export markets until around 1965, with its export share often exceeding 50 percent. After 1965, North America has become their major exporting market, but its share has not exceeded 50 percent, except for Korea in 1970 and 1972, and for Taiwan in 1985, as both countries tried to diversify their markets. In addition to the similarity in the pattern of direction on the export side, there is the similarity in summary statistics. For both countries, the standard deviation, the mean, and the coefficient of variation statistics are very close.

On the import side, during and after the Korean War, Korea received a large amount of the United Nations Aid, as shown by imports from "others" in Table 11.3. The United States was then the major supplier for Korea and Taiwan until the early 1960s, and afterward, Japan and other Asian countries substituted the United States as the major sources of imports, often exceeding 50 percent share.

11.4 Empirical Tests of Similarity

Real GDP and real exports for Japan are graphed in Fig. 11.2 and those for Korea and Taiwan in Fig. 11.3. The data are from 1885 to 1940 for Japan and from 1960 to 1982 for Korea and Taiwan, as shown by the range of the dotted lines in Fig. 11.1. The sources of data for Figs. 11.2 to 11.7 and Tables 11.4 to 11.9 are given in Appendix 11A. The data cover approximately 50 percent, 36 percent, and 16 percent of the phase 1 time period of the development of Japan, Korea, and Taiwan, respectively. They include phase 2 of all three countries, and cover part of the third phase of the development. Note that the data for Japan are in terms of million

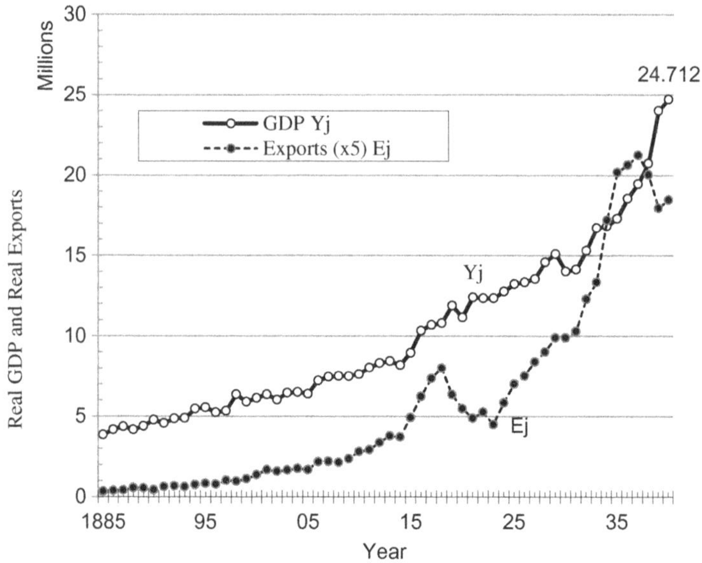

Figure 11.2: Real GDP and Real Exports
Japan 1885–1940, 1934–36 = 100, in Million Yen

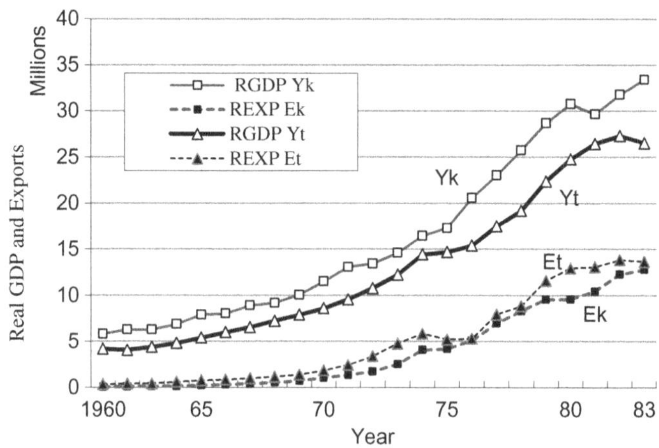

Figure 11.3: Real GDP and Real Exports
Korea and Taiwan 1960–1982, in Million US$

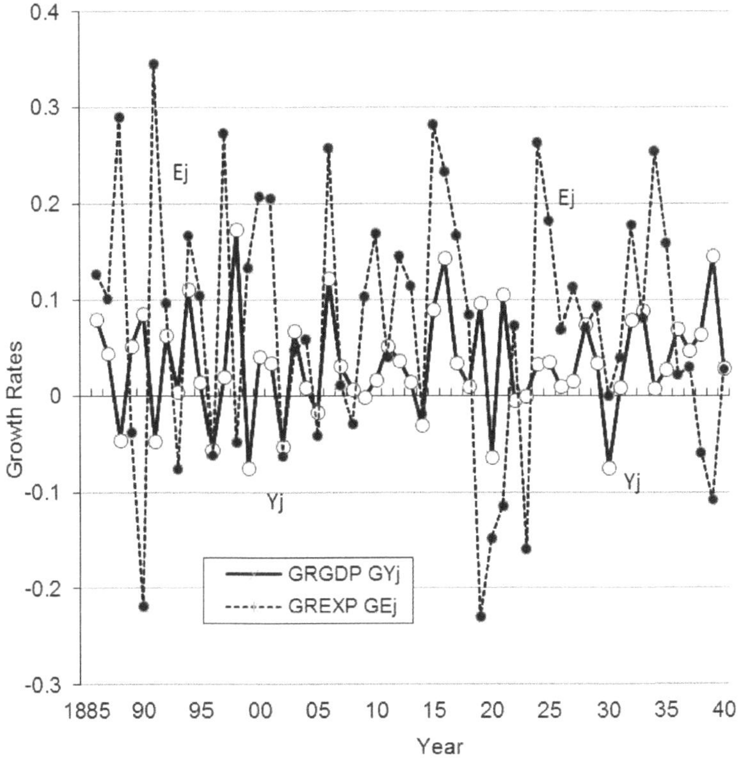

Figure 11.4: Growth Rates of RGDP and RExports
Japan, 1885–1940, in %

yens while the data for Korea and Taiwan are in terms of million US$ dollars. Thus, Figs. 11.2 and 11.3 are not strictly comparable. Despite the differences in the units of measurements and time periods, we see that the shapes and relative positions of both real GDP and real exports are similar for the three countries.

11.4.1 *Similarity in the Patterns of Growth Rates*

The available data for Japan consists of time series data from 1885 to 1940, a total of 56 observations. The data of Korea and Taiwan range from 1960 to 1982, a total of 23 observations. To make these data comparable, we made the following adjustments. First, we find the first difference of the logarithms of real GDP, and also that of real exports. This difference is taken as the growth rate of each variable. The use of growth rates reduces

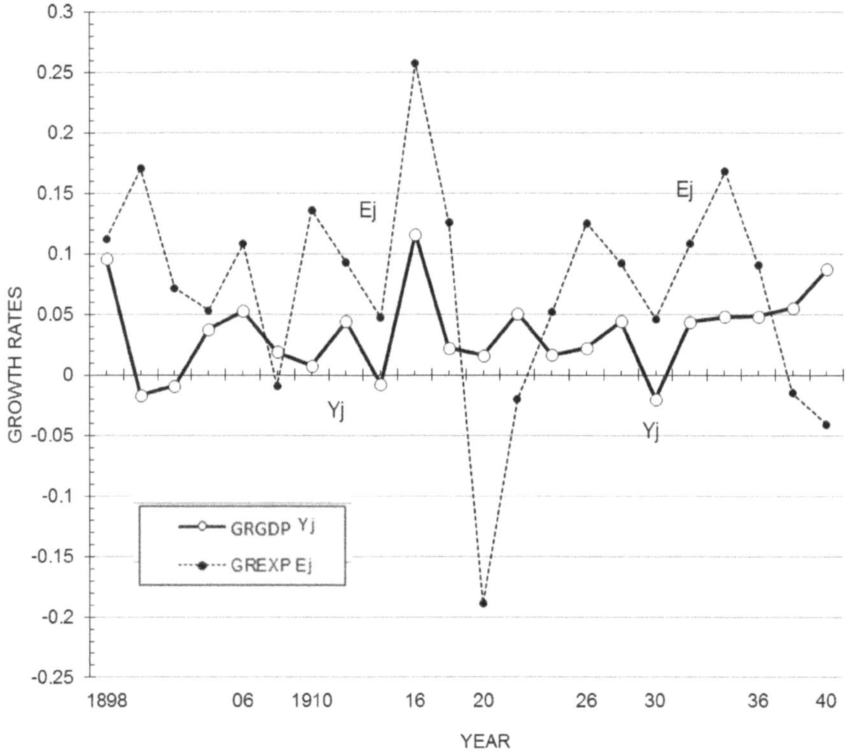

Figure 11.5: Growth Rates of RGDP and RExports Japan 1897–1940 (reduced), in %

the number of observations in each country by one. The results are shown in Figs. 11.4, 11.6, and 11.7. Second, to use the econometric software package that is currently available, we take the Japanese growth rate data from 1897 to 1940, reducing the observations to 44. We reasoned that the data in later years probably are more accurate and important than the earlier ones. This also makes the starting date of the Japanese data more consistent with that of the Korean and Taiwanese data. Third, the growth rate data of Japan from 1897 to 1940 are then reduced to 22 observations by taking moving average growth rate of every two consecutive years, and deleting the average growth rate of every other year. The revised growth rates are shown in Fig. 11.5.

Figures 11.5, 11.6, and 11.7 plot the GDP and export growth rates for the three countries. All figures are now comparable. In each diagram, the export growth rates fluctuate much more than the GDP growth rates.

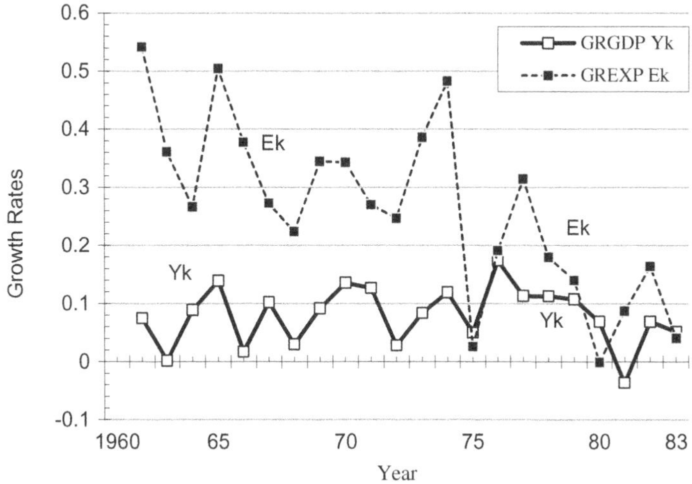

Figure 11.6: Growth Rates of RGDP and RExports Korea, 1960–1982, in %

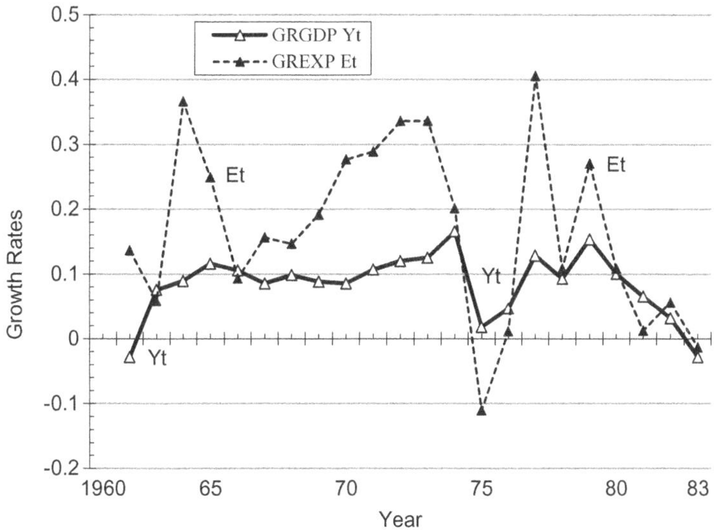

Figure 11.7: Growth Rates of RGDP and RExports Taiwan 1960–1982, in %

All growth rates are mostly positive, and the negative growth rates are generally small in absolute values and short lived.

The shapes of growth rate figures are also similar in the sense that all three countries have more or less the same number of peaks and troughs for each variable, as may be counted from Figs. 11.5. 11.6, and 11.7 as the following table.

	Japan	Korea	Taiwan
Real GDP			
Peak	7	7	5
Trough	6	7	6
Real Exports			
Peak	6	6	7
Trough	7	6	7

11.4.2 *An Econometric Definition of Similarity*

The visual inspection of growth rate figures above and the summary statistics presented in Section 11.3 are some of the basic descriptive statistics methods to inspect the similarities among these three countries. In this section, we would like to propose methods of testing the similarity using recently developed econometric techniques.

We first define "similarity". It is defined in the sense of causality and a system of equations involving the three countries and will be tested by the following methods. First, we apply a causality test to the relationship between real GDP and real exports of Taiwan, Korea, and Japan, respectively. If all countries have the same, or nearly the same, causality directions, then we say the economic development process of Korea and Taiwan and that of Japan has the "similarity of the first kind," as the causality tests are confined to an individual country.

When regression equations are estimated separately, the regression coefficients of different countries are sample statistics from different sampling distributions of the coefficients. Thus, it does not make much sense to compare them directly. We therefore propose to test the null hypothesis that the regression coefficients among the three countries by using seemingly unrelated regressions (Zellner, 1962; Johnston, 1984). If we could accept the null hypothesis, then we may say that the economic development process of Japan and Taiwan, Japan and Korea, or Taiwan and Korea has "similarity of the third kind," as the tests are conducted for all three countries as a group.

The "similarity of the second kind" involves time series analysis related to comparing the time series data taken from each pair of countries. Because of the time and space constraints, the results of the similarity of the second kind will be reported in a separate paper.

Although there are many informal intuitive discussions about the similarity of economic development between Japan and the Asian NICs, few rigorous analyses have been done in the literature. As noted before, there are comparative development studies by Yamazawa and Hirata (1978), Ohkawa md Ranis (1985), and especially, Fei *et al.* (1985). However, their analysis is mostly descriptive. We believe that this chapter advances the research in this area a step further by using the econometric tests, the microcomputer programs of which became generally available only in the last decade.

11.4.3 *Tests of Similarity of the First Kind*

Similarity of the first kind is defined here as the case in which two countries have the same causality direction between real GDP and real exports. The tests of causality between GDP and exports for Korea and Taiwan are given in Hsiao (1987). Some problems of using "causality tests" are described in Appendix 11B. Briefly, Sims (1972), 541, proposed a test for the existence of unidirectional causality between economic variables. The applications of Sims' test to the case of exports and GDP involve estimation of the following two distributed lag regression equations:

$$Y(t) = a + \sum_{-k}^{m} b(i)E(t-i) + e(t) \tag{11.1}$$

$$E(t) = c + \sum_{-k}^{m} d(i)Y(t-i) + w(t) \tag{11.2}$$

where $Y(t)$ is the logarithm of real GOP at time $t(t = 1, 2, \ldots, \text{n})$, $E(t)$ is the logarithm of real exports at time t, i denotes the lead or lag period, m is predetermined lag length, and $-k$ is a predetermined lead length of a variable. a and c are constant terms, $b(i)$'s and $d(i)$'s are coefficients, and $e(t)$ and $w(t)$ are uncorrelated series of disturbances.

According to Sims, E is exogenous to (or causes) Y if, in Eq. (11.1), the present and past values of E have significant effect on $Y(t)$, but the future values of E namely, $E(t + 1), E(t + 2), \ldots, E(t + k)$, taken as a group of additional explanatory variables, have no influence on $Y(t)$. That is, the $b(i)$'s for $i = -1, \ldots, k$ in Eq. (11.1) are jointly insignificantly different from zero. Y is exogenous to (or causes) E if, in Eq. (11.2), the present and past values of Y have significant effect on $E(t)$, but the future values of Y, namely, $Y(t+1), Y(t+2), \ldots, Y(t+k)$, taken as a group of additional explanatory variables, have no influence on $E(t)$. That is, the $d(i)'$s for $i = -1, \ldots, -k$ in Eq. (11.2) are jointly insignificantly different from zero.

If the test results show E causes Y in Eq. (11.1) and Y causes E *in* Eq. (11.2), then there is a feedback relationship between Y and E. On the other hand, if the test results show E does not cause Y in Eq. (11.1) and, at the same time, Y does not cause E in Eq. (11.2), then there is no causality relation between Y and E.

Theoretically, the length of the lags, m periods, and the leads, k periods, in Eqs. (11.1) and (11.2) should be long. In practice, however, each additional lag or lead period will cause a loss of one sample point in the estimation process. To avoid the serious loss of degrees of freedom we assume $m = k = 3$ for all equations. In fact, for m and k greater than 3, the loss of degree of freedom will be too large for accurate estimations.

We first apply the ordinary least-squares method (OLS) to estimate Eqs. (11.1) and (11.2). We also calculate the probability-value of exact Durbin–Watson d statistic to test the null hypothesis of no positive AR(1) errors in each regression (Judge *et al.*, 1985, 322–333; White and Horsman, 1985).

The calculated probability values range between 0 and 0.035 for all cases. Thus, at the 5 percent significance level, the exact Durbin–Watson test indicates that we reject the null hypothesis of no-autocorrelated errors in all cases. This implies that the existence of AR(1) errors violates the OLS assumption of zero covariance among the disturbances, and the OLS formulas for the variances of the estimators no longer hold. Without correction, we would be unable to test hypothesis accurately (Hsiao, 1988).

To correct this problem, we use the maximum likelihood Cochrane-Orcutt iterative procedure to estimate Eqs. (11.1) and (11.2) with the first-order autoregressive scheme, that is, ML-AR(1) method (Beach and MacKinnon, 1978; Judge *et al.*, 1982, 446–448; White, 1978; White and Horsman, 1985).

Table 11.4 presents the estimated coefficients, t ratios, and R^2 of Eqs. (11.1) and (11.2). From R^2, we then calculate the F-statistics (Kmenta, 1986, 416–418), and determine the causal directions indicated by Sims' test. The results are presented in Table 11.5.

Table 11.4: ML-AR(1) Regression Coefficients for Sims' Test[a]

Equation (1)									Sum of		Periods
	b(-3)	*b(-2)*	*b(-1)*	*b(0)*	*b(1)*	*b(2)*	*b(3)*	Const	*b(i)*	R^2	
Jpn	**0.102**	**-0.051**	**0.070**	**0.028**	**0.164**	**-0.030**	**0.118**	**6.508**		**0.989**	1885-
	(1.7)	*(0.9)*	*(1.3)*	*(0.5)*	*(3.1)*	*(0.6)*	*(2.3)*	*(45.7)*			1940
				0.081	**0.162**	**0.002**	**0.148**	**6.605**	**0.393**	**0.987**	1885-
				(1.5)	*(3.2)*	*(0.04)*	*(2.8)*	*(50)*	*(3.83)*		1940
Kor	**0**	**-0.159**	**-0.139**	**0.182**	**-0.038**	**0.299**	**0.109**	**8.065**		**0.993**	60-82
	(0.0)	*(1.4)*	*(1.3)*	*(1.6)*	*(0.41)*	*(3.0)*	*(1.1)*	*(20.0)*			
				0.189	**-0.078**	**0.203**	**0.001**	**7.370**	**0.315**	**0.991**	60-82
				(2.0)	*(0.9)*	*(2.3)*	*(0.02)*	*(31)*	*(1.75)*		
Twn	**0.072**	**-0.036**	**-0.020**	**0.268**	**0.109**	**0.087**	**0.035**	**5.253**		**0.998**	60-82
	(1.8)	*(0.8)*	*(0.5)*	*(6.4)*	*(2.8)*	*(2.2)*	*(0.95)*	*(33)*			
				0.262	**0.101**	**0.099**	**0.047**	**5.325**	**0.509**	**0.998**	60-82
				(6.4)	*(2.4)*	*(2.3)*	*(1.2)*	*(41)*	*(6.19)*		
Equation (2)									Sum of		Periods
	d(-3)	*d(-2)*	*d(-1)*	*d(0)*	*d(1)*	*d(2)*	*d(3)*	Const.	*d(i)*	R^2	
Jpn	**0.640**	**-0.189**	**0.851**	**0.465**	**0.493**	**0.007**	**0.120**	**-15.284**		**0.989**	1885-
	(2)	*(0.6)*	*(2.8)*	*(1.5)*	*(1.6)*	*(0.02)*	*(0.4)*	*(11.1)*			1940
				0.676	**0.713**	**0.55**	**0.487**	**-15.487**	**2.426**	**0.987**	1885-
				(2.1)	*(2.6)*	*(2)*	*(1.5)*	*(9.8)*	(4.09)		1940
Kor	**0.923**	**0.863**	**0.314**	**1.331**	**0.351**	**-0.632**	**-0.185**	**-21.54**		**0.992**	60-82
	(1.3)	*(1.3)*	*(0.5)*	*(1.8)*	*(0.5)*	*(1.0)*	*(0.3)*	*(11)*			
				1.879	**0.814**	**-0.287**	**0.364**	**-19.2**	**2.77**	**0.989**	60-82
				(2.6	*(1.2*	*(0.45)*	*(0.5)*	*(6.9)*	*(2.00)*		
Twn	**-0.056**	**0.334**	**0.823**	**2.446**	**-0.865**	**-1.026**	**0.263**	**-10.22**		**0.997**	60-82
	(0.2)	*(0.8)*	*(2.1)*	*(6.6)*	*(2.2)*	*(2.2)*	*(0.8)*	*(13)*			
				2.942	**-0.728**	**-0.698**	**0.397**	**-9.914**	**1.913**	**0.995**	60-82
				(7.1)	*(1.6)*	*(1.4)*	*(1.1)*	*(12)*	*(2.19)*		

Notes: Variables are ln(RealGDP) and ln(RealExports).
(a) The regression equations with first-order autoregressive errors are estimated by the maximum likelihood method [ML-AR(1)]. The absolute value of t ratio is in parenthesis beneath each regression coefficients.

Table 11.5: The F-test for Sims' Causality Test

Regression Equation	F-value (a)	Causal Direction
Equation (11.1)	F value	
Japan	$F(3,42) = 1.892$**	E is exogenous to (or causes) Y
S. Korea	$F(3,9) = 0.634$**	Same as the above
Taiwan	$F(3,9) = 0.706$**	Same as the above
Equation (11.2)		
Japan	$F(3,42) = 3.370$*	Y is exogenous to (or causes) E
S. Korea	$F(3,9) = 0.976$**	Same as the above
Taiwan	$F(3,9) = 1.600$**	Same as the above

Notes: Variables are in In(realGDP) and In(RealExports).
(a) At the 5 percent significance level the critical value for $F(3,40)$ is 2.84 and for $F(3,9)$ is 3.86. At the 1 percent significance level, the critical value for $F(3,40)$ is 4.31.
**We could accept the null hypothesis at the 5 percent significance level.
*The F-value is between the critical values at the 5 percent and the 1 percent significance levels. We could accept the null hypothesis at the 1 percent significance level.

In Eq. (11.1), the F statistic is used here to test the null hypothesis that there is no joint influence from the future values of exports on current GDP, that is, to test; $H_0 : b(-3) = b(-2) = b(-1) = 0$ against the alternate hypothesis that H_0 is not true. The F values, 1.892, 0.634, and 0.706, are below their respective critical values at the 5 percent significance level. Thus the F test shows that we could accept the null hypothesis in all cases, that is, exports causes GDP in these three countries. Since the sum of the coefficients of current and past export variables represents the long-run export elasticity, we have calculated and presented it in the column "Sum of $b(i)$" in Table 11.4. The long-run export elasticities are 0.393, 0.315, and 0.509 for Japan, Korea, and Taiwan, respectively. Note the closeness of these long-run export elasticities.

On the other hand, in Eq. (11.2), the F statistic is used here to test the null hypothesis that there is no joint influence from the future values of GDP on the current exports, that is, to test $H_0 : d(-3) = d(-2) = d(-1) = 0$ against the alternative that H_0 is not true. In Korea and Taiwan, the F values, 0.976 and 1.6, are below their respective critical values at the 5 percent significance level. The F test shows that we could accept the null hypothesis, that is, Y causes E in these two countries. For Japan, the F value is 3.37, which is between the critical values 2.84 and 4.31. Hence, the F test shows that we should reject the null hypothesis at the 5 percent significance level, but we could accept the null hypothesis at the 1 percent significance level. Based on these results, we may say that Y causes E is true, or nearly true, in all three countries. Since the sum of the coefficients of

Table 11.6: OLS Regression Coefficients for Sims' Test[(a)]

Equation (1)										Observtion-
b(-3)	*b(-2)*	*b(-1)*	*b(0)*	*b(1)*	*b(2)*	*b(3)*	Const.	*DW-d*	R^2	Periods
Japan										
0.068	**-0.086**	**0.042**	**0.009**	**0.126**	**-0.077**	**0.069**	**0.02**	**2.32**	**0.186**	1885-
(1.0)	*(1.3)*	*(0.7)*	*(0.1)*	*(2.1)*	*(1.2)*	*(1.1)*	*(1.2)*			40
			0.016	**0.093**	**-0.070**	**0.082**	**0.022**	**2.53**	**0.126**	1885-
			(0.3)	*(1.6)*	*(1.2)*	*(1.4)*	*(1.8)*			40
Korea										
0.099	**-0.034**	**-0.084**	**0.158**	**-0.285**	**0.058**	**-0.113**	**0.158**	**1.66**	**0.615**	1960-
(0.9)	*(0.3)*	*(0.9)*	*(1.6)*	*(2.7)*	*(0.5)*	*(1.0)*	*(3.2)*			82
			0.188	**-0.258**	**0.059**	**-0.185**	**0.159**	**1.67**	**0.518**	1960-
			(2.5)	*(3.1)*	*(0.7)*	*(2.2)*	*(3.6)*			82
Taiwan										
0.036	**-0.090**	**-0.097**	**0.195**	**0.006**	**0.025**	**-0.063**	**0.098**	**2.87**	**0.905**	1960-
(1.2)	*(2.8)*	*(2.9)*	*(6.0)*	*(0.2)*	*(0.8)*	*(1.9)*	*(4.8)*			82
			0.204	**0.051**	**0.061**	**-0.017**	**0.044**	**1.95**	**0.652**	1960-
			(4.0)	*(1.0)*	*(1.3)*	*(0.4)*	*(2.0)*			82
Equation (2)										
b(-3)	*b(-2)*	*b(-1)*	*b(0)*	*b(1)*	*b(2)*	*b(3)*	Const.	*DW-d*	R^2	Periods
Japan										
0.568	**-0.259**	**0.78**	**0.427**	**0.495**	**0.035**	**0.17**	**0.004**	**1.81**	**0.167**	1885-
(1.5)	*(0.7)*	*(1.8)*	*(1.0)*	*(1.1)*	*(0.08*	*(0.4)*	*(0.08)*			40
			0.256	**0.195**	**0.054**	**0.147**	**0.054**	**0.54**	**0.013**	1885-
			(0.6)	*(0.4)*	*(0.1)*	*(0.4)*	*(1.3)*			40
Korea										
-0.086	**-0.062**	**-0.024**	**0.364**	**-1.037**	**-1.642**	**-0.489**	**0.534**	**1.35**	**0.360**	1960-
(0.1)	*(0.1)*	*(0.03)*	*(0.4)*	*(0.9)*	*(1.7)*	*(0.5)*	*(1.7)*			82
			0.398	**-0.978**	**-1.595**	**-0.488**	**0.507**	**1.36**	**0.359**	1960-
			(0.5)	*(1.2)*	*(2.2)*	*(0.7)*	*(2.9)*			82
Taiwan										
0.119	**0.75**	**1.4**	**3.068**	**-0.155**	**-0.480**	**0.571**	**-0.331**	**2.23**	**0.826**	1960-
(0.2)	*(1.1)*	*(1.9)*	*(4.2)*	*(0.2)*	*(0.6)*	*(1.1)*	*(1.1)*			82
			2.363	**-1.118**	**-1.248**	**0.128**	**0.173**	**1.64**	**0.725**	1960-
			(3.8)	*(1.9)*	*(1.9)*	*(0.3)*	*(1.3)*			82

Notes: Variables are the growth rates of real GDP and real exports.
(a) The regression equations are estimated by the ordinary least-squares method (OLS). The absolute value of t ratio is in parenthesis beneath each regression coefficient.

current and past income variables represents the long-run income elasticity, we have also calculated and presented it in the column "Sum of $d(i)$" in Table 11.4. The long-run income elasticities are 2.426, 2.770, and 1.913 for Japan, Korea, and Taiwan, respectively.

The above test is performed on the values of natural logarithm of variables. Another method of avoiding the problem of autocorrelation in errors is to use the growth rates of variables, as recommended by Granger and Watson (1984, 1006–1008). For this approach, in Eqs. (11.1) and (11.2), $Y(t)$ is taken as $Y(t) = \ln[\text{real GDP}(t)] - \ln[\text{real GDP}(t-1)]$. Similarly, $E(t)$ is taken as the first difference of the logarithm of real exports of two consecutive years to obtain the growth rate of real exports. The OLS estimated results using the growth rates of variables are reported in Tables 11.6 and 11.7. The causality directions for all three countries are exactly the same as in Table 11.5, where we use the logarithm of the variables.

Table 11.7: The F Test for Sims' Causality Test

Regression Equation	F-value (a)	Causal Direction
Equation (11.1)		
Japan	$F(3, 41) = 1.009^{**}$	E is exogenous to (or causes) Y
S. Korea	$F(3, 8) = 0.670^{**}$	Same as the above
Taiwan	$F(3, 8) = 7.110^{*}$	Same as the above
Equation (11.2)		
Japan	$F(3, 41) = 2.534^{**}$	Y is exogenous to (or causes) E
S. Korea	$F(3, 8) = 0.005^{**}$	Same as the above
Taiwan	$F(3, 8) = 1.545^{**}$	Same as the above

Notes: Variables are the growth rates of real GDP and real exports.
(a) At the 5 percent significance level, the critical value for $F(3, 40)$ is 2.84 and for $F(3, 8)$ is 4.07. At the 1 percent significance level, the critical value for $F(3, 8)$ is 7.59.
** See note ** in Table 11.5.
* See note * in Table 11.5.

Thus from the results in Tables 11.5 and 11.7, we may conclude that there is a bidirectional causality between GDP and exports. The economic development experienced by the three countries has similarity of the first kind.

11.4.4 *Tests of Similarity of the Third Kind*

Similarity of the third kind is defined here as the case in which we can accept the null hypothesis that the three countries have the same coefficients in a model of seemingly unrelated regressions (SUR).

Let the SUR model be

$$y = \hat{e} * b + u \tag{11.3}$$

where $y = (y^1, y^2, y^3)^T$ is a $(22 \times 3) \times 1$ column vector and y^i is a 1×22 row vector of the growth rates of real GDP of the *ith* country, $i = 1$ for Japan, $i = 2$ for Korea, and $i = 3$ for Taiwan, and $\hat{e}$ is a $(22 \times 3) \times (2 \times 3)$ matrix of the form,

$$\hat{e} = \begin{bmatrix} E^1 & 0 & 0 \\ 0 & E^2 & 0 \\ 0 & 0 & E^3 \end{bmatrix}$$

where E^i is a 22×2 matrix with the first column of E^i; consisting of ones, and the second column consisting of growth rates of real exports of the *ith* country. b is a 6×1 column vector of the constant terms and slope coefficients, and $u = (u^1, u^2, u^3)^T$ is a $(22 \times 3) \times 1$ column vector of disturbance terms of the three countries.

If we assume $E(u) = 0$ and $E(uu^T) = \sigma^2 I$, where I is the identity matrix, the ordinary least-squares estimation of b in (11.3) will be the same as the ordinary least-squares estimation of each individual equation in the model. Instead we will assume that

$$E(u^i) = 0, \quad E(u^i u^{jT}) = \sigma_{ij} I$$

for $i, j = 1, 2, 3$. This means that, for each country $(i = j)$, the disturbance terms are homoscedastic. For each pair of countries $(i \neq j)$, the disturbance terms are correlated due to the similarity in economic policies, social tradition and historical backgrounds described in Sections 11.2 and 11.3.

It should be noted that since we are dealing with historical experience in different periods, Japan on the one hand, Korea and Taiwan on the other, "correlations" here should not be interpreted as actual contemporaneous interactions among these three countries. Rather we consider that they are correlated with one another in the sense that Japan occupied Taiwan and Korea in the prewar period, and the latters "learned" from Japan in the postwar period.

The coefficient vector b in model (11.3) is estimated by using Zellner's SUR method (Zellner, 1962; Johnston, 1984, 337–340; VAR Econometrics, 1985). The results are shown in the first part of Table 11.8. The slope coefficients show the effect of changes in the growth rate of exports on that of real GDP, and the constant terms show the effect of other factors that are

Table 11.8: Seemingly Unrelated Regression Coefficients for $y = \hat{e} * b + u$

Country name	Const. term	Slope b	R^2	*SEE* (a)	*DW-d* (b)
Japan	**0.0296**	**0.0791**	**0.0312**	**0.0356**	**2.0379**
	(3.24)(c)	*(1.02)*			
S. Korea	**0.0566**	**0.0872**	**0.0696**	**0.0498**	**1.9452**
	(2.75)	*(1.28)*			
Taiwan	**0.0446**	**0.2344**	**0.4232**	**0.0392**	**1.351**
	(3.6)	*(4.14)*			

Null Hypothesis (d)	p-value (e) for H_0	Test Result
$H_0 : b_1 - b_2 = 0$	0.9369	Accept H_0 at 5% signif. level.
$H_0 : b_1 - b_3 = 0$	0.104	Same as the above
$H_0 : b_2 - b_3 = 0$	0.0975	Same as the above

Notes:
(a) SEE is the standard error of estimation.
(b) *DW-d* is Durbin–Watson d statistic.
(c) The absolute value of t ratio is in parentheses.
(d) b_i is the slope coefficient of the growth rate of real exports for the ith country, and $i = 1, 2, 3$ for Japan, South Korea, and Taiwan, respectively.
(e) It is also called the prob-value for testing H_0. See Wonnacott and Wonnacott (1977), 246–247 and 269–271.

not accounted for by changes in the growth rate of exports. The slope coefficients are all less than 0.24, and are very close between Japan and Korea, but Taiwan's is about three times larger than that of Japan and Korea.

Since the estimated coefficients themselves are random variables, strictly speaking, it does not make much sense to compare the value of the coefficients. Thus, we perform a statistical test of the null hypothesis that the slope coefficients of Japan and Korea, Japan and Taiwan, and Korea and Taiwan, respectively, are the same. The calculated probability values for the testing are reported in the second part of Table 11.8. The test results show that we could accept the null hypothesis at the 5 percent significance level for all three restrictions.

In the previous section, our causality tests showed that each of the three countries has a bidirectional causality between GDP and exports. Hence we also estimate the sets of regression equations of the form,

$$e = \hat{y} * d + v \tag{11.4}$$

where, similar to (11.3), $e = (\mathrm{e}^1, \mathrm{e}^2, \mathrm{e}^3)^{\mathrm{T}}$ is a $(22 \times 3) \times 1$ column vector of the growth rates of real exports, and $\hat{y}$ is a $(22 \times 3) \times (2 \times 3)$ matrix similar to $\hat{e}$, except that it now consists of Y^1, Y^2, and Y^3. The first column of Y^i consists of ones and the second column, the growth rates of real GDP of the ith country.

The coefficient vector d in (11.4) is again estimated by using the SUR method and the results are reported in the upper part of Table 11.9. The estimated slope coefficients are again very close between Japan and Korea, but are different between Japan and Taiwan, as well as Korea and Taiwan. To test the null hypothesis that the slope coefficients are identical for each pair of three countries, a set of linear restrictions is imposed on the SUR model. The probability values for the hypothesis testing are reported in the lower part of Table 11.9. The results again show that we could accept the null hypothesis for all three restrictions.

Table 11.9: Seemingly Unrelated Regression Coefficients for $e = \hat{y} * d + v$

Country	Constant term	Slope d	R^2	SEE (a)	DW-d (b)
Japan	**0.0548**	**0.49**	**0.0317**	**0.0919**	**1.5015**
	(2.06)(c)	*(0.91)*			
S. Korea	**0.2238**	**0.4787**	**0.0587**	**0.1508**	**0.9378**
	(4.04)	*(0.82)*			
Taiwan	**0.0308**	**1.6302**	**0.4206**	**0.107**	**1.7851**
	(0.75)	*(3.92)*			

Null Hypothesis (d)	p-value (e) for H_0	Test Result
$H_0 : d_1 - d_2 = 0$	0.9886	Accept H_0 at 5% sig. level.
$H_0 : d_1 - d_3 = 0$	0.0906	Same as the above
$H_0 : d_2 - d_3 = 0$	0.0957	Same as the above

Notes: (a), (b), (c), and (e) are the same as those in Table 11.8. (d) d_i is the slope coefficient of the growth rate of real GDP for the ith country, and $i = 1, 2, 3$ for Japan, South Korea, and Taiwan, respectively.

Since the null hypothesis that the effects of the growth rate of real exports on the growth rate of real GDP, and vice versa, are the same for all countries, we may conclude that economic development experience of these three countries satisfies what we call the similarity of the third kind.

11.5 Some Concluding Remarks

We have shown the similarities and differences in industrialization of Japan, Korea, and Taiwan. Despite some differences, we have found similarity in their phases of development, the industrial origin of output, the commodity composition of trade, and the direction of trade. Even the patterns of growth rates over the period under study show very strong similarity. The evidence of these similarities is, however, mainly based on the visual appeal for the patterns and changes in real GDP and real exports, using either diagrams or statistical summaries.

This chapter goes a step further and introduces the concept of similarity that can be tested by econometric methods. Thus "similarity of the first kind" is defined as the case in which every country has the same causality direction between the variables, and "similarity of the third kind" is defined as the case in which the null hypothesis that the regression coefficients are equal could be accepted when all countries are considered to be correlated historically. All the test results show strongly and consistently that Japan, Korea, and Taiwan do have similarity of the first kind as well as the third kind.

A more detailed interpretation of such similarities is beyond the scope of this chapter. However, we would like to point out that, in addition to the similar cultural tradition and historical background, as we have described in Section 11.2, the strong resemblance of postwar development of Korea and Taiwan vis-a-vis prewar Japan may also stem from the competitive minds of the Korean and Taiwanese people. The fierce resistance of both peoples against Japanese colonialism until the end of WWII, the rapid economic recovery of Japan after the war, and advancement of "Japan as Number One" (Vogel, 1979), etc., have probably stimulated Koreans and Taiwanese alike to imitate and work harder to catch up with those they feel to be arrogant but not unsurpassably bright former colonists (Tsurumi, 1977, 211). "If the Japanese can do, we can do too" has been a common catch phrase among many Korean and Taiwanese entrepreneurs and businessmen. They imported Japanese technology, read Japanese books on management, and found direction of operations by looking at the Japanese. We submit that this is the major reason that their economic performance has been so similar to Japan, and even better than Japan in rapidity.

It has been reported that Japan has 9 out of the 10 world's largest banks, 4 out of the 5 largest insurance companies, and the 4 largest investment houses. Despite the difficulties encountered in recent years, both Korea and Taiwan are already advancing toward the status of developed countries. If Japanese achievement is any indication of the future of Korea and Taiwan, we may envision that the emulation and competition among these three countries may indeed lead to a new era that "the 21st Century will be the Century of Japan, Korea, and Taiwan" (Nakajima, 1986).

Appendix 11A: Sources of Data

For Korea, annual data on GDP (in millions of US dollars) and GDP price deflator (1975 is the base year) from 1960 to 1982 were collected from *National Accounts Statistics Yearbooks* published by the United Nations. Taiwan's GDP from 1960 to 1982 were collected from *Statistical Yearbook of the Republic of China*, and GDP price deflators were calculated using the data from *Taiwan Statistical Data Book, published* by the Council for Economic Planning and Development, Taiwan.

For Korea and Taiwan, export data (in millions of U.S. dollars) were collected from *Direction of Trade Statistics* yearbooks published by the International Monetary Fund, except that Taiwan's data for 1977 to 1982 were collected from the *Statistical Yearbook* quoted above. Export price deflators for Korea were collected from *National Accounts Statistics* yearbooks. Since there were no export price deflators for Taiwan, Taiwan's wholesale price indexes were used as the proxy for export price deflators. The GDP and export data are then calculated in real values.

The Japanese data from 1885 to 1940 were taken from Ohkawa, *et al.* (1974): GDP (in 1934–1936 prices), 227; exports of goods and services at current prices, 194–195; export deflators (1934–1936 = 100), 232.

Appendix 11B: Some Technical Notes on the Econometric Methods

1. As pointed out by one of the referees, the term causality used in this chapter is frequently referred to as "causality in the sense of Granger and Sims" (Greenberg and Webster, 1983, 147) or simply "Granger Causality" (G-causality, hereafter). When a regression in which current value of variable Y is regressed on the past, current, and future X, as suggested by Sims (1972, 545), the G-causality is often called the "exogeneity test" (Geweke, 1984, 117) or Sims' causality test. However, use of the term causality for G-causality, the equivalence between G-causality and exogeneity, and the usefulness of the concept of G-causality have been the subject matter of recent controversies (Geweke, 1982; Leamer, 1985; Wu, 1983; Greenberg and Webster, 1983, 154). Thus, it should be noted that the term "causality" used in this chapter refers to G-causality.

   There are several econometric methods of testing G-causality (Greenberg and Webster, 1983, 147–156; Geweke, 1984, 1122–1127). The most common ones are the Sims' test, as used in this chapter, and Granger's test (Granger, 1969; Geweke, 1984, 1122–1123). The results for different tests are compared in Geweke (1984, 1127–1133; 1982, 223–225) and the pros and cons of the tests in general are given in Greenberg and Webster (1983, 150–154). Generally speaking, Sims' test "will tend to reject the null more frequently under the alternative" as well as "under the null hypothesis" (Geweke, 1982, 225). Hsiao (1987) has reported the results for Granger's test using the same variables for Asian NICs. For Taiwan and South Korea, the results are "E does not cause Y" and "Y does not cause E" (Hsiao, 1987, Table 1). The same results are obtained by using the Japanese data for 1885–1940, no specific direction in G-causality for all countries. Thus, the "similarity of the first kind" among these three countries still holds even in terms of Granger's test. In this chapter, however, we have reported only the results of the Sims' test since they are more consistent with our expectations and interpretations.

2. Our definition and test of the "similarity of the third kind" are not based on any previous causality tests. We simply formulate the SUR model as (11.3) and ask whether the null hypothesis of the same slope coefficients holds for any pair of two countries among Japan, Korea, and Taiwan. Thus, equations in (11.3), as noted by another referee, are not a system of simultaneous equations. They are merely a set of regression equations that is related by nonzero correlation coefficients of the disturbance terms.
3. A referee also suggested that "it is more appropriate to call similarity of I and II 'similarity in causal structure' and 'similarity in overall structure' since we are comparing various countries with respect to these attributes." The suggestion is well taken. However, since we do not complete the formulations and testing of "similarity of the second kind," we feel that it would be better to reconsider the specific terminologies in a subsequent paper.

Appendix 11C: Illustration of Table 11.1 and Table 11.2

The similarity of the industrial origin of NDP in Table 11.1 can be seen clearly using the following chart, Fig. 11C1. Note in Fig. 11C1 the rising trend of manufacturing sector (Mfg), declining trend of the agricultural sector (Agr) and horizontal trend of the service sector (Svc) during the three periods for all three countires. The black circle shows the average

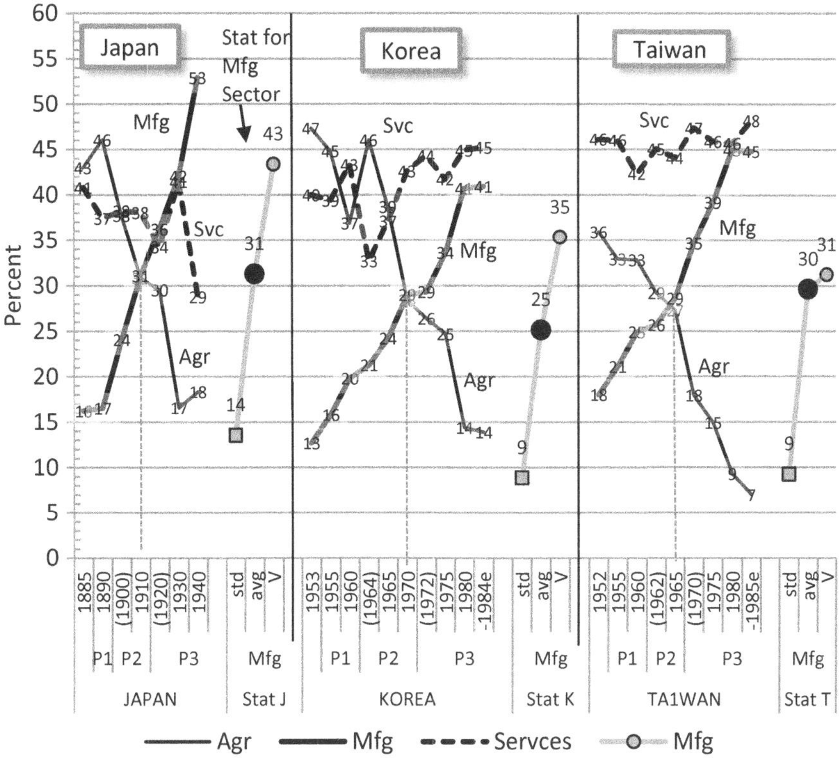

Figure 11C1: Illustration of Table 11.1: Industrial Origin of NDP

percentage of the manufacturing sector throughout the three periods for Japan, Korea, and Taiwan. They are very close to each other: 25 percent for Korea, 30 percent for Taiwan, and 31 percent for Japan.

The three panels in the chart also show that the critical turning point of economic development (the percentage of the manufacturing sector in NDP equals to that of the agricultural sector) occurred for the three countries at around 30 percent for both sector and around 1910 for Japan, 1970 for Korea, and 1965 for Taiwan.

Figure 11C2 illustrates Exports part of Table 11.2. Note the very similar increasing trend of exports of manufacturing goods (XMfg) and similar decreasing trend of exports of agricultural goods (XAg) during the three periods for all three countries. The black circle shows the average percentage (Avg) of the exports of manufacturing goods throughout the three periods

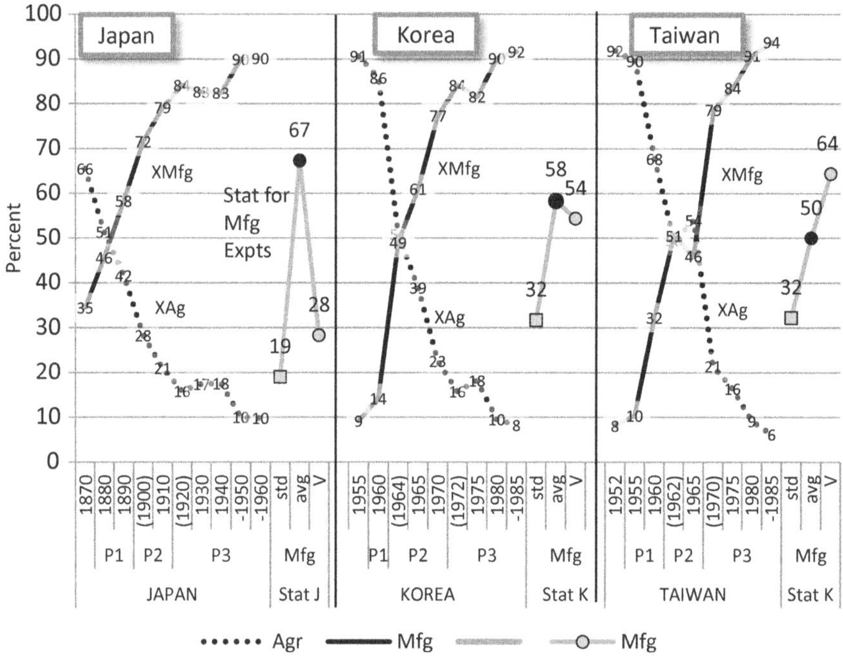

Figure 11C2: Illustration of Table 11.2: Commodity Composition of Trade — Exports

for Japan, Korea, and Taiwan, respectively. They are very close to each other, 25 percent for Korea, 30 percent for Taiwan, and 31 percent for Japan.

Figure 11C3 illustrates Imports part of Table 11.2. Despite the difference in classification of the import categories between Japan on the one hand and Korea and Taiwan on the other (Food vs Consumption, Manufacturing vs Capital) the similarity between Japanese development on the one hand and Korean and Taiwanese development on the other can still be detected from the three panels, although all the three categories of Japan fluctuated erratically during the three periods. The black circle shows that the average percentage (Avg) of the imports of manufacturing goods throughout the three periods for Japan was 47 percent, while that of Korea and Taiwan were mere 24 percent and 25 percent, respectively. Note the very close similarity between Taiwan and Korea in terms of both trend and statistical summaries during the three periods.

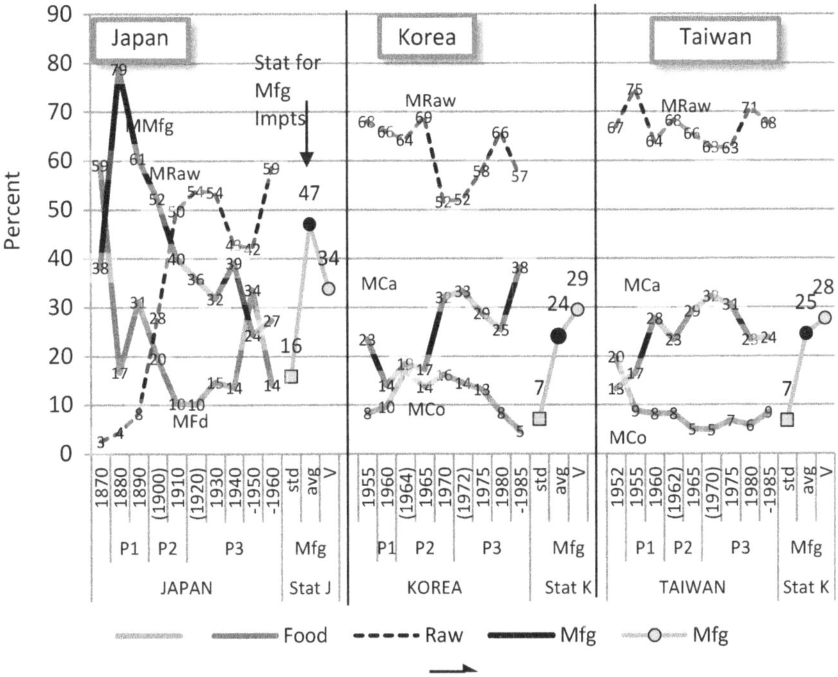

Figure 11C3: Illustration of Table 11.2: Commodity Composition of Trade — Imports

Acknowledgments

This study has been one of the main concerns of the first author since he attended the "Comparative Analysis (CA) Project" (see Ohkawa and Ranis, 1985, 1) seminars, while he was a Fulbright-Hayes Research Fellow at the Institute of Economic Research, Hitotsubashi University, Tokyo, during the spring of 1976. He is grateful to Professor Kazushi Ohkawa for allowing him to attend the seminars, and to Professor Motoaki Moriya of Kansai University, Michihiro Ohyama of Keio University, and Gary Saxonhouse of the University of Michigan for help in the literature search and encouragement at various stages of development. In completing this paper, both authors have benefited from discussions with Professors Robert McNown and Donald Waldman, and from the research assistance of Soen Jae Kim and Chi Meng, all of the University of Colorado at Boulder. Detailed comments and suggestions by three referees are also appreciated.

In preparing this chapter, we have redone the charts and tables using Microsoft Excel program, Appendix 11C is added for visual appeal of Tables 11.1 and 11.2. All errors of omission and commission are naturally the authors'.

References

(BOK) Bank of Korea. *Economic Statistic Yearbook*. 1960, 1962, 1966, 1971, 1974, 1976, 1985, 1987.

Beach, C. and J. MacKinnon (1978). "A Maximum Likelihood Procedure for Regression with Autocorrelated Errors." *Econometrica*, 46(1): 51–58.

Clark, C. (1957). *Conditions of Economic Progress*, 3rd ed. London: Macmillan.

Fei, J.C.H., K. Ohkawa and G. Ranis (1985). "Economic Development in Historical Perspective: Japan, Korea, and Taiwan." Chapter 3 in Ohkawa and Ranis, 1985, listed in this References section.

Geweke, J. (1982). "Causality, Exogeneity, and Inference." In W. Hildenbrand (ed.), *Advances in Econometrics*. Invited papers for the Fourth World Congress of the Econometric Society at Aix-en-Provence, September 1980. Cambridge: Cambridge University Press.

Geweke, J. (1984). "Inference and Causality in Economic Time Series Models." In Z. Griliches and M. D. Intriligator (eds.), *Handbook of Econometrics* (Chapter 19, Volume 2). Amsterdam: North-Holland, 1984.

Granger, C.W.J. (1969). "Investigating Causal Relations by Econometric Models and Cross-Spectral Methods." *Econometrica*, 37(3): 424–438.

Granger, C.W.J. and M.W. Watson (1984). "Time Series and Spectral Methods in Econometrics." In Z. Griliches and M.D. Intriligator (eds.), *Handbook of econometrics* (Chapter 17, Volume 2). Amsterdam: North-Holland, 1984.

Greenberg, E. and C.E. Webster, Jr. (1983). *Advanced Econometrics: A Bridge to the Literature*. New York: Wiley.

Hall, J.W. (1970). *Japan, from Prehistory to Modern Times*. New York: Dell Publishing Co.

Ho, S.P.S. (1978). *Economic Development of Taiwan, 1860–1970*. New Haven: Yale University Press.

Hsiao, F.S.T. and M.C.W. Hsiao (1983). "Some Development Indicators of Taiwan: A Comparative Study." *Journal of Economic Development*, 8(1) (July): 45–58.

——— and ——— (1984). "Direct Foreign Investment and Economic Development — The Taiwanese Experience." *Bulletin of North America Taiwanese Professors' Association*, 4(2) (December): 7–15.

——— and ——— (1988). "Energy and Income Relationship of the Asian NICs: An Econometric Analysis." In M.J. Dutta (ed.), *Asian Industrialization: Changing Economic Structures* (239–256). *Research in Asian Economic Studies*, 1, Part B. Greenwich. CT: JAI Press.

Hsiao, M.C.W. (1987). "Tests of Causality and Exogeneity Between Exports and Economic Growth: The Case of Asian NICs." *Journal of Economic Development*, 12(2) (December): 143–159.

Inoue, Kiyoshi (1966). *Japanese History* (in Japanese). Volume 3, Iwanami Shinsho, No. 500c. Tokyo: Iwanami Shoten.

Johnston, J.J. (1984). *Econometric Methods*, 3rd ed. New York: McGraw-Hill.

Judge, G.G., W.E. Griffiths, R.C. Hill, H. Luetkepohl and T. Lee (1982). *Introduction to the Theory and Practice of Econometrics.* New York: John Wiley.

______ (1985). *The Theory and Practice of Econometrics*, 2nd ed. New York: John Wiley.

Kanamori, H. (1968). "Economic Growth and Exports." In L. Klein and K. Ohkawa (eds.), *Economic Growth, The Japanese Experience Since the Meiji Era* (Chapter 10). Homewood, Illinois: Richard D. Irwin.

Kanamori, H. (1964). "Economic Growth and Trade Structure." In A. Koizumi and M. Shinohara (eds.), *Japan's Trade* (in Japanese). *Japanese Economic Series* (Chapter 1) (2–52). Tokyo: Seilin Shoin Shinsha.

Kavoussi, R. M. (1985). "International Trade and Economic Development: Recent Experience of Developing Countries." *The Journal of Developing Area*, 379–392.

Kojima, M., N. Kasai, T. Watanabe and T. Tanaka (1980). *Japan and Asia's Middle Developing Countries* (in Japanese). Tokyo: Sangyo Keizai Kenkyu Kai.

KDI (1975). *Korea's Economy, Past and Present.* Seoul: Korea Development Institute.

Kmenta, J. (1986). *Elements of Econometrics*, 2nd ed. New York: Macmillan.

Kuznets, S. (1966). *Modern Economic Growth, Rate, Structure, and Spread.* New Haven: Yale University Press.

Lau, L. (1986) (ed.). *Models of Development. A Comparative Study of Economic Growth in South Korea and Taiwan.* San Francisco: ICS Press.

Leamer, E. E. (1985). "Vector Autoregression for Causal Inference." In K. Brunner and A. H. Meltzer (eds.), *Carnegie-Rochester Conference Series on Public Policy*, 22 (255–304). North Holland.

Myers, R. H. (1986). "The Economic Development of the Republic of China on Taiwan, 1965–1981." Chapter 2 in Lau (1986), listed in this References section.

Nakajima, M. (1986). *The 21st Century is for Japan, Taiwan, Korea-East Asia Leads the World Today* (in Japanese). Tokyo: Daiichi Kikaku Shuppan.

Oh, I. (1970). *Taiwan: Its History in Agony* (in Japanese). Tokyo: Kobundo.

Okkawa, K. and G. Ranis with L. Meissner (eds.) (1985). *Japan and the Developing Countries, A Comparative Analysis.* Oxford: Basil Blackwell.

Ohkawa, K., N. Takamatsu and Y. Yamamoto (1974). *National Income.* In K. Ohkawa, M. Shinohara and M. Umemura (eds.), *Estimates of Long-term Economic Statistics of Japan Since* 1868, Volume I. Tokyo: Toyo Keizai Shimposha.

Ohyama, M. (1967). "Foreign Trade and Economic Development." In Keio Gijuku Economic Association (ed.), *Modernization of Japanese Economy* (in Japanese) (Part B of Section 3, 133–152). Tokyo: Toyo Keizai Shinpo Sha.

Scitovsky, T. (1986). "Economic Development in Taiwan and South Korea, 1965–1982." In Chapter 4 of Lau (1986), listed in this References section.

Sims, C. A. (1972). "Money, Income, and Causality." *American Economic Review*, 62(4): 540–552.

(TSDB) (1975, 1986). *Taiwan Statistical Data Book.* Council for Planning and Development, Executive Yuan, Republic of China, Taiwan.

Tsiang, S.C. and R.I. Wu (1985). "Foreign Trade and Investment as Boosters for Take-off: The experiences of the Four Asian Newly Industrializing Countries." In W. Galenson (ed.), *Foreign Trade and Investment, Economic Development of the Newly Industrializing Asian Countries* (Chapter 7). Madison, WI: The University of Wisconsin Press.

Tsurumi, E.P. (1977). *Japanese Colonial Education in Taiwan*, 1895–1945. Cambridge, MA: Harvard University Press.

VAR Econometrics (1985). *RATS* (Regression Analysis of Time Series). Minneapolis, MN: VAR Econometrics.

Vogel, E. F. (1979). *Japan As Number One: Lessons for America.* Cambridge, MA: Harvard University Press.

White, K. J. (1978). "A General Computer Program for Econometric Methods: SHAZAM." *Econometrica*, 46(1): 239–240.

White, K.J. and N.G. Horsman (1985). *SHAZAM: The Econometrics Computer Program User's Reference Manual.* Vancouver, Canada: University of British Columbia.

Wonnacott, T.H. and R.J. Wonnacott (1977). *Introductory Statistics for Business and Economics*, 2nd ed. New York: John Wiley.

Wu, D. (1983). "Test of Causality, Predeterminedness and Exogeneity." *International Economic Review*, 24(3): 547–558.

Yamazawa, I. and A. Hirata (1978). "Industrialization and External Relation: Comparative Analysis of Japan's Historical Experience and Contemporary Developing Countries' Performance." In *Papers and Proceedings of the Conference on Japan's Historical Development Experience and Contemporary Developing Countries Phase II.* Tokyo: International Development Center of Japan, 1978, 181–211.

Yajima, K. (1986). *The Complete Scope on the Taiwanese Economy* (in Japanese). Tokyo: Nihon Keizai Tsusinsha.

Yamaguchi, K. (1968). *Japanese Economic History* (in Japanese). Tokyo: Tsukuma Shobo.

Zellner, A. (1962). "An Efficient Method of Estimating Seemingly Unrelated Regressions and Tests for Aggregation Bias." *Journal of the American Statistical Association*, 57(298) (June): 348–368.

Chapter 12

Economic Liberalization and Development — The Case of Lifting Martial Law in Taiwan

12.1 Introduction

The lifting of martial law in 1987 was hailed as a great transition of Taiwanese politics and society. While some limitations still exist in continuing Nationalist Party (KMT) dominance of the central government and the government news media, as well as the slow pace of privatization of public enterprises, the political transformation was swift and peaceful. However, its impact on the Taiwanese economy, which has been liberalizing gradually and consistently since the mid-1960s, is not clear and still not properly examined. This paper examines the indexes of civil liberties, political rights, and economic freedom to investigate the impact of democratization and liberalization on the Taiwanese economy.

To our knowledge, no study has addressed these economic questions empirically or theoretically, either for Taiwan or for developing countries in general, using time series analysis. Empirically, it is difficult to study economic transition over time, since long-run economic statistics of reasonable quality are not available in most developing countries. Fortunately, Taiwan has been blessed with rich economic and industrial statistics, which enable us to apply the advanced econometric methods on complicated economic analysis.

In Sections 12.2, we trace the origin of the authoritarian regime in Taiwan from the prewar period, and relate how it was continued after the World War II. We then show in Section 12.3 how Taiwan's liberalization was first prompted by the foreign influences in the early 1960s, and then continued to the following three decades through export promotion policy. We reason that as the economy developed and the language problem eased, the younger generation of Taiwanese, who were educated under the Chinese system, started socially and politically assertive. Diplomatic setbacks and external events finally led to the lifting of martial law in 1987. Section 12.4 presents external and internal factors which accelerated democratization and liberalization after 1987.

Section 12.5 defines three kinds of freedom, which are measured quantitatively by some world watch organizations, and confirm the progress of freedom in Taiwan since mid-1977. Section 12.6 examines some of the previous studies on the impact of liberalization on economic performance and structural changes.

To investigate the impact of the lifting of martial law on economic activities using time series analysis in Sections 12.7 and 12.8, we have chosen six important and popular economic series: Real GDP, real GDP per worker, real money supply, real government expenditures, inward direct foreign investment, and outward investment. Since time series regression analysis requires stationarity of the series, we first test these series for the stationarity with structural changes in Section 12.7. We assume that the lifting of martial law in 1987 is a big bang of liberalization and test statistically whether it has significant influences on the Taiwanese economy. Thus, in Section 12.8, we examine the statistical significance of one time change in 1987 and structural changes in the constant term and slope of these time series before and after 1987.

As shown in the first several sections, the Taiwanese economy has been opening up continuously since the mid-1960s, the post-martial law era may be considered as a gradual transition of the Taiwanese economy instead of a discrete big bang break. Hence, we also examine in Section 12.8 the possibility of smooth transition of these six series, using nonlinear smooth transition model of logistic functions. Some concluding remarks are in the last section.

12.2 The Origin of the Authoritarian Regime in Taiwan

Modern Taiwanese economic development started after Taiwan was ceded from China to Japan in 1895. For fifty-one years until the end of the World War II in 1945, Japan developed Taiwan from a feudalistic pre-modern economy into a modern capitalist society. Guided by Taiwan's comparative advantage in the Japanese prewar empire, Japanese capitalists invested heavily in developing Taiwanese agriculture (Hsiao, F., 1997).

For six agricultural products (Bananas, canned pineapples, sugar, sweet potatoes, rice, peanuts) Taiwan ranked within the ten largest producers in the world by the end of the 1930s (ibid., 507). After the outbreak of the Manchurian Incident in 1931, Taiwan's industrialization started in earnest. A major hydraulic power plant was completed in 1934, and triggered the development of industry of aluminum, shipping, pulp, fertilizer, oil and fat, and others (Hsiao and Hsiao, 1996, Section 1.3.3). Before World War II, the Taiwanese economy completed the phase of primary-export-led growth, and the industry was already in the stage of import substitution, during which economic policy of self-sufficiency was adopted. Basic social and economic infrastructure, like modern transportation, communication, schools for all levels, irrigation and flood control, and electric power generating facilities were already in place at the end of the WWII (Ho, 1978; Lin, 1973; Hsiao and Hsiao, 1996). According to Maddison's data (1995), by the early 1940s, real GDP per capita of Taiwan, along with Korea, was higher than all the Asian countries, except Japan[1] (Hsiao and Hsiao, 1999a, Fig. 1).

As the Sino-Japanese War erupted in 1937, Taiwan entered into the period of wartime controlled economy and society. Japan's declaration of war against the Allied Forces in 1940 caused the total mobilization of national resources and complete control of the Taiwanese economic and social activities (Lin, 1996). When the war ended in 1945, the Nationalist Chinese took over Taiwan and confiscated major Japanese industries and reorganized them as government and KMT Party enterprises. The Taiwanese economy was mostly in ruin due to allied air raids, and inflation was rampant. The Nationalist Government was defeated in the Civil War in China and reestablished itself on Taiwan in 1949. Martial law was declared in that year, and Wartime Temporary Provisions was declared and the Constitution was suspended. Under these conditions, the government perpetuated the strictly controlled economy of the Japanese wartime period (Twu, 1975, 499) under the pretence of "recovering the Chinese mainland." It continued and exploited Japanese colonial laws and institutional arrangements, while additional control measures were

[1]In a report to the United States Congress, Conlon Associates (1959), 139, wrote that "Taiwan did not enter the post war era without advantages. Progress under Japan had been extensive. Prior to World War II, the Taiwanese had a standard of living second only to that of Japan itself in Asian. The people had acquired many industrial and agrarian skills. The years immediately after 1945, however, were years of chaos. . . ."

introduced.[2] The government had huge deficit spending for defense and refugees and the future was bleak. The outbreak of the Korean War in 1950 and the beginning of the Containment Age, however, prompted the resumption of U.S. aid to Taiwan. It stabilized the economy and protected Taiwan from falling to Chinese communists.[3]

Elsewhere we have divided Taiwanese postwar economic development into six stages: The Chaotic Period (August 1945–1949), the Transition Period (1950–1953), the Recovery and Import Substitution Period (1954–1963), Take-off and Export Promotion Period (1964–1973), the Second Import Substitution Period (1974–1980), Accelerated Growth and High-tech Industrialization Period (1980–) (Hsiao and Hsiao, 1996, Section 1.10). As the names imply, each period corresponds to the gradual opening and liberalization of the economy.

In the 1950s, the KMT government control of the Taiwanese economy and politics was omnipresent and omnipotent.[4] In production, it even monopolized daily items like liquor, beer, tobacco, sugar, salt, and about 90 percent of petroleum and its products. It had a majority of shares in the production of food, chemicals and chemical products, metal and metal products, and others, which included from bagasse board to shipbuilding. In the distribution and financial sectors, the government monopolized railroads, all the communication facilities, commercial and development banks, and external trade (ibid.). The government monopoly of the economy also reflected in the government revenues and expenditures. In the 1950s

---

[2]See Chen (1996) and Huang (1996). Cheng and Haggard (1992), 3, aptly observed, "Taiwan's decolonization took the form of a wholesale transfer of power and resources from a defeated Japan to a soon-to-be-defeated KMT . . . the new political order in Taiwan in the immediate postwar period resembled in many ways a colonial one. An outside power, the KMT, established political control over the domestic politics of a subject people largely excluded from political representation."

[3]"From June 1951 to June 1965, $1,465 million of economic aid was earmarked for Taiwan, averaging about $100 million a year, . . . or about 6 percent of the Taiwanese GNP during this period . . ." (Hsiao and Hsiao, 1996, Section 1.5.2.3). During that period, "Taiwan remains heavily dependent upon American aid . . . . (It) helped to produce substantial improvements in the Taiwan economy as in its military defenses. . . . On a per capita basis, few countries in the world have received so much American aid." (Conlon Associates, 1959, 139).

[4]The monopoly of government and KMT Party enterprises in Taiwan has continued well into the 1990s, despite the intermittent talks of privatization. See Chen *et al.* (1991); Chou (1992); Chu (1992). Also see reports by Underwood (1997) and feature articles on "Slicing up the Taiwan Pie," "In-depth Look at the Newly Liberalized Telecommunications, Power, Petroleum and Banking Industries," in *Topics*, The American Chamber of Commerce in Taipei, 28(2), March 1998.

and long afterward, government revenues relied mostly on indirect taxes and monopolies. Almost 80 percent of the central government expenditures, or 65 percent of central and local government expenditures, were on defense and general administration (ibid.).

During 1950s, however, some new infrastructures for future development were laid. These include the following events: massive U.S. economic and military aid was infused into the country, especially in the electric power industry and agricultural development (Hsiao and Hsiao, 1996), the Seventh Fleet kept peace and stability in Taiwan area, land reform was implemented in 1949 and almost completed in 1953 (Hsiao and Hsiao, 1996, Section 1.5.2.3), inflation was practically subsided (ibid.), the first four-year economic plan was launched in 1953 (Li and Yeh, 1982). Thus, by 1959, the U.S. Agency of International Development (AID) "projected 'an accelerated economic development program' for Taiwan, based upon a belief that the conditions of rapid progress already were in existence and that a stronger effort should be made by the Chinese government to create in Taiwan a 'showcase' of the achievement possible by a free economy" (Jacoby, 1966, 134). The director of the U.S. AID Mission then proposed an 8-Point Program of reform. It included "noninflationary fiscal and monetary policies, tax reform, unification of foreign exchange rates, liberalized exchange controls, establishment of utility commission and of investment banking machinery, and also the sale of government enterprises to private owners" (ibid., 134).

After "discussing" with the KMT government, and using U.S. aid as leverage, the proposal was elaborated into the 19-Point Program of Economic and Financial Reform early in 1960 (ibid., 134–135). "It added actions to encourage saving and private investment, fully utilize government production facilities, remove subsidies, raise public utility rates, liberate trade regulations and hold the military expenditures to the real 1960 level" (ibid., 135). The Program was subsequently adopted by the KMT government in its Third Four-Year Economic Plan, 1961–1964, and a Statute for Encouragement of Investment was enacted in that year to execute the Program.[5] Thus, the twenty-five year long wartime strictly

[5]Hsu (1997), 55–57. The Statute was revised more than ten times during the three decades, and expanded from 35 to 80 items. The major contents consisted of tax reduction, procurement of industrial land, and coordinated development of public enterprises (ibid., 57). The statute's effectiveness of encouraging investment was mixed (ibid., 88).

controlled economy in Taiwan since 1937 finally began to change in the 1960s. The Statute was originally intended for 10 years. It was extended two more decades, and finally was substituted by the Statute of Industrial Upgrading in 1990.

12.3 Continuous Liberalization and Democratization

The economic and financial reform programs paved the way for export expansion,[6] which has continued until today. However, economic liberalization proceeded only gradually.[7] Export processing zones were started in 1966. In the 1970s, import controls were relaxed in 1970, the bond market was established and rice-fertilizer barter program was discontinued in 1974, and a floating exchange rate system was introduced in 1978. In the 1980s, trade mark and patent laws were amended in 1982, tariffs and import controls were further reduced and capital market was liberalized in 1983. Reform had accelerated in the mid-1980s, bank interest rates were deregulated and the labor standard law was published in 1985, value-added tax, which is fairer than tariffs, was implemented in 1986.

In general, the wartime authoritarian controlled economy and the government policy priority of "recovering the mainland," rather than promoting local economic and social development[8] kept Taiwan's industrial sector from recovering fully to the prewar peak of the Japanese period until the end of the 1950s.[9] When it recovered, however, the possibility of "an accelerated economic development" for Taiwan was envisaged,

---

[6]Elsewhere we have pointed out that the advance to export expansion policy was not so much due to small domestic market nor shortage of natural resources, as not all smaller countries adopt export expansion policy (WDR, 1987; Hsiao and Hsiao, 1996, Section 1.11).

[7]The following chronology from 1952 to 1995 is based on Li (1988), Appendix. For the summary table of financial reform before 1997, see Hsu and Yang (1997), 168.

[8]Jacoby (1966), 137, 144, 169, 221, 223. In evaluating the "extent of leadership commitment to economic development" among 74 developing countries in the period of 1957–1962, Adelman and Morris (1967) placed Taiwan only at 55 percentile, slightly better than average. Their evaluation of Taiwan's economic indicators (18 variables) is generally higher than that of political system indicators (7 variables) during that period. (Hsiao and Hsiao, 1998b).

[9]Hsiao and Hsiao (1998a), 98. Using DYMIMIC (Dynamic Multiple Indicators and Multiple Causes) econometric model, Hsu (1997), 82, reported that the degree of industrialization in the postwar Taiwan *exceeded* the Japanese period only after 1966. Taiwanese standard of living did not recover to the prewar peak until the mid-1960s (Hsiao and Hsiao, 1998a; Wu, 1991).

and economic reform was brought about by external influences.[10] Rapid economic growth then ensued. The reform began with consolidating the multiple exchange rates into a single rate, and subsequent reform programs have been catered to the purpose of promoting exports. The success of export promotion policy is due to the fact that, among other factors, Taiwanese economic development was parallel to the growth of Japanese multinational corporations, and the subsequent formation of the Pacific trade triangle among Japan, Taiwan, and the United States.[11]

Along with the progress of economic liberalization came the political reform. In the 1950s, the Chinese who replaced the Japanese in the government did not speak Taiwanese, and the Taiwanese became the silent majority. The terror of the 228 Incident of 1947 further silenced and alienated most of the Taiwanese.[12] However, the language problem eased gradually after the next generation of Taiwanese, who were educated under the Chinese system, started being socially and politically active in the mid-1970s (Hsiao and Hsiao, 1996, Section 1.10.3). They were middle class intellectuals who were exposed to the Western democracy and society (Cheng and Haggard, 1992, 10–11). They started questioning the legitimacy of the authoritarian regime and formed political opposition groups. External events also played a decisive factor in spurring political reform. Taiwan was expelled from the United Nations in 1971, Japan and the United Kingdom severed diplomatic ties with Taiwan in 1972, and the United States followed suit in 1979. After winning several local elections, the opposition and the ruling party confronted in the Kaohsiung incident in December 1979. The subsequent struggle of the opposition and concession of the ruling party led to the formation of the Democratic Progressive Party (DPP) in 1986, the first new political party in postwar Taiwan. The big bang event of lifting the 38-year martial law ensued in July 1987 (ibid., 15–16). An observer of the event wrote that "the

---

[10]Hsiao and Hsiao (1996), Section 1.11. The importance of external factors in Taiwan's economic and political transition was also emphasized in Shiau (1994).

[11]Hsiao and Hsiao (1996), Section 1.13; M. Hsiao (1998); Twu (1995).

[12]An anthropological study of a small village, Liu Ts'o, in the middle Taiwan, indicates that from 1945 to 1970, only two small factories appeared. However, dramatic changes occurred after 1970, approximately 20 small-scale factories had emerged (Hu, 1983, 391–392; Hsiao and Hsiao, 1999b). We submit that the change is attributable to the rise of Chinese speaking Taiwanese youths (Hsiao and Hsiao, 1999b).

changes have been sudden... as 20 years of reform occurring, in 12 months."[13]

12.4 Post-1987 Reform

After 1987, the pace of both political democratization and economic liberalization accelerated.[14] In 1991, the "Temporary Provisions" was abolished and the "Period of National Mobilization for Suppression of the Communist Rebellion" was terminated, ending the 42-year long state of war with the Chinese communist government. In 1994, the governor of Taiwan and the mayors of Taipei and Kaohsiung were directly elected by popular votes, instead of being appointed by the "Central Government." Finally, the president and the vice president of Taiwan were elected directly by the Taiwanese people for a four-year term in 1996. In 1997, the newly elected National Assembly voted to reduce the power of the "provincial government" of Taiwan, a step considered to be eliminating the fiction of Taiwan being a province of China.[15]

A similar pace of reform occurred in the economic front. Externally, the change of global trade policy environment accelerated the process of economic liberalization in Taiwan. To curb the persistent trade deficits of the United States and trade surpluses of Japan, Germany, and to a lesser degree, Taiwan and South Korea, the Plaza Agreement of G5 in 1985 allowed an orderly devaluation of the U.S. dollar, and urged the accessibility of the market of the developing countries. In 1988, the U.S. Congress passed the Omnibus Trade and Competitiveness Act to require the U.S. government to make investigation on foreign trade barriers of the U.S. exports, and to negotiate with, or even retaliate against, the offenders by provoking Super 301 provision. In 1989, Taiwan was dropped from the

[13]King (1988), 234. King wrote further that "Observers generally credit President Chiang Ching-kuo... as the architect of the reform. But... the growing influence of pragmatic foreign-educated bureaucrats within the ruling Nationalist Party, or KMT, had at least nominal influence on the process."

[14]The following two paragraphs are based on *Facts on File, Far Eastern Economic Review*, and *Asia and Pacific Review*, various years.

[15]The speed of liberalization and democratization after 1987 seems outpaced many Taiwan observers. In the early 1990s, after studying "liberalization, democratization, and the role of the KMT", Meaney (1992), 115–116, listed 11 counterindicators of liberalization or democratization in Taiwan. She expected that "Comparing the situation in Taiwan to the regimes studied in the literature on transitions, the potential for a halfway house of liberalization without full democratization appears high."

offender's list by agreeing to appreciate its currency sharply against the dollar, and proposed to cut tariffs on "4,800 agricultural, consumer and industrial products to open Taiwan's market wider to foreign traders."[16]

Realizing the significant change in international trading environment and relieving of foreign exchange constraint, in July 1987, the Taiwan government eased foreign exchange controls, which had lasted 38 years, and allowed no limits on outward investment up to US$ 5 million, and no limits on the amount of imports payment. Tariffs were cut on some 2,500 products. In 1988, import tariffs were reduced on an, average of 50 percent for 3,500 items, including automobiles, color television sets, and videocassete recorders. A new banking law was promulgated in 1989. Commercial banks' interest rates were completely deregulated.[17] Private banks are allowed to open and invest in the stock market. A new foreign trade law was passed in 1993 to liberalize trade for the purpose of Taiwan's application to join the World Trade Organization (WTO) and developing Taiwan as an Asia-Pacific Regional Operation Center (APROC). In 1994, Taiwan allowed the foreign banks to open offices and branches.

In general, after the lifting of martial law, both democratization and liberalization proceeded hand-in-hand through internal and external pressures. However, democratization appears to happen in a big bang, while liberalization occurred gradually. Changes in Taiwan's democratization and liberalization processes are reflected in various freedom ratings by world watch organizations. Figure 12.1 shows three indexes of freedom: Civil liberties (icl), political rights (ipr), and economic freedom (ief). The terms will be explained in the following section. All three indexes increased over time. Note that, icl is generally lower[18] than ief before 1987, but it became higher after 1987. In the following sections, we will define icl and ief, and examine the effects of icl and ief on economic growth.

---

[16]Hsiao and Hsiao (1995). Also see Baldwin (1993).

[17]The following is a very good example of gradual nature in economic liberalization in Taiwan. Before 1960, there was only one rate for bank deposit and bank loan. In 1975, the bank deposit rate was set by the Central Bank, while the Banking Association, with the approval of the government, determined the bank loan rate. In 1985, each commercial bank set its own loan rates within certain upper and lower limits. In 1986, the requirement of the upper limit was lifted, and in 1989, the requirement of the lower limit was also lifted. Thus, after 1989, all banks can set their own interest rates. Hsu and Yang (1997) 168, Table 5.4.

[18]Note that since the freedom indexes are ordinal numbers, it does not make sense to compare the two indexes without normalizing the indexes to the unit interval.

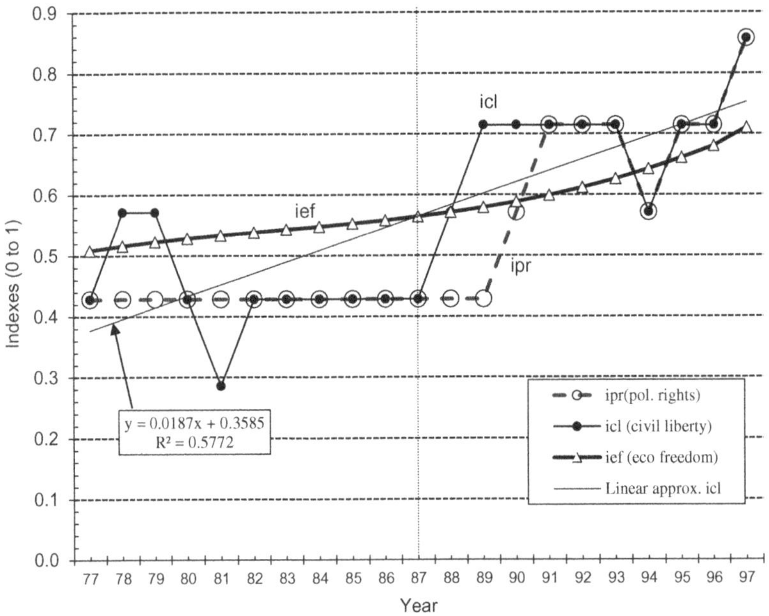

Figure 12.1: Indexes of Political Rights (ipr), Civil Liberties (icl) and Economic Freedom (ief) in Taiwan

12.5 Quantitative Measurements of Freedom

There are several definitions and measurements of democracy and freedom (Siermann, 1998). Here, we adopt the Gastil approach, which provides long-run consistent ratings. We took the indexes for civil liberties and political rights from "The Comparative Survey of Freedom" published in January–February issues of *Freedom Review* from 1983 to 1997, supplemented by Gastil (1982) for ratings from 1977 to 1982. Civil liberties are defined as "the freedoms to develop views, institutions and personal autonomy apart from the state" (FR, 1966, 6). It has thirteen checklist items, including the independence of the news media, freedom of opinion and religion, right of fair trial, and the number of political prisoners (Gastil, 1979, 15–24). The light line in Fig. 12.1 shows the civil liberties index over the years.

We also considered political rights, which "enable people to participate freely in the political process," that is, "the polity chooses the authoritative policy makers and attempts to make binding decisions affecting the national, regional or local community" (ibid., 5–6). It has eight to nine checklist items, including the existence of significant opposition parties and openness of voting procedures. They are rated on a seven-category scale, shown as the heavy dotted line[19] in Fig. 12.1. Note that, for Taiwan, the index of political rights (ipr) is either lower than or equal to the index of civil liberties (icl), however, they generally move together.

In the freedom ratings, the average of category numbers for civil liberties and political rights in each country is then classified into three major categories, "free," "partly free," and "not free." As may be expected from the previous three sections of this paper, Taiwan was rated "not free" from 1973, the year the ratings started, to 1976 (Gastil, 1982, 40), "partial free" from 1977 to 1996, and finally has become "free" after 1997. Taiwan is one of a few countries that has gone through, and advanced through, all these three categories since 1973.[20]

Economic freedom index (ief) is a weighted average of 17 components: Money and inflation (four items), government operations and regulations (six items), takings and discriminatory taxation (three items), and restrictions on international exchange (four items) compiled by Gwartney *et al.* (1996, xv) for 104 countries. Three kinds of weighting methods[21] for the 17 components are used: The Equal Impact Index, Survey Index 1 and 2, each ranges from zero (least free) to 10 (most free) for each component and each country. Figure 12.1 draws the Survey Index 1 for Taiwan. Dividing the original rating by 10 has normalized the index. Since the ratings are conducted for 1975, 1980, 1985, 1990 and 1995 only, the ratings of the intermediate years are interpolated by fitting a cubic function of time (t) using these five points:

$$\text{ief} = 4.140 + 1.045\text{t} - 0.318\text{t}^2 + 0.417\text{t}^3 \qquad (12.1)$$

The ief (the marked solid line) in Fig. 12.1 shows a near perfect fit, showing a rising trend of economic freedom over the years, slowly at the early years,

[19] The Survey rates civil liberties and political rights from 1 (the most free) to 7 (the least free) for each country. To facilitate our regression analysis below, we have changed the order from 1 (the least free) to 7 (the most free), and normalized the number to percentage by dividing by 7. Hence each category advances by 0.14 point.

[20] Also see Hsiao and Hsiao (1983), 51, 54. Several countries have been in and out of the three categories through out the years, indicating that a political system changes with time. However, China is one of a few countries which has been consistently "not free."

[21] Equal impact index (Ie) assigns each component a weight inverse to its standard deviation across countries. Survey index 1 (Isl) is the average of the weights given by 18 experts on each component. Survey index 2 (Is2) assigns each component a subjective country weight in accordance to the size of a correlation coefficient (Gwartney, 1996, 37–41). The difference among these three ratings is not significant for Taiwan (ibid., 210).

rapidly after 1987. Using equation (12.1), we have extrapolated the indexes for the last two years. As can be seen from the diagram, like the index for political rights (ipr), the ief index increased steadily. In fact, Taiwan is one of a few countries that have the index of economic freedom advanced from middle-rated countries in 1977 to one of the 15 highest-rated countries in the world[22] in 1995.

We may point out that Taiwanese experience of transition from authoritarian to democratic regime is not unique. In fact, Taiwan follows the world trend. In 1986, the political freedom in the world was evenly divided into "free," "partly free" and "not free" countries: 56, 56, and 55. The composition changed considerably in 1996. 76 countries were free, 62, partly free, and 53, not free (Karatnycky, 1996, 5). The condition of freedom in a country can change over the years. Taiwan is one of a few countries that its gain of freedom has been proceeded linearly upward.

12.6 Some Previous Studies on the Impact of Liberalization

There are many studies related to economic performance and liberalization. The consensus is that they are generally positively related. Recently, Aswicahyono *et al.* (1996) study the case of Indonesian liberalization since the mid-1980s. They found that there is no clear tendency of industrial concentration by domestic and foreign enterprises due to freer market entry and rising import competition. There are a decline in state enterprises, an increase in the private sector, slight changes in the firm size, steady growth in medium-sized firms at the expense of larger firms, and little impact on spatial distribution of manufacturing activity. Finally, they found that the total factor productivity (TFP) growth for selected industries was increasing, but it is not clear what the impact of liberalization was on TFP.

In Taiwan, while there are some discussions on the impact of liberalization, few related specifically to the effects of martial law on the economy, Chou *et al.* (1997) applied single country computable general equilibrium model to assess the effects of trade liberalization (in their case, joining GATT) on Taiwan. They showed that, from 1971 to 1986, and to 1992, the average tariff rate in Taiwan was reduced from 12.25 percent to

[22]Gwartney (1996), 64. In Gwartney (1996), there is a slight numerical discrepancy between the indexes of Taiwan listed in page 64 and those in country table in page 210. However, the conclusion here does not change.

6.96 percent, and to 4.87 percent; the import duty rate was also reduced from 13.51 percent to 9.31 percent, and to 6.74 percent. Their most optimistic simulation shows that multilateral liberalization of Taiwan by joining GATT will increase real GDP by 1.09 percent and total consumption by 2.88 percent. However, the agricultural and motor vehicle sectors will be adversely affected.

The above two studies do not specifically deal with the impact of economic liberalization due to a sudden change in the political climate, like the lifting of martial law. Chang (1996a, 1996b) is more specific. He compares the impact of liberalization before and after the mid-1980s, especially 1987. He observes that, after 1987, the Taiwanese economy has changed "quite visibly" (Chang, 1996a, 26), without, quite curiously, ever attributing the changes to the lifting of martial law. The real GDP share of manufacturing industry, which faced the rising labor cost due to the labor protection law, peaked at 38 percent in 1986–87, and then declined to about 31 percent in 1993 and after. On the other hand, rising consumer income expanded the service sector. Its real GDP share increased from 49 percent to about 58 percent during the same period. Liberalization enhances competition in domestic and foreign markets, resulting in industrial specialization. Thus, inside the manufacturing industry, the real GDP share of capital goods and durable consumer-goods industries exceeded the share of the non-durable consumer-goods industry for the first time in 1989 (39% vs. 37%). By 1994, the gap increased steadily to 44 percent vs. 29 percent, reflecting the technological advancement of the economy (ibid., 29–32).

Liberalization lifts the import restriction and local content requirements. Real imports of final goods contracted by 0.1 percent per year in 1981–1986, but expanded at 20.7 percent per year in 1986–1991. Real imports of intermediate goods also grew from 7.7 percent in 1981–1986 to 12.8 percent in 1986–1991. In the tradable sector, it was from 8.6 percent to 12.8 percent, and in the non-tradable sector, it was from 2.6 percent to 17.3 percent, while in the service sector, it was from 0.4 percent to whopping 17.4 percent (ibid., 34–37). At the same time, "the import contents of domestic final demand expanded from 15.0 percent in 1986 to 36.8 percent in 1991" (ibid., 40), among them, the tradable sector changed from 24 percent to 47 percent, non-tradable sector from 11 percent to 32 percent, and service sector from 7 percent to 29 percent.

Liberalization also accelerated industrial restructuring by changing the sources of industrial growth. On the input side, during 1981–1985, "of the 6.7 real GDP growth of all industries, labor productivity gain contributed 51.9 percent, employment increase contributed 37.4 percent, and employment structural change contributed 10.7 percent." In contrast, during 1986–1994, average real GDP growth rate was 8.1 percent, and the above percentages changed to 64.8 percent, 19.4 percent, and 15.8 percent, respectively (ibid., 45–46). Thus, after liberalization, the effect of labor productivity gain on real GDP growth becomes a predominant factor. On the demand side (using the Syrquin model of input–output analysis, Chang (ibid.), 48–49, also found that 1981–1986 was characterized by strong foreign demand and weak domestic demand. The situation reversed in 1986–1991. It featured weak foreign demand and strong domestic demand.

Using a similar input-output analysis, Hsu-Ku (1998) compared the industrial structures of the 1962–1987 period and the 1988–1997 period without, like Chang, attributing the changes to the lifting of martial law. He found that the income elasticities of demand, the labor productivity growth rates, and the labor reallocation effects for both agricultural and industrial sectors all decreased while those of the service sector increased.

While the above studies of the impact of liberalization provide a valuable insight and help us understand the expected results of changes in economic environment and policy reform, the major problem is that, as in any input–output models or simulation models, the analyses are based on descriptive statistics, no statistical inferences are applied. The calculated results of the variables naturally differ from year to year or period to period. They may increase or decrease. Even if one finds that the change is large, it may not be statistically significant, implying that the change is merely due to some random factors not related to the lifting of martial law. On the other hand, although the change may seem to be small, it may be statistically significant, meaning that the change is due to some systematic factors, like the lifting of martial law, and the results of changes in underlining basic social and economic characteristics. Thus, we propose a time series analysis and test the structural changes of the variables statistically.

12.7 Tests of Stationarity with Structural Changes

We have seen that all three indicators of freedom in Taiwan have improved over time. We also have seen that political rights and civil liberties increased suddenly in 1987 and afterward. We would like to know whether these political events in 1987 affect the structure of the economy.

In this section we examine the changes in the Taiwanese economy before and after 1987 by testing the following six economic time series. They are some of the important variables in the process of the Taiwanese economic development, namely, total output (gdp), output per worker or labor productivity (ypw), monetary policy indicator (m1), fiscal policy indicator (expd), external resources (dfi), and outward investment (outinv). The data are defined as follows:

gdp = real GDP at 1991 prices (NT$ million)
ypw = real GDP per worker (NT$)
dfi = approved inward private direct foreign investment, including "foreign" and "overseas Chinese" investment (US$ million)
outinv = approved outward investment (US$ million)
m1 = real money supply M1 (NT$ million), a proxy for monetary policy
expd = real total expenditures of all levels of government (NT$ million)

The six time series are all in natural logarithm. The original annual data from 1977 to 1997 are obtained from TSDB (1998). The sample includes the data 10 years before and 10 years after 1987. We have chosen the year 1977 as the beginning year, which is at the mid-point of the second import substitution period (1974–1980), to eliminate the shock of the first oil price crisis.[23] The series ypw is calculated from the real GDP (that is, deflated by GDP deflator) divided by the number of persons of working age (15–64). The series m1 and expd are the nominal money supply (M1) and the total government expenditures. Both nominal series were divided by the GDP deflator (1991 = 1), respectively, to obtain real M1 and real expd series.

The Perron test in time series (Perron, 1989) is an appropriate method to examine the stationarity (no unit-root) of time series with the structure changes due to the lifting of martial law in 1987. We test unit-root with one-time break and changes in the intercept and slope of each time series. The test equation is,

$$y_t = a_o + \mu_1 DP_t + \mu_2 DL_t + a_2 t + \mu_3 t * DL_t + a_1 y_{t-1} + \Sigma_{i=1}^{k} \beta_i \Delta y_{t-i} + \epsilon_t \tag{12.2}$$

[23]In Taiwan, the second oil price crisis (1979) was much less sever than the first (1973), as per capita GDP growth rate did not dip, the inflation rate was well in control, and balance of trade did not become negative (Hsiao and Hsiao, 1996, Section 1.10.3.2).

where y_t is natural logarithm of a time series, DP_t is a pulse dummy variable, taking 1 at the year 1987 (for one-time break, $t_B = 1986$) and 0 otherwise. It is the dummy variable for the possibility of one-time pulse or break in the year 1987. DL_t is a level dummy variable, taking 1 for 1987 and after, and 0 otherwise. It is the dummy variable for changes in the level of y_t for 1987 and after as compared with the level before 1987. Variable t is time trend, $t * DL_t$ is an interaction variable to measure the structural change in the slope (* shows multiplication), y_{t-1} is the one-period lag dependent variable, and Δy_{t-i} is the ith lag of the first-difference of dependent variable. The value of lag length k is chosen by following the method suggested in Perron (1989) and Enders (1995). λ in Table 12.1 is the proportion of the observations prior to the break to the total number of observations.

For a unit-root test, the null hypothesis is H_0: $a_1 = 1$ against the alternative hypothesis, H_1: $a_1 < 1$. All other coefficients are tested for the null hypothesis of the coefficient being zero against the alternative hypothesis that the coefficient is non-zero. The OLS estimated coefficients, the t-statistics, and adjusted coefficients of determination (adj R^2) are listed in Table 12.1. For convenience, the numerical results in Table 12.1 are summarized and interpreted in Table 12.2.

From Table 12.2, we find that three series, gdp, ypw, and dfi are stationary, as the null hypothesis of a unit-root can be rejected either at 1 percent or 5 percent level. The other three series, outinv, m1, and expd, are non-stationary. The gdp series is a trend stationary series with significant structural changes in constant term and slope, without significant pulse. The ypw series is also a trend stationary series with significant structural changes in the constant, slope, and pulse. The dfi series is not trend stationary, and has no significant structural changes in constant, slope, or pulse. For other series, m1, expd, and outinv, we cannot reject the null hypothesis of a unit-root at the 10 percent level. They are not stationary series, but have significant structural changes in constant, slope (m1), and pulse (expd). The regression results of these non-stationary series should be interpreted with caution.

The Perron test shows the properties of time series. We found all the series, except dfi, present structural changes of one kind or other. These structural changes can be considered as those induced by the lifting of martial law in 1987. However, the general practice is to reexamine the structural changes without the terms of testing unit-root in equation (12.2). For this purpose, we will present the next two sections.

12.8 Tests of Structural Changes with Regression

We first assume that the structural changes in the above time series are due to a big bang effect in 1987 by using linear regression with time and dummy variables. The model is,

$$y_t = a_o + \mu_1 DP_t + \mu_2 DL_t + a_1 t + \mu_3 t^* DL_t + \epsilon_t \tag{12.3}$$

Table 12.1: Perron Test for a Unit-Root and Structural Changes, 1977–1997

		lag	const	DP	DL	t	t*DL	y_{t-1}	adj
	Coeff	k	a_0	μ_1	μ_2	a_2	μ_3	a_1	R^2
	Series	tB = 1986							
1	gdp	0	13.5	-0.019	0.159	0.066	-0.006	0.059	0.999
			(4.36)	*(-0.80)n*	*(3.47)*	*(4.21)*	*(-2.18)*	*(-4.33)b*	
2	ypw	5	14.99	-0.090	0.491	0.087	-0.034	-0.263	0.999
			(7.13)	*(-4.64)*	*(7.91)*	*(7.55)*	*(-7.04)*	*(-7.08)a*	
3	dfi	6	17.51	0.985	3.087	1.095	-0.375	-3.506	0.920
			(5.36)	*(2.00)n*	*(1.94)n*	*(2.74)n*	*(-1.70)n*	*(-4.37)b*	
4	outinv	0	1.401	-1.298	2.503	0.203	-0.074	0.182	0.935
			(2.32)	*(-1.72)n*	*(2.29)*	*(2.48)*	*(-0.74)n*	*(-3.70)*	
5	ml	1	9.432	-0.073	0.795	0.096	-0.054	0.260	0.987
			(2.17)	*(-0.46)n*	*(2.51)*	*(3.48)*	*(-3.47)*	*(-2.20)*	
6	expd	0	6.902	-0.260	0.339	0.035	-0.011	0.467	0.968
			(2.42)	*(-2.15)*	*(1.84)*	*(1.67)n*	*(-0.62)n*	*(-2.39)*	

Notes: 1. t-value is in the parentheses, n = not significant at 10 percent level.
2. For all coefficients, except a_1, the null hypothesis is that the coefficient = 0 in the t-test.
3. a and b denote that we can reject H_0: $a_1 = 1$ (a unit-root) at 1 percent and 5 percent level, respectively. At $\lambda = 0.5$, the critical values are -4.90, -4.24, and -3.96 at 1 percent, 5 percent, and 10 percent level, respectively. See Perron (1989).

Table 12.2: Summary of Perron Test

				Structural Change		
		Stationarity	Trend	Pulse	Cons	Slope
Series/Coeff		$a_1 < 1$	a_2	μ_1	μ_2	μ_3
1	gdp	y**	y***	n	y***	y**
2	ypw	y***	y***	y***	y***	y***
3	dfi	y**	n#	n	n	n
4	outinv	n	y**	n#	y**	n
5	m1	n	y***	n	y**	y***
6	expd	n	n#	y**	y*	n

Notes: y = yes, n = no.
***, **, and * = significant at 1 percent, 5 percent, and 10 percent level, respectively. # = significant at 15 percent level.

The estimated results are presented in Table 12.3. Among the six series, each one has two estimated results. Part A estimates equation (12.3) with all independent variables in the equation, and Part B re-estimates the equation by dropping the insignificant variables. Thus, the interpretation of structural changes should be based on the results in Part B. The numerical results are summarized in the last three columns. We found that there are pulses only in the government expenditure (expd) and outward investment (outinv). There are no pulses in other series, that is, no significant dips in 1987. All the series have an upward shift in constant term, and the level of the series is significantly different before and after 1987. There are, to our surprise, downward shifting in the slopes of real GDP (gdp), real money supply (m1), and inward direct foreign investment (dfi). For these three series, the growth rates have decreased after 1987. There also has downward shifting tendency in the slopes of real GDP per worker (ypw) and outward foreign investment (outinv), but they are not significant.

In general, there are different responses of economic time series to the lifting of martial law. While the level of the series has increased, the growth rate has decreased after 1987. The decrease in growth rates may be due to factors other than the lifting of martial law, such as increases in land price,

Table 12.3: OLS Regression with Time and Dummy Variables, 1977–1997

		Cons	DP	DL	t	t*DL	Adj.	DW	Pls	Stct
	Coef	a_0	μ_1	μ_2	a_1	μ_3	R^2	-d	87	Chg
	Series									
1A	gdp	14.311	-0.023	0.188	0.073	-0.010	0.998	1.651		
		(0)	*(0.30)n*	*(0)*	*(0)*	*(0)*				
1B	gdp	14.311		0.170	0.073	-0.009	0.998	1.703		cons
		(0)		*(0)*	*(0)*	*(0)*				slope
2A	ypw	11.955	-0.023	0.124	0.051	-0.002	0.997	1.698		
		(0)	*(0.32)n*	*(0)*	*(0)*	*(0.50)n*				
2B	ypw	11.957		0.098	0.050		0.998	1.794		cons
		(0)		*(0)*	*(0)*					
3A	dfi	5.318	0.069	1.118	0.148	-0.073	0.902	1.220		
		(0)	*(0.85)n*	*(0.05)*	*(0)*	*(0.12)n*				
3B	dfi	5.318		1.171	0.148	-0.076	0.907	1.244		cons
		(0)		*(0.02)*	*(0)*	*(0.08)*				slope
4A	out-inv	2.059	-1.544	2.358	0.184	-0.008	0.935	2.061		
		(0)	*(0.04)*	*(0.04)*	*(0.01)*	*(0.93)n*				
4B	out-inv	2.077	-1.521	2.277	0.180		0.938	2.054	P	cons
		(0)	*(0.03)*	*(0)*	*(0)*					
5A	m1	12.950	-0.081	1.011	0.099	-0.049	0.983	1.652		
		(0)	*(0.48)n*	*(0)*	*(0)*	*(0)*				
5B	m1	12.950		0.948	0.099	-0.046	0.984	1.926		cons
		(0)		*(0)*	*(0)*	*(0)*				slope
6A	expd	12.851	-0.316	0.297	0.072	-0.003	0.966	1.826		
		(0)	*(0.02)*	*(0.14)n*	*(0)*	*(0.84)n*				
6B	expd	12.858	-0.307	0.264	0.070		0.968	1.796	P	cons
		(0)	*(0.02)*	*(0.02)*	*(0)*					

Notes: P = Pulse 1987; Strt Chg = Structure Change in constant and or slope. p-value is in the parentheses, p = 0 means that the coefficient is significant at less than 1 percent level. *n* = not significant at 10 percent level.

shortage of labor supply and rapid wage increase, resulting in increase in Taiwanese outward foreign direct investment to China and Southeast Asia, and decrease in domestic capital formation.[24] Clearly, after mid-1980s, the Taiwanese economy has gradually matured, and the growth rate of series, especially real GDP, has started to taper off.

Our finding of the decrease in the growth rate of real GDP and real per worker GDP is not consistent with the findings from the cross-country data compiled by Gwartney *et al.* (1996), xxiii. They reveal that, so far as economic freedom is concerned, the effect is clearly positive. The 1994 per capita GDP of six persistently high-rated countries from 1975 to 1995 are Hong Kong, Switzerland, Singapore, the United States, Canada, and Germany. The average per capita GDP[25] is US$ 16,600. They then compare these with the nine persistently low-rated countries during the same period. The nine countries are Somalia, Zambia, Hungary, Romania, Brazil, Syria, Uganda, Zaire, and Zimbabwe. The average per capita GDP is only US$ 2,600. The average growth rate for persistently high-rated countries is 2.6 percent, while that of persistently low-rated countries is −0.6 percent. Thus, from this very crude comparison, we may expect a positive correlation between increase in economic freedom and per capita GDP growth rate. As we have pointed out in the previous section, their cross-country analysis does not take other factors into consideration and relation between economic growth and liberalization may also depend on the stage of economic development.[26]

---

[24]We owe this explanation to a referee. Chang (1996a), 26, has pointed out that the Taiwanese economy reversed its characteristics after 1987. "Export expansion slackened while domestic demand strengthened; imports shot up.... The dampening of exports reversed manufacturing-industry growth, resulting in as appreciable reduction in its share of real GDP.... The rapid expansion of domestic demand spurred vigorous development of the service sector..." A slowdown in exports may result in slowdown in GDP growth rates. However, Chang also found that, for shorter period, the real GDP growth rate was 6.7 percent from 1981 to 1985 and 8.1 percent from 1986 to 1994 (ibid., 47), as compared with our estimated results which shows 7.3 percent from 1977 to 1986 and 6.4 percent from 1987 to 1997 (see equation 1B in Table 12.3).

[25]GDP per capita figures are measured in 1985 U.S. dollars, and are updates of the Summers and Heston data derived by the purchasing power parity method (Gwartney, 1996, xxiii).

[26]In the original version of this paper, we have presented a section on the relationship between civil liberties, economic freedom, and endogenous growth. Since our data consist of only 20 years, we have decided to treat the impact of freedom on long-run economic growth in a separate paper.

12.9 Tests of Smooth Transition

The tests of structural changes we have applied in the previous section assume that the changes occurred in 1987. Could these changes also be interpreted as a smooth transition? In this section, we would like to take a step further to examine this possibility. We will employ the logistic smooth transition regression model (LSTR) explained in Granger and Terasvirta (1993) to test the six time series. There are advantages of using the LSTR model. First, it does not require to set a priori assumption on specific time of the break. Second, the mid-time of transition, the speed of adjustment, and the structural changes of level and slope are all incorporated into one model. The model is specified as follows:

$$y_t = b_1 + b_2 f_t(\gamma, \tau) + b_3 t + b_4 t f_t(\gamma, \tau) + \epsilon_t \tag{12.4}$$

where $f_t(\gamma, \tau) = \{1 + exp[-\gamma(t - \tau)]\}^{-1}$ is a logistic function of time in the unit interval. The coefficient γ is the smoothness parameter. If it is positive and small, then the model transition occurs smoothly. The coefficient τ is the location parameter that determines the mid-point of transition.

Table 12.4 shows the estimated results of the six time series using the nonlinear least squares method (NLS). The results are summarized in the last column of the table. We find that the estimated γ is positive and significant in gdp, ypw, m1, and outinv series. Hence, we may say that real GDP, real GDP per worker, real money supply, and outward foreign investment may also be interpreted as having a smooth transition from 1977 to 1997.

For real GDP and real money supply, smooth transition occurred in both constant term and slope. As in the previous section, the level moved up and the growth rate decreased smoothly. For real GDP per worker and outward foreign investment, smooth transition occurred only in the constant term, that is, only the level moved upward smoothly. These findings are consistent with those we have found in Table 12.3. As we have observed in the previous sections, economic liberalization occurred slowly over three decades. Thus, we consider that the interpretation of the smooth transition, rather than the big bang, is more appropriate for these economic variables. Notice also that for these four series, the mid-point of transition, τ occurs at 9 to 11. Since we assign t = 0 at 1977, the implied τ is around 1986 to 1988. This means that the smooth transition has occurred around the mid-point of the sample, which is what we have expected.

The estimated γ for inward direct foreign investment (dfi) and government expenditures (expd) are not significant at the 10 percent level, hence,

Table 12.4: Logistic Smooth Transition Regression (LSTR), 1977–1997

	Coeff	Cons b_1	Adj cons b_2	Rate of transi γ	mid-time τ	t b_3	Adj slope b_4	Adj R^2	DW −d	Results
	Series									
1	gdp	14.316 *(0)*	0.188 *(0)*	2.175 *(0.11)*	9.488 *(0)*	0.071 *(0)*	−0.008 *(0.02)*	0.999	1.56	near s.t. *(cons, slope)*
2	ypw	11.962 *(0)*	0.123 *(0)*	1.922 *(0.06)*	9.311 *(0)*	0.05 *(0)*	0.001 *(0.85)n*	0.998	1.650	s.t. *(cons)*
3	dfi	5.186 *(0)*	−2.77 *(0.11)*	2.199 *(0.21)n*	14.675 *(0)*	0.19 *(0)*	0.107 *(0.25)n*	0.937	1.788	not s.t.
4	outinv	2.143 *(0)*	4.251 *(0.02)*	1.223 *(0.11)*	10.732 *(0)*	0.15 *(0.07)*	−0.088 *(0.44)n*	0.949	2.19	near s.t. *(cons)*
5	m1	13.013 *(0)*	0.938 *(0)*	2.253 *(0.02)*	8.953 *(0)*	0.08 *(0)*	−0.024 *(0.05)*	0.992	1.78	s.t. *(cons, slope)*
6	expd	12.858 *(0)*	0.676 *(0)*	14.56 *(1.00)n*	11.239 *(0.96)n*	0.070 *(0)*	−0.023 *(0.08)*	0.986	1.22	not s.t.

Notes: p-value is in the parentheses. n = not significant at 15 percent level. s.t. = smooth transition.

there is no smooth transition. In view of deregulation and openness of the domestic market for foreign investment, sudden claims of entitlement by people, and increase in expenditures for social and economic infrastructures, inward direct foreign investment and government expenditures increased suddenly and considerably after 1987. These factors may contribute to the non-smooth transition of these series.

12.10 Some Concluding Remarks

In this paper, we have examined the origin of Taiwan's authoritarian regime by tracing back to the Japanese period, and discussed the external and internal factors which prompted the authoritarian regime to reform its economic policy for rapid economic growth. We also considered the process of economic liberalization and the external and internal factors that led to the lifting of martial law. We see the accelerated liberalization and democratization after martial law was lifted in 1987. Our observations that economic liberalization occurred gradually and democratization happened rather abruptly have been confirmed by the indexes of civil liberties, political rights, and economic freedom compiled by some international organizations which compared various aspects of freedom in other countries. We then reviewed some literature on the impact of economic liberalization on economic performance and structural changes. We found that the previous findings are valuable and informative in understanding the impact. However, they are mainly analysis of descriptive statistics, devoid of statistical inferences.

We have chosen six economic time series to test their stationarity and structural changes. Among them, three series, real GDP, real per worker GDP, and direct foreign investment are trend stationary. They show no one-time pulse in 1987, but have increase in the constant term. The growth rates of real GDP and direct foreign investment decreased after 1987, but no change for the growth rate of real per worker GDP. The first two series also show a smooth transition over time, but not for the third series.

The other three variables, namely, real money supply M1, total government expenditures, and outward investment are not trend stationary. Hence, the regression results must be interpreted with caution. For levels, all three of them increased with statistical significance, and for the growth rate, all have decreased, but only the money supply has decreased statistically significantly. In general, all six series we have tested show increase in the constant terms, but either no change or decrease in the growth rates after 1987. Increase in constant terms means that the levels of the values of these six time series data have increased after martial law was lifted. However, their rates of growth have not increased probably due to changes in international trading environment not specifically related to the lifting of martial law.

Acknowledgments

The revised version of this paper has benefited from discussions with the participants of the International Conference on The Transformation of an Authoritarian Regime: Taiwan in the Post-Martial Law Era, organized by the Taiwan Study Promotion Committee, Institute of Taiwanese History, Preparatory Office, Academia Sinica, Taipei, Taiwan, April 1999. We thank the Committee members, especially, Dr. Ts'ui-jung Liu, for their hospitality, and Drs. Chu-yuan Cheng, Yun-peng Chu, Chao-cheng Mai, and Tzong-shian Yu for comments and suggestions. Comments by two referees are also useful. In preparing for this Chapter, the chart and tables have been reformatted using the Microsoft Excel program. All errors of omission and commission are ours.

References

Adelman, I. and C.T. Morris (1967). *Society, Politics, and Economic Development, A Quantitative Approach.* Baltimore: The Johns Hopkins University Press.

Aswicahyono, H.H., Kelly Bird and Hal Hill (1996). "What Happens to Industiral Structure When Countries Liberalise? Indonesia since the Mid-1980s." *The Journal of Development Studies*, 32(3): 340–363.

Baldwin, Robert E. (1993). "Trade Policy in a Maturing Taiwan Economy." Conference on the Evolution of Taiwan within a New World Economic Order, Conference Series, No. 25, 199–220. Taiwan: Chung-Hua Institution for Economic Research.

Chang, Wen-po (1996a). "The Impact of Economic Liberalization on the Pattern of Economic Growth." *Industry of Free China*, 85(3): 25–62.

______ (1996b). "The Impact of Economic Liberalization on the Industrial Growth in Taiwan." *Quarterly Journal of the Bank of Taiwan*, 47(2): 52–70.

Chen, Ching-chih (1996). "The Legacy of Japanese Socio-political Control System in Post-war Taiwan." Paper presented at Conference on the Japanese Legacy in Post-Colonial Taiwan, sponsored by the Joint Center for East Asian Studies, Washington University and University of Missouri. St. Louis.

Chen, Shih-meng S., Chung-cheng Lin, C. Y. Cyrus Chu, Ching-hsi Chang, Jun-ji Shi and Jin-tian Liu (1991). *Disintegrating KMT-State Capitalism, A Closer Look at Privatizing Taiwan's State- and Party-Owned Enterprisies.* Taipei, Taiwan: Taipei Society.

Cheng, Tun-jen and Stephen Haggard (1992). "Regime Transformation in Taiwan: Theoretical and Comparative Perspectives." In Tun-jen Cheng and Stephen Haggard (eds.), *Political Changes in Taiwan.* Boulder: Lynne Rienner Publishers.

Chou, Ji, Yun-Peng Chu, and Shiu-Tung Wang (1997). "Effects of Trade Liberalization on Taiwan: A Computable General Equilibrium Analysis." *Asian Economic Journal*, 11(2): 169–186.

Chou, Tian-cheng (1992). "Small-and-Medium Enterprises on the Fringe of the Power" (in Chinese). In H. Hsiao *et al.* (1992), cited in this References section (Chapter 5).

Chu, Yun-peng (1992). "Oligopolistic Economy and Authoritarian Political Regime" (in Chinese). In H. Hsiao *et al.* (1992), cited in this References Section (Chapter 7).

Conlon Associates (1959). *United States Foreign Policy: Asia*, Studies no. 5. Prepared at the request of the Committee on Foreign Relation, United States Senate, Washington, D.C., U.S. Economic Liberalization and Development 375 Government Printing Office.

Enders, Walter (1995). *Applied Econometric Time Series.* New York: John Wiley & Sons, Inc.

Freedom Review (FR, previously, *Freedom at Issue*) 1996, 27(1) (January–February).

Gastil, Reymond D. (1979). *Freedom in the World, Political Rights and Civil Liberty*. Freedom House.

——— (1982). *Freedom in the World, Political Rights and Civil Liberty*. Westport, CT: Greenwood Press.

Granger, C. W. J. and T. Terasvirta (1993). *Modelling Nonlinear Economic Relationship*. Oxford: Oxford University Press.

Gwartney, James, Robert Lawson and Walter Block (1996). *Economic Freedom of the World, 1975–1995*. Canada: The Fraser Institute.

Ho, S.P.S. (1978). *Economic Development of Taiwan, 1960–1970*. New Haven: Yale University Press.

Hsiao, Frank S.T. and Mei-Chu W. Hsiao (1983). "Some Development Indicators of Taiwan: A Comparative Study." *Journal of Economic Development*, 8(1): 45–58.

——— and ——— (1995). "Globalization of the Taiwanese Economy and U.S.-Taiwan Trade Relations." In Cheng F. Lee (ed.), *Advances in Pacific Basin Business, Economics, and Finance* (Vol. 1, 197–214). Greenwich, CT: JAI Press. (Ref. Chapter 10).

——— and ——— (1996). "Taiwanese Economic Development and Foreign Trade." In W.C. Kirby and J.M. Greene (eds.), *Harvard Studies on Taiwan: Papers of the Taiwan Study Workshop*. John King Fairbank Center of East Asian Research, Harvard University, 1995. Reprinted in John Y.T. Kuark (ed.), *Comparative Asian Economies* (211–302). JAI Press, 1996. (Ref. Chapter 1).

——— and ——— (1998a). "Colonial Linkages in Early Postwar Taiwanese Economic Development." In William C. Kirby and Michael S. Weiss (eds.), *Harvard Studies on Taiwan, Papers of the Taiwan Studies Workshop* (Vol. II, 91–117). Cambridge, MA: The Fairbank Center for East Asian Research, Harvard University. (Ref. Chapter 5).

——— and ——— (1998b). "International Comparisons of Taiwanese Economic Growth: Long-run Trends and Postwar Initial Conditions." Working Paper, Department of Economics, University of Colorado at Boulder. Published as "Miracle Growth in the Twentieth Century — International Comparisons of East Asian Development," *World Development*, 2003, 31(2): 227–257.

——— and ——— (1999a). "Falling Behind but Catching Up in the Long Run-On Capitalistic Development of Taiwan and Korea." Economic Research Center Discussion Paper, No. 110, School of Economics, Nagoya University, Nagoya, Japan. February 1999. Working Paper Series, No. 9907, Center for Research on Economic and Social Policy, University of Colorado at Denver, March 1999. Published as "Catching-up and Convergence: On the Long Run Growth in East Asia" in *Review of Development Economics*, 8(2) (May 2004): 223–236.

——— and ——— (1999b). "The Historical Traditions of Taiwanese Small-and-Medium Enterprises." In Fu-san Huang and Ka-im Ang (eds.), *Taiwan's Commercial Traditions*. 524 Taipei, Taiwan: Academia Sinica. (Ref. Chapter 6).

Hsiao, Frank S. T. (1997). "Colonialism or Comparative Advantage? — On Agricultural Development in Colonial Taiwan." Paper presented at the Taiwan Studies Workshop, The Fairbank Center for East Asian Research, Harvard University, and National Taiwan University, 1996. *Proceedings of the National Science Council, Part C: Humanities and Social Sciences*, 7(4) (October): 497–513. Taipei, Taiwan. (Ref. Chapter 4).

Hsiao, Hsin-huang, Yun-pong Chu, Jia-dong Hsu, Zhong-ji Wu, Tian-Cheng Chou, Ji-li Yan, Yun-han Chu, and Zhong-chen Lin (1992). *Dissecting Taiwanese Economy: Monopoly and Exploitation Under an Authoritaran Regime.* Taiwan Research Fund Series No. 2, Taipei, Taiwan: Taiwan Research Fund.

Hsiao, Mei-Chu W. (1998). "Pacific Trade Triangle and the Growth of Korea and Taiwan-Cointegration and Causality Analysis." Working paper, University of Colorado at Denver.

Hsu, Jia-dong and Ya-hui Yang (1997). "Taiwanese Financial System and Economic Development" (in Chinese). In Yu and Lee (eds.) (1997) (149–190), cited in this References section.

Hsu, Song-ken (1997). "A Study of the Contribution of Industrial Policy in Taiwan during 1960–1990" (in Chinese). In Yu and Lee (eds.) (1997) (51–93), cited in this References section.

Hsu-Ku, Yuan-hong (1998). "An Analysis of Labor Reallocation and Industrial Adjustment in Taiwan." *Industry of Free China*, 88(6): 49–64.

Hu, Tai-li (1983). "The Emergence of Small-scale Industry in a Taiwanese Rural Community." In June Nash and Maria P.E. Kelly (eds.), *Women, Men, and the International Division of Labor.* Albany: State University of New York Press.

Huang, Fu-san (1996). "The Japanese Legacy and the Nationalist Chinese Rule in Postwar Taiwan." Paper presented at Conference on the Japanese Legacy in Post-Colonial Taiwan, sponsored by the Joint Center for East Asian Studies, Washington University and University of Missouri. St. Louis.

Jacoby, Neil H. (1966). *U.S. Aid to Taiwan, A Study of Foreign Aid, Self-help, and Development.* New York: Frederick A. Praeger.

Karatnycky, Adrian (1996). "Democracy and Despotism: Bipolarism Renewed?" *Freedom Review* 27(1) (January–February): 5–12.

King, Bob (1988). "Taiwan." *The Asia and Pacific Review.* Essex, U.K.: World of Information, 232–236.

Li, K.T. (1988). *The Evolution of Policy Behind Taiwan's Development Success.* New Haven: Yale University Press.

______ and Wan-an Yeh (1982). "Economic Planning in the Republic of China." In Kwoh-ting Li and Tzongshian Yu (eds.) (1982), *Experiences and Lessons of Economic Development in Taiwan* (103–130). Taipei, Taiwan: Academia Sinica.

Lin, Ching-yuan (1973). *Industrialization in Taiwan, 1946–72: Trade and Import-Substitution Policies for Developing Countries.* New York: Praeger.

Lin, Ji-wen (1996). *A Study on War Mobilization System During the Last Stage of the Japanese Occupation Period (1930–1945)* (in Chinese). Taipei: Tao-Hsiang Publishing Co.

Maddison, Angus (1995). *Monitoring the World Economy, 1820–1992*. Paris: Development Centre, OECD.

Meaney, Constance S. (1992). "Liberalization, Democratization, and the Role of the KMT." In Tun-jen Cheng and Stephen Haggard (eds.), *Political Changes in Taiwan*. Boulder: Lynne Rienner Publishers.

Perron, Pierre (1989). "The Great Crash, The Oil Price Shock, and the Unit Root Hypothesis." *Econometrica*, 57(6) (November): 1361–1401.

Shiau, Chuan-Jenq (1994). "The Transformation of Authoritarianism in Postwar Taiwan: Democratization and Liberalization." In Stuart S. Nagel (ed.), *Asian Development and Public Policy* (Chapter 12). NY: St. Martin Press.

Siermann, Clemens L.J. (1998). *Politics, Institutions, and the Economic Performance of Nations*. Northampton, MA: Edward Elgar.

Taiwan Statistical Data Book (TSDB) (1998). Council for Economic Planning and Development, Taiwan, Republic of China.

Twu, Jaw-Yann (1975). *Taiwan under Japanese Imperialism* (in Japanese). Tokyo: The Tokyo University Press.

——— (1995). "The Asian Growth Triangle: Structure, Change and Perspective." *International Economic Conflict Discussion Paper* 81. Economic Research Center, School of Economics, Nagoya University.

Underwood, Laurie (1997). "Inside the Ruling Party's Moneymaking Machine — KMT, Inc." *Topics: Issues on International Business in Taiwan*, 12–23. Taiwan: The American Chamber of Commerce in Taipei, May.

World Bank (1987). *World Development Report, 1987* (WDR). World Bank. NY: Oxford University Press.

Wu, Tsong-min (1991). "Long-run Fluctuations in Aggregate Outputs of Taiwan and Changes in Economic Structure" (in Chinese). In Kuo-ji Li (ed.), *Modern Taiwanese History* (609–636). Taipei: Taiwan Sheng Wenshian Weiyuanhui.

Yu, Tsong-shian and Joseph Lee (eds.) (1997). *Economic Policy and Economic Development — An Evaluation of Taiwanese Economic Development* (in Chinese). Taipei: Chung-hua Institution for Economic Research.

Chapter 13

Diminishing Returns and Asian NIEs — How They Overcome the Iron Law

13.1 Introduction

There are a great deal of studies on the four Asian NIEs (hereafter NIEs) — South Korea, Taiwan, Hong Kong, and Singapore in recent years. They are often characterized by sustained rapid economic growth for over three decades (OECD, 1979; Page, 1994; World Bank, 1993; Park and Park, 1989). Since the late 1960s, they quickly entered the world production process, fended off oil crises, repulsed the competition from other developing countries, and resisted the rise of protectionist pressures in the developed countries. By 1996, Korea was admitted to the prestigious OECD countries.

Table 13.1 compares per capita GNP and its growth rate[1] in U.S. dollars for Asian NIEs, ASEAN-4, and some other countries. According to the 2000–2001 World Development Report classification (World Bank, 2000, 275, footnotes), by 1999, ASEAN countries, except Indonesia, belong to lower middle-income countries (US$ 755 to 2,996); Korea is an upper middle-income country (US$ 2,997 to 9,265). Taiwan, Hong Kong and Singapore belong to high-income countries, whose per capita GNP is US$ 9,266 or more. From 1980 to 1999, the average annual per capita income of Asian NIEs increased 5.5 to 6.7 times (col. (8), Table 13.1), almost four times faster than average middle-income countries (1.4%), or twice faster than that of Japan and the United States (2.7%), while that of ASEAN-4 increased (at 2%) slightly above average rate of low income economies (1.6%). So far as Asian NIEs are concerned, (absolute) convergence of their

[1]Taiwan's growth rates are calculated from TSDB (1996), 32. The growth rate is the ordinary least squares estimate b in equation In y_t = a + bt.

Table 13.1: GNP, per capita GNP, and Growth Rates

Selected Countries and Regions

	GNP/pc	'80, '93			GNP/pc	'99			GNPpc gr rates		
Units	US$	US$	ratio	*'93*	US$	(b)	(c)	ratio	%	%	
Year, Period	1980	1993	93/80	*rkg*	1999	*rkg1*	*rkg2*	99/80	60-80	80-93	+/-
	(1)	(2)	(3)	*(4)*	(5)	*(6)*	*(7)*	(8)	(9)	(10)	(11)
Middle IEco	1400	2480	1.8		2000			1.4	3.8	0.2	-3.6
NIEs											
Korea	**1520**	**7600**	**5.0**	*29*	**8490**	*52*	*26*	**5.6**	**7.0**	**8.2**	**1.2**
Singapore	4430	19850	4.5	*14*	29610	*9*	*6*	6.7	7.5	6.1	-1.4
Taiwan (a)	**2344**	**10850**	**4.6**	*24*	**13248**	*43*	*22*	**5.7**	**6.4**	**5.7**	**-0.7**
Hong Kong	4240	12767	3.0	*25*	23520	*20*	*13*	5.5	6.8	5.4	-1.4
ASEAN-4											
Thailand	670	2110	3.1	*55*	1960	*103*	*55*	2.9	4.7	6.4	1.7
Indonesia	430	740	1.7	*85*	580	*151*	*86*	1.3	4.0	4.2	0.2
Malaysia	1620	3140	1.9	*39*	3400	*83*	*41*	2.1	4.3	3.5	-0.8
Philippines	690	850	1.2	*164*	1020	*132*	*71*	1.5	2.8	-0.6	-3.4
Low IEco	260	380	1.5		410			1.6	1.2	3.7	2.5
Low & Middle IEco		1090			1240			1.1	(d)	0.9	
EA and Pacific		**820**			**1000**			**1.2**	**(d)**	**6.4**	
South Asia		310			440			1.4	(d)	3.0	
LAm and Carib		2950			3840			1.3	(d)	-0.1	
Eur & Cent Asia		2450			2150			0.9	(d)	-0.3	
Sub-Saha. Africa		520			500			1.0	(d)	-0.8	
Middle East & N. Africa		-			2060				(d)	2.4	
China	290	490	1.7	*99*	780	*141*	*77*	2.7	-	8.2	
India	240	300	1.3	*112*	450	*163*	*95*	1.9	1.4	3.0	1.6
Industrial market	**10320**	**23090**	**2.2**						**3.6**	**2.2**	**-1.4**
Japan	9890	31490	3.2	*2*	32230	*6*	*3*	3.3	7.1	3.4	-3.7
USA	11360	24740	2.2	*5*	30600	*8*	*5*	2.7	2.3	1.7	-0.6
Total Ctries	125					*206*	*128*				

Notes: Low IEco = Lowe Income Economies; IEco = Income Economies, LAm and Carib = Latin America and Caribbean.
(a) TSDB (2000); (b) Ranking given by WDR (1999), including all countries not listed in WDR (2000). Taiwan is added in the ranking. (c) Ranking of the countries listed in WDR (2000). (d) 99/93

Sources: WDR (1982, 1995, 2000).

per capita GNP to that of the industrial countries are conclusively shown in the table.

In terms of the level of GNP in 1999 (WDR, 2000/2001), the contrast is even more staggering. Few people know that the economic scale of Korea (ranked 13th in the world order, not shown in the table) is about 40 percent of that of China (ranked 7th). At the GNP level of US\$ 290.82 billion (TSDB, 2000, 13), the economic scale of Taiwan (17th) is almost the same as that of Russia (16th at US\$ 332 billion), as much as 30 percent of China (7th at US\$ 980.2 billion), and larger than Argentina (18th) and Switzerland (19th). Fewer people are aware that the domestic economic activity of the tiny city-state Hong Kong (25th at US\$ 161 billion) is larger than Poland (26th), and much larger than that of Malaysia (40th at US\$ 77 billion) and the Philippines (39th at US\$ 78 billion). Singapore's economic activity (35th at US\$ 95 billion) is also slightly larger than that of the Philippines and Malaysia.

From 1960 to 1980 (Column (9)), and also from 1980 to 1993, the average annual GNP per capita of the four Asian NIEs grew continuously from low of 5.4 percent to high of 8.2 percent (Column (10)), almost two times faster than those of the developed economies, and much faster than those of any other group of developing countries in the world.[2] The contrast is clearer in the 1980–1993 period, during which the average annual growth rate of middle-income countries recorded a mere 0.2 percent.

The Asian NIEs as well as the vast economies of the United States and Japan that ranked number one and number two in the world, respectively, have worked like magnets. They lead other developing countries in the Pacific, and to a lesser extent, the Southeast Asian countries, to a massive positive growth of 6.4 percent. All other developing areas, especially Middle East and North Africa area (−2.4%), experienced a negative growth. For these other developing countries, convergence of per capita GNP to that of the developed countries is simply out of the question, as the developed countries have experienced respectable positive growth in both periods (3.6% and 2.2%, respectively). The sustained economic growth and vitality of East Asian countries are clearly revealed in Table 13.1. Here is an evidence of East Asian "miracle."

[2]In recent years, WDR changed its reporting format and does not supply long-run growth rates of the countries. Hence, the latest figures are not available. This may not be a problem since Krugman's argument is based on some statistical results before 1993.

In 1994, however, Krugman (1994) has presented a contrarian view. With the risk of oversimplification, his argument may be summarized syllogistically: one, the NIEs' economic growth has been input-driven, that is, not attributable to technical progress or "efficient growth," and presents no economic miracle; two, such growth "is inevitably subject to diminishing returns," similar to what the former Soviet economy had experienced, which eventually collapsed; three, therefore, there may not be "an Asian-centered world economy and geopolitics."

Krugman's first argument is based on total factor productivity (TFP) growth rate studies of other economists. We have discussed it elsewhere.[3] This paper examines mainly his second argument, and to a lesser degree, the third point. While there are many discussions about Krugman's contention, there seems to be no thorough and systematic studies related to the role of diminishing returns in the Asian NIEs. We would like to show that, despite recent setback in economic growth due to the financial crisis which makes his argument ominous, the Asian NIEs still have a long way to go to catch up with the OECD countries, especially Japan and the United States. While the measured TFP may be small, we shall show that the NIEs have been climbing up the technology ladder, the very factor that has enabled the NIEs to maintain their international competitiveness over the past three decades. They have absorbed technology through enhancement of education, openness through vigorous trade with Japan and the United States, and by attracting direct foreign investment, in addition to nurturing native technology through R&D. After they recover fully from the Asian financial crisis, barring from unforeseen political disturbance and world recession, there seems no reason why they could not resume solid growth in the future.

In Section 13.2, three major strategies are suggested to delay diminishing returns. We assess the progress of education in the Asian NIEs and the ASEAN countries, and review the recent literature on the effects of openness on technology transfer and the total factor productivity growth. Section 13.3 emphasizes the features of the Pacific trade triangle formed among the NIEs, Japan, and the United States. The NIEs' industrial upgrading to higher-value-added manufactured good exports is examined. Section 13.4 introduces revealed comparative advantage (RCA) index to

[3]Hsiao and Hsiao (1996). Abe (1996) has made a survey of the related literature in Japanese and English, including our paper.

show the industrial upgrading of the NIEs as a whole. We then discuss the difference in performance among the product groups and countries. Section 13.5 ascertains empirically the technology transfer is an increasing function of direct foreign investment, and points out that the increased outflows of direct foreign investment among the Asian countries, especially from the NIEs to the Southeast Asian countries. These features have enhanced intra-and inter-regional economic integration in recent years, and have contributed to today's dynamic economic activities in the Asian Pacific region, as compared with the Latin America and Sub-Saharan African countries.

We then in Section 13.6 introduce a simple model to show the coefficients of learning between Taiwan and Korea with Japan and the United States, and also Japan with the United States, to partially explain the difference in economic growth. The coefficients of learning are introduced and estimated using polynomial distributed lag model.

The last section concludes with an observation that technology not only transferred to the NIEs, native technology also began to burgeon through research and development. Thus, barring unforeseen political instability and economic disaster, the evidence suggests that it is rather difficult to imagine that, like the former Soviet economy, the economic vitality in the Asian Pacific region will cease in the foreseeable future.

13.2 On Diminishing Returns

The second part of Krugman's syllogism is that the law of diminishing returns will eventually set in for input-driven growth, as experienced by the former Soviet economy. This can be seen from the neoclassical assumptions on the production function $Q = AF(N, K)$, where output (Q) is produced from labor (N), capital (K), and technology or total factor productivity (A). If marginal productivities of factors are positive, and the law of diminishing returns of factors and constant returns to scale hold, then, we may write the production function in per capita magnitude,

$$q = Af(k) \tag{13.1}$$

where $q = Q/N$, the output-labor ratio or average labor productivity, $k = K/N$, the capital-labor ratio, and $f(k) = F(1, k)$. Hence, differentiating with respect to k, we have

$$q' = Af_k(k) > 0, \quad q'' = Af_{kk}(k) < 0 \tag{13.2}$$

where $q' = dq/dk$, $f_k = df/dk$, the marginal productivity of capital,[4] and the law of diminishing returns of the capital-labor ratio holds. If the total factor productivity (TFP) A is held constant (that is, TFP growth rate $(dA/dt)(1/A) = 0$) in (13.1), then, an increase in the output-labor ratio q implies an increase in the capital-labor ratio k. However, (13.2) implies that function $f(k)$ is a strictly concave function of k. As the capita-labor ratio k increases, q will increase at a decreasing rate, and it eventually will cease to increase. This will occur when k is very large.

However, even if k is small, in the neoclassical growth model of capital accumulation, the steady state growth of average labor productivity, q, eventually converges to the growth rate of TFP under the law of diminishing returns (at the well-known Solow's Cross). Constancy of TFP or a small growth rate of TFP means no growth, or almost no growth, of the average labor productivity. Krugman thinks that this is what happened in the former Soviet economy, and will happen to the NIEs.

In both cases, the law of diminishing returns is the culprit of bringing the economy to halt. A check of the empirical implication of the law in the above two equations is revealing. According to the Asian Productivity Organization (1995), among the Asian NIEs, the output-labor ratio q in (13.1) increased between 42 percent and 56 percent from 1985 to 1993. Now, q' in (13.2) is the real rate of return on capital, or the real interest rate. According to IMF (1994), from 1970 to 1992, the (simple) average real interest rate[5] among three Asian NIEs (excluding Hong Kong) was 6.3 percent, among the ASEAN-4 was 8.3 percent, while that of Japan was 4.1 percent, and the United States, 4.5 percent. Thus, the real interest rates were generally higher among the NIEs and the ASEAN-4 during the past two decades.

However, according to (13.2), since the real interest rate is a decreasing function of the capital-labor ratio k, the high real interest rate among these

---

[4]Since $Q = AF(N, K)$, by constant returns to scale, we have $Q = NAF(1, k) = ANf(k)$, where $f(k) \equiv F(1, k)$. Hence, $\partial Q/\partial K = NAF_K(1, k)/N = Af_k(k) = Adf/dk = q'$. Note the difference between K and k. Thus, q' is the marginal productivity of capital, and under perfect competition in the capital market, it must be equal to the real interest rate. Furthermore, $\partial Q^2/\partial K^2 = AF_{KK}(1, k)/N = Af_{kk}(k)/N$. Hence, the law of diminishing returns in Q, $F_{KK}(1, k) < 0$, implies f_{kk} (k) < 0.

[5]The real interest rate q' is defined as the interest rate on short and intermediate term loans minus the inflation rate of the wholesale price index. We calculate the simple average from the table given in EPA (1995), 189. Similar calculation is given in Knoester and Mak (1994), who estimate it by the nominal long-term interest rate net of the inflation rate of the consumer price.

Asian countries with constant TFP would have implied a low capital-labor ratio, and hence by (13.1), a low output-labor ratio. This is contrary to the fact that the labor productivity q has increased. Thus, so far as the neoclassical model is concerned, it is more natural and convincing to assume that TFP in the NIEs must have been increased so to maintain higher per capita output.[6]

As we will show in detail below, this indeed has been the case. In this paper, we do not dispute the iron law of diminishing returns, but ask whether the law can be postponed or avoided, and if so, whether the NIEs and the ASEAN countries are geared to do so. This question also relates closely to the characteristics of the growth of the NIEs, even the growth of Asian countries in general, and provide a sharp contrast with the former Soviet economy.

According to the endogenous theory of economic growth,[7] the law of diminishing returns may be put off temporarily or permanently by increases in endogenously determined quality of labor or capital or both, and upgrading of engineering/production and management/marketing technology (A in (13.1)). Quality of labor can be improved through education, on-the-job training (Washio (1986); Lucas (1993)), and students returning from abroad (reversed brain drain). Introducing more efficient machine and equipment can enhance the quality of capital. A country's technology can be elevated through domestic research and development activities and transfer of technology through international trade and investment. These improvements in quality of labor, capital, and technology are closely related and interdependent. In short, there are three major strategies to delay diminishing returns: Improvement in education, expansion in domestic research and development, increase in openness of the economy, including promotion of exports, imports, and direct foreign investment. These are some of the major factors which have not been considered explicitly in formal models of TFP growth, which is generally defined as the residual

[6]This argument is presented in an appendix of EPA (1995), using the Cobb-Douglas production function. Note that higher real interest rate also implies higher opportunity cost of educational investment and equipment investment. The fact that these two kinds of investment being higher in the NIEs implies higher rate of capital returns for these two kinds of investment in these countries. On the other hand, it may also be argued that higher capital cost fosters efficient allocation of capital, and encourages the choice of higher-return investment projects, thus spurs economic growth (ibid., 189).

[7]For a recent comprehensive survey on the U.S. productivity growth and neoclassical and new growth theories, see Stiroh (2001).

after the percentage contributions of labor and capital are accounted for in the growth rates of output.[8]

Instead of using formal models, there are no lack of them (e.g., see Hsiao and Hsiao, 1996), this paper presents mainly a qualitative analysis of the factors determining TFP with emphasis on education, openness, and direct foreign investment, research and development activity of East Asian development. These are some factors not easily and accurately measured by the conventional neoclassical model, resulting in small growth rate of TFP and leads to Krugman's pessimistic prediction. A formal analysis can be found elsewhere.

13.2.1 *Education*

Recent research suggests that one of the important reasons that the Asian NIEs achieved rapid growth is a special initial condition that they had better educated labor force when their economies started to take off in the 1960s. Increase in the general educational level means easier and faster acceptance of new technology, better and smoother adaptation to new organization, thus increasing labor productivity of the economy.[9]

The heavy lines with circles in Fig. 13.1 show[10] the actual ratios of primary, secondary and tertiary enrollments (relative to the corresponding age group) in 1960 for the NIEs, ASEAN-3 (that is, Thailand, Malaysia, and Singapore, but not including Philippines), and Japan. The light lines with triangles are the expected enrollment based on per capita income in 1960. The data are arranged in the decreasing order of the actual primary school enrollment of the group (the heavy circled line). In all cases, actual values were higher than the expected values, except the secondary enrollment ratio

---

[8]Theoretically, the measurement of conventional TFP is based on the assumptions of constant returns to scale, perfect competition in factor markets, perfect mobility and divisibility of factors, no government regulations. "The Solow residual will not measure only technical change. These assumptions are generally not even remotely satisfied in any actual economy." Thus, there is a merit in our descriptive and anecdotal approaches to the analysis of TFP. Note that "other factors that affect the Solow residual include distortions from imperfect competition, externalities and production spillovers, omitted inputs, cyclical fluctuations, nonconstant returns to scale, and reallocation effects" (Stiroh, 2001, 39).

[9]The importance of human capital in the East Asian economic growth has been examined in Lucas (1993).

[10]The figure is based on Table 4 of Rodrick (1996). The regression is run on 118 countries, the dependent variable is the enrollment ratio, and the independent variables are GDP per capita and its square.

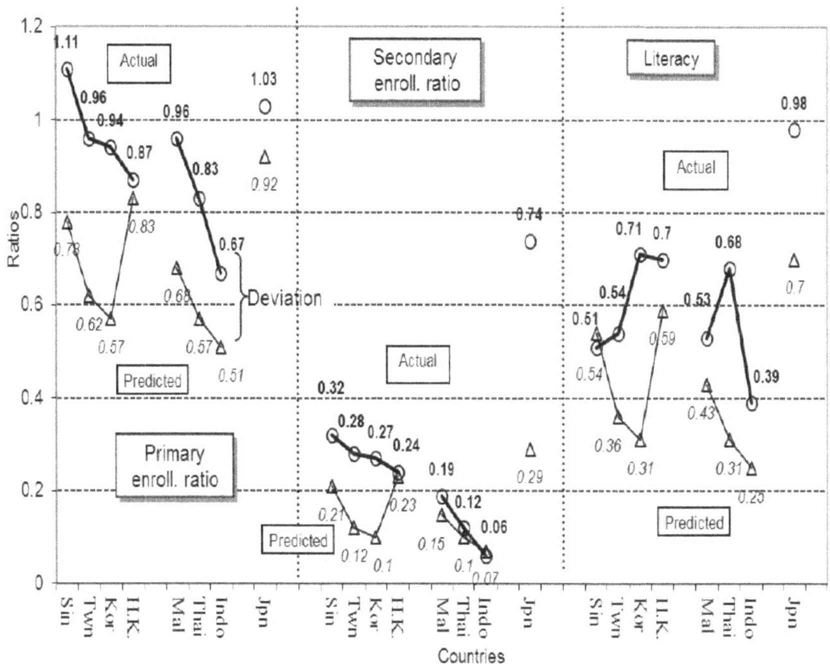

Figure 13.1: Human Capital Indicators
Predicted/Actual Values, 1960

of Indonesia and the literacy ratio of Singapore. Korea had the largest, and Hong Kong had the smallest, deviations between actual and expected values in all categories among the eight countries, followed by Taiwan in the category of primary and secondary enrollments.

The actual primary enrollment of these eight countries in 1960 was already so high that there has been no significant increase afterwards. By the theory of endogenous growth, the availability of "highly educated" labor[11] during the phase of labor intensive industrialization explains at least partially the early development of Taiwan and Korea in the 1950s to the 1970s. Figure 13.2 shows the percentage of age group in secondary and tertiary education. The secondary enrollment in 1960 was low (the light lines with circles), and it grew significantly since then, as shown by the

[11] In Taiwan, by the end of WWII, 81 percent of the boys and 61 percent of the girls among the Taiwanese school-aged children were enrolled in elementary schools (Hsiao and Hsiao, 1995a, Section 1.4). Furthermore, the necessary institutional reform for postwar rapid growth was already established by the end of the war (Hsiao and Hsiao, 2002).

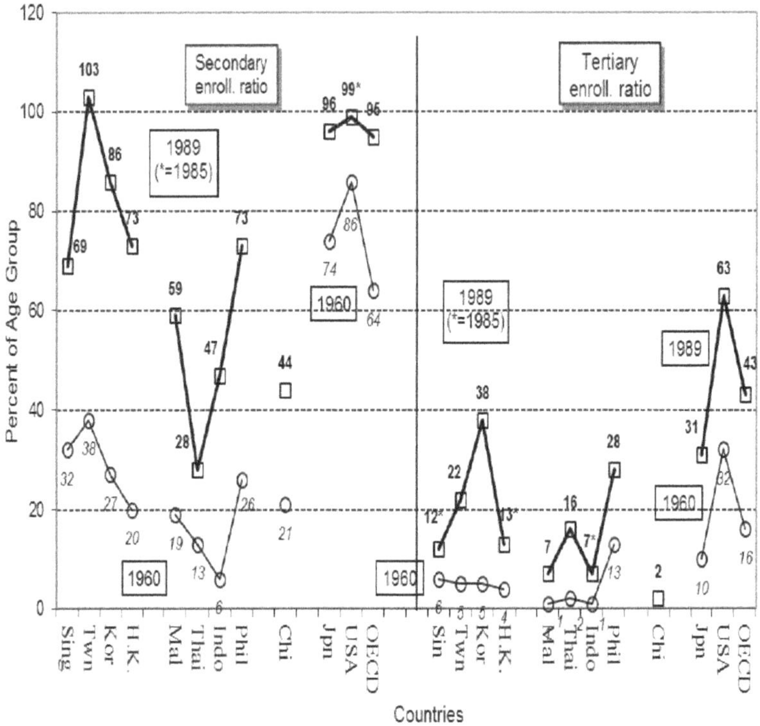

Figure 13.2: Percentage of Age Group in Education
Secondary and Tertiary, 1960 and 1989

Note: 99* means the number is 1985 data.

heavy lines with squares in the left-hand side of Fig. 13.2. By 1989 three NIEs, except Taiwan,[12] were still behind the secondary enrollment ratios achieved by the developed countries, the United States, and the OECD countries' average. All ASEAN-4 countries, except Philippines, are still far behind in the secondary education even in 1989.

The available data also show that the tertiary education in all eight countries also increased in 1989 (the right-hand side of Fig. 13.2). This

[12]Figure 13.2 is based on World Bank (1984 and 1992). The numbers with asterisk are 1985 data, the others are 1989 data. Taiwan's figures are calculated from TSDB (1995, 13, 265). The secondary enrollment age group is generally 12 to 17 years old. Taiwan's figures are based on 15 to 19 age group. There is a discrepancy in Taiwan's secondary education enrollment ratios in Figs. 13.1 and 13.2 due to different sources of data.

explains the postwar initial rapid growth of the Asian NIEs from the side of human capital. However, they all are still far behind the average ratio (43%) achieved by the industrialized countries (OECD), although Korea's tertiary enrollment ratio (38%) is only five percent lower than the average of the OECD countries. So long as the Asian countries still have much room to increase their school enrollments in the secondary and tertiary education, with the future improvement of education, we may expect that the economy and technology transfer will also continue to grow in Asia probably several decades in the future.

Note the general trend of the heavy lines with circle markers. When the actual and expected primary school enrollment ratios are high (Fig. 13.1), so are the secondary and tertiary enrollment ratios (Fig. 13.2), although the trend of tertiary enrollment ratios is not so pronounced. This seems to indicate that the educational system as a whole, not the primary, secondary, or tertiary education, is relevant for economic development. On the other hand, higher level of the primary education, once established, promotes secondary and tertiary education through popular demands and the social emphasis on education.

13.2.2 *Openness*

In the *1987 World Development Report* (World Bank, 1987), among 41 developing economies, South Korea, Hong Kong, and Singapore were classified as the only three countries that consistently maintained strongly outward-looking trade policy and achieved rapid economic growth during 1963–1985. To them we may add Taiwan.[13] In recent years, Sachs and Warner (1995, 1996) argue that the mere act of openness to trade is highly influential on economic growth. In a twenty-year period, they calculate, a country that is always open would grow almost 50 percent faster than a country that is always closed (ibid., 1996). In another paper, Coe, Helpman, and Hoffmaister (1995) have shown that it is more effective in increasing a developing country's TFP the more open it is to trade with the industrial countries, as measured by the import share in GDP. They also found the fact that with whom a country is associated is crucial.

> "A developing country whose trade is more biased towards industrial countries that have large cumulative experiences in R&D has higher productivity."

[13] Ranis (1992). For a recent survey of literature on openness and growth, see Edwards (1993), and Helleiner (1990).

And among the developed countries,

> "The United States has by far the largest domestic capital stock, ... about five time as high as Japan, which is the country with the second largest effect."

Thus, by historical coincidence and geographical proximity, both Korea and Taiwan are indeed very fortunate to associate with the United States and Japan as their major trading partners. Taiwan's ratio of bi-directional trade with both countries to the total trade changed gradually from a whopping 72 percent in the mid-1950s to 51 percent in 1989, and then still fluctuated between 40 percent to 50 percent in the 1990s.[14] To a lesser degree, Hong Kong and Singapore have also traded heavily with the United States and Japan.

There are at least three main channels through which international trade effects economic growth (Grossman and Helpman, 1991; Coe *et al.*, 1995): Imports of intermediate materials and capital equipment, which are not available domestically; cross-border learning of organizational technology and product design; and imitation of production technology (Ito, 1986). These effects basically work through import activities. In the cases of Korea and Taiwan, these benefits from importing industrial raw materials and capital equipment from Japan have been enhanced more than any other countries through cultural similarity and prewar historical linkages (Hsiao and Hsiao, 1995a).

On the export side, especially in cases of exports through component-supply subcontracting and original equipment manufacturing (OEM), the demand for lower prices, faster delivery, and specification contracting from foreign buyers also lead to organizational innovation, industrial upgrading, and off-shore sourcing (Gereffi, 1995).

In the cases of NIEs, due to increasing competition from the ASEAN countries and China, exporters even move beyond OEM to establish original brand name manufacturing in various industries, or retool to export higher value-added products, thereby stimulating economic growth of entire country (Hsiao, M., 1987). In the early 1990s, Korea sold Hyundai (automobile), Leading Edge (computer), and many household appliances

[14] See TSDB (2000). All percentages in this paragraph are calculated in nominal values. In the 1960's and the 1970's, Marxists (especially, Chinese economists) and the Dependencia Scholars described the economies of the newly industrializing countries as shadow, dependent, exploited, or semi-colonial.

under the name of Samsung and Goldstar. Taiwan is also known for Acer and Mitac computers, Giant bicycles, Pro-Kennex tennis rackets, and Travel Fox shoes (Gereffi, 1995; Hobday, 1995, 193). These products are especially aimed at extremely competitive, but almost completely open, U.S. markets, their number one exporting country for over thirty-five years.

Here lies the stark contrast between the East Asian economies and the former Soviet economy. "Soviet's products were exported mainly to 'captive consumers' like the COMECON member countries in East Europe, where transactions were settled with the nonconvertible "transferable Ruble." Low quality products manufactured in the Soviet Union were not marketable in the free world" (Taniuchi, 1995, 10).

Table 13.2 shows the growth of foreign trade among different countries and regions from 1980 to 1991. We first construct a world trade table, the rows of which show exporting countries, and the columns, importing countries. We then calculate the ratio of each country or region between 1980 and 1991, taking the exports (or imports) of 1980 as one. The method is partially shown in the last two columns. They show the world imports in billion U.S. dollars for 1980 and 1991, respectively (the last two columns). The "world" column is then obtained by dividing "Wld91" column by "Wld80" column. For simplicity, all other original data are not presented: only the ratios are shown in the table. Thus, 5.6 in the first column means that the NIEs' intra-regional trade increased 5.6 times from 1980 (that is,

Table 13.2: Growth of Trade among Countries, 1980–1991, 1980 = 1

Ratio					sum					US$ billion	
Exp/imp	NIEs	AS-4	Jpn	Chn	(Asia)	USA	EC	Wld	NIEs80	Wld80	Wld91
NIEs	5.6	3.4	4.2	17.9	5.2	4.0	3.9	4.0	7.0	76.3	303.0
ASEAN	2.7	2.6	1.4	6.2	2.0	2.1	2.5	2.1	8.5	47.1	99.9
Japan	3.5	2.8	—	1.7	3.0	2.9	3.3	2.4	19.1	129.5	314.9
China	7.6	2.7	2.5	—	5.1	6.3	2.9	4.0	4.8	18.1	72.0
sum (Asia)	4.2	3.0	2.3	5.5	3.5	3.2	3.3	2.9	8.5	271.0	789.8
USA	3.2	1.9	2.3	1.7	2.5	—	1.8	1.9	14.2	220.8	421.8
EC	3.7	2.7	4.1	2.8	3.5	2.3	2.2	2.0	8.4	691.2	1368.1
World	3.5	3.0	2.4	3.2	3.0	2.5	1.9	1.9	87.9	1897.6	3577.7
NIEs80										Asia/wld	
(US$ bn)	7.0	8.2	7.7	1.6	24.4	19.0	12.7	76.3		14.3%	22.1%

Notes: AS-4 = ASEAN-4; NIEs80 = 4 NIEs, 1980; Wld80 = World 1980.
Sources: IMF, Direction of Trade Statistics Yearbook, each year. The raw data were compiled in Moon (1993), 18.

from US$ 6.99 billion in 1980, not shown in the table, the same below) to 1991 (at US$ 38.93 billion); similarly 1.9 in the intersection of the "world" row and the "world" column means that world's trade increased 1.9 times from 1980 (at US$ 1,897.6 billion in the "Wld80" column) to 1991 (at US$ 3,577.7 billion in the "Wld91" column).

To perceive the magnitude of trade of the Asian NIEs, the last "NIEs80" row shows the NIEs' exports to each country or region in 1980, and the "NIEs80" column shows the NIEs' imports from each country or region, all in billions of U.S. dollars. The table indicates the vitality and dynamism of Asian countries as a trading block. The intra-regional trade among the NIEs increased 5.6 times, which is almost three times faster than the growth of world trade (1.9 times) and the intra-EC trade (2.2 times). The Asian NIEs' exports to Japan increased 4.2 times (the first row), more than doubling the growth of world trade, and to China, increased whopping 18 times, almost 10 times faster than the world rate. Their exports to the United States (4.0) and EC (3.9) also increased four times, at least two times faster than the growth of world trade, but slower than their penetration to the Japanese market (4.2), during the 1980–1991 period.

Under the pressure from the United States, the domestic markets of the NIEs also opened for imports. Their imports from Japan (3.5 in the first column), USA (3.2), and EC (3.7), increased more than three times, and from China, 7.6 times, all at least 50 percent faster than the world trade.

The "sum" row and the "sum" column show the Asian region as a trading block. NIEs' exports to other Asian countries increased 5.2 times, while their imports from other Asian countries increased 4.2 times. The intra-Asian regional trade increased 3.5 times, about 80 percent higher than the world growth rate. "Asian dynamism" is more revealing in the last two columns. From 1980 to 1991, Asian trade share in the world trade (in the last row) increased from 14.3 percent (=271.0/1897.6) to 22.1 percent (=789.8/3577.7).

By 1991, NIEs' trade volume (US$ 303 billion, the last column) was very close to Japanese trade volume (US$ 315 billion), and catching up with that of the United States (US$ 422 billion). The total amount of trade (US$ 475 billion) of NIEs, ASEAN-4, and China (the last column) exceeded the amount of trade of Japan or the United States, although still far less than the EC countries. However, if we consider the major APEC countries, including Japan and the United States, then the volume of trade among APEC countries (US$ 1212 billion) will be close to that of the EC countries (US$ 1368 billion, the last column).[15] We submit that the mere fact that the NIEs had the ability to sustain its rapid GDP growth for the past three decades through ever increasing exports is a manifestation that resource allocation in the NIEs is, in general, more efficient than the other developing countries, and physical and managerial technologies did play an important role in upgrading the products and enlarging their markets in highly competitive developed countries, especially the United States. These points will be elaborated in the following sections.

13.3 Pacific Trade Triangle and Technology Transfer

13.3.1 *Direction of Trade*

In previous papers (Hsiao and Hsiao, 1989, 1995a, 1995b), we have shown that, from the end of World War II to the 1980s, Korean and Taiwanese trade relies heavily on Japan and the United States: Japan for imports of intermediate goods and capital equipment, and the United States for exports of manufactured goods (also see Park and Park, 1989). Increases in Korean and Taiwanese exports to the United States have paralleled by their increases in import from Japan. The parallel relationship is more pronounced the faster the economy grows, and clearer when we compare the categories of traded commodities. This pattern of trade has been repeated for Korea since the mid-1970s, and for Taiwan since the mid-1960s (Hsiao and Hsiao, 1995a, Section 1.13).

Figure 13.3 dramatizes Taiwan's trade relationship with the United States and Japan, all variables are measured in real value, using the 1986 wholesale price index as the base.[16] The trade amounts and the deficits with both countries from 1952 to 1974 become invisible when the scale is in billions of U.S. dollars. Thus we have plotted the data from 1952 to 1965

---

[15]Table 13.2 shows clearly that trade openness, especially export activities, is an East and Southeast Asian phenomena. The whole region has been involved in trading activities. Thus, it is not tenuous to attribute Taiwan's success of the exports solely to a wise government policy. So far as Taiwan is concerned, see Hsiao and Hsiao (1996).

[16]Figure 13.3 is in real terms calculated from the nominal values in TSDB (1989), 210–212 and TSDB (2000), 210–214, divided by the wholesale price index (WPI) in TSDB (2000), 179. The base year of the WPI published in TSDB (2000) is 1996. We have converted the base year to 1986. Since Taiwan's WPI has been generally stable, especially in the 1990s, the general shape and trend of the figures in real values have similar shape and trend as those in nominal values. Balance of trade (BOT) is commodity exports X (in heavy solid line) minus commodity imports M (in lighter solid line) in Fig. 13.3. Note that Figs. 13.3 and 13.8, which are constructed in the same way as Fig. 13.3, are taken from Hsiao and Hsiao (2002).

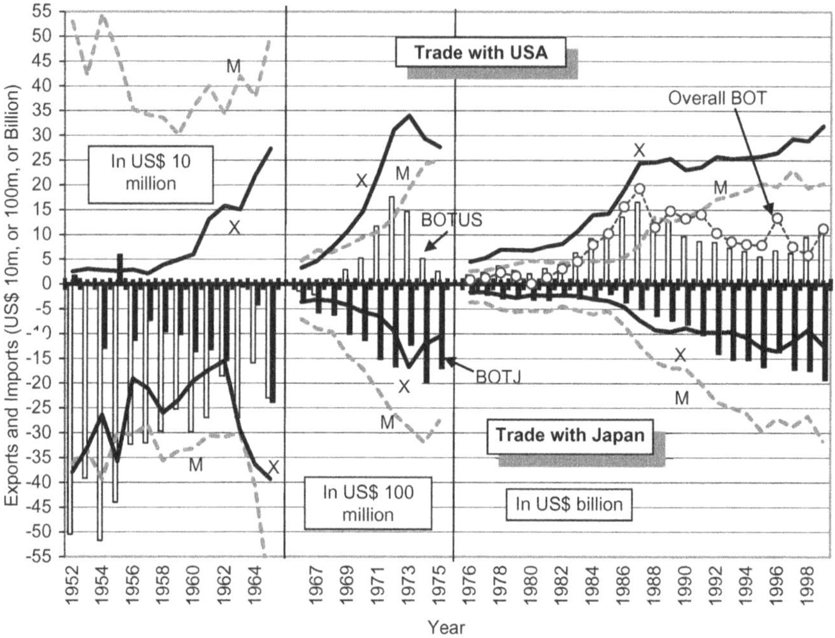

Figure 13.3: The Structure of the Pacific Trade Triangle
The Case of Taiwan Real Exports, Imports, and Balance of Trade

in the units of US$ 10 million (the left panel), and from 1966 to 1975 in the units of US$ 100 million (the middle panel), and after 1975, in the units of US$ billion (the right panel). As shown in the lower part of the diagram, from 1952 to 1999, Taiwan's real imports from Japan (M in the lower part) are steadily increasing, and are consistently higher than Taiwan's real exports to Japan (X in the lower part). This means that Taiwan had persistent increasing trade deficits with Japan since 1953 (except 1955). The dark solid bars in the lower part of the figure show this.

The situation is quite different with the United States. Before 1967, Taiwan also had trade deficits with the United States every year, as shown by the empty bars on the lower part. After 1968, however, Taiwan's real imports from the United States (M in the upper part) have been consistently lower than its real exports to the United States (X in the upper part), bringing about real trade surpluses. The empty bars in the upper part of the figure show this.

After 1968, both deficits with Japan and surpluses with the United States have increased over time with the progress of Taiwan's industrialization. In Fig. 13.3, this is illustrated as an explosion to the two sides of the horizontal axis like a broom. After 1988, exports to the United States slowed down under the watchful eyes of the U.S. government under the Omnibus Trade Competitiveness Act passed in the U.S. Congress in 1988 (Hsiao and Hsiao, 1995b). At the same time, imports from the United States increased considerably, narrowing down the bilateral trade surpluses.

With devaluation of the U.S. dollar and upward revaluation of the Japanese yen, Taiwanese exports to Japan jumped up greatly between 1985 and 1988 but ran out of steam and flattened out afterward. Real commodity imports from Japan, however, continued to accelerate, indicating that the more Taiwan tries to increase its exports, whether to the United States or other countries, the more Taiwan has to rely on imports of materials and capital equipment from Japan. Despite almost desperate efforts by the government,[17] Taiwan simply cannot elude its dependency on Japan!

In another paper (Hsiao, M., 1996), it was found that there is a long-run relationship (cointegration) between Korean and Taiwanese exports to the United States and their imports from Japan. This long-run relationship has enabled the Taiwanese, and for that matter, the Koreans, to learn production and managerial technologies from the two most industrialized countries, and propelled their sustainable endogenous economic growth. They therefore have been able to maximize the benefits of openness and association, as depicted in the literature cited in the previous section on the effects of openness. This relationship alone, that is, without invoking an ambivalent tenet on the effects of government industrial policy,[18] which

[17]The following episode is illuminating. In February 1982, to reduce US$ 3.2 billion trade deficit with Japan, Taiwan surprised the world by unilaterally banning imports from Japan more than 1,500 commodities for an indefinite time, and heavy trucks and diesel engines for one year. Tokyo threatened to cancel Taiwan's preferential tariff and trade status. The ban inflicted serious damage to Taiwanese exports and its national economy. As Tokyo also could not wage a trade war simultaneously with the U.S. and the EEC, both sides reached a compromise and the ban on half of the goods were lifted by November that year. For details, see Arnold (1985), 194–196; Aoki (1985), 157.

[18]Since 1982, the Taiwan government promoted biotechnology aggressively. It failed to thrive, no new drug has been introduced, and there is only one listed biotech firm (Apex Biotechnology) in Taiwan (Chuang, 2000). "Most funding recipients have been large-scale firms that focus not on R&D but on the manufacture of generics or bulk pharmaceutical chemicals" (ibid., 43). In addition to the government misconception and misdirection, we submit that, unlike computer and semiconductor industry, technical transfer from foreign countries, especially from Japan, whose biotech industry is also weak, is not readily available. Chuang reported the lack of government supports of small local R&D firms, and the lack of partnership among university research, government funding, and biotech industry, etc. Few Taiwan scholars discuss this area of government failure.

often conveniently ignores the distortions induced by the policy, seems to be able to explain why Korea and Taiwan, along with Hong Kong and Singapore, are the only developing countries which have achieved and sustained rapid growth after World War II.

13.3.2 *Composition of Trade*

Figures 13.4 to 13.7 dramatize the composition of Taiwanese imports and exports to Japan and the United States. They show five major Taiwanese real imports and exports to Japan and the United States taken from 1982 and also from 1992, respectively.[19] All data are divided by Taiwan's wholesale price index (WPI) with 1986 wholesale price being taken as 100 (TSDB, 1996, 248). Some commodity items have continued since 1969, and others were substituted by new categories, as Taiwanese industrialization progressed. In these figures, an extra space is inserted between 1982 and 1983 to show the differences.

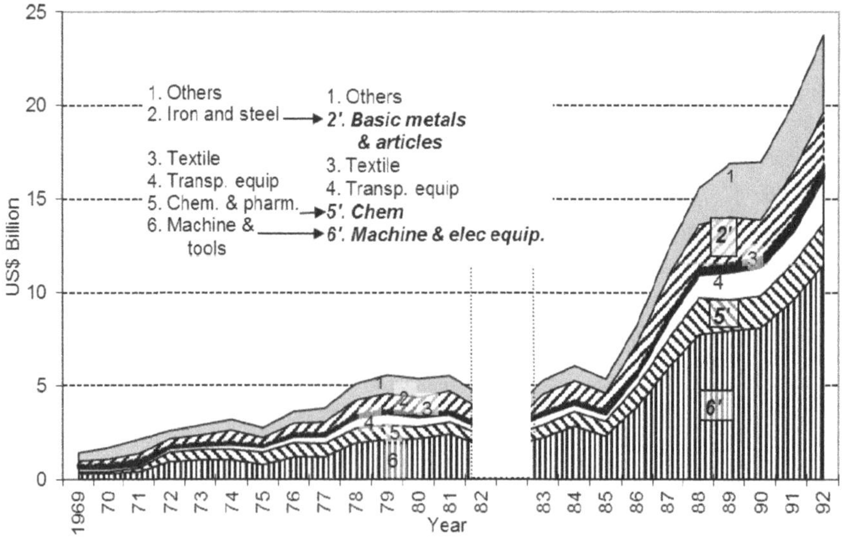

Figure 13.4: Taiwanese Imports from Japan
Five Largest Items, 1982, 1992, in Real Values

[19]TSDB (1989, 1995). The commodity classification used in the figures is based on the Chinese Commodity Classification (CCC) system, which is different from the SITC (Standard International Trade Classification) Code.

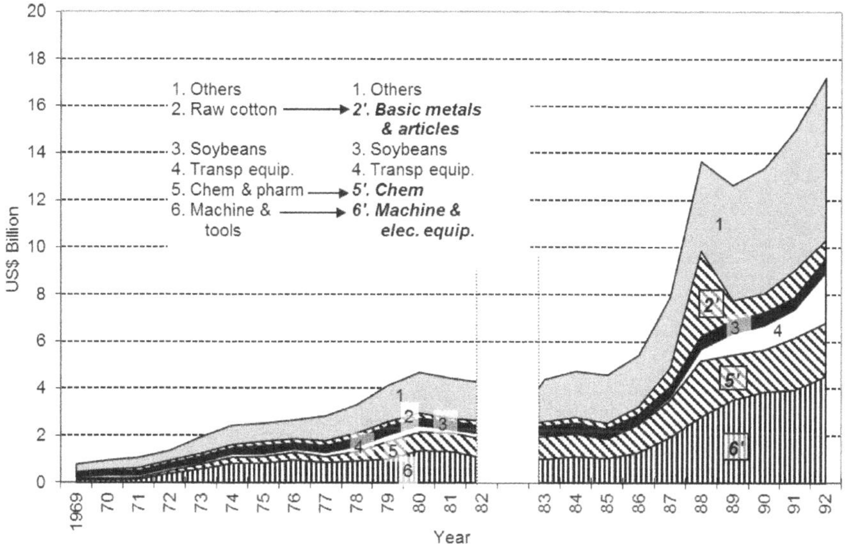

Figure 13.5: Taiwanese Imports from the USA
Five Largest Items, 1982, 1992, in Real Values

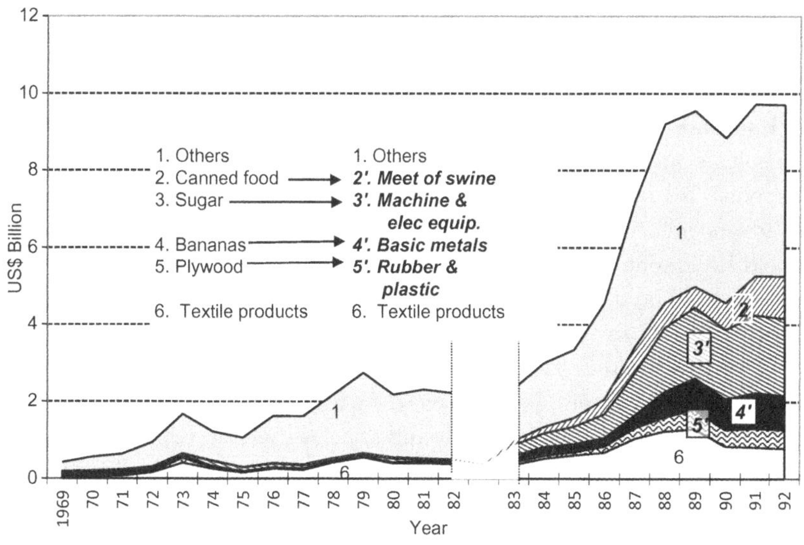

Figure 13.6: Taiwanese Exports to Japan
Five Largest Items, 1982, 1992, in Real Values

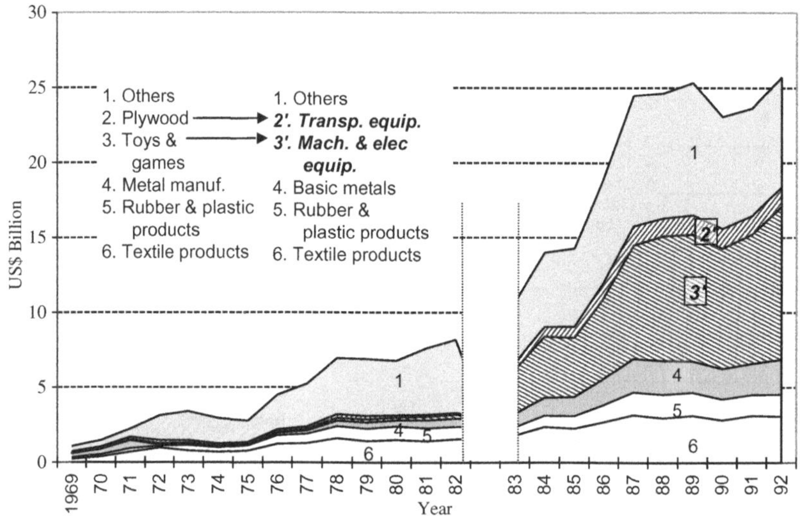

Figure 13.7: Taiwanese Exports to USA
Five Largest Items, 1982, 1992, in Real Values

Imports. On the imports side, Figs. 13.4 and 13.5 show that the five largest items of Taiwanese imports from Japan and the United States are quite stable. All five major imports from Japan and four from the United States before 1982 continued to be so in 1992, except that the name of the category of "iron and steel" (2) was replaced by "basic metals and articles" (*2'*), "Chemicals and Pharmaceutics" (5) by "Chemicals" (*5'*), and "machine and tools" (6) by "machine and electric equipment" (*6'*), reflecting clearly the advancement of technology on the import side. The changes are shown in bold italic fonts in the charts. Furthermore, the proportion of "machine and tools" (6), and "transportation equipment," (4) as well as "basic metals and articles" (2) in the case of imports from Japan and the United States, and "chemicals" (5) in the case of imports from the United States, increased greatly both absolutely and relatively. In Fig. 13.5, imports of raw cotton (2) were upgraded to "basic Metals and articles thereof" (*2'*). These changes clearly reflect the progress in industrialization and upgrading of technology.

Exports. Many more changes occur on the export side. Exports to Japan show a drastic change. Figure 13.6 shows the five largest items of Taiwan's export to Japan. Only textile products (6) continued to be one of the five major export items in both 1982 and 1992. Other items before 1982, namely, plywood (5), bananas (4), sugar (3), canned food (2), were substituted by rubber and plastics (*5'*), basic metals (*4'*), machinery and electric equipment (*3'*), and meat of swine (*2'*) in 1992. Thus, except meat of swine, other items show clearly the increase in the importance of capital and technology intensive export items. The considerable increase of item "Others" (1) also indicates the diversification of exports items to Japan.

In Fig. 13.7, for the Taiwanese exports to the United States, three export items, textile products (6), rubber and plastic products (5), basic metals (4) continued to be important and increasing. They have increased greatly in the 1980s, showing the competitiveness of Taiwanese products in the U.S. markets (Hsiao and Hsiao, 1995b). Furthermore, toys and games (3) along with plywood (2) in 1982 were replaced by machinery and electric equipment (*3'*) and transportation equipment (*2'*) after 1984. Note that these last two high tech items increased greatly during the last decade, so are the "others" (1).

Here again is a clear indication of technological upgrading in a short period of ten years, signifying the vitality of Taiwanese economy in the face of ever changing and competitive world market conditions.

13.4 Revealed Comparative Advantage

These patterns of technological upgrading of trading contents also have taken place in other Asian NIEs. Instead of repeating the same presentation of the previous section, Table 13.3 summarizes the revealed comparative

Table 13.3: Revealed Comparative Advantage of NICs in OECD

No.	Product Group	1965 1	1990 2	diff 3	Country 4
1	Electrical machinery	0	4	+4	TKHS
2	Non-electrical machinery	0	2	+2	TS
3	Metal manufactures	1	2	+1	S
4	Precision instruments	0	1	+1	H
5	Transport equipment	0	0	0	
6	Nonferrous metals	0	0	0	
7	Misc manufactures	4	3	−1	S
8	Clothing	3	3	0	
9	Furniture	3	1	−2	HS
10	Footwear	4	2	−2	HS
11	Chemicals	2	0	−2	TS
12	Textiles	3	1	−2	TH
13	Resource-based products	3	0	−3	(H)

Sources: OECD Series C tape. RCA calculation is based on Chow and Kellman (1993), Tables 2.1 to 2.5.

advantage[20] (RCA) of the NIEs in the OECD market, mostly with the United States and Japan. The RCA for each of the four NIEs in each of the 13 product groups is calculated for every five years starting from 1965 to 1990, a total of six different years, as given in Chow and Kellman (1993, Table 2.1 to Table 2.5). We assign 1 for having RCA (RCA index greater than 1) and 0 for having no RCA (RCA index less than 1).

The table corroborates our observations on technological upgrading of the NIEs through international trade by comparing RCA of exports product groups in 1965 and RCA of those in 1990 for all four economies. The numbers in Columns 1 and 2 show the numbers of economies that have RCA in the corresponding product group. Column 3 shows the difference between the number of economies that has RCA in 1990 and those in 1965. It shows that, in 1990, compared to 1965, in the first four groups of products: Electric Machinery (1), Nonelectrical Machinery (2), Metal Manufactures (3), and Precision Instruments (4), the number of economies which had RCA had increased (positive signs) in each product group. Note the strongest evidence that, as observed in Chow and Kellman (1993, 17), in 1965, none of the NIEs had RCA in Electrical Machinery (1). However, by 1990, all of them had.

In the last six product groups, which are labor intensive, the number of economies which had RCA in 1965 decreased (negative sign) in all product groups in 1990, except Clothing (8) that did not change. This is consistent with our observation of exports composition in the previous section.

More specifically, in 1965, four countries had RCA in Footwear (10), and three had RCA in Clothing (8), Furniture (9), Textile (12), and Resource-based Products (13), and two had RCA in Chemicals (11). However, by 1990, all countries lost their RCA in Resource-based Products (13) and Chemicals (11), no change in Clothing (8), and two lost their RCA in Furniture (9) and Textiles (12), all are labor-intensive products.

Column 4 lists the economies that made the change, or did not make the change (the names in the parentheses). Apparently, the two small city states, Hong Kong (H) and Singapore (S), made the most changes, followed by Taiwan (T), and then Korea (K). This may indicate that the

[20]Here RCA_{ik} is defined as the ith country's commodity k import (M_{ik}) share in country i's total imports (M_i) divided by the OECD's kth commodity import (W_k) share in the total OECD imports (W), that is, $RCA_{ik} = (M_{ik}/M_i)/(W_k/W)$. If it is greater than 1, we say the ith country has RCA of commodity k. If it is less than 1, then the ith country has no RCA of commodity k. See Chow and Kellman (1993), 15.

smaller an economy, the easier or more flexible it is to change its industrial structure.

In general, the increases in RCA of capital and technology intensive exports and reduction of labor-intensive exports show clearly the technical advancement of the Asian NIEs. These are not reflected in total factor productivity analysis.

13.5 The Effects of Direct Foreign Investment

13.5.1 *Inward Direct Foreign Investment*

Along with trade, direct foreign investment (DFI) is another vehicle of technology transfer. It is another method of transferring engineering/production and management/marketing technologies, especially through the presence of foreign personnel employed in foreign or jointly owned firms.[21] The presence of Japanese personnel was undoubtedly more effective in Taiwan and Korea since many Taiwanese and Koreans could speak Japanese during the early stages of postwar economic development (Hsiao and Hsiao, 1995a, Section 1.14.3; Hsiao, M., 1992). While critics like to label DFI as the vanguard of imperialist capitalism and foreign control of the host country, it is also considered as a major channel to bring technological know-how to the host country, creating backward and forward linkages which stimulate the local development of industry under certain conditions (Hsiao and Hsiao, 1995a, Section 1.14).

In this section, we use the Taiwanese case as an example (ibid.) to show DFI activity in the Asian NIEs, and how technology is transferred through DFI. In the early 1950s, among the newly independent former colonies, Taiwan was probably the first country that invited the much-suspected DFI with open arms.[22] Seeing Taiwan's success, other Asian NIEs followed suit, and then China and the ASEAN countries also followed.

The Amount of Inward FDI. Figure 13.8 shows the increase of the approved amount of "real DFI" in Taiwan from 1952 to 1999. As in the

[21]In 1982, there were 916 foreign administrators (1.9% of total administrators) and 849 foreign technicians (2.2% of total technicians) in Taiwan. About 35 percent to 39 percent of foreign employees were in the electronics industry. M. Hsiao (1992), Table 4.

[22]As argued elsewhere (Hsiao and Hsiao, 1995a, Section 1.11), the open door policy was not so much coming out from the far-sightedness of the policy makers, but more to the basic emigre character of Taiwan's KMT government.

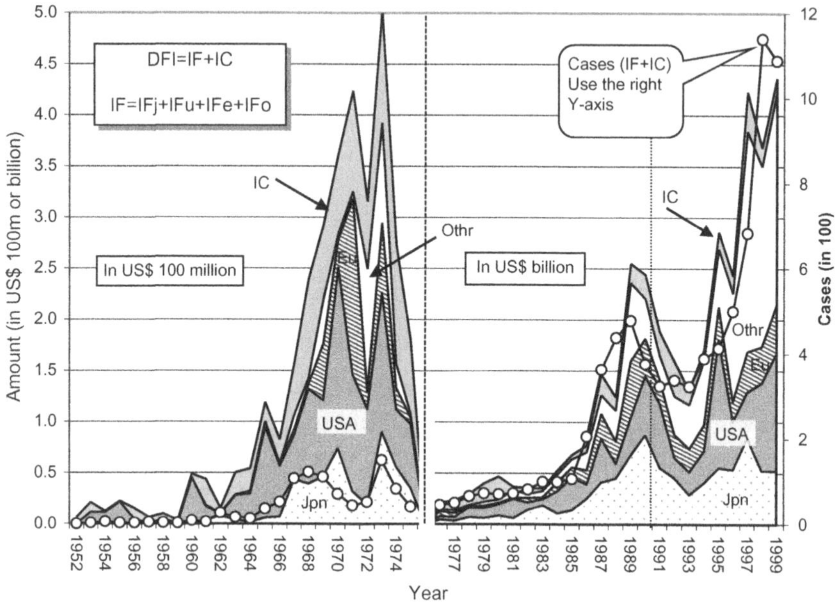

Figure 13.8: Real Direct Foreign Investment in Taiwan Amount Approved and Cases

case of trade statistics, we have converted the data into real terms,[23] using the 1986 wholesale price index as the base. Overseas Chinese investment (IC) is shown in the upper dark band. The rest of the chart shows the (non-overseas Chinese) foreign investment (IF), consisting of investment from Japan, the United States, Europe, and other countries (IF = IFj + IFu + IFe + IFo). IC consists of investment from those overseas Chinese mostly residing in Hong Kong and Japan. Before 1965, IC was an important source of DFI. However, the weight of IC in total DFI decreased after 1965, taken over by IF from the U.S.A. After 1982, IC's weight in total DFI decreased drastically, and became negligible after the mid-1980s.

IF from the U.S.A. (IFu) started in 1953, and was superseded by investment from Japan (IFj) most of the time after 1982 until 1995. In any case, as with trade relations, Japanese and American investments have dominated DFI in Taiwan from 1966 to 1995. Investment from Europe

[23]That is, all data are divided by Taiwan's WPI with 1986 wholesale price being taken as 100 (TSDB, 2000, 179, 258, 260).

(IFe) also has been increasing, and after 1995, "other sources" of foreign investment (IFo) have exceeded all these countries, showing the increases in diversification of Taiwan's inward FDI.

The main areas in the "other sources" category (IFo) are British territories in Central America,[24] which include the Virgin Islands, Bermuda, Belize, and British West Indies. The diagram shows two facts which indicate the resilience of Taiwan in the global economy: the two oil price shocks in 1973–74 and 1979–80 eventually spurred, rather than depressed, DFI; and that Taiwan still can attract and even increase steadily the American and Japanese investments despite strong competition from China and elsewhere in recent years. In fact, as shown in Fig. 13.8, the record amount of DFI (IF + IC) was reached just recently in 1999 at US$ 4.23 billion in real value with 1,089 cases.[25] The Taiwanese economy has never been so strong.

Altogether, from 1952 to 1999, 11,111 cases (shown by the solid line with circles in Fig. 13.8) with the amount of US$ 37 billion (in nominal values[26]) of DFI were approved for IF and IC. Among IF, Japan is the largest contributor with 3,230 cases (US$ 8.3 billion), followed closely by the U.S.A., accounting for 1,694 cases (8.7b), Europe, for 928 cases (4.1b). Other countries were responsible for 2,562 cases (12b). The bulk of DFI has occurred only recently (TSDB, 2000, 260).

In general, from 1952 to 1999, 26 percent of Taiwan's DFI has been in electronic and electric products, totaling US$ 9.4 billion in 1,544 cases. This is followed by "other products," 13 percent, US$ 4.8 billion in 1,927 cases; banking and insurance, 13 percent, US$ 4.6 billion in 502 cases. None or very few DFI were in agriculture, fisheries and livestock, paper and paper products and construction (TSDB, 2000, 261).

Among the foreign investment (IF), the lion's share also goes to electronic and electric products (9.2b/1,339 cases), followed by chemicals (3.7b/470 cases), services (3.2b/1229 cases), foreign trade (2.5b/1,754 cases), and machinery, equipment and instrument (1.6b/431 cases) (ibid.). Indeed, through forward and backward linkages, foreign capital had a

---

[24]Investment Commission (2000), April. We suspect that these so called DFI may be Chinese (mainland) capital registered in Central America, and pose a grave security problem for Taiwan.

[25]In terms of nominal values, the maximum amount was reached two years earlier, in 1997, at US$ 4.27 billion (TSDB, 2000, 258).

[26]In real value of 1986 price, the total amount of DFI comes to US$40 billion.

significant positive effect on the growth of Taiwan's real GDP,[27] and has helped building Taiwan as the kingdom of electronics and computers.[28]

Technology Transfer I. For a developing country like Taiwan, the major objective of inducing DFI is to enhance technological progress and increase the nation's economic activities. In a previous paper (Hsiao, M., 1992), it is shown that, using the 1967 to 1987 data set, the growth of real DFI has had a significant and positive effect on the growth of real GDP. When the growth rate of real DFI increases by 1 percent, it may generate a 0.11 percent increase in the growth rate of real GDP. IF concentrates investment in high-tech and heavy industries, generating more economic activity for the Taiwanese economy.

At least in two surveys in the past, it was shown that foreign firms have a tendency of being three to seven times higher than the national firms to adopt foreign technology. This is shown in Fig. 13.9. In each category, the gray column shows the percentage of total firms surveyed, and the patterned column shows the percentage of firms in the electronic and electric products (or "electronics" in short) industry.

In the 1973 survey of 311 large exporters in Taiwan (the first panel), the percentage of firms adopting foreign technology was 39 percent (76% in the electronic industry). If the firms are divided into national firms (natn'l), minority owned foreign firms (mino), and majority owned foreign firms (majo), then 8 percent, 61 percent, and 91 percent of the firms in each category, respectively (or 24%, 71%, and 100% of the electronics firms), introduced foreign technology.[29] The larger the foreign investment in a firm, the higher the possibility that the firm adopts foreign technology, generating technical progress.

---

[27]In a previous paper (Hsiao, M., 1992, Section 9.2), it is shown that, using the 1967 to 1987 data set, when the real growth rate of DFI increases by 1 percent, it may generate a 0.11 percent increase in the growth rate of Taiwan's GDP.

[28]We have examined the effect of DFI on technology transfer, DFI and Taiwan's television industry in Hsiao and Hsiao (1996), Section 1.14.4, and Hsiao, M. (1992).

[29]The 1973 survey was reported in Schive, (1983), reproduced in Schive, (1990), 26, and Hsiao, M. (1992), Table 3. The 1973 survey included five industries, textile (93 firms, same below), apparel (69), plastic and plastic products (61), metals and its products (26), and electronic an electric product (62). These firms were fast growing exporters with at least one million dollars of annual exports and 80 percent to 90 percent of their outputs were exported. National firms are completely owned by the Taiwanese, the "minority owned firms" are firms in which foreigners own less than 50 percent of the stocks.

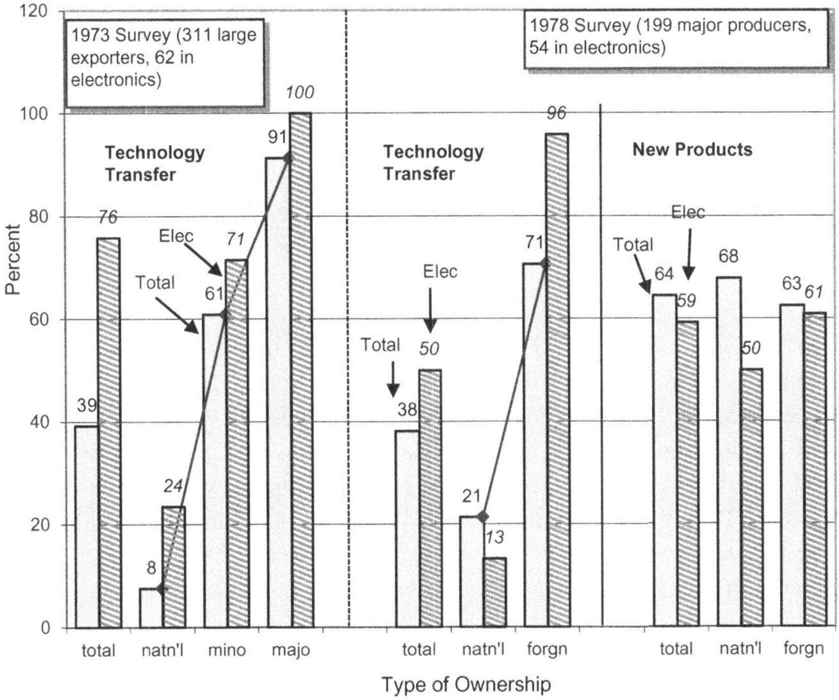

Figure 13.9: The Slanted Structure of Technology Transfer Taiwan, 1973, 1978

Technology Transfer II. Similarly, the middle panel of Fig. 13.9 shows that, in the 1978 survey of 199 major producers,[30] the percentage of firms adopting foreign technology was 38 percent, and among the electronics industry, it was 50 percent. More specifically, the percentage of firms adopting foreign technology was 21 percent for national firms, but 71 percent for foreign firms. The percentage in the electronics industry is lower in the national firms (13%) and much higher in the foreign firms (96%), which are shown by the patterned bars. Thus the empirical rules suggest that technology transfer is an increasing function of DFI (Hsiao,

[30]In the 1978 survey (Schive, 1983, 479), some major products were selected first and then one or two major producers of the products were chosen. The firms were asked whether foreign technology was adopted, and whether its major product was the first product produced in Taiwan. The survey consisted of 8 industries, namely, in addition to the five industries in the 1973 survey, it included automobile and parts, chemicals, and machinery (Hsiao, M., 1992, Table 3).

M., 1992). We have called this the *slanted structure of technology transfer through DFI.* The slant is shown by the black solid lines in Fig. 13.9.

Note that, in the first panel of the diagram, the slope of the first line segment connecting "natn'l" to "mino" is steeper than that of the second line segment connecting "mino" to "majo." It seems to indicate that, so far as technical transfer is concerned, what count is some contacts with the foreign firms, whether the firms are minority- or majority-owned by the foreigners. This again verifies the argument for the openness of the economy.

Technology Transfer III. The last panel of Fig. 13.9 shows the possibility of producing "new products" among the 199 firms surveyed, either through technology transfer, technological cooperation, or research and development. It is interesting to know that, on average, the Taiwanese national firms (68%, "natn'l") have a higher tendency to produce "new products" than the foreign firms (63%, "forgn"), although the difference between the two are not very large, and the electronic industry being excepted (50% vs. 61%).

In any case, contrary to the prediction of the Marxists and other pessimists, the national firms have not been dominated or even crashed by the foreign firms. This indicates the vitality of Taiwanese people, and people in other NIEs, in the face of strong foreign competition. This vitality has in turn contributed to the growth of Taiwanese economy and economies of other NIEs. This part of technical progress is not adequately captured in the usual measurement of total factor productivity.

13.5.2 *Outward Direct Foreign Investment*

As the NIEs grew by the mid-1980s, due to currency appreciation and rising wages, as we have seen in Section 13.4, the NIEs lost its comparative advantages in the labor-intensive industries. Unprecedented outward direct foreign investment of the NIEs took place in the second half of the 1980s. Table 13.4 shows the spurt of such investment in recent years. In a short three-year period, the outward direct foreign investment of the NIEs to ASEAN increased 17 times. Among them, the Taiwanese investment increased 40 times, due to early evaluation of New Taiwan Dollar, earlier liberalization of outward DFI, outward movement of predominantly Taiwanese small-and-intermediate size enterprises, and overseas Chinese connections.

Table 13.4: Outward DFI of NIEs to ASEAN

	Value in US$ million			
Year	1986	1987	1988	Change 88/86
Taiwan	55.4	362.8	2192.6	39.6
Hong Kong	62.8	282.8	820.7	13.1
Korea	23.0	29.9	203.5	8.8
Singapore	150.0	130.8	684.6	4.6
ANICs	231.4	806.3	3901.4	16.9

Sources: Annual Report of Asian Trend, Institute of Developing Economies (1989), as listed in CSE (1989), 13.

With the outward foreign investment, technology also transferred to the developing countries. In the late 1980s, the major Taiwanese investment was in items like toys, Christmas lights, artificial flowers, rubber gloves, etc. The major Korean investment was in textiles, dry goods, etc. (CSE, 1989, 12). However, in the 1990s, more advanced products like machinery, electronic and automobile parts, semi-conductors, etc. have been produced and exported (Shinohara, 1996).

The continuous upgrading of technology embodied in exports not only indicates that, like NIEs in the past, technology has been transferred from NIEs to ASEAN and China through DFI, with much shorter time span. The sustainability of outward investment also demonstrates the establishment of parts and supporting industries of NIEs products, advancement of management and organizational skills, ability of digesting new technology, fostering of the regional foresight and world vision of the entrepreneurs, etc.

Clearly, technology is transferred internationally because some countries possess relative, rather than absolute, technological superiority. Technology, like water, simply flows toward the lower land. Technology that is recently established in NIEs probably is more "appropriate" and easy for adaptation in the less developed countries.[31] Such "natural" transfer of technology can occur only in an open economy.

[31] M. Hsiao (1992), Table 5. Even machinery parts and semiconductors are made locally by multinational investment in ASEAN countries. In 1995, Japan's machinery imports from Malaysia reached 29.4 percent of its machinery exports to Malaysia. In the case of Philippines, it is 30.3 percent. Similarly, NIEs' machinery imports from the ASEAN-4 was about 24.7 percent of their exports to the ASEAN-4 in 1975, the imports increased to 97.3 percent in 1992, mainly through NIEs' DFI in ASEAN-4. Shinohara (1996) calls the development "DFI-led growth" of the 1990s, different from the "export-led growth" of the 1970s and the 1980s.

A good example of DFI and technology transfer is given by Taiwan's television industry (Hsiao and Hsiao, 1995a, Section 1.14.4). It created forward and backward linkages in Taiwan, and thus contributed to Taiwanese industrialization. So was the transistor and condenser parts industry (Kawakami, 1999). It is also a good example of product life-cycle theory in international trade and show clearly how an industry went through the stages of imports to import substitution, and then to exports. To go back to the Krugman's argument, this is not like the former Soviet economy, which skipped these steps and tried to develop heavy industry by using government planning and decrees without due consideration to the demands for the products by users and consumers. In fact, what Krugman really argues is that the industrial policies of the former Soviet government ignored international market forces.

Table 13.5 presents a larger picture of DFI in APEC countries. The last three columns show that NIEs' investment in APEC countries increased almost five times (4.7) from US$ 10 billion in 1989 to US$ 46 billion in 1994. In 1994, most of NIEs investments went to China (US$ 25 billion, same as below)' and ASEAN (16 billion), 12 times and 3 times larger than Japanese investments in the region, respectively, as the Japanese economy was still not fully recovered from recent recession in 1994. Like Japan, the United States also invests more in ASEAN (3.7 billion) than in NIEs (2.3 billion).

In 1994, the total world investment in APEC countries was estimated to be US$ 163 billion, almost 50 percent went to Asian countries (see the

Table 13.5: Investment Matrix in APEC, 1994 (in US$ billion)

from/to	NICs	ASEAN	Jpn	Chn	sum	USA	APEC 1994	APEC 1989	chg 94/89
NICs	0.54	15.95	0.23	24.96	41.67	1.61	45.94	9.84	4.7
ASEAN	0.03	0.77	0	0.69	1.49	0.16	2.37	1.38	1.7
Japan	1.67	4.89	—	2.08	8.64	6.44	17.13	34.13	0.5
China	0.03	0.2	0.01	—	0.24	0.18	0.77	0.24	3.2
sum	2.26	21.81	0.23	27.73	52.03	8.38	66.21	45.59	1.5
USA	2.33	3.7	1.6	2.71	10.33	—	23.14	11.03	2.1
APEC	4.61	25.72	2.18	30.62	63.14	15.22	98.15	59.2	1.7
World	6.27	36.26	4.15	33.77	80.45	50.07	163.1		
% of Wld (a)	3.80	22.20	2.50	20.70	49.30	30.70	100.00		

Note: (a) Percent of the world total.
Source: JETRO (1996), 19.

last two rows). The ASEAN received the lion's share (22%), followed by China (21%) and NIEs (4%). If this trend continues, we may expect continued economic growth in ASEAN and other Southeast Asian countries in the near future. Clearly, both inward and outward direct foreign investments stimulate technology transfer and innovation. These are some factors not measured in the computation of total factor productivity.

13.6 Coefficients of Learning

In the previous sections of this paper, we took the pain to show that, unlike Krugman's assertion, the NIEs have been climbing the technology ladder during the last three decades. They learned and advanced technology through education, foreign trade, and inward and outward direct foreign investment so that they can stay competitive in the world and maintained its rapid growth. This section measures how Taiwan and Korea learned from their mentors and powerful neighbors, Japan and the United States.

13.6.1 *A Simple Model of Learning*

One of the recent concerns in the literature on economic growth is whether the developing countries are catching up with the developed countries in the long run. Catching up can be achieved mainly through technology transfer and spillover between two trading partners through learning. In this section, we would like to set up a simple model of learning between the developing and developed countries.

It is now well known that openness to trade can promote economic growth (Sachs and Warner, 1995). We have observed in section 13.3 that it is also important with which country a developing country is trading. Indeed, the formation of the Pacific trade triangle among Japan, Taiwan and Korea, and the United States has been an engine of growth of Taiwan and Korea (Hsiao, M., 1996). It is generally assumed that the wider the gap of real GDP per capita between the two trading partners, the faster the learning process and the larger the effect of learning. Let y and y^* be real GDP per capita of developing and developed countries, respectively. Then,

$$\ln(\mathrm{y}^*/\mathrm{y}) = \ln \mathrm{y}^* - \ln \mathrm{y}$$

is taken as an indicator of the "advantages of backwardness" (Gerschenkron, 1962), that is, a technological gap which can be exploited by the developing countries like Taiwan and Korea. Following Nelson and Phelps (1966) and more recently Verspagen (1994), the real GDP per capita growth rate of a developing country, denoted as $d(\ln y)/dt$, is proportional to the discrepancy between developed and developing countries' real GDP per capita (in logarithm):

$$d(\ln y)/dt = \alpha(\ln y^* - \ln y) \qquad (13.3)$$

where α is a constant coefficient that measures the degree of learning through technological transfer or imitation of industries in the developing countries.[32] It is the usual speed of adjustment, ranging from zero to one, and may be called more explicitly as the *coefficient of learning* or *catching up*.[33] When $\alpha = 0$, there is no learning and so no growth takes place, and when $\alpha = 1$, the growth rate equals to the income discrepancy (in logarithm).

The above equation may be written in discrete form for statistical estimation:

$$\ln y_t - \ln y_{t-1} = \alpha(\ln y^*_{t-1} - \ln y_{t-1}) \qquad (13.4)$$

We use the data from Maddison (1995), in which GDP per capita is measured in 1990 Geary-Khamis dollars. The data are available from the early 1900s to 1992 for Korea, Taiwan, Japan, and the United States. Thus, we may also compare the learning coefficients of Korea and Japan between the prewar and the postwar periods.

Figure 13.10 shows the values of α for the learning process of pairs of countries, Taiwan with Japan (in a heavy solid line), Korea with Japan (in a dotted line), Japan with the United States (in a light solid line). Similarly, we also calculate the coefficients of learning for Taiwan with the United States, and Korea with the United States. The descriptive statistics of α are presented in Table 13.6.

Ignoring the transition period (1941–1950), for all three periods (total, prewar and postwar), Japan with the United States generally has the highest average value of the coefficients, followed by Taiwan and Korea with Japan, and then Taiwan and Korea with the United States. At the

[32]In addition to trading, technology may be transferred through direct foreign investment and cost-free diffusion (Gomulka, 1990, 161).

[33]In this interpretation, the constancy of a is unrealistic as it implies "least developed country is most innovative" (Gomulka, 1990, 160). However, Hsiao and Hsiao (2000) show that Taiwan and Korea have surpassed the threshold of development before WWII under colonial period, and possessed the ability to absorb foreign technology at the early stage of postwar development.

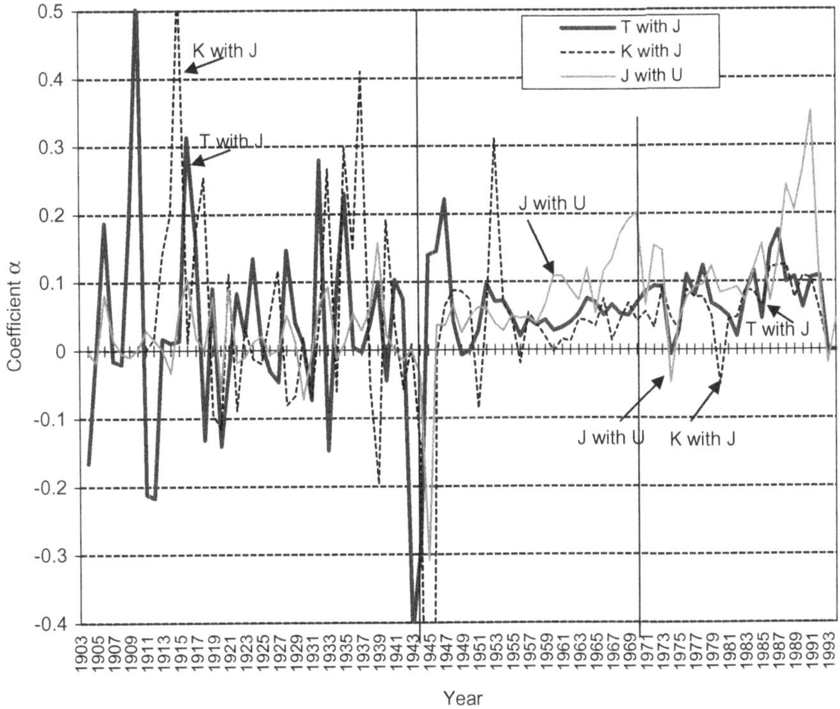

Figure 13.10: Coefficients of Learning
Taiwan and Korea with Japan, Japan with the USA

same time, the coefficient of Japan with the United States fluctuates more (larger standard deviation) than those of Taiwan and Korea with Japan, but less than those of Taiwan and Korea with the United States. This is true for all the three periods. These findings are consistent with our previous observations. They indicate that technology transfer from Japan to Taiwan and Korea is more important than that from the United States to Taiwan and Korea.

Note the difference in the values of coefficient α in the prewar and the postwar periods in Fig. 13.10. For all three cases in the diagram, the range of fluctuation in the prewar coefficients is much larger than the range in the postwar period, showing the erratic nature of the learning process in the prewar period.

Before the war, Taiwan experienced largest fluctuations in the coefficient α, followed by Korea, and then Japan. The positive learning coefficients seem to cancel out the negative ones, although the net results seem to

Table 13.6: Coefficients of Learning

	T/J	K/J	T/U	K/U	J/U
	Total period (1911–1992)				
Grand Max	0.314	0.545	0.123	0.109	0.349
Grand Min	−0.414	−1.220	−0.168	−0.268	−0.309
Grand Average	0.044	0.044	0.025	0.023	0.063
Grand StdDev	0.108	0.181	0.046	0.049	0.084
	Prewar period (1911–1940)				
a Max	0.314	0.545	0.091	0.091	0.158
a Min	−0.217	−0.197	−0.061	−0.081	−0.072
a Average	0.024	0.075	0.008	0.015	0.026
a StdDev	0.128	0.169	0.039	0.040	0.049
	Transition period (1941–1950)				
b Max	0.222	0.088	0.048	0.027	0.067
b Min	−0.414	−1.220	−0.168	−0.268	−0.309
b Average	0.002	−0.107	−0.012	−0.021	−0.015
b StdDev	0.201	0.398	0.075	0.089	0.108
	Postwar period (1951–1992)				
c Max	0.176	0.310	0.123	0.109	0.349
c Min	−0.006	−0.086	−0.004	−0.039	−0.048
c Average	0.069	0.058	0.045	0.039	0.108
c StdDev	0.036	0.058	0.029	0.033	0.072

Notes: Grand = Grand Total. a, b, c show the three subcategories. T/J = Taiwan with Japan, see Table 13.7.
Source: Maddison (1995).

be positive. This explains the slow growth of the prewar period for all three countries. The postwar coefficients behaved quite differently. The coefficients are mostly positive. However, there is a clear difference among the three pairs of the countries. Throughout the three periods, Japan's learning coefficients with the United States are consistently the highest, especially during the late 1960s and late 1980s, followed by Taiwan and Korea with Japan. Taiwan's learning coefficient with the United States is also higher than that of Korea in the prewar and the postwar periods. Apparently, the difference in the learning ability of Taiwan, Korea, and Japan explains at least partly the difference in growth rates of the three countries.[34]

[34]Using Maddison data (1995), Hsiao and Hsiao (2000) have shown that, during the postwar period from 1951 to 1992, the average annual growth rate of real GDP per capita measured in Geary-Khamis dollar of Taiwan was 6.03 percent, higher than any other 57 countries in which long-run data are available. Taiwan's growth rate was above Korea, which ranked 2nd at 5.8 percent, and even that of Japan, which ranked 3rd at 5.57 percent, and almost 2 percent above the 4th country, Thailand (4.07%).

Given the growth rates and the coefficients of learning in the past, in a separate paper (Hsiao and Hsiao, 2000), we have examined whether real GDP per capita of Taiwan and Korea could catch up with that of Japan and the United States in the future. By combining a logistic model of growth and time series analysis using Perron's test of trend stationarity, we were able to show that real GDP per capita of both Taiwan and Korea converges to that of Japan and the United States, although the speed of convergence is slow. Thus, while diminishing returns will eventually set in and the economic growth rate of NIEs may be tapering off, the convergence of the Taiwanese and Korean economies to the advanced countries like Japan and the United States may ultimately realized. In fact, Table 13.1 shows that Singapore's nominal GDP per capita already almost caught up with that of the United States[35] in 1999.

13.6.2 *Estimation of the Long-Run Coefficients of Learning*

When we assume that the growth rate of real GDP per capita, $\ln y_t - \ln y_{t-1}$, is a distributed lag function of the indicator of the advantages of backwardness, $\ln y^*_{t-1} - \ln y_{t-1}$, the long-run learning relationship between two countries can be written as the finite distributed lag model (Greene, 1997, Chapter 17)

$$\ln y_t - \ln y_{t-1} = c + \sum_{j=0}^{k} \beta_j (\ln y^*_{t-j-1} - \ln y_{t-j-1}) + e_t \tag{13.5}$$

where k is the lag length, β_j's are the distributed lag weights, and e_t is the error term. We apply the technique of Almon distributed lag (also called the polynomial distributed lag) to estimate the coefficients β_j's in the model, that is,

$$\beta_j = \sum_{i=0}^{p} \gamma_i j^i$$

where p is the degree of polynomial, and γ_i's are polynomial coefficients. The sum of β_j's is the long-run coefficient of learning, which represents the long-run effect from the discrepancies in the real GDP per capita between an advanced country (Japan or the United States) and the less advanced

[35] In terms of GNP measured at PPP in 1999, Singapore ranked 7th at $27,024, the United States ranked 4th at $30,600. WDR (2000/2001), 275.

Table 13.7: The Long-Run Coefficients of Learning

Taiwan and Korea with Japan and the U.S.

Relation	Total period 1911–92 Long-run				Prewar period 1911–40 Long-run			Postwar period 1951–92 Long-run			
	k	p	Coef.		k	p	Coef.	k	p	Coef.	
Taiwan with Japan	4	1	0.101		7	1	0.176	5	1	0.046	
(T/J)			*(2.45)*	**			*(0.40)*			*(2.04)*	**
Korea with Japan	4	1	0.085		4	1	0.269	7	1	0.052	
(K/J)			*(2.62)*	**			*(1.32)*			*(1.40)*	
Taiwan with USA	7	2	0.006		1	1	0.008	5	1	-0.019	
(T/U)			*(0.25)*				*(0.09)*			*(-1.79)*	
Korea with USA	7	2	0.041		7	2	0.027	2	2	-0.024	
(K/U)			*(1.19)*				*(0.12)*			*(-1.39)*	
Japan with USA	5	2	0.012		3	2	-0.054	7	2	0.026	
(J/U)			*(0.51)*				*(-0.59)*			*(2.41)*	**

Notes: 1. The optimal lag length k is chosen at the minimum AIC from lag 1 period to lag 8 periods.
2. p = degree of polynomial distributed lags.
3. The t-values are in the parentheses.
4. **denotes significant at the 5 percent level.

country (Taiwan or Korea) on the growth rate of real GDP per capita of the less advanced country.

Table 13.7 presents the estimated results of the long-run coefficients of learning for the different pair of countries in three time periods: The total period, 1911–1992; the prewar period, 1911–1940; and the postwar period 1951–1992. The total period includes the transitional period from 1941 to 1950. In the estimation process, we apply the parsimony principle by first assuming that the β_j is a decreasing linear function ($p = 1$) to estimate the model. If this assumption does not hold, then we re-estimate the model by assuming that the β_j is a concave quadratic function ($p = 2$). We have estimated the model from the lag length equals to one to the lag length equals to eight, and the optimal lag length k is chosen by the minimum Akaike information criterion (AIC).

Taiwan with Japan. The most interesting and striking results that we have obtained are the case of Taiwan with Japan. From the total period, the long-run coefficient of β_j is 0.101, which is positive and significant at the 5 percent level. This means historically, Taiwan's GDP per capita growth has benefited from the learning with Japan. In addition, from the postwar period, the long-run learning coefficient is 0.046, which is also positive and significant at the 5 percent level. This implies that Taiwan has continuously learned from Japan, the advanced neighboring country, even after the war. This is consistent with our observations in the previous papers (Hsiao and Hsiao, 1995a, 2002; M. Hsiao, 1992).

Korea with Japan. The results also show ironically that, like Taiwan, Korea also learned greatly from Japan throughout the total period, but when we divided the total period into the prewar and the postwar periods, then the coefficients become not significant.

Taiwan and Korea with the USA. Our results also reveal that both Taiwan and Korea did not seem to learn much from the United States, as their estimated coefficients are generally small, even have wrong sign and insignificant. This probably is the case, since the gaps of the per capita income between Taiwan (and Korea) and the United States are so far apart, at least before the 1990s that the former countries are too far behind to learn advanced technology from the United States, the most advanced country in the world.

Japan and the USA. This interpretation seems consistent with the relationship between Japan and the United States. Overall long-run learning coefficient of Japan with the United States is 0.012 but it is not at all significant. When the total period is divided into the prewar and postwar periods, the prewar coefficient has the wrong sign and is very insignificant, but the postwar coefficient is 0.026 and significant at the 5 percent level, showing Japanese learning from, and catching up with, the United States in the postwar period. Unlike Taiwan or Korea, the GDP per capita difference between Japan and the United States are closer and Japan was able to learn with the United States in the postwar period.

Lastly, note that the values of estimated learning coefficients in Table 13.7 are generally very close to the average coefficients in the descriptive statistics in Table 13.6. No particularly unusual difference between the four statistically significant coefficients in Table 13.7 and the corresponding average coefficients in Table 13.6. All of them have positive sign and are fractions. This seems to suggest that our econometric results are consistent with the sample observations.

13.7 Concluding Remarks

In this paper, we have examined Krugman's second proposition that in an input-driven growth, the law of diminishing returns will eventually set in, as the former Soviet economy once did and collapsed. There are three major strategies to overcome diminishing returns. They are improvement in education, increase in openness, and expansion of domestic R&D. Until the mid-1990s, the NIEs relied mainly on the first and the second strategies to counter diminishing returns and achieved rapid economic growth, the "miracle." We have argued in detail that technology could, and, in fact, did, transfer through import and export activities, and also through inward direct foreign investment in the NIEs.

Is Krugman right in view of recent financial crisis (1997–1998) and the slowdown of the growth rates of the NIEs and Asian countries? Korea and ASEAN-3 countries are severely affected, although other three NIEs had relatively minor recession.[36]

However, Krugman (1997) believes that the crisis has little direct bearing with Asia's long-run growth prospects.[37] In fact, after accepting the rescue packages from international organizations, the financial reform and restructuring programs of these countries seem working, and the recovery from recession already in sight by the end of 1999. The recent prediction of the Asian Development Bank (2000), 242–243, is that the growth rates of real GDP (and real GDP per capita) for Taiwan and Korea in 2000 and 2001 range from 6.0 percent to 7.5 percent (and 5% to 6.4%), respectively. The continuous growth of the NIEs and other ASEAN countries may be expected.

Krugman's argument may be taken as a warning against the lack of R&D in the NIEs. It also points out the limitation of education and openness, after all, as he has aptly observed, it is unrealistic to expect every person in Singapore to earn a Ph.D. However, so long as the NIEs' GDP per capita is still lagging behind the developed countries, the secondary and tertiary enrollment ratios are still low, and technology gaps still exist, the NIEs still could continue rapid growth through education and openness in

[36]Hsiao and Hsiao (2001) have compared the impacts of financial crisis on the Korean and Taiwanese economies. They found that in both countries, the macroeconomic fundamentals are basically similar, except the international financial sector. They also found that a unidirectional causality from the "external short-term debt to international reserves ratio" to foreign exchange rate in the case of Korea, but no causality was found in the case of Taiwan.

[37]The crisis merely indicates that "the doctrine of Asian exceptionalism, however, turned out not merely silly, but dangerous," including the "unabashed government interventionism." After all, the Asian economies do "operate under the same constraints that apply to everywhere else." (Krugman, 1997).

the foreseeable future, although the rate of GDP growth may slow down as the level of GDP increases.

The firms and governments of NIEs are also fully aware of the importance of domestic R&D. New research and development have been introduced, new technical institutions and science zones, like Taiwan's Shinchu Science Developing Park, have been built, and reverse brain drain has been taken place in these countries. In many Asian countries, public enterprises and foreign companies used to lead the nation's economic development in the 1950s and 1960s. But no more. Western educated native private entrepreneurs are the center of economic activities in these market oriented Asian countries (Nikkei, December 1, 1995). We have seen that producers and exporters in the NIEs have moved beyond original equipment manufacturing (OEM) to establish their original brand-name development manufacturing (ODM) in various industries, especially in the fields of computers and communication. The emergence of East Asian companies are so prominent and powerful that even the hard-to-crack Japanese companies started to purchase parts and supplies from non-Japanese Asian firms. As a consequence, Suzuoki (1996) observes the beginning of the collapse of Japan's notorious Keiretsu, although the NIEs' challenge to Japan still at an early stage (Hobday, 1995, 201).

The success of the technological upgrading may be seen again from the Taiwanese story. The left-hand side of Table 13.8 shows the world market share of Taiwan's exports of some high-tech products in 1991 and 1993, ranked from number one to number three in the world export markets. For example, in 1993, Taiwan supplied 76 percent of the world's exports of handheld scanners for personal computers, 62 percent of CPU's, 51 percent of monitors, etc. The Taiwanese achievement is indeed astounding. There were 9 items ranked number one, three items in number 2, and four items number 3, in the world export markets in 1993. In terms of production in 1995, Taiwan produced more than 10 percent of world's personal computers,[38] and the production of keyboards and motherboards ranked number one in the world (Nikkei, February 11, 1996). Table 13.8 also shows that they, along with many others, were still Number One at whopping 65 percent or so of the world share in 1998, although the production of keyboard started to decrease.

[38]Using another source of statistics, in 1994, Taiwan produced 5,147,000 computers, about 10 percent of the total world production, far exceeded Japanese production (about 3.5 million computers). See Asamoto (1996), 115, 118.

Table 13.8: World Market Share and Innovative Activities
The Case of Taiwan

World Market Share Product Name	Year 91 %	93 %	98 %	Trend ↓
No. 1 Ranking				
Scanner (hand-held)	65	76	85	-
CPU	65	62	66	
Monitor	44	51	58	-
Case			75	
Switching Pwr Supply			66	
Keyboard			65	-
Mouse			60	-
Sound Card			49	-
Video Card			40	-
Notebook PC			39	
CD-ROM			36	
Graphic Cards			31	
ABS fiber	28	29	32	*
Sewing machine	25	25		
Frozen processed eel	31	24		
MSG	19	20		
ABS (petrochemical)	15	15		
Bicycles	7	9		
No. 2 Ranking				
Scanner (desk-top)		30		
Uninterrupted Pwr Supply			40	
PTA		18		
Machine mould	3	4		
Bicycles			10	*
No. 3 Ranking				
Scanner (desk-top)	19			
Personal computers	10	9	16	-
Printed circuit board		6		
PS (petrochemical)	26	18		
Lighting diode	9	9		

Innovation 1989-1993 (cases) Industry	Wld rkg	# of Patnt	tech. tran-slatn	tech co-op	copy rghts
Industrial Machine		40	120	36	160
Semiconductor	6	180	116	36	
Machine Tools	7	22	114	75	24
Computer	5	75	113	66	334
Communicatioı	10	21	104	108	246
Laser		65	52		39
Instrument		14	50	57	33
Cnsmer Electronics		18	47	57	1
Anti-pollution		17	47	33	
Food		5	37	35	
Textile		13	22	65	
Pharmaceudicals		15	12	35	
Special Chemicals		21	7	46	
Sum		506	841	649	837
5 yr avg		101	168	130	167

Sources: Special Program on Science and Technology, Summary of Major Achievements, Ministry of Economic Affairs, Republic of China, 1989–1993.

The data on 1998 is from Underwood (1999), and on 1997 (with*) is from Schive and Chang (1999). Negative in the trend column shows decreasing from the 1997 data.

Table 13.9: Technological Competitiveness of the Taiwanese Computer Industry

	Taiwan	Japan	USA
Motherboards	1	2	3
PC, Desk-top	1	2	1
PC, Notebook	2	1	3
LC Display	3	1	4
Software	3	4	1

Sources: Nikkei Business (February 27, 1995). Quoted in Asamoto (1995, 123).

The right-hand side of Table 13.8 shows that, during 1989–1993, Taiwanese achievements were supported by intensive activities in patented innovation (average 101 cases per year, same as below), technical transfer (168 cases), technical cooperation (130 cases), and copy rights (167 cases).

Today, Taiwan's infrastructure of producing personal computers and their peripherals are much better than any developing countries in Asia (Nikkei, February 1996), and, in some area, Taiwan's computer technology is now comparable, if not better, than Japan's.[39] Table 13.9 shows an estimation of technological competitiveness of Taiwanese computer products by the Nikkei Business Journal. Taiwanese made motherboards and desktop personal computers are more competitive than Japan, and their motherboards are as competitive as those made in the United States. Similar statements can be made of Korea (Yu and Choi, 1995). Technology not only has transferred to the NIEs, native technology also begins to burgeon. We should emphasize again that these are something that cannot be measured in the conventional TFP analysis.

So long as the NIEs continue to improve its educational level, maintain exports promotion policy, keep the market open, nurture local research and development, upgrade computer and information technology, preserve macroeconomic stability, especially keep inflation rate moderate (Rodrick, 1996), then, in view of recent studies of the relation between information technology and the U.S. economic growth (Jorgenson, 2001; Stiroh, 2001), there is much better chance for the NIEs and ASEAN-4 to overcome the iron law of diminishing returns and continue its rapid economic growth. Barring unforeseen political disturbances and economic disasters in the region, our analysis suggests that NIEs will continue to grow. Furthermore, through

[39] We owe this point to Takabumi Suzuoki of Japan Economic Times (Nikkei).

increased DFI from Japan and NIEs to ASEAN-4 and other Southeast Asian countries, and increased intra-regional trade in Asia, we expect the Asia and Pacific region to be the world center of economic activity in this century.

Acknowledgments

We would like to thank Professors Teruo Asamoto, Natsuki Fujita, Chi Schive, Messrs. Takabumi Suzuoki and Kenichi Yanagi, for help in references. Comments by a referee and Prof. Song-ken Hsu are most helpful. This paper is dedicated in the memory of our teacher, Professor Mo-huan Hsing. In preparing this chapter, charts and tables were reconstructed using the Microsoft Excel program. All errors of commission and omission are ours.

References

Abe, Shigeyuki (1996). "The Myth of Asian Economy" (in Japanese). *Kokumin Keizai Zasshi*, 174(3) (September): 43–59.

Aoki, Takeshi (1985). *The Pacific Era and Japan* (in Japanese). Tokyo: Yuhi Kaku.

Arnold, W. (1985). "Japan and Taiwan: Community of Economic Interest Held Together by Paradiplomacy." In Ozaki, R.S. and W. Arnold (eds.), *Japan's Foreign Relations* (Chapter 11). Papers presented at the 35th Annual Meeting of the Association for Asian Studies, March 25, 1983, San Francisco. Boulder, CO: Westview Press.

Asamoto, Teruo (1996). *Economic Analysis of Contemporary Taiwan, An Approach of Development Economics* (in Japanese). Tokyo: Keiso Shobo.

Asian Development Bank (2000). *Asian Development Outlook, 2000.* Oxford, UK: Oxford University Press.

Asian Productivity Organization (1995). *Comparative Information on Productivity Levels and Changes in APO Member Countries.* Tokyo: APO Office.

Center of Softening Economy (CSE) (1989). *Softening of Japanese Economy and Asian NIEs.* A Report of the Study Group of 1989 Softening of the Japanese Economy and Coexistence with the Asian NIEs (in Japanese). Tokyo.

Chow, P.C.Y. and M.H. Kellman (1993). *Trade–The Engine of Growth in East Asia.* New York: Oxford University Press.

Chuang, Sharon (2000). "Failure to Thrive." *TOPICS, The Magazine of International Business in Taiwan*, 30(6) (August): 42–46. The American Chamber of Commerce in Taipei.

Coe, D.T., E. Helpman and A.W. Hoffmaister (1995). "North–South R&D Spillovers." NBER Working Paper Series, No. 5048, March.

Economic Planning Agency (EPA). Japan (1995). *Asian Economies 1995* (in Japanese). Tokyo: Ministry of Finance Publishing Bureau.

Edwards, S. (1993). "Openness, Trade Liberalization, and Growth in Developing Countries." *Journal of Economic Literature* (September): 1358–1393.

Gereffi, G. (1995). "Global Production Systems and Third World Development." In B. Stallings (ed.), *Global Change, Regional Response — The New International Contest of Development* (100–142). Cambridge, UK: Cambridge University Press.

Gerschenkron, A. (1962). *Economic Backwardness in Historical Perspective.* Cambridge, MA: Harvard University Press.

Gomulka, Stanislaw (1990). *The Theory of Technical Change and Economic Growth.* London: Routledge.

Green, William H. (1997). *Econometric Analysis*, 3rd ed. Upper Saddle River, NJ: Prentice Hall.

Grossman, G.M. and E. Helpman (1991). *Innovation and Growth in the Global Economy.* Cambridge, MA: The MIT Press.

Helleiner, G.K. (1990). "Trade Strategy in Medium-Term Adjustment." *World Development*, 18(6): 879–897.

Hobday, M. (1995). *Innovation in East Asia, the Challenge to Japan.* Northampton, MA: Edward Elgar.

Hsiao, Frank. S.T. and Mei-Chu W. Hsiao (2002). "Taiwan in the Global Economy — Past, Present, and Future." In Peter C.Y. Chow (ed.), *Taiwan's in the Global Economy — From an Agrarian Economy to an Exporter of High-Tech Products.* Westport, C.I.: Praeger Publishers (Ref. Chapter 2).

——— and ——— (2001). "Capital Flows and Exchange Rates — Recent Korean and Taiwanese Experience and Challenges." Paper presented at the AEA/ACAES joint session at 2001 ASSA annual meeting, New Orleans. January. Published in *Journal of Asian Economics*, 12(3) (Fall 2001): 353–381.

——— and ——— (2000). "International Comparisons of Taiwanese Economic Growth — A Long-Run Perspective." *World Development*, 31(2) (2003): 227–257.

——— and ——— (1996). "Miracle or Myth of Asian NICs' Growth — the Irony of Numbers." In M. Dutta (ed.), *Research in Asian Economic Studies*, 8(8): 51–68. Greenwich, CT: JAI Press.

——— and ——— (1995a). "Taiwanese Economic Development and Foreign Trade." In *Harvard Studies on Taiwan: Papers of the Taiwan Studies Workshop*, Vol. 1. Cambridge MA: The John K. Fairbank Center for East Asian Research, Harvard University, 199–270. Also in *Comparative Asian Economies*, in John Y.T. Kuark (ed.), *Contemporary Studies in Economic and Financial Analysis*, 77 (Part B). An International Series of Monographs, Greenwich, CT: JAI Press, 1996. 211–302. (Ref. Chapter 1)

——— and ——— (1995b). "Globalization of the Taiwanese Economy and U.S.-Taiwan Trade Relations." In C.F. Lee (ed.), *Advances in Pacific Basin Business, Economics, and Finance* (197–214) Vol. 1. Greenwich, CT: JAI Press (Ref. Chapter 10).

——— and ——— (1989). "Japanese Experience of Industrialization and Economic Performance of Korea and Taiwan: Tests of Similarity."

In C.F. Lee and S.C. Hu (eds.), *Taiwan's Foreign Investment, Exports and Financial Analysis*, in *Advances in Financial Planning and Forecasting* (157–190). Greenwich, CT: JAI Press (Ref. Chapter 11).

Hsiao, Mei-Chu W. (1987). "Tests of Causality and Exogeneity between Exports and Economic Growth: The Case of Asian NICs." *Journal of Economic Development*, 12(2) (December): 143–159.

——— (1992). "Direct Foreign Investment, Technology Transfer, and Industrial Development — The Case of Electronics Industry in Taiwan." In *Asian Economic Regime: An Adaptive Innovation Paradigm*, M. Dutta (ed.), *Research in Asian Economic Studies* (145–164). 4A, Greenwich, CT: JAI Press, 1992. (Ref. Chapter 9).

——— (1996). "Pacific Trade Triangle and the Growth of Korea and Taiwan — Cointegration and Causality Analyses." Paper presented at the 1996 Meetings of the Eastern Economic Association, March. Boston, MA.

International Monetary Fund (IMF) (1994). *International Financial Statistics*. Various issues.

Investment Commission (2000). *Monthly Statistics on Overseas Chinese and Foreign Investment, Outward Investment, Outward Technical Cooperation, Indirect Mainland Investment, Guide of Mainland Industry Technology*. April. Taipei, Taiwan: Ministry of Economic Affairs.

Ito, Shoji (1986). "Modifying Imported Technology by Local Engineers: Hypotheses and Case Study of India." *The Developing Economies*, 24(4) (December): 334–348.

JETRO (1996). *1996 JETRO White Paper, Overseas Direct Investment of the World and Japan, Investment* (in Japanese). Tokyo: Japan Exports and Trade Organization (JETRO).

Jorgenson, Dale W. (2001). "Information Technology and the U.S. Economy." *American Economic Review*, 91(1) (March): 1–32.

Kawakami, Momoko (1999). "Formation of Parts Industry in Taiwan — the Spin-out from Japanese Firms." Paper presented at the Japan Society of Taiwanese Studies, June.

Knoester, A. and W. Mak (1994). "Real Interest Rates in Eight OECD Countries." *Rivista Internazionale di Scienze Economiche e Commerciali*, 41(4): 325–344.

Krugman, Paul (1994). "The Myth of Asia's Miracle." *Foreign Affairs*, 73(6) (November/December): 62–78.

——— (1997). "Asia's Miracle is Alive and Well? Wrong, It Never Existed." *Time*, 150(13) (September 29).

Lucas, Robert E. Jr. (1993). "Making a Miracle." *Econometrica*, 61(2) (March): 251–272.

Maddison, Angus (1995). *Monitoring the World Economy, 1820–1992*. Development Centre, Paris: OECD.

Moon, Dae-Woo (1993). "Spread of Industrialization in the Western Pacific: Chain Reaction of Structural Transformation" (in Japanese). *Aziya Kenkyu*, 40(2) (November): 1–34.

Nikkei, *Nikkei Sangyo Sinbun* (Japan Economic and Industry Daily). Various issues.

Nelson, R. R. and E. S. Phelps (1966). "Investment in Humans, Technological Diffusion and Economic Growth." *American Economic Review*, 56: 66–75.

OECD (1979). "*The Impact of the Newly Industrializing Countries on Production and Trade in Manufactures.*" Report by the Secretary-General, Paris: OECD.

Page, J. (1994). "The East Asian Miracle: Four Lessons for Development Policy." In S. Fischer and J.J. Rotemberg (eds.), *NBER Macroeconomics, Annual 1994*. Cambridge, MA: The MIT Press.

Park, Y.C. and W.A. Park (1989). "Changing Japanese Trade Patterns and The East Asian NICs." In P. Krugman (ed.), *Trade with Japan, Has the Door Opened Wider?* (Chapter 3). Chicago: The University of Chicago Press.

Ranis, G. (ed.) (1992). *Taiwan — From Developing to Mature Economy*. Boulder, CO: Westview Press.

Rodrick, D. (1996). "Understanding Economic Policy Reform." *The Journal of Economic Literature*, 34(1) (March): 9–41.

Sachs, J. D. and A. Warner (1995). "Economic Reform and the Process of Global Integration." *Brookings Papers on Economic Analysis, 25th Anniversary Issue* (1–118).

______ and ______ (1996). "Achieving Rapid Growth in the Transition Economies of Central Europe." HIID Development Discussion Papers, #544. July. 64 pp. Harvard Institute for International Development, Harvard University.

Schive, Chi (1990). *The Foreign Factor, The Multinational Corporation's Contribution to the Economic Modernization of the Republic of China*. Stanford: Hoover Institution Press.

______ (1983). "Direct Foreign Investment, Technology Transfer, and Industrial Development in Taiwan" (in Chinese). In *Proceedings of Conference on Taiwanese Industrial Development*, 2, 471–501. Taipei, Taiwan: The Institute of Economics, Academia Sinica. March.

______ and Hsiang-hsian Chang (1999). "High-tech Industry and Economic Development in Taiwan" (in Chinese). *Industry of Free China*, 89(2) (February): 13–34.

Shinohara, Miyohei (1996). "What is Happening in Asian Economies? — Transition to DFI-led Growth" (in Japanese). *Ajiken World Trend*, 10 (March): 1–2.

Stiroh, Kevin J. (2001). "What Drives Productivity Growth?" *FRBNY Economic Policy Review*, Federal Reserve Bank of New York, March (37–59).

Suzuoki, Takabumi (1996). "From Flying Geese to Round Robin: The Emergence of Powerful Asian Companies and the Collapse of Japan's Keiretsu." Discussion Paper, Program on U.S.-Japan Relations, Harvard University.

Taniuchi, Mitsuru (1995). "An East Asian Growth and Efficiency Gains: A Critique of Krugman's 'The Myth of Asia's Miracle." *APO Productivity Journal* (Winter): 3–16.

TSDB (1989, 1995, 1996). *Taiwan Statistical Data Book*, various issues. Council for Economic Planning and Development, Republic of China. Taiwan.

Underwood, Laurie (1999). "The Park that Chips Built." *TOPICS, The Magazine of International Business in Taiwan*, The American Chamber of Commerce in Taipei. April 29(3).

Verspagen, B. (1994). "Technology and Growth: The Complex Dynamics of Convergence and Divergence." In G. Silverberg and L. Soete (eds.), *The Economics of Growth and Technical Change, Technologies, Nations, Agents* (154–181). Brookfield, Vermont: Edward Elger.

Washio, Hiroaki (1986). "The Provision of Manuals and Japanese Private Technology Transfer." *The Developing Economies*, 24(4) (December): 326–333.

World Bank (1984, 1987, 1992, 1993, 2000/2001). *World Development Report* (WDR). New York: Oxford University Press.

——— (1993). *The East Asian Miracle, Economic Growth and Public Policy.* A World Bank Policy Research Report. New York: Oxford University Press.

Yu, Jisoo and Jeong-Wook Choi (1995). "Transformation from Low-Tech to High-Tech: The Case of Samsung Group." *APO Productivity Journal* (Winter): 41–56.

Lightning Source UK Ltd.
Milton Keynes UK
UKOW06n2047070415

249243UK00003B/81/P

9 789814 618502